The
Tin Pan Alley
Song Encyclopedia

Two tunesmiths in the Tin Pan Alley offices of H.W. Savage, New York, New York, 1903. Copyright © Museum of the City of New York. Courtesy of the Museum of the City of New York, The Byron Collection.

THE
TIN PAN ALLEY
SONG ENCYCLOPEDIA

Thomas S. Hischak
2

GREENWOOD PRESS
Westport, Connecticut • London

Library of Congress Cataloging-in-Publication Data

Hischak, Thomas S.
  The Tin Pan Alley song encyclopedia / Thomas S. Hischak.
    p. cm.
  Includes bibliographical references (p.) and index.
  ISBN 0–313–31992–8 (alk. paper)
  1. Popular music—United States—Encyclopedias. I. Title.
  782.42164'0973—dc21
  ML102 .P66H57 2002   2002023250

British Library Cataloguing in Publication Data is available.

Library of Congress Catalog Card Number: 2002023250
ISBN: 0–313–31992–8

First published in 2002

Greenwood Press, 88 Post Road West, Westport, CT 06881
An imprint of Greenwood Publishing Group, Inc.
www.greenwood.com

Printed in the United States of America

The paper used in this book complies with the
Permanent Paper Standard issued by the National
Information Standards Organization (Z39.48–1984).

10 9 8 7 6 5 4 3 2 1

For Bill Whiting

Contents

Preface ix

Glossary of Terms xiii

Songs **1**

Alternate Song Titles 429

ASCAP's Hit Parade 435

NEA's Hit Parade 437

Tin Pan Alley Standards from Stage and Screen 439

Selected Bibliography 449

Index 457

Preface

Tin Pan Alley cannot be found on any map. Yes, there was a stretch of Twenty-eighth Street between Fifth Avenue and Broadway in New York City that was sardonically referred to as Tin Pan Alley during the first decades of the twentieth century. But that is like calling Broadway a street in Manhattan or describing Hollywood as a thoroughfare in California. Tin Pan Alley was more than a location. It was a state of mind, a fanciful dream, a never-neverland and where anyone could become a millionaire by capturing a familiar sentiment in thirty-two bars and set America singing. It was also a business, a bustling enterprise where semi-literate immigrants and necktie salesmen peddled songs just as their relatives were peddling fruit and kitchen utensils on the street a few blocks away. Tin Pan Alley was a barometer that gauged the public's temperament, providing songs about the latest inventions, dance steps, crazes, people in the news, local and world events, even slang expressions and catchphrases. The fact that the Alley was often responsible for creating these very phenomena was not missed by anyone. As America went, so did Tin Pan Alley; the reverse was also true.

I say *was* because Tin Pan Alley doesn't exist anymore. The music business thrives today, but the Alley has been dead for five decades. David Ewen pinpoints the heyday of Tin Pan Alley as 1885 to 1930 but, like any empire, it stretched beyond its golden age. In the first half of the nineteenth century, popular song was not easily measured or accounted for. Printed sheet music of Stephen Foster's songs sold in the thousands, but most people performing or singing along had no use for musical notation. By the middle of the century the parlor piano became the focal point of the music business, and sheet music sales became the accepted method of measuring success. The sale of player piano rolls by the turn of the century and the introduction of records, then radio, in the following decades were all effective ways of determining just how popular a song was. But regardless of the media, the source was Tin Pan Alley, a group of music publishers who commissioned, bought, plugged, and distributed songs as quickly as the public demanded them.

By 1903 hundreds of these publishers were housed in former brownstone apartments on Twenty-eighth Street, their offices a labyrinth of little rooms with tunesmiths banging away on cheap pianos. When all the windows were open, the noise must have been both annoying and exhilarating. Here was the musical voice of America being hammered out in a factory just like any other industry. Journalist Monroe Rosenfeld is credited with coining the phrase "Tin Pan Alley." Writing a series of articles for the *New York Herald*, Monroe used the expression (which he probably stole from songwriter Harry Von Tilzer) to describe Twenty-eighth Street, and the term quickly came to mean the popular music business in America. By 1919 most publishers had moved uptown with the migrating theatre district and settled in the Brill Building on Broadway at Forty-ninth Street. The place Tin Pan Alley existed only those nineteen years, but the music business would continue to thrive in the same manner until the 1950s. Radio, vaudeville, Broadway, sound movies, long-playing records, even television would contribute to the Alley's ongoing demand for songs. It seemed like it would go on forever. But it didn't.

Rock-and-roll is often blamed for the death of Tin Pan Alley but there is more to the story than that. The Alley had survived the invasion of ragtime, blues, jazz, swing, country-western, and other new and upsetting musical movements: Why should rock be any different? The waning of the old-time music business started years before "Rock Around the Clock." By the late 1930s, for example, the emphasis started to shift from the song to the performer. Tin Pan Alley had always been about the song. A performing star was useful in promoting one's product. When the star became the product, the music publishers suffered. Soon the record companies were the most likely to benefit from a hit song, and the music business found itself in a new business. When the parlor piano slowly faded away, so too did the heart of Tin Pan Alley. By the 1950s, when popular music started to concentrate on singers who performed their own songs, the product became a package. But it is difficult to sell a package with one of the components missing. Did anyone really want to own the sheet music to an Elvis Presley song? Or, for that matter, how often did one want to hear a Presley song sung by someone else? The Alley found itself unnecessary. Add to that the divergent ways that theatre music and popular music traveled, the strict separation between the kinds of music enjoyed by different generations, and the move away from lyric-based songs to rhythm-based music, and it was clear that the old music business was no longer.

Although Tin Pan Alley is long gone, it has left a rich and living legacy. Old scratchy 78s of Al Jolson singing may not be part of contemporary American pop culture, but very often the songs he sang are. If it was the individual songs that made the Alley thrive, it is those very songs that keep it alive today. It is thrilling to think of how many of the 1,228 songs in this book are still familiar to Americans, how many of them show up in films and on Broadway, and how many of them are still being recorded each year. It is also interesting to see how so many of these songs have been reinterpreted over the years, a waltz favorite becoming a jazz hit or a fox trot ballad becoming a rock bestseller. Tin Pan Alley was all about the songs and it is the songs that live on.

This book is a companion to the earlier *The American Musical Theatre Song Encyclopedia* and *The American Musical Film Song Encyclopedia*, hoping to describe and explain some of the thousands of popular songs that did not come from the stage or the screen. There is some overlap with the previous volumes. Songs that premiered on Broadway or in the movies but didn't find recognition until they were Tin Pan Alley hits are included. Successful numbers from the other media are also included if their subsequent history on the Alley is outstanding. But most of the songs covered here were written and introduced as individual numbers, hoping to capture the public's attention by way of vaudeville, sheet music, piano rolls, nightclubs, concerts, or records.

As with the previous books, selecting which songs to include has been an unsatisfying experience. The chronological boundaries I have chosen are from the pre–Civil War years to the end of the 1950s. A handful of important songs from colonial times and from the early decades of the new nation are included, but the rest of the entries fall into the one hundred years that saw the rise, golden age, and decline of Tin Pan Alley. An effort has been made to cover major songwriters, performers, musical styles, types of songs, and time periods. While all of the songs discussed enjoyed some popularity at one time, this is not a parade of hits. Many songs flourished for only a short time, others were longtime standards, and still others were forgotten only to be revived again by a future generation. For the most part, the songs included are American. But British songs that were widely popular in the States and foreign-language songs that were translated and became Tin Pan Alley hits are considered as well. Concert songs, hymns, religious Christmas carols, college songs, classical pieces, children's tunes, and other numbers outside of popular music are not discussed unless they crossed over to find success on the Alley.

In the appendices are listed hundreds of songs from Broadway and Hollywood that are not considered in this book but can be found in the previous song encyclopedias. Song titles are notoriously inconsistent on Tin Pan Alley, so a list of alternate titles is included to help locate numbers by one of their other names. I have also added two "hit parade"

lists that might be of interest to the reader and a selected bibliography
that will point the way to dozens of books that further explore Tin Pan
Alley, the songs, and the songwriters. Finally, a glossary of terms that
are used in describing the entries is presented before the encyclopedia
to help the reader understand the terminology as it is used in this book.

I would like to acknowledge the continued help from the staff at the
Cortland Free Library and the Memorial Library at the State University
of New York College at Cortland. William Whiting has been invaluable
again in checking the text, the staff at Greenwood Press has been efficient
and helpful during every step of the process, and the assistance of Richard and Nancy Kroot and Mark Cerosaletti is much appreciated. Finally,
I am pleased to publicly acknowledge the untiring support and understanding of my wife Cathy and our children Mark and Karen.

Glossary of Terms

ballad   A term with too many meanings in music and literature, a ballad in popular music is any sentimental or romantic song, usually with the same melody for most stanzas. Most Tin Pan Alley songs are ballads, and so were many of the big hits from films and Broadway musicals. A *narrative ballad* is closer to poetry's definition of the term (a song that tells a story), and Tin Pan Alley has seen many hits of this type, often in the genre of folk songs or sentimental ballads with extended narratives in the verse.

crossover hit   A song that was released in one field, such as country-western or rhythm-and-blues, but then enjoyed popular recordings in another field is said to have crossed over. A pop song by a celebrated songwriter was often performed by various kinds of artists, but when a cowboy song, for instance, was picked up and successfully recorded by opera singers or theatre performers, it was considered a crossover hit.

interpolation   A song added to a theatre production or a movie musical that was not written by the same songwriters who penned the rest of the score is termed an interpolation. They remain very common in films where a Tin Pan Alley standard was often added to a score or to the background soundtrack. There are also many cases of an Alley favorite being interpolated into a Broadway score, particularly in the years before the integrated musical came along with *Oklahoma!* (1943).

list song   Any song, serious or comic, that is structured as a list of examples or a series of items. It is sometimes called a "laundry list" song, although the result, hopefully, is much more interesting than that.

lyric   A line from a song or the entire set of lines written for a song is the lyric. The person who pens the words of a song is known as a *lyricist*. The plural form *lyrics* refers to the words to all the songs a lyricist has written for a theatre or film score; one writes a *lyric* for a song and the *lyrics* for the score. In this book, when a songwriter is not referred to specifically as a lyricist or a composer, it can be assumed that he or she wrote both music and lyric for the song.

pastiche song   Any song that echoes the style, either musically or lyrically, of an earlier era is a pastiche number. Such songs were written to spoof the past or to recapture the flavor of a past style of songwriting.

refrain   The main body of a song is called the refrain. It is the section that follows the *verse* and repeats itself with the same melody and/or lyric. The most familiar part of a popular song is usually the refrain section. The refrain is sometimes called the *chorus*, but the later term is too often confused with a group of singers, so it is not used in this book.

release   A section of the *refrain* that departs from the repeated melody is a release. It usually explores a new musical line that may or may not have been suggested in the main melody. The release (sometimes called the *bridge*) helps keep a song from being too predictable or monotonous.

song form or **structure**   Although there were no set rules for writing for Tin Pan Alley, songwriters knew what worked and what the public wanted, so many songs over the decades followed a similar structure. Most songs consisted of a *verse* and a *refrain*, sometimes going back and forth between the two. In later years, the verse was used as the introduction and the refrain as the body of the song. While the length of the verse varied widely from song to song and period to period, the refrain was more uniform. The most standard song form was AABA; that is, the first two stanzas were musically identical, the third was a variation on it or a separate *release*, then the final stanza repeated the initial melody of the first two sections. Also, thirty-two measures was considered the traditional length for a popular song. But there are hundreds of examples in this book of Tin Pan Alley songs that broke away from this structure and length.

specialty song   A song that is written to highlight a particular performer's unique talents is said to be a specialty number. Some specialty songs that were written and recorded by one star later found success with other artists as well.

standard   A song that is popular on its initial release and remains popular over a number of years is classified as a standard. There are many cases of a song finding little success at first and reaching the rank of standard years later. There are also standards that fell out of favor after some years, then found a new audience and popularity decades later.

Tin Pan Alley Technically, a stretch of Twenty-eighth Street in New York City between Fifth Avenue and Broadway where the greatest concentration of music publishers was situated during the first two decades of the twentieth century. But the expression has wider implications, often meaning the popular music business itself. A Tin Pan Alley song is one written primarily for publication, recording, or broadcast rather than for the musical theatre or a film musical. Yet many songs from Broadway and Hollywood went on to become Tin Pan Alley hits as well.

torch song In popular music a torch song is usually a sentimental song involving unrequited love. Torch songs can range from a suicidal blues number to a comic or sarcastic commentary on lost love.

verse The introductory section of a song is called the verse. The melody is usually distinct from that of the *refrain* that follows, and verses during the twentieth century tend to be shorter. Most songs are known more for their refrains than for their verses. In the 1800s the verses tended to be long and narrative. Later the verses got shorter and more succinct, usually setting up the premise for the idea explored in the refrain. Verses were considered requisite for most Tin Pan Alley songs, though many times a recording might omit the song's verse and start with the more popular refrain. But a superior verse sets up the song's important images and theme and gives the number its full potency.

Your Hit Parade First a radio program (from 1935 to 1950), then a television show (1950 to 1959), this weekly look at the popular music industry was the gauge that both the public and those in the music business used to identify song hits. The show featured songs that had sold the most sheet music or records the previous week, ranked the top sellers, and then had its resident artists perform the songs. To be included in *Your Hit Parade* for several weeks running was evidence of a song's high popularity.

The
Tin Pan Alley
Song Encyclopedia

A

" 'A' You're Adorable" (1941) is a plucky list song in which an admirer goes through the alphabet finding doting adjectives ('B'—so beautiful, 'I'—the idol of my eye, and so on) to heap on his beloved one. Sometimes listed as "The Alphabet Song," the number was written by Buddy Kaye, Fred Wise, and Sid Lippman in 1941, but they could not interest anyone in recording it until Jo Stafford and Gordon MacRae made a duet version in 1949 that was moderately popular. It was Perry Como's record with the Fontaine Sisters that brought the naive ditty wide recognition. Over the years it has been recorded by Mike Douglas, Emile Ford and the Checkmates, Tommy Sands, Rosemary Clooney, Jimmy Dorsey, Claire Hogan, and Dean Martin.

"The Aba Daba Honeymoon" (1914) is the perennial favorite that came from vaudeville but found its greatest success decades later when Debbie Reynolds and Carlton Carpenter sang it in the film *Two Weeks With Love* (1950). Arthur Fields (lyric) and Walter Donovan (music) wrote the nonsense number about the courtship, wedding, and honeymoon of a monkey and a chimpanzee in the Congo, the two sweethearts proclaiming their love in jungle gibberish. Ruth Roye introduced the tune at the Palace Theatre in New York, and a later record by Arthur Collins and Byron Harlan was at the top of the charts. Paul Whiteman and his Orchestra played the number in the film *King of Jazz* (1930), and Willie Solar sang it in *Diamond Horseshoe* (1945). But it was the Reynolds-Carpenter recording that sold over a million discs and kept the song on *Your Hit Parade* for nine weeks. There have been other recordings by such diverse talents as Reynolds, Hoagy Carmichael and Cass Daley, Freddie Martin, the Chenille Sisters, Maria Muldaur, and the Three Stooges.

"Absence Makes the Heart Grow Fonder (For Somebody)" (1929) is a crooning ballad that Gene Austin introduced on record, but it was Bernie Cummins and his Orchestra who popularized it with their bestselling disc. Harry Warren composed the dreamy music, and Sam Lewis and Joe Young came up with the heartfelt lyric. Orrin Tucker's 1941 disc revived interest in the song, and over the years there have been recordings by Tom Gerun, Art Gillham, Loudon Wainwright III, Lou Reid, Marty Grosz, Horace Henderson, and Dean Martin. The torchy ballad was heard in the film *Spring Is Here* (1930), and a duet version by Tiffany Anders and Boyd Price was featured in *Grace of My Heart* (1996).

"An Ace in the Hole" (1926) is a lusty saloon song by George D. Mitchell and James E. Dempsey that was a favorite sing-along number in speakeasies in the Roaring Twenties. The swinging tune slyly comments on the flashy dressers and men-about-town who are all talk but have little dough in their pockets. Tommy Lyman popularized the song after performing it in some upscale clubs, and it has been recorded often, most memorably by Lee Wiley with Billy Butterfield's Orchestra in 1957. Other recordings were made by the University Six, Ella Fitzgerald, Connie Francis, Chick Bullock, Red McKenzie, Clancy Hayes with Bob Scobey's Frisco Band, Anita O'Day, Lu Watters, Mabel Mercer, and more recently, Barbara Carroll and Andrea Marcovicci. The song can be heard in the films *Frisco Sal* (1945) and *Naked Alibi* (1954).

"Across the Alley From the Alamo" (1947) is an uptempo cowboy song by Joe Greene with an odd tale to tell. In San Antonio, a Navajo and his pinto pony entertained passersby with their cheery smiles and songs. But one day they got dressed up and went for a walk along the railroad tracks, a train was heard, and the two never returned. This rather somber story is set to surprisingly chipper music with a Latin flavor and pleased audiences enough for both the Mills Brothers and Stan Kenton (vocal by June Christy) to have hit records. There were also discs by Bob Wills and his Texas Playboys, George McClure, the Moms and Dads, Hank Thompson, the Pine Valley Cosmonauts, and Patti Austin.

"Address Unknown" (1939) is a tearful ballad about a lover who has moved on, with only returned letters to remember him by. Carmen Lombardo, Johnny Marks, and Dedette Lee Hill collaborated on the song, taking the title from a bestselling book of the era. Guy Lombardo and the Royal Canadians introduced and recorded the number, but it was a celebrated disc by the Ink Spots that made the song popular. There were also recordings by Hank Snow, Red Nichols, Don Gibson, Marty Robbins, Eric Mingus, Jimmy Scott, and Roy Acuff.

"Adios" (1931) became the Latin-flavored theme song for Enric Madriguera and his Orchestra with a hit recording in 1931. Yet Glenn Miller and his Orchestra revived interest in it with an even more successful record in 1941, and it remained popular throughout the war years. Madriguera composed the gentle music, and Eddie Woods penned the somber farewell lyric. Long a favorite of Spanish artists such as Xavier Cugat, the song was also recorded by Carol Bruce, Ray Anthony, Percy Faith, Stan Kenton, the Ray Charles Singers, Tony Pastor, Gisele MacKenzie, the Ray Conniff Singers, Laurindo Almeida, Syd Lawrence, and the orchestras of Mantovanni, Andre Kostelanetz, and Claude Thornhill. The song was featured in the film bio *The Glenn Miller Story* (1953).

"Adios Muchachos" (1929) is the well-known Latin number that says farewell in an upbeat, rhythmic manner. Julio Sanders composed the lilting music, and Cesar Vedani wrote the Spanish lyric. In 1951 an English lyric by Dorcas Cochran retitled the number "I Get Ideas," and a disc by Tony Martin revived interest in the song. Other recordings over the years, in Spanish and English, include those by Xavier Cugat, Louis Armstrong, Peggy Lee, Andy Russell, Jane Morgan, Lester Lanin, Mantovanni's Orchestra, the Ray Conniff Singers, Carlos Gardel, and many other Spanish singers and bands.

"After All, You're All I'm After" (1933) is one of composer Arthur Schwartz's rare Tin Pan Alley hits not to come from a Broadway musical. Edward Heyman (lyric) collaborated with him on the playful love song, which was introduced by John Boles in the nonmusical play *She Loves Me Not* (1933). When Bing Crosby sang it in the 1934 film version of the play, the song caught on. As the title indicates, the lyric is a play on words, and Schwartz's music is both mystifying and animated. Notable recordings were made by McKinney's Cotton Pickers, Ray Noble (vocal by Al Bowlly), and Don Redman.

"After I Say I'm Sorry (What Can I Say?)" (1926) is a gentle ballad standard by Walter Donaldson and Abe Lyman that tearfully asks a lover to forgive and accept a heartfelt apology. Lyman and his Orchestra introduced the song, which has had many recordings over the years, including those by Josephine Baker, Pee Wee Russell, Ella Fitzgerald, Frank Sinatra, Bobby Hackett, Dinah Washington, Helen Forrest, Juanita Hall, Buddy Morrow, the Nat King Cole Trio, and more recently, Carol Sloane and John Pizzarelli. The ballad can be heard in the background in the films *Love Me or Leave Me* (1955) and *Pete Kelly's Blues* (1955).

"After My Laughter Came Tears" (1928) is a torchy ballad by Charles Tobias and Roy Turk about the sudden crash of emotions when a love affair ends. The song was introduced by organist Jesse Crawford but became popular because of a record by Cliff Edwards. Later there were notable discs by Big Miller, Bob Barnard, and Ray Charles.

"After the Ball" (1892) is arguably the most famous and most durable popular song to come out of the nineteenth century and one of the first Broadway songs to become a Tin Pan Alley hit. Charles K. Harris wrote the number for vaudevillian Sam Doctor to sing in his act, but the singer forgot the lengthy lyric the first time he attempted it, and the audience laughed him off the stage. Then Harris paid singing star J. Aldrich Libbey $500 to sing it in the Broadway hit *A Trip to Chinatown* (1891) when it played Milwaukee and bribed orchestra conductor Frank Palma a box of cigars to orchestrate it for her. According to Harris, the presentation of the song was followed by a moment of silence in which the desperate author thought he had failed again. But then the crowd burst into applause for five minutes and would not let the show go on without an encore. The ballad's popularity spread quickly (aided by Helene Mora's performance of it in vaudeville and John Philip Sousa playing it at the 1893 world's fair in Chicago), selling over 5 million copies of sheet music (the most ever sold yet for a song) and earning Harris $10 million. Although the memorable refrain is still known today, the long narrative verse is mostly forgotten, yet it was an important part of the song's popularity. Inspired by a quarreling couple that Harris observed as they parted company at a dance in Chicago, the lyric told of an old man who counsels his young niece in matters of love and explains to her why he never wed. Years earlier, at a fancy dress ball, he saw his sweetheart embrace and kiss another man, so he left the ball and never saw the woman again. It was only years later that he learned that the man was her long-lost brother. While the tale is typical of the sentimental story-ballads prevalent at the time, "After the Ball" has such an unpretentious sense of power that the thirty-two-bar refrain still entrances even without the sixty-four-bar verse. The language may be antique at times ("many a heart is aching"), but Harris's sweeping waltz melody has not dated. The number was added to every subsequent production of *A Trip to Chinatown* and is also included in every production of *Show Boat* (1927) as the number Magnolia (Norma Terris) sings on stage on New Year's Eve and launches her career. In the films of *Show Boat* it was sung by Irene Dunne in the 1936 version and Kathryn Grayson in the 1951 remake. The ballad was performed by Alice Faye in *Lillian Russell* (1940), Scotty Beckett in *The Jolson Story* (1946), and Gloria Jean in *There's a Girl in My Heart* (1950), as well as in the background of *Back in the Saddle* (1941), *Star!* (1968), and other period movies. Among the hundreds of recordings over the years, distinctive ones were made by the Knickerbocker Serenaders, Ace O'Donnell, the Blue Sky Boys, Frances Black,

Max Bygraves, William Bolcom and Joan Morris, the Banjo Kings, Guy Lombardo and the Royal Canadians, John Fahey, and Johnny Cash.

"After You Get What You Want, You Don't Want It" (1920) is Irving Berlin's wry commentary on worldly wishes that the team of Van and Schenck introduced in vaudeville and first recorded with great success. But most remember it from Marilyn Monroe's slinky interpretation in the film *There's No Business Like Show Business* (1954). The clever number has been recorded on occasion, most significantly by Nat King Cole.

"After You've Gone" (1918) is the early and highly influential jazz standard that remains an improvisation favorite for both singers and musicians. The African American team of Henry Creamer (lyric) and Turner Layton (music) wrote the short (only twenty measures long) but potent rhythm ballad that also has a touch of the blues in it. Creamer's lyric, a lover's plea to his honey not to leave because she'll regret it later, uses a Negro dialect in spots ("you'll miss the bestest friend you ever had") but is more concerned with simple and unadorned fervor. Turner's music contains accents that are of the beat so that the effect is both bluesy and sprightly. Marion Harris introduced the song with a recording in 1918, but it was Al Jolson who popularized it by singing the ballad at the Winter Garden Theatre. Later Bessie Smith, Sophie Tucker, Paul Whiteman and his Orchestra, and Louis Armstrong each made classic recordings of the number. Though never quite forgotten, "After You've Gone" was revived with a celebrated disc by the Benny Goodman Sextet, one of his first recordings. Other noteworthy records over the years were made by Fats Waller, Johnny Dodds, Mel Tormé and Cleo Laine, Joe Venuti, Teddy Wilson, Joe Williams, Jack Teagarden, Django Reinhardt, Lionel Hampton, and Gene Krupa. Linda Hopkins performed it in the Broadway musical bio *Me and Bessie* (1975), Thais Clark sang it in the Off-Broadway revue *One Mo' Time* (1979), and Hopkins reprised it with Bernard Manners in the Broadway show *Black and Blue* (1989). On screen it was performed by Gene Austin, Candy Candido, and Coco in *Sadie McKee* (1934), Marsha Hunt in *Unholy Partners* (1941), Judy Garland in *For Me and My Gal* (1942), Constance Moore in *Atlantic City* (1944), the Goodman Sextet in the animated *Make Mine Music* (1946), Jolson dubbing for Larry Parks in *Jolson Sings Again* (1949), Shirley MacLaine and a male trio in *Some Came Running* (1958), Armstrong in *The Five Pennies* (1959), and Leland Palmer in *All That Jazz* (1979), as well as on the soundtracks for *Git Along Little Doggies* (1937), *Ghost Catchers* (1944), *Paper Moon* (1973), and other films.

"Again" (1948) is a flowing ballad with a Latin flavor that Ida Lupino introduced in the film *Road House* (1948). Dorcas Cochran (lyric) and

Lionel Newman (music) wrote the catchy song in which a swain proclaims to a sweetheart that a love like theirs comes once in a lifetime and couldn't happen again. Vic Damone revived the ballad in 1954 with a record that sold over a million copies. Other discs were made by Doris Day, Mel Tormé, Gordon Jenkins (vocal by Joel Graydon), and Art Mooney (vocal by Johnny Martin and Madely Russell). The number can also be heard in the movies *Island in the Sun* (1957), *Best of Everything* (1959), and *Damnation Alley* (1977).

"Aggravatin' Papa (Don't You Try to Two Time Me)" (1922) is the caustic warning for amorous fidelity that Sophie Tucker, Bessie Smith, and Marion Harris popularized in the no-nonsense, tell-it-like-it-is manner in which they excelled. The sassy number was written by Roy Turk, J. Russel Robinson, and Addy Britt and was introduced by the Original Dixieland Jazz Band. Other notable recordings were made by Alberta Hunter, Lil Green, the Original Memphis Five, Fletcher Henderson, and Lizzie Miles.

"Ain't Misbehavin' " (1929) is the timeless jazz lament of a faithful lover who stays at home listening to the radio and is "savin' my love for you" even though the lusty music and the sly tone of voice make one question the sincerity of the sentiment. One of the song's distinctive qualities is its contagious use of changing harmonies and, as Gerald Bordman has written, its "plaintive undertones that hint at the stylings of much of the music that would come out of Broadway for the next few years." The famous rhythm ballad was written by Thomas "Fats" Waller, Harry Brooks (music), and Andy Razaf (lyric) for the nightclub show *Hot Chocolates* (1929), which was so popular it moved to Broadway, where it ran six months. Margaret Simms, Paul Bass, and Russell Wooding's Jubilee Singers sang the number, and in the orchestra pit was the young musician Louis Armstrong, making his New York debut, whose trumpet solo of the piece brought him recognition. Armstrong later recorded the song with Seger Ellis and his Orchestra, but the most popular disc was Waller's vocal and piano solo, and the number became his theme song. Other memorable records were made by Ruth Etting, Bill Robinson, Teddy Wilson, Kay Starr, Nat King Cole, Dinah Washington, the Three Suns, Helen Forrest, Sarah Vaughan, Eartha Kitt, Hank Williams Jr., Carol Channing, and Karen Akers. The number was included in several movies, including *Ain't Misbehavin'* (1955), and was sung by Waller in *Stormy Weather* (1943), Mary Beth Hughes in *Follow the Band* (1943), Armstrong in *Atlantic City* (1944), Dan Dailey in *You Were Meant for Me* (1948), Armstrong and Mickey Rooney in *The Strip* (1951), Jane Russell, Jeanne Crain (dubbed by Anita Ellis), and Alan Young in *Gentlemen Marry Brunettes* (1955), and

Burt Reynolds in *Lucky Lady* (1975). It was also performed on Broadway by the cast of the Waller revue *Ain't Misbehavin'* (1978).

"Ain't Nobody Here But Us Chickens" (1947) is a boogie-woogie gem by Alex Kramer and Joan Whitney that takes its title from an old joke about a thief in the hen house. The farcical lyric describes the sounds coming from a chicken coop ("don't point that gun!") when a farmer goes to investigate noises from the hen house one night. Both the lyric ("hobble, hobble, hobble") and the furious music have all the chaos of clucking hens. A recording by Louis Jordan and his Typami Five popularized the comic ditty, and there were also discs by Phil Harris, B.B. King, Sanford Clark, James Brown, Pat Boone, and more recently, Lisa Stansfield, Mark Murphy, and Patti LuPone. In the Broadway revue *Five Guys Named Moe* (1992) it was performed by Kevin Ramsey and Milton Craig Nealy.

"Ain't She Sweet?" (1927) is one of those carefree and naively silly love songs from the 1920s that captures the era's frivolity. Milton Ager composed the Charleston-like music, and Jack Yellen provided the slaphappy lyric, a series of rhetorical questions about the fine qualities of his dearie. The short lyric phrases sit on the dancing music beautifully and the famous near-rhyme "I ask you very confidentially" is inspired daffiness. Paul Ash and his Orchestra introduced the song in a Chicago nightclub, and Ben Bernie and his Orchestra made the first recording, but the number really caught on when Lillian Roth, Eddie Cantor, Sophie Tucker, Annette Hanshaw, and other stars sang it on the vaudeville circuit. Over a million copies of sheet music were sold, and it was a favorite in clubs, college campuses, and at dances. Interest in the number was revived in the 1940s because of a hit recording by Jimmie Lunceford and his Orchestra, and two decades later it was a Top 20 hit for the Beatles. Other estimable recordings over the years include those by the Dixie Stompers with Fletcher Henderson, Paul Whiteman's Rhythm Boys (including a young Bing Crosby), Harry Richman, Gene Austin, Bob Hannon and Johnny Ryan, Benny Carter, Tiny Hill, Les Brown, Harry James, Bunny Berigan, Bob Wilson and his Varsity Rhythm Boys, Jive Bunny and the Mastermixers, Mel Powell, Frankie Lyman and the Teenagers, and Fabian. Dan Dailey, Jeanne Crain, and Barbara Lawrence sang it in the film *You Were Meant for Me* (1948), Eddie Duchin played it on the soundtrack of *The Eddy Duchin Story* (1956), and it was heard in the background in a handful of movies, including *Margie* (1946) and *Picnic* (1955). On Broadway, it was performed by Desiree Coleman, Mel Johnson Jr., and the ensemble of the musical *Big Deal* (1986).

"Ain't That a Shame" (1955) is a crossover hit that Antoine "Fats" Domino had in the rhythm-and-blues field, but it was even more popular when Pat Boone had a chart hit with it in the pop category, his first success and the one that launched his career. Domino collaborated with Dave Bartholomew on the rhythmic lament about lost love ("you said goodbye . . . ain't that a shame!"). The Four Seasons revived the number in 1963, and the group Cheap Trick had success with it in 1979. Other records include those by Roy Eldridge, Ella Mae Morse, Frankie Valli, Max Morath, Ronnie Hawkins, Ike and Tina Turner, Hank Williams Jr., Charlie Rich, and the Dells. Domino sang it in the film *Shake, Rattle and Rock!* (1956), and his recording was heard in *American Graffiti* (1973). The song is sometimes listed as "Ain't It a Shame."

"Ain't We Got Fun" (1921) is a Roaring Twenties favorite and a vibrant archetype of the decade with its zesty music and ridiculous lyric. Richard A. Whiting was the composer, and Gus Kahn and Raymond B. Egan penned the carefree exclamation of a young couple enjoying the high life even as the bill collector is knocking at their door. The classic line "the rich get rich and the poor get children" is particularly funny because the previous rhyme causes the listener to expect the word "poorer" at the end of the phrase. Arthur West introduced the number in a satirical stage revue, but it was the vaudeville team of Van and Schenck that popularized it, along with Billy Jones, Ruth Roye, Eddie Cantor, and others in variety. The ditty was applauded again in the 1950s because of its interpolation in a handful of movie musicals. Doris Day and Danny Thomas sang it in the Kahn bio *I'll See You in My Dreams* (1951), Day reprised it with Gordon MacRae and Russell Arms in *By the Light of the Silvery Moon* (1953), and Cantor sang it on the soundtrack for *The Eddie Cantor Story* (1953). "Ain't We Got Fun" was also used in the background to set the period in many films, most memorably *On Moonlight Bay* (1951) and *The Great Gatsby* (1974), and it was sung by the casts of the Broadway musicals *A Day in Hollywood—A Night in the Ukraine* (1980) and *Big Deal* (1986). Al Jolson, Carmen Cavallaro, Margaret Whiting, Debbie Reynolds, Peggy Lee, Rex Stewart, Ray Noble (vocal by Al Bowlly), Mitch Miller and, most recently, Jessica Molasky, are among the many who recorded the vivacious song.

"Alabamy Bound" (1925) was a favorite railroad song that, like many 1920s tunes, used a southern dialect filled with affection for back home. Ray Henderson wrote the spirited music, and B.G. DeSylva and Bud Green penned the lyric about a southbound train. Al Jolson, Eddie Cantor, and Blossom Seeley featured the song in their acts, and before long it had sold over a million copies of sheet music. Both Jolson and Cantor later recorded it, as did Fletcher Henderson, Bing Crosby, the Banjo

Kings, Bob Crosby and his Orchestra, Lucille Hegamin, Jo Ann Castle, Sonny Criss, Dean Martin, Bobby Darin, and Ray Charles. The Ink Spots sang it in the movie *The Great American Broadcast* (1941), then the Nicholas Brothers danced to it. The number was also heard in the films *Broadway* (1942), *Babes on Broadway* (1942), *Is Everybody Happy?* (1943), *Show Business* (1944), and *With a Song in My Heart* (1952). "Alabamy Bound" was also associated with the beloved singer Nora Bayes, who sang it at a 1928 benefit at the Bowery Mission House in New York. It was her last public appearance; four days later she died.

"Alexander's Ragtime Band" (1911) was not only the most famous song in America in its day, but it did more than perhaps any other tune to change the direction of popular music. Irving Berlin wrote a ragtime ditty called "Alexander and His Clarinet" (music by Ted Snyder) in 1910 but discarded it except for a few of the lyric phrases. Instead of making it a rag, Berlin rewrote the number as a syncopated piece *about* ragtime and wrote a terse lyric encouraging all to go and listen to a fictitious bandleader who was all the rage. Berlin intended the song for the annual *Friar's Frolic* but instead submitted it to some vaudeville performers, all of whom rejected it. The number was finally played at the Columbia Burlesque House, but no one seemed to notice it. It was not until Emma Carus performed it in a Chicago vaudeville theatre that it started to catch on, thanks also to vaudeville turns by Eddie Miller, Helen Vincent, Ethel Levey, and Sophie Tucker. Within a month over a million copies of sheet music were sold, and soon it was being played in theatres, restaurants, dance halls, and concert houses across America and in Europe as well. This widespread popularity in a day before radio was unprecedented, and Berlin became the most famous songwriter in the country, a position he held for decades. As many (including Berlin) have pointed out over the years, the song is not a true ragtime. There is some syncopation in the music, but it is more of a march with plenty of breathing space in the notes and the lyric to make it easily sung. The verse and refrain are beautifully balanced, and despite the often-cited complaint that Berlin only writes in one key, the verse starts in C major and ends in C minor, then shifts into F major for the refrain. This was one of the earliest pop songs to change keys when moving from verse to refrain, and the effect is still potent. Philip Furia has pointed out that although the music is not ragtime, "the *words* are ragged." For example, Berlin changes the accent on the word "natural" in order to rhyme with "call." The lyric pays homage to Stephen Foster's "Old Folks at Home" with a reference to the Swanee River and even echoes other nineteenth-century ballads. But there is nothing sentimental or nostalgic about "Alexander's Ragtime Band." It swings and sways as few songs do and remains a captivating piece of popular music. Arthur Collins and Bryon Harlan were the first to record the song, followed by such classic discs as those by Prince's Orchestra in 1912, Bessie Smith in 1927, the Boswell Sisters in 1935, Louis Armstrong in 1937, Bing Crosby and Connee Boswell in 1938, and Crosby and Al Jolson in 1947. Other significant records were made by Johnny Mercer with the Pied Pipers, the Andrews Sisters, Bunk Johnson's New Orleans Band, Benny Goodman, Miff Mole and Red Nichols, the Hoosier Hot Shots, Judy Garland, Julie Andrews, Al Goodman, and more recently, Michael Feinstein and Mandy Patinkin. On screen, the song was performed by Alice Faye in *Alexander's Ragtime Band* (1938) and Ethel Merman, Dan Dailey, Donald O'Connor, Johnnie Ray, and Mitzi Gaynor in *There's No Business Like Show Business* (1954), as well as in the background of many movies, most recently *Titanic* (1997).

"All Alone" (1924) is a torchy love song by Irving Berlin and one of his autobiographical ballads that mesmerize with their simplicity. So upset about not being able to marry heiress Ellin MacKay because of her family's animosity, Berlin penned this straightforward lament about a lover who pines for his sweetheart and wonders if she is as lonely as he is. The song was interpolated in the 1924 edition of the *Music Box Revue* on Broadway, where it was performed by Oscar Shaw and Grace Moore singing on telephones on opposite sides of the stage. But it was tenor John McCormack's singing the ballad on the radio that propelled it to hit status, selling a million copies of sheet music and 160,000 player piano rolls. Al Jolson, Paul Whiteman, Abe Lyman, Judy Garland, Red Garland, Artie Shaw, Frank Sinatra, Connee Boswell, Doris Day, Thelonious Monk, and Pat Boone are among the many who had successful records of the song. "All Alone" was sung on screen by Alice Faye in *Alexander's Ragtime Band* (1938) and by Bing Crosby and the chorus in *Blue Skies* (1946).

"All By Myself" (1921) is an early Irving Berlin ballad and one of his biggest hits of the decade. The lyric is a lament of a lonely soul who plays solitaire and watches the clock on the shelf. Charles King introduced the number at the Palace Theatre in New York, and Ted Lewis and Frank Crumit were the first to record it. Sheet music sales went into the millions, and over 150,000 piano rolls were also sold. Notable recordings over the years include those by Bob Wills, Ella Fitzgerald, Fats Domino, the McGuire Sisters, Gene Krupa, Connie Francis, Della Reese, Shirley Bassey, and more recently, David Osborne and Michael Ball. Bing Crosby crooned the ballad in the film *Blue Skies* (1946).

"All Coons Look Alike to Me" (1896) is a classic example of a "coon song," Negro folk tunes that were popular in the nineteenth century, and one that is quite accomplished despite its unfortunate title. In fact, if the word "coons" was replaced by "men," it remains a clever protestation by an African American woman that all of her persistent suitors hand her the same old line. (The number was originally titled "All Pimps Look Alike to Me.") The song was written by Ernest Hogan, an educated black vaudevillian who first performed it on stage, and it was soon picked up by white singers (as most "coon songs" were). But years later Hogan stated that he regretted ever writing the song because it was wrongly interpreted to mean that all African Americans were facially the same. A very early and rather primitive recording was made by Len Spenser in 1897.

"All I Have to Do Is Dream" (1958) is the harmonizing ballad that the Everly Brothers had great success with in the late 1950s. Boudleaux Bryant, a classically trained violinist who toyed around with pop music, wrote the soothing number about having a darling in one's arms just by dreaming it; but the poor suitor finds that he is dreaming his life away. Every few years the song was revived with a new record of note: Richard Chamberlain in 1963, Glen Campbell and Bobbie Gentry in 1970, the Nitty Gritty Dirt Band in 1975, and Andy Gibb and Victoria Principal in 1981. There were other recordings by Gary Lewis and the Playboys, the Persuasions, Roy Orbison, Frankie Avalon, Jan and Dean, Billie Jo Spears, Linda Ronstadt, and the Lettermen. Juice Newton sang it in the film *Shoot the Moon* (1988), and the Everly recording was heard in *Stealing Home* (1988).

"All I Want for Christmas (Is My Two Front Teeth)" (1946) was a novelty hit in the postwar years and still shows up occasionally at Christmastime. Donald Gardner wrote the seriocomic lament of a kid whose two front baby teeth have fallen out and are not yet replaced with adult teeth; the child is tired of lisping and hopes to be able to whistle once again. The innocent complaint appealed to a war-weary public and was very popular. It was introduced by the Satisfiers on Perry Como's radio show, and before long, everyone was singing it. Noteworthy records were made by Jive Bunny and the Mastermixers, Ray Charles, the Chipmunks, George Strait, Nat King Cole, and the Andrews Sisters with Danny Kaye. Ironically, the biggest seller of all was a parody version by Spike Jones and his City Slickers, which climbed to the top of the charts. The number is sometimes listed as "My Two Front Teeth."

"All My Love" (1950) is a gushing ballad based on Ravel's *Bolero* with a French lyric by Henri Coutet that promises total and exclusive affection forever after. Mitchell Parish did the English lyric, and Paul Durand adapted Ravel's lengthy composition into a standard pop song format. Jacqueline Francois introduced the number, but it was Patti Page's hit record that popularized it in America. Other discs were made by Andy Russell, Bing Crosby, Doris Day, Cliff Richard, Dinah Shore, Bobby Hackett, Dick Haymes, Big Miller, the Four Tops, Vikki Carr, and the orchestras of Billy Vaughn, Guy Lombardo, and Percy Faith.

"All of Me" (1931) is a gently swinging song of surrender that offers heart, soul, and body to a loved one. The Seymour Simons (lyric) and Gerald Marks (music) number manages to be upbeat even though there is something alarmingly defeatist about the offer. The very casualness of the recurring line "why not take all of me?" makes the lyric distinctive, and Marks's music is restrained even while seeming expansive. Vaudevillian Belle Baker introduced the song, but early recordings by Paul Whiteman (vocal by Mildred Bailey) and Louis Armstrong, as well as its use in the background of the film *Careless Lady* (1932), helped make it widely known. It enjoyed a modest revival with Count Basie's 1943 record and with Johnnie Ray's 1952 disc, but it was Frank Sinatra's rendition of "All of Me" in the movie *Meet Danny Wilson* (1952) that made it more popular than ever. (Sinatra's record at the time was the most successful of all the versions.) Other artists who made prominent discs include Kate Smith, Russ Columbo, Connee Boswell, Martha Tilton, Nick Lucas, Jimmy Dorsey and his Orchestra (vocal by Helen O'Connell), Duke Ellington, Louis Jordan, Frankie Laine, Billie Holiday, Charlie Parker, Billy Eckstine, the King Sisters, Tony Bennett, Dean Martin, and Willie Nelson. Gloria DeHaven sang it in the film *Down Among the Sheltering Palms* (1953), Diana Ross performed it in the Holiday bio *Lady Sings the Blues* (1972), and it was featured in *Bird* (1988) and *Sweet and Lowdown* (1999). In the Broadway revue *Swing!* (1999) "All of Me" was sung by Everett Bradley and Ann Hampton Callaway.

"All of My Life" (1944) is a simple, heartfelt ballad by Irving Berlin that expressed the yearning for domestic bliss that preoccupied war-weary Americans. The penchant lyric pleads for "the right" to take care of and love one for the rest of their lives, hoping to make their world "as simple as a nursery rhyme." Kate Smith introduced and popularized the ballad, and there were also noteworthy records by Bing Crosby (with John Scott Trotter's Orchestra), the Three Suns, Sammy Kaye (vocal by Billy Williams), Harry James, Tony Bennett, Sarah Vaughan, and more recently, Andrea Marcovicci.

"All or Nothing at All" (1940) is the fervent appeal for uncompromising love that Jack Lawrence and Arthur Altman wrote with the hope of selling it to one of the Big Bands. Harry James liked it and recorded it with his contracted vocalist Frank Sinatra, but the record failed to sell. Two years later, after Sinatra had gone solo and was the nation's hearthrob, the James record was rereleased, and it sold over a million copies. Sinatra would sing the ballad throughout his career and recorded it on three other occasions. Joe Foley's disc in 1954 revived interest in the song. Other significant records were made by June Christy, Jimmy Dorsey, Chet Baker, Dick Haymes, Al Hibbler, the Frank Wess Quartet, John Coltrane, Billie Holiday, George Shearing, Billy Daniels, and recently, Diana Krall, Robert Habermann, and Bobby Caldwell. "All or Nothing at All" was heard in the films *Doughboys in Ireland* (1943), *Weekend Pass* (1944), where the Delta Rhythm Boys performed it, *This Is the Life* (1944), and *Missing* (1982), where a Bob Eberly recording was heard.

"All the Things You Are" (1939) was chosen as the all-time favorite song by a poll of American composers in 1964, and the decades since then have done little to diminish the high opinion people have of it. Oscar Hammerstein (lyric) and Jerome Kern (music) wrote it for the Broadway musical *Very Warm for May* (1939), which only managed to run fifty-nine performances, but the ballad gradually caught on and has become a beloved standard. It is a straightforward love song that praises the qualities of one's intended, yet the perfect blending of words and music make it exceptional. Hammerstein's lyric is enthrallingly romantic ("you are the promised gift of springtime") without crossing over into mawkishness, while Kern's music is ingenious and boldly adventurous. Kern wrote the odd but effective key and tempo changes for his own satisfaction and often stated that he never thought the song could become popular because it was too complex for the layman's ear. Yet the melodic line captivates even as one is aware of its strangeness. As James R. Morris explains, the refrain "flows gently downward for a full sixteen bars," the bridge provides "relief from the long-breathed principal theme," and the conclusion is "wonderfully satisfying . . . rounded off in a four-bar tag that is passionate and climatic." The ballad was sung by a quartet (Hiram Sherman, Frances Mercer, Hollace Shaw, and Ralph Stuart) in the Broadway show, but usually it is performed as a solo, most of the great singers having sung it sometime in their career. The song remained on the *Hit Parade* for eleven weeks, and its sheet music and record sales remain healthy to this day. Among the many memorable recordings are those by Gordon MacRae, Dick Haymes, Ella Fitzgerald, Frank Sinatra, Betty Johnson, Helen Forrest, Zoot Sims, Artie Shaw, Tommy Dorsey (vocal by Jack Leonard), Charlie Parker, Art Pepper, Dave Brubeck, Frankie Masters, Jessye Norman, and more recently, Ann Hampton Callaway, Scott Hamilton, and José Carreras. *Very Warm for May* was turned into the film musical *Broadway Rhythm* (1944) where Ginny Simms performed the ballad, Tony Martin crooned it in the Kern bio *Till the Clouds Roll By* (1946), and Mario Lanza sang it in *Because You're Mine* (1952).

"All This and Heaven Too" (1939) is a gushing ballad written by Eddie DeLange (lyric) and Jimmy Van Heusen (music) as a promotion song for the 1939 Bette Davis film of the same name. Early recordings by Jimmy Dorsey (vocal by Bob Eberly), Tommy Dorsey (vocal by Frank Sinatra), and Charlie Barnet (vocal by Larry Taylor) made it well known, and over the years it has appealed to a variety of artists. DeLange's lyrics might be a bit lofty, but Van Heusen's rhythmic music, according to Alec Wilder, "does pleasant, unstartling as well as unexpected things." Mel Tormé, Dick Todd, Gene Krupa, Duke Ellington, Ellyn Rucker, Lew Tabackin, and Bucky and John Pizzarelli are among those with distinctive recordings of the ballad.

"Aloha Oe" (1878) is probably the most famous song to come out of Hawaii; a few bars of it played in a movie or a show still conjures up visions of the tropical islands. Queen Liliuokalani of Hawaii, the islands' last reigning monarch, wrote the enticing number, which took three decades before it became popular in the States. "Aloha" means both hello and good-bye in Hawaiian, but the phrase "Aloha Oe" translates best as "Farewell to Thee," which is sometimes used as the song's title. The lyric fervently hopes to return someday not only to one's inamorato but to the islands themselves. Recordings early in the new century made the song familiar by 1908, and of all the discs made later, Bing Crosby's was the bestselling one. Harry Owens and his Orchestra, the Brothers Cazimero, Billy Vaughn, Joe "Fingers" Carr, Burl Ives, Enoch Light, Les Paul, Arthur Lyman, Dorothy Lamour, Don Ho, Andy Williams, Kim Kahuna and the Royal Palms Orchestra, and countless other Hawaiian bands have recorded the song. It was sung on screen by Bobby Breen in *Hawaii Calls* (1938), Jeanette MacDonald in *I Married an Angel* (1942), and Elvis Presley in *Blue Hawaii* (1962).

"Along the Navajo Trail" (1942) is a cowboy song that paints a bucolic picture of the west, yet it was written by Hollywood songwriters for the movies. Larry Marks and Dick Charles collaborated on a pseudocowboy ballad called "Prairie Parade" for the film *Laugh Your Blues Away* (1942). Lyricist Eddie DeLange rewrote the lyric as "Along the Navajo Trail," about a cowboy on the trail who sits by a fire at night and listens to the music of nature such as the blowing wind and the calling of the coyotes. Roy Rogers introduced the revised song in the movie *Don't Fence Me In* (1945), and it immediately found favor. Rogers crooned it again in *Along the Navajo Trail* (1945), and Gene Autry sang it in *The Blazing Sun* (1950). A hit recording by Bing Crosby with the Andrews Sisters helped propel the ballad to hit status, followed by notable records by Autry, Dinah Shore, Glenn Miller, Gene Krupa, Buddy Stewart, Sammy Kaye, Frankie Laine, Bob Wills and his Texas Playboys, and Johnny Bond.

"Along the Santa Fe Trail" (1940), which predates its companion piece "Along the Navajo Trail," is both a love song and a tribute to the beauty of the western frontier. Will Grosz composed the flowing music, and Al Dubin and Edwina Coolidge collaborated on the lyric that compares the beauty of the canyon and the desert (which angels supposedly painted at night) to that of his sweetheart whom he wishes was riding alongside him on the trail. It was first used in the background of the film *Santa Fe Trail* (1940), but when Glenn Miller (vocal by Ray Eberly) recorded it, the ballad was in demand. Bing Crosby, Sammy Kaye, Dick Jurgens, Artie Shaw, Guy Lombardo, Johnny Desmond, and Earl Hines were among the many who recorded it. Once "Along the Navajo Trail" hit the charts, the original "trail" song was interpolated into the western movie *Song on the Range* (1944) to remind audiences of its earlier success.

"Always" (1925), one of Irving Berlin's most cherished ballads, was written sometime in the early 1920s and put in the proverbial trunk until the songwriter pulled it out to use in the Marx Brothers' Broadway musical *The Cocoanuts* (1925). But director George S. Kaufman disliked the ballad (he mockingly referred to it as "I'll be loving you—Thursday"), and back into the trunk it went. When Berlin finally got to marry heiress Ellin MacKay in 1926, he presented the song (and any future royalties) to his bride. It turned out to be quite a profitable wedding present. While the facile lyric and the lazy waltzlike music strike some as mawkish, the song does have a unique and unexpected shift from F major to A major in the eleventh measure that is far from routine. Belle Baker, Gladys Clark and Henry Bergman introduced the number in vaudeville, and it was soon heard in clubs, records, and later on the radio. Early discs were made by Vincent Lopez, George Olsen, Nick Lucas, and Henry Burr, and the song enjoyed a big revival in the 1940s, thanks to Big Band records by Benny Goodman, Gordon Jenkins, Guy Lombardo, and Sammy Kaye. Other artists who have recorded it with success include Deanna Durbin, Eileen Farrell, Erroll Garner, Ruby Braff, Dinah Shore, the Ink Spots, Grace Moore, Sarah Vaughan, Rosemary Clooney, Pat Boone, and more recently, Mandy Patinkin, Andrea Marcovicci, and Michael Feinstein with Liza Minnelli. Betty Avery sang it with Ray Noble's Orchestra in the film *The Pride of the Yankees* (1942), Durbin performed it in *Christmas Holiday* (1944), and it was done as a choral number in *Blue Skies* (1946). "Always" is also heard in every production of Noel Coward's comedy classic *Blithe Spirit* (1941), where it is used as a running joke throughout the play.

"Amapola (Pretty Little Poppy)" (1924) is a captivating Spanish song by Joseph M. Lacalle that was first published in America in 1924 but found celebrity when Albert Gamse wrote an English lyric comparing one's lover to a flower. The new version was introduced by Deanna Durbin in the movie *First Love* (1939). A 1940 recording by Jimmy Dorsey (vocals by Helen O'Connell and Bob Eberly) went to the top of the charts, and the song was on *Your Hit Parade* for nineteen weeks. Dorsey performed it in the film *The Fleet's In* (1942), and it was also heard in *Can't Help Singing* (1944) and *Saddle Pals* (1947). The ballad was recorded by Gene Autry, Doris Day with Les Brown's Band, Connee Boswell, Mantovanni's Orchestra, Xavier Cugat (vocal by Carmen Castillo), José Carreras, Placido Domingo, and many Spanish singers and bands.

"Amazing Grace" (c. 1779) is the traditional hymn favorite that crossed over to become a prominent success on Tin Pan Alley as well. While the tune itself is centuries old and has been traced to various sources, the lyric that has come down to us was written by John Newton, a British navy deserter and slave ship captain who discovered the Scriptures late in life and became a minister. Newton arranged the music and penned the lyric about rebirth and a new life that "saved a wretch like me." The five stanzas explored the different ways God turned his life around (he was like a blind man, now he can see; he was lost, now he is found), and the simple, unadorned words have found their place in many different kinds of churches. The hymn was particularly popular at revivals and tent meetings in the nineteenth century, but it survived throughout the twentieth century on hundreds of recordings and such variations as a swing version, Hawaiian version, and Scottish and Welsh bagpipe versions. The revival song had a revival of its own in 1971 when Judy Collins's recording climbed the charts, and the next year a disc by the Royal Scots Dragon Guards (solo by Tony Crease) was in the Top 20. It has been heard in movies as diverse as *Alice's Restaurant* (1969), *Coal Miner's Daughter* (1980), and *Gettysburg* (1993). Among the distinctive records made over the years are those by Mahalia Jackson, Al Hirt, Vera Lynn, Paul Robeson, Odetta, Lawrence Welk, Charlie Rich, Diana Ross, George Beverly Shea, LeAnn Rimes, Glen Campbell, Joan Baez, Phil Coulter, Jim Nabors, and Rod Stewart.

"America" (1832) is more familiarly known by its opening phrase "My Country 'Tis of Thee," and in the days when every school day began with singing it, it was the most performed song in America, even surpassing "Happy Birthday." The music has been traced to the German hymn "Heil, Dir im Siegerkranz," which later became the British anthem "God Save the King" (lyric attributed to Henry Carey), but its new American lyric is well documented. Samuel Francis Smith, a student at the Andover Theological Seminary, was asked to write a simple song for a children's chorus to perform. Going through a book of old hymns, Smith came across the original German song and, not knowing it had become a British anthem, used the melody for his heartfelt lyric celebrating the homeland, from its mountains to its forefathers, coining the expression "Pilgrims' Pride" along the way. The new song was first sung by children in Boston's Park Street Church on Independence Day 1832 and was published later that year in a collection of church music. It would eventually be sung at other patriotic gatherings, memorials, graduations, funerals, army camps, war bond rallies, and of course, schools across the land. Recordings over the years have mostly been by choral groups, such as the Mormon Tabernacle Choir, and church singers, such as Mahalia Jackson. "America" has been played in the background of many films for patriotic flavor, and it was given a warm rendition by the cloth cast of *The Muppet Movie* (1979).

"America the Beautiful" (1895) has a history that is quite the opposite of its patriotic companion "America" in that the lyric was written first, and it took years before an appropriate melody was found to go with it. During an 1893 visit to the western states, poet Katherine Lee Bates was inspired by the view from Pike's Peak and put her thoughts down in a poem that was printed in a Boston periodical in 1895. Several people put the poem to music over the next few years, but the most satisfying was a theme from Samuel A. Ward's concert piece "Materna." The resulting song became popular in the new century, selling plenty of sheet music and being recorded for the first time in 1925 by Louise Homer. Bates's images throughout the song are highly poetic ("amber waves of grain") yet make for a singable lyric as well. In addition to many military bands and choral recordings, there have been distinctive recordings by Frank Sinatra, Tony Sarno, Charlie Rich, Boxcar Willie, Gene Autry, Ray Charles, George Beverly Shea, Elvis Presley, and even the Chipmunks. Jane Froman provided the singing voice for Susan Hayward in the Froman movie bio *With a Song in My Heart* (1952), and Haley Mills and the chorus sang it in *Pollyanna* (1960). The patriotic ballad was also sung by Lynn Thigpen and the cast in the Broadway revue *Tintypes* (1980).

"Among My Souvenirs" (1927) is a flowing ballad that, according to John S. Wilson, "raised the sentimental song from the maudlin depths in which it had been wallowing in the few years before." British publisher Lawrence Wright composed the graceful music under the pen name of Horatio Nicholls, and American lyricist Edgar Leslie wrote the sorrowful lyric in which a spurned lover is left to look through the souvenirs of memory. While it is filled with self-pity, the voice of the lonely one is more reflective and knowing than pathetic. The standard was introduced in Great Britain by Jack Hylton and his Orchestra and in America by Paul Whiteman (vocals by Jack Fulton, Charles Gaylord, and Austin Young) whose recording was a hit. There were also early discs

by Ben Selvin, the Revelers, and Roger Wolfe Kahn, with successful re-
vival records by Connie Francis in 1959 and a country version by Marty
Robbins in 1976. Other recordings include those by Louis Armstrong,
Helen Humes, Joni James, Slim Whitman, Judy Garland, Frank Sinatra,
Vera Lynn, the Lennon Sisters, Vic Damone, and Burl Ives. "Among My
Souvenirs" figured predominantly in the background in the film *Paris*
(1929), and Hoagy Carmichael sang it in *The Best Years of Our Lives* (1946).

"Anchors Aweigh" (1906), the rousing fight song that encourages one to
set sail and attack the enemy, is the official anthem of the U.S. Naval
Academy, and hearing a few bars of it played immediately brings to
mind the navy itself. Alfred Hart Miles, a cadet in the class of 1907, wrote
the vigorous lyric, and Royal Lovell collaborated with Charles A. Zimmerman, bandmaster at the Annapolis campus, on the pulsating march
music, which was written for the Army-Navy football game of 1906. For
years it was only heard at football games, not getting published until
1926 even though the U.S. Navy Band first recorded it in 1921. The anthem reached its peak of popularity during World War Two but still
remains one of the most recognized of patriotic songs. Paul Tremaine
and his Orchestra was the first nonmilitary group to record it, and they
were followed by many marching bands and versions by Bob Crosby,
Rudy Vallee, the Firehouse Five Plus Two, the Robert Shaw Chorale,
Glenn Miller, and others. Heard on the soundtrack of many war films,
"Anchors Aweigh" was also sung by Nelson Eddy and the chorus in
Rosalie (1937), a choral version was conducted by José Iturbi in *Anchors
Aweigh* (1945), and Eileen Farrell provided the vocals for Eleanor Parker
in *Interrupted Melody* (1955).

"And the Angels Sing" (1939) is an entrancing ballad about angels re-
acting to two lovers, Johnny Mercer's delicate lyric repeating the title
phrase throughout with great effect. The song had started out as an instrumental piece by trumpet player Ziggy Elman called "Fralich in
Swing," and the composer recorded it. But it was Mercer's lyric that
made the number soar, and a recording by Benny Goodman (vocal by
Martha Tilton, trumpet solo by Elman) brought the song wide recognition, putting it on *Your Hit Parade* for twelve weeks. Sixteen years later,
Goodman, Tilton, and Elman reprised their performance in the movie
bio *The Benny Goodman Story* (1956). In the meantime, there had been
dozens of recordings, including memorable ones by Bing Crosby, Glenn
Miller, Jan Savitt (vocal by Bon Bon), Louis Armstrong, Les Brown,
Count Basie (vocal by Helen Humes), and Mercer himself. Later discs
were made by Lawrence Welk, Elaine Stritch, Steve Lawrence and Eydie
Gorme, Ella Fitzgerald, Louis Prima and Keely Smith, Herb Alpert and
the Tijuana Brass, and Barry Manilow. "And the Angels Sing" was also

featured on Broadway in the Mercer revue *Dream* (1997). The song was always a particular favorite of Mercer's, so the title phrase is inscribed on his tombstone in his native Savannah, Georgia.

"Angelina (The Waitress at the Pizzeria)" (1944) is a catchy Italian-flavored number that also has a bit of boogie-woogie to it. Allan Roberts and Doris Fisher wrote the bubbly song in which a beau keeps ordering different kinds of Italian food at a restaurant so that he can be near the waitress Angelina, whom he adores. Despite the merry list of all the menu items he orders, she "never listens to my song." Louis Prima's playful recording popularized the number, and there have also been discs by Harry Belafonte, Joe Venuti, Herb Alpert, Mel Tormé, the Braxton Brothers, and Jimmy Rosselli. The amusing ditty can also be heard in the film *People Are Funny* (1946).

"Angry" (1923) is the terse title for a pleasing, rhythmic love song by Dudley Mecum (lyric), Jules Cassard, and Henry and Merritt Brunies (music) in which a wooer pleads with his beloved one not to be angry about his looking at another girl. The number was introduced with a recording by the New Orleans Rhythm Kings with Jelly Roll Morton at the piano, but acclaim came with a disc by Ted Lewis and his Orchestra with Art Gillham on the keys. A decade later it was revived with a hit record by Bob Crosby and his Orchestra, to be followed by estimable discs by Tiny Hill and his Orchestra in 1939 (Hill made it his theme song) and Kay Starr in 1951. Other artists who recorded "Angry" include Perry Como, Ray Miller, Bob Scobey's Frisco Band, Earl Hines, Rosemary Clooney, the Moms and Dads, the Buffalo Bills, Muggsy Spanier, and Ray Anthony with Kenny Trimble.

"Any Bonds Today?" (1941) is a patriotic song by Irving Berlin that flourished during the war years and then disappeared as its timeliness wore off. The genial number that encourages Americans to buy savings bonds to help the war effort ("scrape up the most you can") was introduced by Barry Wood on the radio and became the official song of the U.S. Treasury Department's bond campaign. It was sung all over (even Bugs Bunny, using the voice of Mel Blanc, sang it in cartoons), and there was a popular recording by the Andrews Sisters with Jimmy Dorsey's Orchestra. Duke Ellington and Jack Mudurian also made noteworthy discs and Bing Crosby sang it in the Berlin-scored movie musical *Blue Skies* (1946). Berlin updated the lyric throughout the war to include recent developments, including a 1942 version called "Any Bombs Today?"

"April in Paris" (1932) is an intoxicating ballad that magically combines the love for a city with the realization that the love for a person is what makes springtime and Paris so special. Vernon Duke wrote the music, which is boldly different from the usual song format both melodically and harmonically, especially with its sudden key changes in the opening section. E.Y. Harburg penned the beguiling lyric that uses short, haiku-like phrases to paint a picture with a series of specific and unforgettable images, such as clusters of cafe tables and blossoming chestnut trees. There are few rhymes in the lyric, and those that are there are quiet and understated. The song was written for the Broadway revue *Walk a Little Faster* (1932), where it was introduced by Evelyn Hoey, but it got little attention, probably because Hoey had laryngitis on opening night and barely got through the number. It wasn't until chanteuse Marion Chase and others began to perform it in clubs or early records were made by Marion Harris, Freddy Martin, and Henry King that it went on to become one of the most popular ballads of the 1930s. "April in Paris" enjoyed a revival in 1951 when Count Basie's jazz version was a hit, and the number became a favorite of jazz musicians. Other memorable records were made by Rosemary Clooney, Ella Fitzgerald and Oscar Peterson, Bill Evans, Artie Shaw, Frank Sinatra, Joe Pass, Pete Fountain, Gloria Lynne, the Sauter-Finnegan Orchestra, Stan Kenton, Charlie Parker, and Thelonious Monk. The ballad was used in the film *Countdown* (1968), Parker's recording was heard on the soundtrack of his bio *Bird* (1988), and the song was sung by Doris Day in *April in Paris* (1952), Ann Blyth (dubbed by Gogi Grant) in *The Helen Morgan Story* (1957), and Bob Hope in *Paris Holiday* (1958).

"Are You Havin' Any Fun?" (1939) is a lively song of celebration that echoed the festive temperament of the nation as the depression was waning. Sammy Fain composed the spirited music, and Jack Yellen wrote the playful lyric that asks a rich man why he is worrying about everything and not enjoying life with all his money. The number was introduced by Ella Logan in the Broadway revue *George White's Scandals* (1939), and later in the show it was reprised by the Kim Loo Sisters, the Three Stooges, and a chorus of girls with the lyric printed on their hats so that the audience could join and sing along. Major recordings of the song were made by Logan, Tommy Dorsey (vocal by Edythe Wright), Lee Wiley, Elaine Stritch, Tony Bennett with Count Basie's Orchestra, and Fain himself.

"Are You Lonesome Tonight?" (1927) is a straightforward love song that takes the form of a letter asking a sweetheart after they have parted if one is missed. Roy Turk and Lou Handman collaborated on the ballad, which is sentimental without a trace of cynicism in either words or music. Vaughn Deleath introduced the song with a hit record, followed by early discs by Henry Burr and Little Jack Little. Blue Barron and his

Orchestra revived the ballad in 1950 with a successful recording, and Elvis Presley's 1960 record went to the top of the charts. The number found favor again when Donny Osmond recorded it in 1974. Other versions over the years include those by Al Jolson, Doris Day, Benita Hill, the Lettermen, Leon Redbone, Vera Lynn, Connie Francis, the Moms and Dads, Engelbert Humperdinck, Ken Griffin, Roger Whittaker, and Merle Haggard. Ronnie McDowell provided the singing voice for Kurt Russell who sang it as Presley in the film bio *Elvis* (1979), and Val Kilmer performed it in *Top Secret* (1984).

"Around the World" (1956) was written to promote the film *Around the World in Eighty Days* (1956), but only Victor Young's entrancing music was heard on the soundtrack. Harold Adamson penned the lyric that had nothing to do with Jules Verne's tale, instead describing a lover wandering the globe searching for his darling. The musical theme quickly became popular because of the movie and through orchestral versions by Young and Mantovanni, but it took awhile for vocal discs to catch on. Jane Morgan, Eddie Fisher, Bing Crosby, Nat King Cole, and the McGuire Sisters are among those who recorded it. "Around the World" was also performed by the cast of the Off-Broadway revue *The Taffetas* (1988).

"As Long as I Live" (1934) was one of composer Harold Arlen's first songs to be recorded, a nimble ballad that has not dated. Ted Koehler wrote the ardent lyric in which a devotee claims not to have diamonds to bestow but will love and take care of her his whole life long, even boasting that he'll take care of his health so that it is a long lifetime. Arlen's music has been described by James R. Morris as "a swinging danceable song in the straight AABA form" yet there is a surprising contrast moving from the verse to the refrain. The number was introduced in the revue *Cotton Club Parade* (1934) where it was sung by sixteen-year-old Lena Horne and Avon Long. Benny Goodman's 1941 record was a big seller, and Horne's 1944 disc is exceptionally accomplished. Other recordings were made by George Shearing, Maxine Sullivan, June Christy, Johnny Johnston and the Satisfiers, Billy Eckstine, Ella Fitzgerald, Ernestine Jackson, Julie Wilson, and more recently, Elisabeth Welch, Billy Stritch, and Weslia Whitfield.

"At a Georgia Camp Meeting" (1897) is a cakewalk classic that Frederick Allen Mills wrote as a reaction to and a protest against the "coon songs" that still proliferated in vaudeville. Mills's high-strutting number, about an outdoor religious revival where there is preaching, music, and chocolate cake for all, attempts to portray a more realistic picture of African Americans. In the words of Alec Wilder, it is "a strong, memorable tune, very much in the ragtime, cakewalk tradition" and the song has some-times been attributed as inventing the cakewalk. But its musical main theme is based on a Civil War song "Our Boys Will Shine Tonight," and evidence of cakewalks have been found previous to Mills's piece. When no publisher would buy the song, Mills printed it himself under the name of Kerry Mills, and soon he became a Tin Pan Alley publishing giant. "At a Georgia Camp Meeting" was introduced in vaudeville by the song-and-dance team of Genaro and Bailey, and their cakewalk per-formance of the number was immediately a sensation. Vern Ossman also brought it recognition, and John Philip Sousa helped by including the song in his repertoire for several years. Distinctive recordings were made by Bessie Smith, Kid Ory's Creole Jazz Band, Bunk Johnson, the Fire-house Five Plus Two, Lu Watters, Jim Cullum, and Sidney Bechet. The song has been added to the background soundtrack for several movies over the years, including *Show Boat* (1936), *San Francisco* (1936), *Birth of the Blues* (1941), *Stormy Weather* (1943), and *Pretty Baby* (1978).

"At a Perfume Counter (On the Rue de la Paix)" (1938) is a romantic ballad about a Paris rendezvous that Morton Downey and Wini Shaw each introduced in Manhattan nightclubs. The Edgar Leslie (lyric) and Joe Burke (music) song was popularized by a hit record by Jimmy Dorsey (vocal by Bob Eberly), and there was also a successful disc by Blue Bar-ron (vocal by Russ Carlyle). Dave Brubeck made a celebrated jazz re-cording of the number years later.

"At Dawning (I Love You)" (1906) was a concert song that crossed over into the popular music market because of admired recordings by John McCormack, Paul Robeson, and other singers. Nelle Richmond Eberhart penned the simple lyric that uses nature images to express a paramour's early morning devotion to his beloved that continues all day long. The composer was Charles Wakefield Cadman, who was greatly influenced by Native American songs, and there is a flavor of that sound in this ballad. Organist Jesse Crawford, Nelson Eddy, the Victor Herbert Or-chestra, John Charles Thomas, Coleman Hawkins, and Mary Garden are among the many who have recorded it.

"At Sundown" (1927) is an entrancing ballad that describes the coming of night with every breeze "sighing of love undying." Composer Walter Donaldson wrote both music and lyric for the atmospheric piece, and it was introduced by Cliff Edwards at the Palace Theatre. An early record-ing by George Olsen and his Orchestra went to the top of the charts, and within a year, various discs of the song sold over 2 million copies, as well as hefty sales in sheet music. It was a favorite of Ruth Etting's and both Jimmy and Tommy Dorsey. Other recordings of note are those by

Bobby Hackett, Matt Dennis with Paul Weston's Orchestra, Bing Crosby, Mildred Bailey, the King Sisters, Bud Freeman, Les Brown, Betty Carter, Dave Whitney, Spiegle Willcox, and Percy Humphrey. Marsha Hunt sang it in the film *Music for Millions* (1944), the Bobby Brooks Quartet crooned it in *This Is the Life* (1944), both Dorseys performed it in *The Fabulous Dorseys* (1947), Doris Day sang it in the Etting bio *Love Me or Leave Me* (1955), and Frank Sinatra gave it his own distinctive interpretation in *The Joker Is Wild* (1957). The ballad can also be heard in *Glorifying the American Girl* (1930), *The Bells of Capistrano* (1942), *Margie* (1946), and other movies.

"A-Tisket, A-Tasket" (1938) was long associated with Ella Fitzgerald, who wrote the novelty number with Al Freeman (a.k.a. Van Alexander) and introduced it at Manhattan's Savoy Ballroom with Chick Webb and his Orchestra. Fitzgerald was only fifteen years old at the time, and it launched her career, her record selling over a million discs. The silly, rhythmic lyric, about singing the blues because of losing a green and yellow basket, came from a nursery rhyme that Fitzgerald recalled from her not-so-distant childhood. Yet the jazzy way the song asks and answers questions ("was it red?"—"no no no no") is very adult, and the sassy music is almost suggestive. Continually popular on children's records, the song was also recorded by Red Garland, Etta Jones, Oscar Peterson, Sarah Pillow, Glenn Miller, Terry Blaine, Milt Jackson, Fats Waller, Tommy Dorsey, Lars Erstrand, Sara Hickman, and Spider Saloff and Ricky Ritzel. Fitzgerald sang it in the film *Ride 'Em Cowboy* (1942), and June Allyson and Gloria DeHaven did a duet version in *Two Girls and a Sailor* (1944).

"Aura Lee" (1861) is an atypical Civil War song in that it is more sentimental and romantic than military or patriotic. W.W. Fosdick (lyric) and George R. Poulton (music) are credited for writing the ballad in which a beau hears the charms of his sweetheart Aura Lee sung by a blackbird in spring. "Aura Lee" has had a long and interesting history since it was first sung by Union and Confederate soldiers. West Point Academy adopted it as its graduation song in 1865, changing the title to "Army Blue." For the rest of the century it was a favorite of barbershop quartets because of its harmonizing possibilities. In 1956 it was revised and retitled by Elvis Presley and Vera Matson as "Love Me Tender" and served as the title song for the Presley film, his recording of the new-old ballad selling over a million discs. Other hit records of the new version were made by Richard Chamberlain in 1962 and Percy Sledge in 1967. Recordings of "Aura Lee" over the years include those by the Cumberland Three, Tony Williamson, Connie Francis, John Harford, Simon and Verity Grace, and choral groups such as the Mormon Tabernacle Choir.

Hollywood has used all three versions of the song: "Army Blue" was featured in the West Point film *The Long Gray Line* (1955); "Aura Lee" was sung by Frances Farmer in *Come and Get It* (1936) and heard in a handful of Civil War movies; and "Love Me Tender" was performed by Pat Boone in *All Hands on Deck* (1921), by Presley in the documentaries *Elvis: That's the Way It Is* (1970) and *Elvis on Tour* (1972), and by Linda Ronstadt in *FM* (1978).

"Autumn in New York" (1934) is the celebrated paean to New York City and "the promise of new love" by Vernon Duke, one of the few songs in which he provided both music and lyric. The music seems rhythmically simple, yet it is surprisingly complex with an ambitious verse and a richly textured refrain that is difficult to sing. In fact, some in the music business felt it was too tricky for the public to like. But Duke's expansive lyric, about getting a new lease on life once fall arrives and the city comes to life, is highly pleasing, and it eventually became a favorite. Ironically, the song was hardly noticed when introduced by J. Harold Murray in the Broadway revue *Thumbs Up!* (1934), and it wasn't until a recording by Louella Hogan years later that the ballad caught on. Memorable among the hundreds of recordings made are those by Frank Sinatra, Bud Powell, Carmen Cavallaro, Jeri Southern, Jo Stafford, Bill Mays, Mel Tormé, Art Van Damme, Marian McPartland, and Bobby Short. More recently the song was heard sung on the soundtracks of the films *When Harry Met Sally* (1989) by Harry Connick Jr. and *Autumn in New York* (2000) by Yvonne Washington.

"Autumn Leaves" (1950) is a popular ballad that originated in France but, once it caught on in America, became a perennial favorite. The Jacques Prevert (lyric) and Joseph Kosma (music) song was titled "Les Feuilles Mortes" and was featured in the film *Les Portes de la Nuit* (1946). In 1950 Johnny Mercer wrote a captivating English lyric about a dejected suitor who cannot help recall his lost love each year when the leaves start to fall. Bing Crosby and Jo Stafford recorded it as a duet, but the disc did not sell. In 1953 Roger Williams and his Orchestra made an instrumental recording, and it sold over a million copies. The Crosby-Stafford disc then became successful, followed by scores of others, including those by Nelson Riddle (vocal by Monica Lewis), Stan Getz, Buddy Morrow (vocal by Tommy Mercer), Nat King Cole, the Lennon Sisters, Andy Williams, Roscoe Lee Brown, Louis Prima, Frank Sinatra, Dizzy Gillespie, Mabel Mercer, Portia Nelson, Willie Nelson, Natalie Cole, Andrea Marcovicci, and Lee Lessack, as well as just about every "easy listening" orchestra. Nat King Cole sang it on the soundtrack of the film *Autumn Leaves* (1956), Kelly Smith and the chorus performed it in *Hey Boy! Hey Girl!* (1959), and Paula Cole was heard singing it in *Midnight in the Garden of Good and Evil* (1997).

"Avalon" (1918) has remained popular over the decades because of its tearful lyric and engaging music. Vincent Rose composed the flowing music that was so similar to the opera aria "E lucevan le stelle" in *Tosca* that Giacomo Puccini sued the songwriters and won a $25,000 settlement. B.G. DeSylva and Al Jolson wrote the lyric about returning to the town of Avalon on Santa Catalina Island where one first found and then later lost a true love. Jolson interpolated the number into his Broadway musical *Sinbad* (1918) and was the first of many to record it. His was followed by discs by Helen Morgan, Teddy Wilson, Kenny Baker, Harry Reser and the Cliquot Eskimos, the Pied Pipers, Benny Goodman, Jimmie Lunceford, Chet Atkins, Al Hirt, and Nat King Cole with Count Basie's Orchestra, which was a hit in 1959. Years later Cole's daughter Natalie recorded the ballad, and more recently there has been a disc by Harry Connick Jr. Jeanette MacDonald and Robert Young sang "Avalon" in *Cairo* (1942), Jolson reprised it on the soundtrack for Larry Parks to sing in *The Jolson Story* (1946), Ann Blyth (dubbed by Gogi Grant) performed it in *The Helen Morgan Story* (1957), and it was heard in *Margie* (1946) and *The Benny Goodman Story* (1956).

B

"Baby Face" (1926) is a Roaring Twenties favorite that is still familiar to the public, both words and music overflowing with silliness and carefree abandon. Benny Davis's lyric, said to be inspired by the appealing baby face of silent screen star Clara Bow, boasts about the charms of his sweetie, from her rosy cheeks to her curly hair and her "turn'd up nose." Harry Akst wrote the vivacious Charleston-like music that is contagiously danceable. Jan Garber and his Orchestra (vocal by Davis) introduced the song with a recording that sold well, but it was Eddie Cantor who propelled the number to fame. Other early records were made by Jack Smith with the Clark Sisters and orchestra versions by Ben Selvin, Henry King, and the Ipana Troubadours (vocal by Lewis James). The lively ditty was revived by a 1948 disc by Art Mooney and his Orchestra that sold a million copies and put the number in the *Hit Parade* for nine weeks. Later revivals came with Little Richard's record in 1958, Bobby Darin in 1962, and the Wing and a Prayer Fife and Drum Corps in 1976. In between were notable recordings by Al Jolson, Tiny Hill, Jan Garber, Lou Reed, Bobby Vee, the Revelers, Tom Jones, Tiny Tim, and more recently, Cris Groenendaal. Mary Eaton sang "Baby Face" in the film *Glorifying the American Girl* (1930), Jolson provided the singing for Larry Parks in *Jolson Sings Again* (1949), Julie Andrews performed it in *Thoroughly Modern Millie* (1967), and it was heard in the background of many films, including *Baby Face* (1933), *Stop, You're Killing Me* (1952), and *She's Working Her Way Through College* (1952).

"Baby, Won't You Please Come Home?" (1922) is a "very sweet late-at-night song," as Alec Wilder described it, that became a jazz standard because of its interesting musical line. The lyric is also unusual, pleading for a loved one to return with knowing sassiness ("daddy needs mama") rather than desperate bathos. Charles Warfield and Clarence Williams wrote the number in 1919, but it didn't get published until four years later when Eva Tanguay (with Williams at the piano) popularized it in clubs and on record. The Mills Brothers revived interest in the song in 1932 with a hit record, and Jerry Vale did the same thing in the early 1960s. Of all the jazz musicians who have recorded the piece, Jimmie Lunceford's disc is considered the finest. Fletcher Henderson, Bessie Smith, Eva Taylor, George Thomas with McKinney's Cotton Pickers, Louis Armstrong, Cab Calloway, Oscar Klein, Ray Charles, and Jane Horrocks are among the artists to also record it. "Baby, Won't You Please Come Home?" was also heard in the film *Crazy House* (1943), was sung by Jo Stafford and Nat King Cole in *That's the Spirit* (1945), and was performed by Jeri Lynn Fraser in *Two Tickets to Paris* (1962)

"Back Home in Tennessee" (1915) is composer Walter Donaldson's first hit song, a tribute to a state he had never seen. But it was one of the top songs of that year and has been a popular favorite in the state ever since. William Jerome penned the patronizing lyric, and Al Jolson introduced the number on stage and in clubs. An instrumental version by Prince's Orchestra popularized the song, which remained a standard for some years. More recently it was recorded by Freddy Gardner and Lee Clayton. The success of this state song encouraged Donaldson to write an even bigger hit, "Carolina in the Morning," about another state he had never visited.

"Back in the Saddle Again" (1938) was cowboy singer Gene Autry's theme song throughout his career and a classic example of the lazy, contented kind of prairie song that appealed to Americans during the war years. Movie actor Ray Whitley collaborated with Autry on the number about riding the range where "a friend is a friend" and the cattle feed on "jimson weed" and where "the only law is right." As the story goes, Whitley was awakened early one morning by the studio who needed him on the set for a western. He remarked to his wife, "Well, it looks like I'm back in the saddle again." She thought it was a perfect title for a cowboy song, and by the end of the day, Autry and Whitley completed the number. Over the years some question has been raised over Autry's contribution to the song, some noting that he had an agreement to pay Whitley for songs, then add his own name to the authorship. "Back in the Saddle Again" was introduced in the film *Border G-Man* (1938), and Autry sang it in *Rovin' Tumbleweeds* (1939), *Melody Ranch* (1940), and *Back in the Saddle* (1941), as well as on records, radio, and later television. More recently the familiar Autry recording was heard on the soundtrack of the film *Sleepless in Seattle* (1993). There were also discs by Art Kassel and his Orchestra, Charlie Daniels, Riders in the Sky,

Merle Travis, Don Edwards, Johnny Bond and the Willis Brothers, Herb Jeffries, and Gary Nichols.

"Back Water Blues" (1927) was one of many blues numbers that proliferated during the 1920s, but this one is notable because singer Bessie Smith wrote both the music and lyric herself. She recorded the song, a painful lament of a woman left behind in a nowhere town, with James P. Johnson at the piano, and it was later recorded by such blues artists as Dinah Washington, Viola McCoy, Big Bill Broonzy, Lonnie Johnson, Leadbelly, Josh White, Long John Baldry, and LaVern Baker.

"Ballad for Americans" (1939) differs from other patriotic songs written during the 1940s because of John Latouche's lively yet fervent lyric that avoids jingoism and celebrates the simple and precious gifts of freedom. The lengthy number, narrated by a "nobody who's everybody," recounts highlights from American history, then goes on to salute the many ethnic types that make up the citizens of the country. Earl Robinson wrote the inspiring music, and the number, then titled "Ballad for Uncle Sam," was introduced by Gordon Clarke in the Works Progress Administration (WPA) theatre revue *Sing for Your Supper* (1939). It was first heard with its revised title on the radio show *Pursuit of Happiness*, followed by live and record versions by Bing Crosby and Paul Robeson. The patriotic ballad was also featured in two movies, *Babes on Broadway* (1941) and *Born to Sing* (1942).

"The Ballad of Davy Crockett" (1954) was one of the few Tin Pan Alley hits to come from television, in this case the popular *Davy Crockett* adventure series that had everyone singing the song and buying raccoon skin hats. The Tom Blackburn (lyric) and George Bruns (music) song is a narrative ballad that relates the history of Crockett with more legend than facts, such as his killing a bear when he was only a child. Fess Parker played Davy and sang the song in the television show and in the movies *Davy Crockett, King of the Wild Frontier* (1955) and *Davy Crockett and the River Pirates* (1956). Parker, Bill Hayes, and Tennessee Ernie Ford each recorded the song, and each version sold over a million discs. By the end of the decade there were twenty-three different recordings made, selling over 10 million copies. Surprisingly, this all-American tune was an international bestseller as well. There were records made in several countries, including over twenty different versions in France, and it was the biggest-selling song in Japan for awhile. Billy Cotton, the Cliff Adams Singers, Eddie Fisher, the Wellingtons, Eddy Arnold, the Kentucky Headhunters, and Mannheim Steamroller were among the others who recorded the ballad in America.

"Ballerina" (1947) is a Latin-flavored number encouraging a dancer to spin and whirl for an audience even though the one she loves has left her and is not there to see her perform. Bob Russell and Carl Sigman wrote the melodious song, which is sometimes listed as "Dance, Ballerina, Dance," and it stayed on the *Hit Parade* chart for seventeen weeks, primarily because of Vaughn Monroe's record, which sold nearly 2 million discs. A decade later the song was revived by a popular recording by Nat King Cole with Nelson Riddle's Orchestra. There were also applauded versions by Bing Crosby, Buddy Clark with Dick Jones' Orchestra, Jimmy Dorsey (vocal by Bob Carroll), Mel Tormé, Luis Arcaraz, and Lawrence Welk.

"Ballin' the Jack" (1913) is one of those dance songs in which the lyric gives you directions on how to do the steps. Although the "Ballin' the Jack" dance has faded from memory (the lyric makes no attempt to explain what the title phrase means), the song has remained a ragtime favorite. Chris Smith composed the catchy music, and Jim Burris wrote the rhythmic lyric that describes a dance that is all the rage in Georgia. More than perhaps any other dance song, this one gives such specific directions that it is possible to do the steps as you listen to it. Billy Kent and Jeanette Warner introduced the number in vaudeville, but it was Eddie Cantor who popularized it when he performed it in a Texas vaudeville theatre. It was added to the road company of the musical *The Girl from Utah* in 1914 and was interpolated into Broadway's *The Passing Show of 1915*. When Judy Garland and Gene Kelly sang the song in the film *For Me and My Gal* (1942), it enjoyed a revival of interest and made *Your Hit Parade*, aided by a bestselling disc by Georgia Gibbs. Later the number was long associated with Danny Kaye, who sang it on records, in clubs, on radio and television, and in the film *On the Riviera* (1951). There was yet another revival of "Ballin' the Jack" in the 1960s with a twist version by Chubby Checker. Other recordings over the years include those by Prince's Orchestra, Fats Domino, the Three Suns, Red Nichols, Bunk Johnson, Jelly Roll Morton, a duet version by Martha Tilton and Hal Derwin, and George Lewis and his Ragtime Band. Dean Martin sang it in the film *That's My Boy* (1951), and it was included in the Off-Broadway musical bio *Jelly Roll* (1996).

"Baltimore Oriole" (1944) is a jazz favorite that tells a fable about an oriole and a "two-timin' blackbird" that is both humorous and touching. Paul Francis Webster wrote the whimsical lyric and Hoagy Carmichael composed the slow jazz music that is unusual in that it is written in 4/4 time yet consists mostly of quarter note triplets. In fact, the music is so meandering and casual that the song seems to sneak up on the listener rather than overpowering one. "Baltimore Oriole" was written for the film *The Ghost Catchers* (1944) but was not used. Carmichael sang it in the movie *To Have and Have Not* (1944), where it was also heard several times in the background, and it was used again in *The Stork Club* (1945), so audiences became familiar with it before any recordings were released. Carmichael made a splendid record with Frances Langford, Carmen McRae's 1958 version revived interest in the song, and there were also discs by the Four Freshmen, Barbara Lea, Amanda McBroom, Lorez Alexandria, the Rick Hollander Quartet, Sheila Gordon, and Keith Ingham.

"The Banana Boat Song (Day-O)" (1956) was not only Harry Belafonte's theme song, which he sang in clubs, on records, and on radio and television; it also started a calypso and West Indies craze in the States in the 1950s. Erik Darling, Bob Carey, and Alan Arkin collaborated on the number that has been advertised as calypso but is closer to a West Indies folk song. The lyric describes working on a Caribbean banana boat all day and longing for quitting time because "I wanna go home." The pulsating number is punctuated by the wail of "Day-O" throughout, and the song is sometimes titled by that phrase. The Tarriers introduced the song with a successful record and sang it in the film *Calypso Heat Wave* (1957), but it was Belafonte's recording that made both him and it famous. His album *Calypso* was the first pop LP by a single artist to sell over a million copies. There were other chart records by the Fontane Sisters, Steve Lawrence, and Sarah Vaughan. Long popular on children's records, "The Banana Boat Song"was also recorded by Nat King Cole, Xavier Cugat, Taj Mahal, the Kinks, and Stan Freberg, whose 1957 parody version was popular. The celebrated Belafonte recording was heard in the film *Beetlejuice* (1988).

"The Band Played On" (1895) is the simple but unforgettable waltz number that has remained a standard for over a century. The nostalgic song tells of Matt Casey who waltzed with a "strawberry blonde" at a neighborhood dance, the two of them still whirling on the dance floor after all the others had left. The sparkling lyric uses the recurring phrase "and the band played on" (often listed as the song's title) to propel the number, and it ties the whole composition together beautifully. There is some contention over the true authorship of the piece. John E. Palmer took the main musical theme from a German street band he heard playing for coins from passersby. Vaudevillian Charles B. Ward is credited as the coauthor, though it is believed he made only minor alterations to the song and claimed credit because his performing it at Hammerstein's Opera House encouraged a publisher to print it. It is also thought that Ward paid Palmer for the song outright and never shared his profits from it with Palmer. And they were considerable profits, the song selling over a million copies of sheet music within a few years and recorded hundreds of times. The nostalgic number was so popular that the *New York World* published both music and lyric in one edition of the newspaper. "The Band Played On" enjoyed a revival of interest in 1941 when Guy Lombardo's recording went to the top of the charts. Other prominent recordings were made by Dan Quinn, the Jesters, Connie Francis, Ace O'Donnell, Max Bygraves, Mitch Miller, Jack Mudurian, Mandy Patinkin, and Wynton Marsalis. James Cagney, Rita Hayworth, and the chorus sang it in the film *The Strawberry Blonde* (1941), Dennis Morgan crooned it in *Cattle Town* (1952), and it was heard in the background of several period movies, including *Lillian Russell* (1940) and *Swingtime Johnny* (1943).

"The Banks of the Dee" (c. 1770) was one of America's first sentimental ballads, one that became popular during the Revolutionary War and was a favorite throughout the nineteenth century. John Tait is credited with the lyric about a Scotsman's farewell to his lassie before joining the British troops going to fight in the American colonies. The music is based on the Irish folk song "Langolee," which dates to the 1760s. Though largely forgotten in the twentieth century, there were recordings by Jack Elliott, the High Level Ranters, Louis Killen, and Mason Williams.

"Barnacle Bill the Sailor" (1929) is a silly novelty number about a crusty old sailor that was based on some bawdy sea chanties. Musicians Carson Robison and Frank Luther wrote the song, and Luther popularized it on disc. The song was later given a historic recording by Luther and Robison with Hoagy Carmichael, Bix Beiderbecke, Benny Goodman, Tommy Dorsey, Gene Krupa, Joe Venuti, and other famed talents. Carmichael and Beiderbecke also made their own discs, as did Louis Jordan and the Tympany Five, the Controllers, the Texas Troubadours, Ella Jenkins, Glenn Ohrlin, and Louis Prima and Keely Smith.

"Barney Google" (1923) is one of those 1920s nonsense songs so prevalent at the time, yet this one hung on for decades. Billy Rose (lyric) and Con Conrad (music) wrote the silly number about Barney with the "goo-goo-googly eyes," based on a newspaper comic strip in favor at the time. Little Barney had a wife "three times his size" who sued him for divorce and took all his money, and he ended up sleeping with the horse. Eddie Cantor introduced the ditty in vaudeville with some success, but no publisher would consider it. So Rose convinced the team of Olson and Johnson to put it in their act (with a horse costume, no less), and it was such a big hit that audiences demanded sheet music. The team of Jones and Hare made one of the first recordings, followed by many others, including those by Georgie Price, Charles Ventura, the Firehouse Five Plus Two, the Charles Baum Orchestra, and Spike Jones and his City Slickers.

"Basin Street Blues" (1928) is the slow blues favorite that salutes the street in New Orleans where the "dark elite always meet." Spencer Williams (with uncredited help from a young Benny Goodman) wrote the scintillating number that Louis Armstrong introduced in a 1928 recording that immediately became a classic, being reissued in 1938 and again in 1948. Jack Teagarden's 1931 record, in which he played trombone and the Charleston Chasers did the vocals, was responsible for popularizing the song, and it was helped by Goodman's 1934 disc and, the biggest seller of all, Bing Crosby's 1937 recording with Connee Boswell and John Scott Trotter's Orchestra. Other memorable versions over the years were made by Pee Wee Hunt, Ella Fitzgerald, Ruby Newman, Pete Fountain, Johnny Guarnieri, Shirley Horn, Bob Wills, Duke Ellington, Dave McKenna, Willie Humphrey, and Al Hirt. Armstrong reprised "Basin Street Blues" in three films: *New Orleans* (1947), *The Strip* (1951) with Teagarden, and *The Glenn Miller Story* (1954) with Gene Krupa.

"Battle Hymn of the Republic" (1862), as its title states, is both a war song and a hymn. Although it is usually associated with the Civil War, the song has managed to inspire generations of Americans because of its surging music and flowery but potent lyric. Phrases from the song, such as "mine eyes have seen the glory," "His terrible swift sword," and "where the grapes of wrath are stored," have entered literary and popular language and have served as everything from campaign cries to book titles. The music, while far from easy to sing, builds in momentum as few hymns can and still has the power to move listeners. Poet Julia Ward Howe was visiting Washington, D.C., in 1861 and was invited to review the troops in nearby Virginia when the Confederates attacked and the Union soldiers were forced to retreat. As they straggled in, they sang "John Brown's Body," which prompted an army chaplain to request Howe to write a more appropriate lyric for the tune. That night in her hotel room, Howe wrote all five stanzas of the hymn, and it was published as a poem in the *Atlantic Monthly* in 1862. The editor, who suggested the title to Howe, paid her $5 for her effort. William Steffe took the tune of "John Brown's Body" and another folk song, "Glory Hallelujah," and wrote the music we are familiar with today. Throughout the rest of the war, the song was sung in the North in army camps, at patriotic rallies, even on the battlefield. In later years it became a national favorite not necessarily associated with just the North. The first popular recording of the song was made by the Columbia Stellar Quartet in the 1910s, and it has remained a favorite of singers and choral groups on record. The 1959 disc by the Mormon Tabernacle Choir with the Philadelphia Orchestra sold over a million copies. Andy Williams also had a hit with it in 1968. Jeanette MacDonald sang "The Battle Hymn of the Republic" with a choir in the film *San Francisco* (1936), Louis Armstrong and Danny Kaye performed a distinctive version in *The Five Pennies* (1959), and it has been heard in the background for many movies, such as *Stars and Stripes Forever* (1952) and *How the West Was Won* (1962). Elvis Presley performed the hymn many times in his career, singing it in the documentary *Elvis on Tour* (1972); Kurt Russell, impersonating Presley, sang it in *Elvis* (1979).

"Be Honest with Me" (1940) is a genial western-flavored song by Gene Autry and Fred Rose that pleads for romantic fidelity. Autry introduced it in the film *Ridin' on a Rainbow* (1941) and sang it again in *Sierra Sue* (1941). It was heard in *Strictly in the Groove* (1942) and in *Flaming Bullets* (1945), where Tex Ritter sang it. Autry's record was the top seller, but discs by Bing Crosby and Freddie Martin and his Orchestra were also successful. Billy May, Roy Acuff, Carl Perkins, Riders in the Sky, Roy Rogers and Dale Evans, Jim Reeves, and Bobby Darin were among the others who have recorded it.

"Beale Street Blues" (1917), a blues standard that was first published as "Beale Street," was written by W. C. Handy and introduced by Prince's Orchestra. Beale Street is the Memphis neighborhood where Handy grew up, and the autobiographical song draws on the locale in its lyric. Although it has a traditional blues structure, the number became a special favorite of jazz musicians over the years, in particular with a disc by Jack Teagarden and his Orchestra. Alberta Hunter revived interest in the song in 1927, just as Joe Venuti and Eddie Lang did in 1932 and Guy Lombardo and the Royal Canadians did in 1942. Other outstanding versions were made by Jelly Roll Morton, Duke Ellington, Wingy Manone, Bob Crosby, Tommy Dorsey, Nat King Cole, Eartha Kitt, Pearl Bailey, and Lena Horne. The number was heard in the film bio of Handy, *St. Louis Blues* (1958), and in *The Great Gatsby* (1974). Mitzi Gaynor performed it in *The I-Don't-Care Girl* (1953), and Kenny Ball sang it in the British film *Ring-a-Ding Rhythm* (1962).

"Beat Me Daddy, Eight to the Bar" (1940) is a boogie-woogie favorite by Don Raye, Hughie Prince, and Eleanor Sheehy that requests a lively eight-counts-to-the-measure tune to dance to. Will Bradley and his Orchestra (vocal by Ray McKinley) introduced and popularized the energetic number, which was also a hit for the Andrews Sisters. Freddie Slack, Glenn Miller, Red Nichols, Ray Anthony, Ella Fitzgerald, Jim Cullum, and George Shearing are among those who also recorded it. In the Broadway musical *Big Deal* (1986), the number was performed by Bernard J. Marsh and the ensemble. The use of a family member in the title was in the tradition of the earlier "Swing, Brother, Swing" and the later "Bounce Me Brother With a Solid Four" and "Scrub Me Mama With a Boogie Beat," both of which were also recorded by Bradley and McKinley.

"Beautiful Brown Eyes" (1951) is a flowing waltz based on a traditional melody with unknown sources. Cisco Houston wrote and performed a version of the ballad in vaudeville in the early years of the twentieth century, but the song had pretty much disappeared until Alton Delmore, Arthur Smith, and Jerry Capehart created a new adaptation in 1951, and Rosemary Clooney had a hit record with it. Although the title suggests another gushing ballad about a beautiful girl, the lyric is actually the lament of a woman who fell in love with the seductive blue eyes of Willie, married him, lost him, and married another man, and now, seven years later, she unhappily claims she will "never love blue eyes again." Notable recordings of the song were made by Jimmy Wakely and Les Baxter, Art Mooney and his Orchestra, Jimmy Martin, Burl Ives, Solomon Burke, the Brothers Four, Billy Walker, Connie Francis, Chet Atkins, and Roy Acuff. "Beautiful Brown Eyes" can be heard on the soundtrack of the film *Endangered Species* (1982).

"Beautiful Dreamer" (1864) is Stephen Foster's cherished ballad written at the end of his career and one of the most beloved songs in American popular culture. The enticing music has the flavor of a lullaby as the poetic lyric sings the praises of a sleeping woman who he wishes will "wake unto me." Some of Foster's phrases ("starlight and dewdrops are waiting" and "over the streamlet vapors are borne") may seem a bit purple for contemporary tastes, but the dreamy melody makes it all palatable. Published in 1864 after Foster's death, the song was sold by publishers as having been written a few days before he died. In fact, Foster had written it in 1862, and no one printed it until a shrewd publisher saw a way to capitalize on the songwriter's demise. "Beautiful Dreamer" has been heard in a score of movies, including *Go West* (1940) sung by Diana Lewis, *Rhythm Round-Up* (1945), *Golden Girl* (1951), *Saginaw Trail* (1953) and in the Foster bios *Swanee River* (1939), sung by Al Jolson, and *I Dream of Jeanie* (1952). Of the hundreds of recordings, there were eminent ones by Bing Crosby, Kate Smith, Bobby Darin, Floyd Cramer, John Carter, Phil Coulter, Richard Crooks, Dick Curless, Phil Haynes, Andre Kostelanetz, Hank Snow, Slim Whitman, Roy Orbison, Marty Robbins, Jessica Molasky, and Natalie Cole.

"A Beautiful Lady in Blue" (1935) is a rather routine love song that provided hits for two Jans: Jan Peerce introduced it on radio in 1936, and his subsequent recording was popular; and Jan Garber and his Orchestra made a recording that went to the top of the charts. Sam Lewis (lyric) and J. Fred Coots (music) wrote the amorous salute to a woman dressed in blue, and it was also recorded by Ray Noble, Johnny Johnston, Billy Vaughn, and Putney Dandridge.

"Beautiful Love" (1931) is an emotive and heartfelt ballad that was written by Haven Gillespie (lyric), Victor Young, Wayne King, and Egbert Van Alstyne (music). Wayne Young and his Orchestra introduced and popularized the number, followed by successful recordings by James Melton, Young's Orchestra (vocal by Donald Novis), and Lewis James. Interest in the song was revived when Allan Jones sang it in the movie *Sing a Jingle* (1944), and dozens of recordings followed, including discs by Art Tatum, Eddie Daniels, George Shearing, Helen Merrill, Joe Pass, Bill Evans, Shirley Horn, Percy Faith, Mario Lanza, and more recently, Weslia Whitfield.

"Beautiful Ohio" (1918), an elegant waltz that celebrates the natural beauty of the state, is mostly known today as the background music used in acrobatic acts in the circus. Robert A. King, using the pseudonym of Mary Earl because he was under contract to a publisher, wrote the music for an "alley-oop" (acrobatic) act in vaudeville, but when Ballard MacDonald later added the affecting lyrics, it became popular not only in Ohio but across the country, selling 5 million copies of sheet music. King's publisher found out the identity of Mary Earl and took all of his earnings, as specified in the contract. But the song was such a big seller they later relented and paid him $60,000. Early recordings of the waltz were made by Henry Burr, the Waldorf-Astoria Dance Orchestra, Fritz Kreisler, and Sam Ash and his Orchestra. Jeanette MacDonald sang it in the film *Cairo* (1942), and it can be heard in the background in other movies as well. As time passed, the lyric was often dropped, and the instrumental version became a circus favorite. Noteworthy disc versions were made by Glenn Miller, Paul Whiteman, Laurie Franks, Roger Flanagan, Tony Martin, Chet Atkins, the Moms and Dads, Frankie Yankovic and his Yanks, and Marty Robbins.

"Because" (1902) is a concert song that crossed over to become a Tin Pan Alley hit, then remained a standard for decades, becoming a favorite at weddings. Guy d'Hardelot (a.k.a. Helen Guy) composed the lush, operatic music, and Edward Teschemacher penned the hymnlike lyric that claimed a beloved came to him, spoke to him, and gave him a reason for living. The musical prayer concludes by crediting God with sending his true love to him. Enrico Caruso introduced the ballad in concerts and on record, and opera tenor Richard Crooks included it in all his concerts, recording it in 1930. When Deanna Durbin sang "Because" in the film *Three Smart Girls Grow Up* (1939), it became popular all over again, and her recording sold well. A decade later Perry Como had an ever bigger hit with the song, selling over a million discs. Frankie Laine, Richard Tauber, Jerry Vale, José Carreras, and Placido Domingo also made successful recordings of it. The number was performed by an unidentified singer in the movie *Thrill of a Romance* (1945), Mario Lanza gave it his full voice in *The Great Caruso* (1951), and opera star Lauritz Melchior did the same in *The Stars Are Singing* (1953).

"Because of You" (1940) took awhile to catch on, but once it did, the ballad fostered many hit records and remained popular for two decades. Dudley Wilkinson composed the poignant music, and Arthur Hammerstein wrote a tender lyric about the darling who came along and "filled my life with song." A 1941 record by Larry Clinton (vocal by Peggy Mann) was moderately popular, and there were orchestra versions by Horace Heidt and Tommy Tucker as well. But the song faded from view until it was interpolated into the nonmusical film *I Was an American Spy* (1951) for Ann Dvorak to sing, and the number shot to the top of the *Hit Parade* eleven times. Tony Bennett recorded it in 1952, and it became his first hit, going to the Number One spot on the charts. There were also discs by Jan Peerce, Johnny Desmond, Jackie Wilson, Tracie Spencer, Kenny Rankin, Sammy Davis Jr., Al Hibbler, Mel Tormé, and Bobby Vinton. "Because of You" can also be heard in the background of the film comedy *Let's Make It Legal* (1951).

"Bedelia" (1903), advertised by its publisher as "the Irish Coon Song Serenade," sold more than 3 million copies of sheet music in its day and remained a sentimental favorite for years. Jean Schwartz composed the lilting music that was based on Irish folk tunes, and William Jerome wrote the lyric, a wooing song delivered to a lass from "Killarney with a Tipperary smile." The text is rather slangy for its time (the title girl's name is rhymed with "I want to steal ya"), and Jerome even pays tribute to a fellow songwriter when the lyric states "I'll be your Chauncey Olcott." Vaudeville singer Emma Carus helped popularize the song, and it became even more celebrated when Blanche Ring interpolated it into her Broadway musical *The Jersey Lily* (1903). Alice Faye sang "Bedelia" in two films, *Broadway to Hollywood* (1933) and *Hello, Frisco, Hello* (1943), and it was also heard in the period movies *Mother Wore Tights* (1947) and *The Eddie Cantor Story* (1953). Recordings of note were made by the Knickerbocker Serenaders, Jan Garber and his Orchestra, Billy Murray, George J. Gaskin, the Hayden Quartet, Arthur Pryor's Band, the Buffalo Bills, Paddy Noonan, and Bobby Short.

"Beer Barrel Polka (Roll Out the Barrel)" (1939) is the polka favorite of the war years that is still widely known today. The zesty number, mistakenly thought of as a German song, was based on a popular 1934 Czech ballad, "Skoda Lasky" by Wladimir A. Timm, Vasek Zeman (lyric), and Jaromir Vejvoda (music), that translated as "Lost Love." Lew Brown wrote an English lyric about a celebration in a beer garden ("we'll have a barrel of fun") and punctuated it with "zing!" and "boom!" to make it an ideal party song. Will Glahe and his Musette Orchestra introduced the number to America, and thanks to records by Sammy Kaye and his Orchestra and a top-selling disc by the Andrews Sisters, it quickly became one of the most popular songs of the year. The number was interpolated into the Broadway musical *Yokel Boy* (1939) and was sung on screen by Lucille Ball in *Dance, Girl, Dance* (1940) and the Andrews Sisters in *Follow the Boys* (1944), as well as heard in *At the Circus* (1939), *Eve of St. Mark* (1944), and *From Here to Eternity* (1953). Recordings were also made by Myron Floren with Lawrence Welk, Liberace, Glenn Miller, Merle Travis, Willie Nelson, Frankie Yankovic and his Yanks, Six Fat Dutchmen, and just about every other polka band that ever cut a record.

"Bei Mir Bist Du Schoen (Means That You're Grand)" (1937) is another song favorite mistakenly thought to be German, but it is a Yiddish ditty that proclaims that there is no better way to describe how wonderful you are than this title expression that translates as: "To me, you are beautiful." Sholom Secunda and Jacob Jacobs wrote the number for the Yiddish musical *I Would If I Could* (1937) where it was introduced by Aaron Lebedeff. Secunda sold the song to Sammy Cahn and Saul Chaplin for $30, and their partial-English version was introduced on a recording by the Andrews Sisters that went to the top of the charts and launched both Cahn's and the Sisters' careers. The song remained on *Your Hit Parade* for nine weeks, but Secunda got none of the $3 million it earned. When the copyright expired in the 1960s, he reacquired the rights and finally started to get a percentage of the royalties. The merry number was sung by Priscilla Lane in the movie *Love, Honor and Behave* (1938), it was heard in *Take It Big* (1944), and the Andrews Sisters reprised it in *Follow the Boys* (1944). The song was revived with a 1959 recording by Louis Prima and Keely Smith, and there were also discs by Guy Lombardo, Benny Goodman, Kate Smith, the Clark Sisters, Ella Fitzgerald, the Village Stompers, and Steve Lawrence and Eydie Gorme. It was also sung by the cast of the Off-Broadway revue *Bei Mir Bist Du Schoen* (1961).

"The Bells of St. Mary's" (1917) is a nostalgic ballad that recalls the sound of the bells coming from a church and how they seem to be calling one back home. The English song by A. Emmett Adams (lyric) and Douglas Furber (music) became popular in America, particularly with glee clubs and concerts bands. There was an early recording by Frances Alda in 1920, but the number never became a hit record until Bing Crosby sang it in the film *The Bells of St. Mary's* (1945). Other records were made by Vera Lynn, Ted Heath, Lee Andrews and the Hearts, Douglas Dillard, Bobb B. Soxx and Blue Jeans, Connie Francis, Kenny Baker, the Drifters, Ken Griffin, Chet Atkins, and Andy Williams, and it often is included on Christmas albums.

"Bésame Mucho" (1944) is a passionate, hot-blooded Mexican song by Consuelo Velazquez that was a romantic favorite in the 1940s. Sunny Skylar wrote the English lyric about a fervent declaration of love but kept the Spanish title (which roughly translates as "kiss me deeply"). Velazquez's music is rhythmic and pulsating, and the tune joined the list of Latin hits in the era. Jimmy Dorsey and his Orchestra (vocals by Kitty Kallen and Bob Eberly) popularized the song with a Number One chart record, and Abe Lyman and his Orchestra also had success with it. Andy Russell made a test record with George Siravo's Orchestra, and when it was released, it sold a million copies. In 1957 Russell recorded it again, as did Josephine Baker, Xavier Cugat, James Booker, the Flamingos, Nat King Cole, Mantovanni's Orchestra, Sammy Davis Jr., Steve Lawrence and Eydie Gorme, Charo, Bill Evans, the Ray Conniff Singers, Dave Brubeck, Charlie Byrd, Diana Krall, and Richard Clayderman. Charlie Spivik and his Orchestra played it in the movie *Follow the Boys* (1944), and the Davis recording was heard in *Moon Over Parador* (1988).

"The Best Is Yet to Come" (1959) is a hot, jazzy number by Broadway songwriters Carolyn Leigh (lyric) and Cy Coleman (music) that promises even better things now that the two sweethearts have met and fallen in love. Tony Bennett introduced the piquant number and had a hit record with it, but it was jazz musicians and singers who kept it in their repertoire for several years. Other discs were made by Peggy Lee, Ella Fitzgerald, Ann Margaret, Mel Tormé, Sarah Vaughan, Frank Sinatra, Shirley Horn, Dick Curless, Rosemary Clooney, Nancy Wilson, Johnny Mathis, Helen Baylor, Bobby Caldwell, and more recently, Jane Harrocks, and Ann Hampton Callaway. It was used in the film *Nine and a Half Weeks* (1986), and the Wilson recording was heard in *What Women Want* (2000).

"Between the Devil and the Deep Blue Sea" (1931) is a vibrant rhythm song that was way ahead of its time as it forecasts the swing and later jazz movements in popular music. Ted Koehler wrote the lucid lyric about an indecisive lover who is both enamored and annoyed by her beau and feels caught in the middle of love and hate. Harold Arlen composed the innovative music in which the verse swings and the release moves into a riff section. The number was introduced by Aida Ward in the Cotton Club revue *Rhythmania* (1931), and it was popularized by Bill Robinson, Cab Calloway, and Louis Armstrong. The last two recorded it, as did the Boswell Sisters, Eddy Duchin, Carmen McRae, Ella Fitzgerald, Bob Crosby, Woody Herman, Carmen Cavallaro, Elliot Lawrence, and more recently, Julie Wilson, Sylvia McNair with André Previn, and Kenny Drew. But a disc by Benny Goodman (vocal by Helen Ward) is considered the finest version and remains a jazz classic. Bonnie Bedelia sang the song in the movie *They Shoot Horses, Don't They?* (1969), and the Armstrong recording was used in *The Cotton Club* (1984).

"Bill" (1918), one of the finest torch songs in American popular music, had a difficult history before it was finally presented as part of the musical theatre classic *Show Boat* (1927) and went on to become a Tin Pan Alley standard as well. Jerome Kern composed the leisurely and reflective music that has all sorts of little surprises along the way. P.G. Wodehouse wrote the piquant lyric, a terse, self-aware torch song with none of the maudlin sentiment often found in torchy laments. The lyric is also remarkably conversational. The description of Bill as less than ideal hints at a smile underneath the woe, and the singer can only conclude that she loves him "because—I don't know—because he's just my Bill." The number was originally written for the Broadway musical *Oh, Lady! Lady!* (1918) but was cut because it was considered too slow for its position in the show. It was later given to Marilyn Miller to sing in *Sally* (1920), but again it was not working and was eliminated. When Kern and Oscar Hammerstein were writing the score for *Show Boat*, they drew on some old favorites, such as "After the Ball," for period flavor but couldn't find a torch song that seemed appropriate. Kern remembered the discarded ballad, and with a few lyric changes, it was given to Helen Morgan to sing and it stopped the show. Because Hammerstein wrote the book and most of the lyrics for *Show Boat*, "Bill" has often mistakenly been credited to him. Morgan reprised the song in the added footage for the silent version of *Show Boat* in 1929 and in the full-sound version in 1936. Ava Gardner (dubbed by Eileen Wilson) performed the number in the 1951 version, and Ann Blyth (dubbed by Gogi Grant) sang it in the musical film bio *The Helen Morgan Story* (1957). Of the hundreds of women who have recorded "Bill," there are memorable discs by Morgan, Helen Humes, Peggy Lee, Dinah Shore, Joni James, Lena Horne, Margaret Whiting, Marni Nixon, Maxine Sullivan, Helen Forrest, and more recently, Cleo Laine, Andrea Marcovicci, Teresa Stratas, Lonette McKee, and Audra McDonald.

"Bill Bailey, Won't You Please Come Home?" (1902) is the early ragtime classic that became a favorite of banjo, honky tonk piano, and Dixieland jazz performers, as well as a popular sing-along standard. Hughie Cannon wrote the bubbly number about a black woman who is hanging out laundry and singing to her absent husband Bill to come back home. She admits she drove him off "wid nothing but a fine tooth comb," but Bill hears her lament and returns, driving a big fancy automobile. The story behind the song is part of Tin Pan Alley folklore. Cannon was an alcoholic who ended up in the poorhouse, and he loved to socialize in taverns. One night Bill Bailey, an African American vaudeville singer, came into the bar and complained that his angry wife had locked him out of the house. Cannon gave Bailey some money to stay in a hotel that night and promised him that she would be begging him to return before long. John Queen introduced the number in a minstrel show in Newburgh, New York, and it was first recorded by Arthur Collins and then Kid Ory. But it was Louis Armstrong playing it in clubs that made the song all the rage, and it was performed in vaudeville by the team of Jimmy Durante and Eddie Jackson, as well as other singing comics. Before long thousands of copies of sheet music were sold, and there were song sequels (by other authors) such as "I Wonder Why Bill Bailey Don't Come Home" and "Since Bill Bailey Came Back Home." Although it remained a familiar favorite, the song got a new boost with a hit recording by Pearl Bailey in the 1950s and one by Bobby Darin in 1960 that sold a million discs. Other notable recordings were made by Armstrong, Durante and Jackson, the Preservation Hall Jazz Band, King Curtis, Earl Hines, Guy Lombardo, Pete Fountain, Nellie Lutcher, Bob Scobey, Sarah Vaughan, Della Reese, Ella Fitzgerald, the Dixieland Ramblers, Brenda Lee, Earl Hines, Patsy Cline, and Wayne Newton. "Bill Bailey" was heard in such period movies as *The Strawberry Blonde* (1941) and *Meet Me at the Fair* (1952), Danny Kaye and Armstrong performed it in *The Five Pennies* (1959), and it was sung by Donna Butterworth in *Paradise Hawaiian Style* (1966) and by Glynis Johns in *Papa's Delicate Condition* (1963). In the Broadway revue *Tintypes* (1980), Lynn Thigpen performed the famous ditty.

"A Bird in a Gilded Cage" (1900) may be the stuff of parody today, but at the turn of the century, it was a Tin Pan Alley blockbuster, selling over 2 million copies of sheet music and ranking as one of the most successful of all sentimental ballads. Harry Von Tilzer composed the tinkling music, a few bars of which bring to mind all the banality of old-time "mellerdrama." Arthur J. Lamb wrote the lyric first as a poem, describing the plight of a young woman who wed an old, rich man "for wealth, not for love" and was now a prisoner in her "gilded cage." In the original lyric the woman was the millionaire's mistress, but Von Tilzer insisted that it be a married woman as not to risk offending the public. As the legend tells it, Von Tilzer tested the song one night in a brothel; when the hardened prostitutes broke down and wept, he knew he had a hit. Vaudeville singer Jerry Mahoney popularized the song, and soon every parlor piano had the sheet music. The expression "gilded cage" stuck and still remains in the common vernacular. Von Tilzer wrote a sequel titled "The Mansion of Aching Hearts" about the inability of gold and riches to buy happiness, and it was popular for awhile before fading away. "A Bird in a Gilded Cage" was used in a handful of 1940s movies, such as *Ringside Maisie* (1941), *Coney Island* (1943), *Hello, Frisco, Hello* (1943), and *Above Suspicion* (1943), in which it was crooned by Fred MacMurray and Joan Crawford. It was also sung in the Broadway revue *Tintypes* (1980). Not often recorded anymore, the ballad can be found on discs by Beatrice Kay with Ray Bloch's Orchestra, Virginia O'Brien, the Banjo Kings, Ronnie Lane and Slim Chance, the Buffalo Bills, and William Bolcom and Joan Morris.

"Black and Blue" (1929) is one of the most haunting and disturbing ballads to find a home on Tin Pan Alley. When sung complete with the verse, the bluesy lament by Andy Razaf (lyric), Thomas "Fats" Waller, and Harry Brooks (music) is the painful cry of a dark-skinned black woman who has been rejected because her darling prefers lighter-skinned women. But the song is usually sung without the verse, and it becomes a poignant number about racial injustice, asking, "What did I do to be so black and blue?" (The song is sometimes listed with this question as the title.) The double meanings of "black" and "blue" in the lyric are very effective: The singer has the blues, has black skin, and is emotionally bruised. Razaf's indelible lyric also notes that "my only sin" is the "color of my skin." The torch song was introduced by Edith Wilson in the "all-Negro" revue *Hot Chocolates* (1929), then popularized by Waller in clubs and on records. It became an Ethel Waters specialty in the 1920s, and her recording is a blues classic. There were also records by Louis Armstrong, Frankie Laine, Gene Krupa, Jack Teagarden, Dinah Washington, Red Nichols, Roy Eldridge, Sidney Bechet, Lionel Hampton, and Dave Brubeck. "Black and Blue" was considered too disturbing to be put in film musicals, but it has been heard on Broadway in the revues *Ain't Misbehavin'* (1978) and *Black and Blue* (1989) and Off-Broadway in *Slow Drag* (1997).

"Black Is the Color of My True Love's Hair" (c. 1875) is a traditional American folk song from the Appalachian region that probably originated in Elizabethan England and was brought over by early colonists. The ballad is a simple yet affecting paean to a mistress with dark hair, fair lips, the "bluest" eyes, and the "daintiest" hands. Both pop and folk singers have recorded the song, including Nina Simone, the O'Neal Brothers, Kendra Shank, Jo Stafford, Patti Page, Marc Johnson, the

Johnny Griffin Quartet, Joan Baez, Helen Merrill, the Norman Luboff Choir, and Burl Ives. Mark Dinning sang it in the movie *Hootenanny Hoot* (1963), and the Simone recording was heard in *Point of No Return* (1993).

"Blue Again" (1930) is an elegant ballad by Dorothy Fields (lyric) and Jimmy McHugh (music) about an on-and-off relationship filled with fighting, breaking up, and getting back together. Fields repeats the word "again" effectively throughout, everything happening again and again, and Alec Wilder describes the music as "a delicate melody, almost like something written for a formal dance," Evelyn Hoey introduced the number on Broadway in *The Vanderbilt Revue* (1930), and it was popularized by Guy Lombardo and the Royal Canadians. It was also a specialty of the Ipana Troubadours on radio, concerts, and records. Other prominent discs were made by Duke Ellington (vocal by Sid Gary), Louis Armstrong, Red Nichols, Marion Harris, the Revelers, Barbara Lea, Lee Morse, Glen Gray and the Casa Loma Orchestra, and the Manhattan Transfer.

"Blue Champagne" (1941) is a Big Band number that Jimmy Dorsey (vocal by Bob Eberly) recorded, and it went to the Number One spot on the charts. The dreamy serenade, written by Grady Watts, Frank Ryerson, and Jimmy Eaton, remained popular throughout the 1940s, with recordings by Glenn Miller and the Army Air Corps Band, Charlie Ventura, Ted Heath, Frankie Carle, Tex Beneke, Teri Thornton, Charlie Spivak, Dick Haymes, and Anita O'Day. A disc by the Manhattan Transfer in 1975 revived interest in the number.

"Blue Moon" (1934) is a rare Rodgers and Hart song not written for a play or film, and ironically, it became a huge hit and sold more sheet music than any other number by the team. Richard Rodgers composed the tender music for a lyric by Lorenz Hart called "Prayer" to be sung by Jean Harlow in the movie *Hollywood Party* (1934). When it was cut from the film, Hart rewrote the number as "Manhattan Melodrama" as the title song for a film, but again it was cut from the final print. With a third lyric titled "The Bad in Every Man," the song was sung by Shirley Ross in that same *Manhattan Melodrama* (1934), but it made little impact and was quickly forgotten. A studio head liked the tune and told Hart he would promote the number if he could come up with a title that was more commercial. So Hart wrote "Blue Moon," a simple but heartfelt lyric that addresses the moon that watches over as two lovers are reunited. It is an atypical Hart lyric, being more sentimental than sophisticated, and the lyricist did not think very highly of the number himself, calling the title a spoof of every moon-spoon-croon ballad ever written. But the public was not so critical, and a record by Glen Gray and the

Casa Loma Orchestra went to the top of the charts. Benny Goodman also had a hit with the song, and it was revived with success in 1949 by Mel Tormé and by Billy Eckstine, and again in 1961 with a million-seller by Elvis Presley and a Number One hit by the Marcels. Other noteworthy discs were made by Tony Bennett, Carmen McRae, Jo Stafford, Helen Ward, Tex Beneke, Billie Holiday, Chet Baker, Ella Fitzgerald, Julie London, Oscar Peterson, Dave Brubeck, Ray Anthony, Mandy Patinkin, and Bob Dylan. Harpo Marx played it on the harp in the film *At the Circus* (1939), Tormé reprised it in *Words and Music* (1948), Jane Froman was heard on the soundtrack of *With a Song in My Heart* (1952), Joan Crawford (dubbed by India Adams) performed it in *Torch Song* (1953), Mary Kay Place and Robert DeNiro did a duet version in *New York, New York* (1977), the group Sha Na Na was heard singing it in *Grease* (1978), the Marcels with Bobby Vinton and Sam Cooke were on the soundtrack of *An American Werewolf in London* (1981), and Dudley Moore performed it in *Arthur* (1981), "Blue Moon" has been heard in the background in several movies, including *Hollywood Hotel* (1938), *Malaya* (1949), *East Side, West Side* (1949), *Rogue Cop* (1954), *This Could Be the Night* (1957), *8 ½* (1963), *Babe* (1995), and *Apollo 13* (1995). Also, Kim Criswell sang it in the Off-Broadway show *Slow Drag* (1997).

"Blue Prelude" (1933) is mostly remembered as the theme song for Woody Herman and his Orchestra in the 1940s, but the slow blues number was introduced by Isham Jones and his Orchestra much earlier. Joe Bishop composed the delicate music, and bandleader Gordon Jenkins wrote the lyric, a farewell song in which a dejected admirer promises to leave town and work out his grief elsewhere, commenting, "[W]hat is love but a prelude to sorrow?" Glen Gray and the Casa Loma Orchestra and George Hall (vocal by Loretta Lee) both had popular recordings of the ballad, and there were also records by Jenkins, Lena Horne, Boyd Raeburn, Clyde McCoy, Jan August and the Harmonicats, Adrian Rollini (vocal by Howard Phillips), Nancy Wilson, Zoot Sims and Jimmy Rowles, Bing Crosby, the Ames Brothers, and Marian McPartland.

"Blue Skies" (1926) is the perennial song favorite by Irving Berlin in which the lyric explores the various implications of the word "blue," from a color to a bird to a feeling. Although the song is in the standard AABA structure, the shifts from minor to major keys (the verse is a very bluesy minor, while the refrain is an optimistic major) make it very inventive and, consequently, a favorite of jazz musicians. The song was introduced when Belle Baker interpolated it into the Rodgers and Hart musical *Besty* (1926) because she needed a different solo piece. The number went over so well on opening night that Baker was forced to do twenty-four encores before the audience was satisfied. "Blue Skies" immediately got around, the first recording by Ben Selvin and his Orchestra climbing to the top of the charts. Other early hit discs were made by Harry Richman, Al Jolson, and the orchestras of George Olsen and Vincent Lopez. Johnny Long revived the still-popular number in 1941, Benny Goodman did the same in 1946, and Willie Nelson's 1978 recording sold a million copies. Other highly regarded records were made by Josephine Baker, Ben Webster, Ella Fitzgerald, Artie Shaw, Pete Fountain, Erroll Garner, Maxine Sullivan, Dinah Washington, Perry Como, Lou Rawls, Bobby Darin, and more recently, Andrea Marcovicci, Kiri Te Kanawa, and Susannah McCorkle. Jolson sang the song in the first sound film, *The Jazz Singer* (1927), Alice Faye and Ethel Merman did a duet version in *Alexander's Ragtime Band* (1938), Bing Crosby crooned it in *Blue Skies* (1946), and Crosby reprised it with Danny Kaye in *White Christmas* (1954).

"Blue Turning Gray Over You" (1930) is a jazzy blues number by Andy Razaf (lyric) and Thomas "Fats" Waller (music) that plays off the double meaning of "blue" to create a nimble lament. Louis Armstrong introduced the song on record, followed by early discs by Waller and Lee Morse. Later recordings of distinction were made by Earl Hines, James P. Johnson, Gene Krupa, Charlie Barnet, Harry James, Nat Shilkret, Sidney Bechet, Ringo Starr, and Frankie Laine.

"Blue Velvet" (1951) is a wailing torch song that Tony Bennett popularized with his slightly lisping croon, which comics of the day loved to mimic. Bernie Wayne and Lee Morris wrote the lament in which one recalls a lost lover who wore blue velvet that went with her blue eyes. When Bobby Vinton revived the song in 1971, his record was a bestseller. There were also discs by Ray Anthony, Lawrence Welk, the Moonglows, Gene Ammons, Brenda Lee, Johnny Tillotson, the Paragons, Red Garland, and Johnny Hodges. The Bennett recording was heard in the movie *The Last Picture Show* (1971), and Vinton's was on the soundtrack of *Blue Velvet* (1986).

"Blueberry Hill" (1940) is a country-blues favorite by Al Lewis, Larry Stock, and Vincent Rose that has a strong sexual connotation but seemed to slip by the censors to become a hit. The lyric is about two sweethearts who met in the moonlight on Blueberry Hill and, now that they are no longer together, recall how each "found my thrill" that night. The song caught on when it was interpolated into the film *The Singing Hill* (1941), where it was sung by Gene Autry. This was followed by hit records by Glenn Miller (vocal by Ray Eberly), and Kay Kyser that kept the number on *Your Hit Parade* for fourteen weeks. When Fats Domino revived it in 1957, his recording sold a million copies. "Blueberry Hill" was also a specialty of Louis Armstrong whose 1949 version with Gordon Jenkins' Orchestra was popular and became a hit again when it was released in the late 1950s. Brenda Lee, the Oscar Peterson Quartet, Elvis Presley, Pat Boone, Duane Eddy, Cliff Richard, Andy Williams, the Walker Brothers, Johnny Cash, and Carol Sloane are among the many who also recorded it. Domino reprised it in the film rockumentary *Let the Good Times Roll* (1973), and the song was often crooned by Ron Howard in the long-running television series *Happy Days*.

"Blues in My Heart" (1931) is a ballad in the blues mode that Fletcher Henderson and his Orchestra introduced but found favor through a record by Ethel Waters with Herman Chittison. The Irving Mills (lyric) and Benny Carter (music) number was recorded by a variety of artists in the 1930s and 1940s, some of the most notable discs by Bert Lown, Mildred Bailey, Chick Webb, Cab Calloway, Eddie Davis, Marty Grosz, Ray Noble (vocal by Al Bowlly), Lee Sims, the Browns, Greta Keller, and Scott Hamilton.

"Body and Soul" (1930) is the morose torch song by Edward Heyman, Robert Sour, Frank Eyton (lyric), and Johnny Green (music) that became popular in Europe before becoming a hit in the States. The sensual lyric offers both body and soul for love but cynically "turns away romance." Green's composition is distinctive, its musical line being both innovative and appealing. The series of musical fragments that do not resolve until the title phrase set the style for many other 1930s songs. The lyric structure is also unusual, the release providing the information usually presented in the verse. (Some radio stations thought the number too lewd for air play, so the final line of the lyric was changed from "I'd gladly surrender myself" to "my castles have crumbled.") Green wrote the number for Gertrude Lawrence, who sang it on BBC radio, and a recording by British bandleader Bert Ambrose was a hit overseas. American producer Max Gordon heard the song and interpolated it into his Broadway revue *Three's a Crowd* (1930), where it was sung by Libby Holman and danced by Clifton Webb and Tamara Geva. The first recording in America was by Leo Reisman with Eddy Duchin at the piano, then a Number One record by Paul Whiteman (vocal Jack Fulton), and they were followed by dozens of others over the years. Long a favorite of jazz musicians, it was given a classic interpretation by Coleman Hawkins on tenor sax in 1940. The Benny Goodman Trio made their first record with the song. Other significant discs were made by Ruth Etting, Helen Morgan, Louis Armstrong, Martha Raye, Ben Webster, Dave Brubeck, Ella Fitzgerald, Gordon MacRae, Sarah Vaughan, Carmen McRae, Ozzie Nelson, and Bill Evans. Ida Lupino sang "Body and Soul" in the film *The Man I Love* (1946), Ann Blyth (dubbed by Gogi Grant) performed it in *The Helen Morgan Story* (1957), and it was heard on the soundtracks of *Her Kind of Man* (1946), *Body and Soul* (1947), *The Eddy Duchin Story* (1956), *They Shoot Horses, Don't They?* (1969), and *Radio Days* (1987). On Broadway, it was sung by Ruth Brown in the revue *Black and Blue* (1989).

"The Bonnie Blue Flag" (1861) was the most popular Civil War song in the South after "Dixie," and it was sung by Confederate troops in camps, while marching, and even in battle. Henry McCarthy composed the flowing music, based on an old Irish tune called "The Jaunting Car." Annie Chambers-Ketchum penned the patriotic lyric about the events leading up to succession and the glory of the flag adopted by South Carolina, a blue banner "that bears a single star." The song was first performed by McCarthy in New Orleans in 1861, and it remained a Southern favorite throughout the war and for some time after. In 1955, William Engvick (lyric) and Jessie Cavanaugh (music) adapted the piece into a new number called "Bonnie Blue Gal," and it was recorded by Lawrence Welk's Orchestra with the Mitch Miller Singers. The tune can be heard in the background of some Civil War movies, most memorably *The Horse Soldiers* (1959).

"Boo-Hoo" (1937) is a silly torch song that was a surprise hit in the late 1930s and remained on *Your Hit Parade* for eleven weeks. Edward Heyman, Carmen Lombardo, and John Jacob Loeb wrote the novelty number about a distraught fiancé who has been left at the alter by his betrothed and is crying out, "I'll tell my mama on you!" The ditty was introduced and popularized by Guy Lombardo (vocal by Carmen Lombardo), and Fats Waller also had a big hit with it. Others who recorded the song were Mal Hallet, Count Basie, Jimmy Dorsey, Bert Kaempfert, Benny Goodman, Wingy Manone, and Jimmy Rushing. The wailing number can be heard in the movies *Dead End* (1937) and *Stars on Parade* (1944).

"Bounce Me Brother With a Solid Four" (1941) is a swing favorite that celebrates the rhythm of 4/4 time ("play it again!") and its dancing possibilities ("let's dance!"). Don Raye and Hughie Prince wrote the vivacious number, and it was popularized by the Andrews Sisters. It was also recorded by Woody Herman, Tom Cunningham, and the team of Will Bradley and Ray McKinley, who made records of the other "family" swing songs "Beat Me Daddy, Eight to the Bar," "Swing, Brother, Swing," and "Scrub Me Mama With a Boogie Beat." The Andrews Sisters performed "Bounce Me Brother With a Solid Four" in the film *Buck Privates* (1941), and it was also heard in *One Exciting Week* (1946) and *Willie and Joe Back at the Front* (1952). Ann Hampton Callaway and trumpeter Douglas Oberhamer performed the number in the Broadway revue *Swing!* (1999).

"Brazil" (1939) is perhaps the most famous samba song to hit Tin Pan Alley and a Latin standard that remained popular for decades. Ary Baroso wrote the music and the original Portuguese lyric, which was titled "Aquarela do Brazil," in his native country. S.K. Russell penned an English lyric about the South American country, and it was introduced by Eddy Duchin and his Orchestra on record and on the soundtrack of the Disney animated movie *Saludos Amigos* (1943). Carmen Miranda sang it in *The Gang's All Here* (1943), Nan Wynn performed it in *Jam Session* (1944), and it was heard on the soundtracks of *Road to Rio* (1956), *The Eddy Duchin Story* (1956), and three movies titled *Brazil* (1943, 1944, and 1985). Hit recordings of the samba were made by Xavier Cugat (vocal by members of the band) and Jimmy Dorsey (vocal by Helen O'Connell and Bob Eberly). Les Paul made a unique recording in 1948 using multitrack guitars that was a hit, as was a 1975 disco version by the Ritchie Family. In addition to just about every rhumba band, "Brazil" was also recorded by Billy Vaughn, Josephine Baker, Bo Thorpe, Perez Prado, Percy Faith, the Dinning Sisters, Ethel Smith, Frank Ifield, the Ventures, and more recently, Julia Migenes.

"Break the News to Mother" (1897) is a maudlin but powerful ballad that Charles K. Harris wrote after seeing the stage drama *Secret Service* (1896) in which a dying drummer boy in the Civil War whispers the title phrase to a black house servant. Harris's lyric tells of a young Union soldier who rushes forward to save the flag when it falls in battle and is mortally wounded in the process. Carried back to camp, he pleads with his fellow soldiers to tell his mother "not to wait for me . . . I love her . . . I'm not coming home." Harris was pleased with the song but felt sure that no one wanted a Civil War song thirty years after the event, so he put it away. When the Spanish-American war broke out, "Break the News to Mother" was published and became popular right away. Troops sang it on the battlefield, and citizens at home played it on their parlor pianos. The ballad was revived again during World War One. Sometimes listed as "Just Break the News to Mother," the song can be heard in the period films *The Floradora Girl* (1930) and *Wait Till the Sun Shines, Nellie* (1952).

"The Breeze and I" (1940) is a Latin-flavored torch song in which a jilted one joins the breeze in sighing over a lost love. The song began as a solo piano piece by Ernesto Lecuona titled "Andalucia Suite." Tutti Camarata adapted the music and Al Stillman wrote the lyric, and the ballad was popularized by Jimmy Dorsey (vocal by Bob Eberly) with a 1940 record that hit Number One on the charts and placed it on the *Hit Parade* for thirteen weeks. Xavier Cugat and Vic Damone each had successful discs of the song, which was also recorded by Art Blakey, Dinah Shore, Coleman Hawkins, Wes Montgomery, the Flamingos, and Curtis Fuller, Ethel Smith performed it on the organ in the movie *Cuban Pete* (1946), and it was heard in *On the Riviera* (1951).

"Breezin' Along With the Breeze" (1926) is a lighthearted travel song by Haven Gillespie, Seymour Simons, and Richard A. Whiting about a rover who's "trailin' the rails" and happy to be free and easy. Al Jolson popularized the number, and Lou Brese took it as the theme song for his orchestra. Danny Thomas sang it in the first remake of *The Jazz Singer* (1953), Lucille Ball and Desi Arnaz did a duet version in *The Long, Long Trailer* (1954), Ann Blyth (dubbed by Gogi Grant) performed it in *The Helen Morgan Story* (1957), and it was also heard in *Shine On Harvest Moon* (1944) and *Pete Kelly's Blues* (1955). The happy-go-lucky song was recorded by Abe Lyman, Nellie Lutcher, Josephine Baker, the Revelers, Red Nichols, the Hoosier Hot Shots, Bing Crosby, the Four Lads, the Smoothies, and the piano duo of Marlene Fingerle and Arthur Schutt.

"Brother, Can You Spare a Dime?" (1932) has been called the unofficial theme song of the depression because it struck a chord with so many Americans. David Ewen notes that it is the "one song more than all the others [that] sounded the keynote" of those difficult years. While many popular songs of the era sought to cheer the public up and offer hope for the future, this one was brutally honest as it offers a forceful message while still remaining understated. E.Y. Harburg wrote the piercing lyric in which a veteran from World War One stands in line for a piece of bread, asking how he went from a wartime hero to one of society's cast-offs. The voice is more dazed and confused than bitter as he asks how he descended from saving the world to panhandling for a dime. Jay Gorney composed the haunting music that moves from recitative form in the verse to a wailing march in the refrain. Gorney based his main musical theme on a Russian-Jewish lullaby, but it moves forward irregularly with bits of syncopation. As James R. Morris points out, the "combination of rhythm and harmony establishes a sense of uncertainty, countered by the classic, even conventional melodic architecture of the AABA" pattern. The song was written for the Broadway revue *Americana* (1932), but the producers thought it too disturbing for escapist entertainment, and it was nearly cut in rehearsals. The songwriters held firm, and on opening night it was sung by Rex Weber and the chorus. Audiences, at the lowest point of the depression, immediately seized on the gripping number. Just as many were threatened by the song, particularly the Republican administration with an election only a month away. Attempts were made to ban the anthem from radio play, but it was already proving popular, thanks to recordings by Bing Crosby and Rudy Vallee. "Brother, Can You Spare a Dime?" did not disappear after the depression. In 1985 Tom Waitts sang a slightly revised version as an anthem for the homeless and unemployed, and the number is still used today as the theme song for the National Coalition of the Homeless. The number can be heard in the background of 1930s films, such as *Embarrassing Moments* (1934), and later movies set during the depression, such as *They Shoot Horses, Don't They?* (1969). Notable recordings over the years include those by Leo Reisman, Al Jolson, George Dosher, Ike Quebec, Maxine Sullivan, the Weavers, Ronnie Lane, Connie Francis, Dave Brubeck, Don McLean, Phil Harris, Eartha Kitt, Tom Jones, Judy Collins, Mandy Patinkin, and Peter, Paul and Mary.

"Buffalo Gals (Won't You Come Out Tonight?)" (1844) is one of America's oldest and most popular cowboy songs, dating back to minstrel shows before the Civil War (the tune is mentioned in Mark Twain's *Tom Sawyer*) when it was called "Lubly Fan." Cool White wrote the version familiar today, and he introduced it with the Virginia Serenaders on the minstrel circuit. The invitation to go out dancing with the "Dolly with a hole in her stocking" was so popular that cities often localized the lyric and sang variations such as "Pittsburgh Gals" and "Louisiana Gals." In 1944 Terry Shand, Jimmy Eaton, and Mickey Leader rewrote the song as "Dance With a Dolly (With a Hole in Her Stocking)," and it was on the *Hit Parade* for fifteen weeks, thanks to records by Russ Morgan (vocal by Al Jennings), Tony Pastor, and Evelyn Knight. The traditional version was sung by the Jimmy Wakely Trio in the movie *Strictly in the Groove* (1942) and heard in *Cow Town* (1950), while the new version was used in *On Stage, Everyone* (1945) and sung by the Andrews Sisters in *Her Lucky Night* (1945). The Sons of the Pioneers, Woody Guthrie, Rosemary Clooney, Malcolm McLaren, Roy Acuff, Pete Seeger, and dozens of children's and sing-along records have featured the merry number over the years.

"The Bully Song" (1895) is a strutting, vigorous number that was one of the first song hits in the new ragtime idiom. The uninhabited lyric boasts about looking for the bully (a "red-eyed river roustabout") who is terrorizing the neighborhood. It was written for May Irwin, who belted it out first in vaudeville and then in the Broadway musical *The Widow Jones* (1895) where the number became her trademark and she became known as "the stage mother of ragtime." The song was commonly referred to as "May Irwin's Bully Song," and it was sometimes listed that way. Charles E. Trevathan is credited with the music and lyric, but the authorship is questioned. It is believed Trevathan based his song on a black urban folk song that was never published or even written down. And a St. Louis saloon song set on the waterfront predates Trevathan's composition, and it is known that he visited St. Louis soon before 1895.

(The lyric even refers to the levee.) The popularity of the song waned after Irwin died, so in many ways it really was "May Irwin's Bully Song."

"By the Beautiful Sea" (1914) is the perennial quickstep favorite that remains one of the most recognized tunes in American pop culture. Harry Carroll composed the zesty music that dances up and down the scale like the waves on a beach, and Harold Atteridge penned the agile lyric that celebrates a vacation by the seaside. The number was introduced in vaudeville by the Stanford Four and was interpolated into the Broadway revue *The Passing Show of 1914*, where it was sung by Muriel Window. Healthy sheet music sales and early records by the Heidelberg Quintet, Ada Jones, Billy Watkins, and Prince's Orchestra soon had all of America singing the spirited tune. Judy Garland, George Murphy, Ben Blue, and the chorus performed the ditty in the period film *For Me and My Gal* (1942), Constance Moore sang it in *Atlantic City* (1944), and it was heard in the background in several movies, including *The Story of Vernon and Irene Castle* (1939), *Coney Island* (1943), *Some Like It Hot* (1959), and *They Shoot Horses, Don't They?* (1969). Recordings over the years ranged from traditional versions (the Firehouse Five Plus Two) to satirical ones (Spike Jones and his City Slickers), as well as those by Eddie Cantor, Barney Kessel, Ronny Whyte, and more recently, Alison Fraser, Jackie Cain, and Roy Kral.

"By the Light of the Silvery Moon" (1909) is the crooning standard that has long been a favorite of glee clubs, barbershop quartets, and singalongs. Gus Edwards composed the dreamy soft-shoe music, and Edward Madden wrote the smooth lyric depicting a moonlit romance. The verse is a series of short phrases that set up the scene, even with stage directions and dialogue, then the refrains rolls along with all of the rhymes but one rhyming with "moon." The whole lyric is a cliché now with its moon-June-croon rhymes, but it is still a beautifully constructed piece of Tin Pan Alley songwriting. Child star Georgie Price introduced the song in a kiddie show in vaudeville, but it got more notice when it was interpolated into the *Ziegfeld Follies of 1909*, where it was sung by Lillian Lorraine. Early records were made by Billy Murray, Ada Jones, and the Peerless Quartet, and later ones by Guy Lombardo, Johnny Winter, Burl Ives, Fats Waller, the Banjo Kings, Les Paul and Mary Ford, Little Richard, Louis Prima, and Julie Andrews. None was more popular than a 1942 disc by Ray Noble and his Orchestra that sold a million copies. The song has been heard in dozens of movies as well. It was sung by Clark Gable and the chorus in *Idiot's Delight* (1939), Bing Crosby in *Birth of the Blues* (1941), Alice Faye in *Hello, Frisco, Hello* (1943), Scotty Beckett in *The Jolson Story* (1946), Jane Powell in *Two Weeks With Love* (1950), and Doris Day and Gordon MacRae in *By the Light of the Silvery*

Moon (1953) and in the background in such films as *The Broadway Hoofer* (1929), *Ruggles of Red Gap* (1935), *The Story of Vernon and Irene Castle* (1939), *Babes on Broadway* (1942), *Flame of the Barbary Coast* (1945), *Sunbonnet Sue* (1945), and *Always Leave Them Laughing* (1949).

"Bye Bye Blackbird" (1926) is an unusual rhythmic song with a distinctive musical pattern and a breezy lyric that seems to retain its freshness decade after decade. Mort Dixon wrote the catchy lyric, a series of nonsequitors about waiting all winter with the blackbird singing the blues outside the door. But now that spring is here, it is time to find a true love and bid the bird farewell. Ray Henderson composed the music, which is punctuated with quarter rests throughout, stopping the melody and the lyric in an effective way. Georgie Price sang it in vaudeville and made it his theme song, but it was Eddie Cantor who popularized the number. There were early records by Nick Lucas, Gene Austin, and the orchestras of George Olsen and Leo Reisman, followed by dozens of later ones. A Russ Morgan disc revived the song in 1949, yet it had never completely fallen out of favor. Just a sampling of the artists who recorded it includes Frank Froeba and His Boys, Six Hits and a Miss, Dean Martin, Mitch Miller, Sammy Davis Jr., Trini Lopez, Miles Davis, Vikki Carr, and Liza Minnelli. Frankie Laine sang it in *Rainbow Round My Shoulder* (1952), Marilyn Monroe performed it in *River of No Return* (1954), Cantor provided the singing voice for Keefe Braselle in *The Eddie Cantor Story* (1953), Peggy Lee sang it in *Pete Kelly's Blues* (1955), Ty Hardin and Jerry Van Dyke did a duet version in *Palm Springs Weekend* (1963), and Jason Robards growled it in *Melvin and Howard* (1980). It can also be heard in *When My Baby Smiles at Me* (1948), *The Helen Morgan Story* (1957), and sung by Joe Cocker on the soundtrack of *Sleepless in Seattle* (1993). The number was sung and danced by the cast of the Broadway revue *Fosse* (1999).

"Bye Bye Blues" (1930) has remained a favorite of tap dancers and softshoe hoofers for several decades because of its deliberate rhythmic quality. Bert Lown, Chauncey Gray, David Bennett, and Fred Hamm collaborated on the lively farewell song that says "so long" to sorrow since a sweetie has smiled on one, causing bells to ring and birds to sing. Lown and his Orchestra introduced the song at the Biltmore Hotel, and soon after Leo Reisman helped popularize it. It was revived by Cab Calloway in 1941 and by Les Paul and Mary Ford in 1953. Other noteworthy discs along the way were made by Count Basie, Benny Goodman, Dinah Shore, Frankie Trumbauer, Andy Ross, Merle Travis, Dizzy Gillespie, Peggy Lee, Larry Elgart, and Julius LaRosa.

C

"**Cabin in the Cotton**" (1932) is a southern-style ballad that, like most songs about the south, paints an idyllic picture of rural life back home. Mitchell Parish (lyric) and Frank Perkins (music) wrote the number that was interpolated into the revue *George White's Music Hall Follies* (1932) and was later used in the film *George White's Scandals of 1934*. The song was popularized by a hit record by Bing Crosby with Lennie Hayton's Orchestra, followed by discs by Cab Calloway with Bennie Payne, Johnny Hamp, Harry "Singing Sam" Frankel, Carol Gibbons, Barron Lee and the Blue Rhythm Band, and Russ Carlson and the High Steppe. The ballad, sometimes listed as "There's a Cabin in the Cotton," was revived years later with a record by Neal Hefti (vocal by Frances Wayne).

"**The Caissons Go Rolling Along**" (1908) is the official song of the U.S. Artillery and has become the unofficial theme song for the U.S. Army in toto. Just a few measures of the famous march bring to mind the military even though caissons (wagons) have long since disappeared. Edmund L. Gruber, a West Point graduate of the class of 1904, wrote the patriotic number while serving in the Artillery Corps in the Philippines. The marching song encourages the troops to pull the wagons "over hill, over dale" and to "call off your numbers loud and strong." Although used by the military soon after it was written, the song was not known to the general public until John Philip Sousa did an arrangement of it called "The Field Artillery March" and played it in a concert in the New York Hippodrome. Because he popularized the march, many wrongly credited Sousa with writing the original song. Most recordings of the number are by marching bands and chorale groups, most notably the Robert Shaw Chorale, Bob Crosby, Andre Kostelanetz, Steve Rapson, Jenks Tex Carman, John McDermott, Gene Krupa, and the Mormon Tabernacle

Choir. Nelson Eddy sang it in the movie *Rosalie* (1937), and it was heard in dozens of other films over the years, most memorably *Ice-Capades Revue* (1942), *The Heat's On* (1943), and *Four Jills in a Jeep* (1944). The march is sometimes listed as "Over Hill, Over Dale" or "The Caisson Song."

"Caldonia (What Makes Your Big Head So Hard?)" (1945) is a jaunty swing number by Fleecie Moore that was popularized by Louis Jordan and his Tympani Five with a record that sold a million copies. The ribald lyric concerns a "lean and lanky" gal named Caldonia who had big feet and is unfaithful, but one loves her all the same for what she's "puttin down." Woody Herman's recording was also very successful, as was a disc by Erskine Hawkins (vocal by Ace Harris). Other major records were made by Carl Perkins, Dale Hawkins, Muddy Waters, Louis Prima, the Chevalier Brothers, Bill Haley and the Comets, and B.B. King. Jordan reprised "Caldonia" in the film *Swing Parade of 1946* (1946), and it was also heard in *No Love, No Leave* (1946). The song, sometimes listed as "Caldonia Boogie," was performed in the Broadway revue *Five Guys Named Moe* (1992) as a sing-along number with the audience led by Doug Eskew.

"California, Here I Come" (1923) was long associated with Al Jolson but has survived as perhaps the most popular song about the state. B.G. DeSylva, Jolson (lyric), and Joseph W. Meyer wrote the forceful number about leaving the cold and snow and returning to one's home in California, and it was introduced by Jolson who interpolated it into the 1923 tour of his Broadway hit *Bombo* (1921). Although his name appeared on the sheet music, it is questionable if Jolson actually helped write the song. But he did popularize it and made it a hit in the 1920s and again in the 1940s when he provided the singing voice for Larry Parks in the movie *The Jolson Story* (1946), his new recording selling a million copies. Jolson also sang it in *The Singing Kid* (1936) and *Rose of Washington Square* (1939) and for Parks in *Jolson Sings Again* (1949). Jolson's rival George Jessel sang "California, Here I Come" in the film *Lucky Boy* (1929), Benny Goodman and his Orchestra performed it in *Hollywood Hotel* (1938), and Jane Froman sang it on the soundtrack for Susan Hayward in *With a Song in My Heart* (1952). It can also be heard in *Billion Dollar Scandal* (1933), *Torchy Blane in Panama* (1938), *You're My Everything* (1949), and *They Shoot Horses, Don't They?* (1969). The number became the theme song for both Abe Lyman and his Californians and the California Ramblers, and there were other noteworthy recordings by Eddie Cantor, Georgie Price, Cliff Edwards, Ben Pollack, Eddie Condon, Mabel Mercer, Freddy Cannon, Bob Grant, and Ray Charles.

"Can You Tame Wild Wimmen?" (1918) is a delightful novelty song in which a put-upon male asks the title question of a lion tamer. Andrew B. Sterling (lyric) and Harry Von Tilzer (music) wrote the silly ditty, and it was recorded with success by Billy Murray and Arthur Fields. The amusing number is all but forgotten today.

"Canadian Sunset" (1956) is a slightly swinging song about finding true love on the ski slopes while vacationing in Canada. Norman Gimbel wrote the atmospheric lyric, and jazz pianist Eddie Heywood composed the sweet-sounding music that has a touch of a cowboy song about it. The number was popularized by an instrumental record by Hugo Winterhalter and his Orchestra with Heywood at the piano, and soon after Andy Williams recorded it; both discs sold over a million copies each. There were also recordings by Woody Herman, Archie Bleyer, Earl Bostic, Etta Jones, Floyd Cramer, Jo Ann Castle, Tony Martin, the Four Aces, Dean Martin, Keely Smith, Billy Vaughn, George Shearing, Richard Chamberlain, and Anne Murray.

"Caravan" (1937) is an enticing ballad by Irving Mills (lyric), Juan Tizol, and Duke Ellington (music) that manages to have a sense of both romance and danger. The lyric paints an exotic picture of two lovers together under the moon in a desert caravan. Ellington and his Orchestra introduced and popularized the song, and it was revived with a hit record by Billy Eckstine in 1949 and again by Ralph Marterie in 1953. Other versions of note were made by Barney Bigard, Dizzy Gillespie, Les Paul, Nat King Cole, the Mills Brothers, the Ventures, Coleman Hawkins, Les Brown, Lawrence Welk, and Bunny Berigan and his Orchestra. The Berigan version was used on the soundtrack of the film *Sweet and Lowdown* (1999), and a recording by the Arthur Lyman Group was heard in *Ocean's Eleven* (2001). On Broadway, Gregg Burge and the ensemble sang it in the revue *Sophisticated Ladies* (1981), and the Gotham City Gates performed an instrumental version in the revue *Swing!* (1999).

"Careless" (1939) is a plaintive ballad about a wooer whose intended is taking him for granted, not only acting "careless" but also seeming to "care less" for him. Lew Quadling, Eddy Howard, and Dick Jurgens are the credited authors, but it is believed that Irving Berlin helped with the lyric. The play on words in the song is certainly in the Berlin style. Jurgens and his Orchestra (vocal by Howard) popularized the number with a top-of-the-chart record, and Glenn Miller (vocal by Ray Eberly) also had success with it. Tommy Dorsey, Phil Harris, Dinah Shore, Tony Martin, Teddy Powell, Woody Herman, Lena Horne, Vera Lynn, and Ella Fitzgerald were among the many who also recorded it.

"Careless Hands" (1949) is a rhythmic ballad with a memorable lyric about letting one's heart fall into the hands of someone who is not careful with it. The singer complains that her lover held her dreams "like worthless grains of sand" in his hand and, not being able to hold on to love, let it slip through his fingers. Carl Sigman and Bob Hilliard wrote the felicitous song, and it was popularized by a record by Mel Tormé with Sonny Burke's Orchestra that went to the top of the charts. Sammy Kaye (vocal by Don Cornell) also had a bestseller version. Other highly regarded recordings were made by Bing Crosby, Jimmy Dorsey, Larry Clinton, Kitty Kallen, Bob and Jeanne, Jerry Lee Lewis, Tex Ritter, and Slim Whitman.

"Careless Love" (1921) is a celebrated slow blues with uncertain origins. It is a standard blues number in music and lyric ("see what love has done to me"), yet it has a folk element to it as well. It is believed the song originated in the mountains of the American South and was sung by white inhabitants. But later a blues version was sung by African American workers in Missouri. To add to the mystery, the number has also been published as "Careless Love Blues" and "Loveless Love" (with different authors listed each time) and later became a jazz and hillbilly favorite. W.C. Handy and Spencer Williams are the credited composers with Martha E. Koenig usually listed as the lyricist. Recordings (under the various titles) were made by Lee Morse, Ethel Waters, Fats Waller, Noble Sissle, the Yale Glee Club, Bessie Smith, Lee Wiley, the Four Tunes, Billie Holiday, Lena Horne, and the Mills Brothers. The song enjoyed a revival of interest when Nat King Cole and Eartha Kitt sang it in the Handy movie bio *St. Louis Blues* (1958), and later Ray Charles performed it in the British film *Blues for Lovers* (a.k.a. *Ballad in Blue*) (1966).

"Carolina in the Morning" (1922) is the dreamy standard by Gus Kahn (lyric) and Walter Donaldson (music) that longs to return home to the South where the morning dew is "pearly early" and the morning glories twine around your door. Donaldson's flowing music alternates back and forth between two notes (a device he used that same year in "My Buddy"), while Kahn's lyric is warm and evocative with a gentle southern drawl to it (he rhymes "Carolina" and "finer"). Kahn had never been to either of the Carolinas, but both states embraced the number, as did the whole nation. The ballad was introduced in vaudeville by Lillian Frawley and was quickly interpolated into the Broadway revue *The Passing Show of 1922*, where it was performed by the comedy team of Willie and Eugene Howard. The song gained further attention because of a top-selling record by the team of Van and Schenck, and Paul Whiteman and his Orchestra also helped popularize it. Although "Carolina in the Morning" was never totally forgotten, it was revived when Al Jolson sang it on the soundtrack of the movie bios *The Jolson Story* (1946) and *Jolson Sings Again* (1949). It was also sung on screen by June Haver and Betty Grable in *The Dolly Sisters* (1945), Robert Alda, Ann Sothern, and Bobbie Ellis in *April Showers* (1948), and Patricia Wymore in the Kahn bio *I'll See You in My Dreams* (1952). Others who made discs of the song include Ray Noble, Benny Goodman, Red Nichols and his Five Pennies, the Golden Gate Quartet, Pat Flowers, Freddie Cannon, Bob Grant, Judy Garland, and more recently, Barbara Cook.

"Carolina Moon" (1928) combines two of Tin Pan Alley's favorite romantic elements: a glowing moon and down south. Benny Davis and Joe Burke wrote this waltzing ballad that recalls how the moon shone in Carolina the night two lovers parted and now asks the moon to keep shining on until they are reunited. Gene Austin introduced the number, which later became the theme song for Morton Downey on radio and in concerts. Guy Lombardo and the Royal Canadians also had a hit with it. Among the others who recorded the lyrical piece were Smith Ballew, Jesse Crawford, Basil Fomeen, the Ernie Felice Quartet, Thelonious Monk, Connie Francis, Dean Martin, Perry Como, and Maureen McGovern. It was heard in the movie *Twenty Million Sweethearts* (1934), and Gene Autry sang it in *Carolina Moon* (1940).

"Carry Me Back to Old Virginny" (1878) was a longtime staple in minstrel shows, yet it remained popular after that kind of entertainment died out and was made the official state song of Virginia in 1940. James Bland, an African American songwriter, drew on his memories of a peaceful plantation on the James River and wrote the nostalgic number about an old slave who wishes to be brought back to the South where he was born. The song was introduced by minstrel performer George Primrose, and soon several minstrel troupes were performing it. "Carry Me Back to Old Virginny" was recorded as early as 1915 by Alma Gluck and was later sung on disc by such artists as Marian Anderson, Bunk Johnson, Jo Stafford, Rufus Thomas, Helen Traubel, Randy Brooks, Jeanette MacDonald, the Mills Brothers, and the Sons of the Pioneers. MacDonald and Nelson Eddy sang it in the film *Maytime* (1937), Alice Faye, Tyler Brooke, and a male quartet performed it in *In Old Chicago* (1938), Roy Rogers crooned it in *Heart of the Golden West* (1942), Jane Froman dubbed it for Susan Hayward to sing in *With a Song in My Heart* (1952), and it was heard in *Sing, Baby, Sing* (1936), *Hullabaloo* (1940), *Juke Box Jenny* (1942), *The Merry Monahans* (1944), *Golden Girl* (1951), and other movies.

"Carry Me Back to the Lone Prairie" (1934) is the cowboy standard that, ironically, had its biggest hit when sung by an opera singer. Carson T.

Robison wrote the tearful folk song about a dying cowboy who asked to be carried back to the west so he can be buried "where the wind blows free." Robison adapted the song from an 1850 folk tune titled "The Ocean Burial" (which had been taken from a poem by E.H. Chapin), and he introduced it on the radio with his Buckaroos. But the ballad didn't catch on until opera tenor James Melton sang it in the film *Stars Over Broadway* (1935), and his disc version was a hit. Among the recordings that followed were those by Eddy Arnold, Gene Autry and Mary Lee, Johnny Bond, Dick Curless, Roy Rogers and the Sons of the Pioneers, Cisco Houston, Burl Ives, the Carter Family, and Johnny Cash. The song goes under a variety of titles, including "The Dying Cowboy," "Bury Me Not on the Lone Prairie," and even "The Ocean Burial." The ballad can be heard in many western films, including *Sing Me a Song* (1937), *Stagecoach* (1939), *Ridin' on a Rainbow* (1941), and *Cow Town* (1950).

"Casey Jones" (1909) is one of America's most cherished railroad songs and a musical testament to a folk hero who stands as a symbol of heroism in railroading. The narrative ballad is based on a real person and an actual event. Train engineer John Luther Jones, nicknamed "Casey," substituted for a sick friend one day in 1900 and drove the Cannonball Ltd. out of Memphis, heading south, but met with a fatal crash in Mississippi. As the lyric explains, he was "scalded to death by the steam . . . with his hand on the throttle," but he bravely "run her till she leaves the rail." Wallace Saunders, a black engineer who worked with the real Casey, wrote a poem about the incident, and it was printed in a magazine. Vaudevillians T. Lawrence Seibert (lyric) and Eddie Newton (music) took the poem and wrote the song version in 1909. It was popularized in vaudeville by the Leighton Brothers, and there were early hit recordings by the American Quartet, Billy Murray, and Arthur Collins and Bryon Harlan that turned the legend into a song standard. Prominent records were also made by Wingy Manone, Mississippi John Hurt, Vernon Dalhart, Jack Teagarden, the New Christy Minstrels, Johnny Cash, and a parody version by Spike Jones and his City Slickers. Gene Autry sang "Casey Jones" in the film *Sunset in Wyoming* (1941), and Bibi Osterwald performed it with the chorus in the Broadway revue *Sing Out, Sweet Land* (1944).

"The Cat Came Back" (1893) is a novelty number that still shows up in school song books and on children's records. Henry S. Miller wrote the simple childlike melody and the droll lyric about a persistent "yeller" cat that always returns home to "Old Mister Johnson" even though he keeps trying to get rid of it. The amusing number was introduced by Billy Rice of Haverly's Minstrels at Tony Pastor's in New York and was soon a favorite in vaudeville. Norman Blake, Roy Gaines, Lee Moore,

Merle Travis, Cisco Houston, Dave Holt, and Bill Harrell and the Virginians are among those who recorded the ditty.

"Catch a Falling Star" (1957) was a huge hit for Perry Como in the late 1950s, his record selling over a million copies. Paul J. Vance and Lee Pockriss wrote the rhythmic yet dreamy ballad that suggested you catch a star, keep it in your pocket, and "save it for a rainy day." Then, when you find your true love, you'll have a "pocketful of starlight" to set the mood. In addition to his solo version, Como also made a recording with the Ray Charles Singers. Other discs of note were made by Anthony Moore, Lawrence Welk, Bridget St. John, and Francoise Hardy. Jason Graae sang the ballad in the Off-Broadway musical *Forever Plaid* (1990), and the song was heard on the soundtrack of the film *Never Been Kissed* (1999).

"C'est Si Bon (It's So Good)" (1950) is most associated with Eartha Kitt, who had her first hit record with it and included her sexy, slinky version of it in her concerts for decades. The popular French song by Andrez Hornez (lyric) and Henri Betti (music) was given an English lyric by Jerry Seelen about how satisfying life can be, but most singers, including Kitt, performed it mostly in French and got the idea across with no problem. The carefree, sidewalk café music bounces along so enticingly that there were several instrumental recordings over the years, particularly with accordions and harmonicas. The number was first popularized in America by Johnny Desmond, but Kitt's 1953 record with Henri René's Orchestra climbed the charts. She reprised the song in the film *New Faces* (1954), and it was also heard in *Love in the Afternoon* (1957) and *Two Tickets to Broadway* (1954), where it was sung by Joey Dee and the Starliters. After Kitt's, the most popular recording in America was by Danny Kaye. Other artists to record it include Yves Montand, Louis Armstrong, Perez Prado, Buddy Collette, Earl Grant, Caterina Valente, the Chantels, Dionne Warwick, Barbra Streisand, and Conway Twitty. Karen Curlee sang "C'est Si Bon" in the Off-Broadway revue *The Taffetas* (1988).

"Chains of Love" (1951) is a rhythm-and-blues hit by Ahmet Ertegun (lyric) and Van "Piano Man" Walls (music) that crossed over into the pop market. The song was introduced on record by Big Joe Turner with Walls at the piano, but it was later revived three times with even more success: by Pat Boone in 1956, the Drifters in 1965, and Bobby Bland in 1969. Other recordings were made by Pinetop Perkins, Sam Cooke, Mickey Gilley, Jimmy James and the Vagabonds, Johnny Burnette, Jimmy Hughes, and Lou Rawls.

"The Champagne Waltz" (1934) was a favorite of ballroom orchestras in the 1930s and 1940s that celebrated the joys of a romantic waltz together. Con Conrad, Ben Oakland, and Milton Drake wrote the graceful number, and it was popularized by Jack Denny and his Orchestra and Glen Gray and the Casa Loma Orchestra. The waltz enjoyed revived interest when Veloz and Yolanda danced to it in the film *The Champagne Waltz* (1937). Six Fat Dutchmen and Myron Floren each made noteworthy recordings of the song as well.

"Chances Are" (1952) was one of Johnny Mathis's biggest hits and in many ways served as his unofficial theme song for years. Al Stillman (lyric) and Robert Allen (music) wrote the crooning ballad that listed certain signs of behavior and noted that "chances are" it is true love. Although none came close to Mathis in terms of popularity, there were also major records by Bob Marley and the Wailers, David Osborne, the Ray Conniff Singers, Julie London, Marieann Meringlo, Liza Minnelli, and Scott Robinson. The song was heard on the soundtrack of the movie *Chances Are* (1989).

"Charleston" (1923) started a dance craze in the 1920s that ran strong for five years and surpassed all previous songs in its effect on dance floor patrons. James P. Johnson and Cecil Mack collaborated on the frantic song, the lyrics proclaiming that this new dance step put Carolina "on the map" and explaining how to perform the dance that is a "la-pazoo." Few recall the words today, but the effervescent music is what defined the era. The number is made up of its short, propulsive bursts of music that accommodated the halting dance, and soon other songs were written to the same tempo so that there was a whole repertoire of "Charleston"-like songs. Both the song and the dance step were introduced in the all-black musical revue *Runnin' Wild* (1923), where Elisabeth Welch performed the knee-twisting, high-stepping number. When Joan Crawford sang and danced the "Charleston" in the film *Our Dancing Daughters* (1928), it launched her screen career. The number was also featured in *Margie* (1946) and *Tea for Two* (1950), where it was danced by Billy De Wolfe and Patrice Wymore. The song can also be heard in the background of dozens of movies set in the Roaring Twenties. Recordings over the years, most of which have been instrumentals, include those by Paul Whiteman, Bob Wilson and his Varsity Rhythm Boys, Jive Bunny, Django Reinhardt, Louis Prima, Richard Greene, Lester Lanin, the Charleston Chasers, Willie Smith, Ernie Fields, James P. Johnson, and Sidney Bechet and a parody version by Spike Jones and his City Slickers. As popular as the Charleston step became, it was eventually replaced by the Black Bottom, Varsity Drag, and other trendy dances.

"Charmaine" (1926) is a sentimental waltz that was inspired by the character of a French girl in the silent movie *What Price Glory?* (1926). Erno Rapee had written the music back in 1914 when still in Hungary, and it was later used repeatedly in the musical score for the movie. Audiences were immediately drawn to it, so Lew Pollack added a gushing lyric about a French sweetheart named Charmaine, and the song became popular on records and with sheet music sales. Guy Lombardo had a hit disc a decade later, and when Mantovanni's Orchestra recorded a lush version in 1951, it sold a million copies, gave the orchestra its first bestseller, and started a vogue for graceful string orchestras. Over the years the number has become a favorite of jazz musicians as well. Other significant recordings of "Charmaine" include those by Billy May, Frank Sinatra, Mantovanni's Orchestra, Erroll Garner, Gracie Fields, Tex Beneke, the Ink Spots, Bill Haley and the Comets, Max Bygraves, the Bachelors, Peter Bocage with the Creole Serenaders, Jimmie Lunceford, Gene Ammons, Arnett Cobb, Jerry Murad and the Harmonicats, Neal Hefti, Skitch Henderson, the Four Freshmen, and Vic Damone. Harry James and his Orchestra performed it in the movie *Two Girls and a Sailor* (1944), and it was heard in *Margie* (1946), the sound version of *What Price Glory?* (1952), *Thoroughly Modern Millie* (1967), *One Flew Over the Cuckoo's Nest* (1975), and *The Green Mile* (1999), where the famous Lombardo recording was used.

"Chattanoogie Shoe Shine Boy" (1950) is an energetic boogie-woogie number by Henry Stone and Jack Stapp about a youth shining shoes in rhythm to the music, slapping his rag to the beat of the tune. Red Foley popularized the song with a record that went to the top of the charts, and Bing Crosby had a bestseller as well. Frank Sinatra, Phil Harris, the Statler Brothers, Tommy Duncan, Pat Boone, Freddy Cannon, Perez Prado, and Gene Austin also recorded it. Sometimes listed as "Chattanooga Shoe Shine Boy," the song was interpolated into the movie *Indian Territory* (1950).

"Cheatin' On Me" (1925) is a mournful but rhythmic blues that Sophie Tucker introduced on stage and later recorded. Jack Yellen (lyric) and Lew Pollack (music) wrote the lament about a gal who finds out about her beau's unfaithfulness. Ben Bernie made an early recording that became a hit, and Jimmie Lunceford (vocal by Trummy Young) revived it with success in 1953. Other records were made by Johnny Taylor, Fats Waller, Maxine Sullivan, Tampa Red, Jimmy Hart and his Merrymakers, Hank Thompson, Billy Butterfield, and Dean Martin. The number is sometimes listed as "I Know My Baby Is Cheatin' On Me."

"Cherie, I Love You" (1926) is a romantic ballad that has managed to resurface and get attention every other decade or so. Lillian Rosedale Goodman wrote the straightforward proclamation of love, and it was introduced by opera singer Grace Moore in concert and on records. Soon after it became a hit record for Ben Bernie (vocals by Paul Hagan and Jack Pettis). In the 1940s it was revived when Kaaren Verne sang it in the film *All Through the Night* (1942) and when it was recorded by Fred Waring's Pennsylvanians and by Ross Gorman and his Orchestra. In the 1950s there were also noteworthy discs by Pat Boone, Frankie Laine, and Nat King Cole.

"Cherokee (Indian Love Song)" (1938) was one of bandleader Ray Noble's biggest hits of his career. Not only did he write both music and lyric for the chipper swing number, but his band's recording was a best-seller as well. Despite the bright and carefree music, the lyric is a fervent proclamation of love by a Native American to a beautiful Cherokee maiden, and the words have not dated well. But most recordings over the years were instrumentals, such as a disc by Charlie Barnet in 1939 that was a chart hit. There were also records by the George Shearing Trio, Herbie Fields, Clifford Brown, Joe Pass, Earl Bostic, Dianne Reeves, Don Byas, Art Pepper, Glenn Miller, Marian McPartland, and Vassar Clements. Barnet reprised the number for the movie *Jam Session* (1944), and Gene Krupa performed it on the soundtrack for *The Gene Krupa Story* (1959).

"Cherry Pink and Apple Blossom White" (1951) is the driving, rhythmic number that seems at odds with its gentle, flowery lyric about spring. The song came from France where Jacques Larue (lyric) and M. Louigay (music) wrote the piece in a pop style. It was heard in an instrumental version as the theme song for the American film *Underwater!* (1955) and attracted enough interest that Mack David added an English lyric about the blossoming of spring and new life. Perez Prado and his Orchestra recorded a very Latin version of the song, and it sold a million copies; so, ironically, the French tune became a Latin-flavored favorite. Alan Dale made a vocal version with Dick Jacob's Orchestra that was successful, but the song was still considered a south-of-the-border piece. Jerry Murad and his Harmonicats revived "Cherry Pink and Apple Blossom White" in 1961, and their disc was popular. Other notable records were made by Xavier Cugat, Earl Bostic, the Ventures, Billy Vaughn, the Thunderbirds, Liberace, Harry James, Al Hirt, Lawrence Welk, and Gisele MacKenzie. The song can also be heard in the movie *Jinxed* (1982).

"Chester" (1778) is, as described by David Ewen, "America's first great war song." New England colonist William Billings was a friend of Paul

Revere and Samuel Adams and active in the independence movement. He set out to write a patriotic song that would move his fellow Americans to fight the British, so he took the stately and formal music from an old hymn and wrote a fervent lyric that was filled with fire yet was religious and God fearing. Billings's three stanzas urge the citizens not to fear the tyranny of the king and to trust "in New England's God" so that victory will be theirs. Strangely, there is no mention of anyone named Chester in the whole song, and the anthem is sometimes titled after its opening line, "Let Tyrants Shake Their Iron Rod." The song caught on (particularly in New England), and it inspired the colonists so much that it was later described as the "Marseillaise of the Revolutionary War." Although "Chester" has not remained as familiar as "Yankee Doodle" and some other early American songs, its music was used by composer William Schuman for his two symphonic works, *William Billings' Overture* and *New England Triptych*.

"Chew-Chew-Chew (Chew Your Bubble Gum)" (1939) is a mindless little novelty number by Chick Webb, Buck Ram, and Ella Fitzgerald that merrily advertises the joy of chewing gum. A record by Fitzgerald with Webb's Orchestra was surprisingly popular, and there were many other discs as well, including those by Larry Clinton, Duke Ellington, Don Redman, the Quintones with Barney Bigard's Orchestra, McKinney's Cotton Pickers, and Holly Robinson.

"Chicago (That Toddling Town)" (1922) is the tuneful salute to the Windy City that has become the unofficial theme song for the Illinois metropolis. Fred Fisher wrote the catchy melody and the wry lyric that boasts "you lose the blues" in Chicago even better than you can in New York. The place is so unique, the lyric states, that a man was even seen dancing with his wife. The zippy number was first heard in vaudeville throughout the 1920s and sold thousands of copies of sheet music. Ben Selvin and his Orchestra was the first name band to play it, and there were early hit records by Paul Whiteman's Orchestra, Al Jolson, and Billy May. In the late 1930s Tommy Dorsey revived the tune with a bestselling record, and Frank Sinatra revived it again in 1957 when his recording was a hit. The uptempo number has also had discs by Bob Scobey's Frisco Band, Jack Mudurian, Earl Hines, Rosemary Clooney, Coleman Hawkins, Tony Bennett, and Sammy Davis Jr. In Hollywood a few measures of "Chicago" set the locale in many a film, including *Little Giant* (1933), *The Story of Vernon and Irene Castle* (1939), *Roxie Hart* (1942), *Oh, You Beautiful Doll* (1949), *Beyond the Forest* (1949), *In the Good Old Summertime* (1949), *With a Song in My Heart* (1952), and *The Joker Is Wild* (1957). The song was to be used in the Broadway musical *Chicago* (1975), but director Bob Fosse cut it and used it later in his show *Big Deal* (1986), where it was sung by the ensemble.

"The Children's Marching Song" (1958) is a simple counting song better known by the opening phrase of each stanza, "This Old Man," and is sometimes listed by its recurring nonsense refrain "Nick Nack Paddy Whack." The lyric finds rhymes for each of the numbers (one: thumb; two: shoe; and so on) and is easily and quickly learned. Malcolm Arnold wrote the childlike ditty, based on an old English song for children, and it was introduced in the movie *The Inn of the Sixth Happiness* (1958), where it was chanted by Ingrid Bergman and a chorus of young orphans. In addition to being sung in nursery schools and camps, the song shows up on dozens of children's records. Mitch Miller and his Chorus and Orchestra made a record that was surprisingly popular, and Cyril Stapleton's disc with a children's chorus also sold a lot of copies. Other recordings were made by Kenny Rankin, Pete Seeger, Doris Day, Ella Jenkins, and even the Three Stooges.

"China Boy" (1922) is a pseudo-oriental lullaby in which an Asian child is sung to sleep with the assurance that "Buddha smiles on you." Dick Winfree and Phil Boutelje wrote the song that was little known until it was popularized by Paul Whiteman and his Orchestra in 1929. The number was revived in 1936 with a hit record by the Benny Goodman Trio. Other distinctive recordings were made by Red Nichols and his Five Pennies, Gene Krupa, Lawrence Welk, Eddie Condon, Willie Humphrey, Teddy Wilson, Oscar Peterson, Lionel Hampton, Sidney Bechet, Bud Freeman, Bix Beiderbecke, Jack Teagarden, the Firehouse Five Plus Two, Muggsy Spanier, and Stephane Grappelli. The gentle ballad can be heard in the movies *Diamond Horseshoe* (1945), *The Stork Club* (1945), *The Benny Goodman Story* (1956), and *The Impostors* (1998), where the Condon recording was used.

"Chinatown, My Chinatown" (1906) is the durable standard about New York City's Chinatown district, a place where hearts beat faster once the evening comes. William Jerome (lyric) and Jean Schwartz (music) wrote the number in 1906, but it attracted no attention until Eddie Foy interpolated it into his Broadway revue *Up and Down Broadway* (1910) to replace a Chinatown number that wasn't working. The American Quartet made the first recording of the peppy little ditty, and it was revived with success in the 1930s, first by Louis Armstrong in 1932, then soon after by the Mills Brothers, then in 1935 by Ray Noble and his Orchestra. Other records of note over the years were made by Slim and Slam, Tommy Dorsey and the Clambake Seven, Jack Teagarden, Fletcher Henderson, Glen Gray and the Casa Loma Orchestra, Joe Newman, the Hi-

Lo's, Dan Block, Louis Prima, and Chris Connor. Al Jolson sang it on the soundtrack of the movie bio *Jolson Sings Again* (1949), and Bob Hope performed it with children in *The Seven Little Foys* (1955). It can also be heard in *Bright Lights* (1931), *Git Along Little Doggies* (1937), *Is Everybody Happy?* (1943), *Nob Hill* (1945), *Young Man With a Horn* (1950), and other films.

"Chiquita Banana" (1946) is one of the rare Tin Pan Alley hits to come from a commercial jingle. Leonard MacKenzie, Garth Montgomery, and William Wirges took a popular radio commercial for the Chiquita company and turned it into a Latin number explaining the wonderful things you can do with bananas (use them in a salad or a pie, for example) but warning you that they should never be put in the refrigerator. Xavier Cugat introduced the new version in the movie *This Time for Keeps* (1947), and it was followed by recordings by Roberto Inglez, Edmundo Ros and his Rhumba Band, Johnny Bothwell, Buddy Clark, Bud Freeman, and Jack Mudurian. Christy Romano sang the silly number in the film *Everyone Says I Love You* (1996).

"Chloe" (1927) is a sonorous ballad by Gus Kahn (lyric) and Neil Moret (music) in which a distraught paramour calls out to his lost love Chloe, wandering with outstretched empty arms and hoping that she will hear his heavy sighs. Moret's graceful music makes the turgid lyric bearable, and the number remained popular for three decades. Lee Barton Evans introduced the love song, but it was Paul Whiteman who popularized it, and years later Louis Armstrong revived it with a 1953 hit recording. Duke Ellington, Eva Taylor, Bunk Johnson, Dinah Shore, Al Jolson, Benny Goodman, Joe Pass, the Dorsey Brothers, Ry Cooder, and Red Allen were among the many who recorded it. The lyric seemed ripe for parody, and in 1945 Spike Jones and his City Slickers made a slapstick recording and performed it in the film *Bring on the Girls* (1945). The title is sometimes spelled "Chlo-E" to indicate the wailing nature of the song.

"The Christmas Song" (1946) is the rather vague title for the beloved holiday song that lists very specific images of domestic happiness: a fire in the hearth, Yuletide carols heard, turkey cooking, mistletoe hanging, and so on. More familiarly known by its opening line "Chestnuts Roasting on an Open Fire," the Christmas favorite was written by Robert Wells (lyric) and Mel Tormé (music). Tormé introduced the modern carol on records and sang it in concerts for many years after. Of the hundreds of recordings made later, none sold more copies than a disc by Nat King Cole in the 1940s. He recorded it again with Nelson Riddle's Orchestra in 1954, and it was a hit all over again. Another unusually popular recording was that by Doris Day with Les Brown's Band of Renown. Returning every December, "The Christmas Song" continues to be one of the most popular nonreligious holiday songs in America.

"Clap Hands! Here Comes Charley!" (1925) is a vibrant rhythm number that has found favor during each decade of the twentieth century. Joseph Meyer wrote the pulsating music, and Billy Rose and Ballard MacDonald penned the active lyrics about the rousing welcome that greets a good-time Charlie when he arrives at a party. The energetic song was introduced in vaudeville by the team of Salt and Pepper and was first recorded by Johnny Marvin. The number was revived in the 1930s by Chick Webb and his Orchestra, by Charlie Barnet (who made it his theme song) in the 1940s, and by Jimmy Dorsey in the 1950s, and it found an audience again when Ben Vereen performed it in the movie *Funny Lady* (1975). Other recordings were made by Ella Fitzgerald, Benny Goodman, Lester Young, Eddie Peabody, Red Norvo, Count Basie, Fletcher Henderson's Dixie Stompers, and Dexter Gordon. "Clap Hands! Here Comes Charley!" can also be heard in the film *Tahiti Honey* (1943).

"Clementine" (1884) is the traditional song of the American west that has as many possible authors as it does possible titles. The lyric can be traced to a poem called "Down By the River Lived a Maiden" that was published in 1863. A song titled "Oh, My Darling Clementine" was published in 1884 with Percy Montrose credited with both the music and lyric. But the same song came on the market in 1885 with the title "Clementine" and Baker Bradford listed as the author. The story the ballad tells has stayed basically the same over the years: A miner and his daughter Clementine head out west, she falls into the ocean and drowns, and the father grieves for her in the churchyard where she is buried. The lyric is filled with colorful regionalisms such as "dreadful sorry," and the tale of woe is told so simply and honestly that it doesn't strike the listener as maudlin. Although "Clementine" had long been a piece of folklore, interest in the song was revived when it was used throughout the film *My Darling Clementine* (1946) and many new recordings appeared. It was also heard in *The Big Sombrero* (1949). A new version by Woody Harris became a hit in 1960, and Bobby Darin's swinging interpretation a few years later was also a bestseller. Among the major records made of "Clementine" are those by Duke Ellington, the Weavers, Bix Beiderbecke, Bobby Hackett, Joe Venuti, Connie Francis, Yves Montand, and Johnny Cash, not to mention many children's records.

"Cold, Cold Heart" (1951) is the country-western standard that has crossed over and been recorded by jazz and pop artists as well. Hank Williams wrote and introduced the torchy number about a sweetheart who hangs on to the memory of a past love and makes it impossible for a new lover to melt the other's cold heart. Williams's recording was popular, but it was Tony Bennett's 1952 disc made with Mitchell Ayers' Orchestra that sold a million copies. Other notable discs were made by Eddie Dean, Margaret Whiting, Charlie Rich, Dinah Washington, Del Shannon, Midge Ure, Jerry Lee Lewis, Connie Stevens, Johnny Cash, and B.J. Thomas. Gene Autry sang the ballad in the movie *Apache Country* (1952), Hank Williams, Jr., provided the singing voice for George Hamilton in the bio *Your Cheatin' Heart* (1964), and the original Williams recording was heard on the soundtrack for *The Last Picture Show* (1971).

"Columbia, the Gem of the Ocean" (1843) is an old-style but still recognized patriotic song that celebrates the land of the free and boasts that "thy banners make tyranny tremble." The authors are listed as David T. Shaw and T.A. Beckett, but it is not clear which, if either of them, is actually responsible for the song. Shaw, an actor at the Chestnut Street Theatre in Philadelphia, asked Beckett to write a patriotic song for an upcoming theatrical benefit. Shaw claimed he gave Beckett a completed lyric, but Beckett later argued that it was only an outline and was unusable. Then it was discovered that the song was clearly taken from the British anthem "Britannia, the Pride of the Ocean." When it was published, only Shaw's name appeared on the sheet music. Nevertheless, the patriotic number has been sung through many decades and many wars and remains an elegant and fervent piece of songwriting. It can be heard in several movies, most memorably *In Old Monterey* (1939), *Thousands Cheer* (1943), and *The Music Man* (1962).

"Come Down, Ma Evenin' Star" (1902) is the song most associated with the flamboyant star and fashion icon Lillian Russell. The ballad is a bittersweet cry to the heavens from a socialite who longs to be a real star in the sky rather than a superficial star in society. The tale behind the song is as melodramatic as the lyric. Composer John Stromberg wrote the ballad for Russell to sing in the musical burlesque *Twirly Whirly* (1902) but changed his mind about it, not showing the sheet music to anyone. A few weeks later he committed suicide in his apartment, and the song was found in his pocket. Robert B. Smith quickly wrote the lyric, and it was added to the show. On opening night Russell broke down and wept as she tried to sing it. Soon it became her signature song, and she recorded it in 1912, the only existing record she ever made. The ballad can be heard in the film *Broadway to Hollywood* (1933), was sung by Alice Faye in the bio movie *Lillian Russell* (1940), and was performed by Andrea King in *My Wild Irish Rose* (1947).

"Come, Josephine, in My Flying Machine" (1910) was one of the first popular songs about air travel, and it remained a favorite during the early years of aviation. Alfred Bryan (lyric) and Fred Fisher (music) took their inspiration from the Wright Brothers and the newfangled flying contraptions to write an enticing waltz that invited one's dearie to take to the air with him. The merry song was introduced in vaudeville by Blanche Ring, who made a recording of it in 1910. Other early discs were made by Ada Jones, Billy Murray, and the American Quartet. The number can be heard in such period films as *The Story of Vernon and Irene Castle* (1939), *Oh, You Beautiful Doll* (1949), and *Titanic* (1997). Spike Jones and his City Slickers made a parody version that was more familiar to the public than the long-forgotten original.

"Come On-a My House" (1950) was Rosemary Clooney's theme song on radio, television, and in concerts, yet the number had a long and unusual history before it was associated with her. Playwright William Saroyan and his cousin Ross Bagdasarian took an auto trip across New Mexico sometime in the 1930s and together wrote the tuneful little ditty welcoming one inside the house for candy and other treats. Depending on how the singer interprets the lyrics, it can also be an invitation for sexual favors. The cousins put the song away and forgot about it until Saroyan needed a number for his nonmusical play *Son* (1950). The Off-Broadway play got little attention, and the song would have disappeared again had not singer Kay Armen liked it and recorded it. In 1951 Mitch Miller convinced Clooney to record it, orchestrating it himself with a harpsichord as the accompaniment. It became Clooney's first hit record, going to the top of the charts, and she reprised it in the movie *The Stars Are Singing* (1953). Julie London, Della Reese, Frank Devol, Big Kahuna and the Copa Cat Pack, and John Pizzarelli are among those who also recorded the bouncy ballad.

"Comin' in On a Wing and a Prayer" (1943) is a slightly swinging hymn about a lost pilot who puts his trust in the Lord as he tries to reach Paris by air. The unlikely hit song was written by Harold Adamson (lyric) and Jimmy McHugh (music) and was based on a true incident. Sonny Bragg, a celebrated football star who was a pilot in the air force during World War Two, told McHugh about an experience he had in North Africa when his plane was in trouble, and he felt "we came in on one engine and a prayer." Eddie Cantor introduced the number in a USO (United Service Organization) show at an air force base, and the song was immediately in demand. A record by the Song Spinners went to the Number One spot on the charts, over a million copies of sheet music were sold, and it remained on *Your Hit Parade* for eighteen weeks. The gospellike number was also recorded by Bing Crosby, Bob Grant, the Four Vagabonds, Perry Como, the Golden Gate Quartet, Willie Kelly, Ry Cooder, Ann Shelton, Lisa Richard, Phil Heywood, and Malcolm Gets.

"Coquette" (1927) is a popular ballad that was inspired by a 1927 hit play of the same name. Carmen Lombardo and Johnny Green (in his first published song) wrote the adoring music, and Gus Kahn penned the lyric in which a wooer asks "little Coquette" why she flirts and breaks so many hearts. He warns her that someday she might fall as hard as he has and someone just might break her heart. Guy Lombardo and the Royal Canadians introduced the song on the radio in 1927, and Rudy Vallee sang it on the air waves with great success. A record by Billy Eckstine revived interest in the song in 1953, and Fats Domino had a popular recording in 1958. Other discs were made by Bob Crosby, the Dorsey Brothers, Teddy Wilson, Frankie Laine, Eddy Howard, Charlie Parker, Nat King Cole, and John Pizzarelli. Tony Martin sang "Coquette" in the film *Easy to Love* (1953), and it was also heard in *Coquette* (1929), *Cockeyed Cavaliers* (1934), and *They Shoot Horses, Don't They?* (1969).

"A Cottage for Sale" (1930) is a pleasing pastoral ballad about an idyllic cottage on the hill where two sweethearts lived. But she has left, so the shades are drawn and the cottage is put up for sale. Larry Conley wrote the effective lyric, and Willard Robison composed the delicate music that begins on a high note, then winds down gracefully into a touching conclusion. The song was introduced by Robison and his Deep River Orchestra and was revived by Billy Eckstine in 1945, but the most popular of the many recordings was done by Frank Sinatra. Among the other artists who made discs were Ruth Etting, Guy Lombardo, Judy Garland, Ray Anthony, Mel Tormé, Nat King Cole, Paul Small, the Revelers, Bernie Cummins (vocal by Frank Munn), Phil Brito, Maxine Daniels, Gracie Fields, Harry Cool, Errol Garner, and Roberta Flack.

"The Cowboy Serenade" (1941) is a tearful cowboy lament that is highly sentimental and yet strangely affecting. Rich Hall wrote the somber ballad about a dying cowpoke ("the sun's almost set") who smokes his last cigarette and asks someone to sing his favorite prairie song, complete with a repeated "yipee-ky-ay." The song was published only after Tony Martin introduced it on the radio in 1941, and it was popularized further by Kay Kyser (vocal by Harry Babbitt) and by Gene Autry who sang it in the film *Cowboy Serenade* (1942). Glenn Miller (vocal by Ray Eberly) also had a hit record of it. Other discs were made by Gene Krupa (vocal Howard Dulany), the Charioteers, Russ Morgan, Art Jarrett, Barry Wood, Craig Chambers, and Roy Rogers. The ballad is subtitled "While I'm Smokin' My Last Cigarette" or sometimes "While I'm Rollin' My Last Cigarette."

"Cry" (1951) is a wailing ballad by Churchill Kohlam that was a giant hit for Johnnie Ray and started a vogue for similarly mournful songs in the 1950s. The tearful lament says it is okay to cry when your endeared one abandons you or when you are down on your luck or have a bad dream. The title word and some others are wailed in the singing of the song, forecasting the long-winded sounds that would become a favorite later in rock-and-roll. Kohlam was a night watchman for a Pittsburgh dry cleaning company who wrote the number for an amateur songwriting competition in 1951. Ray's recording later that year sold 2 million copies and was associated with the young singer for the rest of the decade. Yet the song has proved to be popular with other artists as well. Ray Charles's 1965 record was a hit, and it was also successful for Ronnie Dove in 1966 and for country singers Lynn Anderson in 1972 and Crystal Gayle in 1986. Others who recorded the ballad include the Knightsbridge Strings, Connie Francis, Roy Orbison, the Ray Conniff Singers, Brenda Lee, and Jimmy Roselli. The wailer was heard in the movie *As Long as They're Happy* (1955), and Ray Charles reprised it in the British film *Blues for Lovers* (a.k.a. *Ballad in Blue*) (1965). "Cry" was featured in two Off-Broadway revues: Tia Speros performed it in *The Taffetas* (1988) and Stan Chandler sang it in *Forever Plaid* (1990).

"Cry Me a River" (1953) is an unusual torch song in which the spurned lover gets a form of sweet revenge. When a former beau returns to say he is lonely and wants to be forgiven, she suggest he "cry me a river" because she once "cried a river over" him. Arthur Hamilton wrote the "wailing ballad" that allows the singer plenty of long notes to cry and sing, and it was popularized by Julie London. Janice Harper revived the number in 1960, and Joe Cocker brought attention to in 1970 in concert and on records. Among the many artists who also recorded it are Dinah Washington, Dexter Gordon, Dinah Shore, Shirley Bassey, Ray Charles, Vic Damone, Ella Fitzgerald, Barbra Streisand, and more recently, Betty Buckley, Diana Krall, Michael Ball, and Harry Connick Jr. London sang it in the movie *The Girl Can't Help It* (1956) and Cocker performed it in the concert film *Joe Cocker: Mad Dogs and Englishmen* (1971). In the Broadway revue *Swing* (1999), Laura Benanti sang the ballad, while trombonist Steve Armour joined in with the wailing.

"The Cubanola Glide" (1909) is a dance song that turned into an early ragtime hit on Tin Pan Alley. Vincent P. Bryan wrote the lyric about a new dance step, the Cubanola Glide, and Harry Von Tilzer composed the ragged music that caught the fancy of both musicians and dancers. It was written for Sophie Tucker to sing in the *Ziegfeld Follies of 1909*, but the number was cut, so Tucker introduced it in vaudeville. The next year the song was interpolated into the Broadway musical *The Girl from Rector's* (1910), where it was sung by Harriet Raymond. Early records by Billy Murray, Arthur Collins and Bryon Harlan, and Prince's Orchestra helped spread its popularity. But, like many dance songs, it faded away in time as dancing trends changed. The number can be heard in the movie *Flame of the Barbary Coast* (1945) and Alice Faye sang it in *Fallen Angel* (1945).

"The Curse of the Dreamer" (1899) was one of Paul Dresser's most popular ballads, though it is not so well known today. The story behind the song adds to its dramatic appeal. When Dresser's promiscuous wife left him and their young child for another man, Dresser was heartbroken and wrote a bitter ballad that he titled "The Curse." It was such a personal effort that he made no attempt to have it published. But when he eventually tracked the unfaithful woman down, he sang it to her, and she relented and returned home with him. But the marriage was not saved; after a time she left him again. Dresser then rewrote the ballad, gave it a happy ending, and it was published as "The Curse of the Dreamer." One wonders if the considerable profits from the song did much to soothe Dresser's grief.

D

"Daddy" (1941) is a swinging rhythm number by Bobby Troup in which Daisy Mae asks her sugar daddy for a diamond ring, furs, a new car, and other necessities because he "oughta get the best for me." The song is punctuated with a recurring "Hey! Daddy!" which holds the number together lyrically and musically. Joan Davis and Jinx Falkenburg introduced the song in the movie *Two Latins From Manhattan* (1941), but it was popularized by a Number One chart record by Sammy Kaye and his Orchestra, the musicians providing the vocals. The tune remained on *Your Hit Parade* for fifteen weeks and was later recorded by such artists as Joan Merrill, the Andrews Sisters, Gertrude Lawrence, Glenn Miller, Helen Ward, Ted Heath, Harry James, the Statler Brothers, Julie London, Vaughn Monroe, Della Reese, and Troup himself. "Daddy" was heard in the film *I'll Be Yours* (1947), Joan Blondell sang it in *The Blue Veil* (1951), it was performed by Jane Russell and Jeanne Crain (dubbed by Anita Ellis) in *Gentlemen Marry Brunettes* (1955), and the Andrews Sisters recording was used on the soundtrack of *1941* (1979). The number was also sung in the Off-Broadway revue *Swingtime Canteen* (1995).

"Daddy Has a Sweetheart and Mother Is Her Name" (1912) is a coy ballad about domestic bliss that Gene Buck (lyric) and Dave Stamper (music) wrote for Lillian Lorraine to sing in the *Ziegfeld Follies of 1911*. But A.L. Erlanger, the powerful showman who was an investor in the show, did not like Lorraine or the song, so both were cut. But Lorraine introduced the number in a variety program at Hammerstein's Victoria Theatre, and it was an immediate hit. A million copies of sheet music were sold with Lorraine's picture on the cover, and Ziegfeld apologized and got the star to sing it in the *Ziegfeld Follies of 1912*. Edna Brown (better known later as Elsie Baker) made an early recording of the song.

"Daddy Wouldn't Buy Me a Bow-Wow" (1892) is a comedy number by Joseph Tabrar that is written from a young child's point of view, and it was so popular that it started a vogue for baby-talk songs. The silly lament concerns a kid who brings a cat to school, explaining that she wanted to bring a dog, but her father won't let her have one. The facile lyric even allows the child to shout "bow wow wow wow wow . . ." to express her enthusiasm for dogs over cats. The comic ditty was introduced by the English comedienne Vesta Victoria at Tony Pastor's in New York, and thousands of copies of sheet music found their way to parlor pianos. Jessie Matthews sang the number in the British film *Evergreen* (1934), and the song can still be heard ocassionally on children's records.

"Daddy, You've Been a Mother to Me" (1920) is a sentimental ballad by Fred Fisher that praises a loving father. The song was a popular favorite in vaudeville in the 1920s, and there were some early records by Henry Burr and Lewis James. The ballad was featured in the period films *Mother Wore Tights* (1947) and *Oh, You Beautiful Doll* (1949), and more recently it was recorded by Jimmy Roselli.

"Daisy Bell" (1892), more familiarly known as "A Bicycle Built for Two," remains one of the most recognized tunes from the nineteenth century. The proposal song by Henry Dacre offers his fiancée Daisy a two-seater bike because he "can't afford a carriage," yet the simple and naive declaration of love ("I'm half crazy over the likes of you") is very winning. There is a touch of Irish dialect in the lyric ("give me your answer, do"), and Dacre's waltzing music still manages to entrance. The story behind the song seems as nostalgic as the number itself. The Englishman Dacre decided to try and make his fortune writing songs in America, so he emigrated to New York with his worldly belongings, including his bicycle. At customs he had to pay duty on the bike, and one of his friends commented that it was a good thing it wasn't one of those "bicycles built for two" or he would have to pay twice as much. The phrase inspired Dacre to write his first song in America, but cycling here was not yet a widely popular recreation, and no publisher would buy it. Ironically, the song first caught on in England (where cycling was more prevalent) after Kate Lawrence sang it in a music hall. Luckily for Dacre, bicycle manufacturers in America were just introducing a new model of bike that was safer and easier to handle, especially for women with their long skirts. Just as the sport was gaining favor, Tony Pastor introduced the song in New York at his music hall, and both song and sport took off. Some claim "Daisy Bell" did more to promote cycling than any other factor; what is for certain, it spawned a multitude of other cycling songs in the 1890s. Jennie Lindsay was among the vaudeville stars who featured it in their acts, and some years later an early record by Dan Quinn was at the top of the charts. Other significant recordings were made by the Banjo Kings, Dale Miller, Ace O'Donnell, Dinah Shore, John Bolcomb and Joan Morris, Merle Travis, John Faye, Chet Atkins, JoAnne Pullout, John Colville, and Mitch Miller, not to mention many children's records. "Daisy Bell" can be heard in the movies *My Gal Sal* (1942), *Bowery to Broadway* (1944), *Shine On Harvest Moon* (1944), *A Foreign Affair* (1948), *One Sunday Afternoon* (1948), *There's a Girl in My Heart* (1949), and others, but modern audiences will recall it as the song that H.A.L. the computer sang as he was dying in *2001: A Space Odyssey* (1968).

"Dallas Blues" (1918) is a blues standard, difficult to distinguish from other place name blues numbers but memorable enough to recognize upon hearing it. Hart A. Wand (lyric) and Lloyd Garrett (music) wrote the song, and it was given dozens of recordings, including those by Marie Cahill, Ted Lewis, Wingy Manone, Louis Armstrong with Lugs Russell, Glen Gray and the Casa Loma Orchestra, Woody Herman, Fats Waller, George Lewis, Floyd Dixon, Andy Kirk and Clouds of Joy, Leadbelly, and Muggsy Spanier.

"Dancing on the Ceiling" (1930) is an entrancing song by Rodgers and Hart in which a woman fantasizes that her admirer dances above her bed when she is sleeping. Lorenz Hart wrote the imaginative lyric after hearing Richard Rodgers's sublime melody, proclaiming that it had the feeling of weightlessness. The number was written for the Broadway musical *Simple Simon* (1930) but was cut before opening. So the team put it into their score for the London musical *Evergreen* (1930), where it was sung by Jessie Matthews and Sonny Hale. The song caught on in England, and British bandleader Jack Hilton had a hit recording of it. It took longer to become popular in America, but once it did, there were many recordings, including discs by Frank Sinatra, Mabel Mercer, Jerk Southern, Ray Anthony, Chet Baker, Bob Kane, Lionel Hampton, Russ Peterson and the High Hats, Ella Fitzgerald, Peggy Lee, Johnny Mathis, the Ray Conniff Singers, and more recently, Dawn Upshaw. Matthews reprised the song in the film version of *Evergreen* (1934), and it was also heard on the soundtrack of the Rodgers and Hart movie bio *Words and Music* (1948).

"Dancing With Tears in My Eyes" (1930) is a torchy standard in which a dejected lover dances with another but cannot hide the woe inside because "my heart is calling you." Al Dubin (lyric) and Joe Burke (music) wrote the dancing ballad for the movie *Dancing Sweeties* (1930), and it was recorded but cut from the final print because the studio deemed it "not good enough." Rudy Vallee introduced the ballad on radio, and it became one of the most successful songs of the year. Early recordings were made by Ruth Etting, Nick Lucas, Nat Shilkret, and others, and the number was revived in 1952 with a hit record by Mantovanni's Orchestra. Among the other artists who recorded it were Joe Venuti, Lew White, Wayne King, Kate Smith, the Three Suns, and Jack Teagarden. The song can be heard briefly in the film *Broadway Hostess* (1935).

"Danny Boy" (1913) is the Irish folk standard that crossed over to become a Tin Pan Alley hit several times throughout the twentieth century. The haunting, heartbreaking song is a farewell to Danny, who must leave because the pipes are calling him away, from the lass left behind in the glen who will wait for him to come back when summer returns. There is a tragic subtext to the lyric as well, the girl telling him that should she die she will not sleep in peace until he comes to her. Fred Weatherly is credited with the song, but it was based closely on an 1855 Irish piece called "Londonderry Air." Weatherly's version was introduced in concerts and on records by the contralto Ernestine Schumann-Heink, and its fame soon spread to various parts of the world. In America the ballad was revived by a hit instrumental recording by Glenn Miller and his Orchestra in 1940. There were also successful revival discs in 1959 by Conway Twitty, in 1961 by Andy Williams, in 1965 by Patti La Belle and the Blue Belles, and in 1967 by Ray Price. Other memorable versions were made by Gracie Fields, the Flamingos, Duane Eddy, Jim Reeves, Harry Belafonte, Glen Yarbrough, Jimmie Rogers, James Gaul, and more recently, Carly Simon. Fields sang it in the British film *Shipyard Sally* (1940), and it can be heard on the soundtracks of many Hollywood movies, including *Little Nellie Kelly* (1940), *He Laughed Last* (1956), *Can't Stop the Music* (1980), and *Memphis Belle* (1990).

"Dardanella" (1919) is a unique ballad with an oriental flavor about an exotic girl from Asia Minor "with the harem eyes." The music has a slightly syncopated fox trot tempo, yet there is a recurring bass rhythm that is very unique and foreshadows the boogie-woogie sound of later years. Even more unusual, the music's rising and falling scales continue fearlessly over this rhythm, making for a complex and pulsating effect. The song started as a piano rag by Johnny S. Black called "Turkish Tom Tom." Felix Bernard adapted the music into pop song format, and Fred Fisher wrote a mystical and romantic lyric. It was introduced by Ben Selvin and his Orchestra on a record that sold over 1 million discs. The song also sold over 5 million copies of sheet music. "Dardanella" was also the focus of two famous court battles. Bernard sued Fisher because he only got $100 for his contribution, but he lost the case. Fisher, in turn, sued Jerome Kern in 1921, claiming that Kern's hit song "Ka-lu-a" had a melody taken directly from "Dardanella." The matter was settled out of court. Among the many recordings of "Dardanella" are those by Bing

Crosby, Vaughn Monroe, Louis Armstrong, Ted Strutter, Borrah Minnevitch and his Harmonica Rascals, Bix Beiderbecke, the Three Suns, Bobby Hackett, Alvino Rey, Jerry Murad's Harmonicats, Islam Jones, and the Herbie Fields Quintet. The enticing ballad can also be heard in the movies *Baby Face* (1933), *Stella Dallas* (1937), *Two Girls and a Sailor* (1944), and the Fisher bio *Oh, You Beautiful Doll* (1949).

"The Daring Young Man on the Flying Trapeze" (1868) is arguably the most famous circus song in American popular music, yet its roots are British. George Leybourne (lyric) and Alfred Lee (music) are the credited songwriters, but the authorship is suspect, a very similar ditty having been sung in London music halls by comic singer Joe Saunders earlier in the 1860s. The music is a contagious waltz that is very circuslike, and the lengthy lyric (inspired by the famous trapeze artist Léotard) tells an involved tale about a girl who falls for a high wire artist. She joins the circus and runs off with him, eventually becoming part of his act, but ends up doing all the performing while he takes it easy. The song was first heard in America in vaudeville, popularized by Johnny Allen in 1870, and then became a favorite of circus clowns. In 1933 Walter O'Keefe adapted the number, retitled it "The Man on the Flying Trapeze," and sang it in vaudeville, on radio, and later in a 1939 record that was a hit. Rudy Vallee also sang it on radio, and his record version was a bestseller, putting the old song on the *Hit Parade*. In addition to many kids' records, there were major discs, using both titles, by Eddie Cantor, Cliff Edwards, Ace O'Donnell, Don Redman, the Banjo Kings, Spike Jones and his City Slickers, and Les Paul and Mary Ford. Vallee reprised the song in the movies *George White's Scandals* (1934) and *Too Many Blondes* (1941), Clark Gable and a group of bus passengers sang it in *It Happened One Night* (1934), Dick Powell crooned it in *Twenty Million Sweethearts* (1934), and Gene Autry sang it in *Under Fiesta Stars* (1941). Playwright-novelist William Saroyan used the celebrated song for the title of his first published novel, *The Daring Young Man on the Flying Trapeze* (1934).

"Darkness on the Delta" (1933) is a jazz-influenced ballad by Marty Symes, Al Neiburg (lyric), and Jerry Livingston (music) that paints a moody, dreamy picture of life down south. Mildred Bailey introduced the song, and it was Livingston's first of many hits. Recordings of note were made by Islam Jones, Ted Fio Rito, George Lewis, Chick Bullock, Del Lampe, Thelonious Monk, the Dukes of Dixieland, the Moms and Dads, Tim Laughlin, and Chet Atkins. Sometimes listed as "When It's Darkness on the Delta," it was heard in the movie *South of Dixie* (1944).

"The Darktown Strutters' Ball" (1917) is one of the giants of Tin Pan Alley, a ragtime classic that has found success in all media with all kinds of artists and remains as vivacious today as when it first caught the public's attention during World War One. The song was written by Shelton Brooks, who recalled a dance at a 1915 exposition in San Francisco. The lyric is a promise to a sweetheart to pick her up in a taxicab and go to the Darktown Ball where they play the "Jelly Roll Blues" and do all sorts of dances, such as the Buck and Wing and Walking the Dog. The music has, as described by Alec Wilder, a "flexible, pliant, yet swinging air about it." The strong, driving verse flows easily into a refrain that has useful breaks built into it so that the orchestra can go into a riff or a dancer could tap away between lyric phrases. The vibrant number was introduced by the Original Dixieland Jazz Band, but it was popularized by Sophie Tucker in vaudeville. Hundreds of recordings were made over the decades with major revivals in 1927 by Ted Lewis, in 1948 by Alan Dale and Connie Haines, and in 1954 by Lou Monte. Of the many other discs made, there were eminent ones by Jelly Roll Morton, Bob Grant, Red McKenzie and the Mound City Blue Blowers, George Hartman, Ella Fitzgerald, Harry Roy, Bunk Johnson's New Orleans Band, Fats Waller, Charlie Barnet, Ray Anthony, Benny Goodman, George Wettling's Chicago Rhythm Kings, Ruby Newman, and Hoagy Carmichael. It was either sung or played on the soundtrack of several films, including *The Story of Vernon and Irene Castle* (1939), *Babes in Arms* (1939), *Broadway* (1942), *Coney Island* (1943), *Atlantic City* (1944), *Incendiary Blonde* (1945) *The Dolly Sisters* (1945), *Little Boy Lost* (1953), and *The Trouble With Girls* (1969). In 1964, ASCAP (American Society of Composers, Authors, and Publishers) named "Darktown Strutters' Ball" as one of the sixteen best popular songs written during the organization's fifty-year history.

"Darling, Je Vous Aime, Beaucoup" (1935) is a hit American ballad by Anna Sosenko that is sung in both French and English. The number is an overt love song declaring affection in halting French and wishing she knew more of the language in order to express herself better. Sosenko was the manager for the singer-pianist Hildegarde and wrote the ballad for her client's specific talents. Hildegarde introduced it, recorded it, sung it in concerts for years, and made it her theme song. When Nat King Cole revived it in 1955, his recording sold over a million copies. Forty years later his daughter Natalie Cole recorded it as well. Other discs were made by Hubert Laws, the Cliff Adams Singers, Bing Crosby, Buddy Collette, Django Reinhardt, Dean Martin, the Chateaus, and the Red Garland Trio. The song was sung by Simone Simon in the film *Love and Hisses* (1938) and was heard in *Naughty Nanette* (1945).

"Darling Nelly Gray" (1856) is a sentimental ballad that had a very inflammatory affect on audiences in the years right before the Civil War. The lyric tells about the runaway slave Joseph Selby who lies dying in

an Ohio station in the underground railroad and bids farewell to Nellie
Gray, the slave girl he loves who was taken from him in Kentucky. It
was written by Benjamin Russell Hanby, a student at Otterbein College
in Ohio, who based the lyric on a true story of a slave girl who was sold
and separated from her betrothed. Hanby sent the song to a music publisher but never knew it had been published until he heard it sung at a
concert. The popularity of the ballad helped fuel antislavery sentiments,
and some believed the widespread appeal of the song did as much as
the book *Uncle Tom's Cabin* to create public sympathy for Negro slaves
in the South. "Darling Nellie Gray" was still being sung and recorded
in the twentieth century and there were discs made by Bing Crosby, the
Mills Brothers, Maxine Sullivan, Johnny Gimble, Louis Armstrong, Tiny
Hill, and George Lewis. The song can also be heard in the movies *The
Sarong Girl* (1942) and *The Sting* (1973).

"Darling, Not Without You" (1936) is a crooning ballad by Edward Heyman, Al Sherman (lyric), and Abner Silver (music) that assures a sweetheart of complete devotion. Dolly Dawn popularized the song on record,
and there were also successful discs by Ted Weems (vocal by Perry
Como), Artie Shaw (vocal by Peg La Centra), Red Allen, and Ruby Newman.

"Darn That Dream" (1939) is a swinging lament that complains about
dreaming of one's beloved each night, but she disappears when he
awakes. The lover curses the dream for teasing him like that and argues,
"I'd welcome a nice old nightmare!" This unusual lyric is supported by
music that has a tricky melody, the notes hard to find correctly in spots.
Eddie DeLange (lyric) and Jimmy Van Heusen (music) wrote the wry
number for the Broadway musical *Swingin' the Dream* (1939), a jazz interpretation of *A Midsummer Night's Dream*, that failed to run despite the
major talents involved. In the show the song was performed by Louis
Armstrong, Maxine Sullivan, Bill Bailey, the Dandridge Sisters, the
Rhythmettes, and the Deep River Boys. Unfortunately that illustrious
cast did not get to record the song, but when Benny Goodman (vocal by
Mildred Bailey) did, the disc went to the top of the charts. Other records
were made by Tommy Dorsey (vocal Anita Boyer), Paul Whiteman (vocals by Joan Edwards and the Modernaires), Dinah Shore, Art Pepper,
Doris Day, Billie Holiday, Dexter Gordon, Charlie Barnet, Teresa Brewer,
Chet Baker, Miles Davis, Erskine Butterfield, Don Elliot, and more recently, Karen Ziemba.

"The Daughter of Rosie O'Grady" (1918) is the rare Tin Pan Alley sequel that was nearly as popular as the original. Monty C. Brice (lyric)
and Walter Donaldson (music) wrote the Irish waltz that was clearly a

follow-up to the 1896 favorite "Sweet Rosie O'Grady." Again the lyric was full of praises for an Irish lass, and the melodic tune took the form of a waltzing clog dance. Pat Rooney Jr. introduced the ballad at the Palace Theatre, and he was associated with it for the next fifty years, often performing a clog step as he sang it. Rooney reprised the song in the movie *Show Business* (1944), Gordon MacRae sang it in *The Daughter of Rosie O'Grady* (1950), and it was heard in *The Dance of Life* (1929) and *When My Baby Smiles at Me* (1948).

"Day By Day" (1946) is a poignant ballad about falling deeper and deeper in love with each passing day and hoping to go through life together day by day through the years. Sammy Cahn (lyric), Paul Weston, and Alex Stordahl (music) wrote the song, and it was introduced in a record by Frank Sinatra with Stordahl's Orchestra. Jo Stafford (with Weston's Orchestra), Les Brown (vocal by Doris Day), Bing Crosby, and Mel Tormé and the Mel-Tones all had successful discs, and there were other versions by Carmen McRae, Ella Fitzgerald, Ray Anthony, Ted Heath, Dick Haymes, and the Four Freshmen. The song is not to be confused with the popular hymn from the stage musical *Godspell* (1971) also titled "Day By Day."

"Day In—Day Out" (1939) was a favorite of Big Bands and their vocalists throughout the 1940s. Johnny Mercer wrote the captivating lyric about thinking of one's darling every day and all day. (Parts of the lyric foreshadows Mercer's later "Come Rain or Come Shine.") Rube Bloom composed the slightly swinging music that uses ascending scales against repeated notes in a very satisfying manner. The song is rather long for Tin Pan Alley (fifty-six measures) but develops its musical themes beautifully and emphasizes the "day in—day out" temperament of the lyric. An early recording by Bob Crosby (vocal by Helen Ward) went to the Number One spot and put the ballad on the *Hit Parade* for ten weeks. Frank Sinatra's recording was even more popular, and Lena Horne's 1957 disc was also a hit, and the number was associated with her for many years. Other noteworthy records were made by Artie Shaw (vocal by Helen Forrest), Tommy Dorsey, Al Donohue, Ella Fitzgerald, Tony Martin, Mel Tormé, Art Tatum, Judy Garland, Duke Ellington, Billie Holiday, Joni James, Nat King Cole, and Peggy Lee. Margaret Whiting sang the number in the Mercer Broadway revue *Dream* (1997).

"Daybreak" (1942) is a flowing ballad that produced three hit records when it was introduced: Tommy Dorsey (vocal by Frank Sinatra), Harry James (vocal by Johnny McAfee), and Jimmy Dorsey (vocal by Bob Eberly). Ferde Grofé composed the music, which he adapted from the "Mardi Gras" section of his 1926 orchestra piece *Mississippi Suite*. Harold

Adamson penned the evocative lyric that describes a new day beginning with mist on the meadow, a new sun providing new hope, and another daydream about an endeared one. Kathryn Grayson sang the ballad in the film *Thousands Cheer* (1943), and there were other distinctive recordings by Dick Haymes, Al Hibbler, Frank Ifield, Chet Baker, Vera Lynn, and Dinah Washington.

"De Camptown Races" (1850) is Stephen Foster's catchy nonsense song that is still one of the most recognized tunes in popular music. The spirited song about horse racing is perhaps Foster's happiest and most buoyant composition with plenty of "do-dah"s in the lyric to give the number the flavor of a galloping horse. It was introduced by Christy's Minstrels and soon became a staple in the repertoire of many minstrel troupes. (Sometimes Christy was wrongly credited as the author of the ditty.) With altered lyrics, Abe Lincoln used it as his campaign song around the time of the famous Lincoln-Douglas debates. Long a favorite on children's records, the number has also been recorded by such varied artists as Al Jolson, Frank Sinatra, Johnny Mercer and Jo Stafford with the Pied Pipers, Dave Brubeck, Red Allen, Frank Luther and the American Square Dance Orchestra, Robert White, the Hi-Lo's, Andre Kostelanetz, Spike Jones and his City Slickers, and the Mormon Tabernacle Choir. Among the dozens of movies that featured it were *Wake Up and Live* (1937), *Babes in Arms* (1939), *Swanee River* (1939), *Hi Buddy* (1943), *Stormy Weather* (1943), *Song of the Sarong* (1945), *Riding High* (1950), *I Dream of Jeannie* (1952), *Walking My Baby Back Home* (1953), and *Primary Colors* (1998). The song is sometimes listed as "Camptown Races" or "Gwine to Run All Night."

"Dear Hearts and Gentle People" (1950) was a hit in the middle of the twentieth century, but its roots go back nearly a hundred years earlier. When Stephen Foster died in 1864 a piece of paper was discovered in his pocket with the words "Dear hearts and gentle people" written on it. Musicologists had long noted the phrase that Foster probably intended as a title or part of a lyric, but it wasn't until 1950 that Bob Hilliard (lyric) and Sammy Fain (music) wrote a song inspired by the words. The tender ballad longs for one's home back in Tennessee and expresses love for the people in the town. They read the Bible every weekend, they "never ever let you down," and one hopes to return some day and build a dream home there. Bing Crosby's recording sold a million discs and, along with a bestseller by Dinah Shore, helped the song stay on *Your Hit Parade* for fifteen weeks. There were other memorable records by Doris Day, Gordon MacRae, Jim Reeves, Bob Crosby and the Bobcats, Gene Autry, and Perry Como. Autry also sang it in the film *Beyond the Purple Hills* (1950).

"Dear Old Girl" (1903) is a song of lament about a lost love by Richard Henry Buck (lyric) and Theodore F. Morse (music) that sold thousands of copies of sheet music during the first two years after its publication. The ballad was further popularized by early records by J.W. Myers, the Haydn Quartet, and Harry MacDonough. Arthur Godfrey revived interest in the number when he featured it on his television show in the 1950s. There were later notable records by the Sons of the Pioneers, Bing Crosby, the Buffalo Bills, and Jimmy Roselli. The song can be heard in the movies *Sing a Jingle* (1943) and *Flame of the Barbary Coast* (1945).

"Dear Old Southland" (1921) is a heartfelt and jazzy ballad about a home south of the Mason-Dixon Line that Henry Creamer (lyric) and Turner Layton (music) based upon the Negro spiritual "Deep River," which had been revived in 1917. Sidney Bechet introduced the number, but it was popularized by records by Paul Whiteman and Vernon Dalhart. A disc by Benny Goodman revived the song in 1939, and many more recordings followed. Among the artists to record "Dear Old Southland" were Louis Armstrong with Bessie Smith, Gene Krupa, Duke Ellington, the California Swing Cats, Paul Robeson, Teddy Wilson, Johnny Hodges, and Al Hirt.

"Dearie" (1950) is a charming soft-shoe number that lightly spoofs nostalgia even as it takes pleasure in it. Bob Hilliard and David Mann wrote the amusing song that takes the form of a series of questions asked by one spouse to another about the good old days. After asking whether the other recalls waltzing to Sousa's band, watching John L. Sullivan in the ring, listening to a crystal set, and other quaint activities of old, the response is yes, so the spouse concludes, if you can remember these, "well dearie, you're much older than I." The comic lyric continues for six refrains as the list of archaic incidents explores a cornucopia of the past. "Dearie" was popularized by a recording by Ray Bolger and Ethel Merman, but it was also a hit for Guy Lombardo and Jo Stafford with Gordon MacRae. Bing Crosby and Andrew Parks with Vicki Lewis also recorded it.

"The Death of Floyd Collins" (1925) is a sobering example of how popular songs were often written about current events, capitalizing on the dramatic situation much as made-for-TV movies exploit similar topics today. Floyd Collins was a Kentucky farmer and cave explorer who was trapped 125 feet below the surface, his legs wedged between the rocks. While friends and relatives tried to free him, the media had a field day, and the story appeared in newspapers across the country. The press and spectators gathered on the Kentucky farm to gawk, but rescue efforts failed and Collins died. Rev. Andrew Jenkins (lyric) and Irene Spain (music) turned the event into a song, and sheet music was put on sale while the incident was still fresh in the public's mind. Within a few years both Collins and the song were pretty much forgotten, but Vernon Dalhart sang the narrative ballad throughout his career, recording the song fifteen times on fifteen different labels. Other discs were made by "Fiddlin' " John Carson and Ronnie Hawkins.

" 'Deed I Do" (1926) is a cool jazz standard that answers the age-old question "Do I love you?" with the slangy affirmative of the title. Fred Rose composed the smooth, rhythmic music, and Walter Hirsch wrote the zesty lyric that plays with "d" alliteration throughout. The song was popularized by Ben Bernie and his Orchestra in clubs, and Johnny Marvin was the first of many to record it. Lena Horne revived interest in the number with her slinky interpretation in 1948. Other memorable discs were made by Jack Teagarden, Peggy Lee, Ruth Etting, Bunny Berigan, Ben Pollack, Charlie Barnet (vocal by Mary Ann McCall), Joe Pass, Ella Fitzgerald and Count Basie, Helen Humes, Lee Wiley, Claude Thornhill, Jay McShann, and Tommy Dorsey (vocal by Edythe Wright). The song can be heard in the movie *When You're Smiling* (1950).

"Deep in a Dream" (1938) is a romantic ballad that was featured on *Your Hit Parade* for fourteen weeks because of its steady radio play rather than any blockbuster records. Eddie DeLange (lyric) and Jimmy Van Heusen (music) wrote the warm song about love putting one in a dreamlike trance, and it was popularized by Artie Shaw and his Orchestra. Other records of note were made by Bob Crosby (vocal by Marion Mann), Woody Herman (vocal by Connee Boswell), Guy Lombardo, Russ Morgan, Cab Calloway, Skinnay Ennis, Jeri Southern, Frank Sinatra, Chet Baker, Milt Jackson, and Marlene Ver Planck.

"Deep in the Heart of Texas" (1941) is the clapping participation song that remained one of the most popular tunes throughout the 1940s and is still widely recognized today. June Hershey penned the lyric that paid tribute to the Lone Star State in short phrases that were punctuated by four rapid claps, and Don Swander wrote the animated music that left room for the clapping after every eighth note in the refrain. A 1942 record by Alvino Rey (vocals by Skeets Hurfurt and Bill Schallen) went to the top of the charts, and a later disc by Horace Heidt and his Orchestra sold a million discs, keeping the song on the *Hit Parade* for twelve weeks. When Bob Wills made a western-swing version of the song, it became a country favorite as well. Other well-known recordings include those by Bing Crosby, Max Bygraves, Perry Como, the Merry Macs, Fats Domino, Roy Acuff, the Ray Conniff Singers, Gene Autry, and Ray Charles. The song was performed or heard in the background in dozens of films in the 1940s and 1950s. It was sung by Autry in *Heart of the Rio Grande* (1942), Dennis Day in *I'll Get By* (1950), Howard Keel in *Texas Carnival* (1951), Wendell Cory (in French) in *Rich, Young and Pretty* (1951), Thelma Ritter and Susan Hayward (dubbed by Jane Froman) in *With a Song in My Heart* (1952), and Glenn Ford, Eddie Albert, and Marlon Brando in *Teahouse of the August Moon* (1956), as well as on the soundtracks of *Deep in the Heart of Texas* (1942), *Hi, Neighbor* (1942), *King of the Cowboys* (1943), *Thirty Seconds Over Tokyo* (1944), *How to Marry a Millionaire* (1953), and other movies.

"Deep Purple" (1934) is a lilting ballad by Mitchell Parish (lyric) and Peter DeRose (music) that found itself revived decade after decade by a variety of artists. The torchy number is about watching the sky turn purple and the stars come out, all of it reminding one of a lost love who appears in "deep purple dreams." DeRose wrote the piece as an instrumental, and it was introduced by Paul Whiteman's Orchestra with moderate success. Parish added the lyric in 1939, and the new song was popularized by Larry Clinton (vocal by Bea Wain). Interest in the ballad was revived by Bing Crosby in the 1940s, by Billy Ward and his Dominoes in 1957, by Nino Tempo and April Stevens in 1963, and by Donny and Marie Osmond in 1976. Other memorable recordings were made by Jimmy Dorsey, Don Baker, Helen Forrest, Frankie Carle, Percy Faith, Ella Fitzgerald, Benny Carter, Ray Anthony, Chet Baker, Earl Bostic, Vic Damone, Pat Boone, Paul Weston, the Norman Luboff Choir, and Peggy Lee. Doris Roberts used it as her theme song on her radio show and billed herself as the "Deep Purple Girl." The number was also a favorite of Babe Ruth, who had DeRose come and sing it to him on his birthday during the last ten years of his life. "Deep Purple" was heard in the film *Lake Placid Serenade* (1944), and it was sung by Andre De Shields and the company of the Broadway revue *Stardust* (1987).

"Deep River" (1917) is a traditional Negro spiritual of unknown origin that was popularized in the late nineteenth century by a troupe of ex-slaves who toured America and Europe to raise money for Fisk University in Nashville. The emotive lyric expresses a desire to cross over the deep River Jordan to get to the "campground" ("paradise" in some versions) on the other side. Henry Thacker Burleigh wrote a standardized version in 1917, and the old song was more popular than ever, especially with choral groups. When musical numbers were added to the 1929 silent film of *Show Boat*, "Deep River" was sung by the black ensemble. Among those who recorded the poignant ballad were Paul Robeson, Ezio Pinza, Marian Anderson, Artie Shaw, Jack Teagarden, Tommy Dorsey, Fats Waller, Morton Gould, Eddy Arnold, George Beverly Shea, Jim Cullum, and Johnny Mathis. In 1921 Henry Creamer (lyric) and Turner Layton (music) adapted the spiritual into a jazz piece called "Dear Old Southland," and it also was very popular.

"Der Fuehrer's Face" (1942) was a rarity on Tin Pan Alley: a comic propaganda song from a cartoon short that became a hit. G. Oliver Wallace wrote the slapstick lampoon about Adolf Hitler, and it was sung by Donald Duck (voice of Clarence Nash) in the animated short subject *Donald Duck in Nutzi-Land* (1942). The comic number was reprised in another cartoon, *Der Fuehrer's Face*, later that same year. The two shorts were seen by thousands of moviegoers, but it was a record by Spike Jones and his City Slickers that sold a million and a half discs and made the song a coast-to-coast favorite. Carl Grayson and Willie Spicer did the vocals on the Jones record, doing a Bronx cheer every time the dictator's name was mentioned, and Jones filled the recording with odd sound effects and incongruous musical notes to create a chaotic effect. It was the City Slickers' first record, and it launched their career.

"Diana" (1957) was the first published song and first record for sixteen-year-old Paul Anka, and few singers or songwriters have had a more successful start. Anka, as a fifteen-year-old living in Ottawa, Canada, fell hopelessly in love with a girl named Diana, who was three years older, so he wrote a ballad describing the situation. Anka's recording sold a million discs, was the top-selling song in North America for thirteen weeks, and during the next six years received over 300 different recordings in twenty-two different countries. The autobiographical song is somewhat in the "wailing" style, but the lyric is deeply personal, and its sincerity rings true. Although Anka used an amplified guitar in the style of the new rock-and-roll sound, the song was still firmly in the Tin Pan Alley ballad tradition. Bobby Rydell revived the number in 1965 with his successful recording, and there were also discs by Johnny O'Keefe, the Ventures, Frankie Lymon and the Teenagers, Bobby Vee, the Bachelors, and Conway Twitty.

"Did I Remember?" (1936) is the Oscar-nominated ballad by Harold Adamson (lyric) and Walter Donaldson (music) that was featured on *Your Hit Parade* for sixteen weeks. Alec Wilder describes the music as having an "open and free melody . . . direct and unbusy, containing no notes of less duration than a quarter note." Jean Harlow (dubbed by Virginia Verrill) and Cary Grant introduced the number in the movie *Suzy* (1936), and there were early hit discs by Dick Powell, Billie Holiday, Shep Fields, and Tommy Dorsey (vocal by Edyth Wright). Other highly regarded records were made by Gracie Fields, Jane Froman, Etta Jones, Frank Ifield, and Marty Grosz.

"Dinah" (1924) is arguably the most famous song to come from a night-club show. The celebrated rhythm ballad was written by Sam Lewis, Joe Young (lyric), and Harry Akst (music) for the floorshow *Plantation Revue* (1924) where Ethel Waters introduced it and was associated with it for years. The contagious music is relaxed and unpretentious as the catchy lyric sings the praises of bride-to-be Dinah Lee who came from Carolina, with "her Dixie eyes blazin'." Sung in a playful southern accent, the title rhymes with "China," "finer," Carolina," and "ocean liner." Waters reprised the song in the Broadway revues *Africana* (1927) and *Blackbirds of 1930* and made a recording that is considered a jazz classic. Eddie Cantor interpolated the number into his musical *Kid Boots* (1923) after it had been running a year, and he also sang it throughout his career. Early records by Cliff Edwards, Louis Armstrong, and Fletcher Henderson helped popularize the song, then it was revived with a bestselling disc by Bing Crosby in 1932, as well as hits by the Boswell Sisters in 1935 and Fats Waller in 1936. Fanny Rose Shore sang the number on a radio station in Nashville, and it started her career; she changed her name to Dinah Shore because of the number, and it was her theme song for decades. Other notable records were made by Jan Garber, Josephine Baker, Jimmie Lunceford, Count Basie, Sam Donohue, Frankie Carle, Basil Fomeen, the Mills Brothers, Ruby Braff, the Benny Goodman Quartet, Danny Kaye, and Rick Nelson. It was sung by Crosby in the movie *The Big Broadcast* (1932), Jeanette MacDonald in *Rose Marie* (1936), Gene Autry in *Round-Up in Texas* (1937), and Cantor, George Murphy, Constance Moore, and Joan Davis in *Show Business* (1944), as well as on the soundtracks of *Hello, Everybody* (1933), *Lemon Drop Kid* (1934), *Hit Parade of 1941* (1940), and *Broadway* (1942).

"The Dipsy Doodle" (1937) is a nonsense song about a nonsense dance that bandleader Larry Clinton wrote and used as the theme song for his orchestra. The silly ditty has been recorded many times, most memorably by Tommy Dorsey (vocal by Edythe Wright), Glenn Miller, Chick Webb (vocal by Ella Fitzgerald), Sammy Kaye, the Milt Herth Trio, Ernie Fields, and the Golden Gate Quartet. Johnny Maddox revived the song in 1953, and even British comic Graham Chapman cut a record version. The tune can be heard in the films *Since You Went Away* (1944) and *Angela's Ashes* (1999).

"Dixie" (1859) started as a minstrel song, grew to become a national anthem during the Civil War, and today is the theme song for the American South. Ironically, "Dixie" was written by a northerner, Daniel Decatur Emmett, whose wife was from the South. On a cold and rainy day, she commented to her husband that she wished she was back in Dixie, and Emmett was intrigued by the term, which was rarely used at the time, especially in the North. He wrote the lyric about the yearning to be back home ("wish I were in the Land of Cotton") yet also stressed a pride in the land ("take my stand to live and die in Dixie"), which gave the song the flexibility to be both domestic and militant. It was introduced in the North as a "walkaround" number for Bryant's Minstrels in 1859 before Mrs. John Wood brought it south in a concert tour. When the song was performed in Charleston in 1860, it started to catch on as a regional anthem. By the time the Civil War broke out, "Dixie" was adopted by the Confederate Army as its national song and was played and sung at rallies, parades, in camps, and even on the battlefield. (Colonel Pickett had his men sing it to boast morale before their famous charge at Gettysburg.) Interestingly enough, even Northerners liked the tune, and it was a favorite of Abraham Lincoln's; he stated that the song belonged to the whole country and insisted it be played when Lee surrendered at Appomattox. For decades after the war, some felt that "Dixie" was still nationalistic, but most of America enjoyed it for the tuneful, pleasing number that it is. Of the hundreds of recordings, major discs were made by such artists as Dinah Shore, Jerry Lee Lewis, Bing Crosby, Boxcar Willie, Ace Cannon, Eric Clapton, Peter Allen, and Elvis Presley, not to mention many choral groups and marching bands. ("Dixie" remains the victory fight song for several southern colleges.) The anthem can be heard in dozens of period movies, from *Gone With the Wind* (1939) to *Rio Grande* (1950) to *Stars and Stripes Forever* (1952) to *Gettysburg* (1993), and it was sung by Crosby in *Dixie* (1943), Mitzi Gaynor in *Golden Girl* (1951), Susan Hayward (dubbed by Jane Froman) in *With a Song in My Heart* (1952), and Kurt Russell in *Elvis* (1979). Among the titles the song has been listed under are "Wish I Were in the Land of Cotton," "Dixieland," and "I Wish I Was in Dixie's Land."

"Do I Worry?" (1941) is a carefree ballad by Stanley Cowan and Bobby Worth that remained popular throughout the 1940s and has resurfaced on occasion since then. The song was introduced by the Ink Spots on a bestselling record, and there were also hit records by Tommy Dorsey (vocal by Frank Sinatra) and Bea Wain. Other discs were made by Claude Thornhill, Harry James, Derrick Harriott, Max Bygraves, the Platters, Brenda Lee, and Pat Boone. It was heard in the film *In the Groove* (1941), the Ink Spots reprised it in *Pardon My Sarong* (1942), and Bobby Brooke sang it in *Honeymoon Lodge* (1943).

"Do Nothin' Till You Hear From Me" (1943) is a jazzy ballad in which a parting lover asks his sweetheart not to fall in love with someone else after he's gone. The standard began as an instrumental piece called "Concerto for Cootie" that Duke Ellington wrote and recorded in 1940 to highlight his trumpeter Cootie Williams. Bob Russell added the sly lyric in 1943, and Ellington introduced that version on record as well. Hit discs by Woody Herman and his Orchestra and Stan Kenton (vocal by Red Dorris) made the song popular, so "Concerto for Cootie" was rereleased as "Do Nothin' Till You Hear From Me" and it was also a hit. Other memorable discs were made by Billie Holiday, Al Hibbler, Johnny Hodges, Count Basie, Gary Grant, Joe Pass, Zoot Sims, Anita O'Day, Ella Fitzgerald, Joe Augustine, Diana Krall, Quincy Jones, and Leslie Uggams. The number was heard on the soundtrack of the movie *New York, New York* (1977), and Gregory Hines sang it in the Broadway musical revue *Sophisticated Ladies* (1981).

"Does the Spearmint Lose Its Flavor on the Bedpost Over Night?" (1924) is a silly novelty number from the 1920s that was still being sung four decades later. Ernest Breuer wrote the hoedownlike music, and Billy Rose and Marty Bloom penned the comic lyric that asked the musical question of the title, as well as inquiring if "you swallow it in spite" when your mother doesn't allow chewing gum. Harry Richman introduced the ditty in concert, and the team of Ernest Hare and Billy Jones recorded it with success. The lyric (and sometimes the title) had to be changed to "Does Your Chewing Gum Lose Its Flavor on the Bedpost Over Night?" for radio play because of complaints from other gum companies that it was free advertising for Spearmint. The song was revived in 1961 with a record by the British singer Lonnie Donegan and his Skiffle Group, and a successful disc was also made by the Re-Bops.

"Doggie in the Window" (1953) may be the simplest and most juvenile song ever to reach the top position in *Your Hit Parade*, but this little ditty by Bob Merrill remains as familiar today as any classic nursery rhyme or traditional American folk song. Sometimes titled "How Much Is That Doggie in the Window?" or "That Doggie in the Window," the short song was popularized by a Patti Page record that went to the top of the charts. In addition to many children's discs, it was also recorded by Homer and Jethro, the Persuasions, and Wylie Gustufson. The well-known Page recording was heard in the cult film *Pink Flamingos* (1972), and it was sung by the cast of the Off-Broadway musical revue *The Taffetas* (1988).

"Don't Blame Me" (1933) is the scintillating jazz standard that crossed over to become a favorite in various fields. Jimmy McHugh composed the sparse yet expansive music, and Dorothy Fields penned the direct, potent lyric arguing that it is "not my fault" that one falls under the spell of a lover. The uptempo ballad was introduced by Jeanette Leff in the stage revue *Clowns in Clover* (1933) and popularized by Walter Wolfe King first in Chicago. Early records by Guy Lombardo and the Royal

Canadians and Ethel Waters made it a coast-to-coast success, and it was revived by Nat King Cole in 1948. Other distinctive recordings were made by Leo Reisman, Irene Taylor, Rudy Vallee, Andy Russell, Erroll Garner, Bing Crosby, Keely Smith, Paul Weston, Frankie Laine, Bill Coleman, Charlie Parker with Miles Davis, the Norman Luboff Choir, Sarah Vaughan, the Everly Brothers, and more recently, Barbara Cook. It was featured in a handful of films, being sung by Freddie Stewart in *Freddie Steps Out* (1946), Betty Garrett in *Big City* (1948), Vic Damone in *The Strip* (1951), Constance Towers in *Bring Your Smile Along* (1955), and Leslie Uggams in *Two Weeks in Another Town* (1962). Also, Ann Miller and Eddie Pruett performed it in the Broadway revue *Sugar Babies* (1980).

"Don't Fence Me In" (1944) is a very atypical Cole Porter ballad that is about the wide-open prairie rather than the sophisticated world of penthouses and nightclubs. Porter intended the number to be a spoof of a sentimental cowboy song, but it was taken at face value by performers and the public. His lyric, based on a poem by Montana miner Robert Fletcher, is the woeful lament of a jailed cowboy who longs for the open spaces of the land. The number was written in the early 1930s for a film that was never produced, and it was cut from another movie before the final print. The cowboy ballad was finally heard in the film *Hollywood Canteen* (1944), where it was sung by Roy Rogers and the Sons of the Pioneers. Rogers's recording, as well as a Number One hit by Bing Crosby with the Andrews Sisters, kept the song on the *Hit Parade* for sixteen weeks. There were other prominent recordings by Kate Smith with Four Chicks and a Chuck, the Banjo Kings, Gene Autry, Johnny Mercer, Louis Armstrong, Hoyt Axton, Marian McPartland, and recently, Rebecca Luker and Susannah McCorkle. Rogers reprised the ballad in the films *Don't Fence Me In* (1945) and the Porter bio *Night and Day* (1946), and it was featured in the Off-Broadway revue *Swingtime Canteen* (1995).

"Don't Get Around Much Anymore" (1942) is the cool jazz standard about a dejected admirer who stays at home listening to the radio, reading books, and missing a lost lover. Duke Ellington originally composed it as an instrument piece called "Never No Lament," but it didn't catch on until Bob Russell added the slangy lyric, omitting the personal pronouns (as in the title phrase). Ellington introduced the new version with Al Hibbler as vocalist, and it was also recorded with success by Glen Gray and the Casa Loma Orchestra and the Ink Spots. The song was long associated with comic Jimmy Savo whose burlesque version of it was popular in vaudeville and nightclubs for years. Among the other artists who recorded the ballad were Nat King Cole with Count Basie's Orchestra, Ella Fitzgerald, Bob Grant, Joe Williams, Judy Garland, Hank Crawford, Oscar Peterson, Little Anthony and the Imperials, Barbara

Hendricks, and more recently, Natalie Cole, Vicki Stuart, and Harry Connick Jr. On Broadway, Gregory Hines sang the song in the Ellington revue *Sophisticated Ladies* (1981), Cheryl Freeman and Tonya Pinkins performed it in the musical *Play On!* (1997), and it was heard in the movies *So's Your Uncle* (1943) and *When Harry Met Sally* (1989).

"Don't Let's Be Beastly to the Germans" (1945) was a timely comic song by Noel Coward that was very popular in its day even though Coward's was the only major recording. With the tide turned and an end in sight for World War Two, Coward wrote this satiric number suggesting that the Allies should show kindness to "the Hun" and hold no grudge. The tongue-in-cheek lyric ("treat the rats with charity") appealed to both British and American audiences who were tossed between bitterness and relief. Although it was written for the London revue *Flying Colors* (1943), the song was cut, and it found success through Coward's recording and concert appearances.

"Don't Sit Under the Apple Tree (With Anyone Else But Me)" (1939) was one of the first and most durable song hits of World War Two, expressing a sentiment that was on the mind of many GIs and their girls back home. Sam H. Stept composed the swinging music, and Lew Brown and Charles Tobias wrote the lyric pleading a sweetheart not to go back to the place where they fell in love with anyone else. While the words could have been interpreted as a sentimental 1890s ballad, Stept's gentle boogie-woogie music and the jiving "no, no, no!" in the lyric made it all very modern. The song was introduced in the Broadway musical *Yokel Boy* (1939), but it became all the rage when the Andrews Sisters sang it in the movie *Private Buckaroo* (1942). Their record went to the top of the charts, as did one by Glenn Miller (vocals by Marion Hutton, Tex Beneke, and the Modernaires). Other noteworthy discs were made by Kay Kyser, Paula Kelly, Bob Grant, Laine Nelson, Bob Crosby, the Coleman Hawkins Quartet, Jive Bunny and the Mastermixers, Barry Manilow, and Vicki Stuart. Eleanor Parker (dubbed by Eileen Farrell) sang the song in the film *Interrupted Melody* (1955), it was heard on the soundtrack of *Come See the Paradise* (1990), and the Andrews Sisters recording was heard in both *Red Sky at Morning* (1970) and *The Story of Us* (1999). Ann Hampton Callaway and the cast performed it in the Broadway musical revue *Swing!* (1999).

"Don't Take Your Love From Me" (1941) is a tearful ballad by Henry Nemo that was introduced and popularized by Mildred Bailey and went on to become a hit record for Artie Shaw (vocal by Lena Horne), Alvino Rey (vocal by Yvonne King), Glen Gray and the Casa Loma Orchestra (vocal by Eugenie Baird), and the Three Suns. Nemo's music is freewheeling and easygoing, but his lyric lists painful subtractions (if you take a star from the sky, a wing off a bird, a petal from a rose, and so on) that cause grief and compares them to one's love going away. Etta James, Doris Day, Earl Hines, Frank Sinatra, the Calvanes, Billy Eckstine, Kay Starr, the Cadillacs, the McGuire Sisters, and Randy Travis were among the many who also recorded the ballad.

"Don't Worry 'Bout Me" (1939) is an intriguing farewell song where the lyric expresses one idea but the music and the subtext says quite the opposite. Ted Koehler wrote the sentimental lyric assuring a departing inamorata that he will be fine and not to fret about it, but Rube Bloom's sad music is full of longing, making the number both tense and touching It was introduced in the revue *Cotton Club Parade* (1939) by Cab Calloway and was followed by dozens of recordings, none more successful than one by Frank Sinatra. Other memorable discs were made by Hal Kemp, Les Brown (vocal by Miriam Shaw), Duke Ellington, Horace Heidt, Ginny Simms, Count Basie (vocal by Helen Humes), Bob Crosby (vocal by Marion Mann), Zoot Sims, Stan Getz, Rosemary Clooney, Art Van Damme, Savannah Churchill, Teddy Wilson (vocal by Sarah Vaughan), June Christy and the Keytones, Pat Boone, and Tony Bennett.

"Down Among the Sheltering Palms" (1914) is a harmonizing favorite by James Brockman (lyric) and Abe Olman (music) with an exotic locale and feel to it. The song is a lyrical and romantic invitation to meet under the swaying palms at eight o'clock, and its gently swooning quality has made it a specialty of barbershop quartets over the years. In fact, it was first popularized by the Lyric Quartet and enjoyed a revival three decades later by Sammy Kaye and his Orchestra. There were also notable records by Al Jolson, the Boswell Sisters, Barney Kessel, Kid Ory and his Creole Jazz Band, Jo Ann Castle, Kay Starr, Horace Heidt, Earl Hines, and Dinah Shore. It was heard in the movies *Oh, You Beautiful Doll* (1949), *Down Among the Sheltering Palms* (1953), and *Some Like It Hot* (1959), and Keenan Wynn sang it with a quartet in *That Midnight Kiss* (1949).

"Down By the O-Hi-O" (1920) is a folk ballad by Jack Yellen (lyric) and Abe Olman (music) that tells a tragic tale. A beau asks his girl to take a stroll along the Ohio River, and he talks about their wedding day to come and how they will settle in a cabin by the riverside. But she refuses his offer, so he drowns her in the river and is mourning her loss as the sheriff arrests him. The team of Van and Schenck popularized the narrative ballad first in vaudeville and then in the *Ziegfeld Follies of 1920*. There were early records by Billy Murray and Billy Jones, Milton Brown and his Musical Brownies, and the Blue Sky Boys. Two 1940 records by the Andrews Sisters and the Smoothies revived the country-flavored song and there were later discs by Spike Jones and his City Slickers and the Moms and Dads. The Blue Sky Boys record was heard in the movie *Paper Moon* (1973) and the Andrews Sisters' disc was on the soundtrack of *1941* (1979).

"Down By the Old Mill Stream" (1910) is a barbershop quartet favorite that lends itself to four-part harmony more effectively than perhaps any other. Tell Taylor wrote the swooning ballad whose music gently ascends and descends the scale as its lyric nostalgically recalls a past, youthful love. The sweethearts are now old, but they fondly remember the mill stream where they fell in love. Arthur Clough introduced the ballad on stage, and in a few years over 5 million copies of sheet music were sold. In addition to quartets, the song was popular at sing-alongs, and often standardized gestures were used to act out the words. In the 1940s the Mills Brothers recorded the ballad in a more swinging style, and many other newer artists (including some jazz musicians) recorded the old standard. Well-known discs were made by Bing Crosby, Benny Goodman, Gene Krupa, Jimmie Lunceford, Harry James, the Three Peppers, Marty Grosz, Sidney Bechet, Nat King Cole, the Dukes of Dixieland, Mitch Miller, and Jimmy Roselli. It was also heard in the films *Her Master's Voice* (1936), *War of the Wildcats* (1943), and many period movies looking for nostalgic background music.

"Down By the Riverside" (c. 1865) is a tradition Negro spiritual that is also one of the earliest antiwar songs in American popular music. The gently swinging gospel number pledges to lay down both sword and shield by the river's edge and promises to "study war no more." Although its origins go back to the Civil War days, it was not formally published until Paul Barnes adapted it into a Tin Pan Alley song in 1900. A 1954 recording by Bing and Gary Crosby revived the number as a Dixieland jazz-flavored song. In addition to glee clubs, gospel choirs, and jazz groups, it has been recorded with success by Elvis Presley, Louis Armstrong, the Dukes of Dixieland, Turk Murphy, Conrad Janis, Bunk Johnson, Mahalia Jackson, Pete Seeger, George Lewis and his Ragtime Band, Jim Robinson, Mindy Carson, Chris Barber, Patsy Cline, and the Neville Brothers. It was sung by Ottilie Patterson in the British movie *Ring-a-Ding Rhythm* (1962), Alan Bates in *A Kind of Loving* (1962), and Elvis Presley in *Frankie and Johnny* (1966). The number is sometimes listed as "I Ain't Gwine Study War No More."

"Down in the Valley" is the traditional American folk song with unknown origins that has been in published form since 1917 but probably goes back far into the nineteenth century. The gentle ballad encourages one to "hang your head" over the "valley so low" and to hear the wind

blow. Subsequent stanzas are about a new day breaking and a proclamation of love as well. The song conjures up visions of the American
landscape and has been used for its atmospheric effect in many movies
from *Moonlight and Cactus* (1944) to *Bound for Glory* (1976). Gene Autry
sang it in *Cow Town* (1950), and a parody of the celebrated song was
used in *Bye Bye Braverman* (1968). A 1944 recording by the Andrews
Sisters gave the already-familiar number a new boost, but it had always
been a favorite of folk singers and cowboy balladeers. Major recordings
were made by Autry, Tex Ritter, Leadbelly, Otis Redding, the Browns,
Solomon Burke, Pete Seeger, Connie Francis, Slim Whitman, Ike and Tina
Turner, and Ray Charles.

"Down Went McGinty (To the Bottom of the Sea)" (1888) is a comic
list song that was a favorite in vaudeville, particularly with Irish singers.
Joe Flynn wrote the farcical number about the accident-prone Irishman
Dan McGinty who kept falling down coal chutes, off of high walls, and
so on, eventually sinking deep into the ocean, all the while "dressed in
his best suit of clothes." The silly number was introduced by the comic
team of Flynn and Sheridan in a Brooklyn theater, and soon it was being
performed by every Irish comic in the business. It was most associated
with vaudevillian Maggie Cline who included it in her act for many
years. The song's jaunty, Irish-flavored music is often used in the background in movies, and it was sung in *South Sea Rose* (1929) and by Will
Rogers in *David Harum* (1934).

"Down Where the Wurzburger Flows" (1902) is not about a river but a
brand of beer and this rowdy drinking song long outlived the brewing
company that inspired it. Harry Von Tilzer wrote the catchy sing-along
melody, and Vincent P. Bryan penned the lyric that encouraged one to
drown your troubles and cares by getting too drunk to remember. Nora
Bayes introduced the merry number in vaudeville, and she had such a
hit with it that she was called the "Wurzburger girl" and made it her
signature song until she found a bigger hit with "Shine On, Harvest
Moon." Tilzer collaborated with lyricist Andrew B. Sterling on a song
sequel called "Under the Anheuser Bush" in 1903, and it also was very
popular.

"Down Yonder" (1922) took thirty years to catch on, but when it did, it
made up for lost time. L. Wolfe Gilbert wrote the vibrant levee song that
urges one to return to one's home down south. He introduced it in a
vaudeville house in New Orleans in 1922 and managed to get some
major stars (Al Jolson, Sophie Tucker, Eddie Cantor, and Belle Baker) to
put it in their vaudeville acts. But nothing seemed to happen to the song,
and no publisher was interested. Gilbert founded his own company to

publish it, but the sheet music did not sell and the song fell into obscurity. In 1952 Dell Wood made a recording that sold 1 million discs, put the song on the *Hit Parade* for eighteen weeks, and spurred twenty different recordings in the 1950s. Bing Crosby, Bill Monroe, Buddy and Ella Johnson, Merle Travis, Johnny and the Hurricanes, Roy Clark, the Nitty Gritty Dirt Band, Flatt and Scruggs, and Willie Nelson are among those who have recorded it since the acclaimed Wood disc.

"Dream" (1945) is one of the handful of hit songs that Johnny Mercer wrote both music and lyric for, and in many ways, this ballad is his most evocative. The simple but rich melody was first heard as the closing theme for the Chesterfield radio show in 1945, and the music was so alluring that Mercer was encouraged to write a lyric for it. Like the melody, the lyric is direct and unadorned, suggesting that when you are blue, one should realize that things are not as bad as they seem, "so dream dream dream." The song was popularized by the Pied Pipers, whose record sold a million copies, and by a Frank Sinatra disc that was also a big hit. In 1954 the Four Aces revived interest in the number with their recording. Other versions were made by Jimmy Dorsey, the Clark Sisters, Ray Anthony, Ella Fitzgerald, Les Brown, Dean Martin, the Norman Luboff Choir, Les Elgart, the Moms and Dads, and more recently, Andrea Marcovicci. The ballad was heard in the movie *Mother Is a Freshman* (1949) and was sung by Fred Astaire and the chorus in *Daddy Long Legs* (1955), Beverly D'Angelo in *In the Mood* (1987), and Brad Mehldau in *Midnight in the Garden of Good and Evil* (1997). It was also sung by the cast of the Broadway Mercer revue *Dream* (1997).

"Dream a Little Dream of Me" (1931) is a simple but melodic little ballad that managed to resurface every once in a while and become a hit all over again. Wilbur Schwandt and Fabian André wrote the felicitous music, and Gus Kahn penned the smooth and alliterative lyric ("I'm longing to linger till dawn, dear"), which observes the fading stars and proclaims that her dreams about him are not fading, hoping he is dreaming about her as well. The song was introduced by Wayne King and his Orchestra, but Kate Smith popularized it when she sang it on her first radio broadcast in 1931. Frankie Laine turned it into a popular favorite again with his 1950 record. Then it became an even bigger success with a 1968 disc by Mama Cass Elliott with the Mamas and the Papas. Others who have recorded the ballad include Jack Owens, Ella Mae Morse, Louis Armstrong, Joe Augustine, Nat King Cole, Doris Day, Ella Fitzgerald, Dean Martin, Roger Williams, and more recently, Karen Akers and Jane Horrocks. Robert Lindsay sang it in the movie *Bert Rigby, You're a Fool* (1989), and the admired Elliott recording was heard in *Beautiful Thing* (1996).

"A Dreamer's Holiday" (1949) is a hyperbolic description of a fantasy vacation that includes everything from riding on butterflies to eating rainbow candy bars. Mabel Wayne composed the lazy, gliding music, and Kim Gannon wrote the lyric that argued that anything is possible when you dream. Perry Como made the song a hit, and there were also accomplished records by Ray Anthony, Buddy Clark, Bing Crosby, Gordon Jenkins, Randy Brooks, Eddy Arnold, Charlie Shaffer, and Willie Nelson.

"Drifting Along With the Tide" (1921) is a very early George Gershwin song, written when he was a struggling demonstrator on Tin Pan Alley. Arthur Jackson penned the graceful lyric about a free and easy lifestyle, and the number was interpolated in the Broadway revue *George White's Scandals of 1921* where it was performed by Lloyd Garrett and Victoria Herbert. While no blockbuster, the song attracted some attention and was used in the London musical *Mayfair and Montmartre* (1922). Years later expert recordings of the ballad were made by Bobby Short, Jack Brent, and Susannah McCorkle.

"Drifting and Dreaming" (1925) was a 1920s version of the earlier atmospheric hit "On Moonlight Bay," both songs painting an idyllic scene with a full moon shining over a lake with two lovers in a canoe. Haven Gillespie wrote the picturesque lyric, and Egbert Van Alstyne, Erwin Schmidt, and Loyal Curtis collaborated on the music, a surprisingly rhythmic melody that pushes forward and is not as aimless as the title suggests. Orrin Tucker and his Orchestra popularized the number and made it their theme song, and it was also a hit for George Olsen and his Orchestra. Les Brown and his Band of Renown revived the ballad with a bestselling record in 1950. Other memorable discs were made by Guy Lombardo, Vaughn Monroe and the Moon Maids, Carson Robison and Bud Billings, Basil Fomeen's Orchestra, Vera Lynn, Burl Ives, Les Paul and Mary Ford, Pat Boone, Billy Vaughn, Jimmy Bryant, Bert Kaempfert, Ken Griffin, and Cleo Laine with James Gaul. Because of its bucolic nature, the song also became a favorite of Hawaiian bands.

"Duna" (1914) is an Irish standard that waxes poetical about the place of the title back in Ireland. Marjorie Pickhall and Josephine McGill wrote the sentimental favorite, which was big in sheet music sales and was recorded by Charles Hackett, Robert White, Gabor Csupo, and Sydney MacEwan, as well as a multitude of Irish singers and bands.

"Dust Off That Old Pianna (Oh, Suzanna)" (1935) is a pastiche of a turn-of-the-century sing-along song, encouraging folks to gather around the old parlor piano and sing some jazzy tunes from the good old days.

Irving Caesar, Sammy Lerner, and Gerald Marks collaborated on the bouncy number, and it was popularized by Ozzie Nelson (vocal by Harriet Hilliard). Other recordings of note were made by the New Orleans Rhythm Kings, Eddie Cantor, Fats Waller, Bob Hannon, George Hall (vocals by Loretta Lee and Sonny Schuyler), Lew Stone, and Wingy Manone.

E

"Early Autumn" (1949) is a tender ballad that describes the coming of fall (a summer pavilion all boarded up, the foliage turning russet, frost appearing, and so on) and the feeling of remorse as one ponders on the true love discovered last spring. Woody Herman and Ralph Burns wrote the number as an instrumental piece called "Summer Sequence," and Herman recorded it with Stan Getz on tenor sax. Johnny Mercer added the poignant lyric in 1952, and Herman and his Orchestra rerecorded it as "Early Autumn." Jo Stafford had a successful disc with it. Claude Thornhill, Anita O'Day, Sylvia Syms, Ella Fitzgerald, Harry Allen and the John Pizzarelli Trio, Ray Anthony, Ben Webster, Fran Warren, Stan Kenton, and Anita Kerr are among those who also recorded it.

"East of the Sun (And West of the Moon)" (1935) is one of the very few songs written for a college show that went on to become a standard. Princeton student Brooks Bowman wrote the lilting ballad that described the location where two lovers wish to build their dream house, and it was introduced in the university's Triangle Club show *Stags at Bay* (1935). The song got noticed, and soon Hal Kemp (vocal by Bob Allen) had a hit with it. Other early records were made by Bob Crosby and Arthur Tracy, but the biggest seller of all was a 1941 disc by Tommy Dorsey (vocals by Frank Sinatra and the band). Other records of note were made by Helen Forrest, Billie Holiday, George Shearing, Dick Haymes, Paul Weston, Tom Croakley, Billy Daniels, Bud Powell, Charlie Parker, and Sarah Vaughan. Sadly, the ballad was Bowman's swan song as well as his debut. When he graduated from Princeton he was given a Hollywood contract to write songs for the movies, but Bowman died in a car accident while driving out to California.

"Easter Parade" (1933), one of Irving Berlin's most cherished holiday songs, took awhile before it became the perennial favorite it is today. Berlin first wrote the tune as "Smile and Show Your Dimple" in 1918, but it never caught on. While preparing the score for the lavish Broadway revue *As Thousands Cheer* (1933), he recalled the tune and wrote a new lyric for a song to be used in a production number about the Easter procession down Fifth Avenue. Marilyn Miller and Clifton Webb led the ensemble in the number, and audiences quickly accepted it as a holiday standard. Several recordings and hefty sheet music sales followed, and the never-forgotten song enjoyed revivals in 1942 with Harry James and in 1947 with Guy Lombardo, both records selling over a million discs. Other distinctive recordings were made by Bing Crosby, Al Jolson, Kate Smith, Andy Russell, Freddy Martin, Henry King, Leo Reisman (vocal by Webb), Jimmie Lunceford, Dave Bartholomew, Red Nichols and his Five Pennies, Ruby Braff, Roy Rogers and Dale Evans, Liberace, Rise Stevens, Sarah Vaughan, Perry Como, and Kiri Te Kanawa. On screen, it was sung by Don Ameche in *Alexander's Ragtime Band* (1938), Crosby in *Holiday Inn* (1942), and Judy Garland and the chorus in *Easter Parade* (1948).

"Easy Come, Easy Go" (1934) is a low-key farewell song that suggests two lovers part as easily as they first met, showing no regret or remorse. The smooth ballad was written by Edward Heyman (lyric) and Johnny Green (music) for the movie *Bachelor of Arts* (1934), but it was only heard on the soundtrack and attracted little attention. The song was later popularized by two hit records: Lee Wiley with Green's Orchestra and Eddy Duchin (vocals by the De Marco Sisters). There were also notable discs by Helen Merrill, Al Bowlly, Anita O'Day, and Bobby Short. The somber ballad was used as a recurring theme throughout the film *They Shoot Horses, Don't They?* (1969) and included a vocal treatment by Lynn Willis.

"Easy Living" (1937) is a jazz standard by Leo Robin (lyric) and Ralph Rainger (music) about how easy going life is since one fell in love. It was written as the title song for the movie *Easy Living* (1937), but only the music was used in the background, so the number wasn't noticed until Billie Holiday recorded in that same year with Teddy Wilson. Her disc was popular, and Holiday recorded it again in 1947. Peggy Lee's 1953 recording revived interest in the ballad, and there were also discs by Dave McKenna, Sonny Stitt, Count Basie, Clifford Brown, Stan Getz, Joe Pass, Marian McPartland, and André Previn. The cool jazz number can be heard in the films *Remember the Night* (1940), *Easy Living* (1949), and *Chinatown* (1974).

"Easy Street" (1940) is a sly, self-mocking song by Alan Rankin Jones with a slow, slightly swinging melody. The languid ballad is about the longing to live on easy street where no one works, there are no weekly payments to make, and you can even ignore opportunity when it knocks. The tone of the lyric is quite droll (he doesn't want to look for a job because he's scared someone might hire him), and the way the title phrase moves to a different pitch each time it is repeated is unique. Jimmie Lunceford and his Orchestra featured it and recorded the number with success, and later there were outstanding versions by Martha Tilton, Sonny Dunham, Guy Lombardo, and Elaine Stritch. The offbeat song was also recorded by Billy May, Duke Ellington, the Pied Pipers, June Christy, Pearl Bailey, and Julie London.

"Easy to Love" (1934) is the romantic Cole Porter standard that has bounced back and forth from the stage to Hollywood to Tin Pan Alley during its lifetime. Porter wrote the climbing ballad for the Broadway musical *Anything Goes* (1934), but it was cut in rehearsals because leading man William Gaxton complained that he couldn't reach the high notes. After he went to Hollywood, Porter included the song in his score for the movie musical *Born to Dance* (1936), and it was used throughout, though rarely in full voice. James Stewart sang it (barely) to Eleanor Powell who danced to it, Reginald Gardiner mimed it, Frances Langford briefly reprised it, and Buddy Ebsen tapped to it. The full qualities of the ballad were not appreciated until it was recorded by such artists as Langford, Hal Kemp (vocal Bob Allen), Shep Fields (vocal by Dick Robertson), Teddy Wilson, Billie Holiday, and others. It was sung by opera tenor Lauritz Melchior in the film *This Time for Keeps* (1947), and Tony Martin crooned it in *Easy to Love* (1953). Also on screen it was heard in the Porter bio *Night and Day* (1946) and in *A Life of Her Own* (1950). "Easy to Love" was eventually heard on Broadway in the revue *A Day in Hollywood—A Night in the Ukraine* (1980), and Howard McGillin sang it in its originally intended spot in the 1988 revival of *Anything Goes*. Among the many who have recorded the ballad over the years were Dick Jurgens (vocal by Eddy Howard), Judy Garland, Maxine Sullivan, George Shearing, Doris Day, Polly Bergen, Lee Wiley, Dinah Shore and Buddy Clark, Sammy Davis Jr., Bill Evans, Ella Fitzgerald, Charlie Parker, Vic Damone, Shirley Bassey, and more recently, Ann Hampton Callaway and Harry Connick Jr.

"Ebb Tide" (1953) is a skillful song whose music follows the pattern of a rushing tide for dramatic effect. The number began as an instrumental piece written by harpist Robert Maxwell that starts off in dreamy mode, then builds and cascades before quieting down again. Frank Chacksfield had a hit record of the composition in England, so Carl Sigman added a lyric about the tide rushing in and compared it to a lover's returning and kissing a sweetheart, the climax then moving into a mellow afterglow. Vic Damone had a hit with the new vocal version, as did Roy Hamilton. The Platters revived it in 1960, Lenny Welch had success with it in 1964, and a 1966 Righteous Brothers disc made the Top 10 list. Other memorable recordings were made by Charlie Applewhite, Tony Martin, Frank Sinatra, Connee Boswell, Rosemary Clooney, Percy Faith, Lawrence Welk, Pat Boone, Kim Kahuna and the Royal Palms Orchestra, Gisele MacKenzie, and Robert Goulet. The Platters's recording was used in the movie *Sweet Bird of Youth* (1962), and the song was also heard in *The Walking Stick* (1970).

"Either It's Love or It Isn't" (1947) is a gliding fox trot by Allan Roberts and Doris Fisher about not compromising when it comes to love. The lyric poses a series of ultimatums: Either it's real or it isn't, he does not want her arms and lips if her heart isn't included, one is either true or not true. The song was introduced by Lizbeth Scott in the film *Dead Reckoning* (1947), which led to many recordings, most notably those by the Pied Pipers and June Hutton with Paul Weston's Orchestra, Frankie Carle (vocal by Marjorie Hughes), Charlie Ventura, Harry Cool, and Betty Carter.

"El Rancho Grande (My Ranch)" (1934) is a Mexican song by Silvano R. Ramos that became a hit cowboy ballad in the States when Bartley Costello added an English lyric in 1939 about escaping from the big "city's rattle" and heading out west to a ranch of one's own. Bing Crosby's recording of the new version was a hit, and the song was revived as "El Rancho Rock" (with a new lyric by Ben Raleigh) in 1958 by the Champs. In addition to many Spanish artists, the ballad was also recorded by Gene Autry, Bob Chester, Tito Guizar, Jan Savitt, Louise Massey and the Westerners, Ethel Smith, Dean Martin, Dave Brubeck, and Pearl Bailey. Autry sang it in the movies *Mexicali Rose* (1939) and *Rancho Grande* (1940), Roy Rogers, Dale Evans, and Gabby Hayes performed it in *My Pal Trigger* (1946), and it was heard in *The Texas Rangers* (1936), *The Gay Senorita* (1945), and *Mexicana* (1945). The number is often listed as "Alla en El Rancho Grande."

"Elmer's Tune" (1941) is one of those songs that sings about the song being sung. Elmer Albrecht, Sammy Gallop, and Dick Jurgens wrote the number as a lively Big Band instrumental and named it after Albrecht, who came up with the basic melody. Jurgens and his Orchestra recorded it, and so did Lew Quadling. The three songwriters then added a lyric posing several questions: Why are the stars blinking? What makes a person want to fall in love? What puts the "kick in a chicken?" The answer in each case is this song. The vocal version was a big hit for Glenn Miller (vocals by Ray Eberly and the Modernaires), and the song stayed on *Your Hit Parade* for fifteen weeks. It was also successful on the country music charts, and several records were made in that category as well. Del Wood's piano version in 1953 revived the number, and Peggy Lee's disc with Benny Goodman was her first record. Other prominent recordings were made by Bob Wills and his Texas Playboys, the Andrews Sisters, Bob Crosby, Count Basie, Kay Kyser, Ray Anthony, Al Hirt, Ella Fitzgerald, and Tex Beneke.

"Elsie From Chelsea" (1896) is a chipper ditty by Harry Dacre that has all of the unpretentious charm of a turn-of-the-century romance. A swain gives his seat up to a young woman on the streetcar, then falls in love with her, from that point on not being able to think of "nobody elsie." Both the girl's name and her neighborhood are spelled out in the bouncy number, which is as naive as it is touching. Bonnie Thornton introduced it in vaudeville, and it remained popular until more sophisticated songs about more sophisticated girls appeared on Tin Pan Alley.

"Enjoy Yourself (It's Later Than You Think)" (1950) is the rhumba-flavored song that urges one to enjoy life "while you're still in the pink" and not to worry the years away. Herb Magidson wrote the bright, optimistic lyric, and Carl Sigman composed the playful Latin music. Guy Lombardo and the Royal Canadians (vocal by Kenny Gardner) had the bestselling record, but it was also a success for Doris Day, the Mills Brothers, and Louis Prima. In the movie *Everyone Says I Love You* (1996), the merry song was sung by Patrick Cranshaw and a chorus of elderly ghosts.

"Especially for You" (1939) is a heartfelt ballad of devotion by Orrin Tucker and Phil Grogan that Tucker recorded successfully with a vocal by "Wee" Bonnie Baker. Other early and leading discs were made by Jimmy Dorsey (vocal by Helen O'Connell), Jack Teagarden (vocal by Linda Keene), and Vincent Lopez (vocal by Sonny Schuyler). Woody Herman, Jason Donovan, Kylie Minogue, and Kenny "Babyface" Edmonds are among the others to record it.

"Every Day (I Have the Blues)" (1950) is a mild blues number that found favor with country singers and jazzmen as well as blues artists. Peter Chatman wrote the longing ballad, and it was introduced by Lowell Fulson on record, but nothing much happened with the song until 1955 when there were hit recordings by Count Basie (vocal by Joe Williams) and B.B. King. Billy Stewart's disc revived the song in 1967, and it was heard in the film *The Buddy Holly Story* (1978). James Cotton, Sonny

Rhodes, Jimmy Rushing, the Marshal Tucker Band, Juanita Williams, Pee Wee Crayton, T-Bone Walker, and Doc Severinson and his Band are among those who also recorded the song.

"Every Little Movement (Has a Meaning All Its Own)" (1910) is a captivating dance song that was ahead of its time and has remained a favorite with dancers because of its quirky but pleasing rhythm. Otto Harbach (lyric) and Karl Hoschna (music) wrote the sparkling number about communicating through dance for the Broadway musical *Madame Sherry* (1910), where it was sung and danced by cast members Frances Demarest, Jack Gardner, and Lina Abarbanell. Soon it was used both by vaudeville acts and ballroom dancers. A 1935 recording by Jimmy Dorsey revived interest in the number, and it later showed up in a handful of films. Judy Garland and Connie Gilchrist performed it in *Presenting Lily Mars* (1943), Robert Alda and the chorus sang it in *April Showers* (1948), Jack Smith crooned it in *On Moonlight Bay* (1951), and it was heard in *Shine On Harvest Moon* (1944) and *The Jolson Story* (1946). Garland and Doris Day each made outstanding records of the song.

"Everybody Loves My Baby (But My Baby Don't Love Nobody But Me)" (1924) is a rhythmic favorite that was on everybody's lips in the 1920s and found a revival of success in the 1950s as well. Jack Palmer wrote the slangy lyric that sings the praises of a dearie (she's his "sweet pattotie") and her steadfast faithfulness. Spencer Williams composed the catchy music that is simply a riff repeated three times but done with resplendent effect. The song was introduced by Clarence Williams' Blue Five with Louis Armstrong on trumpet and was popularized by Ruth Etting, who recorded it and kept the number in repertoire for several years. There were other early records by Aileen Stanley, Gene Rodemich, and the Goofus Five. When Doris Day sang the song in the Etting movie bio *Love Me or Leave Me* (1955) it became popular again. Noteworthy recordings over the years were made by Orrin Tucker, the Boswell Sisters, Gene Krupa, Fats Waller, Bob Grant, Earl Hines, Glenn Miller, the Pied Pipers, Al Hirt, and Eli Newberger. The Temperance Seven performed it in the British film *Ring-a-Ding Rhythm* (1962), Alan Weeks and the ensemble sang it in the Broadway musical *Big Deal* (1986), and it was featured in the Off-Broadway shows *One Mo' Time* (1979), sung by Topsy Chapman, and *Slow Drag* (1997), sung by Liza Sadovy.

"Everybody Loves Somebody (Sometime)" (1948) is most associated with Dean Martin whose 1964 record sold a million copies and who used it as his theme song in concerts and on his television show. Irving Taylor (lyric) and Ken Lane (music) wrote the matter-of-fact ballad for Frank Sinatra, who recorded it with Nelson Riddle's Orchestra in 1948, but the record never sold well and Sinatra did not keep it in his repertoire. Occasionally recorded, the song was little known until Martin revived it in the 1960s. Other discs were made by Dinah Washington, Wayne Newton, Andy Williams, the Ray Conniff Singers, Barbara Windsor, and Michael Ball.

"Everybody's Doin' It (Now)" (1911) is a ragtime classic that was about a new dance craze in which one throws one's "shoulders in the air" and snaps one's fingers. Irving Berlin wrote the vigorous number, which had early records by the Columbia Quartette, Arthur Pryor's Band, and the team of Collins and Harlan but found more favor in dance halls. Like most dance songs, it fell into obscurity when dance styles changed, but interest was revived in the song when Alice Faye, Dixie Dunbar, and Wally Vernon performed it in the movie *Alexander's Ragtime Band* (1938). It was heard in *The Fabulous Dorseys* (1947) and sung by Judy Garland and the chorus in *Easter Parade* (1948). Memorable records were made by Tommy Dorsey (vocal by Edythe Wright), Bix Beiderbecke, the Chazz Cats, and Marty Grosz.

"Everybody's Makin' Money But Tschaikovsky" (1942) was a comic commentary on the state of Tin Pan Alley in the 1940s. A series of pop songs based on classical pieces of music was flooding the market, so the team of Krippens, Roe, and Broad wrote this novelty number about the long-dead composers, whose works were in public domain, and were being cheated out of song royalties. The humorous number was introduced by Les Brown (vocal by Betty Bonney), and it found some popularity for a few years.

"Everything Happens to Me" (1941) is an amusing lament by Tom Adair (lyric) and Matt Dennis (music) that lists examples of bad luck that have befallen, including an endeared one walking out forever. The droll torch song has a defeatist point of view, but the tone is self-mocking and fun, filled with delicious phrases such as "catchin' colds and missing trains." The song was introduced and popularized by Tommy Dorsey (vocal by Frank Sinatra), and it soon became a favorite of both pop singers and jazz musicians. Among the many who recorded it were Carmen McRae, Bill Evans, Erroll Garner, Ella Fitzgerald, Dave Brubeck, Patti Page, Paul Desmond, Nat King Cole, Scott Hamilton, Billie Holiday, Rosemary Clooney, the Ed Blackwell Trio, Chet Baker, Julie London, Wynton Marsalis, and Patti LuPone.

"Ev'ry Time We Say Goodbye" (1944) may not be a typical Cole Porter ballad with its straightforward and deeply heartfelt sentiment, but it is among his best songs. The unusual shifts in key give the song's melody a haunting quality, and the lyric about dying a little each time they must part is indelible. The most famous moment in the farewell song is near the end, when the lyric states how one's emotion moves from "major to minor," and the music shifts into a minor chord on the phrase. Nan Wynn introduced the song in the long-forgotten revue *Seven Lively Arts* (1944), but it lives on in many recordings, most significantly one by Benny Goodman (vocal by Peggy Mann). Other records were made by Stan Kenton (vocal by Anita O'Day), Lena Horne, Thelma Carpenter, George Paxton (vocal by Alan Dale), Hildegarde, Charlie Spivak (vocal by Irene Daye), Carmen McRae, Maxine Sullivan, Jeri Southern, Ella Fitzgerald, the Four Freshmen, Mel Tormé, June Christy, John Coltrane, Polly Bergen, Bobby Short, and more recently, Carly Simon, Cleo Laine, Weslia Whitfield, and Ann Hampton Callaway.

"Exactly Like You" (1930) is a breezy, tuneful number that became a hit despite the fact that it is difficult to sing and goes beyond the usual pop song requirements. Dorothy Fields wrote the casual lyric about finding the perfect mate, one who matches the kind she imagined in her dreams. Jimmy McHugh composed the appealing music that has a wide range (an octave and a fifth) and is vocally demanding with little breathing space as it moves from one section to another. Harry Richman and Gertrude Lawrence introduced the song in the Broadway show *International Revue* (1930), but it really caught on in 1936 with a recording by Benny Goodman. Ruth Etting, Connee Boswell, Count Basie, Scatman Crothers, Harry James, Bob Crosby, Louis Armstrong, Eddy Duchin, Carmen McRae, Ted Heath, Gene Krupa, Fran Warren, Oscar Peterson, and Andy Williams are among the many who recorded it over the years, and there have been recent discs by Barbara Cook and Patrick Wilson with Marcus Neville. Carmen Cavallaro provided the keyboard skills for Tyrone Power when he played it in the movie bio *The Eddy Duchin Story* (1956), and the song was also heard in *The Gene Krupa Story* (1959). Ann Jillian and the chorus performed the number in the Broadway revue *Sugar Babies* (1979).

F

"Falling Leaves" (1940) is an atmospheric ballad about autumn by Mack David (lyric) and Frankie Carle (music) that was introduced by Horace Heidt and his Orchestra with Carle at the piano. The number was popularized by Glenn Miller (vocal by Ray Eberly), whose disc was a bestseller, and Miller's orchestra recorded it again after the war with Tex Beneke conducting. Other noteworthy records were made by Jimmy Dorsey (vocal by Bob Eberly), Wayne King, Bettine Clemen, Cliff Waldron, Frances Black, Terri Wells, and Kenny Drew.

"Farewell Blues" (1922) is a blues standard with many recordings over the years in the fields of jazz and country as well as rhythm-and-blues. Paul Joseph Mares, Elmer Schoebel, and Leon Rappolo wrote the number, and there was an early record by the Friars' Society Orchestra, a group that would become more famous when they changed their name to the New Orleans Rhythm Kings. Among the varied artists who recorded "Farewell Blues" were Paul Whiteman, Ted Lewis, Eva Taylor, Glenn Miller, Cab Calloway, Isham Jones, Count Basie, the Charleston Chasers, Woody Herman, Eddie Condon, the Goofus Five, Django Reinhardt, Flatt and Scruggs, Pete Fountain, and Hank Snow. The song was heard on the soundtrack of the movie *Deliverance* (1972).

"Fascination" (1904) is a slow and graceful waltz that was popular on and off during the twentieth century. French songwriter F.D. Marchetti wrote the gypsy number as "Valse Tzigane" for a café band, and it was soon picked up by string orchestras and recorded both in Europe and America, though rarely with the lyric. By World War Two the song pretty much faded away. When the music was used on the soundtrack of the film *Love in the Afternoon* (1957), audiences were again entranced by the number. That same year Dick Manning added an English lyric about how one glance at a true love was so bewitching that "it was fascination," and Jane Morgan recorded it, the disc selling over a million copies. Julie London, Dick Jacobs, the Lennon Sisters, Billy Vaughn, Dinah Shore, Lawrence Welk, Jerry Murad's Harmonicats, Carmen Cavallaro, Keely Smith, Al Martino, and Liberace were among the many who recorded it. The popular Morgan disc was heard on the soundtrack of *Diner* (1982).

"The Fatal Wedding" (1893) is a sentimental and highly melodramatic ballad, the kind that was fashionable in the 1890s but would fade away with the new century. The narrative ballad tells of a wedding ceremony interrupted by the arrival of the groom's first wife with her sick baby. The infant dies in the mother's arms, the groom commits suicide, and after the double funeral the two women comfort each other and go off to live together. H.W. Windom penned the heart-wrenching lyric, and Gussie Davis, Tin Pan Alley's first successful African American composer, wrote the affecting music, even including a section of Mendelsohn's *Wedding March* in the piece. Recordings of interest were made by the Carter Family and Grandpa Jones.

"The Ferry Boat Serenade" (1940) is an Italian favorite that became a huge hit for the very un-Italian Andrews Sisters. Eldo di Lazzaro wrote the flowing ballad as "La Piccinina," and it was introduced in America in an orchestra version by Gray Gordon and his Orchestra. But when Harold Adamson wrote an English lyric about a moonlight ride on a ferry boat and it was recorded by the Andrews Sisters, the disc went to the top of the charts. There were also successful records by Alvino Rey (vocal by the King Sisters), Kay Kyser, and Duke Ellington.

"Fever" (1956) is a rhythm-and-blues hit that appealed to a variety of artists and was much recorded during the second half of the twentieth century. John Davenport and Eddie Cooley wrote the rhythmic number about love being a feverish illness that burns all day and all night, and it was popularized by Little Willie John with a top-selling record. Peggy Lee had a similarly successful disc in 1958, and Earl Grant did well with it the next year. The number was revived by the McCoys in 1965 and by Rita Coolidge in 1973. Other estimable records were made by Sarah Vaughan, the Ventures, Elvis Presley, Wanda Jackson, Shirley Horn, King Curtis, Helen Shapiro, Frances Faye, Dion, Tom Jones, Ann Murray, and Michael Ball. Keely Smith, Louis Prima, Sam Butera, and the Witnesses sang it in the movie *Hey Boy, Hey Girl* (1959), and the Willie John version was heard in *The Big Town* (1987). Carter Calvert sang "Fever" in the Broadway revue *It Ain't Nothin' But the Blues* (1999).

"Find Out What They Like" (1929) is a sassy number by Andy Razaf (lyric) and Thomas "Fats" Waller (music) that was perhaps too sassy for most audiences, and radio play was limited. The smooth jazz song urges one to seek out a honey's favorite weakness, find out "how they like it," and then let them have it "just that way." The sexual connotations were unmistakable, yet the song comes across more comic than sultry. Memorable recordings were made by Waller, Pat Flowers, Edith Wilson, and Teresa Brewer. On Broadway it was sung by Nell Carter and Amelia McQueen in the Waller revue *Ain't Misbehavin'* (1978).

"Fine and Dandy" (1930) was one of the first anti–Great Depression songs that tried to cheer up audiences with a chipper and optimistic point of view. Paul James wrote the tangy lyric about life being "sugar candy" when a beloved one is near, and Kay Swift composed the sparkling music that is very rhythmic and bouncy, even though it all stays within the range of one octave. The song was introduced in the Broadway musical *Fine and Dandy* (1930) by Joe Cook and Alice Boulden, but theatregoing had dropped so much during the depression that the song had to be popularized by radio play and records. Among the many who made discs were Art Tatum, Louis Armstrong, Teddy Wilson, Buddy Rich, Erroll Garner, Mel Tormé, Chet Baker, Doris Day, Steve Allen, Marian McPartland, Debbie Reynolds, Pat Suzuki, Eydie Gorme, and Barbra Streisand.

"The First Time I Saw You" (1937) is a romantic ballad about love at first sight that Allie Wrubel (lyric) and Nat Shilkret (music) wrote for the film *The Toast of New York* (1937), where it was sung by Frances Farmer. A favorite on the radio at the time, the number was given distinctive recordings by Bunny Berigan (vocal by Ford Leary), Charlie Barnet, Emery Deutsch, Jimmie Lunceford (vocal by Dan Grissom), the Paragons, and Gracie Fields. The ballad can be heard in the movies *Go Chase Yourself* (1938), *Law of the Underworld* (1938), and *Out of the Past* (1947).

"Fit as a Fiddle (And Ready for Love)" (1932) is a vigorous number by Arthur Freed, Al Hoffman, and Al Goodhart that celebrates one's energy and overflowing good health ever since falling in love. The hoedownlike music is very playful, and the lyric has the familiar phrase "with a hey-nonny-nonny and a hot-cha-cha" in the release. Harry Richman introduced the ditty in the revue *George White's Music Hall Varieties* (1932), followed by lots of air play and records, the most successful being a bestseller by Fred Waring's Pennsylvanians. The number was revived when Gene Kelly and Donald O'Connor performed it in the movie *Singin' in the Rain* (1952), and it was also featured in *Married before Breakfast*

(1937) and *Bert Rigby, You're a Fool* (1989). Annette Hanshaw, Kay Starr, Red Ingle, the Charleston Chasers, Doris Day, and the Three Suns are among the many singers and bands who recorded the lively song.

"Five Foot Two, Eyes of Blue (Has Anybody Seen My Girl?)" (1925) is a vivacious number that epitomizes the Roaring Twenties and its carefree dance songs. Ray Henderson, right before he teamed up with De Sylva and Brown, wrote the bouncy music, and Sam Lewis and Joe Young collaborated on the farcical lyric that is actually a torch song asking if anyone knows where his departed sweetie is. Much of the lyric is a description of the missing girl, listing her height, eyes, "turned up nose, turned up hose," and her ability to love ("oh! what those five feet could do!"). The comic lyric also asks the rhetorical question, "could she, could she, could she coo?"—making it sound like the slang expression "kootchy-coo." Gene Austin popularized the number, his record hitting the top of the charts. Al Jolson kept it in his act for years, and in 1948 Art Mooney and his Band had a bestselling disc. Major recordings were also made by the Dorsey Brothers, Billy May, Bing Crosby, the California Ramblers, Nick Lucas, Phil Harris, Louis Prima, Dean Martin, and Mitch Miller. The song is often used in the background for films set in the 1920s, such as *Has Anybody Seen My Gal?* (1952) and *Love Me or Leave Me* (1955), and the Lucas recording was used in *The Great Gatsby* (1974).

"Five Guys Named Moe" (1941) is a vibrant boogie-woogie number by Larry Wynn (lyric) and Jerry Bresler (music) about a singing quintet who came out of nowhere to become the "talk of rhythm town." The delightful novelty song was popularized by Louis Jordan and his Tympani Five, and there were also notable recordings by Joe Jackson, the Chazz Cats, and the Chevalier Brothers. On Broadway it was performed by the cast of the Jordan revue *Five Guys Named Moe* (1992).

"The Five O'Clock Whistle" (1940) is the jazzy standard about quitting time that proved a big seller for Glenn Miller (vocal by Marion Hutton). Josef Myrow, Kim Gannon, and Gene Irwin collaborated on the ballad, and it enjoyed dozens of recordings, most memorably those by Erskine Hawkins, Duke Ellington (vocal by Ivie Anderson), Woody Herman, Count Basie, Ella Fitzgerald, Ray McKinley with Will Bradley's Orchestra, George Shearing (vocal by Mel Tormé), Red Garland, and Oscar Peterson.

"Flamingo" (1941) is a crossover hit that was most associated with Herb Jeffries, who introduced it on disc with Duke Ellington's Orchestra and kept it in his repertoire for years, later recording it on his own. The exotic number about a tropical climate crossed over to Big Bands, rhythm-and-blues, and jazz artists. Edmund Anderson's lyric was often dropped as Ted Grouya's felicitous music was featured in many instrumental recordings. Earl Bostic and his Band revived the number in 1951, and Herb Alpert and the Tijuana Brass did the same thing in 1966. Others who made discs of the song include Les Brown, Jimmie Lunceford, Carmen McRae, Kenny Burrell, Buddy Rich, Dave Brubeck, Tony Martin, Andre Kostelanetz, and Mantovani's Orchestra.

"The Flat Foot Floogie (With a Floy Floy)" (1938) is a novelty number about a new dance that is "a new way to ruin the rugs." Slim Gaillard, Slam Stewart, and Bud Green wrote the moderately swinging number and punctuated the lyric with plenty of nonsense phrases ("floy floy . . . flou flou"). It was popularized on record by the coauthors, the team of Slim and Slam, but the song was also a favorite in dance halls and on radio broadcasts. Noteworthy records were made by Fats Waller, Count Basie, Wingy Manone, the Mills Brothers, Benny Goodman, Woody Herman, the Milt Herth Trio, Will Hudson, and Charlie Parker.

"Fly Me to the Moon" (1954) is the romantic standard that couldn't find success until a title change was made eight years after it was written. Bart Howard wrote the song as "In Other Words" with a fanciful lyric about knowing what it must be like in the heavens just by holding and kissing a sweetheart. It is a lush and hyperbolic lyric but somehow stops short of the ridiculous, helped by such memorable phrases as "let me see what spring is like on Jupiter and Mars." The number was introduced as "In Other Words" by Felicia Sanders, and there was an early recording by Kaye Ballard, but the song wouldn't sell. Mabel Mercer started singing it in clubs with success, but Howard found out that audiences could not remember the title, it being buried in the middle of the song. In 1962 he retitled it "Fly Me to the Moon," after the opening line of the song, and hoped to capitalize on all the interest generated by the new space program in America. Immediately the ballad started to sell, and it was revived with success by Tony Bennett in 1965 and Buddy Womack in 1969. There was even a Latin version called "Fly Me to the Moon Bossa Nova" by Joe Harnell that was a bestseller. Over one hundred different recordings were made, including those by Dinah Washington, Keely Smith, Ray Anthony, Anita O'Day, Frank Sinatra, Nat King Cole, Judy Garland, June Christy, Trini Lopez, John Gary, Bobby Darin, Portia Nelson, and Jack Jones. Tia Speros sang the song in the Off-Broadway revue *The Taffetas* (1988).

"Flying Home" (1941) is a swing standard that started out as an instrumental composed by bandleaders Benny Goodman and Lionel Hampton. Goodman's Sextet (including Hampton) popularized the number, and

Hampton made it the theme song for his orchestra and recorded it two more times (under the title "Flyin' Home"). Sid Robin added a lyric about a homecoming, and Ella Fitzgerald was among the singers who recorded the new song. In the movie *A Song Is Born* (1948), the number was given a delicious treatment by Goodman, Louis Armstrong, Tommy Dorsey, Charlie Barnet, and Mel Powell. "Flying Home" was also heard on the soundtracks of *Memphis Belle* (1990) and *Malcolm X* (1992). Other versions were made by Barnet, Pee Wee King, Red Norvo, Les Brown, Duke Ellington, Arnett Cobb, Herbie Mann, Oscar Peterson, Johnny Guarnieri, Art Tatum, Will Bradley, Chris Connor, and Roy Eldridge.

"Fools Rush In (Where Angels Fear to Tread)" (1940) is a tender ballad warning of the dangers of falling in love too quickly. But the wooer can't help it and asks the admired one to "open your heart and let this fool rush in." Johnny Mercer wrote the piquant lyric, and Rube Bloom composed the music, basing his theme on an earlier melody of his called "Shangri-La." Mildred Bailey introduced the ballad, but it was two hit records by Glenn Miller (vocal by Ray Eberly) and Tommy Dorsey (vocal by Frank Sinatra) that made the song famous. It was revived in 1960 with a bestselling record by Brooks Benton and again by Rick Nelson in 1963. Other notable records were made by Mercer, Rosemary Clooney, Harry James (vocal by Dick Haymes), Al Martino, Kay Kyser (vocal by Ginny Simms), Keely Smith, Jo Stafford, Louis Armstrong, Louis Prima, Tom Jones, and Elvis Presley. The Clooney recording was heard in the movie *Midnight in the Garden of Good and Evil* (1997), and the John Pizzarelli Trio performed it on Broadway in the Mercer revue *Dream* (1997).

"For All We Know" (1934) is a tearful farewell song by Sam M. Lewis (lyric) and J. Fred Coots (music) that is filled with indecision, wondering what the future will bring and if the two lovers will ever meet again. Morton Downey introduced the ballad on his radio program, and it was revived by a popular Andrews Sisters recording in 1942. Other highly regarded discs were made by Billy Vaughn, Isham Jones (vocal by Joe Martin), Kay Kyser, Hal Kemp (vocal by Bob Allen), Nick Lucas, Guy Lombardo and the Royal Canadians, Nat King Cole, the Four Freshmen, Matt Monro, Sonny Til and the Orioles, and Nina Simone. The song can also be heard in the movies *Hi, Good Lookin'!* (1944) and *New York, New York* (1977).

"For Me and My Gal" (1917) is the perennial favorite about wedding day bliss that was also a forerunner of the jazz age. Edgar Leslie and E. Ray Goetz wrote the snappy lyric about bells ringing and birds singing as two turtle doves go off to their wedding, and George W. Meyer composed the adventurous music. Although it is a traditional thirty-two-measure song with only a one-octave range, the music is surprising and effective as it moves through its ABAC structure, ending in a unique and unexpected way. The number was popularized in vaudeville where such stars as Al Jolson, Sophie Tucker, Eddie Cantor, Van and Schenck, Belle Baker, and George Jessel sang it. Over 3 million copies of sheet music were sold, and it was still a staple on parlor pianos when Judy Garland and Gene Kelly sang it in the film *For Me and My Gal* (1942). The movie spurred more sheet music sales and many new recordings (including their duet version that was a big hit). Jolson, who sang it throughout his career, reprised it on the soundtrack for Larry Parks in the movie *Jolson Sings Again* (1949). Among the artists who have recorded it over the years were Bing Crosby, Cliff Edwards, Bob Grant, Dick Shannon and his Society Sextet, Les Elgart, Arthur Godfrey, the Chordettes, Perry Como, the Cliff Adams Singers, Freddy Cannon, Tiny Tim, and Harry Nilsson. When composer Meyer's wife died, he had the title of the song inscribed on her tombstone.

"For Sentimental Reasons" (1947) is the affectionate paean to a loved one, asking for her heart not for logical reasons but for emotional ones. Deke Watson (one of the Ink Spots) wrote the direct and plaintive lyric, and William Best composed the graceful music. Eddy Howard and his Orchestra introduced the ballad, but it was a record by Nat King Cole that went to the Number One spot on the charts and made the ballad a nationwide favorite. Sam Cooke's 1958 disc was also a major hit and revived interest in the song. Dinah Shore, Charlie Spivak (vocal by Jimmy Saunders), Etta Jones, Tommy Dorsey, Hildegarde, Ella Fitzgerald with the Delta Rhythm Boys, Dexter Gordon, Anita Ellis, Red Ingle, and the Cleftones were among the many who recorded it, and there have been more recent discs by Natalie Cole, Linda Ronstadt, and Kathy Lee Gifford. The most unusual of the many recordings is a parody version called "For Seventy Mental Reasons" sung by Country Washburne.

"For You" (1931) is a hyperbolic declaration of love by Al Dubin (lyric) and Joe Burke (music) that lists all the impossible things one will do for a sweetheart: gather stars from the heavens, weave a carpet out of clover, turn dew drops into a string of pearls, and so on. Glen Gray and the Casa Loma Orchestra (vocal by Kenny Sargent) popularized the song, and being their first hit record, it launched the group's career. In 1956, two bestselling discs by Nat King Cole and Rosemary Clooney revived the song's popularity, and Ricky Nelson did the same thing in 1964, his version making the Top 10 list. Other major records were made by Jo Stafford, Kay Starr, Perry Como, Erroll Garner, Louis Prima and Keely Smith, George Shearing, and Louis Jordan and the Tympani Five. The ballad can also be heard in the films *Holy Terror* (1931) and *A Shot in the Dark* (1941).

"For Your Precious Love" (1958) is a gushing ballad by Arthur and Richard Brooks and Jerry Butler that managed to stay popular through the early decades of rock-and-roll by keeping one foot in Tin Pan Alley and let the other foot rock. Butler introduced the ballad with the Impressions, and it was the first of five hit recordings of the song. Garnett Mimms and the Enchanters revived it with success in 1964, and there were subsequent hits by Oscar Toney Jr. in 1967, Jackie Wilson with Count Basie's Orchestra in 1968, and Linda Jones in 1972. The heartfelt number crossed over to various fields and was recorded by such artists as Otis Redding, Johnny Taylor, Virgil Shaw, Byron Lee and the Dragonaires, Barbara Mason, Aaron Neville, Spyder Turner, and Curtis Mayfield. The Mimms recording was heard in the movie *American Me* (1992) and the Butler version in *A Bronx Tale* (1993).

"Forever and Ever" (1949) was a popular Swiss song that became a Tin Pan Alley hit when Russ Morgan and his Orchestra had a top-selling record in 1949. Franz Winkler wrote the delicate music and the original German lyric for "Fliege mit Mir in Die Heimat," which was popular in Europe. Malia Rosa penned an English lyric about two lovers making up a quarrel and promising never to part again, and it was introduced by Gracie Fields. After the Morgan record, there were also discs by Perry Como, Margaret Whiting, Dinah Shore, Dick Curless, Floyd Cramer, Engelbert Humperdinck, Merle Haggard and Bonnie Owens, and the Ventures.

"Forgive Me" (1927) is a pleading ballad by Jack Yellen (lyric) and Milton Ager (music) that Ruth Etting popularized in nightclubs and with a hit record. There was also an early disc by Gene Austin that was successful. Eddie Fisher revived the number in 1952 with a Top 10 record, and Al Martino did almost as well with his 1962 version. Peggy Lee, Gene Autry, Bert Kaempfert, Gene Chandler, Noleen Batley, and Pat Boone were among the others who recorded it. The ballad can be heard in the movie *Bells of Capistrano* (1942).

"Four Winds and the Seven Seas" (1949), an expansive ballad about wandering the wide world, was the first hit song for lyricist Hal David. Don Rodney composed the lush music, and the song was popularized by Sammy Kaye and his Orchestra (vocal by Tony Alamo) with a chart disc. Among the other artists to record the ballad were Mel Tormé with Frank DeVol's Orchestra, Guy Lombardo (vocal by Don Rodney), Rosemary Clooney, Vic Damone, Herb Jeffries, and Cynthia Crane.

"Frankie and Johnny" (c. 1870) is the celebrated folk song about a woman who shoots her unfaithful lover (sometimes her husband) because "he done her wrong." It is estimated that several hundred versions of this song have been sung during the past 130 years, and the narrative ballad's origins are as debatable as Frankie's course of action. The earliest versions go back to the 1870s, but a 1902 ballad called "He Done Her Wrong" by Hughie Cannon was based on a true event in St. Louis in 1891 when Albert Britt was shot by his lover Frankie Baker. (In several versions of the song the cheating lover is called Albert instead of Johnny.) Mama Lou, an African American singer in St. Louis, was singing a variation of the tale for white audiences in the 1890s. A "Frankie and Johnny" song was not published until 1912, and variations of that version (with the philosophic conclusion that "there ain't no good in men") were heard in vaudeville and on early records. (The first known disc of the song was by Palmer Jones in Kansas City around 1916.) Ted Lewis made the first widely distributed recording in 1927, and there have been prominent versions by Frank Crumit in 1927, Guy Lombardo and the Royal Canadians in 1942, Johnny Cash in 1959, Brooks Benton in 1961, Sam Cooke in 1963, and Elvis Presley in 1966. Sammy Cahn wrote a revised lyric for Sammy Davis Jr. to sing in the film *Meet Me in Las Vegas* (1956), and Fred Karger, Alex Gottlieb, and Ben Weisman collaborated on a version for Presley, Harry Morgan, Donna Douglas, and Sue Ann Langdon to perform in *Frankie and Johnny* (1966). The ballad was associated with Lena Horne for several years, and there were other distinctive recordings by Louis Armstrong, Coleman Hawkins, Duke Ellington with Bing Crosby, Mississippi John Hurt, Margaret Whiting and Jack Smith, Sidney Bechet, Jimmie Rodgers, the Village Stompers, and Jerry Lee Lewis. Mae West sang a version in *She Done Him Wrong* (1933), Helen Morgan another in *Frankie and Johnny* (1936), and on Broadway Burl Ives, Alma Kaye, Jack McCauley, and Ted Tiller performed it in the revue *Sing Out, Sweet Land!* (1944).

"From This Moment On" (1950) is one of Cole Porter's most accomplished rhythm ballads as it celebrates new life and new love and only "whoop-dee-doo" songs instead of the blues. Porter wrote the number for the Broadway musical *Out of This World* (1950), but it was cut out of town because the director felt it was slowing the show down. But the joyous number was noticed when it was added to the film version of *Kiss Me Kate* (1953), where it was sung and danced by Ann Miller, Tommy Rall, Bobby Van, Bob Fosse, Carol Haney, and Jeannie Coyne. Frank Sinatra's subsequent recording popularized it further, and many other records followed, including those by June Christy, Lena Horne, Count Basie, Rosemary Clooney, Judy Garland, John Coltrane, Ella Fitzgerald, Ernie Andrews, John Gary, Sarah Vaughan, Bobby Short, Doris Day, and more recently, Linda Eder and Susannah McCorkle.

"Frosty the Snow Man" (1951) has become a Christmas season favorite even though there is no mention of the holidays in the lyric. Jack Rollins composed the tuneful music, and Steve Nelson penned the lyric about a snowman who magically comes to life. The number was popularized by Gene Autry, whose record sold over a million copies, and there were early hit records by Nat King Cole and Guy Lombardo as well. A popular staple in schools and on children's records, the simple musical tale has also been recorded hundreds of times by artists as varied as Bing Crosby, Brenda Lee, the Dixieland Ramblers, the Chipmunks, Porter Wagoner, the Jackson Five, Glen Campbell, the Four Freshmen, the Ray Conniff Singers, and the Brady Bunch.

"Full Moon (Noche de Luna)" (1942) is a Mexican ballad that found success on Tin Pan Alley during the era of the Big Bands. The original Spanish-language song was written by Gonzalo Curiel and Marcelene Odette, but the number about a romantic lunar evening caught on in America after Rob Russell wrote an English lyric for it. Three bands had bestselling records of the ballad in the 1940s: Jimmy Dorsey (vocal by Bob Eberly), Orrin Tucker (vocal by Bob Haymes), and Benny Goodman (vocal by Peggy Lee). The song was also recorded by Ray Herbeck, Kenny Goldberg, Tony Pastor, Jackie Cain and Roy Kral, and many Latin artists.

"Full Moon and Empty Arms" (1946) was one of several hit songs in the 1940s that were based on a classical piece of music. Buddy Kaye and Ted Mossman adapted Rachmaninoff's third movement of his Piano Concerto #2 in C Minor and wrote a torchy lyric about being left in the moonlight without one's true love. Frank Sinatra and Ray Noble (vocal by Snooky Lanson) both had bestselling records of the "new" ballad, and there were also discs by Nelson Eddy, the Platters, Billy Vaughn, the Norman Luboff Choir, Caterina Valente, Oscar Peterson, Jerry Vale, and Erroll Garner.

G

"**A Garden in the Rain**" (1929) is a felicitous romantic ballad that came from England and stayed on Tin Pan Alley for decades. Carroll Gibbons composed the gentle music, and James Dyrenforth penned the bucolic lyric about two lovebirds watching the raindrops fall and the blossoms drink; then they move on their way once the drizzle stops and the sun comes out. Rudy Vallee introduced the song to Americans, and Gene Austin popularized it with a hit record. The ballad was revived by Perry Como in 1946 and again by the Four Aces in 1952. Other notable discs were made by Billy Eckstine, George Olsen's Band (vocal by Fran Frey), Earl Burtnett's Orchestra, Jane Froman, Willard Robison, Jerry Gray, Frank Sinatra, Blue Barron and his Orchestra, Sarah Vaughan, and Vic Dana.

"**Gee Baby, Ain't I Good to You?**" (1929) is a cool jazz number that lists all of the luxuries (fur coat, diamond ring, Cadillac car, and so on) that an admirer has given his honey because love makes him treat her right. Don Redman wrote the smooth music and collaborated with Andy Razaf on the animated lyric. McKinney's Cotton Pickers (with Redman on alto sax) introduced the song with a successful record, and Nat King Cole revived it with his own hit disc in 1946. Other artists who recorded it include Roy Eldridge, Joe Williams, Kenny Burrell, Helen Merrill, Ruth Brown, Rita Moreno, and Sammy Davis Jr.

"**Georgia on My Mind**" (1930) is one of Hoagy Carmichael's most haunting melodies, a very conversational tune that borders on the monotonous (singers often talk-sing the number) but uses its 4/4 time signature to keep the song moving forward. Stuart Gorrell wrote the lyric, which laments the loss of a sweetheart named Georgia; yet the song makes just as much sense as a homesick ballad about the state of Georgia. In fact, it was suggested to Carmichael that he write a song about the state, but he claimed his sister Georgia was the inspiration for the music. Regardless, it later became the official state song. Mildred Bailey's 1931 recording popularized the song (she made an even finer version in 1941), and it was soon picked up by Louis Armstrong, Ethel Waters, Billie Holiday, Frankie Laine, Fats Waller, Maxine Sullivan, Bix Beiderbecke, Brenda Lee, Lou Rawls, James Brown, and Carmichael himself. Ray Charles's 1960 recording was Number One on the charts, and it is that version that is most recalled today. The Righteous Brothers and Wes Montgomery also had success with it in the 1960s, while Willie Nelson's 1978 record was highly regarded. "Georgia on My Mind" can be heard in the films *When You're Smiling* (1950) and *The Big T.N.T. Show* (1996) where it was sung by Charles, Carmichael's recording was used effectively on the soundtrack of the depression-era film *Paper Moon* (1973), and Vince Giordano and the Nighthawks were heard singing it in *Ghost World* (2001).

"Get Happy" (1930) was Harold Arlen's first published song, his first hit, and one of the finest rhythm songs of the 1930s. Arlen was a rehearsal pianist for the Broadway musical *Great Day* (1929) and was getting bored playing the same dull two-bar vamp used in the accompaniment, so he started to improvise. Lyricist Ted Koehler heard him, encouraged Arlen to put the theme into song form, and wrote a sparkling lyric about celebrating and getting "ready for the judgment day." The revivallike number was added to the score of the short-lived *9:15 Revue* (1930), where it was sung by Ruth Etting, and considerable sheet music sales followed. Although it had never fallen out of favor, "Get Happy" was given new life when Judy Garland sang it in the movie *Summer Stock* (1950); she recorded it and sang it in concerts for several years, and it has been associated with her ever since. Other memorable discs were made by Nat Shilkret, Benny Goodman, Dizzy Gillespie, June Christy and the Kentones, Charlie Parker, Frank Sinatra, Ella Fitzgerald, Barbara Carroll, Leslie Uggams, and Maureen McGovern. Harry James provided the trumpet playing of the hallelujah number for Kirk Douglas in the film *Young Man With a Horn* (1950), it was sung by Susan Hayward (dubbed by Jane Froman) in *With a Song in My Heart* (1952), a Latin version of it was heard in *Cha-Cha-Cha Boom!* (1956), and Jane Horrocks sang it in *Little Voice* (1998).

"Ghost of a Chance With You" (1932) is a heartsick ballad by Ned Washington, Bing Crosby (lyric), and Victor Young (music) about being in love with but not noticed by the popular and much-adored sweetheart. Crosby introduced the number on record, and it quickly caught on. Cab

Calloway and Ted Fio Rito each had successful early recordings, and when Bea Wain revived it in 1939, many more discs were made. Among the more prominent were ones by Will Bradley (vocal by Carlotta Dale), George Shearing, Lionel Hampton, Bobby Hackett, Andy Kirk, Lester Young, Carmen McRae, Charlie Ventura, Billie Holiday, Slim Gaillard, Dexter Gordon, Frank Sinatra, Sarah Vaughan, the Three Suns, Patti Page, and more recently, Linda Ronstadt and Diana Krall. Maurice Chevalier sang the ballad in the film *Folies-Bergère* (1935), it was heard in *A Millionaire for Christy* (1951), and the number was used effectively in the Broadway play *Side Man* (1999). The song is sometimes listed as "I Don't Stand a Ghost of a Chance With You."

"G.I. Jive" (1944) is a breezy number about a day in the life of an enlisted man, from reveille in the morning until he drops off to sleep in his bunk at lights out. Johnny Mercer wrote the sprightly music as well as the lyric, a series of short, terse phrases that use military initials such as M.P., Q.T., K.P., P.U.T., and the title G.I. Mercer recorded it himself, and his disc was a bestseller. Louis Jordan and the Tympani Five also had a chart record of the song. Rosemary Clooney, Sonny Dunham, Glenn Miller, Duke Ellington, and the Squadronaires were among the others who recorded it. Laura Benati, Geralyn Del Corso, and Caitlin Carter performed the number in the Broadway revue *Swing!* (1999).

"Gimme a Little Kiss, Will Ya, Huh?" (1926) is an unusual love song in that it uses a childlike lyric to express adult affection. Maceo Pinkard composed the soft-shoe melody, and Roy Turk and Jack Smith wrote the nimble lyric. A little boy asks a little girl for a peck on the cheek; then the scene shifts to the grownup man pleading for a kiss from the adult woman, still using his childish words. Guy Lombardo and the Royal Canadians introduced the number at a hotel club in Cleveland, but composer Smith, often billed as "Whispering" Jack Smith because of his intimate, breathy way with a song, popularized it with a record that hit the top of the charts. April Stevens revived the song in 1951, and there were also discs by Billy Jones, Teddy Powell, the Norman Petty Trio, Jean Goldkette, Gene Krupa (vocal by Buddy Stewart), Ken Griffin, and Jerry and Patti Lewis. Deanna Durbin sang it in *Lady on a Train* (1945), and it was featured in *Has Anybody Seen My Gal?* (1952).

"Girl of My Dreams" (1927) is a lazy waltz urging a beloved to come back and let him hold her again so that their life will be complete. The romantic standard was written by Sunny Skylar and first recorded by Seger Ellis. The next year Gene Austin made a record with "whistling" provided by Bob McGimsey, and it was very popular. Other artists who made discs of the song include Blue Steele and his Orchestra, Willard

Robison, the Pied Pipers, Etta James, Frankie Carle, the Firehouse Five Plus Two, Harry James, Gene Autry, Buddy Clark, Charles Mingus, Tennessee Ernie Ford, Perry Como, Jerry Vale, Vic Damone, Chuck Mangione, and Jimmy Roselli. The number was heard in the movie *Up the River* (1930), and Autry sang it in *South of the Border* (1939).

"Git Along Little Dogies" (c. 1880) is the traditional American folk song whose author is unknown, but it was being sung by cowboys as early as the 1880s. The merry riding song encourages the herd of cattle to keep moving, especially the young dogies (calves). The lyric contains the famous refrain calling out "yip-pee ti-yi-yo," which becomes a sort of yodel. The song was rarely written down but passed along orally, and there were records by Tex Ritter, Roy Rogers and the Sons of the Pioneers, the Weavers, Ramblin' Jack Elliott, Woody Guthrie, and Pete Seeger, and it is included on many children's records. Gene Autry sang it in the film *Git Along Little Dogies* (1937).

"Give Me a Heart to Sing To" (1934) is a desperate plea for love, the wooer insisting that his song cannot be understood without her heart. Ned Washington (lyric) and Victor Young (music) wrote the number in 1934 for Helen Morgan to sing in the movie *Frankie and Johnny* (1936), but censorship problems kept the film from being released for two years. In the meantime Guy Lombardo (vocal by Carmen Lombardo) made a successful recording, and the number started to become popular. Other discs were made by Morgan, Thelma Carpenter, Arthur Tracy, and Red Nichols.

"Gloomy Sunday" (1936) had one of the most bizarre reputations of any song from Tin Pan Alley. Hungarian songwriters Laszlo Javor (lyric) and Rezso Seress (music) wrote a sad ballad titled "Szomoru Vasarnap" that became popular in Europe, the song's publishers selling it as "The Suicide Song" because several dejected lovers killed themselves by jumping off bridges after hearing it. Sam M. Lewis wrote an English lyric about a disappointed wooer who has decided to end it all. Paul Robeson recorded it in England, and the orchestras of Paul Whiteman, Henry King, Vincent Lopez, and Hall Kemp made American recordings. Word of the European suicides spread, and some radio stations in the States refuse to air even an instrumental version of the ballad, fearing that the same thing might result. By 1941 the furor died down, and Billie Holiday had a bestselling disc of the supposedly deadly song. There were also recordings by Artie Shaw, Charlie Barnet, Billy Eckstine, Etta Jones, Peter Nero, and Rick Nelson. Listening to it today, it is hard to understand why the number was thought to be so dangerous. Seress's music is indeed somber, using minor keys throughout, but the song seems no more depressing than many other torch songs. Ironically, the composer committed suicide in 1968.

"The Glory of Love" (1936) is the easygoing philosophical song by Billy Hill suggesting that a little giving in, laughing, and sometimes breaking your heart is all part of the "story of" love. Rudy Vallee introduced the number on record, but it was a bestselling disc by Benny Goodman (vocal by Helen Ward) that made the song famous. The number also became a rhythm-and-blues hit in 1951 with a top record by the Five Keys. Other recordings of note were made by Hildegarde, the Platters, Frank Ifield, Jimmy Durante, Count Basie, the Dukes of Dixieland, Otis Redding, the Lettermen, Patti Page, Mel Tormé, the Velvetones, P.J. Proby, and the Dells. Dean Martin crooned the ballad in the movie *The Silencers* (1966), Jacqueline Fontaine was heard singing it on the soundtrack of *Guess Who's Coming to Dinner* (1967), and Bette Midler sang it in *Beaches* (1988).

"The Glow Worm" (1907) is the catchy novelty song that has an unusual history. The piece started as a dance composition by Paul Lincke for a 1902 German operetta. The tuneful little melody that ascended and descended the scale was quite memorable, and it was soon played by dance bands across Europe. In America is was turned into a song called "The Glow Worm" with a lyric by Lilla Cayley Robinson about two lovers who find their way through the dark with the help of the glittering glow worms. It was interpolated into the Broadway musical *The Girl Behind the Counter* (1907), where it was sung by May Naudain, and soon sheet music sales boomed as piano students used the merry number as a favorite finger exercise. There were also records (in particular a successful disc by Lucy Isabelle March with the Victor Orchestra) and appearances in dance halls (Anna Pavlova danced to it in one of her programs), but as the years passed it seemed only piano students were familiar with it. In 1952 one of the Mills Brothers heard a little girl play it on the piano and asked Johnny Mercer to write a more swinging, up-to-date lyric. Still titled "The Glow Worm," the Mercer lyric was smoother and more colloquial than the Robinson song, and he even added some modern references, such as comparing the worms to neon lights. The Mills Brothers' recording was a bestseller, and the song was soon heard everywhere. Mercer, Lester Lanin, Bing Crosby, Dean Martin, the Three Suns, Chet Atkins, the Max Roach Quartet, Frankie Carle, Jo Ann Castle, and Frankie Lymon and the Teenagers were among the many who recorded it. There was a Latin version by Jackie Davis called "Glow Worm Cha-Cha-Cha," and even two parody records, by Spike Jones and his City Slickers and Fuller's Novelty Orchestra, were popular. The earlier version was used in the movies *The Story of Vernon and Irene Castle* (1939) and *I Wonder*

Who's Kissing Her Now (1947), and Janet Leigh sang the Mercer version in *Walking My Baby Back Home* (1953).

"Go Tell It on the Mountain(s)" (c. 1865) is the upbeat Negro spiritual of unknown authorship that has remained popular since the Civil War. There are many versions of the song, but the variations are slight. The music is joyous and rhythmic, and the celebratory lyric urges everyone to shout out the good news that "Jesus Christ is Lord!" In many later versions, used as a Christmas hymn, the announcement is that "Jesus Christ is born!" In addition to many children's discs, choir records, and Christmas albums, the song has also been recorded by such artists as Jessye Norman, Frank Sinatra, the Revels, Odetta, Bob Marley and the Wailers, Mahalia Jackson, Smokey Robinson and the Miracles, the Robert Shaw Chorale, Bobby Darin, Simon and Garfunkle, and Garth Brooks.

"God Bless America" (1938) is the simple, unadorned but deeply cherished song by Irving Berlin that remains among the most performed and recorded of patriotic songs. Berlin wrote the hymnlike number for the all-soldier revue *Yip Yip Yaphank* (1918), but he deleted it from the score because he thought it too syrupy even for a wartime show. In 1938 Kate Smith asked Berlin if he had a new song she could sing on an Armistice Day radio broadcast. With the threat of war in Europe growing, Berlin wanted to provide a quiet song about peace and pride in one's country. He dusted off "God Bless America" and made a few lyric changes. The seldom-sung verse concerns the gathering storm in Europe and sets up the famous refrain that asks God to watch over and guide the United States forever. Smith sang the song on November 11, 1938, with great success and it was identified with her for decades, but there were many other recordings and performances as well. Among the most memorable discs were those by Bing Crosby, Margaret Whiting and the Pied Pipers, Barry Wood and the Lehrman Engel Singers, Connie Francis, Anita Bryant, and many military bands, church groups, and orchestras. Both political parties used it at their conventions in 1940, and the song grew even more acclaimed during World War Two. Berlin copyrighted the song in 1939, having all royalties go into the God Bless America Fund, which benefits the Boy and Girl Scouts of America. By the 1950s there was a movement to have "God Bless America" replace "The Star Spangled Banner" as the official national anthem, but Berlin discouraged the change. Smith reprised the number in the movie *This Is the Army* (1943), Deanna Durbin sang it in *Hers to Hold* (1943), Crosby reprised it in *Blue Skies* (1946), Lotte Lehmann and Margaret O'Brien (dubbed by Marni Nixon) performed it in *Big City* (1948), and it has been heard on the soundtracks of several movies, from *Can't Help Singing* (1944) to *The Deer Hunter* (1978). Berlin himself sang "God Bless America" on a few occasions, most memorably on television in 1968 on his eightieth birthday and at the White House in 1974 in honor of some released prisoners from the Viet Nam War; the latter was his last public appearance. The song enjoyed a resurgence of popularity in 2001 after the attack on the World Trade Center, particularly with a top-selling recording by Celine Dion.

"God Bless the Child" (1941) is the bluesy lament that was most identified with Billie Holiday who cowrote it, recorded it, and sang it in concerts for years. Arthur Herzog Jr. and Holiday collaborated on the quiet but indelible number that has some hymn qualities yet is also a sorrowful blues as well. The pungent lyric points out that the world is unfair—the rich get everything, the poor get nothing, but God blesses the child "who's got his own." The ballad was recorded throughout the 1940s and 1950s, then was revived in 1968 with a hit record by Blood, Sweat and Tears. Among the prominent discs made were those by Ella Fitzgerald, Joe Pass, Rosemary Clooney, Ruth Brown, Sonny Rollins, Aretha Franklin, Julie London, Eydie Gorme, Stevie Wonder, Crystal Gayle, Barbra Streisand, Lou Rawls, Liza Minnelli, and Ritchie Havens. On screen Diana Ross sang it in the Holiday bio *Lady Sings the Blues* (1972), and it was heard in *All the Fine Young Cannibals* (1960) and *Satisfaction* (1988). Vivian Reed performed "God Bless the Child" in the Broadway revue *Bubbling Brown Sugar* (1976).

"Golden Earrings" (1947) is a soft ballad with an exotic flavor that proved to be a big success for Peggy Lee. Victor Young wrote the lazy fox trot music, and Jay Livingston and Ray Evans penned the adroit lyric about an old gypsy legend that says a girl will come to you and love you if you give her magical golden earrings. The song was introduced in the film *Golden Earrings* (1947), where it was sung by Murvyn Vye. Lee's blockbuster record popularized it, and Dinah Shore also had a hit version. Other artists who have recorded the ballad include Frank Sinatra, the Ventures, Gene Pitney, the Platters, and Willie Nelson.

"Golden Slippers" (1879) is a contagious folk song favorite that is also one of the earliest and best rhythm numbers in American music. James Bland, the first major African American songwriter, wrote the zesty song about the preparations for a wedding (including the special shoes the bride will wear) as a "walk-around" number for the Original Georgia Minstrels. The song went over so well it was quickly grabbed up by minstrel troupes across the country. Often listed as "Oh, Dem Golden Slippers," the number was seen less and less on the stage with the new century, but sheet music and record sales continued for decades. Among the major recordings are those by Carson Robinson and his Pleasant

Valley Boys, the Sons of the Pioneers, Fats Waller, Don Reno and Red Smiley, the Blue Sky Boys, Al Hirt, Flatt and Scruggs, and Roy Clark. The song was heard in the movie *Tulsa Kid* (1940), and it was sung by Mitzi Gaynor, Dale Robertson, and James Barton in *Golden Girl* (1951).

"Gone With the Wind" (1937) is a ballad standard that has no association with the famous 1939 movie. The titles of bestselling books often were used for Tin Pan Alley songs, and *Gone With the Wind* was so popular that it inspired a handful of songs long before the movie version was made. This was the most durable, with sad and flowing music by Allie Wrubel and a lyric by Herb Magidson about a failed romance that has disappeared like a leaf in the wind. The number was popularized by Horace Heidt and his Orchestra, whose recording went to the Number One spot on the charts. About the same time there was a successful disc by Claude Thornhill (vocal by Maxine Sullivan). Other recordings were made by Dick Haymes, Al Goodman's Orchestra, Mel Tormé, Art Tatum, Martha Raye, Billy May, Benny Carter, Paul Weston, Stan Getz, and Frank Sinatra.

"Gonna Get Along Without You Now" (1952) is a slangy farewell song by Milton Kellem that launched Teresa Brewer's career. The number argues that she got along fine before he came along, so she ought to do just as well now that he's gone. Brewer's recording with Ray Bloch's Orchestra was her first to make the charts, and a disc by the teen sisters Patience and Prudence McIntyre in 1956 made it to the Top 10. The song was also well known in the 1960s because of hit records by Skeeter Davis, Tracy Dey, and Trini Lopez. More recently it has been recorded by Viola Wills and Maureen McGovern.

"Goober Peas" (1864) is a slapstick Civil War song that was sung by troops from both the North and South, concentrating on the more human and everyday aspect of soldiering. The authorship is credited to "Johnny Reb," and the point of view is that of the Confederates as it describes all the soldiers sitting by the roadside, happy to be eating delicious peas rather than fighting. Yet when the battle begins, the General comes upon the Yankee camp and reports that they are eating goober peas, too. The merry tune, sometimes listed as "Eating Goober Peas," was given estimable recordings by the Kingston Trio, Burl Ives, Kirk Browne, the Cumberland Three, Rusty Dragon, Jim Cosgrove, and Arthur Smith.

"Good, Good, Good (That's You—That's You)" (1944) is a spirited declaration of love that has more than a touch of jive in it. Doris Fisher and Allan Roberts wrote the vivacious number that produced two hit records in the 1940s by Xavier Cugat (vocal by Del Campo) and by Sammy Kaye (vocals by Nancy Norman and Billy Williams). Phil Harris and Leslie Brooks sang the ditty in the movie *I Love a Bandleader* (1945).

"A Good Man Is Hard to Find" (1917) is a slightly swinging torch song by Eddie Green that cautions women to hang on to a faithful man because "you always get the other kind." The uptempo blues number was first sung in vaudeville by Green, Alberta Hunter, and others, but it didn't gain wide popularity until Sophie Tucker put it in her act and gave it her unique sassy interpretation. Over the years there have been memorable recordings of it by Eddie Condon, Bessie Smith, Helen Humes, Ted Lewis, Pee Wee Russell, Marion Harris, Fats Waller, Bix Beiderbecke, Juanita Hall, and Rosemary Clooney. Frank Sinatra and Shelley Winters did a duet version of the song in the film *Meet Danny Wilson* (1952).

"Good Morning Heartache" (1946) is a haunting blues number that is more pessimistic than the usual torch song. Irene Higginbotham, Ervin Drake, and Dan Fisher collaborated on the sorrowful song that greets misery each day since a lover has walked out, even welcoming heartache and inviting it to "sit down." Billie Holiday introduced and popularized the ballad with a recording that is considered a classic. Years later when Diana Ross played Holiday in the movie bio *Lady Sings the Blues* (1972) and sang it, her record was also a hit. Other distinctive versions were made by Ruth Brown, Etta Jones, Chris Flory, Freddie Jackson, Dinah Washington, Joe Williams, Nancy Harrow, Natalie Cole, and Ann Hampton Callaway.

"Good Night Ladies" (1853) is perhaps the most famous farewell song in American music, a simple tune with the gentlemen bidding good night to the women before the men merrily go on their way. (The song is just as often called "Merrily We Roll Along.") The origin of the music is uncertain, but minstrel producer E.P. Christy is credited with the lyric, and the song does appear on minstrel programs throughout the nineteenth century. The catchy number was also a favorite sing-along on college campuses. In 1911 Harry H. Williams and Egbert Van Alstyne adapted the number into Tin Pan Alley format, and that is the version most used today. It was heard in the films *Git Along Little Dogies* (1937) and *Swingtime Johnny* (1943), and the Buffalo Bills sang it in the 1957 Broadway musical and the 1962 movie version of *The Music Man*.

"Goodbye" (1935) is the forgettable title of an unforgettable farewell song by Gordon Jenkins that conjures up heartrending melancholy as two parting lovers decide to say farewell rather than good-bye. Jenkins's music is morose yet has a driving rhythm that is surprisingly appealing.

The number became popular as the closing theme for Benny Goodman's concerts, and later if was favored by jazz artists. Among the many recordings are those by Goodman (vocal by Helen Ward), June Christy, Duke Ellington, Erroll Garner, Rosemary Clooney, Frank Sinatra, Chet Baker, Bill Evans, Stan Getz, Charlie Barnet, Michael Callen, the Barbara Carroll Trio, and Gene Ammons. Some interest in "Goodbye" was revived with Linda Ronstadt's 1985 recording with Nelson Riddle's Orchestra. The Goodman version was heard in the movies *The Benny Goodman Story* (1956) and *Radio Days* (1987).

"Goodbye Blues" (1932) was the jazzy theme song of the Mills Brothers that they sang in concerts, on record, and on film. Dorothy Fields, Arnold Johnson (lyric), and Jimmy McHugh (music) wrote the number for the harmonizing brothers, and their recording in which the four of them vocally imitate the instruments in a band was a bestseller. They reprised the farewell number in the movies *The Big Broadcast* (1932) and *Strictly Dynamite* (1934). Skeets McDonald, Rosemary Clooney, Benny Carter, T-Bone Walker, and Fletcher Henderson are among those who also recorded it.

"Goodbye Dear, I'll Be Back in a Year" (1941) was a novelty number by Mack Kay that found some attention but quickly disappeared at the declaration of war after Pearl Harbor. Before the United States entered the war, men were drafted into the army for a one-year tour of duty—hence, the promise indicated in the lyric. The farewell song was recorded with success by Horace Heidt and his Musical Knights, but no one was much interested in the number after 1941.

"Goodbye, Little Darlin', Goodbye" (1940) is a cowboy farewell song that Gene Autry wrote with Johnny Marvin to sing in the movie *South of the Border* (1937). The rustic piece was recorded by Autry, Dick Robertson, Bing Crosby, Boxcar Willie, Wayne King, Glenn Miller, Larry Sparks, Troy Shondell, and Johnny Cash.

"Goodbye Mama, I'm Off to Yokohama" (1942) was a novelty number that was quickly put together as a musical reaction to the attack on Pearl Harbor and the beginning of the war with Japan. J. Fred Coots wrote the patriotic farewell number right after the December 7 attack, and the song was published, recorded, and on the charts within two months. The most popular version was by Teddy Powell (vocals by Dick Judge and Peggy Lee). As the war wore on, the sunny optimism of the song was less appealing, and it was pretty much forgotten in a few years.

"Goodbye, My Lady Love" (1904) is a rousing cakewalk number by Joseph E. Howard in which a beau bids a fond farewell to a "turtle dove" who has been unfaithful to him, but he is confident that she will return and "love me tenderly." The lighthearted song was introduced and popularized by Ida Emerson in vaudeville, and it was a favorite at parlor pianos for several years. Oscar Hammerstein and Jerome Kern interpolated it into their musical *Show Boat* (1927), where it was sung by Sammy White and Eva Puck for authentic period flavor. The song is included in most productions of the classic musical, and it was performed by White and Queenie Smith in the 1936 film version. "Goodbye, My Lady Love" was also heard in the period movie *I Wonder Who's Kissing Her Now* (1947). In addition to various *Show Boat* cast recordings, a superb disc of the song was made by William Bolcom and Joan Morris.

"Goodnight, Irene" (1936) is a morose folk song that has managed to charm audiences for years with its appealing waltz music and sincere lyric. John Lomax and Huddie Ledbetter (better known as Leadbelly) wrote the number while Leadbelly was serving time in the Louisiana State Prison. The poignant ballad describes the despair a suitor feels since he parted from his beloved Irene and how he considers jumping into the river to drown himself. Leadbelly and others recorded it, but the song didn't catch on nationally until 1950 when a record by the Weavers with Gordon Jenkin's Orchestra sold a million discs. Sadly, Leadbelly died right before the recording was released, so he never saw his song go to the top of the charts. Other memorable records were made by Jo Stafford, Frank Sinatra, Boxcar Willie, Gordon MacRae, Ernest Tubb and Red Foley, Nat King Cole, Les Paul and Mary Ford, Mississippi John Hurt, the Village Stompers, Bobby Vee, and the Kingston Trio. Roger E. Mosley (dubbed by HiTide Harris) sang the torchy number in the film bio *Leadbelly* (1976), and it was heard in *Bound for Glory* (1976). Charles Bevel and Dan Wheetman performed "Goodnight, Irene" in the Broadway revue *It Ain't Nothin' But the Blues* (1999).

"Goodnight, Sweetheart" (1931) is the fox trot standard that for years was traditionally played as the last number at a dance. Ray Noble, Jimmy Campbell, and Reg Connelly collaborated on the fluent farewell song that offers comfort to a dear one, asking her not to cry as they part and promising that "sleep will banish sorrow." The song was introduced in England where Henry Hall's BBC Orchestra played it on the radio. Rudy Vallee introduced the number to American audiences with a bestselling record, and it was quickly interpolated into the Broadway show *Earl Carroll's Vanities of 1931*, where it was sung by Milton Watson and Woods Miller. Guy Lombardo and the Royal Canadians also had a chart record of the ballad, and over the years there have been noteworthy discs by

Wayne King, Del Courtney, Al Bowlly, Gordon MacRae, Fats Domino, the Flamingos, Ella Mae Morse, Dean Martin, and Julius LaRosa. The song has also been heard in several movies. Noble's orchestra played it in *The Big Broadcast of 1936* (1935), Vallee reprised it in *The Palm Beach Story* (1942), Gene Autry sang it in *Stardust on the Sage* (1942), Kenny Baker crooned it in *Stage Door Canteen* (1943), and it was on the soundtrack of *Angel's Holiday* (1937), *Holiday in Mexico* (1946), *You Were Meant for Me* (1948), and *Miller's Crossing* (1990).

"Goodnight, (Well) It's Time to Go" (1954) is an uptempo farewell song that was a rhythm-and-blues hit for the Spaniels. Calvin Carter and James Hudson originally wrote the number as "Goodnight, Sweetheart, Goodnight," but it became popular under its new name. The McGuire Sisters, Joe Resiman (vocal by Sonny Gale), and the Platters each had a successful record of it. The celebrated Spaniels disc was heard on the soundtrack of the movie *American Graffiti* (1973), Tom Selleck, Steve Guttenburg, and Ted Danson sang it in *Three Men and a Baby* (1987), and it was heard in *W.W. and the Dixie Dancekings* (1975) and *La Bamba* (1987).

"Goody-Goody" (1936) is a jumping song of sweet revenge by Johnny Mercer and Matty Malneck about a swain who, saying he knew how to play with fire without getting burned, left his dearie and went out and got his heart broken by someone else. Now she is celebrating and singing, "I hope you're satisfied, you rascal you!" Mercer got the title from a menu in a Chinese restaurant, and he also added, "Oh, yeah? Oh, yeah?" to punch the lyric in time to the music. A disc by Benny Goodman (vocal by Helen Ward) was popular and put the song on *Your Hit Parade* for twelve weeks. It was back in vogue twenty years later with a hit record by Paula Kelly and the Modernaires. Other commendable discs were made by Mercer, Freddy Martin, Bob Crosby, Ella Fitzgerald, Frank Sinatra, Sylvia Syms, Frankie Lyman and the Teenagers, the Hi-Lo's, Caterina Valente, and Paul Peterson. The Goodman version can be heard in the film bio *The Benny Goodman Story* (1956).

"Got a Date With an Angel" (1931) is a British ballad that happily anticipates a rendezvous with a special heartthrob. Clifford Grey and Sonny Miller wrote the giddy lyric ("I'm on my way to heaven!"), and Jack Waller and Joseph Tunbridge composed the harmonious music. A recording by Ray Noble and the New Mayfair Orchestra introduced the song in England, and it was popularized in America by a bestselling disc by Hal Kemp (vocal by Skinnay Ennis). Later Ennis formed his own band and used the ballad as his theme song. Among the other artists to record the number are Les Brown, Kitty Kallen, Pat O'Malley, the Sauter-

Finegan Orchestra, Helen Carr, Lawrence Welk, the Four Freshmen, Phil Harris, and Ian Whitcomb.

"Grandfather's Clock" (1876) is a perennial favorite of children's records and schools because of its distinctive use of tempo and rests that are both playful and instructive. Henry Clay Work wrote the narrative ballad about a clock that was purchased the day grandfather was born, ticked away merrily for years, then "stopped short, never to run again" the day the old man died. What makes the woeful tale so much fun is the ticking pattern in the accompaniment and the dramatic way that pattern is broken with the repeat of "stopped short." The song was introduced by the Hyer Sisters Colored Minstrels in New Haven in 1876, and it quickly found favor, eventually selling over a million copies of sheet music. (The number became a favorite of piano students as well.) Sometimes listed as "My Grandfather's Clock in the Hallway," the song was revived on Tin Pan Alley in 1938 with a hit record by Gene Krupa and his Orchestra. There have also been recordings by the Sons of the Pioneers, Hank Snow, Doc Watson, Jo Ann Castle, and Minnie Pearl. "Grandfather's Clock" can also be heard in the film *Collegiate* (1936).

"Great Day!" (1929) is an effervescent come-to-meeting song that was also a blues chaser during the depression. Billy Rose and Edward Eliscu wrote the fiery lyric harking to the sound of Gabriel's trumpet and claiming there will be another great day tomorrow. Vincent Youmans composed the rhythmic music that is rather subdued for a revival number yet is highly effective as it punches up all the "Amens!" in the lyric. Lois Deppe and the chorus introduced the song in the short-lived musical *Great Day* (1929), but the number managed to catch on, thanks to a successful record by Paul Whiteman and his Orchestra. Other notable discs were made by Benny Goodman, Bing Crosby, Glenn Miller, Allan Jones, the Staple Singers, Sarah Vaughan, Andre Kostelanetz, Leon Russell, and Jessye Norman. Interest in the song was revived when Barbra Streisand performed it in the movie *Funny Lady* (1975).

"Green Eyes" (1931) is a Cuban song that became a rhumba hit on Tin Pan Alley. Adolfo Utrera (lyric) and Nilo Menéndez (lyric) wrote "Aquellos Ojos Verdes" in their native Cuba, and it was introduced by Don Azpiaza and his Havana Casino Orchestra. Soon its contagious rhumba melody was picked up by Latin bands in the States. Eddie Woods and E. Rivera collaborated on an English lyric that is very enigmatic. A suitor is entranced by his mistress's "cool limpid green eyes" and describes them as a "pool where love lies," yet the lady's eyes seem to be indifferent to him and he wonders if she wants him at all. The new version was recorded by Xavier Cugat and others, but it never became a bestseller until Jimmy Dorsey (vocals by Helen O'Connell and Bob Eberly) revived it in 1941 with a chart record that sold over a million copies. Other artists who made discs of the ballad include Anita O'Day, Perez Prado, the Ventures, Abbe Lane, Desi Arnaz, Ray Anthony, Steve Lawrence and Eydie Gorme, and many Spanish-language performers. Dorsey, O'Connell, and Eberly reprised the number in the film bio *The Fabulous Dorseys* (1947), and it was heard in *When Johnny Comes Marching Home* (1942) and *Memphis Belle* (1990).

"Grizzly Bear" (1910) is a bizarre dance song that started a trend of dance steps named after animals, such as the Bunny Hop and the Turkey Trot. The lyric by Irving Berlin gives instructions on how the step is done, two partners hugging each other bear-style and rocking back and forth to George Botsford's music. Sophie Tucker introduced the song in vaudeville, and there were early records by the American Quartet and Arthur Collins. Like most dance songs, it disappeared when interest in the dance waned. But the number can be heard in the film *Wharf Angel* (1934) and *Hello, Frisco, Hello* (1943), where it was sung by Alice Faye and danced by Jack Oakie and June Haver.

"Guess I'll Hang My Tears Out to Dry" (1944) is a torch song standard by Sammy Cahn (lyric) and Jule Styne (music) in which a rejected lover can't get back into life but feels it is time he tried. It was written for the musical *Glad to See You* that closed in Philadelphia in 1944 before it reached Broadway. But Dinah Shore recorded it, and the song was soon famous. Other noteworthy discs were made by Harry James (vocal by Kitty Kallen), Eileen Farrell, Bill Mays, Frank Sinatra, Della Reese, Mel Tormé, Carol Burnett, Ray Charles, and more recently, Judy Kuhn, Michael Feinstein, K.T. Sullivan, and Linda Ronstadt. The number is sometimes listed as "I Guess I'll Hang My Tears Out to Dry."

"Guilty" (1931) is a delicate ballad that confesses to loving a sweetheart and dreaming of her all the time, admitting that "if love's a crime, then I'm guilty." Gus Kahn (lyric), Richard A. Whiting, and Harry Akst (music) wrote the number, and it was popularized by Ruth Etting in clubs and on records. There were also early discs by Russ Columbo, Ozzie Nelson, and Gene Austin. In the late 1940s the ballad was revived by successful records by Margaret Whiting and Ella Fitzgerald with Eddie Heywood. Sammy Kaye, Johnny Desmond with the Page Cavanaugh Trio, Tony Martin, the Statler Brothers, and Ray Noble (vocal by Al Bowlly) are among the artists that also recorded it.

"A Guy Is a Guy" (1952) is a sly narrative ballad by Oscar Brand that tells how a strange man followed a lady home one day, kissed her on the doorstep, then ended up walking down the aisle with her. The title phrase is repeated throughout the narrative, a droll commentary on the nature of men, and making the song perfect for sing-alongs. Brand adapted the number from a bawdy ditty called "A Gob Is a Gob" that GIs sang in World War Two and that was descended from an eighteenth-century song of ribaldry called "I Went Down to the Alehouse (A Knave Is a Knave)." Doris Day recorded the tune with Paul Weston's Orchestra, and it went to the top of the charts. Outstanding versions were also made by Ella Fitzgerald and Peggy Lee.

"The Gypsy" (1945) is a euphonic English song by Billy Reid that is both musically and lyrically intriguing. A suitor suspects that his betrothed is unfaithful, so he keeps going to a gypsy caravan where the fortune teller says that she is true. He doesn't believe her, but he has become dependent on the gypsy's lies. The Ink Spots popularized the song in America with a Number One record that put it on the *Hit Parade* for twenty weeks. There were also memorable discs by Dinah Shore, Sammy Kaye (vocal by Mary Marlowe), Guy Lombardo (vocal by Hildegarde), Frank Sinatra, Louis Armstrong, Bix Beiderbecke, and the Platters. The most haunting recording is an instrumental by Charlie Parker. It was recorded the day Parker was suffering from a drug overdose and, having completed the taping, collapsed in a nervous breakdown that put him in a mental institution.

"The Gypsy in My Soul" (1938) is an uptempo standard that originated from a college musical revue. Moe Jaffe (lyric) and Clay Boland (music) were students at the University of Pennsylvania when they wrote the rhythmic song for the annual Mask and Wig Club show *Fifty-Fifty* (1938). The freewheeling number exclaims that if one feels fancy free, has the urge to wander, and hears something calling him away, it must be the gypsy in his soul. The student song got published, and dozens of recordings were made over the years, including those by Mildred Bailey, Margaret Whiting, Jan Savitt (vocal by Bob Bon), Marian McPartland, Clyde McCoy, Jeri Southern, Art Van Damme, Dick Haymes, Eydie Gorme, Sammy Davis Jr., and a duet version by Judy Garland and Liza Minnelli.

H

"Hail, Hail, the Gang's All Here" (1917) may have a British melody, but with an American lyric, it became one of the most recognized of all party songs, particularly popular with U.S. troops during World War Two. The melody is the celebrated "Come Friends Who Plough the Sea" choral from Gilbert and Sullivan's *The Pirates of Penzance* (1879). Theodore Morse (using the pen name D.A. Estrom) took Arthur Sullivan's music and added a simple sing-along lyric celebrating togetherness. (Some believe that the lyric was actually written by Morse's wife Dolly and that D. Estrom is close to Dolly Morse's name spelled backwards.) The first known recording was made by Irving Kaufman, but the song would be preserved on many children's records and sung in many gatherings over the years. Guy Lombardo and the Royal Canadians always included it in their New Year's Eve celebrations.

"Hair of Gold, Eyes of Blue" (1948) is an uptempo cowboy song by Sunny Skylar about a cowhand from Butte, Montana, who met a "pretty queen" in Santa Fe, fell in love, and vowed to "make her mine." The genial number was introduced by Jack Emerson but was popularized by a bestselling record by Gordon MacRae. There were other discs by Jack Lathrop, Art Lund, and Frank Sinatra and a popular instrumental version by the Harmonicats.

"Hallelujah!" (1927) was composer Vincent Youman's first and one of his most popular songs. While stationed at a naval base during World War One, Youmans wrote out the contagious melody and had the Navy Band play it. Soon John Philip Sousa's Band was performing it, but it didn't take the form of a song until Leo Robin and Clifford Grey added the celebratory lyric about chasing away the blues and singing "Hallelujah" even though "Satan lies awaitin'." The rhythm ballad was interpolated into the Broadway musical *Hit the Deck* (1927), where it was sung by Stella Mayhew and the chorus as a revival number. While the music remained a favorite of Navy Bands, the new song was heard in the two movie versions of *Hit the Deck*, sung by Marguerite Padula in 1930 and by Tony Martin, Russ Tamblin, and Vic Damone in 1955. Among the many who recorded the vibrant number were Benny Goodman, Teddy Wilson, Red Garland, Ella Fitzgerald, Glenn Miller, Lee Wiley, Art Van Damme, Charlie Parker, and Charles Mingus.

"Hand Me Down My Walking Cane" (c. 1865) is a traditional American spiritual that compares dying and going to heaven to grabbing a cane and catching the midnight train now that "all my sins are taken away." Often sung but rarely written down, the song was given a Tin Pan Alley version by Paul Tremaine and his Orchestra in 1930. Over the years the joyous hymn has also been recorded by the Boswell Sisters, the Sons of the Pioneers, Roy Acuff, Fats Waller, Sonny Burgess, the Osborne Brothers, Jerry Lee Lewis, and many choral groups.

"A Handful of Stars" (1940) is a jazz standard about a dreamy night that Jack Lawrence and Ted Shapiro wrote, basing the melody on a thirteen-note musical phrase that Shapiro wrote during breaks when he was playing for Sophie Tucker. The glowing number was popularized by Glenn Miller (vocal by Ray Eberly) on record, and there were other early hit discs by Jimmy Dorsey (vocal by Bob Eberly), Artie Shaw (vocal by Anita Boyer), and Ina Ray Hutton's All-Male Orchestra (vocal by Stuart Foster). Long a favorite of jazz musicians, the song was later recorded by Stan Getz, Serge Chaloff, Eddie Higgins, Dave McKenna, and Mel Tormé with Rob McConnell and the Boss Brass. "A Handful of Stars" can be heard in the movie *Hullabaloo* (1940).

"Hands Across the Table" (1934) is a short (only sixteen bars) but highly atmospheric ballad that conjures up a picture of two lovebirds after dinner in a restaurant with the lights low, the music playing softly, and their hands joined together on the table. Mitchell Parish (lyric) and Jean Delettre (music) wrote the song for the musical revue *Continental Varieties* (1934), where it was sung by Lucienne Boyer, but it was popularized by several bands, most successfully by Hal Kemp (vocal by Skinnay Ennis). Other notable discs were made by Eddy Duchin, the Dorsey Brothers Orchestra (vocal by Kay Weber), Lud Gluskin, Joe Reisman (vocal by Paul Small), Lee Wiley, Buddy Clark, Sylvia Syms, Fats Domino, Gloria Lynne, Johnnie Ray, and Tina Louise. The number was heard in the film *Hands Across the Table* (1935), and on Broadway Michele Bautier sang it in the Parish revue *Stardust* (1987).

"Happy as the Day Is Long" (1933) is a happy-go-lucky rhythm number that has no use for "lovey dovey" songs and expresses happiness because of little everyday things like having your suit pressed, your shoes shined, and plenty of peace of mind. Ted Koehler wrote the carefree lyric, and Harold Arlen composed the sparkling music that (very unusual for him) uses repeated notes effectively. The lively tune was introduced by Henry "Rubber Legs" Williams in the Harlem revue *Cotton Club Parade* (1933). A recording by Duke Ellington (vocal by Ivie Anderson) helped the song to find an audience, and there were other memorable discs by Fletcher Henderson, Joe Haymes, Adrian Rollins (vocal by Howard Phillips), Leo Reisman, the Washboard Rhythm Kings, and more recently, Weslia Whitfield.

"Happy Birthday to You" (1893) is probably the most frequently sung song in the English-speaking world. Louisville schoolteacher Patty Smith Hill originally wrote the lyric as "Good Morning to All," and set to Mildred J. Hill's simple melody, it was sung by her students at the beginning of each school day. It was published as a children's song in 1893 and was eventually sung in schools across the country. How the innocent little ditty became the birthday song of choice is not quite clear, but no song ever went more places and stayed as popular. (It is estimated that Western Union messenger boys have sung it over a million times.) Most people mistakenly think that the short jingle is in the public domain, but the songwriters had their song copyrighted, and to this day a royalty must be paid if it is sung on stage, television, radio, or film. Countless movies have included it, and the song was even featured at times, such as Shirley Temple singing it in *Little Miss Broadway* (1938), Tony Martin, Vic Damone, Russ Tamblyn, and the chorus performing it in *Hit the Deck* (1955), and Julie Andrews having fun with it in *10* (1979).

"Happy Days Are Here Again" (1929) is perhaps the best of the anti-depression songs to be embraced by the American public during the 1930s, and it remained a favorite song of optimism for decades after. Milton Ager's music is bright and tuneful yet very flexible, being effective as a rousing number or as an inspiring ballad. Jack Yellen wrote the spirited lyric that bids farewell to bad times and urged everyone to "sing a song of cheer" again. The song was written for the movie *Chasing Rainbows* (1930), but the studio cut it out of the script before it was filmed. A few days after the stock market crash, George Olsen's Orchestra played it at Manhattan's Pennsylvania Hotel ballroom, and the downhearted patrons reacted to it with enthusiasm. When it was played in the Roosevelt Hotel in Hollywood, studio producer Irving Thalberg heard it and asked why they didn't have such great songs in their movies. When told it had been cut from one of his own films, Thalberg had the number put back into *Chasing Rainbows*, where it was sung by Charles King, Bessie Love, and the ensemble. The movie was not a success, but "Happy Days Are Here Again" caught on quickly and became one of the most performed songs of the decade. Franklin D. Roosevelt used it as his campaign song in 1932 (it would later be used by Harry Truman and John F. Kennedy for their presidential campaigns as well), and it was adopted as the theme song for the popular weekly radio show sponsored by Lucky Strike. The earliest recordings were made by Ben Selvin and Leo Reisman, to be followed by dozens of others over the years. Among the major discs were those by George Shearing, Jim Bailey, the Casa Loma Orchestra, Jack Hylton, Judy Garland, Guy Lombardo, and Barbra Streisand. Fred Allen, Raymond Walburn, and Andrew Tombes sang it in the film *Thanks a Million* (1935), and it was also used in *Git Along Little Dogies* (1937), *Beau James* (1957), *This Earth Is Mine* (1959), *Night of the Iguana* (1964), *M*A*S*H* (1970), and others. In the Broadway musical *Big Deal* (1986), the number was performed by Larry Marshall, Desire Coleman, Mel Johnson Jr., and the ensemble. A 1963 ASCAP Poll cited "Happy Days Are Here Again" as one of the sixteen all-time *Hit Parade* songs.

"Happy-Go-Lucky You (And Broken Hearted Me)" (1932) is a heartfelt torch song by Al Goodhart, Al Hoffman, and J.F. Murray that Bing Crosby popularized with a record made in his typically smooth and crooning style. The number was also a hit for Glen Gray and the Casa Loma Orchestra (vocal by Kenny Sargent) and Ray Noble (vocal by Al Bowlly). Other records of note were made by Charles "Buddy" Rogers and his Orchestra, Smith Ballew, Russ Carlson and the High Steppe, and Bobby Gordon.

"The Happy Wanderer" (1954) is a catchy traveling song from Austria that had everyone in America singing (and yodeling) in the 1950s. Friedrich Wilhelm Moeller wrote the hiking song as "Der Froehliche Wanderer," and it was soon being sung across Europe. When the Oberkirchen Children's Choir from Germany toured the States and sang it, Americans latched onto the happy tune. Antonia Ridge wrote an English lyric about wandering across the countryside with a knapsack on one's back and retained the yodeling refrain "Val-De Ri, Val-De Ra" (which is sometimes listed as the song's title). Frank Weir and his Orchestra popularized the new version, and soon there were dozens of records, the song becoming a particular favorite of children's choirs and polka bands. Henri Rene, Nelson Riddle (vocal by Tommy Leonetti), Louis Prima, Bill Staines, Myron Floren with Lawrence Welk, and Frank Yankovic and his Yanks were among the artists who made disc versions. More recently, it was sung by the cast of the Off-Broadway revue *The Taffetas* (1988).

"Harbor Lights" (1940) is a tearful English song in which two separated lovers view the lights in the harbor, which remind them of the miles that stand between them. Jimmy Kennedy wrote the sorrowful lyric, and Will Grosz (using the pen name Hugh Williams) composed the slow and mournful music. Roy Fox and his Orchestra popularized the number in Britain, and Rudy Vallee did the same in America. In 1959 Sammy Kaye and his Orchestra revived the ballad with a recording that reached the top of the charts and put the number on the *Hit Parade* for twenty-nine weeks. The Platters revived it again in 1960 with their successful disc, and Dinah Washington had a hit record as well. Other noteworthy recordings were made by Claude Thornhill, Emery Deutsch, Frances Langford, Guy Lombardo, Ralph Flanagan, Kim Kahuna and the Royal Palms Orchestra, Bing Crosby, Ray Anthony, and Willie Nelson. An instrumental version of the ballad was used effectively on the soundtrack of the movie *The Long Voyage Home* (1940).

"Hard-Hearted Hannah (The Vamp of Savannah)" (1924) is a silly novelty song that was a favorite in vaudeville, then decades later on, records. Jack Yellen, Bob Bigelow, and Charles Bates wrote the slapstick lyric about a coldhearted gal ("she's the polar bear's pajamas!") who breaks men's hearts, destroys their lives, even kills them; Hannah has even been known to pour water on a drowning man. Milton Ager composed the merry music that moves at "a barrellhouse tempo." Frances Williams introduced the ditty in vaudeville, and there were early records by Belle Baker and Cliff Edwards. In the 1950s the number was revived through hit records by Peggy Lee and the Ray Charles Singers. Other discs were made by Dolly Kay, Ray McKinley, Lucille Hegamin, Bud Freeman, Fletcher Henderson, Margaret Whiting, Barbara Cook, and Nancy Sinatra. Ella Fitzgerald sang the number in the movie *Pete Kelly's Blues* (1955).

"Has Anybody Here Seen Kelly?" (1909) is an English comedy song that was fully Americanized once it crossed the sea. C.W. Murphy and Willie Letters wrote "Kelly from the Isle of Man" about an itinerant Irishman who stumbles across the countryside of Great Britain. The lyric was full of British names and customs and seemed an unlikely candidate for Tin Pan Alley. But in 1909 William C. McKenna rewrote the lyric, changing Kelly to an Irish immigrant newly arrived in New York who takes off and can't be found. The singer asks the musical question of the new title and mentions American locations while pleading with his listeners for information. The new version was heard in vaudeville, but it didn't become widely popular until Nora Bayes sang it in the Broadway musical *The Jolly Bachelors* (1910). Bayes also made an early recording of the song that helped promote sheet music sales. Alice Faye, Jack Oakie, and the chorus performed the number in the film *Hello, Frisco, Hello* (1943).

"Have I Stayed Away Too Long?" (1943) is a poignant ballad by Frank Loesser in which a neglectful lover asks a series of questions about returning to his girl: If he returned tonight would she take him back? Should he come to her door or stay away? Has it been too long a separation this time? Perry Como introduced and popularized the song, but because of the gentle cowboy ballad flavor in Loesser's music, it became a favorite of country-western artists. Tex Grande and his Range Riders, Hank Snow, Tex Ritter, Bob Wills, Jim Reeves, Bobby Bare, Dominique Eade, Johnny Bond, and Willie Nelson are among those who recorded it with success.

"Have I Told You Lately That I Love You?" (1944) is a tender, domestic ballad by Scott Wiseman that asks a loved one if he's mentioned of late how much he cares for her. Gene Autry's early recording was a bestseller, then it was picked up by a variety of artists, including Bing Crosby with the Andrews Sisters, Tony Martin and Fran Warren, Billy Vaughn, Vera Lynn, the Sons of the Pioneers, Tony Bennett, Foy Willing, Coleman Hawkins, Floyd Cramer, Elvis Presley, Al Martino, Jim Reeves, Ricky Nelson, Eddy Arnold, Ringo Starr, Barbra Streisand, and Kenny Rogers. The warm ballad can be heard in the movies *Sing, Neighbor, Sing* (1944) and *Coal Miner's Daughter* (1980).

"Have You Ever Been Lonely? (Have You Ever Been Blue?)" (1933) is a Big Band ballad that was later taken up by country-western singers and became a tearful favorite. Peter De Rose composed the emotive music, and George Brown (a.k.a. Billy Hill) wrote the pleading lyric in which an admirer asks forgiveness from a sweetheart, hoping for a second chance and wondering if she has ever felt the way he does now. Paul Whiteman and his Orchestra popularized the song, and there were also early band recordings by Ted Lewis and Ray Noble (vocal Al Bowlly). The ballad was revived in the 1960s by Jerry Vale, but by then it had become a staple with country artists. Among those who recorded it were Nellie Lutcher, Chet Atkins, Ernest Tubb, Della Reese, the Beverley Sisters, Slim Whitman, Patsy Cline, Max Bygraves, Ruby Murray, the Browns, and Jim Reeves. The heartsick ballad can be heard in the film *Oklahoma Annie* (1952).

"Hawaiian War Chant" (1936) is one of the most celebrated Hawaiian songs with over one hundred versions recorded, most of them instrumentals. Johnny Noble and Prince Leleiohaku of Hawaii composed the pulsating drum music, and Ralph Freed wrote the English lyric about a "sunny little melody" that was started by the natives in Waikiki and soon gathered together all the boys and girls, "swinging it like a tropical storm." A 1939 record by Tommy Dorsey and his Orchestra popularized the song, and it was revived in 1946 with a parody version by Spike Jones and his City Slickers, in 1951 by the Ames Brothers, and soon after by a jazz vocal recording by Dave Lambert. Eminent among the many recordings were discs by Kim Kahuna and the Royal Palms Orchestra, Guy Lombardo, Billy Vaughn, Ted Heath, Teresa Brigh, the Ventures, and Ella Fitzgerald. Harry Owens and his Royal Hawaiians played it in the movie *It's a Date* (1940), and the number was heard in several other films, such as *Moonlight in Hawaii* (1941), *Ship Ahoy* (1942), *Song of the Islands* (1942), and *Song of the Open Road* (1944).

"He Was Too Good to Me" (1930) is one of Rodgers and Hart's most beguiling ballads, yet it took awhile before it caught on. Lorenz Hart's torch song lyric is very ambiguous, the jilted lady describing the fine qualities of her lover but coming to the wry conclusion that "he was too good to be true." Richard Rodgers's music is just as intriguing, providing a sweeping melody within a narrow range (one note more than an octave). The number was written for the Broadway musical *Simple Simon* (1930) to be sung by Lee Morse, but both Morse and the song were cut before opening. The song was then slated for the *Nine-Fifteen Revue* (1930), but again it was cut. So the songwriters had the ballad published, and it slowly found an audience. Among the artists who recorded it were Jeri Southern, Helen Merrill, Nina Simone, Carmen McRae, Mabel Mercer, Eydie Adams, Dinah Shore, Dorothy Loudon and more recently, Barbara Cook, Carly Simon, Dawn Upshaw, K.T. Sullivan, and Natalie Cole.

"Head Over Heels in Love" (1937) is a clever number by American songwriters Mack Gordon (lyric) and Harry Revel (music) that was introduced in a British film and then worked its way to Tin Pan Alley. Gordon's lyric is particularly expert, using repeated words and phrases effectively. A lovesick inamorato describes his recent behavior (singing instead of talking, dancing rather than walking, missing meals, being unable to sleep, and so on), then admits that he likes it. Jessie Matthews sang the song in *Head Over Heels* (1937) and recorded it as well. Discs by Tommy Dorsey and Lud Gluskin popularized the ballad in America, and there were also records by Ozzie Nelson, Jack Smith, Flatt and Scruggs, and Paul Adkins and his Borderline Band.

"Heart and Soul" (1938) became, along with "Chopsticks," the most overplayed song by beginning pianists, but the number is also a hearty ballad as well. Frank Loesser wrote the ardent lyric about falling completely—both heart and soul—for a special someone, and Hoagy Carmichael composed the rhythmic music that makes for an ideal finger exercise because of the chord progressions that run throughout it. The number was written as a Tin Pan Alley piece but was first interpolated into the movie short *A Song Is Born* (1938), where it was played by Larry Clinton and his Orchestra. Clinton's record (vocal by Bea Wain) hit the top of the charts, and the song would be revived often over the next three decades: by the Four Aces in 1952, Johnny Maddox in 1956, Jan and Dean in 1961, and the Cleftones in 1962. Other well-known discs were made by Loesser, Carmichael, Gene Krupa, Al Bowlly, Frank Ifield, Connee Boswell, Ella Mae Morse, Betty Carter, Floyd Cramer, Vera Lynn, Mel Tormé, the Marshall Tucker Band, Dean Martin, Johnny Bond, Skitch Henderson, the Spaniels, and Dave Brubeck. Krupa and his band reprised it in the movie *Some Like It Hot* (1939), the Cleftones version was heard in *American Graffiti* (1973), and Anne Bancroft sang it in *To Be or Not to Be* (1983). Guy Stroman and the cast performed "Heart and Soul" in the Off-Broadway musical revue *Forever Plaid* (1990).

"Heart of My Heart (I Love You)" (c. 1897) is a sing-along favorite of uncertain authorship that was first sung in saloons in the 1890s. The number nostalgically recalls an old gang of friends who used to gather and sing ("oh, how we could harmonize!") old songs together. The ditty was first published in 1899 with Andrew Mack listed as composer and the words by "Alice." In 1926, Ben Ryan wrote a new version, sometimes titled "The Gang That Sang Heart of My Heart," that was introduced by Tommy Lyman in nightclubs, and it soon became popular in taverns and around the parlor piano. The song seemed to have faded away by World War Two but was revived in 1954 with a Top 10 record by the Three D's (Don Cornell, Alan Dale, and Johnny Desmond). Other discs over the years were made by the Four Aces, Les Elgart, Frankie Laine, Roberta Sherwood, Max Bygraves, Freddy Martin (vocal by Merv Griffin), the Firehouse Five Plus Two, Charlie Daniels, and Mitch Miller. Lou Monte was heard singing it in the film *Donnie Brasco* (1997).

"Heartaches" (1931) is a dramatic example of a successful song that faded into obscurity, then was revived to become an even bigger hit. Al Hoffman composed the tender music, and John Klenner wrote the lyric, a tearful lament by a spurned suitor who cannot escape from the memory of a lost love. The song was popularized by a 1932 record by Ted Weems and his Orchestra featuring a whistling section by Elmo Tanner. The song was popular enough that Weems recorded it again in 1937, but by the end of the decade, it was pretty much forgotten. In 1947 a disc jockey in Charlotte, North Carolina, came across the Weems record and out of curiosity played it on the air. The station was deluged with calls asking about the melancholy ballad, and the song caught on again; the Weems disc was reissued, and it sold 3 million copies. The number became a hit yet again in 1961 with a successful record by the Marcels.

Other significant discs over the years were made by Harry James, Billy Vaughn, Al Bowlly, Joe Alexander, Frankie Laine, Ruby Braff, Jimmy Rushing, Eddy Arnold, Connie Francis, Lawrence Welk, Kenny Ball, and Pat Boone. The song can also be heard in the movie *Heartaches* (1947).

"Hearts and Flowers" (1899) is a turn-of-the-century hit ballad whose music and very title later became clichés for melodramatics. Mary D. Brine penned the gushing lyric in which a beau proposes to Marguerite in her garden. She is hesitant, worrying that weeds might spring up in her life, but he assures her, pleading "let my heart your garden be." Finally she accepts, asking him to "give seeds of love to me." Theodore Moses Tobani composed the fussy, weepy music, which was taken from a section of *Wintermarchen* (1891) by Hungarian composer Alphonse Czibulka. It became a favorite melody for pianists to play during melodramas and silent films, especially when the heroine pleads with the villain or when a beloved character lies dying in bed. The song can be heard in the talking movie *Stolen Harmony* (1935).

"Hello, Frisco!" (1915) is a Tin Pan Alley song written to capitalize on a current news event, yet it managed to stick around for quite awhile. Louis Hirsch composed the cheerful music, and Gene Buck wrote the lyric that celebrated the inauguration of transcontinental telephone service by having two sweethearts talk to each other coast to coast. It was interpolated into the *Ziegfeld Follies* (1915), where it was sung by Ina Claire and Bernard Granville, and the tangy number was the hit of the show. There were early duet recordings by Elida Morris and Sam Ash, and Olive Kline and Reginald Werrenrath, and sheet music sales boomed. Alice Faye, John Payne, Jack Oakie, and June Havoc performed the song in the movie *Hello, Frisco, Hello* (1943), and it was also heard in *Wharf Angel* (1934), *The Story of Vernon and Irene Castle* (1939), and *The I-Don't-Care Girl* (1953). "Hello, Frisco!" was interpolated into the score for the 1976 Broadway revival of *Going Up!* where it was sung by Pat Lysinger and four aviators.

"Hello! Ma Baby" (1899) was one of the first telephone songs and, as described by David Ewen, "one of the earliest significant ragtime numbers." The vibrant ditty was written by vaudevillians Joe Howard and Ida Emerson as a cakewalk specialty. The exaggerated lyric, written in Negro dialect, is the declaration of love to a girl he's never seen, but he talks to his "ragtime gal" every day on the telephone because his "heart's on fire." The music is a succession of eighth and quarter notes bouncing back and forth so that the syncopated rhythm is very distinct and innovative. Philip Furia has also pointed out that the words are syncopated as well, the emphasis put on the first syllable of "hello" rather than the usual second. The result is a playful and memorable piece of early rag-time. Howard got the idea for the song when he heard an African American porter use the title phrase on the phone to his sweetheart. Within two weeks the song was written, and Howard was performing it on stage. He later made a recording of the number and sang it throughout his whole career, which lasted into the 1950s. Other major recordings were made by Bing Crosby, the Banjo Kings, and Chet Atkins. The song was heard in such period films as *Hello, Frisco, Hello* (1943), *Nob Hill* (1945), and *I Wonder Who's Kissing Her Now* (1947), and it was sung by the cast of the Broadway revue *Tintypes* (1980).

"Henry's Made a Lady Out of Lizzie" (1928) is a topical novelty song by Walter O'Keefe about the rising popularity of Henry Ford's Tin Lizzies. It was the first automobile advertised as a family car, and its middle-class respectability was gently spoofed in the song. O'Keefe performed the number in vaudeville and on the radio for years, and there was a distinctive recording made later by the Happiness Boys (Billy Jones and Ernie Hare).

"Here Comes Santa Claus (Down Santa Claus Lane)" (1947) is the seasonal favorite by Gene Autry and Oakley Haldeman that announces Santa's arrival for Christmas. Autry's recording sold a million copies, and he reprised it in the movie *The Cowboy and the Indians* (1949). The success of the song was only eclipsed by his record of "Rudolph the Red Nosed Reindeer" two years later. Other memorable discs of the song were made by Bing Crosby, Eddy Arnold, the Andrews Sisters, Doris Day, Elvis Presley, Pat Boone, Keely Smith, Glen Campbell, Diana Ross and the Supremes, and Willie Nelson and a parody version by Spike Jones and his City Slickers.

"Here's That Rainy Day" (1953) is a torch song standard that was rescued from obscurity to become a favorite of nightclub singers. Johnny Burke wrote the succinct lyric of regret, wishing one had saved those "leftover dreams" for a rainy day because love is gone and now they are needed. Jimmy Van Heusen composed the intriguing music, which Alec Wilder calls "a difficult song, almost demanding its harmony's presence for a singer not to get lost in the complex line." The number was written for the Broadway musical *Carnival in Flanders* (1953), where it was sung by Dolores Gray. But the flop show closed after six performances, and it wasn't until nightclub singers began using it that the ballad started to become admired. Among those who recorded the song are Frank Sinatra, Julie London, June Christy, Vic Damone, Judy Garland, Mike Douglas, Art Pepper, André Previn, Benny Carter, Nancy Wilson, Dizzy Gillespie,

Kenny Rogers, and more recently, Ann Hampton Callaway and Judy Kaye.

"He's a Good Man to Have Around" (1929) is a saucy song of admiration that was most associated with Sophie Tucker, who sang it on stage, film, and records. Jack Yellen (lyric) and Milton Ager (music) wrote the hot jazz number for Tucker to sing in the movie *Honky Tonk* (1929), and it was a hit also for Billy Murray with the Yuban Radio Orchestra and Libby Holman with the Cotton Pickers. Later there were estimable records by Kay Starr, Alberta Hunter, the Original Memphis Five, Herman Kenin, and Jimmie Noone.

"He's Got the Whole Wide World in His Hands" (1958) is a traditional gospel number that was turned into a Tin Pan Alley hit in the 1950s. The country hymn, about God having children and all kinds of people in his care, has uncertain origins. In 1958 Geoff Love adapted the spiritual into a rousing song, and it was popularized by Roland Hayes in concert and through a record by thirteen-year-old Laurie London that went to the Number One position on the charts. Mahalia Jackson had a hit with it around the same time, and dozens of discs followed, including those by Etta James, the Isley Brothers, Nina Simone, Perry Como, Marian Anderson, Odetta, George Beverly Shea, Leslie Uggams, Roberta Flack, and Kathleen Battle. The song remains a favorite with folk sing-alongs, banjo groups, choirs, and children's records.

"He's My Guy" (1942) is a Big Band ballad that was well known from records and films in the 1940s. Don Raye (lyric) and Gene De Paul (music) wrote the swinging song of affection, and it was popularized by Harry James (vocal by Helen Forrest). Other successful band discs were made by Tommy Dorsey (vocal by Jo Stafford), Freddie Slack (vocal by Ella Mae Morse), and Dick Stabile (vocal by Gracie Barry). Among the many other female artists to record the ballad were Ella Fitzgerald, Etta Jones, Peggy Lee, Sarah Vaughan, Marion Montgomery, Dinah Washington, Doris Drew, and Nancy Wilson. "He's My Guy" can also be heard in the movies *Laugh Your Blues Away* (1943), *Never a Dull Moment* (1943), *Follow the Band* (1943), *Hi'ya, Chum* (1943), *He's My Guy* (1943), and *Undercover Girl* (1950).

"He's 1-A in the Army and He's 1-A in My Heart" (1941) is an early military draft song of World War Two that Redd Evans wrote to romanticize the image of a man in uniform. Like many of the war effort songs of the era, this one promoted the idea that girls were attracted to GIs and that a man classified 1-A (the highest eligibility rank) by the draft board also ranks high in females' hearts. The number was popularized by a record by Harry James (vocal by Helen Forrest), and there were also discs by Les Brown (vocal by Betty Bonney), Johnny Long, and the King Sisters.

"Hey, Good Lookin' " (1951) is one of Hank Williams's few cheerful songs and also one of his most popular, his record selling over a million copies and the number crossing over from country to different fields. The sexy wooing song uses food imagery throughout, asking a sweetie, "what's cookin'?" and suggesting she "cook something with me." A duet version by Frankie Laine and Jo Stafford was also very successful, and there were other notable discs by Boxcar Willie, Del Shannon, Norman Petty, Charlie Rich, Kitty Kallen, Roy Buchanan, Ethel Merman, Floyd Cramer, Connie Stevens, Johnny Cash, Ray Charles, and Tennessee Ernie Ford. Hank Williams Jr. sang "Hey, Good Lookin' " on the soundtrack for George Hamilton in the movie bio *Your Cheatin' Heart* (1964) and the original Williams record was heard in *The Last Picture Show* (1971).

"High Hopes" (1959) is the Oscar-winning song by Sammy Cahn (lyric) and Jimmy Van Heusen (music) that Frank Sinatra and Eddie Hodges introduced in the movie *A Hole in the Head* (1959). Van Heusen's music is peppy and tuneful, in the mode of a children's ditty, especially in the soaring refrain. Cahn's lyric is also childlike, observing an ant trying to do the impossible (move a rubber plant) and optimistically commenting that he believes he can do anything and so should you. The song came about because the studio was worried about the rushes of the non-musical film in production. Sinatra and Hodges were not bonding as the father-son relationship ought to, and it was suggested that a song between the two would help. The Sinatra-Hodges duet recording was very popular, and there were also discs by Bing Crosby, Connie Francis, Doris Day, and Sammy Hagar and lots of children's records. "High Hopes" was John F. Kennedy's campaign song during the 1960 presidential election.

"High Noon (Do Not Forsake Me, Oh My Darling)" (1952) is a classic ballad from a classic film western, and one helped the other to celebrity. Early screenings of the movie were disappointing, and audience reaction was not very favorable. Dimitri Tiomkin, who wrote the soundtrack score, suggested to the studio that a narrative ballad at the beginning of the film might help set up the story. He wrote the flowing, western-flavored music, and Ned Washington provided the lyric that told of a crucial gunfight on the sheriff's wedding day. Tiomkin had Frankie Laine record the ballad, and it was released four months before the movie opened. The song was an immediate hit, and it helped promote the film as well. Tex Ritter sang it on the soundtrack of *High Noon* (1952),

and the number took the Oscar for Best Song. There were other recordings of note by Dick Curless, Johnny Bond, Frank Chacksfield, King Curtis, Connie Francis, the Browns, Billy Vaughn, Faron Young, Skitch
Henderson, Peter and Gordon, Duane Eddy, and Merle Travis.

"Hindustan" (1917) is one of the many pseudo-oriental songs about exotic places that were so popular after World War One, this one managing
to remain popular for several decades. Oliver Wallace and Harold Weeks
wrote the number about the mysterious language of India, and it was
introduced in the musical revue *Joy Bells* (1917). The first recording was
by Joseph C. Smith and his Orchestra in 1918, followed by booming sheet
music sales. Bob Crosby revived the song in 1939, Alvino Rey did the
same in 1941, and Ted Weems had a hit with it in 1948. But the biggest
seller was a duet version by Bing Crosby and Rosemary Clooney. Among
those who also recorded it were Joe Venuti, Glen Gray and the Casa
Loma Orchestra, Frankie Carle, Artie Shaw, the Firehouse Five Plus Two,
Bob Scoby's Frisco Band, Caterina Valente, the Three Suns, and Alex
Welsh and his Jazz Band. "Hindustan" can be heard in the movie *The
Dolly Sisters* (1945).

"Hinky Dinky Parlay Voo" (1924) is a novelty number that Al Dubin,
Irving Mills (lyric), Irwin Dash, and Jimmy McHugh (music) wrote,
based on the World War One favorite "Mad'moiselle from Armentiers."
The new version has many stanzas, starting with flirting with a French
miss who hasn't been kissed in twenty years to the difficulties of getting
steak for dinner and how to avoid bombs and nerve gas. The silly ditty
was featured in vaudeville and on sheet music, and there were later
records by the Happiness Boys (Billy Jones and Ernie Hare) and Slim
Jackson. The number, sometimes listed as "What's Become of Hinky
Dinky Parlay Voo?," was also used in the films *The Cockeyed World* (1929)
and *For Me and My Gal* (1942).

"Hold Tight—Hold Tight (Want Some Sea Food, Mama)" (1939) is a
nonsense scat song in which a husband comes home from work and
demands fish for dinner, listing all the kinds he likes and celebrating
with "Foo-ra-de-ack-a-sa!" and similar gibberish. The listed authors were
Kent Brandow and Robinson Ware Spottswood, which were pseudo-
nyms for the five songwriters Leonard Kent, Jerry Brandow, Edward
Robinson, Willie Spottswood, and Leonard Ware. The jazzy number was
popularized by the Andrews Sisters with Jimmy Dorsey's Orchestra, and
it was also a favorite of Fats Waller. Other records were made by Glenn
Miller, the Cliff Adams Singers, Sidney Bechet, Big Sandy and the Fly-
Rite Trio, and Freddy Gardner. The song was used in the movie *Follow
the Boys* (1944), and on Broadway it was sung by Charlaine Woodard in

the Waller revue *Ain't Misbehavin'* (1978) and Alde Lewis Jr. and the female ensemble in the musical *Big Deal* (1986).

"Home (When Shadows Fall)" (1931) is a delicate ballad by Peter Van Steeden and Harry and Geoff Clarkson in which the setting sun always makes one think of a faraway home. Geoff Clarkson was only sixteen years old when he collaborated on the number with his brother Harry and bandleader Van Steeden, and it was introduced in an unusual but effective way. The music publisher arranged to have the song debut on several network radio shows on Thanksgiving eve. The ploy worked, and thousands of copies of sheet music were sold, as well as many different recordings. Among the artists who made discs of the ballad were Mildred Bailey, Arthur Tracy, Louis Armstrong, Irving Kaufman, Benny Bailey, Helen Humes, and Gerry Mulligan. Van Steeden also recorded it and made "Home" his theme song. Nat King Cole revived the song with success in 1950. It can be heard in the films *Home on the Prairie* (1939) and *Moonlight and Cactus* (1944).

"Home for the Holidays" (1955) is the domestic Christmas favorite by Al Stillman (lyric) and Robert Allen (music) about missing home during the holiday season. The poignant song has remained a seasonal standard, and it has always been particularly beloved by enlisted men stationed overseas. Perry Como popularized the ballad with a recording with Mitchell Ayres' Orchestra, and there have been many records since, including commendable ones by Glenn Miller, Joe Pass, the Lennon Sisters, Walter Brennan, Betty Carter, Robert Goulet, the Carpenters, and more recently, Sergio Salvatore, Garth Brooks, and the group Rockapella. The number is sometimes listed as "There's No Place Like Home for the Holidays."

"Home on the Range" (1904) is perhaps the most famous traditional cowboy song in America, yet its origins and authorship have never been authenticated. The easygoing ballad about longing for a home on the prairie "where the deer and the antelope play" probably goes back to the early 1800s, and there is evidence of various versions of the song coming from different parts of the Midwest. The most commonly heard (but probably apocryphal) story says that Kansas homesteader Bewster Higley wrote the lyric as a poem in his cabin in 1873 and had it published in a local newspaper as "Oh, Give Me a Home Where the Buffalo Roam." Some twenty miles away from Higley, guitar player Daniel Kelly supposedly plucked out the melody, and it was handed down for thirty years without being written out. It wasn't until 1919, the story goes, that someone thought of putting the two together. It is known that both music and lyric were published together in 1904 as "Arizona Home" with

William Goodman credited as the sole author. The next year the ballad was included in an anthology of cowboy songs where it was billed as "the cowboy's national anthem," and Higley and Kelly were listed as the authors. This anthology led to its widespread popularity, and the song became so lucrative that Goodman sued the publishers in 1934, failing to prove his ownership and losing the case. Later "Home on the Range" was made the official song of the state of Kansas. The ballad has been consistently sung in schools, camps, sing-alongs, around the parlor piano, and on children's records. Bing Crosby had a bestselling disc in 1933, and other major records were made by Roy Rogers and Dale Evans, Frank Sinatra, Burl Ives, the Banjo Kings, Connie Francis, Gene Autry, and Pete Seeger. It has been heard in dozens of films, including performances by Irene Dunne and Ralph Bellamy in *The Awful Truth* (1937), Jack Oakie in *Song of the Islands* (1942), Deanna Durbin in *I'll Be Yours* (1947), Cary Grant in *Mr. Blandings Builds His Dream House* (1948), the Sons of the Pioneers in *Fighting Coast Guard* (1951), and Neil Young in *Where the Buffalo Roam* (1980). "Home on the Range" can also be heard in *I Loved a Woman* (1933), *Oh Johnny, How You Can Love* (1940), *Song of Nevada* (1944), and other movies.

"Home Sweet Home" (1823), the song that was responsible for a million samplers and coined the domestic motto "Be it ever so humble, there's no place like home," is as American as apple pie, yet it was written and first popularized in Great Britain. When the American actor and playwright John Howard Payne was in London working on an opera, he became so homesick for his family back in the States that he wrote out the lyric to express his feelings. Sir Henry Bishop, the opera's composer, thought the words would make an effective aria, so he composed the melody, and it was sung by Maria Tree in *Clari* (1823). The song became popular in England first; then it crossed over to America, where it became famous thanks to concert performances by Jenny Lind and Adelina Patti. Eventually much of the world adopted it as a favorite domestic ballad. There are two sad and ironic aspects of the song's history. Payne was promised $25 for his lyric, but he never earned a penny from the song. Also, he had been orphaned at the age of thirteen and had never had a real home for most of his difficult life. (In later years he was an ambassador and didn't even live in his native country.) Deanna Durbin sang "Home Sweet Home" in the film *First Love* (1939), Jeanette MacDonald and the chorus performed it in *Cairo* (1942), in *A Date With Judy* (1948) it was sung by Jane Powell, Selena Royale, and Jerry Hunter, and in *Melba* (1953), Patrice Munsel gave it the original operatic treatment. It has been heard on the soundtracks of dozens of movies, including *The Prodigal* (1931), *Let Freedom Ring* (1939), *Can't Help Singing* (1944), *Edward Scissorhands* (1990), and *Gettysburg* (1993).

"Honest and Truly" (1924) is a heartfelt ballad of devotion by Leo Wood (lyric) and Fred Rose (music) that was written as a country song but soon crossed over and became successful in the areas of pop and jazz. Henry Burr popularized the number, and there were noteworthy records by Rose, Jimmie Lunceford, Billy Vaughn, Ralph Flanagan, and Billy May.

"Honey" (1928) is a simple (and somewhat simple-minded) love song that explains the sunniness of the world because he fell in love with his "honey." Seymour Simons and Haven Gillespie collaborated on the slap-happy lyric, and Richard A. Whiting wrote the very playful music that sounds more like a merry children's number than a love song. Rudy Vallee introduced and popularized the ballad on the radio and on record, and his disc reached the top of the charts as the sheet music sold over a million copies in the first two years. Other memorable recordings were later made by Hal Kemp, Bob Wilson and his Varsity Rhythm Boys with the Clare Sisters, Frankie Carle, Sammy Kaye, Connee Boswell, Larry Carlton, the Ruby Braff Trio, Sarah Vaughan, the Four Tops, Kay Starr, and Andy Kirk and his Twelve Clouds. "Honey" can be heard in the movie *Her Highness and the Bellboy* (1945).

"Honeysuckle Rose" (1929) is the sassy standard that has long been a favorite of jazz artists but also reached into various other fields as well. Thomas "Fats" Waller wrote the smooth and slightly swinging music that glides up and down the scale, and Andy Razaf penned the admiring lyric that praises a lover with such exaggeration (the honey bees and the flowers are jealous of her sweetness) that the tone is almost mocking. The song was introduced as a dance number in the nightclub revue *Load of Coal* (1929) but started to catch on when Paul Whiteman and his Orchestra played it on the radio. Hundreds of recordings have been made over the years, among them discs by Waller, Mildred Bailey and the Alley Cats, Red Norvo, Fletcher Henderson, Franke Trumbauer, the Dorsey Brothers, Ella Fitzgerald, Bunny Berigan, Coleman Hawkins, Dinah Shore, Benny Goodman, Lena Horne, Morgana King, Willie Humphrey, and Mary Lou Williams. Willie Nelson's 1980 record revived interest in the standard, and he sang it in the film *Honeysuckle Rose* (1980). The number was heard in *The Marrying Man* (1991) and was performed by Betty Grable in *Tin Pan Alley* (1940), Lena Horne in *Thousands Cheer* (1943), Janet Leigh (dubbed by Paula Kelly) in *Walking My Baby Back Home* (1953), and Diahnne Abbott in *New York, New York* (1977). Josephine Premise and Avon Long did a duet version in the Broadway revue *Bubbling Brown Sugar* (1976), Ken Page and Nell Carter did likewise in *Ain't Misbehavin'* (1978), and Christopher Colquhoun sang it in the Off-Broadway play *Slow Drag* (1997).

"Hot Diggity (Dog Ziggity Boom)" (1956) is the catchy novelty number by Al Hoffman and Dick Manning that describes "what'cha do to me" in nonsense words and bombastic onomatopoeia. The songwriters took the basic melody from the first theme of Alexis Chabrier's "Espana, Rhapsody for Orchestra" and added their own Americanisms to make it one of the most familiar tunes of the decade. Perry Como's disc version sold over a million copies, an unlikely hit for the soft-spoken crooner. The Stargazers, Michael Holliday, and Little Johnny Dickens were among the others that recorded the silly song.

"A Hot Time in the Old Town" (1886), a ragtime classic that has questionable authorship, has remained one of the most recognized of American songs. An apocryphal but legendary story behind the number states that bandleader Theodore M. Metz was touring the South with his musicians when the train passed by a group of African Americans furiously trying to put out a fire in Old Town, Louisiana. One of the minstrel singers commented to Metz, "There'll be a hot time in Old Town tonight." Metz wrote a ragtime march to the phrase, and Joe Hayden came up with a lyric that is not literally about a fire but a joyous anticipation of a revival meeting that is guaranteed to set everyone's souls on fire. Some musicologists point out that a very similar melody was being played in a St. Louis nightclub a few years before Metz wrote his, and having traveled across the country quite a bit, it is not too difficult to believe that he heard it there and used it. Dan Quinn introduced the song in a minstrel show, Josephine Sabel popularized it in vaudeville, then the Heath and McIntyre Minstrels made it their trademark number as they paraded through the streets before a performance. The vivacious song was published in 1896, and soon it was sung across the nation, becoming a particular favorite of the Rough Riders during the Spanish-American War (though personally Teddy Roosevelt disliked it, considering it too coarse). The first recording of the march goes back to ragtime singer Lew Spencer's disc in 1897. Prominent records that followed include those by Bessie Smith, Miff Mole, Guy Lombardo, Bing Crosby, Leon Redbone, Mississippi John Hurt, the Dukes of Dixieland, Jo Ann Castle, and Jan and Dean. The song was played at a slow tempo to hilarious effect in the move *Love Me Tonight* (1932), and it can be heard in several other films, such as *The Floradora Girl* (1930), *Broadway to Hollywood* (1933), *San Francisco* (1936), *Flame of the Barbary Coast* (1945), and *Lucky Lady* (1975), where the famous Bessie Smith recording was heard. Linda Hopkins sang it on Broadway in the musical bio *Bessie and Me* (1975), the cast of the Off-Broadway revue *One Mo' Time* (1979) performed it, and it was sung by Lynn Thigpen and the cast of the Broadway revue *Tintypes* (1980). The song is often listed as "There'll Be a Hot Time in the Old Town Tonight."

"The House I Live In (That's America to Me)" (1942) is a patriotic song that flourished during World War Two and managed to hang on after the war ended. Earl Robinson and Lewis Allan wrote the stirring number that praises democracy for all and the country that is willing to fight to protect it. The song is particularly proud of America's diverse population and the acceptance of all kinds of people. Robinson introduced the number in the Works Progress Administration musical revue *Let Freedom Ring* (1942), and it was first recorded by Paul Robeson. Other memorable discs were made by Conrad Thibault, Roy Hamilton, Mike Douglas, Sarah Vaughan, Josh White, and Sonny Rollins, but the biggest seller was one by Frank Sinatra, who also performed it in the Oscar-winning short film *The House I Live In* (1945). It can be heard in the movie *Follow the Boys* (1944), where the Delta Rhythm Boys sang it.

"How Come You Do Me Like You Do?" (1924) is a Roaring Twenties favorite that was well liked in other decades as well. Gene Austin and Roy Bergère wrote the energetic torch song asking why a darling mistreats one "like you do do do." Austin's recording popularized the song, and Marian Harris also had an early hit with it. Dixieland jazz groups kept the song in their repertoire for years; then the song was revived as a vocal when Betty Grable and Jack Lemmon sang it in the movie *Three for the Show* (1955). Records of note were made by Teddi King, Lil Green, Kid Ory's Creole Jazz Band, Viola McCoy, Tommy Dorsey and the Clambake Seven, Cab Calloway, and John Davidson. The number can also he heard in the film *That's the Spirit* (1945), where it was performed by Peggy Ryan and Jimmy Coy.

"How Deep Is the Ocean?" (1932) is the Irving Berlin standard that was not only one of the most popular songs of the decade but is among his most accomplished compositions as well. The ballad has a simple, controlled melody that stays within an octave, has no extension, is not difficult to sing, yet feels as rich and complex as a concert song. Berlin's lyric is a series of questions not easily answered (asking the depth of the ocean, the height of the sky, the distance from earth to a star, and so on); then they are compared to the question of how much one loves another and how many tears would be shed if one lost that love. The short, terse phrases are very direct (there is not one adjective used in the entire lyric), yet few ballads are as emotionally charged. Berlin wrote the torchy number sometime in the 1920s but put it away, thinking it wasn't good enough. He had it published in 1932, and Bing Crosby popularized it with a successful record. There were also early discs by Ethel Merman, Paul Whiteman (vocal by Joan Edwards), Guy Lombardo, and Rudy Vallee. A 1945 hit record by Benny Goodman (vocal by Peggy Lee) brought further acclaim to the perennial favorite. Of the hundreds of recordings over the years, distinctive ones were made by Dick Haymes, Carmen Cavallaro, Ethel Merman, Artie Shaw, Margaret Whiting with Paul Weston's Orchestra, Dinah Shore, Coleman Hawkins, Les Paul and Mary Ford, Frank Sinatra, Rosemary Clooney, Kay Thompson, Skitch Henderson, and more recently, Michael Feinstein, Ann Hampton Callaway, Andrea Marcovicci, and Susannah McCorkle. The song was heard in the movie *Alexander's Ragtime Band* (1938), Crosby reprised it in *Blue Skies* (1946), and Sinatra did the same in *Meet Danny Wilson* (1952).

"How Dry I Am" (1891) was a novelty favorite during Prohibition, but it was written and published back in 1891. Edward F. Rimbault wrote the lazy music, basing it on a hymn of his called "Happy Day." Phillip Dodridge penned the lyric, a list of rhetorical questions regarding one's sobriety. During the 1920s it was sung at parties, adding hiccups between musical phrases, to make fun of the Great Experiment. Later it would be associated with stage and movie drunks who always sang it as they staggered home from a bar or party. Artie Shaw and his Orchestra had a popular recording, and the number was sung in the movie *Roadhouse Nights* (1930).

"How High the Moon" (1940) is a very early "bop" tune that led the way to improvisations and a new style of jazz. Nancy Hamilton wrote the routine lyric about the moon shining bright and music all around because one is in love. But it is Morgan Lewis's innovative music that used chord progressions so unique that they were later copied by bee-bop artists and jazz musicians. The song's unusual harmonic structure so intrigued early improvisationists that Peter Gammond describes the number as "the theme song of the modern jazz movement." The song was introduced by Alfred Drake and Frances Comstock in the Broadway revue *Two for the Show* (1940) but found popularity with a recording by Benny Goodman (vocal by Helen Forrest) that was a bestseller. In 1951 it was revived by Les Paul and Mary Ford, whose disc sold over a million copies. This version was also one of the first to use an electric guitar and multitrack recording. The number has long been associated with Ella Fitzgerald, who recorded it as a scat number (also a bestseller) and as a slow ballad as well. Other memorable discs were also made by Larry Clinton (vocal by Terry Allen), Lionel Hampton, Charlie Parker, Louis Prima, Chet Baker, Louis Armstrong, Jimmie Rivers and the Cherokees, and the Nat King Cole Trio. The Paul-Ford record was heard in the film *My Favorite Year* (1982), and "How High the Moon" was featured in the Off-Broadway revue *Swingtime Canteen* (1995).

"How Long Has This Been Going On?" (1927) is a romantic standard by the Gershwin Brothers that took a while to catch on but became one of their most beloved love songs. Ira Gershwin wrote the poignant and uncluttered lyric about the discovery and wonderment of first love, and George Gershwin composed the quiet, unfussy music. It was written for the Broadway musical *Funny Face* (1927) but was cut before opening. Producer Florenz Ziegfeld heard the number and liked it enough to put it in his show *Rosalie* (1928), where it was sung by Bobbe Arnst. Although there were some recordings made, the number didn't find success until Peggy Lee and Lee Wiley had popular discs decades later. Of the many recordings made, estimable ones were made by Carmen McRae, Mel Tormé, June Christy and the Kentones, Joe Bushkin, Ben Webster, Louis Armstrong with Oscar Peterson, Rosemary Clooney, Eydie Gorme, Lena Horne, Julie Andrews, Ray Charles, Cher, and Ella Fitzgerald, who recorded it six different times. More recently, there have been discs by Karen Akers, Michael Feinstein, Maureen McGovern, and Rebecca Ryan. The number was sung by Audrey Hepburn in the film version of *Funny Face* (1957), and it was heard in *An American in Paris* (1951) and *Round Midnight* (1986). On Broadway the ballad was performed by Tommy Tune and Twiggy in the musical *My One and Only* (1983).

"How Many Times (Have I Said I Love You)?" (1926) is an Irving Berlin ballad that found recognition in vaudeville before dozens of recordings made it a standard. Another series of questions, the romantic number was introduced by Benny Krueger and his Orchestra, but it was Lillian Roth who sang it in variety and launched its success. Noteworthy recordings over the years were made by Sam Lanin, Jay C. Flippen, Ernest Hare and Billy Jones, Vincent Lopez, Dorothy Collins, Bonnie Tucker with Orrin Tucker's Orchestra, and Aretha Franklin. The Brox Sisters sang it in the movie *The Time, the Place and the Girl* (1929), and it was also heard in *Blue Skies* (1946).

"How Ya Gonna Keep 'Em Down on the Farm (After They've Seen Paree)?" (1919) is a novelty number popular after World War One whose title became a familiar catchphrase that is still used today. Walter Donaldson composed the bubbly music, and Sam Lewis and Joe Young wrote the comic lament about the returning doughboys who will find life on the farm pretty dull after having tasted the city life in France. The verse has a clever lyric that takes the form of a conversation between a man and his wife as they disagree on whether their son will be content on the farm after he returns from Europe. The argument leads to the title question and others, such as, "Who the deuce can parlay-vous a cow?" Nora Bayes introduced the ditty on stage and in an early recording, but it was Sophie Tucker who popularized it in vaudeville. It was also a specialty of Eddie Cantor's who recorded it as well. The song faded away with the passing decades even though the title expression did not. A memorable later disc was made by Jimmy Durante. Judy Garland and a quartet sang it in the movie *For Me and My Gal* (1942), it was heard in *Hi, Buddy!* (1943), and Cantor provided the vocal for the number for Keefe Braselle in *The Eddie Cantor Story* (1953).

"A Hundred Years From Today" (1933) is an uptempo but fatalistic song that suggests that one live, love, and enjoy life today because in a hundred years none of your worries or troubles will matter. The potent little ballad by Ned Washington, Joe Young (lyric), and Victor Young (music) was introduced by Kathryn Perry in the revue *Lew Leslie's Blackbirds* (1933), but Ethel Waters made it famous with her recording with Benny Goodman's Orchestra. There were other discs of note by Jack Teagarden, Glen Gray and the Casa Loma Orchestra (vocal by Lee Wiley), Eddy Duchin, June Christy, Frank Sinatra, Sarah Vaughan, Dean Martin, Doris Day, Johnnie Ray, Barbara Carroll, and Tennessee Ernie Ford. The song was used in the films *The Girl From Missouri* (1934) and *Straight Is the Way* (1934), and the popular Teagarden recording was heard in *King of the Hill* (1993).

I

"I Ain't Got Nobody (Much)" (1915) is a bittersweet number by Roger Graham, Dave Peyton (lyric), and Spencer Williams (music) that James R. Morris describes as "one of the first and best" torch songs in American popular music. Both music and lyric are simple, straightforward, and very effective, the double negative in the title phrase making the ballad conversational rather than operatic or flowery as heard in concert songs. The number was popularized by Bessie Smith in clubs and Sophie Tucker in vaudeville, but the song was mostly associated with African American comic Bert Williams, who kept it in his repertory for years. Marion Harris was among the first to record it (she made discs in 1917 and 1921), and many followed, including those by Louis Armstrong, Earl Hines, Bing Crosby, Cab Calloway, Dick Curless, Coleman Hawkins, the Salt City Six, Leon Redbone, Fats Waller, Wingy Manone, Judy Canova, Woody Guthrie, Jimmy Rushing, the Red Garland Trio, Bobby Darin, Tennessee Ernie Ford, and Sammy Davis Jr. The song was revived with a recording by David Lee Roth in 1985. Crosby reprised the ballad with Woody Herman's Woodchoppers in the film *Paris Honeymoon* (1939), the Village People were heard singing it on the soundtrack of *Just a Gigolo* (1979), and it was used in *Scatterbrain* (1940) and *Atlantic City* (1944).

"I Ain't Got Nothin' But the Blues" (1944) is a slangy torch song by Don George (lyric) and Duke Ellington (music) that lists all the things that are missing (money in his pocket, coffee perking on the stove, a bounce in his shoes, a dream that is coming true), but he does have a case of the blues since his honey left him. Ellington and his Orchestra (vocal by Al Hibbler) introduced and popularized the number, and it became a specialty of Lena Horne's. Other memorable discs were made by Joe Williams, Kenny Burrell, Ella Fitzgerald and Joe Pass, Rosemary

Clooney, Ruth Brown, Lena Horne, Rosemary Vitro, the Vamps, Mose Allison, Lou Rawls, and Marlene Ver Planck. Tonya Pinkins sang the ballad in the Broadway musical *Play On!* (1997).

"I Almost Lost My Mind" (1950) is a rhythm-and-blues standard that also enjoyed success as a straightforward pop song and a country-western ballad. Pianist and blues singer Ivory Joe Hunter wrote the sorrowful lament about losing one's sanity while losing one's true love, and he introduced it with a record that was popular on the rhythm-and-blues charts. In 1956 Pat Boone recorded it as a conventional torch number, and the disc sold a million copies. Among the discs made in various fields were those by Nat King Cole, Fats Domino, Hank Snow, Pinetop Perkins, Jimmy Smith, Joni Jones, Ray Bryant, Eddy Arnold, Connie Francis, Bill Haley, Charlie Rich, Conway Twitty, and Barbara Mandrell.

"I Apologize" (1931) is a tearful ballad that Bing Crosby popularized during the depression, and it returned with success in the 1950s. Al Hoffman, Al Goodhart, and Ed Nelson wrote the pleading song of reconciliation, and there were also early records by Kate Smith, Nat Shilkret (vocal by Paul Small), and Phil Spitalny. Billy Eckstine revived it with a popular 1951 record, and there were also discs by Tony Martin, the Dorsey Brothers, Etta Jones, Anita Baker, Timi Yuro, Claude Hopkins, Engelbert Humperdinck, Clyde Terrell, and Jimmy Roselli.

"I Believe" (1952) is a hymnlike number by Al Stillman, Ervin Drake, Irvin Graham, and Jimmy Shirl that was one of the first songs to become a hit through the new medium of television. The music is solemn and fervent, building to a climax like an anthem. The optimistic lyric cites every raindrop falling, flower growing, candle burning, and prayer answered as proof that life is full of hope. Jane Froman introduced the heartfelt number on the television show *USA Canteen* in 1952, and her 1953 disc became a bestseller, keeping the song on *Your Hit Parade* for twenty weeks. Frankie Laine also had a record that went to the top of the charts. The song was also a big seller of sheet music, as many churches and choral groups included the inspirational pieces in their programs. Other records of note were made by Perry Como, Joni James, Lawrence Welk, Dinah Washington, Pat Boone, the Bachelors, Ray Anthony, the Buffalo Bills, Mahalia Jackson, Julius LaRosa, and the Earls.

"I Can Dream, Can't I?" (1938) is a romantic standard that took a while to find acclaim but after a dozen years became a bestseller. Sammy Fain composed the lilting music, and Irving Kahal wrote the resigned lyric in which a forsaken one realizes how hopeless his case is, but still he dreams of the one he loves. The song compares one's dreams to wine and admits that he is drunk on his dreams. The ballad was introduced by Tamara in the Broadway musical *Right This Way* (1938), which closed after fourteen performances, so the song got little attention. Although there were some early records made by Glen Gray and the Casa Loma Orchestra (vocal by Kenny Sargent), Al Bowlly, and Harry James (vocal by Helen Humes), the number did not catch on until 1950 when the Andrews Sisters made a disc that sold a million copies and kept the ballad on the *Hit Parade* for seventeen weeks. Dozens of other recordings followed, including those by Tommy Dorsey, Tex Beneke leading the Glenn Miller Orchestra, Louis Armstrong, Lee Wiley, Bing Crosby, Dinah Shore, Gordon Jenkins, the Skyliners, Joni James, Clifford Brown, and Mama Cass. More recently the ballad has been recorded by Cleo Laine, Michael Feinstein, and Bobby Short.

"I Can't Believe That You're in Love With Me" (1927) is a slightly swinging love song in which an admirer is astonished that someone "far above me" is in love with him; in fact, everyone else is surprised as well. Clarence Gaskill (lyric) and Jimmy McHugh (music) wrote the number for a Cotton Club revue, where it was sung by Aida Ward. But the song didn't find an audience until it was popularized by Roger Wolfe Kahn and his Orchestra. After many years of record and movie appearances, the ballad was revived with a bestselling Ames Brothers record in 1953. Other noteworthy discs were made by Art Pepper, Bing Crosby with Carmen Cavallaro at the piano, Helen Forrest, Billie Holiday, Eddie Condon, Duke Ellington, Frankie Carle, Doc Cheatham, Mindy Carson, Benny Carter, Count Basie (vocal by Joe Williams), Artie Shaw, June Christy, Nat King Cole, Charlie Parker, Vic Damone, Johnny Mathis, and Morgana King. Claudia Drake sang it in the movie *Detour* (1945), it was sung by May Wynn as the theme song for *The Caine Mutiny* (1954), Connie Francis and Danny Thomas performed it in *Looking for Love* (1964), it was heard in *Thoroughly Modern Millie* (1967), and Forest Whitaker played it on the soundtrack of the Parker bio *Bird* (1988).

"I Can't Face the Music (Without Singing the Blues)" (1938) is a torchy ballad by Ted Koehler (lyric) and Rube Bloom (music) that uses a play on words to express the feeling of rejection a jilted lover feels. An early record by Mildred Bailey with Red Norvo's Orchestra popularized the song, and over the years were many other discs, including those by Teddy Wilson (vocal by Nan Wynn), Billie Holiday, Jimmy Dorsey (vocal by Jane Richmond), Dinah Washington, Larry Clinton (vocal by Bea Wain), Oscar Peterson, and Ella Fitzgerald.

"I Can't Give You Anything But Love (Baby)" (1928), one of Tin Pan Alley's most durable standards, is a perfect blending of words and music with a lyric that bounces along on the notes in a way that makes the whole effect seem like dancing. Dorothy Fields wrote the scintillating lyric after observing a poor couple looking into a display window at Tiffany's, the man slyly saying the title line to his Sweetie. Jimmy McHugh composed the nimble music, and the song was introduced as "I Can't Give You Anything But Love, Lindy" (a tribute to Charles Lindbergh's recent transatlantic flying feat) in the revue *Harry Delmar's Revels* (1928), where it was sung by Bert Lahr and Patsy Kelly. The number was cut soon after opening but was interpolated into the all-black revue *Blackbirds of 1928* with the revised title, and when it was performed by Aida Ward, Lois Deppe, and Adelaide Hall, audiences were immediately taken with the song. Early records by Ethel Waters with Duke Ellington's Orchestra, Gene Austin, Cliff Edwards (whose disc was a bestseller), Billie Holiday with Teddy Wilson, and Fats Waller made the number a nationwide hit. Years later, after Waller had died, his son Maurice claimed that his father composed the music and sold it outright to McHugh. The question has never been satisfactorily resolved, but "I Can't Give You Anything But Love" is so close in style and temperament to later Fields-McHugh songs that the claim is very doubtful. Other commendable records over the years include those by Louis Armstrong, Peggy Lee, Connee Boswell, the Benny Goodman Sextet, Bob Wills and his Texas Playboys, Martha Tilton, Eddy Duchin, Louis Prima, and more recently, Barbara Cook, Sally Mayes, and Malcolm Gets. A novelty disc by Rose Murphy in 1948 substituted "Chee-Chee" for "baby," and Murphy's odd, high-pitched version sold a million copies. The song has been used in several films, sung by Katharine Hepburn and Cary Grant to a leopard in *Bringing Up Baby* (1938), Marlene Dietrich in *Seven Sinners* (1940), Allan Jones in *True to the Army* (1942), Armstrong and Lena Horne in *Stormy Weather* (1943), Armstrong again in *Jam Session* (1944), Gloria De Haven (singing it in French) in *So This Is Paris* (1955), and Ann Blyth (dubbed by Gogi Grant) in *The Helen Morgan Story* (1957), as well as *I Can't Give You Anything But Love* (1940) and *The Eddy Duchin Story* (1956). Rudy Vallee was heard singing it on the soundtrack of *The Grissom Gang* (1971), Waters's record was heard in *The Cotton Club* (1984), and a Billie Holiday recording was played in *The Green Mile* (1999). On Broadway the number was performed by Andre DeShields and Charlaine Woodard in *Ain't Misbehavin'* (1978), Ann Miller and Mickey Rooney in *Sugar Babies* (1980), and the cast of *Black and Blue* (1989).

"I Cover the Waterfront" (1933) is a blues standard that almost disappeared before it had a chance to be heard. Johnny Green composed the morose music that gets quite demanding in the release section as it climbs to dramatic heights. Edward Heyman wrote the moving lyric about standing on the dock, gazing out to sea and hoping for a lost love to return. Like the team's earlier "Body and Soul," the song manages to be both sensual and gloomy at the same time. It was written as the musical theme for the movie melodrama *I Cover the Waterfront* (1933), but the studio cut it before the official release. But Ben Bernie and his Orchestra played the theme on the radio, and it was so well liked that the music was added to later prints of the film. An early disc by Eddy Duchin and his Orchestra was popular, but two hit records by Frank Sinatra and Artie Shaw and his Orchestra made the song famous. Of the many memorable recordings over the years were those by Billie Holiday, Annette Hanshaw, Bert Lown, Louis Armstrong, Eddie Heywood, the Ink Spots, Mel Tormé, Will Osborne, Joe Sullivan (vocal by Helen Ward), Bert Kaempfert, Sarah Vaughan, Buddy Rich, Lester Young, Woody Herman, Ruby Braff, Little Anthony and the Imperials, Sammy Davis Jr., Art Tatum, and Sonny Til and the Orioles. The ballad can be heard in the film *They Shoot Horses, Don't They?* (1969).

"I Cried for You (Now It's Your Turn to Cry Over Me)" (1923) is a jazzy song of revenge by Arthur Freed (lyric), Gus Arnheim, and Abe Lyman (music) that remains unemotional and sly in both words and music. The uptempo number announces that one is over the heartbreak of a love affair, and now that he has found "two eyes that are bluer," he suggests his former mistress start weeping for him, as he once did over her. Lyman and his Orchestra introduced the song, but it was a record by Cliff Edwards that popularized the knowing ballad. Bunny Berigan and his Orchestra revived it in 1938, and the next year there was a distinctive record by Glen Gray and the Casa Loma Orchestra with singer Kenny Sargent, one of the first discs in which a male vocalist was featured with a name band. Bing Crosby had success with the song that same year, and it was revived once again in 1942 by Harry James. Other notable discs were made by Billie Holiday, Andy Russell with Paul Weston's Orchestra, Benny Goodman, Zoot Sims, Ella Fitzgerald, Kay Starr, Louis Armstrong, Della Reese, and Connie Francis. On screen it was sung by Judy Garland in *Babes in Arms* (1939), Helen Forrest with James' Orchestra in *Bathing Beauty* (1944), Ralph Meeker (dubbed by Pat Morgan) in *Somebody Loves Me* (1952), Frank Sinatra in *The Joker Is Wild* (1957), and Diana Ross as Holiday in *Lady Sings the Blues* (1972). The number can also be heard on the soundtrack of *Love Me or Leave Me* (1955).

"I Didn't Raise My Boy to Be a Soldier" (1915) was a topical song that expressed the antiwar sentiments that were widespread in America when World War One first broke out in Europe. The potent number by Alfred Bryan (lyric) and Al Piantadosi (music) warned of a million soldiers dying and a million mothers with broken hearts. The sheet music, illustrated with a gray-haired mother embracing her son while bombs exploded all around them, was a big seller, as were early records by Morton Harvey and the Peerless Quartet. But when America later entered the war, the song was either discarded or the lyric was changed to reflect nonpacifist feelings. There were versions called "I Didn't Raise My Boy to Be a Coward" and a ". . . Slacker" and even a ". . . Molliecoddle." A composer named Cohalin brought a plagiarism suit against the songwriters, claiming the melody was his, and he won a considerable settlement.

"I Don't Care" (1903) is a sassy and free-spirited ditty that was Eva Tanguay's signature song throughout her career. Harry O. Sutton composed the bouncy music, and Jean Lenox wrote the sparkling lyric about a gal who admits she may have no sense of decorum and is too independent and happy-go-lucky for her own good, but frankly, she doesn't care what people say. The vibrant lyric includes some playful multisyllabic rhymes, including "effervescing . . . no distressing . . . no oppressing." There are eight different verses and refrains that list her many unconventional ideas, from her hairstyle to her opinion of William Randolph Hearst to her thoughts about the Russia-Japan War. The number was first heard in the Broadway musical *The Blonde in Black* (1903), where it was sung by Blanche Ring, but it didn't catch on until Tanguay interpolated it into the tour of her show *The Sambo Girl* (1905). She recorded it and sang it in vaudeville, concerts, and clubs for decades. Billed as the "I Don't Care Girl," Tanguay became the most popular female entertainer in vaudeville and later was nicknamed "Miss Tobasco" for her repertoire of similarly spicy songs. "I Don't Care" was revived years later when Judy Garland performed it in the movie *In the Good Old Summertime* (1949), and Mitzi Gaynor sang it in the Tanguay bio *The I-Don't-Care Girl* (1953). Among those who recorded the novelty song were Garland, Eartha Kitt, Webb Pierce, Johnny Otis, and Eydie Gorme. The ditty was also sung by the cast of the Broadway revue *Tintypes* (1980).

"I Don't Care If the Sun Don't Shine" (1949) is a peppy, freewheeling number claiming that the lack of sunshine cannot dampen one's spirits when you have "lovin' in the evening time." Mack David wrote the uptempo song, and it was popularized by a bestselling record by Patti Page. Elvis Presley revived it with success in 1956, and there were also accomplished discs by Louis Prima, Tommy Dorsey, John Layton, Jack Mudurian, and Eddie Fisher. Dean Martin sang it with the chorus in the movie *Scared Stiff* (1953), and the Page recording was heard in *The Adventures of Priscilla, Queen of the Desert* (1994).

"I Don't Know Why (I Just Do)" (1931) is the uncomplicated observation of a devotee who is unable to explain the reasons why he loves his sweetheart. Roy Turk (lyric) and Fred E. Ahlert (music) wrote the simple ballad, and it was introduced by Russ Columbo in clubs and on records. But it was Wayne King and his Orchestra who popularized the number, and Tommy Dorsey and his Orchestra revived it in 1946. Among the many who recorded the song were Stan Getz, Benny Goodman, Roy Eldridge and Dizzy Gillespie, Lillian Roth, Nat King Cole, Frank Sinatra, Dean Martin, Bud Freeman, Tony Martin, Tommy Sands, Max Bygraves, and more recently, Bernadette Peters, John Pizzarelli, and Kathy Lee Gifford. The ballad can also be heard in the movies *Faithful in My Fashion* (1946) and *Young Man With Ideas* (1952).

"I Don't Want to Play in Your Yard" (1894) is a children's ditty that was popular with adult singers as a novelty number in clubs and later on records. H.W. Petrie wrote the simple melody consisting of rising and falling scales, and Philip Wingate penned the petulant lyric in which two little girls, best friends who tell each other all their secrets, have a quarrel, and one threatens the other that she will not be invited to play in her yard. The other responds with the title phrase and plainly states, "I don't like you anymore" and "You'll be sorry when you see me sliding down my cellar door." The number was widely popular (sheet music sales stayed healthy for years), but a song sequel titled "You Can't Play in Our Yard Any More" was a flop. Peggy Lee, Kate Dimbleby, William Bolcomb and Joan Morris, and Lida Husik made recordings of the ditty. James Cagney sang it in the movie *The Oklahoma Kid* (1939), and it was used effectively as a leitmotiv in *Reds* (1981) with a vocal by Heaton Vorse.

"I Don't Want to Set the World on Fire" (1941) is the soulful declaration of love that hopes to "start a flame in your heart" rather than impress the whole world. Eddie Seiler, Sol Marcus, Bennie Benjamin, and Ed Durham collaborated on the number, but it took three years before they could interest anyone in publishing it. Harlan Leonard and his Kansas City Rockets introduced the song on record, and the Ink Spots made it famous, their hit record helping to keep the song on *Your Hit Parade* for fifteen weeks. Dozens of artists also recorded it, including Horace Heidt (vocal by Larry Cotton), the Mills Brothers, Steve Gibson, Harry James, Tommy Tucker (vocal by Ann Arnell), Nat Brandwynne, Donna Wood and the Don Juans, Vera Lynn, the Platters, Guy Lombardo, Dick Todd, Patti Page, Eddy Arnold, Ozzie Nelson, Frankie Laine, Les Elgart, Betty Carter, and Susannah McCorkle. The number was used in the British film *Passport to Pimlico* (1949), and the celebrated Ink Spots recording was heard in *How to Make an American Quilt* (1995).

"I Double Dare You" (1937) is a swinging song of seduction in which an amorist dares one to come close, kiss him, and fall in love. Jimmy

Eaton wrote the sassy, playful lyric, and Terry Shand composed the tuneful, breezy music. The song was introduced and popularized by Freddy Martin and his Orchestra (vocal by Shand), but it was Louis Armstrong who had the biggest hit with the number. Successful discs by the orchestras of Russ Morgan and Larry Clinton also helped keep the song on the *Hit Parade* for twelve weeks. Other records of note include those by Freddy Gardner, Bill Coleman, Woody Herman, the M 'n' M Trio, Brian White's Magna Jazz Band, Rick Fay, Victor Sylvester, and more recently, Weslia Whitfield. The Clinton recording was heard in the movie *Radio Days* (1987).

"I Dream of You (More Than You Dream I Do)" (1944) was a giant hit for Tommy Dorsey (vocal by Freddy Stewart), selling over a million records, and was nearly as successful for Frank Sinatra, Andy Russel, and Perry Como. The romantic fox trot by Marjorie Goetschius and Edna Osser tries to explain to a beloved how much she means to him, playing with words (as in the long title) and lamenting that he's "mean to me" more than "you mean to be." Bing Crosby, Ted Heath, Glenn Miller, Count Basie with Thelma Carpenter, Nat King Cole, Ronnie Heyward, and Jerry Vale were among the many who also recorded it.

"I Faw Down and Go Boom!" (1928), a childish nonsense song that uses baby talk, was a specialty number for Eddie Cantor, who sang it in clubs and on records. James Brockman, Leonard Stevens, and B.B. Donald wrote the silly ditty, and it was also recorded with success by George Olsen and his Orchestra, Fred Hall, and Annette Hanshaw.

"I Found a New Baby" (1926) is the renowned jazz standard that has been interpreted by dozens of artists yet always seems innovative and new. Jack Palmer and Spencer Williams wrote the slick declaration of new love, and it found its way into the repertoire of nearly every jazz band. There were also memorable vocal versions by such artists as Josephine Baker, Nat King Cole, and the Mills Brothers. Other recordings over the years were made by the Chicago Rhythm Kings, Isham Jones, McKinney's Cotton Pickers, Frankie Trumbauer, the New Orleans Feetwarmers with Sidney Bechet, Bud Freeman, Jack Teagarden, Bobby Hackett, Ted Heath, Wild Bill Davison, Harry James, Benny Goodman's Sextet, Lionel Hampton, Erskine Hawkins, Charlie Christian, and Stephane Grappelli. The number, which is often listed as "I've Found a New Baby," was featured in the movie *Sweet and Lowdown* (1944).

"I Get Along Without You Very Well (Except Sometimes)" (1939), a poignant ballad by Jane Brown Thompson (lyric) and Hoagy Carmichael (music), has an interesting and ironic history. When Carmichael was in college, a fellow student gave him a poem to set to music. He composed a melody but put both words and music away and didn't run across them until several years went by. Carmichael wanted to publish and record the song, but he couldn't remember who the lyricist was. So he had the celebrated columnist Walter Winchell read the lyric on the radio, asking for the author to come forward. Forty-eight people claimed to be the lyricist, all of them fakes. But someone recognized the lines and found out that they had been printed years before in *Life* magazine. Through the periodical Carmichael was able to locate the lyricist Thompson living in Philadelphia. In 1940 the song was introduced on Tommy Dorsey's radio show by Dick Powell, but sadly Thompson had died the day before and never heard her words sung. Carmichael's music is atypical of his work, using repeated notes in an intriguing way. The song is also unusually long (sixty-four measures) for a Tin Pan Alley composition. Thompson's lyric is delicate and affecting, claiming to have forgotten a lost love but listing the many things (rain dripping from the roof, a particular laugh heard in the distance, the coming of spring) that remind her of him. "I Get Along Without You Very Well" was popularized through recordings by Dorsey, Red Norvo (vocal by Terry Allen), and Larry Clinton (vocal by Bea Wain). The ballad was revived when Jane Russell sang it in the film *The Las Vegas Story* (1952), and Karen Chandler made it popular again with a 1967 recording. Other prominent discs were made by Mel Tormé, Frank Sinatra, Stan Kenton, Dick Haymes, Eileen Farrell, Maxine Sullivan, Rosemary Clooney, Anita Kerr, Chet Baker, the King Sisters, Petula Clark, and more recently, Carly Simon, Tom Woppat, Linda Ronstadt, Diana Krall, and Carol Merrill.

"I Got a Code in My Doze" (1929) is a novelty number by Arthur Fields, Billy Rose, and Fred Hall that is written in a nasal dialect to add to the comedy. The patient suffering from the flu complains that he can't sleep, doesn't know what medicine to try next, and even laments that his doctor has died. Fields introduced the comic number with Hall's Sugar Babies on record, and it was a favorite party song in its day. The ditty resurfaced when Barbra Streisand sang it in the film *Funny Lady* (1975).

"I Got It Bad (And That Ain't Good)" (1941) is the jazz standard that became a vocal as well as an instrumental favorite even though the demanding music is very difficult to sing accurately. Paul Francis Webster wrote the nimble lyric about having a wild weekend, then sobering up on Monday, realizing once again that a true love has gone and one is left "crying my heart out." Duke Ellington and Edward Kennedy collaborated on the tricky music in which the melody wavers and soars more like a solo instrument than a vocal line. Ivie Anderson introduced the ballad in the California revue *Jump for Joy* (1941), but it was her record with Ellington's Orchestra that brought recognition to the song and the disc became a jazz classic. Other early outstanding records were made by Benny Goodman (vocal by Peggy Lee) and Ella Fitzgerald. The number was heard in the movie *This Could Be the Night* (1957), and a recording by the Oscar Peterson Trio was used on the soundtrack of *Eyes Wide Shut* (1999). On Broadway it was sung by Ethel Beatty in *Bubbling Brown Sugar* (1976), Phyllis Hyman in *Sophisticated Ladies* (1981), and Carl Anderson and Cheryl Freeman in *Play On!* (1997). Among the many other recordings made were those by Rosemary Clooney, Louis Prima, Earl Hines, Doris Day, Ernie Andrews, Roy Lanham and the Whippoorwills, Joe Williams, Don Friedman, Guy Van Duser, Elisabeth Welch, and Nina Simone.

"I Gotta Right to Sing the Blues" (1932) is a jazzy torch song that uses elements of a blues ballad in an intriguing way. Harold Arlen composed the innovative music that contains plenty of "blue" notes that make it a favorite of jazz improvisers. Ted Koehler wrote the potent lyric about a woman who, deceived by her beau, feels justified in her melancholy. The words and music blend eloquently throughout, especially in the section where the notes cascade downward on the lyric "down around the river." The song was interpolated into the Broadway revue *Earl Carroll's Vanities of 1932*, where it was performed by Lillian Shade, but it didn't catch on until early records were made by Louis Armstrong, Cab Calloway, and Benny Goodman (trombone solo by Jack Teagarden). When Teagarden formed his own band seven years later, he adopted the ballad as his theme song. Other commendable discs were made by Lena Horne, Art Tatum, Billie Holiday, Ethel Merman, Frank Sinatra, Carol Bruce, Barbara Lea, Fran Warren, Dorothy Lamour, and K.T. Sullivan. The torchy number was used in the movie *Stallion Road* (1947), and on Broadway it was sung by Constance Moore in *Earl Carroll's Sketchbook* (1946) and by the cast of *Blues in the Night* (1982).

"I Guess I'll Have to Dream the Rest" (1941) is a tender ballad by Mickey Stoner, Martin Block (lyric), and Harold Green (music) about a rejected lover who agrees to part from his idol but plans to continue dreaming about their discarded plans alone. The gentle fox trot was popularized by two records: Glenn Miller (vocal by Ray Eberly and the Modernaires) and Tommy Dorsey (vocal by Frank Sinatra and the Pied Pipers). Harry James, Les Brown with Ralph Young, Tony Martin, Sammy Kaye, Blue Barron, and Dick Haymes were among those who recorded it later.

"I Haven't Got a Worry in the World" (1946) is one of the very few songs that Richard Rodgers and Oscar Hammerstein wrote that wasn't for a musical play or movie. The songwriters were also Broadway producers, and when they presented Anita Loos's comedy *Happy Birthday* (1946) they needed a number for the inebriated Helen Hayes to sing. The merry, carefree number was later recorded by Frances Langford, Hildegarde, and Percy Faith and was popular for a time.

"I Hear You Calling Me" (1908) is a hymnlike ballad by Harold Harford (lyric) and Charles Marshall (music) that moved from the concert hall to Tin Pan Alley. The solemn number about the memory of the call of love was most associated with Irish tenor John McCormack, who made a popular recording in 1927, sang it in concert for years, and reprised it in the movie *Song o' My Heart* (1930). The Irish-flavored song was also recorded by Lucrezia Bori, Richard Tauber, Robert White, Maura O'Connell, the Cliff Adams Singers, and Jonathan Richman.

"I Just Couldn't Take It, Baby" (1934) is the jazzy excuse for having the blues that Mann Holiner (lyric) and Alberta Nichols (music) wrote for the revue *Lew Leslie's Blackbirds* (1934), where it was introduced by Gretchen Branch, Phil Scott, Kathryn Perry, and Eloise Uggams with the Duncan Sisters. Successful records by Ethel Waters with Benny Goodman's Orchestra, Jack Teagarden, and Eddy Duchin brought acclaim to the number, and there were also notable discs by Lionel Hampton, Hal Kemp, Keith Ingham, and Frances Wayne with Neal Hefti's Band.

"I Kiss Your Hand, Madame" (1929) is a popular German ballad by Fritz Rotter (German lyric) and Ralph Erwin (music) about an admirer who longs to kiss the fingertips and capture the heart of the girl he adores. Sam M. Lewis and Joe Young wrote an English lyric, and it was introduced in the States by Rudy Vallee on the radio. Bing Crosby made a record (it was only his second solo release) that brought attention to both the song and the singer. Lanny Ross also had success with it and later made it the theme song for his radio show in the 1930s. Other records were made by Paul Whiteman, Ray McKinley, Donald Novis, Jack Smith, Louis Prima, Merv Griffin, Perry Como, and Tony Martin and a spoof version by Spike Jones and his City Slickers. Crosby reprised it in the movie *The Emperor Waltz* (1948), it was used in *Baby Face* (1933) and *So This Is Love* (1953), and a recording by the Manhattan Transfer was heard in *Just a Gigolo* (1979).

"I Know That You Know" (1926) is a contagious rhythm song that expresses confidence and the knowledge that the one he loves knows it and is willing to return the affection. Anne Caldwell's spirited lyric is matched by Vincent Youmans's sparkling music that uses repeated notes and enticing chord changes. The rousing number was introduced on Broadway where Beatrice Lillie and Charles Purcell sang it in *Oh, Please!* (1926), but it became more popular when Jack Oakie and Polly Walker performed it in the early film musical *Hit the Deck* (1930). Vic Damone and Jane Powell did the duet in the 1955 remake of *Hit the Deck*, it was used in *The Powers Girl* (1943), and Doris Day sang it in *Tea for Two* (1950). Of the hundreds of recordings over the years, Benny Goodman's 1936 disc and one by Nat King Cole in the 1950s were the most celebrated. Other discs were made by Art Tatum, Lester Young, Teddy Wilson, Buster Bailey, Lionel Hampton, Jimmie Noone, Roger Williams, Joe Harnell, Django Reinhardt, and Joe Marsala.

"I Left My Heart in San Francisco" (1954) will forever be associated with Tony Bennett, but the song had a long and troubled history before he made it the standard it is today. In the mid-1940s Douglass Cross wrote a passionate and rather verbose lyric about love in the California city, and George Cory set it to a plaintive but effective melody. No one was interested in the number, and it was not introduced until 1954 by Claramae Turner, never getting much attention. Cross revised his lyric when Bennett asked for a new song that might be appropriate for a San Francisco nightclub engagement. The new lyric lists the aspects of the city (cable cars, the morning fog, the "blue and windy sea") that he loves and climaxes with the knowledge that his love waits for him there. Bennett sang it at the Fairmont Hotel, it met with immediate success, and he and the song have never parted company. The record sold over 3 million copies, Bennett adopted it as his theme song, and the number single-handedly allowed him to resurrect his career and become a crooning star in a time when rock-and-roll was taking over the music industry. Many other artists have also recorded the ballad, including Kate Smith, Louis Armstrong, Judy Garland, Carmen McRae, Frank Sinatra, Andy Williams, Aker Bilk, Count Basie, Roger Williams, Red Garland, Jack Jones, Jerry Vale, the Four Tops, and Wayne Newton. Luciano Pavarotti sang it in the movie *Yes, Giorgio* (1982), and it was heard in *Hard to Hold* (1984).

"I Love a Piano" (1915), one of Irving Berlin's first and best ragtime songs, is a masterwork of ragging words as well as music. The witty number uses the piano as a metaphor for a lovely woman, the keyboard fingered sensually and the pedals fondled as in lovemaking. "Ivories" and "o'er the keys" are ragged, and even the word "piano" is turned into a two-syllable expression at times. Berlin's music is very syncopated (the title phrase is sung as though one is ragging the notes on an instrument), and the descending scale spelling out "p-i-a-n-oh-oh-oh" is unforgettable. The vibrant song was introduced in the Broadway musical *Stop! Look! Listen!* (1915), where it was sung by Harry Fox and the chorus, but it took awhile for the number to catch on. Billy Murray made a noteworthy record in 1915, and Arthur Schutt had a hit with his 1934 disc. "I Love a Piano" was revived when Judy Garland and Fred Astaire sang it in the movie *Easter Parade* (1948), and years later it was performed by the cast of the Broadway revue *Fosse* (1999). Among the many who also made records were Garland, Benny Goodman, Tony Bennett, Blossom Seeley, Barbara Carroll, André Previn, Charles Aznavour and Liza Minnelli, Betty Johnson, Peter Allen, Dorothy Loudon, William Bolcomb and Joan Morris, and more recently, Michael Feinstein and Barbara Cook.

"I Love You Truly" (1901), a wedding favorite for many decades, is the most famous song by Carrie Jacobs Bond, an extremely successful songwriter (one of the most prosperous women in the history of Tin Pan Alley) who wrote, published, promoted, and performed her own work. The brief, simple ballad about mutual love that will help a couple get through "life with its sorrow, life with its tears" was written as a concert piece and was published in a book of art songs in 1901. But when Elsie Baker introduced it in vaudeville in 1906, the number was published as an individual song, and it sold over 1 million copies. Somewhere along the way it became a staple of wedding dances, usually played for the first dance by the bride and groom. The straightforward lyric and the steady fox trot music (Bond calls for "andante con amore" in the sheet music) made the number one of the most beloved love songs of the century, becoming something of a cliché in later years. Hundreds of recordings were made, among them ones by Bing Crosby, Wayne King, Guy Lombardo, Fred Lowery (who whistled it), Phil Spitalny (vocal by "Evelyn and her magic violin"), the Ink Spots, Perry Como, Ray Noble, Helen Traubel, Louis Prima, Ray Anthony, Ace O'Donnell, Jesse Crawford, Connie Francis, the Platters, Lawrence Welk, Allan Jones, and the Firehouse Five Plus Two.

"I May Be Wrong (But I Think You're Wonderful)" (1929) is a bright and snappy love song about a guy who cannot pick a winning number at roulette or choose the right tie to wear but nevertheless has sought out the ideal girl. Harry Ruskin (lyric) and Henry Sullivan (music) wrote the agile number for the Broadway revue *John Murray Anderson's Almanac* (1929), where it was performed by Jimmy Savo and Trixie Friganza. The song was later featured in a handful of films, sung by Dan Dailey in *You're My Everything* (1949), Doris Day in *Young Man With a Horn* (1950), Frankie Laine in *Sunny Side of the Street* (1951), and Jane Wyman in *Starlift* (1951) and heard in *Swingtime Johnny* (1943) and *Wallflower* (1948). Laine's recording was popular, and there were other major discs by Judy Garland, Red Nichols, Charlie Parker, Buddy Rich, the King Sisters, Coleman Hawkins, June Christy, and Dinah Shore, as well as boogie-woogie versions by Stan Kenton and Count Basie.

"I Never Knew I Could Love Anybody (Like I'm Loving You)" (1920), one of the first records made by Paul Whiteman and his Orchestra, is a heartfelt ballad in which a lover is surprised at how deeply he has fallen in love, unable to eat or sleep because he is so preoccupied with her. Whiteman wrote the number with Tom Pitts, Raymond B. Egan, and Roy Marsh, and it helped launch his band's long and influential career. Other laudable records were made by Eddie Cantor, Sonny Til and the Orioles, Eddie Condon, Judy Garland, Don Goldie, Louis Prima, and Tennessee Ernie Ford, and the song was heard in the movies *The Great American Broadcast* (1941), *Strictly in the Groove* (1942), *Honeymoon Lodge* (1943), *Cruisin' Down the River* (1953), and *Pete Kelly's Blues* (1955).

"I Saw Mommy Kissing Santa Claus" (1952) is the highly popular novelty song by Tommie Connor that is an unusual Christmas favorite. The droll lyric takes the point of view of a youngster who sneaks out of his bedroom on Christmas Eve and sees his mother kiss Santa under the mistletoe and tickle him under his beard. The boy's comment that his daddy sure would have been surprised to see such a sight is all part of the naive charm of the song. A record by thirteen-year-old Jimmy Boyd went to the top of the charts and sold nearly 3 million copies, and there were many other discs by child singers and youth choirs. Noteworthy records were made by Perry Como, the Beverley Sisters, Andy Williams, Molly Bee, Mitch Miller, Andy Cooney, the Four Seasons, Bobby Sherman, Tiny Tim, the Jackson Five, and the Carpenters and a parody version by Spike Jones and his City Slickers (vocal by George Rock).

"I Surrender, Dear" (1930) is the song that launched Bing Crosby's career. The crooning ballad by Gordon Clifford (lyric) and Harry Barris (music) is a no-holds-barred capitulation by a devotee to the woman he loves, and it was tailor-made for Crosby's intimate singing style. He introduced the song at the Coconut Grove in Los Angeles with the Rhythm Boys and Gus Arnheim's Orchestra, which led to a movie short called *I Surrender, Dear* (1931). CBS president William S. Paley saw Crosby in the short and signed him to a radio contract. Later the same year Crosby's record caught on, and his remarkable and long-lasting popularity began. Kate Smith sang the ballad on her first radio broadcast as well. Benny Carter's trumpet solo of the song is considered a jazz classic, and there were other memorable recordings by Louis Armstrong, Earl Burnett, Red Ingle, Dick Haymes, Stan Kenton, Harry James, Chet

Atkins, Gordon MacRae, Wild Bill Davison, Artie Shaw, Ben Webster, Joe Venuti with Zoot Sims, and Les Brown. The gentle ballad can be heard in the films *College Humor* (1933), *Sweetheart of the Fleet* (1942), *I Surrender, Dear* (1948), and *Battleground* (1949).

"I Used to Love You But It's All Over Now" (1920) is a driving rhythm song that uses a lively harmony rather than a sorrowful tone to bid farewell to an unfaithful lover. Lew Brown (lyric) and Albert Von Tilzer (music) wrote the number, and it was popularized by a record by Frank Crumit. Other significant discs over the years were made by the Peerless Quartet, Bob Wilson and his Varsity Rhythm Boys (vocals by the Clare Sisters), Bing Crosby, Cliff Edwards, Louis Armstrong, Bob Howard, Jimmie Lunceford, and Nat King Cole.

"I Walk the Line" (1956) is the plaintive ballad by Johnny Cash about behaving himself and staying in line because "you're mine." It was Cash's first hit record, and he sang it throughout his long career, including on the soundtrack of the movie *I Walk the Line* (1970). Don Costa and his Orchestra revived the ballad in 1959, and Jay P. Morgan had a hit with it in 1960. Other artists who recorded it include Burl Ives, Hoyt Axton, the Carter Family, Dick Curless, Dean Martin, the Everly Brothers, Flatt and Scruggs, the Ray Conniff Singers, Shelby Lynne, and Dolly Parton.

"I Wanna Be Loved By You" (1928) is the baby-talk standard that could only have been written and embraced in the Roaring Twenties, yet it is still familiar to audiences today. Bert Kalmar (lyric), Harry Ruby, and Herbert Stothard (music) wrote the coy number for the squeaky-voiced Helen Kane (the "boop-a-doop girl") who sang it with Dan Healy in the Broadway musical *Good Boy* (1928), and it became her signature song. The simple ditty proclaiming affection for "you and nobody else but you" is rather sly and sexy as it remains very juvenile as well. Kane's recording is the most famous, but there were also discs by Lee Wiley, Annette Hanshaw, Ray Anthony, Rose Murphy, Barney Kessel, and Marilyn Monroe, who sang it seductively in the movie *Some Like It Hot* (1959). Other performances on film were made by Carlton Carpenter and Debbie Reynolds (dubbed by Kane) in *Three Little Words* (1950), Jane Russell, Rudy Vallee, and Jeanne Crain (dubbed by Anita Ellis) in *Gentlemen Marry Brunettes* (1955), Ann-Margaret in *The Swinger* (1966), and Jane Horrocks in *Little Voice* (1998).

"I Want a Girl (Just Like the Girl That Married Dear Old Dad)" (1914) is one of Tin Pan Alley's most successful "mother songs" and a longtime favorite of barbershop quartets as well. Will Dillon (lyric) and Harry Von

Tilzer (music) wrote the unabashedly sentimental ballad that yearns for an old-fashioned girl with a true heart. Al Jolson, who had success with several mother songs throughout his career, made this one of his specialties, recorded it, and he sang it on the soundtrack for Larry Parks in the film *The Jolson Story* (1946). The number was also heard in *Tin Pan Alley* (1940), *Guadacanal Diary* (1943), and *Show Business* (1944), where it was performed by Eddie Cantor, George Murphy, Constance Moore, and Joan Davis. Recordings of note were made by Frankie Carle, Bob Schulz and his Frisco Jazz Band, Norrie Cox, Jesse Fuller, the Firehouse Five Plus Two, the Hoosier Hot Shots, the Four Lovers, and Jimmy Roselli.

"I Want My Mama (Mama Yo Quiero)" (1940) is the zesty Portuguese number long associated with Carmen Miranda, both of them coming from Brazil and taking America by storm. Jararaca and Vincente Paiva wrote "Mamae Eu Quero," a lively salute to motherhood with a rhumba beat. Al Stillman wrote the English lyric (with some Spanish phrases inserted), and it was introduced in the Broadway revue *Earl Carroll Vanities* (1940). But it was Miranda who popularized it, singing the number on records, in concerts, on the radio, and in the film *Down Argentine Way* (1940). Mickey Rooney dressed as Miranda and sang it in *Babes on Broadway* (1942), and Jerry Lewis mimed it to the Miranda recording in *Scared Stiff* (1953). The vivacious song was also played by Chico and Harpo Marx on the piano in *The Big Store* (1941), was sung and danced by Harold Nicholas in *Reckless Age* (1944), and was heard on the soundtrack of *Ladies' Man* (1947). Bob Wills, Bing Crosby, Georgie Auld, the Andrews Sisters, Nat Gonella and his New Georgians, Xavier Cugat, and Edmundo Ros and his Rhumba Band were among the many who also recorded it. The number, sometimes listed as "Mama Yo Quiero," has often been spoofed, most recently by the cast of the Off-Broadway revue *Forbidden Hollywood* (1995).

"I Wish I Could Shimmy Like My Sister Kate" (1919) is a Roaring Twenties dance song that managed to survive long after the "shimmy" disappeared from view. Armand Piron wrote the spirited number that envies a younger sister because when she dances the shimmy, gyrating like jello on a plate, all the boys are entranced. The song (and the dance) go back to the late 1910s, but the number was not popular until 1922 when Gilda Gray, Ann Pennington, Bee Palmer, and other dancing favorites started performing it in vaudeville. Early recordings by the Virginians and Harry Reser and his Orchestra helped popularize both the dance and the song. It also became a favorite of jazz instrumentalists in the 1930s and 1940s. The ditty was revived in 1952 with a disc by the Mary Kay Trio that went to the top of the charts. There were other records by Fats Waller, Bobby Hackett, Kid Ory's Creole Jazz Band, Eva

Taylor, the Vagabonds, Fletcher Henderson, Pete Fountain, George Wettling, Marty Grosz, Eddie Condon, the Korn Kobblers, and Clyde McCoy. Betty Grable performed the song in the movie *Wabash Avenue* (1950), Kathryn Grayson sang it in *So This Is Love* (1953), and it was heard in *The Girl Can't Help It* (1956).

"I Wish I Had a Girl" (1908) is an outspoken, unadorned plea for companionship sung by a single soul who envies all the other fellows who have sweethearts. The straightforward ballad was written by Gus Kahn (lyric) and Grace Le Boy (music) and was introduced in burlesque by Mollie Williams. It was Kahn's first published song and the beginning of one of the most prodigious careers in Tin Pan Alley history. Doris Day and Danny Thomas sang it in the Kahn movie bio *I'll See You in My Dreams* (1952), and it was recorded by Day, Al Jolson, and others.

"I Wonder What's Become of Sally" (1924) is a sentimental waltz more reminiscent of the 1890s rather than the Roaring Twenties, yet it was very popular for a while. Milton Ager wrote the gently moving music, and Jack Yellen penned the teary lyric about missing the former neighborhood girl Sally who went off and probably got into trouble in the big city. The admirer mourns her loss and suggests that "if no one wants her now, please send her home to me." The number was a sequel of sorts to a well-known *Follies* song called "Sally, Won't You Come Home," but the new number eclipsed the former one. It was introduced by Gus Van and Joe Schenck at the Palace Theatre; then it became a familiar staple throughout vaudeville. Al Jolson popularized it further on stage and records, a disc by Ted Lewis was also successful, and eventually it sold over a million copies of sheet music. Other prominent recordings were made by Bennie Krueger's Band, Percy Humphrey, Ray Anthony, Dick Haymes, Charlie Spivak, and Perry Como. The ballad was heard in the film *Merry-Go-Round of 1938* (1937) and Ginny Simms sang it in *Night and Day* (1946).

"I Wonder Who's Kissing Her Now" (1909), one of the most popular songs in the history of Tin Pan Alley, remained a favorite for decades and sold over 3 million copies of sheet music. Considered a sentimental cliché today, the number entranced audiences with its flowing music and heartbreaking lyric, making it one of the first conversational and down-to-earth torch song hits. Songwriter-performer Joe E. Howard got the idea for the song when he was in Chicago and he heard a college student say the title phrase to a fellow student. Howard composed the melody and got Will H. Hough and Frank R. Adams to write the lyric, the wistful reflection of a rejected beau about what lies his former honey is telling, who is buying her wine, and whose lips are kissing hers. Henry Woodruff introduced the song in Chicago in the musical *The Prince of Tonight* (1909); then it was interpolated into *Miss Nobody From Starland* (1910) in Milwaukee. But no one had more success with it than Howard himself; it became his signature number, and he sang it in public appearances for fifty years. It was not until 1947 that Harold Orlob, a musical arranger for Howard, came forth and claimed authorship of the music. He sued Howard and won, receiving no money but having his name added to the sheet music credits. Henry Burr made an early recording of the number, and Perry Como revived it in 1947 with Ted Weems' Orchestra. Of the many other discs over the years, memorable ones were made by Wayne King, Fred Froeba, Dick Haymes, the Dinning Sisters, Frank Sinatra, Jimmie Davis, Emile Ford and the Checkmates, Tennessee Ernie Ford, Danny Kaye and the Ken Darby Singers, Bobby Darin, and Ray Charles. Cliff Edwards sang it in the movie *Red Salute* (1935), Mark Stevens (dubbed by Buddy Clark) performed it in the Howard bio *I Wonder Who's Kissing Her Now* (1947), and it was heard in *The Time, the Place and the Girl* (1929) and *Moonlight in Havana* (1942).

"Ice Cream" (1927) is a daffy novelty number by Howard Johnson, Billy Moll, and Robert A. King that is more familiarly known by its shouting subtitle "I Scream, You Scream, We All Scream for Ice Cream." The lyric describes Oogie-wawa College up north "among the Eskimo" where the boys sing this silly and enthusiastic tribute to their favorite dairy product. The ditty was popularized by Fred Waring's Pennsylvanians (featured vocals by Waring and Poley McClintock) and soon became a familiar standard in children's records and songbooks. Other enjoyable recordings were made by George Lewis and his Ragtime Band, the Dixie Stompers, Terry Lightfoot, Percy Humphrey and his Maryland Jazz Band, Lightnin' Hopkins, and the Preservation Hall Jazz Band.

"Ida, Sweet as Apple Cider" (1903) is a catchy little ditty most associated with Eddie Cantor, who performed it in vaudeville as a child and continued to sing it on the radio, in concert, and on records for much of his long career. Minstrel singer Eddie Leonard wrote the tuneful music under unusual conditions. The manager of the minstrel troupe was going to fire Leonard, so he composed the melody, had Eddie Munson write the slaphappy lyric, and he sang it on stage instead of his assigned song. It went over so well with the audience that Leonard not only kept his job, but he took the song with him when he moved up to vaudeville and performed it there for years. He also interpolated the number into the Broadway musical *Roly Boly Eyes* (1919), where he sang it to Queenie Smith. The soft-shoe number has sprightly music that adapts itself to various styles of dance, and Munson's lyric uses arch rhymes ("Ida . . . cider . . . idolize yer") as it pays tribute to a girl back home. After Cantor married a woman named Ida, he turned the song into a tribute of his own, and the number he had sung as a kid rejoined his repertoire. Of the many recordings, the most popular was a disc by Red Nichols and his Five Pennies that sold over a million copies. Other major records were made by Al Jolson, Benny Goodman, Ray Anthony, Frank Sinatra, Glenn Miller, Bing Crosby, the Mills Brothers, Blue Barron, Tex Beneke, and more recently, Lee Newman and Johnny Varro. Mickey Rooney performed it in the film *Babes in Arms* (1939), Kenny Bowers sang it in *Broadway Rhythm* (1944), Cantor provided the vocal for Keefe Braselle in *The Eddie Cantor Story* (1953), and it was heard in *If I Had My Way* (1940) and *Incendiary Blonde* (1945).

"If I Could Be With You (One Hour Tonight)" (1930) is a short (sixteen measures), economic, yet very effective ballad by Henry Creamer (lyric) and James P. Johnson (music) in which a swain regrets letting his beloved go out of his life, dreaming about how much he would love her if she was back with him again. The swinging lament was introduced by Lillian Roth in the quickly forgotten movie *Ladies They Talk About* (1933), but records by Louis Armstrong, Ruth Etting, and McKinney's Cotton Pickers (who made it their theme song) popularized it. Over the years the number became a favorite of jazz musicians because of its tightly packed melody and intriguing possibilities for improvisation. Among the many artists who recorded it were Benny Goodman, Eva Taylor, Maurice Chevalier, Earl Hines, Sidney Bechet, Helen Humes, Count Basie, Doris Day, Kay Starr, Mark Murphy, Nat King Cole, the Buffalo Bills, Jack Teagarden, and Tony Bennett. The song served as the theme song (and was briefly sung by Joan Crawford) in the film *Flamingo Road* (1949), Danny Thomas performed it in the first remake of *The Jazz Singer* (1953), and Frank Sinatra crooned it in *The Joker Is Wild* (1957).

"If I Didn't Care" (1939) is a bluesy ballad by Jack Lawrence that was introduced by the Ink Spots whose record was a bestseller and who reprised it in the movie *The Great American Broadcast* (1941). The breezy lyric argues that a beau wouldn't act the way he does if he didn't love her so. Early records were also made by Count Basie (vocal by Helen Humes), Kate Smith, Gray Gordon (vocal by Cliff Grass), and Van Alexander. It was revived by the Hilltoppers in 1954, Connie Francis in 1958, the Platters in 1961, and the Moments in 1970. Other memorable discs were made by Harry James, Brenda Lee, Chick Webb, Jan Savitt, Mose Allison, Bob Crosby, Peter Skellern, Hank Crawford, and Julia Lee.

"If I Had You" (1929) is a captivating ballad by Ted Shapiro, James Campbell, and Reg Connelly that first became popular in England, where it sold thousands of copies of sheet music that declared it "the Prince of

Wales' favorite fox trot." The ardent lyric boasts that one can do almost anything (climb mountains, cross deserts, become a king, start a new life) if his beloved will be his. The music uses the same four-note phrase over and over again, the effect being both insistent and seductive. Rudy Vallee and his Connecticut Yankees introduced the song in America, and early records by him, Al Bowlly, and Stan Lanin and his Famous Players (including Bing Crosby) popularized it. Later discs of note were made by Margaret Whiting, Art Blakely and the Jazz Messengers, Harry James, Lillian Roth, Artie Shaw, Roy Eldridge and Dizzy Gillespie, Frank Sinatra, Teddy Wilson, Clifford Brown, Nat King Cole, Faron Young, Merle Travis, Kenny Burrell, Sidney Bechet, Diana Krall, and the Platters. The ballad was also heard in the movie *The Hoodlum Saint* (1946) and was sung by Dan Dailey in *You Were Meant for Me* (1948), Tim Roth in *Everyone Says I Love You* (1996), Roy Gerson in *Eyes Wide Shut* (1999), and Neena Freelon in *What Women Want* (2000).

"If I Knew You Were Comin' I'd've Baked a Cake" (1950) is a cheery welcome song by Al Hoffman, Bob Merrill, and Clem Watts that was popularized by Eileen Barton whose record reached the top of the charts and sold over a million copies. The adoring little ballad was also recorded by Georgia Gibbs with Kaminsky's Dixielanders, Ethel Merman and Ray Bolger, the Fontane Sisters, Buddy Strong, Art Mooney, Eve Young and the Homesteaders, Hildegarde, and Lou Monte. The domestic number is also featured in the play *Same Time Next Year*; Charles Grodin sang it in the 1975 Broadway production, and Alan Alda performed it in the 1978 movie version.

"If There Is Someone Lovelier Than You" (1934) is a glittering serenade that hit dead ends on the radio and Broadway before becoming a Tin Pan Alley hit. Howard Dietz wrote the delicate lyric about looking everywhere but not finding anyone as beautiful as his darling. Arthur Schwartz's music, according to Alec Wilder, "moves gracefully, uncontrivedly, and with true creative inevitability." He wrote it for the radio series *The Gibson Family*, but it was never used. The songwriters then put it in their Broadway operetta *Revenge With Music* (1934), where it was sung by Georges Metaxa, but the show failed to run, and the song had to find its audience as an individual song. Later it found acclaim as a jazz favorite, with records by John Coltrane, Bobby Hackett, Mark Levine, Keith Oxman, and others. Schwartz once stated that this was his favorite of his many songs.

"If You Knew Susie (Like I Know Susie)" (1925) is remembered as one of Eddie Cantor's specialty numbers, yet it was originally written for Al Jolson. Joseph Meyer composed the energetic music and B.G. DeSylva penned the lyric, a slangy salute to a gal with "what a chassis!" The repeated "Oh! Oh!" in the lyric is very effective as it bounces along with the music. Jolson introduced the comic ditty in his Broadway vehicle *Big Boy* (1925), but the number did not go over as well as he hoped, so he cut it soon after opening. Cantor picked it up, and it was ideal for his wide-eyed, slyly suggestive singing style. He recorded it, performed it throughout his career, and sang it on the soundtrack for the movie *If You Knew Susie* (1948) and for Keefe Braselle in *The Eddie Cantor Story* (1953). Buddy Doyle, as a young Cantor, sang it in *The Great Ziegfeld* (1936), Gene Kelly and Frank Sinatra did a duet version in *Anchors Aweigh* (1945), George Brent, Dennis O'Keefe, Walter Able, and Don De Fore performed it as a quartet in *The Affairs of Susan* (1945), and Dean Martin crooned it in *The Silencers* (1966). Among the artists who recorded it were Cliff Edwards, Les Elgart, Tiny Hill, Jack Jenny, Johnny Maddox, Jimmy Durante, Lester Lanin, Tennessee Ernie Ford, Mitch Miller, Jack Mudurian, and Max Bygraves.

"I'll Be Around" (1943) is a touching ballad by Alec Wilder that is remarkable for its subtlety and understatement in both music and lyric. A disappointed beau explains that he'll be waiting here for her, no matter how she treats him, hoping that she'll return to him once her new love fades away. Wilder's music is intoxicating, and, as James R. Morris states, "the symmetry and order . . . make it a model of compositional virtue." Cab Calloway and his Orchestra introduced the number, but it was popularized by the Mills Brothers who recorded it several times. Tony Bennett's 1963 disc revived interest in the ballad, and there were also notable records by Billie Holiday, Rosemary Clooney, Buddy Morrow, George Shearing, Peggy Lee, the Spinners, Thelma Carpenter, Ruby Braff, Doris Day, Marian McPartland, and Carol Sloane.

"I'll Be Faithful" (1933) is a direct, emotive declaration of steadfast love. It was written by Ned Washington (lyric) and Allie Wrubel (music) and introduced by Art Jarrett. Jan Garber, Bernie Cummins, Adrian Rollini (vocal by Howard Phillips), and Anson Weeks made early and successful recordings, and Billy Eckstine revived it in the 1950s. Cliff Brunner and the Texas Wanderers, Ivory Joe Hunter, and Dusty Springfield are among the others who recorded it.

"I'll Be Home for Christmas (Though Just in Memory)" (1943) is the perennial favorite that mixes nostalgia for home and for the holidays in a gentle way that avoids mawkishness. Walter Kent, Kim Gannon, and Buck Ram collaborated on the heartfelt ballad that promises a Christmas reunion even if it's only in a dream. Bing Crosby introduced and popularized the number with a record that sold over a million copies. The song became a particular favorite of troops overseas during World War Two and then again during the Korean, Vietnam, and Persian Gulf conflicts. There have been hundreds of recordings by such diverse artists as Perry Como, the Beach Boys, Elvis Presley, Jimmy Buffett, Phil Baker, the Platters, Linda Ronstadt, Reba McEntire, Doris Day, Andrea Marcovicci, Pat Boone, Linda Eder, 98 Degrees, Barbra Streisand, and John Pizzarelli.

"I'll Be Seeing You" (1938) is perhaps the most fondly remembered of all World War Two ballads, yet the song floundered in obscurity before it was discovered by the public. Sammy Fain composed the haunting music that remains somber even as it climbs to its surging climax. Irving Kahal wrote the unforgettable lyric that recalls a love affair in Paris, the suitor still seeing her in the park, in cafés, and other places. The song concludes with the indelible promise that he'll "be looking at the moon but I'll be seeing you." Tamara introduced the ballad in the Broadway musical *Right This Way* (1938), but it got little attention from the press or the public. The show closed after only fourteen performances, and "I'll Be Seeing You" sat for five years unpublished and unrecorded. Kahal died in 1942 and never saw it become a wartime favorite. Bing Crosby's 1944 recording sold over a million copies, and thanks to additional hits by Tommy Dorsey (vocal by Frank Sinatra) and Frances Langford, it remained on *Your Hit Parade* for twenty-four weeks. Hildegarde made it her signature song, and Liberace used it as the closing theme on his radio and concert performances in the 1950s. Other memorable records were made by Fain, Sylvia Syms, Jo Stafford, Mel Tormé, Rosemary Clooney, Maxine Sullivan, Vera Lynn, Etta Jones, Sarah Vaughan, Dinah Shore, Neil Sedaka, Engelbert Humperdinck, Judy Collins, and more recently, Mandy Patinkin, Andrea Marcovicci, Michael Feinstein, and Vicki Stuart. The song can be heard in the movie *See My Lawyer* (1944), and it was sung by the Five Satins in *Let the Good Times Roll* (1973). The cast of the Off-Broadway revue *Swingtime Canteen* (1995) performed it, and Ann Hampton Callaway sang it in the Broadway revue *Swing!* (1999).

"I'll Be With You in Apple Blossom Time" (1920) is a nostalgic ballad that found favor in its initial presentation and was revived successfully off and on for forty years. Neville Fleeson (lyric) and Albert Von Tilzer (music) wrote the adoring number in which a couple looks forward to their May wedding. Nora Bayes introduced it in vaudeville, and it immediately was in demand, helped by early records by Charles Harrison and Ernest Hare. The Andrews Sister made it a bestseller in 1941 with their harmonizing disc, Nat King Cole and Tab Hunter had 1950s versions, and Wayne Newton's 1965 record was high on the charts. Other prominent discs were made by Nat Brandwynne, Jo Stafford with Nat King Cole and Paul Weston's Orchestra, Vera Lynn, Artie Shaw, Harry James, the Bachelors, Chet Atkins, the Platters, Steve Lawrence and Eydie Gorme, and Barry Manilow. The Andrews Sister reprised it in the films *Buck Privates* (1941) and *Follow the Boys* (1944), it was heard in *This Time for Keeps* (1947), and it was sung by the cast of the Off-Broadway musical *Swingtime Canteen* (1995).

"I'll Dance at Your Wedding" (1948) is a breezy fox trot by Herb Magidson (lyric) and Ben Oakland (music) in which a fiance tells his intended that his plans for their nuptials include dancing, drinking a toast to her parents, and kissing all the ladies farewell. Buddy Clark popularized the tune with a record with Ray Noble and his Orchestra, and there were also successful discs by Fats Waller, Tony Martin, Peggy Lee, Frank Sinatra, and Vic Damone.

"I'll Get By (As Long As I Have You)" (1928) is a potent depression chaser that states, in short but flavorful phrases, that lack of money is no problem, now that he has her love to see him through. The music is unusual in the way it seems to awkwardly stop and not resolve itself, then it picks up again and gains strength as it proceeds to the next section. Roy Turk (lyric) and Fred Ahlert (music) wrote the expert ballad, and it immediately became popular, thanks to Ruth Etting and early records by Nick Lucas, Gus Arnheim, the Ipana Troubadours, and Aileen Stanley. The song took on an even deeper meaning after the stock market crash, and a million discs and a million copies of sheet music were sold. "I'll Get By" enjoyed a revival of interest when it was used as the leitmotiv that Irene Dunne sang in the film *A Guy Named Joe* (1943), and the next year Doris Day recorded it with success. It was revived again in 1960 with a hit record by Billy Williams. Other noteworthy discs were made by Harry James (vocal by Dick Haymes), Buddy Clark, Frankie Carle, Bing Crosby, the Ink Spots, Billie Holiday, Teddy Wilson, Ziggy Elman, the King Sisters, Shirley Bassey, and Michael Feinstein. The ballad can be heard in the movies *The Dance of Life* (1929) and *Puttin' on the Ritz* (1930), and it was sung by Dinah Shore in *Follow the Boys* (1944), Dan Dailey in *You Were Meant for Me* (1948), June Haver, Dennis Day, and Gloria DeHaven in *I'll Get By* (1950), Judy Garland in the "Born in a Trunk" sequence in *A Star Is Born* (1954), and Ann Blyth (dubbed by Gogi Grant) in *The Helen Morgan Story* (1957).

"I'll Never Smile Again" (1939) is a bittersweet ballad with a sad history. Ruth Lowe, the pianist with Ina Ray Hutton's all-girl band, wrote the number when her husband of four months suddenly died. The lyric promises a dear one that she won't smile again until he takes her back, but in the context of Lowe's life, the ballad has a truly morose quality as well. The song became famous with a Tommy Dorsey recording (vocals by Frank Sinatra and the Pied Pipers) that climbed the charts. Sinatra reprised the number with the Pied Pipers when he made his screen debut in *Las Vegas Nights* (1941). The Four Aces revived it in 1953 with their hit record, and there were other discs by Glenn Miller, Count Basie, Lillian Roth, Mel Tormé, Anita Kerr, Doris Day, the Four Freshmen, Sarah Vaughan, Patti Page, Johnny Hartman, and Julie London.

"I'll See You in My Dreams" (1924) is a cherished farewell song, a favorite when played as the last number at a dance. For his thirtieth birthday, Isham Jones's wife bought him a piano. That night he sat down and wrote three melodies, this one among them. The music is unusual in its minimal use of notes, Alec Wilder calling it "a model of lyricism and economy that . . . makes the harmony almost irrelevant." Gus Kahn penned the dreamy lyric in which a heartsick lover knows his beloved is gone, but still he envisions her in his imagination. Jones and his Orchestra introduced the song, and their record went to the top position on the charts. Interest in the ballad was revived when Doris Day and Danny Thomas sang it in the Kahn film bio *I'll See You in My Dreams* (1952) and again when Pat Boone had a hit record of it in 1962. Among the other notable discs were those by Lewis James, Carmen Cavallaro, Andy Russell, Mary Martin, Ray Anthony, Bing Crosby, Vaughn Monroe, Guy Lombardo, Buddy Clark, Eddy Duchin, Alice Faye, the Pied Pipers, the Norman Luboff Choir, and Merle Travis. It has been heard in several movies, sung by Jeanette MacDonald in *Follow the Boys* (1944), Bob Crosby in *Pardon My Rhythm* (1944), and Jeanne Crain in *Margie* (1946) and in *Rose of Washington Square* (1939), *Crazy House* (1943), *Destiny* (1944), and *Sweet and Lowdown* (1999), where guitarist Harold Alden played on the soundtrack for Sean Penn.

"I'll Take You Home Again, Kathleen" (1876), the most cherished sentimental ballad of its time, paints a heartbreaking picture of a husband promising to bring his dying wife back to her homeland across the sea. It is one of the most tearful of Irish homesickness ballads yet; ironically, it was never about Ireland and was written by a southerner about Virginia. Thomas Westendorf took his wife from their homeland in Virginia to live in Lexington, Kentucky, at the end of the Civil War. When she was critically ill, he wrote the tender ballad to cheer her up. The number is a response to a well-known song of the day called "Barney, Take Me Home Again," and various versions of Westendorf's lament circulated the country, some very maudlin, others more straightforward. It was introduced to the public by an amateur singer at the Town Hall in Plainfield, Indiana, in 1876 and soon caught on, eventually turning into an

Irish favorite when tenor John McCormack sang it later on record and in many concerts. In addition to many Irish singers and bands, it was recorded by Bing Crosby, Pat Murphy, Phil Coulter, Elvis Presley, Mitch Miller, James Galway, Daniel O'Donnell, Joe McPartland, and Slim Whitman. Deanna Durbin sang it in the movie *For the Love of Mary* (1948), the Sons of the Pioneers performed it in *Rio Grande* (1950), and it was featured in *The Quiet Man* (1952) and other Irish-flavored films. Also, Trey Wilson sang it in the Broadway revue *Tintypes* (1980).

"I'm Always Chasing Rainbows" (1918) was one of the very first Tin Pan Alley hits to come from a classical piece of music but not the last as songwriters learned to use old melodies to create new songs. Harry Carroll adapted Chopin's *Fantaisie Impromptu* into traditional ballad form, the dreamy music complimenting Joseph McCarthy's lyric about waiting "in vain" for true love to come along. Harry Fox introduced it in the Broadway musical *Oh, Look!* (1918), and it stopped the show each evening. Sheet music sales surpassed the 1 million mark, and many recordings were made over the years. Though far from forgotten, the ballad was revived by Perry Como in the 1940s, and the old song stayed on *Your Hit Parade* for twelve weeks. Other well-known records were made by Dick Haymes, Helen Forrest, Tony Martin, Alice Faye, Judy Garland, the Four Freshmen, Frank Sinatra, Tony Bennett, Della Reese, Barbra Streisand, Jerry Vale, and more recently, Barbara Cook, Mandy Patinkin, Dale Kristien, and Harry Nilsson. Garland and Charles Winninger performed it in the movie *Ziegfeld Girl* (1941), Betty Grable and John Payne sang it in *The Dolly Sisters* (1945), and it was heard in *Rose of Washington Square* (1939), *Nobody's Darling* (1943), and *The Merry Monahans* (1944). It was heard again on Broadway when Debbie Reynolds sang it in the 1973 revival of *Irene*.

"I'm Beginning to See the Light" (1944) is the distinctive uptempo ballad that bandleaders Harry James and Duke Ellington wrote with Johnny Hodges and Don George. The music is a riff melody that repeats the same nine-note phrase, each time resolved by the musical theme in the title phrase. The breezy lyric confesses that he never went in for romantic or sentimental things like mistletoe or moonlit nights, but now that he is in love he sees their attraction. A memorable image in the lyric is that of "shadow boxing in the dark" before he saw the light. Both Ellington and James recorded the number, but it was the latter's disc (with vocal by Kitty Kallen) that rose to the top of the charts and kept the song on *Your Hit Parade* for seven weeks. In 1956 Count Basie (vocal by Joe Williams) revived the number with success, and Connie Francis had a best-selling disc in the early 1960s. Other noteworthy records were made by Ella Fitzgerald with the Ink Spots, Mel Tormé, Joya Sherrill (with

Ellington's Orchestra), Earl Hines, Buddy Greco, Billy Eckstine, Ben Webster, Bobby Darin, and Peter Nero. The song can be heard in the movie *Man from Oklahoma* (1945), and it was sung on Broadway by Judith Jamison and Gregory Hines in *Sophisticated Ladies* (1981) and by Lawrence Hamilton and the company in *Play On!* (1997).

"I'm Forever Blowing Bubbles" (1918) is a graceful waltz with a lyric that might be considered banal (he blows bubbles into the air and then watches them burst, just like his dreams) but whose music has continued to entrance for many decades. The song was written by John Kellette and Jean Kenbrovin, the latter a pen name for the songwriters James Kendis, James Brockman, and Nat Vincent. Written for the vaudevillian team of Henry Burr and Albert Campbell, who popularized it, the number was interpolated into the Broadway musical *The Passing Show* (1919), where it was sung by June Clarice. The first recording was by Ben Selvin and his Novelty Orchestra, and the disc was a hit, helping to sell 2 million copies of sheet music. Gordon Jenkins with Artie Shaw revived the ballad in 1950, and there were other records of note by Harry James, the Clark Sisters, Les Paul and Mary Ford, Eddie Condon, the Three Suns, Roy Eldridge, Charlie Parker, Spike Jones, and Lawrence Welk (who added real bubbles when he conducted it). The song was featured in the films *Stella Dallas* (1937), *Men With Wings* (1938), *The Great American Broadcast* (1941), and *On Moonlight Bay* (1951), where it was sung by Jack Smith and Doris Day. More recently the number was used as a leitmotiv in *Sweet and Lowdown* (1999) where guitarist Howard Alden played it on the soundtrack.

"I'm Getting Sentimental Over You" (1932), most remembered as the theme song for Tommy Dorsey and his Orchestra, is a Big Band ballad by Ned Washington (lyric) and George Bassman (music) that admits to being cynical about love, but things are different now that he has met her. Dorsey's record was a bestseller, and the Ink Spots also had a hit with it when they revived the song in 1940. Among the many other recordings were those by Joe Augustine, Count Basie, Ella Fitzgerald, Dick Conte, Frances Langford, Sonny Stitt, Charles Mingus, the Clark Sisters, Bob Ackerman, Bill Evans, the Four Freshmen, Oscar Peterson, Thelonious Monk, Gogi Grant, and more recently, Andrea Marcovicci and Carol Sloane. Dorsey reprised the number in the movies *Du Barry Was a Lady* (1943) and *A Song Is Born* (1948), and his famous recording was heard on the soundtracks of *Radio Days* (1987) and *King of the Hill* (1993). Also, Carol Bruce sang it on screen in *Keep 'Em Flying* (1941).

"I'm Gonna Sit Right Down and Write Myself a Letter (And Make Believe It Came From You)" (1935) is a jazzy, seriocomic ballad that seems bright on the surface (he pretends he is still getting love letters from a girl who has left him), but the charade points to a true aching underneath. Fred Ahlert (lyric) and Joe Young (music) wrote the bittersweet number, and it was popularized by records by Thomas "Fats" Waller and the Boswell Sisters. Connee Boswell later recorded it herself, as did Al Bowlly, Ella Mae Morse, Ted Weems, Johnny Mercer, Nat Brandwynne, Slim Green, Sarah Vaughan, Russ Hamilton, James P. Johnson, Brian Evans, Scatman Crothers, Fabian, Cleo Laine, and Willie Nelson. But the biggest seller of all was a 1957 disc by Billy Williams, which sold 2 million copies. On Broadway Ken Page sang the song in the Waller revue *Ain't Misbehavin'* (1978).

"I'm Just Wild About Harry" (1921) is one of Tin Pan Alley's most durable cakewalks, a vivacious number from the legendary Broadway show *Shuffle Along* (1921) by Noble Sissle (lyric) and Eubie Blake (music). The songwriters originally wrote their merry tribute to mayor candidate Harry as a waltz but decided that white audiences would not accept such a European sound in an all-black show. So they revised the number and made it a sparkling cakewalk, and it has remained popular ever since. Lottie Gee introduced the song in the musical, and it became the hit of the show, soon picked up by dance bands, nightclub singers, and recording artists. There were early discs by Marion Harris and Vincent Lopez and his Orchestra, followed by hundreds of others, including those by Blake, Al Jolson, Thelma Carpenter, Carmen Miranda, Red Nichols, Judy Garland, Horace Heidt, Peggy Lee, and Cleo Laine. The song was also heard in several films, such as *Rose of Washington Square* (1939) performed by Alice Faye and Louis Prima, *Babes in Arms* (1939) sung by Judy Garland and Mickey Rooney, *Broadway* (1942), *Is Everybody Happy?* (1943), *Greenwich Village* (1944), and *Jolson Sings Again* (1949), where Jolson provided the singing voice for Larry Parks. Lynnie Godfrey, Janet Powell, and the female chorus sang it in the Broadway revue *Eubie* (1978).

"I'm Looking for a Guy Who Plays Alto and Baritone and Doubles on a Clarinet and Wears a Size 37 Suit" (1940) is a novelty number about trying to replace a fat musician. The ditty is more famous for its lengthy title than any widespread popularity. Bandleader Ozzie Nelson wrote the music and lyric and had some success with a record he made of it with his band. The playful number is a candidate for the longest song title on Tin Pan Alley.

"I'm Looking Over a Four Leaf Clover" (1927) is the carefree number by Mort Dixon (lyric) and Harry MacGregor Woods (music) that celebrates a wandering, happy-go-lucky philosophy of life. The merry march song encourages one to enjoy life and look at the things that "I over-looked before." It was popularized by Nick Lucas on record and soon became a choral and party favorite. A very influential record was made by Art Mooney and his Orchestra in 1948 using banjos in the arrangement. A disc jockey in Salt Lake City was so taken with the Mooney record that he played it on the air for twenty-four hours straight as a publicity gimmick. Some listeners complained, but the ploy worked, and soon the record was at the top of the charts, selling over a million copies and putting the number on the *Hit Parade* for fourteen weeks. The disc also started a trend for banjo accompaniment in pop songs. Al Jolson included it in his repertoire for years, recording it and singing it on the soundtrack of the movie bio *Jolson Sings Again* (1949). Danny Thomas followed in Jolson's footsteps by singing it in the first remake of *The Jazz Singer* (1953). Of the many records made over the years, estimable ones include those by Ben Bernie, the Revelers, Paul Specht, Arthur Godfrey and the Mariners, Tiny Hill, Alvino Rey, Cody Fox and his Yellow Jackets, Jo Ann Castle, Mitch Miller, the Ames Brothers, and Maurice Chevalier who sang it in French as "C'est le Nature."

"I'm Nobody's Baby" (1921) is a somber ballad that recalls when one was worshipped and loved as a child, but now she is grown, alone, and lonely. Lester Santley, Benny Davis, and Milton Ager wrote the tender lament, and Ruth Etting popularized it on stage. It soon became a favorite of female singers in vaudeville, leading to many records and over a million sheet music sales. Judy Garland revived the number when she sang it in the film *Andy Hardy Meets Debutante* (1940), and her successful record helped keep the song on *Your Hit Parade* for eleven weeks. Other memorable discs were made by Bea Wain, Jane Pickens, Helen Forrest with Benny Goodman's Band, Marion Harris, Connie Haines with Tommy Dorsey's Orchestra, Betty Hutton with Nelson Riddle's Orchestra, Marian Mann with Bob Crosby's Band, Connie Francis, Mindy Carson, Vic Damone, and Della Reese.

"I'm Sitting on Top of the World" (1925) is the kind of optimistic, expansive number that Al Jolson excelled at, and he had great success with the number when he introduced it on record. Ray Henderson wrote the bouncy music, and Joe Young and Sam M. Lewis collaborated on the peppy lyric about having no money or fancy clothes, but because he is in love with a "sweet little honey" he feels like he owns the world. Jolson performed it in the film *The Singing Fool* (1928) and provided the singing for Larry Parks in *The Jolson Story* (1946). Glenn Miller's recording of the song in 1937 was one of his first discs, and Les Paul and Mary Ford's record in 1953 revived the number. Other records of note were made by Isham Jones, Bill Monroe, Doris Day, Frank Crumit, Sam Collins, Bobby

Darin, Jerry Lewis, and Ray Charles. Susan Hayward sang the song in *I'll Cry Tomorrow* (1955), Claude Stroud performed it in *Love Me or Leave Me* (1955), and it was heard in *Has Anybody Seen My Gal?* (1952) and *Thoroughly Modern Millie* (1967).

"I'm the Lonesomest Gal in Town" (1912) is a sly ballad by Lew Brown (lyric) and Albert Von Tilzer (music) about a loverless lady who proclaims "everybody has thrown me down," so she's thinking of stealing another woman's man and "never give him back." The cynical number was a favorite in vaudeville in the 1910s; it was revived with success by Kay Starr in the 1950s, her bestselling record bringing her fame. Bea Wain, Ella Fitzgerald, and Beatrice Kay with Ray Bloch's Orchestra also made distinctive recordings. The song can be heard in the movies *Make Believe Ballroom* (1949) and *South Sea Sinner* (1950).

"I'm Through With Love" (1931) is a melancholy torch song that also has a touch of hope in it, the singer not truly believing the title phrase. Matty Malneck and Jerry Livingston composed the simple and direct melody that depends on little embellishment, and Gus Kahn wrote the pungent lyric, vowing to "care for no one" and stating that his heart is "stocked with icy Frigidaire." Mildred Bailey introduced the song, but it was Bing Crosby who popularized it when he sang it on his first national radio broadcast. The performance made such an impression that it was released as a record and sold thousands of copies. The number was revived in 1938 by Glen Gray and the Casa Loma Orchestra (vocal by Kenny Sargent) and again in 1941 by Dinah Shore. Other notable records were made by Henry Busse, Don Voorhees, Eileen Farrell, Ziggy Elman, Maxine Sullivan, Ray Anthony, Nat King Cole, Ellis Larkins, Charlie Ventura, Sarah Vaughan, Dion and the Belmonts, Lena Horne, Joni James, and Chet Baker. There was also a successful recording by Marilyn Monroe, who sang it in the movie *Some Like It Hot* (1959). It was also heard in the films *Honeymoon Lodge* (1943) and *I'll See You in My Dreams* (1952), Jane Froman dubbed it for Susan Hayward in *With a Song in My Heart* (1952), Bobby Van performed it in *The Affairs of Dobie Gillis* (1953), and Woody Allen and Goldie Hawn sang it in *Everyone Says I Love You* (1996).

"Imagination" (1940) is a dreamy ballad by Johnny Burke (lyric) and Jimmy Van Heusen (music) that quietly celebrates the power of one's imagination, able to make a cloudy day seem like a sunny one and allowing someone you love to love you back. Fred Waring's Pennsylvanians introduced the number, and it was popularized by Glenn Miller (vocal by Ray Eberly), whose record rose to the top of the charts. The affecting song was also recorded by Ella Fitzgerald, Kate Smith, Tommy

Dorsey, Stan Getz, Count Basie, Joe Williams, June Christy, Art Pepper, Carmen McRae, Paul Desmond, Doris Day, Chick Webb, Fran Warren, Chet Atkins, Shirley Bassey, and Frank Sinatra.

"In a Little Spanish Town" (1926) is a pseudo-Latin number that was popular enough to start a vogue for Spanish tunes in the 1920s. Mable Wayne composed the gently rhythmic music, and Joe Young and Sam M. Lewis wrote the reflective lyric, recalling that it was on a night just like this that he fell in love with her in a village in Spain. Jimmy Carr and his Orchestra introduced it, but it was popularized by early records by Paul Whiteman, the Revelers, and Ben Selvin and his Orchestra. Most memorable among the many discs to follow were those by Bing Crosby, Albert Ammons and the Rhythm Kings, Bunny Berigan, Glenn Miller, Joe Bushkin, Benny Carter, Stan Kenton, the Fireballs, Nick Lucas, Lawrence Welk, Ray Charles, Abbe Lane, Gene Autry, and many authentic Spanish bands. David Carroll and his Orchestra revived interest in the number with a successful 1954 record. The ballad was heard in the film *Ridin' Down the Canyon* (1942), and it was sung by Virginia O'Brien, June Allyson, and Gloria DeHaven in *Thousands Cheer* (1943).

"In a Sentimental Mood" (1936) is a Big Band favorite, the music being moody and sexy even as it maintains a cool, jazzy beat. Duke Ellington composed the intoxicating music, and Manny Kurtz and Irving Mills wrote the lyric that describes the sublime mood and the romantic paradise created with a sweetheart's love. Ellington and his Orchestra introduced the number on record, and there were other early discs by Jimmy Dorsey, Ben Pollack, Caspar Reardon, and Benny Goodman. Over the years prominent records were also made by Sonny Rollins, Earl Hines, Art Tatum, Billy Eckstine, Dick Jurgens, the Ray Brown Trio, Joe Augustine, Count Basie, Lawrence Welk, Bill Evans, Ella Fitzgerald, Johnny Mathis, Nancy Wilson, Miles Davis, and Ann Hampton Callaway. On Broadway, Phyllis Hyman sang the ballad in the Ellington revue *Sophisticated Ladies* (1981), and it was performed by Bunny Briggs and Jerome Richardson in *Black and Blue* (1989).

"In a Shanty in Old Shanty Town" (1932) romanticized the shanty towns that sprang up all over America during the depression, and despite the unlikeliness of the subject, the song was a hit. Joe Young, John Siras, and Little Jack Little wrote the sentimental ballad about finding love in humble places, such as a "tumbled down shack by an old railroad track." Little talk-sang the number on radio, and records and the song grew very popular, especially after Ted Lewis and his Orchestra made a record that climbed the charts. It was revived in 1946 with a bestselling disc by Johnny Long and his Orchestra. Ted Black, Red Allen, Singin'

Sam, the Ink Spots, Rose Murphy, Coleman Hawkins, Fats Domino, Jimmy Wakely, Dizzy Gillespie, the M 'n' M Trio, Jerry Lee Lewis, and Dorothy Loudon were among the many who also recorded it. Teddy Joyce sang it in the movie *Crooner* (1932), it was heard in *Roaring Twenties* (1939), and Doris Day performed it in *Lullaby of Broadway* (1951), her subsequent record of the song finding success.

"In My Merry Oldsmobile" (1905), the first successful Tin Pan Alley song about the automobile, was written to commemorate two Oldsmobiles that won a cross-country race from Detroit to Portland, Oregon. Gus Edwards composed the rollicking waltz music, and Vincent P. Bryan penned the lyric, which took the form of a marriage proposal, Johnny whispering to his Sweetie Lucille as they drive along the roads that will take them to a church where they will be wed. Edwards popularized the tune himself in vaudeville, and later there were commendable records by Bing Crosby, Bix Beiderbecke, the Banjo Kings, Les Brown, Archie Bleyer, and Jo Stafford with Paul Weston's Orchestra. The number was also used for radio and television commercials for Olds. Crosby reprised it in the Edwards movie bio *The Star Maker* (1939), Jack Oakie, Peggy Ryan, and Donald O'Connor performed it in *The Merry Monahans* (1944), and it was heard in *Shine on Harvest Moon* (1944), *One Sunday Afternoon* (1948), and *War of the Wildcats* (1943). The happy travel song was also sung by the cast of the Broadway revue *Tintypes* (1980).

"In the Baggage Coach Ahead" (1896) was one of the most morbid of all the sentimental ballads of the 1890s. As a train travels late into the night, a man sits with a crying child on his lap. When the other passengers complain, asking where the mother is and why he doesn't hand the child to her, the father answers, "I wish that I could," and explains that the mother lies dead in a coffin in the next car. The narrative ballad was written by Gussie Davis, an African American who was working as a Pullman porter. One night he came upon a crying child who told him her dead mother was in a coffin in the baggage car. Davis wrote both words and music and sold it outright to a publisher for a few dollars, never benefiting from the thousands of copies of sheet music it eventually sold. The number was introduced by Imogene Comer in her vaudeville act in Boston. Although widely popular for a time, the ballad eventually fell out of favor and was later considered outdated melodrama.

"In the Chapel in the Moonlight" (1936) enjoyed celebrity twice, featured on *Your Hit Parade* in 1936 and again in 1954. Billy Hill wrote the tender ballad that recalled an old moss-covered church that he and his sweetheart used to stroll by. Now that she is gone, he returns to the church at night to listen to the bells chime and to remember her. Shep Fields and his Orchestra popularized the song with a bestselling record, and Ruth Etting and Richard Himber and his Orchestra also had early success with it. Kitty Kallen revived it in 1954, as did the Bachelors in 1965 and Dean Martin in 1967. Among the other artists who made discs were Faron Young, Sonny Til and the Orioles, Henry Red Allen, Sonny Rollins, Chet Atkins, and Patti Page.

"In the Evening By the Moonlight" (1878) is a southern ballad by James Bland that paints a nostalgic picture of the Old South with Negroes sitting in front of their cabins at night, strumming guitars and singing. Bland got the idea for the song after visiting a Virginia plantation, and he wrote the gentle, almost solemn music to capture the lazy peacefulness he found there. Bland introduced it himself with Callaghan's Original Georgia Minstrels, and soon it was a favorite on the minstrel and later the vaudeville circuit. The song is particularly suited to harmonizing, so it also entered the repertoire of barbershop quartets and choral groups. Often used in films for atmospheric effect, the ballad can be heard in *The Strawberry Blonde* (1941), *Miss Susie Slagle's* (1947), *Mother Wore Tights* (1947), *I Wonder Who's Kissing Her Now* (1947), and *My Wild Irish Rose* (1947), where it was sung by Ben Blue. Highly regarded records of the number were made by Bing Crosby, the Cliff Adams Singers, and Nina Simone.

"In the Good Old Summertime" (1902) is the merry standard about summer, the first hit song about a season of the year and one that would be copied many times after. George Evans was reminiscing one day with a friend and referred to the "good old" summers of his youth. Thinking it would make an effective song, he worked out a spirited waltz tune, but unable to write music, he hummed it for singer Blanche Ring, who notated it. Ren Shields provided the lyric, describing summer as an old friend. The song was introduced in vaudeville by J.W. Myers and later was used by the team of Stewart and Gillen. Ring interpolated it into her Broadway musical *The Defender* (1902), and her rendition started the number on the road to success. Still, music publishers were wary of the song, arguing that it could only be sung in the summer months. But they were eventually proved wrong (it sold over a million copies of sheet music), and seasonal ballads cropped up all over Tin Pan Alley throughout the decade, most memorably Shields and Evans's "In the Merry Month of June." Broadway heard "In the Good Old Summertime" again in *In Posterland* (1902), *In the Good Old Summertime* (1904), and *By the Beautiful Sea* (1954). It was also used in several films, including *Doughboys* (1930), *One Sunday Afternoon* (1933), *Babes in Toyland* (1934), *Jeepers Creepers* (1939), and *In the Good Old Summertime* (1949), where it was sung by

Van Johnson, Spring Byington, S.Z. Sakall, and the chorus. Of the many recordings, a 1952 disc by Les Paul and Mary Ford was probably the biggest seller. Other notable records were made by Ace O'Donnell, Judy Garland, the Kirby Stone Four, Connie Francis, the Cliff Adams Singers, and the Buffalo Bills.

"In the Mood" (1938) is perhaps the quintessential Big Band song, a few notes of which immediately transport one to the swing era. Joe Garland wrote the resplendent music, based on an earlier instrumental he wrote with Wingy Manone called "Tar Paper Stomp." Andy Razaf penned the tripping lyric, a conversation between a boy and a girl dancing together, with the music putting her in the mood for a kiss. Edgar Hayes and his Orchestra introduced the song (though Manone had recorded the instrumental version in 1937), but it was Glenn Miller and his Orchestra that made the song famous (and vice versa). Their recording went to the top of the charts, and the number was forever after associated with the band. They reprised it in the movie *Sun Valley Serenade* (1941), Joseph Gershenson's Orchestra imitated them in *The Glenn Miller Story* (1954), and the original Miller record was heard as background in a handful of films, such as *The Gene Krupa Story* (1959), *1941* (1979), and *Radio Days* (1987). Also on screen, Jennifer Holliday sang it in *In the Mood* (1987). Although the Miller version is definitive, there were successful discs by Ernie Fields in 1959, Bette Midler in 1974, and the Henhouse Five Plus Two in 1977. Most recently it was performed by Ann Hampton Callaway, Laura Benanti, and the company in the Broadway revue *Swing!* (1999)

"In the Shade of the Old Apple Tree" (1905) is the bucolic love song by Harry H. Williams (lyric) and Egbert Van Alstyne (music) filled with nature images (such as the blossoms and the "dull buzz of the bee") as a beau returns to the tree under which he and his darling first professed their love. Van Alstyne, who was from the Midwest, missed the apple trees of home and got the idea for the song one day while taking a walk in Central Park (which has no apples trees). Early records by Harry Burr, Albert Campbell, the Haydn Quartette, and Arthur Pryor's Band popularized the number, and over a million copies of sheet music were sold. The gentle waltz was also popular with barbershop quartets, especially after Theodore Westman made a four-part arrangement that became a choral favorite. Duke Ellington's 1933 disc revived the number, and there were other memorable records by Louis Armstrong, the Banjo Kings, the Mills Brothers, Claude Hopkins, Benny Goodman, the Sportsmen, the Ink Spots, Lawrence Welk, and the Four Aces. The ballad can be heard in the movies *Hello, Frisco, Hello* (1943), *The Stork Club* (1945), and *Wabash Avenue* (1950). In 1937 E.Y. Harburg (lyric) and Harold Arlen (music) wrote a sequel and spoof of the number called "In the Shade of the New Apple Tree."

"Indian Summer" (1939) is a rarity for operetta composer Victor Herbert: a true Tin Pan Alley song. While some of his theatre numbers crossed over to popular records and sheet music, this Herbert composition is written in the traditional song format and actually made the *Hit Parade*, even though it was fifteen years after his death. The straightforward music, with none of the expected operetta embellishments, was written in 1919 as a piano piece called "An American Idyll." Twenty years later Al Dubin ran across the composition and wrote a poignant lyric bidding farewell to summer and all the dreams that were still alive back when the season was young. The disenchanted lover is now heartbroken and asks Indian summer to "watch over" his pain. The ballad was popularized by Tommy Dorsey (vocal by Jack Leonard) whose record went to the top of the charts. A disc by Glenn Miller (vocal by Ray Eberly) was also successful. Other records were made by Billy Vaughn, Frank Sinatra, Al Stewart, Ruby Braff, Bing Crosby, Coleman Hawkins, the California Swing Cats, Wardell Gray and Stan Getz, Nelson Riddle, and Tony Bennett.

"Indiana" (1917) is a nostalgic standard by Ballard MacDonald (lyric) and James F. Hanley (music) that later became a jazz and swing favorite. Recordings in the 1920s by Louis Armstrong, Red Nichols and his Five Pennies, and Frankie Carle are considered jazz classics, and Benny Goodman's swing version in the late 1930s is also highly acclaimed. Other distinctive records were made by Duke Ellington, Lester Young, the Bobby Gordon Quartet, Gene Krupa, Joe Williams, the Hi-Lo's, Scott Hamilton, and Bobby Troup. Jane Froman dubbed it for Susan Hayward in the film *With a Song in My Heart* (1952), Danny Kaye sang it while Nichols provided the trumpet playing in the *The Five Pennies* (1959), and it was heard in *Roberta* (1935) and *The Gene Krupa Story* (1959). The number is often listed as "Back Home Again in Indiana."

"Into Each Life Some Rain Must Fall" (1944) is a philosophical ballad by Allan Roberts and Doris Fisher that optimistically tries to belittle life's disappointments. A recording by Ella Fitzgerald with the Ink Spots popularized the song as it reached the top of the charts, and it was revived a decade later by Teresa Brewer with Les Brown's Orchestra. Among the other artists who made discs of the ballad were Kay Starr, Charlie Barnet, the Platters, Sammy Rimington, Noeleen Batley, Laurie Chescoe, Rebecca Kilgore, and Justin Tubb.

"Is It True What They Say About Dixie?" (1936) is a vibrant southern song that Al Jolson sang with success on stage, over the radio, and on records. Irving Caesar, Sammy Cahn (lyric), and Gerald Marks (music) had never been south, but they wanted to write a Dixie number for Jolson, so they put the lyric into a series of questions, asking about the weather, the magnolia blossoms, even the Swanee River. Rudy Vallee also had a major hit with the song, and in the 1940s bands conducted by Jimmy Dorsey and Ozzie Nelson found success with it. Other notable recordings were made by Ted Lewis, Eddy Howard, Bob White and Clyde Brewer, Larry Adler, Frances Langford, Phil Harris, Orrin Tucker and Bonnie Parker, and Dean Martin. The number can be heard in the movie *Sing, Baby, Sing* (1936), Iris Adrian and Robin Raymond performed it in *His Butler's Sister* (1943), and Jolson reprised it on the soundtrack of *Jolson Sings Again* (1949).

"Isle of Capri" (1934) is a gliding English ballad about the Italian island where one fell in love with a girl, but she wore a wedding ring, so he left the isle, which still haunts his memory. It was written by Jimmy Kennedy (lyric) and Will Grosz (music) and introduced in England by Lew Stone (vocal by Nat Gonella). Guy Lombardo and the Royal Canadians were the first to present it in America, but it was a swing version by Wingy Manone in 1935 that popularized it. Over a million copies of sheet music were sold, and the tune became a favorite of glee clubs and harmonizing singing groups. The melody is very similar to a popular Viennese song, and when the authors sued they received a cash settlement. Twenty years later it was revived by the Gaylords with a hit record. Other well-known discs were made by Xavier Cugat, Frank Sinatra, Al Bowlly with Ray Noble's Orchestra, Duke Ellington, Gracie Fields, Bing Crosby, the Firehouse Five Plus Two, Fats Domino, and Dave Bartholomew.

"It Ain't Gonna Rain No Mo' " (1923) is a simple little nonsense song whose roots go back to the South in the nineteenth century, merrily wondering "how in the heck" one can wash one's neck if it never rains. In 1923 Wendell Hall adapted the old tune into Tin Pan Alley format. The record of him singing it as he accompanied himself on the ukelele sold over 2 million discs and over a million copies of sheet music. Often included in children's songbooks and records, the number was also recorded by Joe Thompson, Layton and Johnstone, Mance Lipscomb, Marvin Gaster, and Slim Jackson. The song was also used in the films *Madam Satan* (1930), *Rain or Shine* (1930), and *Has Anybody Seen My Gal?* (1952).

"It All Depends on You" (1925), the first song written by the illustrious team of De Sylva, Brown, and Henderson, argues that all moods, situations, and even fortunes are dependent on her love. When Al Jolson was preparing his Broadway musical *Big Boy* (1925), he wanted to interpolate a new number to fill out his role. B.G. DeSylva and Lew Brown wrote the lyric about romantic dependency, it was given to composer Ray Henderson to write the bubbly music, and the new team was born. Jolson sang the number in the show and recorded it, as did Ruth Etting, and both discs sold well. Etting used it throughout her career, and Doris Day sang it in her movie bio *Love Me or Leave Me* (1955). Jolson reprised it in *The Singing Fool* (1928), and it was sung by Gordon MacRae, Ernest Borgnine, Dan Dailey, and Sheree North in the DeSylva-Brown-Henderson bio *The Best Things in Life Are Free* (1956). Other memorable records over the years were made by Day, MacRae, Paul Whiteman, Ben Bernie, Pee Wee Russell, Nat King Cole, Frank Sinatra, Patti Page, Johnnie Ray, Jaye P. Morgan, Judy Garland and Barbra Streisand, Shirley Bassey, Dorothy Loudon, and George Burns.

"It Don't Mean a Thing (If It Ain't Got That Swing)" (1932) is probably the first song to used the word "swing" in its lyric to denote the new kind of music developing in the early 1930s. The number started as an instrumental piece by Duke Ellington, then Irving Mills added the zesty lyric about the need for more than just music and melody to make a number jump. Mills even punctuated the lyric with lots of "doo wah's" to imitate instruments in the orchestra. Ellington introduced the new song with Ivie Anderson as vocalist, and the record was an immediate success. Ten years later he made a distinctive instrumental record as well. Other artists who made significant discs include Nina Simone, the Boswell Sisters, Lionel Hampton, the Mills Brothers, June Christy, Paul Gonsalves, Louis Armstrong, Ella Fitzgerald, Woody Herman, Mel Tormé, Rosemary Clooney, and Jane Horrocks. The number can be heard in the movies *The Hit Parade* (1937) and *Sweet and Lowdown* (1999), and it has been performed on Broadway by the ensemble in the revue *Bubbling Brown Sugar* (1976), Gregory Hines, Phyllis Hyman, and the company in *Sophisticated Ladies* (1981), a harmonizing quartet in *Play On!* (1997), and Casey MacGill and the Gotham City Gates in *Swing!* (1999).

"It Had to Be You" (1924) is a Tin Pan Alley high point, an effortless classic that captures all of the romance and humanity of popular music in a simple, straightforward love song. Isham Jones composed the radiant music that quietly climbs the scale in each section and then builds to a point that both climaxes and resolves the melody. Gus Kahn contributed what is arguably his finest lyric, the recognition of the necessity of a sweetheart and the realization that no other love will do. Kahn uses simple, masculine rhymes and short but potent phrases throughout. He even lets an idea started in one section remain incomplete ("I finally found somebody who . . ."), only to have it conclude in the next section (". . . could make me be true"). Jones and his Orchestra introduced the song, and during the first year it produced six bestsellers by Cliff Edwards, Paul Whiteman and his Orchestra, Marion Harris, Sam Lanin, Billy Murray, and Aileen Stanley. Although it never fell out of favor, the ballad enjoyed revived interest through records by Artie Shaw in 1941, Helen Forrest and Dick Haymes in 1944, Doris Day in 1951, and Barbra Streisand in 1963. Earl Hines recorded it in 1941, but it didn't become a hit until 1944 because there was a ban on new recordings for a while. Of the hundreds of other discs made over the years, there were memorable ones by Jimmie Lunceford, Henry Busse, Buddy Clark, Vera Lynn, Frank Sinatra, Billie Holiday, Eddy Duchin, Nat King Cole, Kay Thompson, Margaret Whiting, Anita O'Day, Tony Bennett, Andy Williams, and Dorothy Loudon. It is estimated that "It Had to Be You" can be heard in over forty films (including shorts). Among the more notable screen performances are those by Dooley Wilson in *Casablanca* (1942), Nan Wynn in *Is Everybody Happy?* (1943), George Murphy, Constance Moore, and Eddie Cantor in *Show Business* (1944), Betty Hutton in *Incendiary Blonde* (1945), Gene Kelly and Marie McDonald dancing to the number in *Living in a Big Way* (1947), Doris Day and Danny Thomas in the Kahn bio *I'll See You in My Dreams* (1951), Diane Keaton in *Annie Hall* (1977), and Harry Connick Jr. on the soundtrack of *When Harry Met Sally* (1989).

"It Isn't Fair" (1933) is the bombastic lament of a wooer who complains of his dearie's fickle nature, arguing that it's not fair "for you to taunt me." Richard Himber, Frank Warshauer, and Sylvester Sprigato wrote the tearful ballad, and Himber and his Orchestra introduced it on record and made it their theme song throughout the 1930s. Other early discs were made by Hal Kemp, Jack Fulton, and Elmer Feldkamp, and when it was revived by Don Cornell with Sammy Kaye's Orchestra in 1950, the song stayed on *Your Hit Parade* for twelve weeks. Other records of note were made by Dick Haymes, Benny Goodman (vocal by Buddy Greco), Gracie Fields, Dinah Washington, Les Brown, and the Duprees.

"It's a Sin to Tell a Lie" (1936) is a piquant rhythm song by Billy Mayhew that warns one against saying "I love You" too easily because a million hearts have been broken by that lie. Kate Smith introduced the number on radio, and Thomas "Fats" Waller made it a hit with his chart record. The lively ballad was revived in 1955 by Something Smith and the Redheads. Noteworthy discs were also made by Russ Morgan (vocal by Dick Robertson), child singer Bobby Breen, Vera Lynn, Billie Holiday, George Hall (vocal by Dolly Dawn), the Ink Spots, Ruth Etting, Willie Humphrey, Johnny Long, Jimmy Rushing, and Jerry Murad and his Harmonicats. Nell Carter sang "It's a Sin to Tell a Lie" in the Broadway revue *Ain't Misbehavin'* (1978), and the Hall-Dawn record was heard on the soundtrack of the movie *Pennies From Heaven* (1981).

"It's a Wonderful World" (1939) is a ballad of contentment that was first popular with Big Bands and later became a jazz favorite. Harold Adamson (lyric), Jan Savitt, and Johnny Watson (music) wrote the number, and Savitt introduced it with his Orchestra (vocal by Bon Bon) on record and made it their theme song. Charlie Barnet (vocal by Mary Ann McCall), Ray Anthony, Jan Garber, Frank Sinatra, Peggy Lee, Les Brown, Joe Pass, Ella Fitzgerald, and Vic Damone are among those who also recorded it. The song can be heard on the movie soundtrack of *New York, New York* (1977).

"It's All in the Game" (1951) is a ballad that looks at life and love with a practical eye, philosophizing that love means heartbreak, many a tear will be shed, and that is how the game is played. Carl Sigman wrote the knowing lyric, and the music was by Charles Gates Dawes who had composed the melody back in 1921. But Dawes was too busy with his political career (he was vice president of the United States from 1925 to 1929), so he never got around to finding a lyricist until he was retired. Tommy Edwards popularized the number with a record that went to the top position on the charts; when he recorded it again in 1958, that disc was also a hit. Cliff Richards revived the ballad in 1963 with a bestselling record, and the Four Tops had success with it in 1970. Other artists who made recordings of "It's All in the Game" include Dinah Shore, the Lettermen, Ernie Fields, Andy Williams, Sammy Davis Jr., Bobby Vee, and Isaac Hayes.

"It's Been a Long, Long Time" (1945) was perhaps the favorite homecoming love song of World War Two, a straightforward declaration of love and asking for kisses because they have been separated for too long. (The number is sometimes listed by its opening line "Kiss Me Once, Kiss Me Twice, Then Kiss Me Once Again.") Jule Styne composed the easygoing fox trot music, and Sammy Cahn penned the sincere lyric with the matter-of-fact sentiment "you'll never know how many dreams" he has had about her. Phil Brito introduced the ballad on the radio, but it was a bestselling record by Harry James (vocal by Kitty Kallen) that endeared it to audiences and kept the song on *Your Hit Parade* for fourteen weeks. Among the many memorable recordings made over the years were those by Bing Crosby with the Les Paul Trio, Charlie Spivak, Stan Fenton (vocal by June Christy), Keely Smith, Lillian Roth, Louis Armstrong, Chet Atkins, Peggy Lee, Rosemary Clooney, Frank Sinatra, the Ink Spots, Perry Como, Rick Hardeman, Sam Donohue, Shelly Fabares, Floyd Tillman, and more recently, Andrea Marcovicci, Judy Kuhn, and Michael

Feinstein. Dan Dailey, June Haver, and Gloria DeHaven performed the number in the movie *I'll Get By* (1950).

"It's Beginning to Look (a Lot) Like Christmas" (1951) is a seasonal favorite about the signs that the holidays are approaching. Bandleader Meredith Willson wrote the easygoing number, and it was popularized by Perry Como on records. Willson was encouraged by its success to pursue more songwriting, and he scored *The Music Man* (1957) and other Broadway musicals. He interpolated the Christmas song into *Here's Love* (1963) where Janis Paige and Fred Gywnne sang it contrapuntally with Laurence Naismith singing "Pine Cones and Holly Berries." Johnny Mathis, Dionne Warwick, and Dean Martin were among the many who recorded the modern carol.

"It's Never Too Late (To Say You're Sorry)" (1939) is a tender ballad of reconciliation that Carmen Lombardo and John Jacob Loeb wrote for Guy Lombardo and the Royal Canadians. Their record was successful, as were discs by Jan Garber (vocal by Lee Bennett) and Gray Gordon (vocal by Kitty Bradley). Kate Smith, Barry Wood, Tex Ritter, Brenda Lee, the Stanley Brothers, and Frankie Avalon were among the other artists who also recorded it.

"It's Not For Me to Say" (1957) is a bluesy love song by Al Stillman (lyric) and Robert Allen (music) that was introduced in the movie *Lizzie* (1957), where Johnny Mathis sang it on the soundtrack and appeared briefly in a nightclub scene. The film was not a success, but the ballad was, Mathis's record selling a million copies and staying in the Top 10 for many weeks. There were also notable discs made by Nat King Cole, Jane Morgan, Roger Williams, Connie Francis, the Ray Conniff Singers, George Shearing, and in one of her last recordings, Billie Holiday.

"It's Only a Paper Moon" (1932), the first Harold Arlen tune to appear in a movie, is a radiant number about make-believe becoming real because of the power of love. E.Y. Harburg and Billy Rose wrote the breezy lyric about a "Barnum and Bailey world," arguing that an artificial moon and a painted sunset are as good as the real thing "if you believed in me." Arlen's music is gently swinging and yet quirky enough that the song was later picked up by jazz musicians for its improvisational possibilities. Originally titled "If You Believed in Me," the number was written as a recurring theme in the Broadway play *The Great Magoo* (1932). But when it was retitled after the opening line of the refrain and sung by June Knight, Cliff Edwards, and Charles "Buddy" Rogers in the movie *Take a Chance* (1933), the song caught on and enjoyed hit records by Ella Fitzgerald, the Nat King Cole Trio, and the Mills Brothers. Benny

Goodman and his Orchestra revived the number with a successful disc in 1945. Other prominent records were made by Lee Wiley, Sammy Kaye, Vaughn Monroe, Art Blakely, the Four Freshmen, Kenny Drew, the Mystics, Miles Davis, and more recently, Julie Wilson, Harry Nilsson, and Natalie Cole. "It's Only a Paper Moon" was heard in the films *Too Young to Know* (1945), *Paper Moon* (1973), and *Funny Lady* (1975), where it was sung by James Caan, Barbra Streisand, and the chorus girls. The song is sometimes listed as "Paper Moon."

"It's the Talk of the Town" (1933) is an affecting ballad by Marty Symes, Al Neiberg (lyric), and Jerry Livingston (music) about a marriage on the rocks. Everyone in town is talking about a couple's breakup, but one of the partners pleas for a reconciliation. The song was popularized by a record by Glen Gray and the Casa Loma Orchestra (vocal by Kenny Sargent), and there were other early and successful discs by Fletcher Henderson and Red McKenzie. The slow ballad was also recorded by the Dorsey Brothers, Benny Goodman, Harry James, Art Van Damme, Joni James, Hank Jones, Perry Como, the Ravens, June Christy, Bobby Dukoff, Spiegle Willcox, and Dave Brubeck.

"It's Tulip Time in Holland" (1915) was composer Richard A. Whiting's first hit song, though he ended up sharing in none of the profits. Whiting collaborated with lyricist Dave Radford on the slight but catchy tune about spring. Because the young and struggling composer so much wanted a Steinway grand, he sold his share of the rights to a publisher for such a piano. The song caught on and ended up selling 1.5 million copies of sheet music. Mostly forgotten today, the number can be heard in the period movies *Hello, Frisco, Hello* (1943), sung by Kirby Grant and the chorus, and *April Showers* (1948).

"I've Been Working on the Railroad" (c. 1894), probably the most familiar train song in American pop culture, has unknown authors and origins. The traditional folk song has been credited to various sources, from Negro laborers on the levee to Irish immigrant workers on the rails to a popular nineteenth-century hymn. The lyric versions also vary, though it is usually a work song about rising early to labor on railroad construction all day long. The section about Dinah blowing the horn (a signal to stop working) and her sitting in the kitchen and strumming on a banjo was added later, probably around 1894. A longtime favorite in children's songbooks and records, the ditty has also been recorded by Dick Curless, Ella Jenkins, Pete Seeger, the Carter Family, Mitch Miller, Jack Mudurian, and John Denver. It was heard on the soundtrack of several movies, such as *Let Freedom Ring* (1939), Gregory Peck sang it in

Duel in the Sun (1946), and Elvis Presley performed a new arrangement of it by Fred Wise and Ben Weisman in *Viva Las Vegas* (1964).

"I've Got a Crush on You" (1928) is the romantic Gershwin standard from Broadway that did not take its present form until it became a Tin Pan Alley hit. Ira Gershwin wrote a glib and sassy lyric about affection for a "Sweetie pie" that causes a beau to utter, "Mush." George Gershwin composed a snappy melody, and it was introduced by Clifton Webb, Mary Hay, and the ensemble in the short-lived musical *Treasure Girl* (1928). The brothers interpolated it into their later musical *Strike Up the Band* (1930), where it was sung by Doris Carson and Gordon Smith, and they danced to it at a rapid 2/4 time. The song was published, and recordings were made, none quite getting widespread attention. Then Lee Wiley made a disc in which the tempo was slowed down, and the same brash lyrics sounded tender and sentimental. It was a success and in the dozens of recordings that followed, few retained the original's fast and furious tempo. Frank Sinatra had his first popular single with the song, and there were other discs of note by Lester Lanin, Bing Crosby, Zoot Sims, Rosemary Clooney, Roy Eldridge, Wes Montgomery, Sarah Vaughan, Kenny Burrell, Julie London, Helen Ward, Dorothy Dandridge, Oscar Peterson, Marni Nixon, Mantovanni's Orchestra, Jack Jones, and more recently, Carly Simon, Cleo Laine, Linda Ronstadt, and Bobby Short. Benny Carter and his Orchestra were heard playing it in the movie *An American in Paris* (1951), Sinatra reprised it in *Meet Danny Wilson* (1952), Betty Grable, Jack Lemmon, and Marge and Gower Champion performed it in *Three for the Show* (1955), Gogi Grant dubbed it for Ann Blyth in *The Helen Morgan Story* (1957), Ellen Burstyn sang it in *Alice Doesn't Live Here Anymore* (1974), and it was heard on the soundtrack of *Manhattan* (1979).

"I've Got a Feeling I'm Falling" (1929) is a delectable ballad by Billy Rose (lyric), Harry Link, and Thomas "Fats" Waller (music) about the realization of love, facing the prospect with bittersweet emotion. The way the music rises and falls in line with the "falling" in the lyric is quiet but unforgettable. Helen Morgan introduced the ballad in the film *Applause* (1929), but it was popularized by Waller's recording. Other memorable discs were made by Ella Fitzgerald with the Day Dreamers, Gene Austin, Annette Hanshaw, Benny Goodman, the piano duo Fingerle and Schutt, Louis Armstrong, James P. Johnson, and Earl Hines. Nell Carter sang the number on Broadway in the Waller revue *Ain't Misbehavin'* (1978).

"I've Got My Captain Working for Me Now" (1919) is a topical comedy song by Irving Berlin about life after World War One. Johnny Jones was a private in the army but is now employed in his father's business, where he is supervisor of a clerk who used to be his captain. Planning to work the ex-officer to the bone, he merrily proclaims that "everything comes to those who wait." In its way, the ditty is a follow-up to Berlin's earlier "Oh! How I Hate to Get Up in the Morning" (1918) in which an enlisted man dreams of murdering the bugler who plays reveille early each morning. Eddie Cantor introduced "I've Got My Captain Working for Me Now" in the *Ziegfeld Follies* (1919) and recorded it with success, as did Al Jolson, Billy Murray, and the Original Dixieland Jazz Band. The old song was revived after World War Two when Bing Crosby and Billy DeWolfe sang it in the movie *Blue Skies* (1946).

"I've Got the World on a String" (1932) is a gently swinging number by Ted Koehler (lyric) and Harold Arlen (music) that expresses the fanciful way one feels when in love. The image of sitting on a rainbow and having the earth on a string that is tied to one's finger is both ridiculous and sublime, and Arlen's cool and detached music makes it all perfectly natural. Aida Ward introduced the song in the Harlem revue *Cotton Club Parade* (1932), and soon there were popular records by Cab Calloway, Bing Crosby, and Louis Armstrong. Frank Sinatra revived the ballad in 1953, and it was in Jo Stafford's repertoire for years. Among the many other artists who made disc versions were Woody Herman, Mildred Bailey, Lena Horne, Benny Carter, Bobby Hackett, Red McKenzie with the Spirits of Rhythm, Buddy Cole, Hot Lips Page, Julie Wilson, and Ann Hampton Callaway. June Haver and Gloria DeHaven sang it in the film *I'll Get By* (1950), and a Peggy Lee recording was heard in *What Women Want* (2000).

J

"Jalousie (Jealousy)" (1925) is a gypsy tango that originated in Denmark and found success in England before becoming a Tin Pan Alley hit in America. Danish violinist Jacob Gade wrote the pulsating music that became an instrumental favorite in Europe in the 1920s. In 1931 Vera Bloom provided an entrancing lyric in English about two lovers dancing a tango, one seething with jealousy as he suspects there is another in her life. At first the song became known in the States as an instrumental, Leo Reisman's 1932 record being a bestseller and a disc by Arthur Fiedler and the Boston Pops titled "Tango Tzigane" selling a million copies (the first "light classic" record to do so). Harry James had success with it in 1947, but it was Frankie Laine's 1951 record that made the number a vocal hit, selling over a million copies as well. Other noteworthy discs were made by Clark Dennis, Percy Faith, Xavier Cugat, Caterina Valente, and many guitarists, tango bands, and orchestras. The song was heard in the film *Paris Honeymoon* (1939), Kathryn Grayson performed it in *Anchors Aweigh* (1945), and Lucille Norman sang it in *Painting the Clouds With Sunshine* (1951).

"Jamaica Farewell" (1955) is a calypso favorite even though it is unusual for its genre, not being an uptempo number and not about working on the islands. Lord Burgess (a.k.a. Irving Burgie) wrote the ballad, basing his music on an old West Indies folk song. The tender lyric tells of a sailor who found romance in Jamaica but had to leave his beloved in Kingston when his ship sailed. Harry Belafonte popularized the number on records in the 1950s, and there were other discs by the Kingston Trio, Dick Curless, the Brothers Four, Marty Robbins, the Lennon Sisters, Patti Page, Chuck Berry, and Jimmy Buffett. David Engel and Jason Graae sang the emotive song in the Off-Broadway revue *Forever Plaid* (1990).

"Jambalaya (On the Bayou)" (1952) is a country-western hit by Hank Williams that crossed over into the pop market with success. The farewell song explains that one must return to the bayou where his darling awaits him, listing several foods of the region (cod fish pie, jambalaya, and so on) that he looks forward to as well. The number is lighthearted (especially for Williams) and playful, pronouncing "me oh my-o" to rhyme with "bayou." Williams's record was a bestseller, and Jo Stafford's was even more popular. Different revival versions kept the number well known for decades, thanks to Brenda Lewis in 1956, Bobby Comstock in 1960, Fats Domino in 1962, the Nitty Gritty Dirt Band in 1972, and the Blue Ridge Rangers in 1973. Other commendable records were made by Roy Acuff, Pat Boone, the Norman Petty Trio, Connie Stevens, Jerry Lee Lewis, and Gerry and the Pacemakers. Sometimes listed as "On the Bayou," the song was sung on screen by George Hamilton (dubbed by Hank Williams Jr.) in the Williams bio *Your Cheatin' Heart* (1964), and the original Williams recording was heard in *The Last Picture Show* (1971).

"The Japanese Sandman" (1920) was one of many songs written after World War One about faraway and exotic places, few becoming more popular than this lullaby that sold over a million copies of sheet music. Raymond Egan wrote the gentle lyric about the magical powers of a sandman from the mysterious East, and Richard A. Whiting composed the fluent music that has more than just a touch of the Oriental in it. Nora Bayes introduced the song in vaudeville and on records, but it was Paul Whiteman and his Orchestra that made it a hit. Benny Goodman revived it with success in 1935. Other records of note were made by Django Reinhardt, Nat Brandwynne, Russ Morgan, Ray Noble, Artie Shaw, and comic Graham Chapman. Pat Morita and Jack Soo sang it in the movie *Thoroughly Modern Millie* (1967), it was heard in *Rose of Washington Square* (1939) and *They Shoot Horses, Don't They?* (1969), and it was performed by the cast of the Broadway musical *A Day in Hollywood—A Night in the Ukraine* (1980).

"Jealous Heart" (1943) is a slow country boogie by Jenny Lou Carson that took years to catch on, but once it did, it crossed over into various markets. The lyric addresses one's heart, telling it to stop beating so hard from jealousy, blaming it on driving a sweetheart away, and concluding that "I'm the lonely one" because of such a heart. Carson introduced the song on record, but it got more attention when Tex Ritter recorded it. There were also early discs by Hugo Winterhalter (vocal Johnny Thompson), Jack Owens, and Henri René (vocal by Bill Lawrence), but it was an instrumental version by pianist Al Morgan in 1949 that sold the most records. Tab Hunter revived it in 1958, and Connie Francis did likewise in 1965. Other successful discs were made by the Mills Brothers, Ernest

Tubb, Ivory Joe Hunter, Les Paul and Mary Ford, Bill Haley, and Anthony Rivera.

"Jeanie With the Light Brown Hair" (1854) is one of Stephen Foster's most beloved ballads, a heartfelt song of affection that doesn't use a southern dialect or a rural sentiment to achieve its power. Foster wrote the song when he and his wife Jane had separated, the lyric expressing his inability to forget her. (The two were later reconciled.) The music is a bit more rangy than most of his songs, just as the lyric is more flowery ("floating like a vapor on the soft summer air"). Although it was widely popular in the nineteenth century, Foster only earned $217.80 from it in royalties during his lifetime. In 1941, when ASCAP and the radio networks fought over broadcast rights and many royalty-free songs were put on the air, "I Dream of Jeanie With the Light Brown Hair" (as it is sometimes titled) was the most frequently aired song of that year. Don Ameche sang it in the movie *Swanee River* (1939), Martha Raye performed it in *The Farmer's Daughter* (1940), and it was heard in many other movies, such as *I Dream of Jeanie* (1952). John McCormack, Richard Crooks, Bing Crosby, Glenn Miller, the Banjo Kings, Gene Krupa, Maxine Sullivan, Marilyn Horne, and the Mormon Tabernacle Choir are among the many artists who recorded the flowing ballad.

"Jimmy Crack Corn" (1846), often listed as "The Blue Tail Fly," was one of the most popular songs during the Civil War and a staple in minstrel shows for many years after. Daniel Decatur Emmett wrote the merry number about a slave who has waited on his master for years, shooing away the blue tail flies that bothered him. But now life is easy because "my master's gone away." Emmett wrote it for a minstrel show and had no plans to make a social commentary, but some southerners objected to the insolent attitude toward plantation owners. Abolitionists, on the other hand, reveled in the song and sang it as a farcical anthem. (It was a particular favorite of Abraham Lincoln's.) The comic ditty is heard on many children's records, and there were adult versions by Burl Ives, Leadbelly, Kate Smith, Gene Autry, Shorty Warren, the Ventures, the Andrews Sisters, Pete Seeger, Rosalie Allen, Roy Acuff, and others. Ives sang it with the chorus in the Broadway revue *Sing Out, Sweet Land* (1944), and it can be heard in many period films, such as *Under Colorado Skies* (1947).

"Jimmy Valentine" (1911) was a familiar narrative ballad in vaudeville that took its character and story from the celebrated short story "A Retrieved Reformation" by O. Henry. Edward Madden (lyric) and Gus Edwards (music) wrote the number, warning the audience about safe cracker Jimmy who cannot only figure out any lock combination with his fingertips, but he'll also steal your true love's heart away. Edwards introduced the song in his children's variety act, and soon other vaudeville performers picked up on it. The song became the leitmotiv for the movie *Alias Jimmy Valentine* (1928), and Bing Crosby sang it in the Edwards bio *The Star Maker* (1939). It is sometimes listed as "Look Out for Jimmy Valentine."

"Jingle Bells" (1857), the perennial Christmastime favorite, actually has nothing to do with the holidays, instead capturing the joys of riding through the snow in an open sleigh. S.J. Pierpont wrote the spirited song for a local Sunday school entertainment in Boston. After it was published as "The One-Horse Open Sleigh," the number slowly moved from a seasonal song to a holiday song, especially after the use of cars made such an old-fashion mode of transportation seem quaint and nostalgic. Of the hundreds of recordings over the years, there were bestsellers by Benny Goodman in 1935, Glenn Miller in 1941, and Les Paul in 1952, but none sold as many discs as the million-selling version by Bing Crosby with the Andrews Sisters in 1943. Danny Kaye performed the carol in the movie *The Five Pennies* (1959), Patti Page sang it in *Dondi* (1961), and it has been heard in the background in dozens of other films.

"Jingle, Jangle, Jingle" (1942) is an uptempo cowboy song that was widely popular during World War Two and for several years after. Joseph J. Lilley composed the rhythmic music that clops along like a horse, and Frank Loesser wrote the nimble lyric about riding on a horse with one's spurs jingling and feeling glad to be single and free. The ditty was written for the film *The Forest Rangers* (1942), where it was sung by the chorus on horseback, but the number was released early, and by the time the movie opened, the song was already famous because of radio play, sheet music, and records. The two most celebrated discs were those by the Merry Macs and Kay Kyser (vocals by Julie Conway and Harry Babbitt), the latter selling a million copies and keeping the number on the *Hit Parade* for fourteen weeks. Other successful records were made by Gene Autry, Freddie Martin (vocals by Clyde Rogers and Stuart Wade), Nat Gonella and his New Georgians, Tex Ritter and his Texans, and Loesser himself. General Elliot Roosevelt named his flying fortress *Jingle Jangle* during the war, and it became the theme song for the squadron. "I've Got Spurs That Jingle, Jangle, Jingle," as the number is sometimes listed, can be heard in the movie *And the Angels Sing* (1944).

"John Henry" (c. 1873) is a traditional American folk song of unknown authorship about a legendary Negro worker, a giant of a man with the strength of four men. The narrative ballad tells how he was able to drive more rivets than any other man but lost the championship to a steam-driven riveter, so he "died with a hammer in his hand." The work song has long been a favorite of folk singers, but the number has crossed over on occasion and been recorded in other markets. W.C. Handy wrote a version called "John Henry Blues" in 1922, and it was later recorded by Lena Horne and others. Odetta Felious Gordon had a hit disc of the original ballad in the 1960s. Other artists who have made recordings include Woody Guthrie, Harry Belafonte, Flatt and Scruggs, Wayne Erbsen, Big Walter Horton, Leadbelly, and Pete Seeger. Paul Robeson sang "John Henry" in the movie *The Emperor Jones* (1933), and it was heard in *Follow Your Heart* (1936).

"Johnny Doughboy Found a Rose in Ireland" (1941) is an old-time Irish ballad that was actually written during World War Two and appealed to audiences with its old-fashioned sentiments. Al Goodhart composed the lilting music, and Kay Twomey penned the warm lyric about a Yank who fell in love with a girl in Ireland and took her home to New York City, where she grew from an Irish rose to an American beauty rose. Popular both on radio and records, the number had hit records by Kay Kyser (vocal by the Glee Club), Kenny Baker, and Guy Lombardo (vocal by Kenny Gardner). Other acclaimed discs by Freddy Martin and his Orchestra and Dennis Day helped keep the song on *Your Hit Parade* for sixteen weeks. It was also featured in the movies *Ice-Capades* (1941) and *Johnny Doughboy* (1942).

"The Joint Is Jumpin' " (1937) is one of the most vivacious of all party songs, a jazzy celebration of dancing, boozing, and carefree abandon. Andy Razaf, J.C. Johnson, and Thomas "Fats" Waller collaborated on the scintillating number that Waller introduced with his Rhythm Band. The lyric is particularly sassy, as it describes the annoyed neighbors banging on the door and the partygoers philosophizing that "we're all bums when the wagon comes." Noteworthy recordings were made by Gene Sedric and his Honey Bears, Pat Flowers, Jack Sheldon, the Chevalier Brothers, Ricky Ritzel and Spider Saloff, and the Pointer Sisters. Sometimes titled "This Joint is Jumpin'," it was sung on Broadway by the cast of the Waller revue *Ain't Misbehavin'* (1978).

"Judy" (1928) is a sly romantic song that seems worldly wise about one's sweetheart rather than head over heels and irrational about her. Hoagy Carmichael and Sammy Lerner wrote the paean to Judy, a girl who can both build you up and tear you down. While the lyric admits that she "seems a saint and you find she ain't," the innocent and tuneful melody keeps the tone of the song very ambiguous. The number was written in 1928, but its style and sentiments were considered too avant-garde, and it was not published until 1934. Carmichael sang "Judy" with his band on records, and there were other early discs by Glen Gray and the Casa Loma Orchestra (vocal by Pee Wee Hunt) and the Dorsey Brothers. Lionel Hampton and Bob Chester each had success with it in the late 1930s, Alan Dale revived it in 1947, and Lee Konitz and Lennie Tristano had a hit record in 1949. Other major recordings were made by Louis Prima, Frankie Laine, Al Bowlly, and Tony Bennett. The young Judy Garland liked the song so much she used it when she changed her name from Frances Gumm.

"Juke Box Saturday Night" (1942) celebrated the rising popularity of the juke box in soda shops and other public places. Paul McCrane composed the swinging, playful music, and Al Stillman wrote the bouncy lyric about gathering around the juke box and pretending to be listening live to one of the name bands of the day. The song mentions a few Big Bands by name, and musical phrases from their theme songs are incorporated into the music. Although the number was introduced in the revue *Stars on Ice* (1942), it was popularized through records by Glenn Miller (vocals by Marion Hutton, Tex Beneke, and the Modernaires), Harry James, and the Ink Spots. Patsy Kelly revived the song with the Modernaires in 1953. The jumping number can be heard in the movies *Stars on Parade* (1944) and *When You're Smiling* (1950).

"The Jumpin' Jive" (1939) is a scat song favorite long associated with Cab Calloway. He collaborated with Fred Froeba and Jack Palmer on the number, introduced it with his orchestra on a record that was a hit, and featured it in concerts and on television for the next forty years. The song is an energetic celebration of the music, even the lyrics ("hep! hep!") turning into instrumental sounds. Memorable recordings were made by Ella Fitzgerald, Jimmy Dorsey (vocal by Helen O'Connell), Lionel Hampton, Van Alexander, the Andrews Sisters, and Joe Jackson. Calloway reprised the song, while the Nicholas Brothers danced to it in the film *Stormy Weather* (1943).

"Junk Man" (1934) was Frank Loesser's first song hit, contributing the lyrics to the early swing number about the trash man coming down the street. Joseph Meyer composed the animated music, and the song was popularized by Benny Goodman (vocal by Mildred Bailey). Other artists who recorded it include Jack Teagarden, Isham Jones (vocal by Eddie Stone), the Spirits of Rhythm, Banu Gibson, Carl Hagen's Orchestra, Toni Price, and Loesser himself. On Broadway, Debbie Shapiro sang "Junk Man" in the Loesser revue *Perfectly Frank* (1980).

"Just a Gigolo" (1930) is a unique ballad with a bittersweet lyric and an intoxicating melody, both very disarming as well as enticing. The number started as a Viennese pop song called "Schoener Gigolo" by Julius Brammer (German lyric) and Leonello Casucci (music). Irving Caesar wrote an English lyric about a war hero now down on his luck and forced to dance and flirt with rich ladies for a living. He seems to boast about the job, yet it disgusts him, commenting that when he dies people will forget his wartime valor and say that he was "just a gigolo." Irene Bordoni introduced the number in America, and it was popularized by hit records by Ted Lewis and Vincent Lopez. Another early release by Bing Crosby was also successful. Jaye P. Morgan revived the song in 1953, Louis Prima did the same in 1960, and there was a bestselling disc by David Lee Roth in 1985. Harry Richman, Roy Smeck, Louis Armstrong, Marlene Dietrich, and Sid Garry were among the other artists to record it. "Just a Gigolo" was heard in the films *Flying Down to Rio* (1933) and *Lover, Come Back* (1946), the Dietrich recording was played in *Just a Gigolo* (1979), and Howard Alden provided the guitar playing of it for Sean Penn in *Sweet and Lowdown* (1999).

"Just a Memory" (1926) is the dreamy standard by the celebrated trio of B.G. DeSylva, Lew Brown (lyric), and Ray Henderson (music) about a love that used to be. The torchy song recalls the days when he was in love and he dreams of being together again, but both seem to be nothing more than a fading memory. It was written as a Tin Pan Alley number but was soon interpolated into the Broadway musical *Manhattan Mary* (1927), where it caught the attention of the public. The bands of Paul Whiteman and Vincent Lopez (vocal by Frank Munn) were the first to find success with it on records, followed by many other artists, including Vaughn Monroe, Helen Morgan, Duke Ellington with Johnny Hodges, Andy Russell, the Paragons, Gordon MacRae, and Elvis Costello. "Just a Memory" was used in the movie *Look for the Silver Lining* (1949), Sheree North and the chorus performed it in the DeSylva-Brown-Henderson bio *The Best Things in Life Are Free* (1956), and Gogi Grant provided the singing voice for Ann Blyth in *The Helen Morgan Story* (1957).

"Just Before the Battle, Mother" (1863) was a very popular, if unusual, Civil War song in that it has the sentiment of an antiwar song in many ways. George Frederick Root wrote the heart-tugging ballad in which a soldier, just before the battle begins, says farewell to his faraway mother, hoping that she'll remember him with love if he should be "numbered with the slain." The number is highly melodramatic, yet its unadorned sincerity keeps it from becoming maudlin. It was first published in the Christmas issue of a Chicago magazine, *The Song Messenger*, and it immediately was embraced by the public, both North and South. Although accounts of sales at the time are inaccurate, it is estimated that over a million copies of sheet music were sold, one of the top sellers of the era.

Recordings have been made by Jule Zabawa, Kirk Browne, Douglas Jimerson, and the Sons of the Pioneers. The song can also be heard on the soundtracks of some Civil War films, most recently *Gettysburg* (1993).

"Just Friends" (1931) is a knowing ballad by Sam M. Lewis (lyric) and John Klenner (music) about "lovers no more." The short, economic lyric uses short, terse phrases to tell of two sweethearts who have broken up and decided to be "just friends." But deep inside, one of them wishes to be more than pals and comments, "Two friends—but one broken heart." Red McKenzie introduced the ballad, and there were early successful records by Russ Columbo, Jack Denny, Art Jarrett, Ben Selvin, and Morton Downey. Later discs of note were made by Andy Russell, the Dinning Sisters, Glen Gray and the Casa Loma Orchestra (vocal by Kenny Sargent), and Charlie Parker.

"Just One More Chance" (1931) is a crooning plea for forgiveness that was ideally suited to Bing Crosby's singing style, and his recording went to the top of the charts. Sam Coslow (lyric) and Arthur Johnston (music) wrote the ballad that asks a true love for another chance to prove himself. There were many recordings in the 1930s, and it was revived by Les Paul and Mary Ford in 1951. Among the other well-known records were those by Gus Arnheim, Abe Lyman, Ruth Etting, the Harmonicats, Dinah Washington, Cozy Cole, Buddy Clark, Billie Holiday, Coleman Hawkins, Peggy Lee, the Three Suns, and Ernestine Jackson. It was sung on screen by Dick Powell in *College Coach* (1933) and Dean Martin in *The Stooge* (1953), it was heard in *Country Music Holiday* (1958), and the famous Crosby recording was used on the soundtrack of *Paper Moon* (1973).

"Just Tell Them That You Saw Me" (1895) is a sentimental ballad that coined a popular expression in the 1890s. Paul Dresser read a newspaper article about a woman whose life was ruined by a passionate but unwise love affair. He wrote a smooth, flowing melody and a lyric about a girl who falls into ruin in the big city but is too proud to go back home. When an old school friend from her hometown comes across her one day, he asks if he should say anything when he returns home. She sends her love to her mother, then utters the title phrase. Irish singer James Cavanaugh popularized the narrative ballad in vaudeville, and it got around quickly. The title phrase was picked up by newspaper writers and entertainers, and there were even buttons printed with the words "Just tell them that you saw me." Even after the initial popularity of the song waned, the phrase held on for years. Red Smiley made a memorable record of the old ballad.

K

"Keeping Out of Mischief Now" (1932) is a breezy vow of fidelity that has a sly and ambiguous subtext. Andy Razaf (lyric) and Thomas "Fats" Waller (music) wrote the spry number in which a swain resolves to stop flirting and partying, now that he is truly in love. Yet his declaration that reading books and listening to the radio will content him strikes a sarcastic chord. The song is similar in nature to the same songwriters' earlier "Ain't Misbehavin'" (1929), though this one takes the form of a ballad rather than a rhythm number. Waller introduced and popularized the song in clubs and on records, and there were other discs made by Louis Armstrong, Tommy Dorsey, the Coon-Sanders Orchestra, Isham Jones, Nellie Lutcher, Buddy Greco, Sammy Davis Jr., James P. Johnson, Pee Wee Russell, Nat Jaffe, Ralph Sutton, Teddi King, and Dinah Washington. Charlaine Woodard performed it in the Broadway revue *Ain't Misbehavin'* (1978), and the original Waller recording was heard in the film *The Story of Us* (1999).

"Kentucky Babe" (1896) is a down-home country lullaby by Richard Buck (lyric) and Adam Geibel (music) in which a mother sings her child to sleep as the "skeeters" are humming and the "bobolink" is whistling. As gentle as the number is, there is also a Dixieland bounce to the melody. Bessie Davis introduced and popularized the song in vaudeville, and it was soon a favorite of barbershop quartets and glee clubs. Of the many artists who recorded the number were Gene Autry, Maxine Sullivan, Bing Crosby, the Dixie Symphony Four, Laurie Franks, Deborah Henson, and Burl Ives. It was also sung by the cast of the Broadway revue *Tintypes* (1980).

"Kickin' the Clouds Away" (1925) is a vibrant dance song about hoofing through life and kicking aside all your worries. B.G. DeSylva, Ira Gershwin (lyric), and George Gershwin (music) wrote the number for the Broadway musical *Tell Me More!* (1925), where it was performed by Phyllis Cleveland, Esther Howard, Lou Holtz, and the ensemble, and soon it was picked up by many dance bands. Many years later it was heard on Broadway again when Roscoe Lee Browne and the chorus sang and danced it in the "new Gershwin musical" *My One and Only* (1983). Bobby Short and Kaye Ballard each made distinctive records of the song.

"Kingdom Coming" (1862) is a jubilant number comparing the end of slavery with the Second Coming. Henry Clay Work wrote the bright and hopeful number, the lyric in Negro dialect as it describes the "darkeys" celebrating as Lincoln's gunboats approach and all the plantation masters are on the run. The song, sometimes titled "The Year of Jubilo," was introduced by Christy's Minstrels in Chicago, and it quickly became a staple in minstrel troupes in the North. There were also parody versions and sequels, including Work's "Babylon Is Fallen" in 1863. The Civil War ballad has been recorded by the Boll Weevil Jazz Band, the Sons of the Pioneers, Fiddlin' Buck Ryan with Reno and Smiley, Wayne Erbsen, D.C. Hall's New Concert and Quadrille Band, and Tom Varner. "Kingdom Coming" can be heard in the film *The Blair Witch Project* (1999).

"A Kiss Goodnight" (1945) is a cautionary song about an amorous beau who asks for a goodnight kiss, which leads to another, and soon "Casanova" won't "do an about face" and leave. Freddie Slack, Reba Nell Herman, and Floyd Victor wrote the easy jazz number that became popular by way of records by Slack's Orchestra (vocal by Liza Morrow), Woody Herman, and Ella Fitzgerald with Randy Brooks' Orchestra. There were also later discs by Ted Heath, Scott Hiltzik, and Who's on Bass.

"A Kiss to Build a Dream On" (1935) is a melodious request for a goodnight kiss that took several years to find an audience. Bert Kalmar (lyric) and Harry Ruby (music) wrote the ballad as "Moonlight on the Meadow" for the Marx Brothers vehicle *A Night at the Opera* (1935), but it was not used in the movie and the songwriters tried in vain to interest publishers and singers in it. Oscar Hammerstein was impressed with the melody and helped out the writers, giving it its new title and making some other changes in the lyric. The new song was introduced in the film *The Strip* (1951), where it was performed by Kay Brown and Louis Armstrong. The song then caught on, and Armstrong made an outstanding recording that remains definitive. Other discs of note were made by Hugo Winterhalter, Jimmy Dorsey, Benny Bailey, Paula West, Buddy

Tate, Doc Cheatham, Mose Scarlett, the Dukes of Dixieland, Emile Ford and the Checkmates, Jonah Jones, the California Swing Cats, Charlie Byrd, the Manhattan Transfer, Cathi Walkup, and more recently, Mandy Patinkin and Philip Officer. The famous Armstrong recording can be heard in the movies *Sleepless in Seattle* (1993) and *Closer You Get* (2000).

"Kisses Sweeter Than Wine" (1951) is a slow but rhythmic ballad that tells of a couple's courtship, wedding, raising of a family, and old age, all the time proclaiming that her kisses are sweeter than wine. The authorship of the number is cloudy. The music, which was adapted from the old Irish folk song "Drimmer's Cow," is credited to Joel Newman, though many believe it was written by Huddie Ledbetter (a.k.a. Leadbelly) who died before the song was recorded. The lyricist is listed as Paul Campbell, which turned out to be a pseudonym for the Weavers (Pete Seeger, Lee Hays, Fred Kellerman, and Ronnie Gilbert). The Weavers recorded it with Leo Diamond's Orchestra, and it was a hit. Jimmie Rodgers revived the ballad in 1957 with Hugo Peretti's Orchestra, and it was even more successful. Other artists who have made discs of the song include the Kingston Trio, Peter, Paul and Mary, Marlene Dietrich, Andy Williams, the Cliff Adams Singers, Peter Seeger as a solo, the New Christy Minstrels, the Ray Conniff Singers, and Waylon Jennings.

"Kitty From Kansas City" (1921) is a Dixieland jazz favorite by Harry Rose, Jesse Green, Rudy Vallee, and George Bronson that was not a hit when it was first published and recorded. It wasn't until 1930 that a disc by Vallee caught on, and it was heard often during the depression years. Among the others to record the number were the Coon-Sanders Nighthawk Orchestra, the Original Memphis Five, Bob Schulz and the Riverboat Ramblers, the Pasadena Roof Orchestra, and Dave Stickey. The popular Vallee recording was heard in the film *King of the Hill* (1993).

"K-K-K-Katy" (1918), sometimes listed as "The Stammering Song," is a novelty number by Geoffrey O'Hara that sings the praises of Katy, the "g-g-g-girl" waiting at "the k-k-k-kitchen door." Billy Murray popularized the ditty in vaudeville and on record, and it was a favorite of American troops during World War One. The silly piece can be heard in the films *The Cock-Eyed World* (1929) and *Tin Pan Alley* (1940), where it was sung by Jack Oakie, Alice Faye, John Payne, Betty Grable, and John Loder. Memorable records were made by Faye, Buddy Clark, and Phil Liverpool's Band.

"Knock, Knock, Who's There?" (1936) is a novelty number that uses the familiar word game for its lyric idea, asking and answering a series of foolish questions. Bill Tipton, Bill Davies, Johnny Morris, and Vincent

Lopez wrote the silly ditty, and it was introduced by Lopez and his Orchestra with success. Ted Weems (vocal by Red Ingle) also had a hit recording of it. Other discs were made by Stuff Smith, Chu Berry, Fletcher Henderson, Greg Serrato, Mary Hopkin, and Spike Jones and his City Slickers.

L

"**Lady of Spain**" (1931), perhaps played on the accordion more than any other pop song, was an import not from Spain but from Great Britain, where it was introduced by Jack Payne and his Orchestra. Ray Noble and his Orchestra and Roy Fox (vocal by Al Bowlly) made it a hit in America, and there were revivals of the song in 1952 with a million-seller by Eddie Fisher and an instrumental version by Les Paul that was also a bestseller. The tuneful serenade by a cavalier to his Madrid sweetie ("I adore you . . . what else can I do?") was written by Robert Hargreaves, Tolchard Evans, Stanley J. Damerell, and Henry J. Tilsley. Louis Prima, Bing Crosby, Mario Lanza, the Firehouse Five Plus Two, Ethel Smith, George Melachrino, and Winifred Atwell are among the artists who also recorded it, but the number most often brings to mind accordion players, such as the Philharmonica Trio, who made it an indispensable part of their repertoire. "Lady of Spain" can be heard in the movie *Dancers in the Dark* (1932), and Stan Chandler sang it in the Off-Broadway revue *Forever Plaid* (1990).

"**L'Amour, Toujours, L'Amour (Love Everlasting)**" (1922) is a rare case of operetta composer Rudolf Friml having a hit on Tin Pan Alley that did not come from one of his stage works. He wrote the delicate and ornate ballad as an independent piece, and Catherine Chisholm Cushing provided the heartfelt lyric promising a love without end. Recordings over the years were made by Jessica Dragonette, Lily Pons, Maxine Sullivan, Andy Ross, Meredith Willson's Orchestra, Richard Tauber, and Jesse Crawford. Susannah Foster sang it in the movie *This Is the Life* (1944), and it was also heard in *Cain and Mabel* (1936), *Faithful in My Fashion* (1946), and *Flap* (1970).

"The Lamplighter's Serenade" (1942) is an atmospheric number about an old lamplighter who goes about at sunset to light the street lamps and set the mood for romance. Paul Francis Webster (lyric) and Hoagy Carmichael (music) wrote the sonorous ballad, and it was popularized by a bestselling record by Glenn Miller (vocals by Ray Eberly and the Modernaires). Even more successful was a chart record by Bing Crosby. Prominent discs were also made by the Four Freshmen, Ken Griffin, and Frank Sinatra in his first solo record after leaving the Dorsey Brothers' band.

"Last Night When We Were (Very) Young" (1936), one of the finest love songs of the 1930s, had a lot of trouble getting heard by the public and didn't become a hit until the 1940s. E.Y. Harburg (lyric) and Harold Arlen (music) wrote it for the film *Metropolitan* (1935), but the ballad was cut and only part of the music was heard in the background. The songwriters tried to get it into several other movies, but producers either turned it down or cut it from the final print because they considered it too sad. Judy Garland recorded it for *In the Good Old Summertime* (1949), and Frank Sinatra did likewise for *Take Me Out to the Ball Game* (1949), but, in both cases, the number was eliminated from the film, but the recordings went on to become hits. Harburg's quiet and subtle lyric is a tender reflection on the past when life was new and optimistic, as opposed to the present when the world is old and youth has flown away. Arlen's music is very challenging, the series of descending triplets in each section difficult to sing correctly. The effect is that of a complex concert song, even though the whole number stays within the range of one step beyond an octave. Both Harburg and Arlen, at different times in their lives, stated that this was their personal favorite of all their songs. Among the many artists who have recorded it are Lawrence Tibbett, Eileen Farrell, Carmen McRae, Tony Bennett, Sarah Vaughan, Gil Evans, Sylvia McNair, Kenny Burrell, and more recently, Carly Simon and Julie Wilson.

"The Last Round-Up" (1933) was songwriter Billy Hill's first hit, a pop song in the style of a cowboy ballad. An aging cowpoke contemplates death in the song, noting that this is his last round-up and soon he will be heading to that "far away ranch of the Boss" in the sky. Joe Morris introduced the number at the Paramount Theatre in New York and then made a recording with George Olsen's Orchestra that was a bestseller. It was interpolated into the *Ziegfeld Follies* (1934), where it was sung by Don Ross and Willie Howard. Bing Crosby sang the ballad in one of his earliest solo records, and Roy Rogers's disc got him his first movie contract. Other significant recordings were made by Gene Autry, Guy Lombardo and the Royal Canadians, Rudy Vallee, Arthur Tracy, Spade

Cooley, Gene Krupa, Rex Allen, Charles Brown, the Sons of the Pioneers, Richard Himber, Conrad Thibault, and Robert Merrill. Rogers reprised it in the movie *Don't Fence Me In* (1945), Autry sang it in both *The Singing Hill* (1941) and *The Last Round-Up* (1947), Dean Martin crooned it in *The Silencers* (1966), and it was also heard in *Stand Up and Cheer* (1934), *Twenty Million Sweethearts* (1934), and *One Hour Late* (1935).

"The Last Time I Saw Paris" (1940) is unusual in that its songwriters Oscar Hammerstein (lyric) and Jerome Kern (music) very rarely wrote for Tin Pan Alley, preferring to score movies and Broadway musicals instead. But Hammerstein was so upset when the Nazis occupied Paris in 1940 that he was moved to write a lyric about the much-cherished city. He showed it to Kern, who composed a lilting waltz melody that captured the pictures Hammerstein described: lovers walking in the park, birds singing, honking taxicabs, laughter from the sidewalk cafés, and so on. (This writing procedure was also unusual: Kern usually insisted on writing the music first and then having a lyric fashioned to fit it.) Kate Smith introduced the ballad on the radio, and a movie producer heard it, liked it, and interpolated it into the film *Lady, Be Good* (1941), where it was sung by Ann Sothern. It won the Academy Award for best song even though it was not written for any movie; several complained (none more forcefully than Kern and Hammerstein), and the Academy changed the rules so that such a case would not happen in future. Of the many memorable recordings of the ballad are those by Lanny Ross, Hildegarde, Sophie Tucker, Tony Martin, John Charles Thomas, Nat Brandwynne, Buddy Collette, Joni James, Robert Clary, Bud Powell, Skitch Henderson, Sonny Rollins, George Dvorsky, Andrea Marcovicci, Kiri Te Kanawa, and Noel Coward, to whom the authors dedicated the song. Dinah Shore sang it in the Kern film bio *Till the Clouds Roll By* (1946), it was heard on the soundtrack and performed by Odette in French in *The Last Time I Saw Paris* (1954), and Bob Hope sang it in *Paris Holiday* (1958). In the Broadway revue *Jerome Kern Goes to Hollywood* (1986), the ballad was performed by David Kernan.

"Laughing on the Outside (Crying on the Inside)" (1946) is a slow fox trot about the hidden pain a thwarted lover has, still carrying a torch for her while everyone around sees him "having a gay time." Ben Raleigh (lyric) and Bernie Wayne (music) wrote the ballad, and Sammy Kaye (vocal by Billy Williams) introduced it with a hit record. Just as successful was an early disc by Dinah Shore. The Four Aces revived the number in 1953 with Jack Pleis's Orchestra. Notable records were also made by Andy Russell with Paul Weston's Orchestra, Nat King Cole, Tommy Tucker, Les Brown, the Merry Macs, Aretha Franklin, the Harptones, and more recently, Ann Burton and Jimmy Scott.

"**Laura**" (1945), one of the most haunting love songs to come out of Tin Pan Alley, started as just the musical theme for the movie *Laura* (1944) but David Raksin's entrancing music was so unforgettable that a few months after the release Johnny Mercer was asked to write a lyric. Inspired by the elusive nature of the title character in the film, Mercer penned an exquisite lyric about a mysterious woman whom you have never met, yet you seem to recognize her as someone you once saw in a mist or in a passing train, the whole thing being perhaps a dream. Johnny Johnston introduced the song on the radio, and it has been popular ever since. Woody Herman and his Orchestra made an early record that sold a million copies, and there were other hits by Dick Haymes, Stan Kenton and his Orchestra, Ella Fitzgerald, Freddy Martin, and Jerry Wald (vocal by Dick Merrick). Of the hundreds of discs made of the ballad were acclaimed ones by Johnston, Quincy Jones, André Previn, Johnny Mathis, Nat King Cole, Boots Randolph, Art Van Damme, Vic Damone, Charlie Parker, Ralph Marterie, Erroll Garner, and more recently, Betty Buckley, Skip O'Donnell, Lee Lessack, and Carly Simon. Parker's recording was used on the soundtrack of the movie *Bird* (1988), Kevin Mahogany performed it on the soundtrack of *Midnight in the Garden of Good and Evil* (1997), and Jonathan Dokuchitz sang it on Broadway in the Mercer revue *Dream* (1997).

"**Lawd, You Made the Night Too Long**" (1932) is a fervent hymn that was intended for Tin Pan Alley rather than any church, and it was a surprise success. Sam M. Lewis (lyric) and Isham Jones (music) wrote the bluesy prayer about the loneliness of the night when one is unloved, and it was introduced by Guy Lombardo and the Royal Canadians. Louis Armstrong was the first to record it, followed by many other discs, most memorably those by the Boswell Sisters with Don Redman's Orchestra, Paul Whiteman (vocal by Red McKenzie), the Pickens Sisters, Russ Carlson and the High Steppe, and Pat Yankee. The number was also heard in the movie *George White's Scandals of 1934* (1934). Jones's song "Sam, You Made the Pants Too Long" (1933) was a parody of the solemn number, and it was also a hit.

"**The Laziest Gal in Town**" (1927) is a sly Cole Porter number that took over two decades to become a hit. The song is both sexy and antiromantic at the same time, the languorous lady insisting she won't misbehave with her paramour. With a typical Porter wit, she notes that it's not that she wouldn't or shouldn't and "Lord knows, it's not cause I couldn't," but she's just too lazy to make love. Released as an individual song and recorded by Frankie Trumbauer (vocal by Fredda Gibson who later changed her name to Georgia Gibbs), the droll number never caught on and just about disappeared until Marlene Dietrich sang it in the film

Stage Fright (1950). Her record was a success, and there were other notable discs by Mae Barnes, Liz Keever, Hildegarde Knef, Quinn Lemley, and Julie Wilson.

"Lazy" (1924) is a superior Irving Berlin song in which both words and music seem to lag along in keeping with the indolent nature of the title, yet it is far from monotonous or predictable. The music is unusual in that its opening strain never returns, the structure following an ABCD pattern. The song contains one of Berlin's most ingenious lyrics, a series of brief but potent images of a carefree life: a puppy at play, letting the world go by, stretching and yawning, lying in the sun shirking work, counting sheep as a child does, and so on. The Brox Sisters introduced the ballad, but it was Blossom Seeley that made it famous in vaudeville and records. There were other early and successful discs by Al Jolson and Paul Whiteman and his Orchestra. Interest in "Lazy" was revived when Marilyn Monroe, Donald O'Connor, and Mitzi Gaynor sang it in the movie *There's No Business Like Show Business* (1954), both Monroe and Gaynor later recording it. Other commendable discs were made by Ella Fitzgerald, Dick Haymes, Dave McKenna, Bob Crosby, Judy Holiday, Bing Crosby, and more recently, Andrea Marcovicci, Harry Nilsson, and Anne Tofflemire. Crosby reprised it in the movie *Holiday Inn* (1942), Jeanne Crain, Hoagy Carmichael, and a children's chorus performed it in *Belles on Their Toes* (1952), and it was heard in *Alexander's Ragtime Band* (1938) and *Blue Skies* (1946).

"Lazy River" (1931) is a jazzy folk song by Hoagy Carmichael and Sidney Arodin that is sometimes performed as a languid ballad and other times as a zippy jazz piece. The lyric invites one to travel "up a lazy river . . . in the noonday sun" where one can relax and let the rest of the world go by. Carmichael introduced it with a unique record that also featured the Dorsey Brothers, Bix Beiderbecke, Jack Teagarden, Bud Freeman, Joe Venuti, Gene Krupa, and others. The disc was a hit, and Carmichael made the song popular again when he sang it in the film *The Best Years of Our Lives* (1946). "Lazy River" was revived in the 1950s by the Mills Brothers and in 1961 by records by Bobby Darin and Si Zentner and his Orchestra. Of the many other artists who recorded it were Kate Smith, Benny Goodman, Glen Gray and the Casa Loma Orchestra (vocals by the Merry Macs), Rudy Vallee, Ben Bernie, Bing Crosby, the Vagabonds, Phil Harris, Louis Armstrong, the Four Lads, Eddy Howard, and Brenda Lee. Keely Smith, Louis Prima, and the chorus performed the ballad in the movie *Hey Boy, Hey Girl* (1959), and it was heard in *Cowboy Canteen* (1944) and *Bullets Over Broadway* (1994).

"Lazybones" (1933), Johnny Mercer's first hit song, is a classic example of southern dialect used for both a dreamy and lackadaisical effect. A do-nothing sitting in the sun is admonished for his laziness and asked "how you 'spec' to get your day's work done?" As much as one complains to the lazybones, it is clear he isn't listening, and the lyric concludes with the resignation that "he's just made that way." Hoagy Carmichael adapted the music from his previous song "Washboard Blues' (1926), its easygoing melody staying within an octave except for the tag "well, looky here." Mildred Bailey introduced the number on record, but it was popularized by Ben Bernie and his Orchestra (vocal by Bernie), Rudy Vallee, and Glen Gray and the Casa Loma Orchestra (vocal by Pee Wee Hunt). Louis Armstrong's 1939 disc was also a hit. Other noteworthy versions were made by Carmichael, Mercer, Irving Aaronson and the Commanders (vocal by Dick Robertson), the Mills Brothers, Paul Robeson, Leon Redbone, Dave McKenna, John Eaton, the Art Hodes Trio, Hank Snow, Perry Como, Carrie Smith, Max Morath, Crystal Gayle, and Harry Connick Jr. Midge Williams sang "Lazybones" in the film *The Cotton Club* (1984).

"Leanin' on the Ole Top Rail" (1940) is a cowboy ballad with a twist: It takes the point of view of the gal the cowpoke left behind. Nick and Charles Kenny wrote the tender song about a girl who cannot sleep, so she goes outside, leans on the rail of the corral fence, and dreams of the absent cowboy who promised to return. Gene Autry introduced the number in the movie *Ride, Tenderfoot, Ride* (1940) and recorded it as well. But discs by Bob Crosby and Ozzie Nelson (vocal by Rose Ann Stevens) were bigger sellers. There were also successful records by Eddy Arnold, Jimmie Davis, Patsy Montana, Barry Wood, and Patti Page and a duet version by Larry Cotton and whistling Fred Lowery.

"Let a Smile Be Your Umbrella (On a Rainy Day)" (1927) is an optimistic number by Irving Kahal, Francis Wheeler (lyric), and Sammy Fain (music) that later became a popular depression chaser, encouraging one to smile even in adversity and "you won't get wet." The team of Fain and Dunn introduced the song in vaudeville, but it didn't catch on until Roger Wolfe Kahn and his Orchestra made it famous on the radio and on records. There was also a successful early disc by Sam Lanin and his Orchestra (vocal by Irving Kaufman). Other well-known records were made by Fain, Bob Grant, the Andrews Sisters, Frankie Carle, Bert Kaempfert, Fred Burton, and Shari Lewis and on other kid's records. The Duncan Sisters sang the number in the movie *It's a Great Life* (1930), and it was performed by Dan Dailey and Charles Winninger in *Give My Regards to Broadway* (1948).

"Let It Snow! Let It Snow! Let It Snow!" (1946) is the perennial Christmas favorite that is really about winter rather than any holiday. Jule Styne composed the catchy tune, and Sammy Cahn wrote the cozy lyric about the joy of watching the snow fall as one is snug and warm inside by the fire with a sweetheart. A recording by Vaughn Monroe and his Orchestra popularized the number, keeping it on *Your Hit Parade* for thirteen weeks. There were also early hit records by the Boswell Sisters, Woody Herman, and Russ Morgan (vocal by Connee Boswell). Over the years it has been recorded by dozens of artists, including Dick Haymes, Rosemary Clooney, Joe Williams, Dean Martin, the Temptations, Oscar Peterson, Judy Collins, Elaine Stritch, Barbara Cook, the Carpenters, and Garth Brooks.

"Let Me Call You Sweetheart" (1910) is a straightforward declaration of love that became more famous as a sing-along favorite than an intimate ballad. Leo Friedman composed the waltzing music, and Beth Slater Whitson penned the lyric that overtly proclaims affection and asks the other to "whisper that you love me too." It was introduced by the Peerless Quartet whose record was a hit, but the number was even more popular around the parlor piano, selling an astounding 5 million copies of sheet music. Also it quickly became a staple at community sings and other gatherings. Significant recordings over the years include those by Bing Crosby, Wingy Manone, Doris Day, Joni James, Pat Boone, Lawrence Welk, Gene Autry, Ken Griffin, Mitch Miller, Patti Page, and Bette Midler. On screen, the song was performed by Gene Kelly in *Thousands Cheer* (1943), Beatrice Kay in *Diamond Horsehoe* (1945), and Midler in *The Rose* (1979) and heard on the soundtracks of many films, including *Coney Island* (1943) and *Million Dollar Mermaid* (1952).

"Let's All Sing Like the Birdies Sing" (1932) is an English novelty song that originated in the British music hall and came to American celebrity when Ben Bernie and his Orchestra performed it. The merry ditty by Robert Hargraves, Stanley J. Damerell (lyric), Tolchard Evans, and H. Tilsley (lyric) urges one to be cheerful like the birds that sing and even encourages everyone to go "tweet tweet tweet tweet tweet." Both Tommy Dorsey (featuring Heinie Beau on clarinet) and Ted Fio Rito (vocal and whistling by Muzzy Marcellino) had successful discs of the nonsense song, and it has also been featured in many children's records. The number can be heard in the movie *Molly and Me* (1945).

"Let's Dance" (1935) is a moderate swing number by Fanny Baldridge, Gregory Stone, and Joseph Bonime that invites one to take to the dance floor and "go where sweet music weaves her spell." The music is adapted from Carl Maria Von Weber's "Invitation to the Dance." Benny

Goodman and his Orchestra popularized the song, making a hit record and using it as their opening number for years. Goodman and the band reprised it in the film *Sweet and Lowdown* (1944) and he provided the clarinet playing for Steve Allen in the bio *The Benny Goodman Story* (1956). The number was also heard in *The Powers Girl* (1942) and *The Gang's All Here* (1943). Other records of note were made by the Red Hot Swing Cats, Tony Burgos, Clinton Fearon and the Boogie Brown Band, Terry Gibbs, and Renee Busbee Baldwin and the Capitol City Stage Band.

"Let's Fall in Love" (1934) uses a series of questions to a sweetheart to convince her that it is the perfect time for them to take the romantic plunge. Harold Arlen's music is ardent, and Ted Koehler's lyric, according to Philip Furia, has a "brassy pugnacity" that turns "clichés of romantic proposal into an aggressive sales pitch with rhetorical questions." The song was introduced by Art Jarrett in the movie *Let's Fall in Love* (1934), where it was reprised by Ann Sothern, but it was Eddy Duchin and his Orchestra who popularized it with a chart record. In 1967 it was revived by Peaches and Herb, whose disc also went to the top of the charts. Other versions were made by Frank Sinatra, Les Paul and Mary Ford, Lee Wiley, Margaret Whiting, Louis Prima and Keely Smith, André Previn, Barbara Lea, Peggy Lee, Dave Brubeck, and Nancy Sinatra. The ballad has been used in many films, sung by Don Ameche and Dorothy Lamour in *Slightly French* (1949), Robert Cummings in *Tell It to the Judge* (1949), Jack Lemmon and Judy Holiday in *It Should Happen to You* (1954), Jack Jones in *Juke Box Rhythm* (1959), and Bing Crosby in *Pepe* (1960). Carmen Cavallaro provided the piano playing for Tyrone Power in the film bio *The Eddy Duchin Story* (1956).

"Let's Misbehave" (1927) is a Cole Porter song that leaves little room for an innocent interpretation, but it is so playful in its naughtiness that the number became a hit. The melody is tuneful and innocent, while the sly lyric uses references to Adam and Eve and the amorous birds of spring to encourage a partner to lovemaking. The number was published before it was first performed by Irving Aaronson and his Commanders in Paris at La Revue des Ambassadeurs. It was interpolated into the Broadway musical *Paris* (1928) but cut before opening and replaced by the similarly comic seduction song "Let's Do It." Aaronson recorded the number, and it caught on, becoming a favorite in clubs since it was too risqué for the movies. Other memorable discs were made by Ben Bernie, Helene De Lys, Billy Stritch, Eartha Kitt, Johnny Mathis, Bobby Short, and Laurie Franks. "Let's Misbehave" was heard over the opening credits of the film *Everything You Always Wanted to Know About Sex* (1972), Burt Reynolds and Sybil Shepherd sang it in *At Long Last Love* (1975), and the celebrated Aaronson recording was used in both *Pennies From*

Heaven (1981) and *Bullets Over Broadway* (1994). The song was performed by Eileen Rodgers and Kenneth Mars in the 1962 Off-Broadway revival of *Anything Goes*, and John McMartin and Melissa Errico sang it in the Broadway musical *High Society* (1998).

"Let's Put Out the Lights (And Go to Sleep)" (1932) is a warm and cozy picture of domestic tranquility by Herman Hupfield that appealed to depression-era audiences. A married couple, after giving a party and having seen the last guest depart, decide to leave the dirty dishes in the sink and retire for the night. The ballad is so casual and understated that it manages to be romantic and sincere as few popular songs are. Rudy Vallee and his Connecticut Yankees introduced the number at an Atlantic City nightclub with the original lyric stating, "Let's . . . and go to bed." When he later broadcast the song on the radio, the network insisted that it be changed to "and go to sleep" so that no sexual connotation could be taken, and it remained that way in most subsequent performances. The ballad caught on quickly and was interpolated into the Broadway show *George White's Music Hall Varieties* (1932), where it was sung by Harry Richman, Lili Damita, Bert Lahr, and the ensemble. Ozzie Nelson and his Orchestra (Vocal by Harriet Hilliard) had the most popular recording of the number, and there were also well-known discs by Vallee, Ben Bernie, Paul Whiteman (vocal by Ramona), Bing Crosby, Dean Martin, William Bolcom and Joan Morris, and Sarah Vaughan. The Vallee recording was used in the film *Pennies From Heaven* (1981).

"Lights Out" (1935) is a good-night ballad by Billy Hill that was based on the traditional tune "Taps." The gentle number was introduced on the radio by Ozzie Nelson and his Orchestra (vocal by Harriet Hilliard) and was quickly picked up by many bands, often used as the last song of the evening. Among the artists that recorded it were Eddy Duchin, Dick Robertson, Benny Goodman, Spade Cooley, Nat King Cole, Little Jack Little, Victor Young, Greta Keller, and Mezz Mezzrow.

"Linger Awhile" (1923) is a soft and romantic plea to a darling to stay a while longer with one in the moonlight. Vincent Rose composed the delicate music, and Harry Owens wrote the evocative lyric, the song becoming his first of many hits. It was introduced by Lew Gold and his Orchestra, but it was an early record by Paul Whiteman (featuring a banjo solo by Mike Pingatore) that sold 2 million discs and made the number a romantic favorite. Ted Lewis, Earl Hines, Glen Gray and the Casa Loma Orchestra, Ben Webster, Duke Ellington, Clark Dennis, Ruby Braff, Dickie Wells, Lester Young, Sarah Vaughan, and Vic Damone are among the many who also recorded it. Whiteman reprised "Linger Awhile" in the movie *The King of Jazz* (1930), and it was also heard in

The Great American Broadcast (1941), *Give My Regards to Broadway* (1948), and *Belles on Their Toes* (1952).

"Listen to the Mocking Bird" (1855) was a favorite parlor song during the Civil War (Lincoln had it played in the White House often), and families often made bird calls or whistling sounds as they performed it. Septimus Winner, using the pseudonym Alice Hawthorne, wrote the lyric about a dearly beloved named Hallie who lies buried in the valley, where she is serenaded by a nightingale each evening. He published the lyric as a poem in 1855, and soon after it was set to an old tune by Richard Milburn. It is believed that Milburn was either an African American youth who taught himself how to write music or a Negro barber known for whistling his own songs as he played the guitar. Over the years the song sold an amazing 20 million copies of sheet music, though Winner had sold the lyric outright for $50. The song was recorded as early as 1891 by John Yorke Atlee, and years later there were discs by George Lewis, Kenny Roberts, the Sons of the Pioneers, Ralph Stanley, Steve Forbert, the Kentucky Colonels, Lester Flatt, the Nitty Gritty Dirt Band, Fiddlin' Red Herron, and Roy Acuff. The familiar tune can also be heard in several movies, including *The Singing Cowboy* (1936), *Jeepers Creepers* (1939), *Melody Lane* (1941), and *Wait Till the Sun Shines, Nellie* (1952).

"A Little Bit Independent" (1935) is a slangy song of affection about a gal who is very independent in the way she walks, dresses, and dances, yet she is "so easy on the eyes." Joe Burke composed the lilting melody, and Edgar Leslie wrote the casual lyric that rhymes "New York" with "talk" and "walk." Thomas "Fats" Waller introduced the song with a record that climbed to the top of the charts. It was revived in the late 1940s with discs by Dick Haymes and Bob Crosby (vocal by Georgia Gibbs), and again in the early 1950s with hit records by Eddie Fisher and Nat King Cole. Other leading recordings were made by Freddy Martin's Orchestra, Terry Blaine, Eddie Cantor, Jo Stafford, Putney Dandridge, the Mound City Blue Blowers, and Teddy Powell.

"A Little Bit of Heaven (Sure They Called It Ireland)" (1914) is an American-Irish classic that is filled with so much sentiment and good old-fashioned blarney that it is something of a cliché today. But Irish immigrants in the 1910s wept while they sang this romanticized view of the old country. Ernest R. Ball wrote the flowing melody, and J. Keirn Brennan penned the lyric, describing a legend about how Ireland got its name. When a piece of heaven fell into the ocean, the angels thought it looked so grand that they "sprinkled it with stardust" to make shamrocks grow and christened the new isle Ireland. The song was interpolated into the Broadway musical *Heart of Paddy Whack* (1914), where it was sung by Irish favorite Chauncey Olcott. The first known recording was by Charles Harrison, followed by many others by crooners, choral groups, and bands. George MacFarlane and John McCormack each had early bestsellers, and later Bing Crosby had a giant hit with the ballad. Among the other artists who made discs were Robert Brooks, John Carter, Ronnie Dove, Harry James, Joe McPartland, Steve Hall, Connie Francis, Dennis O'Neill, and Frank Parker. On screen it was sung by Gloria Jean in *A Little Bit of Heaven* (1940), Leonard Warren in *Irish Eyes Are Smiling* (1944), and Dennis Morgan in *My Wild Irish Rose* (1947).

"Little Brown Jug" (1869) is one of the earliest and most popular drinking songs in American popular music. The merry number was written by Joseph E. Winner, who used the pseudonym R.A. Eastburn because he feared such a tribute to inebriation might ruin his reputation. The lyric depicts a happily sloshed couple ("she loved gin and I loved rum") who praise the little brown jug of spirits that brings them so much pleasure. While it remained popular throughout the nineteenth century, the song never became a Tin Pan Alley hit until the Weatherwax Brothers Quartet brought it renewed recognition in 1911. Glenn Miller's 1939 disc sold over a million copies, and later there were several boogie-woogie versions on the market. Other well-known records were made by Billy May, Bing Crosby, Les Brown, Glen Gray and the Casa Loma Orchestra, Dick Curless, Tex Beneke, Les Elgart, Myron Floren with Lawrence Welk, Max Gregor, and Sterling Davis. For some odd reason, the number is often included on children's records. Ann Sheridan and a girls chorus performed the zesty song in the movie *Dodge City* (1939), and it was heard in *The Story of Vernon and Irene Castle* (1939), *Jeepers Creepers* (1939), *Twilight on the Prairie* (1944), *The Jackpot* (1950), and *The Glenn Miller Story* (1954).

"The Little Lost Child" (1894), one of the most beloved sentimental ballads of the era, sold more copies of sheet music (over 2 million) than any other song of the decade. The song can also be viewed as the ancestor of the movie musical. Necktie salesman Joseph W. Stern composed the emotive music, and button salesman Edward B. Marks wrote the heart-tugging lyric that was inspired by a newspaper item. A little girl wanders the streets of the big city until she is spotted by a policeman who befriends her and then learns that it is his own long-lost daughter. Della Fox introduced the number in vaudeville, but it was Lottie Gilson who made it famous in her variety act. When Allen May decided to use the song in his performance at the Grand Opera House in Manhattan, he had lantern slides made (some featuring the actual policeman from the news story) that were projected onto a screen as he sang. The idea was copied by others, and for the next twenty years, both the song and slides were a regular feature on the vaudeville circuit.

"Little Man, You've Had a Busy Day" (1934) is a lullaby that took its title from a bestselling book by Hans Fallada. Maurice Sigler and Al Hoffman wrote the lyric, soothing words of affection sung by a mother to her little boy, and Mabel Wayne composed the tender music. The ballad became popular because of early records by Isham Jones (vocal by Eddie Stone), Frank Luther, the Pickens Sisters, and Emil Coleman. Later discs of note were made by Paul Robeson, Herbie Mann, Connee Boswell, Mel Tormé, Count Basie, Chet Baker, Jerry and Patti Lewis, Art Tatum, and Perry Como.

"Little Old Lady" (1937) is a wry tribute to a grandmother, a spry gal who charmed President Grover Cleveland back in 1886 and is still "catching ev'rybody's eye" as she window shops and goes out on the town to have tea. Stanley Adams wrote the whimsical lyric, and Hoagy Carmichael composed the music, written with his own grandmother in mind. The number was intended for the Broadway revue *The Show Is On* (1937), but the producers decided to cut it. E.Y. Harburg liked it so much he wrote a whole sketch around the song, so it was reinstated and sung by Mitzie Mayfair and Charles Walters. Successful records by Shep Fields and his Rippling Rhythm, Ray Noble (vocal by Al Bowlly), and Abe Lyman (vocal by Sonny Schuyler) kept the song on the *Hit Parade* for eleven weeks. Other major discs were made by Carmichael, Dick Robertson, Gracie Fields, Ruby Braff, the Mills Brothers, Elsie Carlisle, Jack Jenny, Glen Gray and the Casa Loma Orchestra, and John Coltrane.

"Little Things Mean a Lot" (1954) is a tearful ballad by Edith Lindeman and Carl Stutz that is most associated with Kitty Kallen, who made it a hit and, at the same time, resurrected her career. The lyric lists those small but important details that mean so much: a phone call, a letter, taking one by the hand as you cross the street, a friendly comment, and so on. Band singer Kallen's career was destroyed in the late 1940s when something happened to her voice. Hoping to make a comeback, she financed her recording with Jack Pleis' Orchestra herself when no record producer was willing to back it. The disc went to the Number One spot on the charts, becoming one of the top songs of the year, and Kallen enjoyed a second lucrative career. She also recorded the number again in 1962 with success. Other accomplished versions were made by Joni James, the Crusaders, Julie London, the Platters, Mindy Carson, the Dominoes, the Beverley Sisters, and Liberace.

"Little White Lies" (1930) is an intriguing and ambiguous ballad in which a spurned lover recalls the night his mistress told him "those little white lies" about how she felt. It is up to the listener to determine if the lies were that she loved him or that she didn't. Composer Walter Donaldson wrote both words and music for Guy Lombardo and the Royal Canadians to introduce, and their record was a hit. But even more successful was a disc by Fred Waring's Pennsylvanians (featured vocal by Clare Hanlon), which prompted big sales in sheet music. This record was eclipsed in the early 1940s by a bestseller by Tommy Dorsey (vocal by Frank Sinatra) and an even bigger hit in 1949 by Dick Haymes and Four Hits and a Miss with the Gordon Jenkins Orchestra that sold over a million copies. Other noteworthy records were made by Ted Wallace (vocal by Elmer Feldkamp), Dinah Shore, George Shearing, Mel Tormé, Skitch Henderson, Ella Fitzgerald with Chick Webb's Orchestra, and Lee Morse and her Bluegrass Boys. "Little White Lies" can be heard in the movie *Lover, Come Back* (1946).

"Lonely Troubadour" (1929) is a crooning ballad of remorse that was introduced, featured, and recorded by Rudy Vallee and remained one of his specialties for many years. John Klenner wrote the number about a forsaken lover who sings his song of regret, and it was also recorded by Ted Lewis, Meyer Davis, Don Voorhees, and Tiny Tim.

"The Lonesome Road" (1928) is a hymnlike song that suggests one stop and look down the road ahead of you and think on your Maker, of Gabriel blowing his horn on that fateful day, and contemplate what you might have done in your past to bring you to this lonely spot. Gene Austin wrote the somber lyric, and Nathaniel Shilkret composed the solemn music, both adapted from an old Negro spiritual of unknown origins. Austin and Ted Lewis (vocals by the Four Dusty Travelers) each recorded the number with success, and Bing Crosby had a hit version in 1939. Other artists who recorded it include Louis Armstrong, Mildred Bailey, Larry Clinton, Anita O'Day, Ace Cannon, Tommy Dorsey, Will Bradley, Frank Sinatra, Paul Robeson, Floyd Cramer, Sonny Stitt, Jimmy Dean, Helen Traubel, Pat Boone, Barbara Lea, Leslie Uggams, and Joan Baez. When songs were needed to be interpolated into the first film version of *Show Boat* (1929), Jules Bledsoe dubbed "The Lonesome Road" for Stepin Fetchit to sing. It was also heard in *Cha-Cha-Cha-Boom* (1956).

"Lost in a Fog" (1934) is a dreamy song about indecision in love that Dorothy Fields (lyric) and Jimmy McHugh (music) wrote for the Dorsey Brothers' Orchestra. The band introduced it at Ben Marden's Riviera nightclub in Fort Lee, New Jersey, with McHugh doing the vocal. Bob Crosby recorded it with the brothers' band, but the bigger seller was a disc by Rudy Vallee and the Connecticut Yankees. Vallee also featured it on his radio show for a while. Connee Boswell, Jane Froman, and Leo Reisman and his Orchestra each had successful records in the 1930s, and there other records of note by Les Brown, the Memphis Boys, Coleman Hawkins, Von Freeman, Barbara Lea, and Ella Fitzgerald. "Lost in a Fog" was also interpolated into the movie *Have a Heart* (1934).

"Louisiana" (1928) is a jazz classic by Andy Razaf, Bob Schafer (lyric), and J.C. Johnson (music) celebrating the region from which jazz flows. The number is most associated with Paul Whiteman whose orchestra made an outstanding record with vocals by the Rhythm Boys and featuring cornet player Bix Beiderbecke. Later Beiderbecke made a solo disc that is acclaimed, and there are other jazz records of distinction by Count Basie, Duke Ellington, Toots Mondello with Ziggy Elman, Pete Bailey, and Pete Kelly's Big Seven. Fred Astaire, Liz Barnez, Ruby Braff, Sammy Duncan, Harry Choates, and Barney Kessel are among the other artists who recorded it.

"Love and Marriage" (1955) is probably the biggest Tin Pan Alley hit to come out of a television special. Sammy Cahn (lyric) and Jimmy Van Heusen (music) wrote the number for a musical version of Thornton Wilder's play *Our Town*, which was broadcast in 1955. Frank Sinatra sang it in the show, and his recording was a big hit. The catchy tune celebrates the harmony of love in marriage, saying they go together "like a horse and carriage" and insisting that you can't have one without the other. Dinah Shore's disc was also popular, and there were other records by the McGuire Sisters, Eddie Fisher, James Moody, Frankie Vaughn, Peggy Lee, Brian Evans, Sherry Winston, Gary Tesca, Rich Little, and Jack Parnell. "Love and Marriage" was also the theme song for the television series *Married With Children*.

"Love Is a Many Splendored Thing" (1955) is the Oscar-winning song whose lyric is as purple and poetic as its title, but audiences embraced the mellifluous number, and it was a major hit. Sammy Fain composed the soaring music, and Paul Francis Webster penned the lush lyric about wandering through Hong Kong looking for the answer to where love is. The refrain answers the query, defining love as multifaceted and can be found in nature as well as in the morning kiss of two lovers in the mist. The number was written for the film *Love Is a Many Splendored Thing* (1955), where it was to be sung by a major recording star on the soundtrack. But Tony Martin, Eddie Fisher, Doris Day, Nat King Cole, and other big names all turned it down, complaining that the ballad was too heavy and old-fashioned. Finally the Four Aces agreed, and the success of the film helped their recording to sell over a million copies. Of the dozens of discs made later, there were notable ones by Fain, Kate Smith, Don Cornell, David Rose, the Platters, Roger Williams, Mantovanni's Orchestra, Dinah Washington, Woody Herman, the Lettermen, Clifford Brown, Jerry Vale, Eric Alexander, Little Anthony and the Imperials, Skitch Henderson, Peter and Gordon, and Kenny Rogers. A choral version of the song was heard in the movie *Grease* (1978), and Guy Stroman, Jason Graae, David Engel, and Stan Chandler harmonized it together in the Off-Broadway revue *Forever Plaid* (1990).

"Love Is the Sweetest Thing" (1933) is an uncomplicated but intoxicating song that revels in the mystery of "love's story" in one's life. Alec Wilder describes the number as a "very pure, as opposed to a sensuous song, and so simple that it's not easy to define why it's so appealing." Bandleader Ray Noble wrote both music and lyric, and before he recorded it with his orchestra, the number was introduced in the British film *Say It With Music* (1932), where it was played by Jack Payne's Orchestra. Payne recorded it, but the disc was not released in the States. Julia Sanderson introduced the ballad in America, and Noble's record with a vocal by Al Bowlly was a hit when it came out soon after. Among the other artists who have recorded it were Hal Kemp, Perry Como, Conrad Thibault, Jack Fulton, George Shearing, Joe Morrison, Ziggy Elman, Max Morath, Rick Nelson, Mario Lanza, and more recently, Mary Hopin and Peter Skellern. Frankie Vaughn sang it in the movie *The Lady Is a Square* (1959), and it can be heard in *Confidential Agent* (1945) and *Come See the Paradise* (1990).

"Love Is the Thing" (1933) is a philosophical ballad by Ned Washington (lyric) and Victor Young (music) that dismisses wealth, power, and fame as unimportant, for "love is still King." Ethel Waters popularized the number with a successful record, followed by discs by Glen Gray and the Casa Loma Orchestra (vocal by Kenny Sargent), Richard Himber (vocal by Joey Nash), and Morton Downey. Other notable records over the years were made by Andy Kirk and his Clouds of Joy, Marty Grosz, Nat King Cole, the King Sisters, Billy Eckstine, Beryl Brooks, Etta Jones, and Lena Horne. It was also heard in the film *The Marrying Man* (1991).

"Love Letters" (1945) is a dreamy ballad about sweet mail "straight from your heart" that keeps a loved one near even though she is far away. Victor Young wrote the warm music, and Edward Heyman penned the adoring lyric, with the beau memorizing every line in her letter, kissing her written name, and knowing he's not alone when he has "the love you write." The Oscar-nominated song was used as the musical theme throughout the film *Love Letters* (1945) but became famous with a bestselling record by Dick Haymes. Ketty Lester revived it with success in

1962, and Elvis Presley made it a hit again in 1966. Patti Page, Boz Scaggs, Perry Como, Liberace, Eydie Gorme, Nat King Cole, Julie London, Skip Farrell and the Dinning Sisters, Smokey Robinson, Vicki Stuart, and Natalie Cole are among the artists who also recorded it. The Lester version was heard in the movie *Blue Velvet* (1986).

"Love Letters in the Sand" (1931), one of Pat Boone's biggest hits, compares a love affair that is over to the amorous messages they wrote each other in the sand, the tide having come in and washed the words away. Nick and Charles Kenny wrote the lyric as a poem, and it was printed in the *Daily Mirror*. Composer J. Fred Coots read the poem while on a train and immediately sought out the authors in order to turn the piece into a song. Russ Columbo's record first brought attention to the ballad, then George Hall and his Orchestra popularized it further as they broadcast weekly on the radio, later adopting the number as their theme song. But it was Boone's 1957 disc that hit the top of the charts, selling over a million copies, and it was forever after identified with him. Other major records were made by Gene Austin, Benny Goodman, Andy Williams, Bill Haley, Jerry Lee Lewis, Earl Bostic, Leon Redbone, Merle Travis, the Moms and Dads, Ken Griffin, and Patsy Cline. Boone reprised it in the movie *Bernardine* (1957), and Tia Speros sang it in the Off-Broadway revue *The Taffetas* (1988).

"Love Lies" (1940) is a Big Band ballad by Ralph Freed, Carl Sigman (lyrics), and Joseph Meyer (music) about the the little deceptions that creep into a romance. The number was a favorite of bands in the 1940s, no recording more successful than that by Tommy Dorsey (vocal by Frank Sinatra). Other memorable discs were made by Larry Clinton (vocal by Terry Allen), Gene Krupa (vocal by Howard Dulany), Richard Himber, the Mills Brothers, Sammy Kaye (vocal by Tommy Ryan), Ralph Sutton, Keith Ingham, and Frances Langford.

"Love Me and the World Is Mine" (1906) is a flavorful ballad of total dedication that took a while to catch on but then remained a favorite for decades. Ernest R. Ball wrote the fervent lyric, declaring that riches and fame mean nothing ("I care not for the stars that shine") because he would still be lonely and dejected if he didn't have her love. Dave Reed Jr. composed the masterful music. Sigmund Spaeth points out, "Even though the range of the melody is a whole tone less than an octave, the scale progression makes a ringing climax of the top notes, sounding much higher than it really is." The song was first played at Proctor's Fifth Avenue Theatre in New York but stirred little interest. It was not until Mande Lambert started singing it in vaudeville and when Trudy Shattuck included it in her act on a cross-country vaudeville circuit that the number caught on, eventually selling over a million copies of sheet music. The celebrated Irish tenor John McCormack kept the ballad in his repertoire for years, and there were distinctive records by Joe Mc-Partland, Arthur Pryor, and William L. Denton. Jeanette MacDonald sang it in the movie *San Francisco* (1936), Dick Haymes performed it in the Ball bio *Irish Eyes Are Smiling* (1944), and it was heard in several other movies, including *Roaring Twenties* (1939), *The Strawberry Blonde* (1941), and *The Eddie Cantor Story* (1953).

"Love Me or Leave Me" (1928), one of the greatest of all American torch songs, was long identified with Ruth Etting. Walter Donaldson composed the "most unusual and marvelously conceived song," which Alec Wilder notes has a strict AABA structure, but "every note is right" as the music travels up and down the scale with some impressive jumps in key." Gus Kahn wrote the torchy lyric, using quiet alliteration ("love . . . leave . . . believe) and assonance ("lonely . . . won't . . . only") throughout. Philip Furia also points out the many uses of the word "time" in the sterling lyric. Etting first sang the number in the Broadway musical farce *Whoopee* (1928), where it was used to fill in during a scene change. Nonetheless, she brought down the house with the number. Etting also sang it in the show *Simple Simon* (1930), on records, and in nightclubs for the rest of her long career. Benny Goodman's Orchestra revived the song in 1934 and again in 1936, and there were later chart records by Lena Horne and Sammy Davis Jr. Other laudable versions include those by Billie Holiday, Nina Simone, Dinah Shore, Billy Eckstine, Dick Haymes, Peggy Lee, Fats Waller, Stan Kenton, Sarah Vaughan, and Perry Como. In the movies it was sung by Constance Dowling in *The Flame* (1947), Patrice Wymore in the Kahn bio *I'll See You in My Dreams* (1952), and Doris Day in the Etting bio *Love Me or Leave Me* (1955). "Love Me or Leave Me" was also heard in *Tell It to a Star* (1945), and the Simone recording was used in *Billy's Hollywood Screen Kiss* (1998).

"Lovelight in the Starlight" (1938) is an atmospheric ballad perfectly suited to Dorothy Lamour's demeanor, and she had great success with it when she sang the song in the film *Her Jungle Love* (1938) and recorded it with Herbie King's Orchestra. Ralph Freed (lyric) and Frederick Hollander (music) wrote the exotic love song, and there were other noteworthy records by Jan Savitt (vocal by Carlotta Dale), Horace Heidt, Ruby Newman, Bunny Berigan, and Charles "Buddy" Rogers (vocal by Bob Hannon).

"Lover Man (Oh, Where Can You Be?)" (1942) is a blues standard that is still identified with Billie Holiday, who sang it in a bestselling 1945 record and included it in her repertoire for years. Jimmie Davis, Roger

Ramirez, and Jimmy Sherman collaborated on the haunting number that is musically very simple and has a narrow range but manages to seem complex and textured because of the rich harmony. The lyric about the suffering she feels ("Oh, what I've been missin' ") parallels Holiday's personal drug abuse problem, including the painful lament "I long to try something I've never had." Oddly, the song was introduced by female impersonator Willie Dukes. After Holiday popularized it, the number was recorded by such artists as Etta Jones, Erroll Garner, Claude Thornhill, Duke Ellington, Art Tatum, Charlie Parker, Stan Kenton, Sarah Vaughan, Steve Allen, Dick Hyman, Linda Ronstadt, and Andrea Marcovicci. Diana Ross sang the torch song in the Holiday film bio *Lady Sings the Blues* (1972), the Holiday recording was heard in *Little Voice* (1998), and on Broadway it was performed by Leslie Uggams in the revue *Blues in the Night* (1982).

"Love's Old Sweet Song" (1884), one of America's favorite songs of nostalgia for nearly a hundred years, was actually an English number by G. Clifton Bingham (lyric) and J.L. Molloy (music). The song has origins going back to the middle of the nineteenth century, but it was not published until 1884 when a London company printed it with Bingham and Molloy listed as authors. The music is both somber and sweet as it travels up and down the scales. The lyric is just as ambiguous, recalling old songs when dusk comes after a weary day and, at the same time, fondly remembering how everyone used to gather around the piano to sing in the old days. The ballad traveled to the States soon after it was published in England, and it eventually found itself played on thousands of parlor pianos. Sheet music sales were strong all the way into the depression. The old ballad was given significant recordings by Bing Crosby, Nelson Eddy, Richard Tauber, Richard Crooks, Deanna Durbin, Phil Coulter, Jesse Crawford, Clarence Whitehill, Rise Stevens, and William Bolcom and Joan Morris. The number was also used for nostalgic atmosphere in many films, including *Maytime* (1937), *Broadway Serenade* (1939), *It Comes Up Love* (1943), *Can't Help Singing* (1944), and *Wait Till the Sun Shines, Nellie* (1952).

"Lovesick Blues" (1922) is a traditional blues number that is more familiar today as a country-western number because of Hank Williams's popular reworking of the song years after it was written. Cliff Friend composed the simple blues melody, and Irving Mills penned the torchy lyric about a heartsick beau who laments, "I'm nobody's sugar daddy now." There were many recordings in the 1920s and 1930s, most memorably those by Bertha "Chippie" Hill, Anita O'Day, and Bill Darnell. In 1949 an unknown Hank Williams revised the music and lyric, used his distinctive yodeling voice on the words "blues," and made a recording that propelled him to fame. (For a while he was billed as the "Lovesick Blues" Boy.) The disc sold a million copies and was forever after thought of as a country tune. Charley Pride, Leon Redbone, Jerry Lee Lewis, the Ventures, Etta James, Slim Whitman, Don McLean, and Patsy Cline were among the many who recorded it with success. The Williams's version was heard on the soundtrack of the movie *The Last Picture Show* (1971), and Jessica Lange was dubbed by Cline's record in the bio *Sweet Dreams* (1985).

"Lucky Lindy!" (1927) is a vivid example of a song that swept the country when its subject matter was topical but later waned into obscurity. After Charles Lindbergh made his historic flight from New Jersey to Paris in 1927, there were many songs written to capitalize on the event. None was more popular than this ditty by L. Wolfe Gilbert (lyric) and Abel Baer (music) that praised "Lindy" for his feat, crossing the ocean regardless whether it was "fair or windy." The number was popularized by Vernon Dalhart, and the merry march song sold thousands of copies of sheet music. By World War Two the song was pretty much forgotten except as a piece of nostalgia. The most celebrated disc was made by Nat Shilkret with the Victor Light Orchestra and Chorus.

"Lullaby in Rhythm" (1938) is a Big Band number that manages to be a lulling lullaby even as it gently swings. Walter Hirsch (lyric), Benny Goodman, Edgar Sampson, and Clarence Profit (music) collaborated on the number, and it was introduced by Goodman and his Orchestra on record with great success. Other early hit versions were made by Nan Wynn, Harry James, Charlie Ventura, Dexter Gordon, and Woody Herman. June Christy, Lucky Thompson, the Four Freshmen, Peggy Lee, Frankie Laine, Patti Page, Dave Brubeck, Scott Hamilton, and Michael Feinstein were among the other artists who later recorded it.

"Lullaby of Birdland" (1952) is a scat jazz classic by George David Weiss (lyric) and George Shearing (music) that is far from a quiet lullaby as it energetically rises and falls across the scale. Shearing and his band were working the celebrated Birdland jazz club in Manhattan, and while he was playing the accompaniment to "Love Me or Leave Me," he improvised a new refrain that developed into a melody all its own. Weiss wrote the lyric that tries to define the kind of music two lovers make when they kiss, coming up with the cooing of birds as the answer. Shearing recorded it, as did Wild Bill Davis, Earl Hines, Erroll Garner, Sarah Vaughan, Johnny Smith, Eartha Kitt, Don Shirley, Stan Getz, Woody Herman, Ralph Marterie, and Nancy Wilson.

"Lullaby of the Leaves" (1932) is a tender ballad by Joe Young (lyric) and Bernice Petkere (music) that conjures up the memory of being a child in the South where the rustling of the leaves in the wind sounded like a sleepy lullaby. The ballad was introduced on the radio by Freddie Berrens and his Orchestra, and there were soon records made by Ben Selvin and Connee Boswell. It was George Olsen and his Orchestra that made the number famous, their disc hitting the top of the charts. "Lullaby of the Leaves" soon became a favorite of jazz musicians, and many recordings followed, including those by Benny Goodman, Art Tatum, Louis Prima, Dizzy Gillespie, the Page Cavanaugh Trio, Marian McPartland, the Ventures, Gerry Mulligan, Barbara Lea, Cal Tjader, and Frances Wayne with Neil Hefti.

"Lush Life" (1938) is a romantic standard with an uncertain origin but a very definite appeal, never having gone out of style over the decades. The verse is unusually long for a modern pop song (twenty-eight measures) and takes the form of a recitative. The refrain, on the other hand, is rather short (twenty-four measures) and very succinct. The lyric, only using the title phrase once (near the end of the refrain), concerns an abandoned lover who keeps up appearances, going to parties and pretending to have a "lush life," but it seems everyone around him is living a lie and are as lonely as he is. Billy Strayhorn is the credited author, and it is believed that he started performing the number in clubs as early as 1939 when he was a singer for Duke Ellington. Some believe it was written by Ellington, who played it at Carnegie Hall in 1948 with Kay Davis doing the vocal. The song was never copyrighted until 1949 with Strayhorn as the sole author. That same year Nat King Cole made the first recording, and it was a hit. (He recorded it again in 1961.) A 1963 disc by John Coltrane on sax and Johnny Hartman doing the vocal is considered a jazz classic. Other major discs were made by Oscar Peterson, Eileen Farrell, Ella Fitzgerald, Joe Pass, Sarah Vaughan, and more recently, Natalie Cole, Linda Ronstadt, and Patti LuPone.

M

"Ma Blushin' Rosie (Ma Posie Sweet)" (1900), the most popular song to come out of the series of Weber and Fields music hall shows, was long associated with Al Jolson. Edgar Smith (lyric) and John Stromberg (music) wrote the Negro dialect number praising a sweetie named Rosie, and it was introduced by Fay Templeton and the chorus in *Fiddle Dee Dee* (1900). Although Templeton made it famous, it was Jolson who had the greatest success with the southern ballad, singing it at the Winter Garden Theatre to acclaim, recording a disc that sold over a million copies, and providing the voice for Larry Parks when he performed it in the film bios *The Jolson Story* (1946) and *Jolson Sings Again* (1949). The song was also used in the movies *Broadway to Hollywood* (1933), *Lillian Russell* (1940), *The Naughty Nineties* (1945), and *The Daughter of Rosie O'Grady* (1950). Bing Crosby had a successful record of the number, and recently it was recorded by Jimmy Roselli. It was also used in the Off-Broadway revue *Groucho: A Life in Revue* (1994).

"Ma! He's Making Eyes at Me" (1921) is a bellowing song announcing that a beau is looking closely, then acting nice, then proposing marriage and kissing her, yet it is ambiguous whether she is boasting or complaining about it to her mother. Con Conrad composed the lively music, and Sidney Clare penned the sassy, exclamatory lyric. They wrote it for Eddie Cantor, who liked it so much he had it interpolated into his Broadway show *The Midnight Rounders* (1921) and recorded it as well. Pearl Bailey made a distinctive and popular recording of the number in the late 1940s, and ten-year-old Scottish singer Lena Zavaroni had a hit with it in 1974. Other records of note were made by Bob Wilson with the Clare Sisters, Dick Robertson, Johnny Otis, Tennessee Ernie Ford, Tiny Hill, Rod Mason, Al Hirt, Oscar Peterson, the Gene Harris Quartet, and

224 Mack the Knife

Leslie Uggams. The song was featured in the movie *Ma! He's Making Eyes at Me* (1940), was sung by Judy Canova in *Singin' in the Corn* (1946), and Cantor dubbed it for Keefe Braselle in *The Eddie Cantor Story* (1953).

"Mack the Knife" (1928) traveled a long and complicated road to Tin Pan Alley, but once it arrived, it was a major hit and remained one of the most unusual of popular songs. Bertolt Brecht (German lyric) and Kurt Weill (music) wrote the sinister ballad, about a murderer who has returned to town with his jackknife and is on the prowl, for the dark music theatre piece *The Threepenny Opera* (1928). Titled "Moritat" (German for "murder deed"), the minor-key ballad is in the style of a seventeenth-century street song with plenty of dissonance and a ghoulish temperament. The music is sixty-four bars and contains two eight-bar themes that are repeated with chilling effect. When *The Threepenny Opera* was translated and produced on Broadway in 1933, the song was titled "The Legend of Mackie Messer." But the show quickly closed, and the song was forgotten. In 1952 composer-lyricist Marc Blitzstein rewrote the number as "Mack the Knife," and beginning with the now-famous phrase "The shark has pretty teeth, dear," the ballad was performed in a concert at Brandeis University. Blitzstein then retranslated the whole score, and *The Threepenny Opera* opened Off Broadway in 1956 for a record-breaking long run. Scott Merrill sang the song, and it caught on, early records being made by the Dick Hyman Trio (who whistled the eerie tune), Richard Hayman and Jan August, and a jazz version by Louis Armstrong. Bobby Darin's 1959 disc was the most successful of the dozens of versions, reaching the top of the charts. Ella Fitzgerald had success with it in 1960, and Frank Sinatra revived it with a hit record in 1986. Other artists over the years who have made recordings include Les Paul, Eartha Kitt, Lawrence Welk, Joe Pass, Peggy Lee, the Stargazers, Archie Bleyer, Rosemary Clooney, Lou Christie, Emily Saxe, Merle Travis, Julie Wilson, Brian Evans, Jimmy Smith, Jo Ann Castle, Sting, and Ute Lemper. Sammy Davis Jr. sang it in the film *The Three Penny Opera* (1962), the Darin recording was used in both *The Big Town* (1987) and *What Women Want* (2000), and the ballad was heard in *Turk 182* (1985), *Mack the Knife* (1989), and *Shadows and Fog* (1992). Also, Jerry Lanning and the company sang it in the Off-Broadway revue *Berlin to Broadway With Kurt Weill* (1972). The song is sometimes listed as "Moritat" and "The Theme From *The Threepenny Opera*."

"MacNamara's Band" (1917) is an Irish favorite that actually came from Ireland, as opposed to most Irish-American hits. Shamus O'Connor composed the spirited Irish jig music, and John J. Stamford penned the colorful lyric that praises an Irish band and goes on to name most of the players in a slapstick manner. The song was first published in London

and found its way to America by the end of World War One. Of
the many recordings over the years, none was more popular in the States
than Bing Crosby's. Other memorable discs were made by the McFarland
Twins, Dennis Day, Jerry Fielding, and Frank Parker and a parody
version by Spike Jones and his City Slickers. "MacNamara's Band" can
be heard in several movies, such as *Doughboys in Ireland* (1943) and
I'll Get By (1950), and is still used today by the various *Riverdance* companies.

"Mairzy Doats" (1943), one of the most celebrated of all nonsense songs,
is simply a rushing together of words ("Mares eat oats, and does eat
oats . . .") to create a baby-talk lyric that sounds like its own language.
Milton Drake, Al Hoffman, and Jerry Livingston wrote the silly number,
basing the idea on an old English nursery rhyme. The idea came to Drake
when his four-year-old daughter came home from school one day and
announced, "Cowzy tweet and siwzy tweet and libble sharksy doisters."
The gibberish song was introduced by Al Trace and his Silly Symphonists on record, but it was a bestselling disc by the Merry Macs that sold
30,000 copies a week for many weeks running. The stately opera singer
Grace Moore included it in her nightclub act throughout the decade, and
there were also records by such diverse talents as the Pied Pipers,
Tommy Ridgley, the Three Stooges, Eric Nagler, and Maria Muldaur, as
well as many children's records. The ditty can be heard in the movie *A
Man Called Peter* (1955).

"Mama Goes Where Papa Goes or Papa Don't Go Out Tonight" (1923)
is a jazzy, red-hot number that was introduced and popularized by that
"Red Hot Mama" Sophie Tucker. Jack Yellen and Milton Ager wrote the
sassy song in which a suspicious wife tells her husband that she will be
going out with him tonight "just to help Papa keep his conscience clear."
Tucker's recording is a comedy gem, and there were also discs by Sam
Lanin and his Orchestra, the Cotton Pickers, Kay Starr, and Ida Cox with
the Coleman Hawkins Quintet. The farcical number was used in the film
When You're Smiling (1950).

"Mambo Jambo" (1950) is the Latin number that started the mambo fad
in America in the 1950s. Raymond Karl, Charlie Towne (lyric), and Perez
Prado (music) wrote the rhythmic song about the latest dance craze, and
Sonny Burke and his Orchestra made it nationally known with their hit
recording. There were also discs by Perez, Xavier Cugat, Enoch Light,
Stan Kenton, Dave Barbour, Myron Floren, Frank Gambale, and Scatman
John, as well as many Latin bands. The vivacious number can be heard
in the movie *Third World Cop* (1999).

"The Man I Love" (1924), one of the Gershwin brothers' most beloved and recorded ballads, was put in and kicked out of a handful of Broadway shows before it finally found success as a Tin Pan Alley song. George Gershwin's music is a series of repeated musical phrases in the refrain (including one that is from his earlier "Rhapsody in Blue") that come together by the conclusion in a highly satisfying way. It is a difficult song to sing because of the shifting harmony that descends chromatically measure by measure to the famous ending. Gershwin thought the ballad had so much trouble catching on because of these chromatics that make the song difficult to hum or whistle. Ira Gershwin's lyric is straightforward and far from flowery as the hopeful lady imagines what her true love will be like and when he might appear. Just as the music in the unforgettable release is bold and a significant departure from the main melody (something not very common at the time), so too the lyric plays with various uses of the word "day" to created a rhythmic pattern all its own. The ballad was written for Adele Astaire to sing in the musical *Lady, Be Good!* (1924) but was cut in previews because it was deemed too slow for such a jazz-oriented show. The song was added to the 1927 version of *Strike Up the Band*, but the musical closed out of town. Again it was added to *Rosalie* (1928), and again it was removed from the score before opening. The number was first heard by the public when Eva Gauthier sang it in a concert in Connecticut with George Gershwin at the piano. Publisher Max Dreyfus liked the song and decided to publish it without waiting for it to be featured in a Broadway show. It was not an immediate hit, but it slowly gained recognition because Helen Morgan was singing it in her nightclub act in various locations. A 1927 record by Marion Harris helped somewhat, but the ballad was finding more success in England where British bands picked up on it right away. "The Man I Love" was even a hit in Paris before Paul Whiteman popularized it in the States. Of the hundreds of recordings made over the years, some of the most memorable ones include Helen Forrest, the Benny Goodman Trio, Gladys Swarthout, Jane Pickins, Hildegarde (with Gershwin at the piano), Eddy Duchin, Rise Stevens, Lena Horne, the King Cole Trio, Joe Bushkin, the Art Van Damme Quintet, Ella Fitzgerald, Lee Wiley, Barbra Streisand, and Michael Feinstein (who sang it as "The Girl I Love."). Broadway may have rejected "The Man I Love," but Hollywood certainly didn't, putting it in at least ten movies. It was sung by Ida Lupino in *The Man I Love* (1946), Doris Day with Harry James' Orchestra in *Young Man With a Horn* (1950), Ann Blyth (dubbed by Gogi Grant) in *The Helen Morgan Story* (1957), Diana Ross in *Lady Sings the Blues* (1972), Liza Minnelli in *New York, New York* (1977), as well as being played by organist Hazel Scott in *Rhapsody in Blue* (1945).

"The Man That Broke the Bank at Monte Carlo" (1892) is a sprightly march by Englishman Fred Gilbert that was popular on both sides of the Atlantic. Gilbert was inspired by a famous con man, Arthur De Courcey Bower, who worked as a shill in gambling casinos. The dapper gent would walk the streets of London and set tongues wagging about his supposed wealth. Gilbert's lyric concerned an American dandy dressed to the nines who struts the streets of Paris with the air of a millionaire, everyone thinking he must have cleaned up at the gambling tables in the south of France; but in reality he is bluffing and his fame is a fraud. Gilbert couldn't get any publisher interested in the song, so he sold it outright to music hall performer Charles Coburn for ten pounds, who performed it with some success. But when Maggie Durham used it in her act and the song caught on, all the royalties went to Coburn, not Gilbert. Records of sheet music sales in Great Britain and America are not accurate, but it seemed every parlor piano in both countries had a copy of the merry song, and it was a favorite at tavern sing-alongs, community sings, and on vaudeville. Even after the popularity of the song waned, the title expression stuck, referring to a debonair but suspect millionaire. In the film *The Magnificent Ambersons* (1942), it was sung by Joseph Cotton, Anne Baxter, Tim Holt, Dolores Costello, and Agnes Moorehead.

"Mañana (Is Good Enough for Me)" (1948) is a comic song about procrastination that might be deemed politically incorrect today because of its stereotypic Hispanic dialect, but it was one of the most successful of the many pseudo-Latin numbers that flooded Tin Pan Alley in the 1940s and 1950s. Singer Peggy Lee and guitarist Dave Barbour wrote the farcical song, using broken English ("the faucet she is dripping") to list the many activities one can put off until another day, such as getting a job or fixing up the crumbling house. Lee recorded it with Barbour accompanying her, and the disc sold a million copies. Edmundo Ros, Dean Martin, Kate Dimbleby, and Pete Rugolo are among the other artists who also recorded it.

"Mandy" (1918) is a contagious cakewalk number by Irving Berlin and still one of his most recognized tunes. The unembellished lyric is a marriage proposal to a gal named Mandy, informing her that he's got a preacher ready and that their life together "would be dandy." The music is short (only eighteen measures with a two-measure tag) but very direct and forceful. Berlin interpolated the song into his all-soldier revue *Yip Yip Yaphank* (1918) on Broadway, where it was done as a minstrel show routine by Dan Healy and John Murphy. The next year it was added to the *Ziegfeld Follies*, where it was sung by the comedy team of Van and

Schenck and danced by Marilyn Miller, Ray Dooley, and the ensemble. "Mandy" appeared on Broadway again in the military revue *This Is the Army* (1942). On screen, Eddie Cantor, Ethel Merman, Ann Sothern, and the chorus performed it in *Kid Millions* (1934), Ralph Magelssen and company sang it in the screen version of *This Is the Army* (1943), Vera-Ellen (dubbed by Trudy Stevens) and John Brascia performed it in *White Christmas* (1954), and it was heard in *Blue Skies* (1946). Mabel Mercer made a specialty of it in her act, and there were major records made by Cantor, Al Jolson, Claude Hopkins, Fats Waller, Rosemary Clooney, Jimmie Lunceford, and the Modernaires.

"Mandy, Make Up Your Mind" (1924) is a Roaring Twenties number that was ideal for dancing the Charleston and also became a favorite of jazz musicians. Grant Clarke, Roy Turk (lyric), George W. Meyer, and Arthur Johnston (music) wrote the vibrant song asking a sweetie to decide and give her heart to one and only one beau. It was introduced by Florence Mills in the Broadway revue *Dixie to Broadway* (1924) and was soon recorded by Paul Whiteman, Clarence Williams (featuring Louis Armstrong and Sidney Bechet), and Fletcher Henderson. Tommy Dorsey and his Orchestra revived the number in 1943, and there were also discs by Eva Taylor, Earl Hines, Wild Bill Davison, Eddie Condon, Mabel Mercer, the Louisiana Washboard Five, and Muggsy Spanier.

"Manhattan" (1921) is Rodgers and Hart's first hit song and one of their very best. Still considered one of the finest ballads ever written about New York, the song manages to be romantic even as it pokes fun at romanticism. Lorenz Hart's lyric has a sly but heartfelt quality that turns the mundane (pushcarts on Mott Street, the subway, Childs Restaurant, and so on) into the sublime. Richard Rodgers's music is filled with unexpected turns in the refrain that are as surprising as they are unforgettable. The unknown songwriters wrote the ballad in 1921 for a show called *Winkle Town* that never got produced. When asked to score *Garrick Gaieties* (1925), a fund-raiser for the Theatre Guild, the team finally got to use "Manhattan," and when Sterling Holloway and June Cochrane sang it, it made the song and the show a hit. Sometimes titled "I'll Take Manhattan" after the opening line of the refrain, the number has been recorded hundreds of times over the years. Just some of the many commendable discs include those by Ben Selvin, the Dorsey Brothers, Lee Wiley, Bing Crosby, Blossom Dearie, Eddy Duchin, Sonny Rollins, Rosemary Clooney, Ethel Merman, Herbie Hancock, Ella Fitzgerald, Tony Bennett, Dinah Washington, Vic Damone, Johnny Mathis, Bobby Short, and more recently, Dawn Upshaw, Weslia Whitfield, Annie Ross, and Mary Cleere Haran. "Manhattan" was sung by Mickey Rooney in the movie *Words and Music* (1948), Tony Martin and Dinah Shore in *Two*

Tickets to Broadway (1951), and Bob Hope and Vera Miles (dubbed by Imogene Lynn) in *Beau James* (1957) and heard on the soundtracks of *Don't Bother to Knock* (1952), *The Eddy Duchin Story* (1956), *Revenge of the Nerds* (1984), and other films.

"Manhattan Serenade" (1928) is an intoxicating ballad about falling in love on a fall evening in New York City. The number began as a piano solo work by Louis Alter, and the slow, romantic fox trot was published in 1928. Paul Whiteman and his Orchestra made it a familiar instrumental piece, the Dorsey Brothers used it often, and it became the theme song for the radio show *Easy Aces* in the 1930s. When Harold Adamson wrote an atmospheric lyric in 1942, the new song began a second and even more successful career. The lyric describes two lovers walking through a moonlit park one autumn as the breezes through the trees create a "Manhattan serenade." Hit records by Tommy Dorsey (vocal by Jo Stafford), Harry James (vocal by Helen O'Connell), and Jimmy Dorsey (vocal by Bob Eberly) popularized the new number and kept it on *Your Hit Parade* for eleven weeks. There were also well-known discs by Andre Kostelanetz, Billy Cotton, Leon Russell, Dinah Shore, the Curtis Fuller Quintet, Helen Forrest, the Four Coins, and Caterina Valente. The song can be heard in the film *Broadway Rhythm* (1944), where it is danced to by the Ross Sisters.

"Marching Through Georgia" (1865) was one of the most applauded songs of the Civil War, albeit only in the North. The title refers to General Sherman's infamous march from Atlanta to the sea and the path of destruction he left in his wake. Henry Clay Work wrote the ballad as a tribute to the general's conquest, but Southerners despised the number, feeling it condoned Sherman's cruelty. (Sherman himself did not like the song, feeling it detracted from his more glorious feats during the war.) The ballad remained popular for many years after the war. It was a favorite of British soldiers going into France during World War One, and American GIs sang it to boost morale when they invaded North Africa in World War Two. But time did not weaken the South's distaste for the song. When it was played at the Democratic convention in 1916, the Southern delegates threatened to walk out until an apology was made. The Kessinger Brothers, Alan Munde and the Country Gazette, Joe Maphis, the Trail Band, Hoot Hester and Sam Levine, and Slim Jackson are among those who recorded the number.

"Margie" (1920) is a cheerful ditty in which a wooer sings the praises of the girl he wants to marry, feeling he must tell all the world about her charms. Benny Davis wrote the adoring lyric, using Eddie Cantor's five-year-old daughter Marjorie as his inspiration, and Con Conrad and J.

Russel Robinson composed the sparkling music. The number was introduced by the Original Dixieland Jazz Band, but Cantor brought it more
recognition when he sang it in concert and interpolated it into his Broadway show *The Midnight Rounders* (1921). Jimmie Lunceford and his Orchestra revived the song on disc in 1938, and there is also a jazz classic
version by trombonist James "Trummy" Osborne with Lunceford's band.
Other notable records were made by Cantor, Gene Rodemich, Ted Lewis,
Frank Crumit, the Smoothies, Frankie Carle, Nat Brandwynne, Barclay
Allen, the Hoosier Hot Shots, and Bob Wilson and his Varsity Rhythm
Boys. "Margie" was heard in the movies *Stella Dallas* (1937), *Hit Parade
of 1941* (1940), and *Margie* (1946) and was sung by Tom Brown and Joy
Hodges in an earlier version of *Margie* (1940), Betty Hutton in *Incendiary
Blonde* (1945), and Keefe Braselle (dubbed by Cantor) in *The Eddie Cantor
Story* (1953).

"Maria Elena" (1941) is a Mexican song that found success on Tin Pan
Alley more than once. Lorenzo Barcelata wrote the ballad in the early
1930s, naming it and dedicating it to the wife of Mexican president Portes
Gil. Some instrumental versions of the tune drifted north to the States,
but when S.K. Russell wrote an English lyric in 1941, it was an immediate
hit with records by Lawrence Welk and his Orchestra and Jimmy Dorsey
(vocal by Bob Eberly). The Dorsey disc went to the top of the charts and
helped keep the song on the *Hit Parade* for an amazing twenty-two
weeks. Barcelata's music is highly romantic and not easily forgotten. The
new lyric is a passionate declaration of love to one who is the "answer
to a prayer." While it remained a Latin staple for orchestras for years,
an instrumental version by the Brazilian brothers Los Indios Tabajares
was a major hit in 1963. Among those who also recorded it were Mantovanni's Orchestra, Chick Henderson, Jan Garber, Marty Robbins, Nat
King Cole, Jerry Murad's Harmonicats, Andy Russell, Pete Fountain, Jack
Schell, Blue Barron, Gene Pitney, and Placido Domingo, as well as many
marimba bands and other Latin artists. "Maria Elena" can be heard in
Bordertown (1935), *Down Mexico Way* (1941), and other films.

"Marie" (1928) is the quintessential Irving Berlin ballad: simple, direct,
sincere, and poignant. The paean to the girl with a gleam in her eyes
uses notes sparingly, but each musical phrase is full-bodied and memorable. Berlin's lyric is poetic yet never flowery, the suitor calling her
name as a form of recitative. And, like much of Berlin's work, the song
does not date because the timeless ideas it contains are expressed simply
and honestly. The waltzing number was written as the background
theme for the early talkie *The Awakening* (1928), then was popularized
by Rudy Vallee on the radio and on records. Tommy Dorsey revived the
song in 1937, rewriting the number into 4/4 time and featuring a vocal

by Jack Leonard and a trumpet solo by Bunny Berigan. The record sold over a million copies and helped launch Dorsey's career after separating from his brother Jimmy and going off on his own. The Four Tunes revived the ballad in 1954, and the Irish group the Bachelors did the same in 1965. Other significant records were made by Nat Shilkret, Basil Fomeen, Frank Sinatra, Louis Armstrong, Dick Haymes, Boots Randolph, Al Bowlly, Les Brown, Keely Smith and Louis Prima, Pete Fountain, Vic Damone, Steve Lawrence and Eydie Gorme, the Ravens, Ray Charles and Betty Carter, and more recently, Andrea Marcovicci and Mandy Patinkin. On screen Stuart Foster, Janet Blair, and the chorus performed "Marie" with Tommy Dorsey's band in *The Fabulous Dorseys* (1947), and it was heard in *Alexander's Ragtime Band* (1938), *A Song Is Born* (1948), and *There's No Business Like Show Business* (1954).

"The Marine's Hymn" (1919), the official song of the U.S. Marine Corps, is a stimulating march with a bold lyric befitting the famed fighting unit. Henry C. Davis is credited with the music, though there is some question about the authorship. The music is clearly based on a melody from Jacques Offenbach's opera bouffe *Genevieve de Brabant* (1868), and the lyricist was probably a marine who went to Mexico City in 1847 as part of a campaign in the Mexican War (hence the reference to the "Halls of Montezuma"). The lyric also mentions the "shores of Tripoli," which refers to a celebrated mission that the marines had against the Barbary pirates of North Africa in 1805. The words and music did not come together until World War One, and the song has remained a patriotic favorite ever since, reaching a peak of popularity during World War Two. In addition to many marching bands and choral groups, the song has been recorded by such varied artists as Roy Acuff, the Robert Shaw Chorale, Jerry Lee Lewis, Gene Krupa, and the Mormon Tabernacle Choir. Eleanor Parker (dubbed by Eileen Farrell) sang it in the movie *Interrupted Melody* (1955), but most of the song's many screen appearances have been orchestral, as in *The Cuban Love Song* (1931), *Guadalcanal Diary* (1943), *Stage Door Canteen* (1943), *Halls of Montezuma* (1950), *Rocky* (1976), and *Full Metal Jacket* (1987). The anthem is sometimes listed as "From the Halls of Montezuma (To the Shores of Tripoli)."

"Maryland, My Maryland" (1861) was briefly the second most popular Civil War song in the South, only "Dixie" surpassing it in demand until fate played a hand in matters: The state of Maryland decided to side with the North, and the patriotic ballad immediately lost favor below the Mason-Dixon Line. James Ryder Randall, an English professor at a Louisiana college, read in the newspaper about a racial riot in Baltimore where Union troops were called in. Randall wrote a poem saluting the fine state of Maryland, urging a call to arms ("the despot's heel is on thy shore"), and it was published first in a Louisiana paper and then in a Baltimore one, the lyric being turned into a broadside to encourage kinship with the Confederacy. The melody from the 1824 German carol "O Tannenbaum (Oh Christmas Tree)" was put to the poem, and the new song was performed for the first time in a Baltimore church in 1862. That same year it was published as sheet music in New Orleans and quickly became a favorite of Southern troops. Once Maryland chose to side with the Union, the ballad was only embraced by Maryland, later becoming the official state song. In the twentieth century the song became a favorite of jazz artists, Louis Armstrong making a classic recording and reprising it in the movie *New Orleans* (1947). The ballad can also be heard in many period films, most prominently in *Gone With the Wind* (1939). Kid Ory and the Creole Jazz Band, Norrie Cox, George Lewis, Bunk Johnson, Coleman Hawkins, Papa Celestin, and Jim Robinson are among the others who made recordings.

"May the Good Lord Bless and Keep You (Till We Meet Again)" (1950) is a Tin Pan Alley hit that takes the form of a hymn. Meredith Willson, some years before he wrote the Broadway musical *The Music Man* (1957), recalled the title expression that his mother used at the end of each session when she taught Sunday school back in Iowa. The bandleader turned the idea into a cordial farewell song, wishing that all your troubles be small ones and that you "walk in sunshine" until the next time we meet. Frankie Laine popularized the song with a hit record. The number was also used as the closing theme for Tallulah Bankhead's radio program *The Big Show* and she sang it each week with her conductor Willson and her guest stars. From all the exposure, sheet music sales reached half a million and the tender ballad was a household favorite. It was also one of the most requested songs by GIs in the Korean War when entertainers came to do USO (United Service Organization) shows in Asia. Among the other artists who recorded the number were Perry Como, Joe McPartland, Faron Young, Bing Crosby, Ernest Tubb, Bryon Lee and the Dragonaires, Boots Randolph, Jim Reeves, Joni James, Johnny Mathis, Jim Nabors, and Tammy Wynette.

"Maybe" (1935) is an affecting ballad by Allan Flynn and Frank Madden that offers a series of possibilities to a former lover: Maybe you'll think about me when you are lonely, maybe the one you are leaving me for will "prove untrue," maybe you will come and ask me to take you back, "maybe I'll say maybe." The Ink Spots had a bestselling record of the song, sheet music sales were substantial, and the number remained on *Your Hit Parade* for thirteen weeks. A duet version by Eddie Fisher and Perry Como revived the ballad in 1952. Other noteworthy discs were made by Vera Lynn, Harry James, Bing Crosby, the Four Coins, the Chantels, Ella Fitzgerald, and the Shangri-Las.

"Maybe It's Because I Love You Too Much" (1932) is one of those Irving Berlin ballads that use repeated notes so effectively. Such a song seems like it would be monotonous but instead is quietly dazzling. A lover feels that her sweetheart is slipping away from her and she questions whether her total infatuation is driving him away. The bands of Leo Reisman (vocal by Fred Astaire), Guy Lombardo, Ray Noble, and Freddy Martin (vocal by Elmer Feldkamp) each had successful records of the ballad, and there were also discs by Nat King Cole, Connee Boswell, Peggy Lee, and Sarah Vaughan. More recently it has been recorded by Nancy Harrow, Michael Feinstein, Andrea Marcovicci, and Bill Bauer.

"Me and My Shadow" (1927) is the quintessential soft-shoe number, a masterful piece of restrained melody that practically dances all by itself. Billy Rose wrote the unusual torch song in which a dejected wooer takes comfort in his shadow, his only friend and one who never fights with him over a girl. Yet as the two buddies are "walking down the avenue" together, both are blue over her loss. Dave Dreyer and Al Jolson are credited with writing the music, though Jolson's part in the collaboration is questionable. Although Jolson performed and recorded it, the song is more associated with bandleader Ted Lewis, who sang it as he conducted his orchestra, keeping the number in his repertoire for years. Over the years it seemed that every hoofer in show business danced to the tune, which is ideal for the soft shoe, the music having built-in spots to improvise some fancy footwork. It was interpolated into the revue *Harry Delmar's Revels* (1927), where it was performed by Frank Fay, and "whispering" Jack Smith made it a specialty of his on the radio. Never falling out of favor, the number was revived in the 1950s with a popular record by Pearl Bailey, who filled in the dance sections with vocal ad libs. Other memorable discs were made by Lee Sims, Ziggy Elman, Judy Garland, Bob Grant, the Sportsmen, Johnny Marvin and Aileen Stanley, Rose Murphy, Liberace, Frank Sinatra, and Sammy Davis Jr. and, more recently, by Mandy Patinkin and Dave McKenna. "Me and My Shadow" was heard in the film *Here Comes the Band* (1935) and was performed by Lewis and his Orchestra in *Hold That Ghost* (1941), Donald O'Connor in *Feudin', Fussin' and Fightin'* (1948), and James Caan (as Billy Rose) in *Funny Lady* (1975). On Broadway Gary Chapman and the cast sang it in the musical *Big Deal* (1986), and it was performed by the ensemble in the revue *Fosse* (1999).

"Mean to Me" (1929) is a penetrating lament that was associated with three of America's most renowned torch singers: Ruth Etting, Helen Morgan, and Billie Holiday. Roy Turk composed the music that quietly works its way up the scale, then when it is about to climax, winds down in a bluesy manner. Fred Ahlert wrote the piquant lyric, complaining that her lover either ignores her or acts coldly to her, yet she still loves him. The title phrase is particularly potent, referring to the mean way he treats her and also how much he means to her. Etting introduced and popularized the number in clubs and on records, keeping it in her repertoire for years. About the same time Morgan started using it as well. Holiday revived the ballad in 1937 with a classic disc with Teddy Wilson and also sang it in clubs. Other records of note were made by Etta Jones, Art Tatum, the Andrews Sisters, Helen Humes, Woody Herman, Ella Fitzgerald with Oscar Peterson, Paul Weston (vocal by Matt Dennis), Valaida Snow, Eddy Howard, and more recently, Linda Ronstadt, Carol Woods, and Karen Saunders. It was sung by Doris Day in the Etting film bio *Love Me or Leave Me* (1955), by Diana Ross in the Holiday bio *Lady Sings the Blues* (1972) and by Nell Carter in the Broadway revue *Ain't Misbehavin'* (1978).

"Meet Me in St. Louis" (1904) has remained popular for nearly a century even though it was written about a long-gone event, the 1904 World's Fair in St. Louis. Penning songs about newsworthy events and people of the day was common, but few topical songs caught on as this one did. Andrew B. Sterling wrote the catchy lyric, and Kerry Mills provided the waltzlike music. It was first popularized in vaudeville by Billy Murray. Soon variety singers Gus Williams, Nora Bayes, Lottie Gilson, Vera King, and Fields and Ward, as well as all of America, were singing it. Oddly enough, the verse of the song has dropped out of popularity over the years, and the ditty is quite a different number without it. The verse tells of a discontented housewife named Flossie who, fed up with her dull husband Louis, packs up her clothes and jewelry and heads for St. Louis and the fair. She leaves a note (the well-known refrain of the song) for Louis to come and try and find her at the fair; hence, the double "Louis" in the refrain is not just an echo but a rhythmic way of addressing her husband. Mills and Sterling got the idea for the double phrase when they were at a bar together, and Mills ordered a mixed drink called a "louis" from the bartender Louie. They liked the repetition of the two Louie's, and Sterling laid out the lyric. (The $200 that Mills paid him for the lyric was the only financial compensation Sterling ever got from the giant hit.) Although it never fell out of favor, the number enjoyed a modest revival of interest when Lucille Fletcher sang it in the film *The Strawberry Blonde* (1941), and it was very popular all over again when Judy Garland and various cast members sang it (without the now-forgotten verse) in the movie musical *Meet Me in St. Louis* (1944). Leon Ames, whose character complained about everybody singing the song in that film, sang it himself in *By the Light of the Silvery Moon* (1953). On stage, Carolyn Magnini sang "Meet Me in St. Louis" in the period revue *Tintypes* (1980), and Donna Kane and the cast sang it in the 1989 Broadway version of the Garland film.

"Meet Me Tonight in Dreamland" (1909) found success first as a romantic ballad and then later as a swing and jazz favorite. Leo Friedman composed the solemn, slow waltz music, and Beth Slater Whitson penned the felicitous lyric that asked for an amorous assignation in the moonlight. Henry Burr popularized the piece, which caught on so quickly that over 2 million copies of sheet music were sold before World War One. Unfortunately, neither songwriter got a penny of royalties since they were employed by the song's publisher and all their work was owned by the company. The ballad was revived when Judy Garland sang it in the movie *In the Good Old Summertime* (1949) and recorded it, and again in 1965 with a hit record by Pat Boone. Other artists who made disc versions include Les Elgart, the Mills Brothers, Eddie Condon, Glen Gray and the Casa Loma Orchestra, Jimmie Davis, Keith Ingham, and Thelonious Monk. The song was also in some period films, such as *The Eddie Cantor Story* (1953).

"Melancholy Lullaby" (1939) is a swinging good-night song that has also been embraced by jazz musicians. Edward Heyman penned the sad farewell lyric, and Benny Carter wrote the morose but rhythmic music. Carter and his Band introduced the number on record, and there were also well-known versions by Glenn Miller (vocal by Bob Eberly), Ginny Simms, and Artie Shaw. "Melancholy Lullaby" was revived in the 1970s by Gordon Giltrap.

"A Melody From the Sky" (1936) is a cowboy ballad that was recorded by a variety of artists in a variety of styles. Sidney D. Mitchell wrote the bucolic lyric about music coming from nature, and Louis Alter composed the warm melody. It was introduced by Fuzzy Knight in the movie *The Trail of the Lonesome Pine* (1936), and the number was nominated for an Academy Award. The song was recorded by such diverse talents as Jan Garber, Eddy Duchin, Roy Rogers and the Sons of the Pioneers, Bunny Berigan (vocal by Chick Bullock), Tex Ritter, Jack Shilkret, Freddy Martin (vocal by Elmer Feldkamp), Mezz Mezzrow, Flip Phillips, and Jimmy Wakely.

"Melody of Love" (1903) is a dreamy waltz by Tom Glazer (lyric) and H. Engelmann (music) that started as a piano piece that was often used by piano students during the early years of the century. An instrumental recording by the Victor Orchestra enjoyed some popularity in the 1920s.

John Klenner wrote a lyric in 1942, calling the number "Whisper That You Love Me," and it was recorded by Kenny Baker with moderate success. The Glazer lyric, describing the choir of angels that are singing about a perfect love, was added in 1955, and the new version became a hit record for the Four Aces. Among the others who made either instrumental or vocal recordings were Billy Vaughn, Frank Sinatra with Ray Anthony's Orchestra, Archie Bleyer, Pee Wee King, Al Martino, Dinah Shore and Tony Martin, Lawrence Welk, the McGuire Sisters, and Bobby Vinton.

"Memories" (1915) is a gentle ballad whose flowing melody is still recognized today because it has been used dozens of times in films as background music going into a flashback or nostalgic reminiscence. Egbert Van Alstyne composed the dreamy waltz music, and Gus Kahn wrote the teary lyric that harkens back to childhood, young love, and the good old days. Jon Barnes Welles popularized the song in vaudeville, and John McCormack recorded it and made it part of his concert repertory for a while. Other significant recordings were made by Vaughn Monroe, Earl Bostic, Bing Crosby, Lawrence Welk, the Moms and Dads, Jimmie Davis, and Max Gregor. In addition to the many movies that used the melody on the soundtrack, the song was sung in *It All Came True* (1940), *Tin Pan Alley* (1940), *Is Everybody Happy?* (1943), *I'll See You in My Dreams* (1952), and *So This Is Love* (1953).

"Memories Are Made of This" (1955) is an uptempo ballad by Terry Gilkyson, Richard Dehr, and Frank Miller that has more than a touch of a western flavor to it. The number lists some of the many things that make memories: a tender kiss, a boy and girl together, two loving lips, two sips of wine, and so on. Dean Martin popularized the song with a record made with the Easy Riders (a pseudonym for the three songwriters) that sold over a million discs. Gale Storm also had a hit record version of the ballad. Notable among the many others who recorded it were Keely Smith, Hank Snow, Eddy Arnold, Jonah Jones, the Ray Conniff Singers, Gene and Debbe, Jim Reeves, Johnny Cash, the Drifters, and Petula Clark. "Memories Are Made of This" was heard in the movie *Windjammer* (1958), and Mario Lanza sang it in *The Seven Hills of Rome* (1958).

"Memories of You" (1930) is a sparkling love song by Andy Razaf (lyric) and Eubie Blake (music) in which everything around one, from sunrise to sunset, reminds you of your beloved. The number has an unusually wide range for a pop song (an octave and a fifth), yet the musical construction is logical and simple. Minto Cato introduced the song in the revue *Lew Leslie's Blackbirds* (1930), and Ethel Waters was the first to record it. But it was a 1938 bestselling disc by Glen Gray and the Casa Loma Orchestra (with a trumpet solo by Sonny Dunham) that made the ballad famous; Dunham later used it as his theme song and recorded it three times on his own. Of the many artists who recorded it over the years were Louis Armstrong, Benny Goodman, Bud Freeman, Joe Augustine, Judy Garland, Art Hodes, Count Basie, Doc Cheatham, Rosemary Clooney, Illinois Jacquet, the Ink Spots, Vaughn Monroe, Ray Anthony, Mel Tormé, Lionel Hampton, Bucky and John Pizzarelli, and Blake himself. The Benny Goodman Trio performed the number in the film bio *The Benny Goodman Story* (1956), and Anita O'Day sang it in *The Gene Krupa Story* (1959). On Broadway, Ethel Beatty sang it in the revue *Eubie* (1978), and it was performed by Dianne Walker, Kevin Ramsey, and Bernard Manners in *Black and Blue* (1989).

"Memory Lane" (1924) is a halting waltz number that uses musical echoes to parallel the memories recalled in the lyric. Larry Spier and Con Conrad composed the dreamy music, and B.G. DeSylva wrote the tender lyric about remembering a past love, "wandering through memory lane" and reliving the past. Early recordings by Fred Waring's Pennsylvanians (featured vocal by Tom Waring) and Paul Specht and his Orchestra popularized the song, and there was a revival of interest when it was used in the movie *In Society* (1944). Other estimable records were made by Kate Smith, Claude Thornhill, Vaughn Monroe, the Statler Brothers, Edwin Starr, Dean Martin, the Three Suns, B.B. King, and Lou Rawls.

"The Memphis Blues" (1912), historically important as the first blues song to be published and the first of its genre to become a mainstream hit, remains a scintillating example of a true blues ballad. W.C. Handy composed the piece in 1909 as a campaign song called "Mr. Crump" in the Negro minstrel style. But in 1912 Handy reworked the song into a piano piece that was arguably the first blues number ever written out in sheet music. He called it "The Memphis Blues" and sold it to a publisher for $50, his first published work. A lyric by George A. Norton was added, and the new song was published in 1913. The verse mentions Handy's name as it describes how one travels to Tennessee to hear the new blues sound. The refrain then celebrates the new sound, a kind of music that "wraps a spell around my heart." The number was introduced by Prince's Orchestra, and it slowly caught on. It was interpolated into the Broadway revue *George White's Scandals* (1926), and there was a hit record by Ted Lewis in 1927. In 1931, Charles Tobias and Peter De Rose wrote a new lyric and revised the music somewhat, and more bands and performers picked up on it. Harry James revived the song in 1947, and the number became a favorite of Big Bands as well. Among the many acclaimed recordings are those by Dinah Shore, Guy Lombardo and the

Royal Canadians, Bing Crosby, Paul Weston (vocals by Johnny Mercer and the Pied Pipers), Lena Horne, Ruby Newman, and Duke Ellington. "The Memphis Blues" was performed by Mae West with Ellington's Orchestra in the film *Belle of the Nineties* (1934), it was featured in the *St. Louis Blues* (1939), was reprised by Crosby in *Birth of the Blues* (1941), and was sung by Nat King Cole and Eartha Kitt in the Handy bio *St. Louis Blues* (1958).

"The Merry-Go-Round Broke Down" (1937) is a short and slapstick novelty number that proved to be ideal for the jitterbug and other dances, so it was performed and recorded by many of the Big Bands. Cliff Friend and Dave Franklin wrote the nonsense song about a carousel that loses power, and its merry music slows to a halt. Guy Lombardo and the Royal Canadians popularized the number, and there were also notable records by Jimmie Lunceford, Red Allen, Dick Robertson, Bill Coleman, Dick Jurgens, Shep Fields, Eddy Duchin, and Terry Stauffer. The silly ditty shows up on many children's records, and even the Three Stooges made a disc of it. It can be heard in the movie *A Slight Case of Murder* (1938).

"Mexicali Rose" (1923) is a mellow farewell song by Helen Stone (lyric) and Jack B. Temey (music) in the form of a cowboy ballad, telling the crying sweetheart Rose not to worry, that he will return to her "some sunny day." The prairie song was introduced by, ironically, the Cliquot Club Eskimos, and it was a steady favorite on the radio for a while. Bing Crosby revived interest in the ballad when he sang it in the film *Rhythm on the Range* (1936) and then recorded it with John Scott Trotter's Orchestra. It was also a success for Gene Autry, who sang it in the movies *Rootin' Tootin' Rhythm* (1937), *Mexicali Rose* (1939), and *Barbed-Wire* (1952), and Roy Rogers, who performed it in *Song of Texas* (1943). Among the other artists to record "Mexicali Rose" were Burl Ives, the Sons of the Pioneers, Vera Lynn, Lawrence Welk, the Mills Brothers, Jerry Lee Lewis, the Moms and Dads, and Don Edwards.

"Mine" (1933) is a contrapuntal (double song) number by the Gershwins that was the only hit to come out of their failed Broadway musical *Let 'Em Eat Cake* (1933). George Gershwin composed the two melodies—one slow and rolling, the other sprightly and bright. Ira Gershwin penned the double lyric—one declaring affection that will continue in "rain or storm or shine," the other a patter about mutual love so great that it's hard to believe they are "a married pair." William Gaxton and Lois Moran sang one part and the chorus the other, and it was the most engaging part of the problematic show. Although it soon closed, the ballad was picked up by several artists, sometimes just performing the first song. *Let 'Em Eat Cake* was a sequel to the hit show *Of Thee I Sing* (1931), and the song was interpolated into the 1952 revival of the latter musical and in later productions as well. Harry Richman, Emil Coleman, Horace Heidt, the Arden-Ohman Orchestra, Percy Faith (vocal by Dorothy Kirsten), Art Van Damme, Herbie Nichols, the Four Freshmen, Vic Damone, and Bobby Short are among those who recorded it, and Bing Crosby and Judy Garland had a duet disc in 1947 that was popular. Robert Alda and Oscar Levant sang it in the Gershwin film bio *Rhapsody in Blue* (1945), and the song was heard on the soundtrack for *Manhattan* (1979).

"Minnie the Moocher" (1931), a scat singing classic, is still associated with Cab Calloway who cowrote it and performed it in every media over a period of fifty years. Irving Mills and Clarence Gaskill collaborated with Calloway on the musical tale of a "hoochy coocher" who hangs around with her inamorato Smokey who takes her to parties in Chinatown and showers her with expensive gifts. But Minnie, who had "a heart as big as a whale," goes off her head one day and is put in a mental asylum, where she dies. This morose story was contrasted by red-hot music and the repeating "hi-de-ho" and other scat sounds so that the whole number comes across as tribal and magnetic. Calloway and his Orchestra introduced the song at the Cotton Club in Harlem and then cut their first record, Calloway providing the vocals but the band joining in on the repeats. The disc was a hit, and Calloway became known as "the Hi-De-Ho Man." (The number is often listed as "The Hi-De-Ho Song.") Calloway made later recordings as well and reprised the piece in the movies *The Big Broadcast* (1932) and *The Blues Brothers* (1980). Although the song was always thought of as Calloway's domain, it was also recorded by Adelaide Hall, Mills Blue Rhythm Band, Duke Ellington, Valaida Snow, and Danny Kaye, who often used it in concert as an audience participation number. Grace Moore sang it in the film *When You're in Love* (1937), and Larry Marshall, as a young Calloway, performed it in *The Cotton Club* (1984).

"Mischa, Jascha, Toscha, Sascha" (1921) is a novelty number by the Gershwins and a rare Gershwin song not written for a Broadway show or film. The amusing ditty is about all the violin virtuosos coming out of Russia and invading Carnegie Hall in the 1910s, in particular the musicians Mischa Elman, Jascha Heifetz, Toscha Seidel, and Sascha Jacobson of the title. George Gershwin composed the furious, mock-Russian music, and Ira Gershwin wrote the wry lyric, the four men celebrating their fame in America, knowing that their very-Russian names and music make them high-brow favorites even though they themselves would prefer playing pop songs "like the syncopations of Uncle Sammy." The brothers wrote the number as a party song and often performed it informally, as did others, particularly when one of the violinists in question was present. But it was not published until 1932 and was rarely recorded, though Paul Whiteman and his Orchestra made a delightful disc of the song. The comic number later became known from musical revues and nightclub performances.

"Miss Otis Regrets" (1934) is a droll and ridiculous ditty by Cole Porter that mocked the good manners of high society and was dedicated to Elsa Maxwell, the queen of social hospitality. A stiff and overly formal butler responds to an invitation to luncheon for his boss. He tells the hostess that his employer Miss Otis cannot attend because the previous night she shot her lover, was arrested, put in jail, then dragged out by an angry mob and lynched. The farcical lyric is delivered with a dispassionate tone and is all the more amusing because the music is so delicate and formal. Porter wrote the number to amuse friends at parties, and his pal Monte Woolley was always asked to sing it at informal gatherings. The number was interpolated into the London musical *Hi Diddle Diddle* (1934), where it was sung by Douglas Byng, and in the States it became known from a sassy recording by Ethel Waters. Other applauded discs were made by Cab Calloway and his Orchestra, the Mills Brothers, Nat King Cole, Ella Fitzgerald, Rosemary Clooney, Marlene Dietrich (in German), the King Sisters, Maxine Sullivan, Alberta Hunter, and Martha Raye. More recently it has been recorded by Bobby Short, Bette Midler, José Feliciano, and Elisabeth Welch. Woolley reprised the song in the Porter movie bio *Night and Day* (1946).

"Miss You" (1929) is a heart-tugging ballad of loneliness by Harry and Charles Tobias that Rudy Vallee introduced on record and then enjoyed a revival of interest during World War Two. Dinah Shore and Bing Crosby each had hit records in the 1940s, helping the song to remain on *Your Hit Parade* for eleven weeks. There were also successful discs by Eddy Howard, Etta James, Billy Vaughn, Claude Thornhill, the McGuire Sisters, Freddy Martin, Harry Sosnik, Maxine Daniels, and Nat King Cole. "Miss You" was used in the movie *Strictly in the Groove* (1942).

"Mississippi Mud" (1927) is an eccentric dance song by Harris Barris and James Cavanaugh that encourages one to "beat your feet" in the oozing mud. Paul Whiteman and his Orchestra popularized the number with a disc featuring vocals by the Rhythm Boys (Barris, Bing Crosby, and Al Rinker) and featuring Bix Beiderbecke on cornet. The same group reprised the song in the early film classic *King of Jazz* (1930). Among the other artists who recorded the rhythmic number were Frankie Trumbauer, Lee Morse, the Charleston Chasers, Connie Haines, Bob Crosby, the Platters, Connie Francis, Barbra Streisand, Ray Charles, and Mason Williams. Lester Lanin and his Orchestra were heard in the movie *Man of the Century* (1999).

"Missouri Waltz" (1914), the official state song of Missouri, is a tender lullaby in which a mother sings her child to sleep with a tune she recalls from her childhood back in the "Show Me" state. Frederick Knight Logan is the credited composer, though it was later learned that he got the melody from John Valentine Eppell, a young African American who used to play it all the time on his guitar. The song was published as a piano piece in 1914, and two years later the lyric was added by J.R. Shannon (a.k.a. James Royce). The new ballad was introduced by the Victory Military Band, and over 1 million copies of sheet music were sold. Notable records of "The Missouri Waltz" were made by Glenn Miller, Frankie Carle, Kay Starr, Billy Vaughn, Paul Whiteman, Six Fat Dutchmen, Lawrence Welk, Acker Bilk, and the Moms and Dads and a popular polka version by Frankie Yankovic and his Yanks. Fred Astaire and Ginger Rogers danced to it in the movie *The Story of Vernon and Irene Castle* (1939), and it was used in *The Merry Monahans* (1944). The number was a favorite of Missourian Harry Truman, and the song was played a lot during his administration.

"Mister Gallagher and Mister Shean" (1922) is an incongruous patter song written and performed by the comedy team of the title, one of the rare cases of a Tin Pan Alley hit about its own authors. Ed Gallagher and Al Shean collaborated on the comic ditty in which they ask each other a series of non sequitur questions, always calling each other by their formal names. The team introduced the duet in vaudeville, and then it was interpolated into the *Ziegfeld Follies* (1922), where they also performed it, later recording the number and using it throughout their careers. Although the duet was well known and was often copied and parodied, it had few recordings. Billy Jones and Ernie Hare made an early disc, and a 1938 record by Bing Crosby and Johnny Mercer was very popular. Years after Gallagher's death, Shean reprised the number with Charles Winninger in the movie *Ziegfeld Girl* (1941) and again with Jack Kenny in *Atlantic City* (1944). The patter song was also used in the Off-Broadway show *Groucho: A Life in Revue* (1994).

"Mister Sandman" (1954) is an uptempo lullaby of sorts by Pat Ballard that asks the sandman to shine its magic beam on a lonely soul and "bring me a dream" of a perfect true love. The torchy number has such a rhythmic force that it is neither somber nor lulling; instead, it lends itself to harmonizing barbershop quartets and other small vocal ensembles. The number was introduced by the Chordettes with Archie Bleyer's

Orchestra on a record that sold a million copies and hit the Number One spot on the charts. The song was revived in 1981 by a popular record by Emmylou Harris, and there was even a parody version called "Mister Santa." Other discs of note were made by the Four Aces, Bobby Vee, the Flirtations, Bert Kaempfert, Les Paul and Mary Ford, Chet Atkins, and Linda McCartney. "Mister Sandman" was sung by the cast of the Off-Broadway revue *The Taffetas* (1988) and was heard in the film *Cry-Baby* (1990).

"Misty" (1954) is a dreamy ballad by Johnny Burke (lyric) and Erroll Garner (music) that describes how the mist surrounds him, and he hears violins when he is near his beloved. Garner was flying from Chicago to New York one misty afternoon and got the idea for the main musical theme while in the air. Afraid he would lose it, he hummed the music to himself over and over again until they landed and he could get to a piano and tape it. The number was an instrumental hit first, with a popular record by the Erroll Garner Trio. Burke added the graceful lyric in 1956, and Garner recorded it again as a song. In 1959 Johnny Mathis had a bestselling disc, and there were successful versions by Lloyd Price in 1963, the Vibrations in 1965, organist Richard "Groove" Holmes in 1966, and Ray Stevens in 1975. Among the other artists to record "Misty" were Doc Cheatham, Kitty Kallen, Earl Hines, Ella Fitzgerald with Duke Ellington, Bobby Troup, Mitch Miller, Sarah Vaughan, Aretha Franklin, and Lesley Gore.

"Mockin' Bird Hill" (1951) is a lighthearted waltz number by Vaughn Horton that imitates the sounds of birds singing in the morning, their insistent "tra-la la twittle dee dee dee" being as welcome as the flowers. Les Paul with Mary Ford and Patti Page with Jim Carroll's Orchestra each sold a million discs, and it was also a success for the Pinetoppers and Russ Morgan and his Orchestra. Other records were made by Burl Ives, Hank Snow, George Jones and Gene Pitney, Lawrence Welk, Slim Whitman, the Moms and Dads, Donna Fargo, Wayne Henderson, and Maria Muldaur.

"Mona Lisa" (1949), the Oscar-winning song that became Nat King Cole's biggest-selling record, almost never happened. Jay Livingston and Ray Evans were asked to write a song that would serve as the musical theme for a spy film, so they came up with a haunting melody that they called "Prima Donna," then changed it to "After Midnight" when the film's title was changed to that. Evans's wife suggested the lyric be about the woman in Leonardo daVinci's most famous painting, but the song-writers thought the idea ridiculous. But to humor her they sketched out a lyric about the "Mona Lisa" and soon found themselves writing about a woman who was as mysterious as the lady in the painting and whose smile was just as enigmatic. The studio accepted the song, but in the film, now titled *Captain Carey, U.S.A.* (1950), only brief sections of it were heard and what little of the lyric was used was in Italian. The songwriters tried to interest Frank Sinatra, Perry Como, Vic Damone, and Nat King Cole in recording it, and all turned them down. But Carlos Gastel urged it on Cole and got him to change his mind. The recording quickly went to the top of the charts and ended up selling over 3 million discs. Many others recorded it as well, and in 1959 it was revived as a rockabilly hit for both Carl Mann and Conway Twitty. Other prominent discs were made by Harry James, Bing Crosby, Art Lund, Doris Day, Emile Ford and the Checkmates, Floyd Cramer, Frank Chacksfield, Ace Cannon, the Ray Brown Trio, Herb Alpert, James Austin, Willie Nelson, James Brown, Natalie Cole, Julio Iglasias, and José Carreras. The celebrated Nat King Cole recording was heard several times throughout the film *Mona Lisa* (1986).

"Mood Indigo" (1931), Duke Ellington's first major hit song, is a slow but steady blues ballad about being in a deep mood of despair since a lover walked out. The number began as an instrumental piece by Ellington, Irving Mills, and Barney Bigard called "Dreamy Blues," and Ellington and his Orchestra recorded it in 1930. It was successful enough that they asked Mitchell Parish to write a lyric, and the new song, now titled "Mood Indigo," was rerecorded by Ellington and became a big hit. (Unfortunately Parish got no payment since he was under contract with the Mills Publishing Company who owned all his work for them.) There were also early records by Jimmie Lunceford, Clyde McCoy, and Gene Krupa that helped popularize the song. In 1954 it was revived through a popular disc by the Four Freshmen. Among the many artists who also recorded "Mood Indigo" were the Boswell Sisters, Andre Kostelanetz, Larry Adler, Buddy Cole, Sonny Greer and the Duke's Men, Cab Calloway, Nina Simone, Lee Morse, Dinah Shore, Louis Armstrong, Ivie Anderson, Sidney Bechet, Chris Barber, Count Basie, Tony Bennett, Patti Austin, Thelonious Monk, and Kenny Ball. Ellington's Orchestra was heard playing it in the movie *Paris Blues* (1961), and it was used on the soundtrack of *The Cotton Club* (1984). Terri Klausner sang "Mood Indigo" in the Broadway revue *Sophisticated Ladies* (1981), and it was performed by Tonya Pinkins in *Play On!* (1997).

"Moon Country (Is Home to Me)" (1934) is an atmospheric ballad about back home in the south that Johnny Mercer (lyric) and Hoagy Carmichael (music) wrote, using their vivid sense of rural life in both the words and music. The homesick number paints an idyllic picture of " 'possum and 'coon country" where the food tastes better and Cindy Lou plays on the piano each night. Carmichael introduced and popularized the song on record, and at the same time Glen Gray and the Casa Loma Orchestra (vocal by Pee Wee Hunt) had a hit with it. Gray rerecorded the number with the Merry Macs in 1939, and again it was a success. Other noteworthy discs were made by Carrie Smith, Nat Gonella, Jim Cullum, Cory Jamison, and Harry Allen.

"The Moon Is Low" (1936) is a sadly romantic ballad by Irving Mills (lyric) and Will Hudson (music) that was typical of the depression years. The atmospheric number about a moonlight night and the memories it conjures up was introduced by the Hudson-DeLange Band (vocal by Ruth Gaylor), and it was often recorded throughout the decade. The Mills Blue Rhythm Band, Fats Waller, Art Tatum, Ben Pollock's Band, Zoot Sims, Joe Sullivan, Shep Fields, Teddy Wilson, Frank Devol, Earl Bostic, Benny Carter and Roy Eldridge, Della Reese, and Bonnie Guitar are among the artists who made discs of the ballad.

"Moon Love" (1939) was one of the most successful pop songs of the era to be based on a classical piece of music. Mack David, Andre Kostelanetz, and Mack Davis collaborated on the number, which took liberally from Tchaikovsky's Symphony No. 5 in E Minor. The highly romantic song was popularized by Glenn Miller, whose record hit the top of the charts, and Paul Whiteman (vocal by Joan Edwards), keeping it on the *Hit Parade* for twelve weeks. Other recordings of note were made by Horace Heidt, Al Donahue, Mildred Bailey, Chet Baker, Vaughn Monroe, Frank Sinatra, Nat King Cole, Della Reese, and Jerry Vale.

"The Moon of Manakoora" (1937) is a Hawaiian standard most associated with Dorothy Lamour, who introduced it in the movie *The Hurricane* (1937). Frank Loesser (lyric) and Alfred Newman (music) wrote the tropical ballad about parted lovers who believe that they will be reunited when the moon rises over the Polynesian isle of Manakoora. Lamour's recording was successful, as were those by Bing Crosby, Ray Noble (vocal by Tony Martin), Van Alexander, and Ruby Newman. Among the many other artists who recorded it were Loesser, Harry James, Sonny Rollins, Anita Ellis, Kim Kahuna and the Royal Palms Orchestra, Burl Ives, the Ventures, Chet Atkins, Lenny and the Thundertones, Jimmy Bryant, Andy Williams, and Vic Damone.

"Moon Over Miami" (1935) is a picturesque romantic ballad by Edgar Leslie (lyric) and Joe Burke (music) about two lovers strolling along the Florida beach, both in a dreamlike trance. Connee Boswell popularized the number on the radio, on records, and in clubs, and Eddy Duchin's disc went to the Number One spot on the charts. There were also early records by George Hall (vocal by Dolly Dawn), Jan Garber, Lud Gluskin, and Dean Hudson, who made it the theme song for his orchestra. Later discs were made by the George Shearing Quintet, Vaughn Monroe, Henry Hall, the Platters, Mezz Mezzrow, Billy Vaughn, Bill Haley and the Comets, Ray Charles, and Jackie Cain and Roy Kral. The song was heard over the credits of the movie musical *Moon Over Miami* (1941).

"The Moon Was Yellow (And the Night Was Young)" (1934) is a "canoe song" standard, a lazy but romantic kind of ballad that was perfect for paddling along with a sweetheart. Edgar Leslie wrote the fanciful lyric about being caught up in "the mystery of it all," and Fred E. Ahlert composed the minor key music that provided that mystery. Bing Crosby popularized the number in clubs and on records, and the Dorsey Brothers (vocal by Kay Weber) also had success with it. The ballad was also given expert recordings by Frank Sinatra, Frances Langford, Eddie Heywood, Les Brown, the Al Haig Trio, Vaughn Monroe, Charlie Byrd, Jimmy Forest, Buddy Cole, Mario Lanza, Bill Challis, and Robert Goulet.

"Moonglow" (1934) is an amorous ballad by Eddie DeLange, Will Hudson, and Irving Mills arguing that it must have been the moon's hypnotic glow that brought a special dearie into one's life. While there were many recordings in the 1930s and 1940s, the song found its greatest success in 1956 when it was briefly heard in the film *Picnic* (1955) and it provided bestselling records for the orchestras of Morris Stoloff, George Cates, and the Boston Pops. Among the many artists over the years to make successful discs were Benny Goodman, Artie Shaw, Glen Gray and the Casa Loma Orchestra, the King Sisters, Art Tatum, Cab Calloway, Ethel Waters, Louis Prima, Frances Langford, Kay Thompson, and Debbie Reynolds. The Benny Goodman Trio reprised it in the movie *The Benny Goodman Story* (1956), and the song was featured on the soundtrack for *Moonstruck* (1987). "Moonglow" has been rediscovered of late with recent recordings by Sam Taylor, Andrea Marcovicci, and Patti DiPardo.

"Moonlight and Roses (Bring Mem'ries of You)" (1925) is an old-fashioned waltz that Ben Black and Neil Moret adapted from Edwin Lemare's organ piece "Andantino in D Flat," and it had no trouble finding success on Tin Pan Alley, becoming a standard. The heartfelt ballad was popularized by Lanny Ross, who sang it on records and the radio, made it his theme song, and kept it in his repertoire for years. John McCormack also featured it throughout his career in concert and on disc. The Three Suns revived it successfully in 1954, and Vic Dana did the same in 1965. Willie Humphrey, Vaughn Monroe, Jim Reeves, Ken Griffin, the Bachelors, and Ivory Joe Hunter were among those who also recorded it. On the screen, it was sung by Betty Grable in *Tin Pan Alley*

(1940), Roy Rogers in *Song of Texas* (1943), and Gloria Jean in *Mister Big* (1943).

"Moonlight in Vermont" (1944), the song that launched Margaret Whiting's career, provides a descriptive picture of the various elements that surround two lovers walking in the moonlight, from the ski trails to the "snow light" to "pennies in a stream." It was written by John Blackburn (lyric) and Karl Suessdorf (music) for the film *Moonlight in Vermont* (1943) but was never used in the final print. Instead it was popularized by Billy Butterfield and his Orchestra (vocal by Whiting) in a record that sold a million copies. It was Whiting's first hit, and she sang it for years, rerecording it in 1954 with Lou Busch's Band. Other recordings of note were made by Billie Holiday, Frank Sinatra, Ella Fitzgerald, the Flamingos, Frankie Laine, Stan Kenton, Skitch Henderson, Joe Pass, and recently, Carol Sloane and George Mraz.

"Moonlight on the Ganges" (1926) is an exotic ballad by Chester Wallace (lyric) and Sherman Myers (music) that sought to capture the mysticism of the India river and appealed to audiences as many pseudo-Asian numbers did on Tin Pan Alley in the 1920s. Paul Whiteman and his Orchestra popularized the number, and there were successful recordings throughout the decade by Sam Lanin, Willard Robison, Jack Denny, the Revelers, Freddie Rich, and Franklyn Baur. Glenn Miller, Johnny Long, Tommy Dorsey, Charlie Spivak, and the Sauter-Finnegan Band made later discs of the ballad, and Vic Dana revived it in 1965, but the biggest-selling version remained one by Frank Sinatra.

"Moonlight Serenade" (1939) is the familiar fox trot standard that became Glenn Miller's theme song, perhaps the most renowned of all Big Band signature tunes. Miller was studying music and playing trombone for Ray Noble's Orchestra when he composed the slow and enchanting music. Miller asked Edward Heyman to write a lyric, but "Now I Lay Me Down to Sleep," as it was titled, struck Miller as too negative, and he discarded the number. When Miller formed his own band in 1940, he asked Mitchell Parish to provide a new lyric, and he came up with a mellow description of a lover standing at the gate in the moonlight and singing to his darling, waiting for the touch of her hand. Miller and the new band recorded the ballad, and it was a bestseller, forever after identified with the group. All the same, "Moonlight Serenade" was a favorite with many bands and singers in the 1940s, and significant records were made by Archie Bleyer, Frank Sinatra, Benny Goodman, Ted Heath, Joe Augustine, Gene Krupa, Jan Savitt, and later, the Ray Conniff Singers, Barry Manilow, and Andrea Marcovicci. The serenade was heard in the film *Crazy House* (1943), Ruth Hampton sang it in the bio *The Glenn Miller Story* (1954), and on Broadway the ensemble performed it in the Parish revue *Stardust* (1987).

"More Than You Know" (1929) is a languid yet stately ballad that seems to tumble forth effortlessly as it explains how one's love is greater than the object of affection can ever realize. Billy Rose and Edward Eliscu wrote the flowing lyric, and Vincent Youmans composed the dulcet music that gets a bit rhapsodic in the release but is always firmly in control. The number was written for the Broadway musical *Great Day* (1929), where it was sung by Mayo Methot, but the show was a flop and the song took a while to catch on. Mildred Bailey brought attention to it in the 1930s, Jane Froman made it a specialty of hers years later, and Perry Como revived it with his early hit record in 1946. Count Basie, Eddie Condon, Erroll Garner, Rosemary Clooney, Lionel Hampton, Blossom Seeley, Helen Morgan, Juanita Hall, Judy Garland, Mario Lanza, Dorothy Loudon, K.T. Sullivan, and Dinah Washington were among those who made memorable recordings as well. "More Than You Know" was interpolated into the movie *Hit the Deck* (1930), was sung by Tony Martin in the 1955 remake, was performed by Ann Blyth (dubbed by Gogi Grant) in *The Helen Morgan Story* (1957), and was sung by Barbra Streisand in *Funny Lady* (1975). Also, Kim Criswell sang it in the Off-Broadway play *Slow Drag* (1997).

"The Morningside of the Mountain" (1951) is a rural ballad by Dick Manning and Larry Stock that found success in two different eras. In the 1950s there were successful records made by Paul Weston and his Orchestra, Merv Griffin, Tommy Edwards, and Jan Garber and his Orchestra. The number was revived in 1974 by the singing duo Donny and Marie Osmond, and their disc made it to the Top 10. The song was picked up by other artists in the 1970s, including the Scandinavian group ABBA.

"M-o-t-h-e-r (A Word That Means the World to Me)" (1915) is an unabashed tribute to mom, spelling out her title and finding sterling qualities for each letter. Howard Johnson (lyric) and Theodore F. Morse (music) wrote the sentimental number, which Sophie Tucker sang in vaudeville with success. Henry Burr made an early recording that was a hit, and soon sheet music sales climbed. The song was associated with the child tenor Bobby Breen who recorded it in 1936 with his high-range birdlike warble that depression audiences adored. Sonny Stitt, Terry Waldo, and the Cliff Adams Singers were among the others who made disc versions. The ballad can be heard in the movies *Up the River* (1930),

Make Way for Tomorrow (1937), *Anchors Aweigh* (1945), *Mother Wore Tights* (1947), and *Young Man With Ideas* (1952).

"Mother Machree" (1910), one of the most popular of all Irish ballads to come out of Tin Pan Alley, is the paean to motherhood by Rida Johnson Young (lyric), Chauncey Olcott, and Ernest R. Ball (music) that became tenor John McCormack's theme song throughout his long career. The gushing lyric proclaims that no one owns the spark in one's heart or the depth in one's soul more than one's mother, and the song goes so far as to praise her wrinkles and the silver in her hair. Olcott introduced the ballad on Broadway in *Barry of Ballymore* (1910) and reprised it in *The Isle o' Dreams* (1913). Taking their cue from McCormack, Irish crooners throughout the century recorded it, including James Melton, Phil Regan, Richard Crooks, Christopher Lynch, Dennis Day, Pat Murphy, Dick Haymes, Louis Browne, and John McDermott. Blanche Thebom and the chorus sang "Mother Machree" in the movie *Irish Eyes Are Smiling* (1944), Day reprised it in *My Wild Irish Rose* (1947), and it was heard in several other period films, including *Rose of Washington Square* (1939), *Doughboys in Ireland* (1943), and *Trouble Along the Way* (1953).

"Mother Was a Lady" (1896) is one of the most potent of the many sentimental ballads that proliferated in the 1890s, this one selling over 2 million copies of sheet music. Joseph W. Stern composed the lilting waltz music that has a touch of the tango in it, and Edward B. Marks wrote the poignant lyric that still packs a melodramatic wallop. The two songwriters were in a German restaurant one day where they overheard some salesmen harassing and insulting a young waitress who finally broke down in tears and anger and proclaimed, "My mother was a lady!" and "You wouldn't dare insult me if my brother Jack were here!" A narrative ballad was constructed from the incident in which a waitress is subjected to similar abuse by two salesmen, she utters the title line, and then she collapses in tears. But it turns out that she is the sister of one of the drummer's best friends and has fallen into dire circumstances, so he begs forgiveness and even proposes marriage to the pathetic girl. Vaudeville favorite Lottie Gilson introduced the ballad at Proctor's Theatre in Manhattan and it was immediately in demand. The number can be heard in the movie *The Floradora Girl* (1930), and years later Jimmie ("the singing breakman") Rodgers made a teary version of the song on record. It is sometimes listed as "My Mother Was a Lady" and even "If Jack Were Only Here."

"Mountain Greenery" (1926) is a radiant tribute to rural living by Rodgers and Hart, that most urban of songwriting teams. Lorenz Hart's lyric urges one to flee from the dust of the city and go out into the countryside "where God paints the scenery." Richard Rodgers's music has a driving rhythm that builds by repeating the first three notes, then makes all sorts of dazzling harmonic shifts in the release. Their usual seamless collaboration is at its best here, Hart breaking up words and phrases in unexpected places and Rodgers letting the music tie it all together, especially in the celebrated section that states that beans could not get "no keener re . . . ception in a beanery." The number was written for the second edition of *Garrick Gaieties* (1926), where it was sung by Sterling Holloway and Bobbie Perkins. The revue is long forgotten, but the song has remained a standard ever since. Of the dozens of recordings over the years, Mel Tormé's disk in the 1950s was the most successful. Other prominent records were made by Frank Crumit, Roger Wolfe Kahn, Red Norvo, Eileen Farrell, Sylvia Syms, Patti Page, the Village Stompers, Tony Bennett, Peter Nero, Billy Stritch, Ella Fitzgerald, Barbara Lea, Morgana King, Barbara Carroll, and Dawn Upshaw. Perry Como and Allyn McLerie sang the happy number on screen in the Rodgers and Hart bio *Words and Music* (1948).

"Mrs. Worthington (Don't Put Your Daughter on the Stage)" (1935) is a comic novelty song by Noel Coward that was widely known even though few performed or recorded it beside the British songwriter himself. The farcical number pleads with a stage mother to not let her untalented offspring go into the theater, stating the case calmly and politely at first (her personality is not "inviting enough") but getting more furious by the end (the "vile" girl is "uglier than mortal sin!"). Coward performed it on radio, records, television, and concerts for decades, his genteel demeanor a perfect contrast to the risible song. Vic Reeves and Richard Conrad are among the few who also recorded the ditty, and it was sung by Harry Groener (as Coward) in the Off-Broadway musical *If Love Were All* (1999).

"Mule Train" (1949) is a catchy western travel song most associated with Frankie Laine who kept it in his repertoire for years and, it is estimated, performed it over 4,000 times. Johnny Lange, Hy Heath, and Fred Glickman wrote the fast-paced rhythm number that urges the mules to "get along!" as the supply train pushes over the prairie with a "clippity clop" that never stops. Bill Butler introduced the song, but Laine's recording popularized it, selling a million and a half copies. The number was interpolated into the film *Singing Guns* (1950), where Vaughn Monroe sang it, and it was nominated for an Oscar (even though it was not written for the movie). Monroe recorded "Mule Train" with success, as did Tennessee Ernie Ford, Bing Crosby, and Gordon MacRae. Other noteworthy discs were made by Gene Autry, the Osborne Brothers, Duane Eddy, Boxcar Willie, Burl Ives, Ronnie Dawson, and Lorne Greene and a parody version by Spike Jones and his City Slickers. Autry reprised it in the movie *Mule Train* (1950), and it can be heard on the soundtrack of *How the West Was Won* (1962) and other westerns.

"The Music Goes Round and Around" (1935), arguably the most successful nonsense song in the history of Tin Pan Alley, describes the path that sound takes as it goes through a French horn. Ed Farley and Mike Riley wrote the vivacious jazz music, and Red Hodgson penned the zesty lyric, which sometimes imitates the horn itself ("Whoa-ho-ho"). Riley and Farley's band introduced the ditty in a New York City nightclub, and it caught on like wildfire; sheet music sales were so vigorous that four printing companies were needed to keep up with the demand. In one month alone, over 2 million copies of sheet music were sold. Tommy Dorsey's Clambake Seven (vocal by Edythe Wright) had an early hit record, as did Hal Kemp (vocal by Saxie Dowell), and in 1943 Riley and Farley's disc became the first bestseller for the new Decca Record Company. Other successful versions of the song were recorded by Louis Armstrong, the Mound City Blue Blowers, Guy Lombardo, the Boswell Sisters, Wingy Manone, Mel Tormé, Ella Fitzgerald, Louis Prima and Keely Smith, and Red Norvo. Riley and Farley reprised it in the movie *The Music Goes Round* (1936), the Ritz Brothers performed it in *Sing, Baby, Sing* (1936), and Danny Kaye sang a duet version with Susan Gordon in *The Five Pennies* (1959). The number can also be heard in *Trocadero* (1944) and *Holiday in Mexico* (1946), and it was performed by Bernard J. Marsh and the ensemble in the Broadway musical *Big Deal* (1986).

"Music, Maestro, Please!" (1938) is a swing torch song by Herb Magidson (lyric) and Allie Wrubel (music) in which an abandoned lover asks the orchestra to play a swing tune and not a waltz because the slower romantic music makes him think of her. Frank and Frances Langford introduced the forceful number, but it was a hit record by Tommy Dorsey (vocal by Edythe Wright) that climbed to the top of the charts and kept the song on *Your Hit Parade* for twelve weeks. It was also one of the top sellers of sheet music that year. Of the many recordings that followed were notable ones by Art Kassell, Kay Kyser, the Benny Goodman Quintet, Art Tatum, Frankie Laine, Sammy Kaye (vocal by Tony Alamo), the Mills Brothers, the Flamingos, Tony Martin, the Starlings, Ella Mae Morse, and more recently, Harry Connick Jr.

"Music! Music! Music! (Put Another Nickel In)" (1950) is a vibrant dance song that celebrates the juke box as much as the sweetheart one wants to dance with. Stephen Weiss and Bernie Baum wrote the uptempo number asking one to feed a coin to the "nickelodeon" so that there will be music for dancing and loving one's honey. Teresa Brewer's recording sold over a million copies, and the number has always been associated with her. But there were also hit records by the Ames Brothers and Freddy Martin and his Orchestra. Of the many discs that followed were ones by Guy Lombardo, the Ahmad Jamal Trio, and Jack Mudurian. The swinging number, sometimes listed as "Put Another Nickel In," was sung by the cast of the Off-Broadway revue *The Taffetas* (1988).

"My Blue Heaven" (1924), one of the most popular songs of the decade and one of the top sellers in Tin Pan Alley history, has charmed the public for years with its warm and cozy picture of domestic bliss. Walter Donaldson composed the felicitous music, and George Whiting wrote the matter-of-fact lyric about a happy husband hurrying home to his wife Molly and their baby, his idea of heaven. Whiting introduced the song himself in vaudeville, but it garnered little attention and nothing much happened to it until Tommy Lyman sang it on the radio and made it his theme song. About the same time the ballad was interpolated into the *Ziegfeld Follies* (1927), where Eddie Cantor sang it with success. Sheet music sales soared, but even more profitable was a 1928 record by Gene Austin, which hit the top of the charts. Austin rerecorded the number on several occasions, selling over 13 million discs in all. (This was an all-time high until Bing Crosby's recording of "White Christmas" came along fourteen years later.) "My Blue Heaven" was revived with success by Jimmie Lunceford in 1939 and by Fats Domino in 1956. At first female singers didn't record the song because the lyric phrase "Molly and me" was difficult to convert; but Mabel Mercer started singing the lyric as written in clubs, and soon other women did the same. Of the hundreds of discs made over the years were memorable ones by Fred Waring's Pennsylvanians, Bob Grant, Bing Crosby, Eddie Condon, Doris Day, Artie Shaw, Jack Smith, Frank Sinatra, Benny Carter, Paul Weston, Benny Goodman, Marlene Dietrich, Maxine Sullivan, Glenn Miller, Coleman Hawkins, Jimmie Davis, Lena Horne, Perry Como, Gracie Fields, Nat King Cole, Pete Fountain, Jerry Lee Lewis, Oscar Peterson, and Rick Nelson. Frances Langford sang it in the movie *Never a Dull Moment* (1943), Betty Grable and Dan Dailey performed it in *My Blue Heaven* (1950), Day reprised it in *Love Me or Leave Me* (1955), Bob Crosby played it in *The Five Pennies* (1959), Peter O'Toole and Carolyn Seymour did a duet of it in *The Ruling Class* (1972), and the Fats Domino recording was heard in *Let the Good Times Roll* (1973). The song can often be heard in the background in films to give a homely atmosphere, as in *Moon Over Las Vegas* (1944), or for satiric effect, as in *M*A*S*H* (1970). On Broadway, it was sung by the cast of the revue *Sing Out, Sweet Land!* (1944).

"My Buddy" (1922) is one of the most sentimental and also beloved songs about friendship, so well known that it is more of a cliché today than a serious ballad. Walter Donaldson composed the catchy music that effectively moves back and forth between two notes. Although it is written in the traditional 3/4 time and thirty-two-bar structure, the song is really two nearly identical songs back to back, the only variation coming in the closing bars. Gus Kahn wrote the affecting lyric in which an old companion has gone away and is sorely missed. Some female singers have performed the number so that it suggests a romantic relationship, but the strength of the lyric lies in its sincere regard for deep friendship. The ballad first gained attention in vaudeville where Al Jolson and others popularized it. Movie theater pianists played it during showings of the silent film classic *Wings* (1927), particularly for scenes depicting the camaraderie between World War One pilots Charles "Buddy" Rogers and Richard Arlen; Rogers later adopted it as his theme song when he started a band. Sammy Kaye and his Orchestra revived the song in 1946 with a hit recording, and it became popular again when Doris Day sang it in the Kahn film bio *I'll See You in My Dreams* (1952). It can also be heard in *In Old Monterey* (1939) and *My Buddy* (1944), where it was sung by Donald Barry. Over the years there have been noteworthy records by Ben Bernie, Kate Smith, Stan Getz, Harry James, Count Basie, Bob Grant, Benny Carter, Chet Baker, Bing Crosby, Coleman Hawkins, Mario Lanza, Bobby Darin, and Nancy Sinatra.

"My Devotion" (1942) is an emotive ballad by Roc Hillman and Johnny Napton in which a lover ardently proclaims the depth and durability of his devotion to his darling. Vaughn Monroe conducted his band and did the vocals on a bestselling record that was his first hit. Also popular were discs by Charlie Spivak (vocal by Garry Stevens), the King Sisters with Alvino Rey, and Jimmy Dorsey (vocal by Bob Eberly). Other significant records were made by Glenn Miller, Keely Smith, Bud Powell, Perry Como, Dinah Washington, Gloria Lynne, and Matt Monro. The King Sisters reprised the number with Rey in the movie *Follow the Band* (1943).

"My Foolish Heart" (1949), one of Billy Eckstine's biggest hits, is a cautionary ballad by Ned Washington (lyric) and Victor Young (music) that warns one's heart about being taken in by the moon and a melodic night, noting that it is very difficult to tell the difference between "love and fascination." The song was written for the film *My Foolish Heart* (1949), where it was sung by Susan Hayward and was nominated for an Oscar. But it was a record by Gordon Jenkins (vocal by Eileen Wilson) that popularized the number. Eckstine's 1950 disc was even more successful, selling over a million copies and pushing the song to the top spot on the *Hit Parade*. Other recordings were made by Margaret Whiting, Mindy Carson, Carmen McRae, Sonny Stitt, Ray Anthony, Harry Allen, the

Bachelors, Elaine Delmar, Gene Ammons, Bill Evans, Vic Damone, Chet Baker, Engelbert Humperdinck, Lucie Arnaz, and Ann Hampton Callaway.

"My Future Just Passed" (1930) explores different meanings of its seemingly meaningless title phrase. George Marion Jr. wrote the witty lyric that plays with words, finding different aspects of "future" and "present" and concludes that once one falls into true love, there is no hope for future lovers. Richard A. Whiting composed the "neatly written, graceful melody with an infectious bounce," as James R. Morris describes it. Charles "Buddy" Rogers introduced the song in the movie *Safety in Numbers* (1930) and recorded it as well. Other notable discs were made by Kay Starr, Teddi King, Chet Baker, Red Nichols, Carmen McRae, Joyce Carr, the Boswell Sisters, Les Paul, and Margaret Whiting.

"My Gal Is a High Born Lady" (1896) is a ragtime classic by Barney Fagan and a popular "coon song" at the turn of the century. Fagan was riding his bicycle one day, and the pattern of the clicking of the wheels gave him an idea for a syncopated rhythm. He then wrote the Negro dialect lyric praising a "dark Venus" who is "none too shady" and has lots of class. Fagan sold the honky-tonk number to a publisher for $100 and never profited any more from the substantial sheet music sales that followed. The song was introduced by Charles Haverly with his Haverly Minstrels but was popularized by Clara Wieland in clubs. Rarely performed or recorded as a vocal since World War One, the infectious ragtime music is still heard on occasion.

"My Gal Sal" (1905), Paul Dresser's last song, is a moderate waltz ballad that laments the loss of "my old pal" Sally who left twenty years ago. The lyric points out that she was unfaithful and far from serious in her affections, but she was "always willing to share." Dresser was ill and living in poverty when he wrote the solemn number and sent it to a publisher. But he died soon after and never lived to see it become one of his most popular works, selling several million copies of sheet music. Byron G. Harlan introduced the ballad, but it was Louise Dresser (a performer who took Dresser's name after he discovered her) who made it a hit in vaudeville. "My Gal Sal" also became a favorite of barbershop quartets and other harmonizing groups. The Buffalo Bills, Bob Willis and his Texas Playboys, Jelly Roll Morton, Burl Ives, the Pied Pipers, Tiny Hill, the Mills Brothers, Miff Mole, Spiegle Willcox, and Lawrence Welk are among those who recorded it. Sometimes listed as "They Called Her Frivolous Sal," the number was sung by Bobby Gordon in the legendary film *The Jazz Singer* (1927) and by Rita Hayworth (dubbed by Nan Wynn) in the Dresser bio *My Gal Sal* (1942).

"My Happiness" (1933) is a romantic ballad that sat around for fifteen years before it caught on, then it went and sold millions of records. Borney Bergantine composed the slow and dreamy music, and Betty Peterson penned the expansive lyric about a wooer who misses his beloved so much that all he can think of is their reunion when "there'll be no blue memories." The songwriters could not get any major or minor talents to record the song until 1948 when Jon and Sandra Steele made a disc that sold a million copies. Soon after the Pied Pipers with Paul Weston's Orchestra recorded it, and that version also was a million seller. A record by Ella Fitzgerald with the Song Spinners was a hit, the number was revived in 1953 by the harmonica group called the Mulcays, and in 1958 Connie Francis had a record reached the Top 10. Fats Domino, Hank Snow, Billy Vaughn, Frank Ifield, Frank Sinatra, Jim Reeves, Pat Boone, Andy Williams, and Max Bygraves are among the many who also made recordings.

"My Heart Tells Me" (1943) is an inquiring ballad by Mack Gordon (lyric) and Harry Warren (music) that warns against a romance, the heart arguing that sorrow and tears will result, but still one asks oneself, "Should I believe my heart or you?" Betty Grable and Phil Regan introduced the wry love song in the movie *Sweet Rosie O'Grady* (1943), then it was recorded by Glen Gray and the Casa Loma Orchestra (vocal by Eugenie Baird), selling over a million discs and keeping the song on *Your Hit Parade* for nineteen weeks. Well-known records were also made by Etta Jones, Glenn Miller, Johnny Otis, Charlie Parker, Harry James, Dick Haymes, Nat King Cole, Tony Bennett, and more recently, George Evans.

"My Honey's Lovin' Arms" (1922) is a jazz classic with an atypical subject for the genre: married happiness. Joseph Meyer composed the free-wheeling music, and Herman Ruby wrote the lyric praising domestic bliss and the happiness to be found in a spouse's arms. Leading records were made by Isham Jones, Red Nichols, the Original Memphis Five, and Duke Ellington; then Benny Goodman revived it with success in 1939. Barbra Streisand's 1963 recording renewed interest in the scintillating number. Among the other artists who recorded it were Wingy Manone, Bud Freeman, Joe Venuti and Zoot Sims, Barbara Lea, Tiny Tim, and Muggsy Spanier.

"My Ideal" (1930), Richard A. Whiting's favorite of his many songs and the one that helped launch the career of his daughter Margaret, has been successful as both a swing number and a slow ballad. Leo Robin wrote the knowing lyric that imagines an ideal mate but also questions if such a perfect person will ever come along. Newell Chase collaborated with Whiting on the music, a short (sixteen measures) but enticing piece that is both economical and expansive. (Whiting commented that he would never be able to top it.) Maurice Chevalier introduced the song in the film *Playboy of Paris* (1930) and then on record, his disc and one by Isham Jones becoming hits. In 1943 Margaret Whiting chose it for her first solo record, and it made her famous. Other discs of note were made by Jimmy Dorsey, Maxine Sullivan, Helen Forrest, Count Basie, Art Tatum, Jeri Southern, Coleman Hawkins, Lee Wiley, Art Blakey, Chet Baker, J.D. Walker, Gene Krupa, Eartha Kitt, Sonny Rollins, and more recently, Jimmy Roselli and Susannah McCorkle. Charles "Buddy" Rogers sang "My Ideal" in the movie *Along Came Youth* (1931), and it was heard in *You Came Along* (1945).

"My Isle of Golden Dreams" (1919) is a Hawaiian standard by Gus Kahn (lyric) and Walter Blaufuss (music) about an exotic tropical island, one of the earliest examples of the genre. Ben Selvin and his Orchestra made an early recording, and all of America was familiar with it in the 1930s and 1940s as the theme song for Phil Spitalny and his All-Girl Orchestra on the popular radio show *Hour of Charms*. Bing Crosby had a hit disc in 1939, and Glenn Miller had success with it in the 1940s. Other recordings were made by Vaughn Monroe, the Browns, Martin Denny, Hank Snow, Les Paul, the Stripling Brothers, Burl Ives, Kim Kahuna and the Royal Palms Orchestra, the Moms and Dads, and Marty Robbins. The number can be heard in *Lake Placid Serenade* (1944) and in the background of other films.

"My Last Affair" (1934) is a song of resolve by Haven Johnson that declares that this is true love and there will be no others in the future. Billie Haywood introduced the number in the Broadway revue *New Faces of 1934*, but little happened to the song until a popular record in 1936 by Jimmie Lunceford (vocal by Dan Grissom). The next year there were successful discs by Mildred Bailey, Teddy Wilson (vocal by Billie Holiday), Ella Fitzgerald with Count Basie, and Lionel Hampton. Sometimes listed as "This Is My Last Affair," it was also recorded by Art Tatum, Billy May, Charles Brown, Red Allen, Joe Williams, Gerald Wilson, and Herbie Steward.

"My Mammy" (1918), forever associated with Al Jolson, was so popular and distinctive that the term "mammy song" was used to describe any number about motherhood in this broad, expansive style, and the expression "mammy singer" referred to the many crooners who imitated Jolson's forceful delivery. Joe Young, Sam Lewis (lyric), and Walter Donaldson (music) wrote the heart-throbbing paean to one's mother in 1918, but not with Jolson in mind. In fact, the song was not picked up by any singer until William Frawley introduced it in vaudeville in 1920. Jolson heard the ballad and liked it enough to interpolate it into his Broadway vehicle *Bombo* (1921), where he sang it in blackface as he went down on one knee and seemed to caress the audience with his outstretched arms. In addition to singing it in his act throughout his career, Jolson recorded it twice (selling well over a million copies) and sang in six movies: *The Jazz Singer* (1927), *Mammy* (1930), *The Singing Kid* (1936), *Rose of Washington Square* (1939), and on the soundtracks for Larry Parks in *The Jolson Story* (1946) and *Jolson Sings Again* (1949). Paul Whiteman and his Orchestra had a successful recording in the 1920s, and the number was revived by Jackie Wilson in 1962 and by the Happenings in 1967. Other artists who have recorded "My Mammy" include the Boswell Sisters, Eddie Cantor, Bing Crosby, Jerry Lewis, and more recently, Kenny Rogers, Liza Minnelli, Cher, Mandy Patinkin, and Jimmy Roselli.

"My Man (Mon Homme)" (1920) was a popular French torch song that was translated into one of Tin Pan Alley's greatest ballads, most often associated with Fanny Brice but a favorite of all the top female performers. "Mon Homme" was written by Albert Willemetz, Jacques Charles (lyric), and Maurice Yvain (music) and introduced by Mistinguett in the revue *Paris Qui Jazz* in 1920. Irene Bordoni brought the number to the States, singing it in the original French, but it didn't catch on until Brice performed it in the *Ziegfeld Follies* (1921) with an English lyric by Channing Pollock. Essentially a comic performer, Brice surprised everyone by her plaintive and aching delivery. While the song is musically rangy and builds to a passionate climax, Brice's interpretation was more matter-of-fact and very touching as she declared her love for a man who may treat her badly but is hers all the same. Brice recorded the number three times and sang it in the films *My Man* (1928) and *The Great Ziegfeld* (1936). Among the many other singers who had success with it, the most memorable were Billie Holiday with Teddy Wilson's Band in 1938, Peggy Lee in 1959, and Barbra Streisand in 1965. The ballad was sung by Alice Faye as a Brice-like performer in the movie *Rose of Washington Square* (1939), Streisand as Brice in the bio *Funny Girl* (1968), and Diana Ross as Holiday in the bio *Lady Sings the Blues* (1972). Other notable records were made by Dinah Shore, Etta Jones, Louis Armstrong, Lionel Hampton, Eartha Kitt, Abbey Lincoln, Erroll Garner, Helen Forrest, Xavier Cugat, Pearl Bailey, Ella Fitzgerald, Shirley Horn, Gogi Grant, and Shirley Bassey.

"My Melancholy Baby" (1912), one of Tin Pan Alley's most beloved and durable ballads, did not take the familiar slow and soothing form that we know today until it had been around for several years. Ernie Burnett composed the innovative music that rises and descends in a smooth symmetrical manner, often moving in unexpected directions and creating an effect that was far ahead of its time. In fact, the music sounds more like an easy jazz piece from the late 1930s than from the ragtime era, and it has been called the first modern torch song. George A. Norton is credited with writing the simple and straightforward lyric that comforts a loved one, asking that he not be melancholy and offering to "kiss away each tear." Some of the lyric phrases have become clichés, yet the words sit on the music with such ease that the number is still very potent. Questions have often been raised about the authorship, several songwriters claiming credit for writing it, but the matter has never been satisfactorily resolved. Walter Van Brunt introduced the song in vaudeville as an up-tempo number, and Paul Whiteman and his Orchestra further popularized it, playing it in a lively and slightly swinging manner. It was singer Tommy Lyman who was the first to perform the ballad in a slow and heartfelt manner, and that soon became the accepted version. Of the hundreds who have recorded the song over the years, memorable discs were made by Gene Austin, Teddy Wilson, Helen Morgan, Bing Crosby, Tommy Edwards, the Pied Pipers, Dinah Shore, Frank Sinatra, Woody Herman, Sonny Rollins, Connee Boswell, Charlie Parker, Dizzy Gillespie, Vic Damone, Bobby Dukoff, Ray Charles, Barbra Streisand, and Karen Akers. On screen, it was sung by Crosby in *Birth of the Blues* (1941), Frances Langford in *Follow the Band* (1943), Benny Fields in *Minstrel Man* (1944), Dick Haymes in *Diamond Horseshoe* (1945), Judy Garland in the "Born in a Trunk" sequence in *A Star Is Born* (1954), and Ann Blyth (dubbed by Gogi Grant) in *The Helen Morgan Story* (1957). The tender number can be heard on the soundtrack in several other movies, including *East Side of Heaven* (1939), *Swing It Soldier* (1941), and *Scarlet Street* (1945). Somewhere during its long history, "Melancholy Baby" (as it is often called) became the number drunks always requested in nightclubs. How this started is hard to determine, though it might have come from the fact that the somber ballad was so often requested in the 1930s and 1940s that it became the cliché choice for such a situation.

"My Old Kentucky Home" (1853), the official state song of Kentucky since 1928, is one of Stephen Foster's most beloved ballads, an idyllic picture of life in the South and a testament to the warmth and security of home. Foster was visiting his cousin's house, the Rowan mansion in Bardstown, Kentucky, when he awoke one morning early (so the tale goes) and looked out onto the fields where mockingbirds were singing and pickaninnies were playing. (The Rowan house was designated a state memorial in 1922 as a tribute to Foster and the song.) Ed Christy introduced the ballad in his famous minstrel show, and sheet music sales soared, selling over 160,000 copies (but Foster saw little of the profits). Although parts of the lyric are not politically correct today (references like "the darkies are gay" are a bit difficult to take), the gentle and gliding music has always been appreciated. Among the more eminent record versions of the song are those by Paul Robeson, the Sons of the Pioneers, Gene Krupa, Morton Gould, Marian Anderson, the Norman Luboff Choir, Lawrence Welk, the Osborne Brothers, Three Dog Night, and Randy Newman. It can be heard in the three Foster film bios, *Harmony Lane* (1935), *Swanee River* (1939), and *I Dream of Jeanie* (1952), and it was given a satiric treatment by the Marx Brothers in *Animal Crackers* (1930). In the Off-Broadway musical *Oil City Symphony* (1988), Mark Hardwick and the cast sang a rowdy version called "My Ol' Kentucky Rock and Roll Home."

"My Prayer" (1939) is a fervent ballad that enjoyed two peaks of popularity, staying on *Your Hit Parade* for fourteen weeks in 1939 and returning in 1956 and staying eleven weeks. British songwriter Jimmy Kennedy adapted Georges Boulanger's violin piece "Avant de Mourir" into ballad form and wrote an ardent lyric asking a loved one to answer one's prayer by staying close by forever. Vera Lynn introduced the song in England, and Sammy Kaye and his Orchestra popularized it in America, making it a favorite dance number through the war years. Glenn Miller (vocal by Ray Eberly) and the Ink Spots each had hit records of it during this time. In 1956 it was revived by the Platters, whose disc hit the top of the charts and sold a million copies, and the song enjoyed new popularity. Major records were also made by Ace Cannon, Ella Fitzgerald, Sonny Til and the Orioles, Roy Hamilton, Ernie Fields, Bert Kaempfert, Jack Hylton, Ruth Brown, the Ray Conniff Singers, Chet Atkins, the Impressions, Bobby Vee, Gene Pitney, and Vikki Carr.

"My Reverie" (1938) is another Tin Pan Alley hit to come from a classical piece of music, in this case Claude Debussy's *Reverie*. Bandleader Larry Clinton adapted the music and wrote the dreamy lyric about being caught up in the mysterious mood of romance. His band introduced the song on record with a vocal by Bea Wain, and the disc was a bestseller (the first for the young bandleader). Its success led to records by Bing Crosby, Mildred Bailey, Nelson Eddy, Helen Forrest, Ray Anthony, Ella Fitzgerald, Dizzy Gillespie, Betty Carter, Della Reese, Quincy Jones, and Caterina Valente. Clinton and his publishers were under the mistaken notion that Debussy's work was in the public domain, so when the late composer's estate sued, the publishers had to settle the claim to the tune of $60,000, more money than Debussy made in his entire career.

"My Silent Love" (1932) is a jazz standard that began as an instrumental piece called "Jazz Nocturne" by Dana Seusse. Edward Heyman added a lyric about the unspoken passion one holds for an idol, and it was popularized by Ruby Newman and his Orchestra. Ishman Jones, Roger Wolfe Kahn, and the Washboard Rhythm Band each had success with it in the 1930s, and it was revived by Eydie Gorme and Julie London with records in the 1950s. Of all the discs made over the years, none was more popular than one by Frank Sinatra. Among the other artists to record the ballad were Carmen Cavallaro, Anita Boyer, Dick Jurgens (vocal by Harry Cool), Fran Warren, Luis Russell, Billy May, Paul Weston, George Shearing, Helen Stewart, Teddy Powell, Peggy Lee, Billy Eckstine, and Carol Sloane. The number can be heard in the film *Sabrina* (1954).

"My Sin" (1929) is a confessional ballad about being guilty of falling in love that B.G. DeSylva, Lew Brown (lyric), and Ray Henderson (music) wrote as an individual number but was interpolated into the film *Show Girl in Hollywood* (1930) before it was published. The song was most associated with Fred Waring's Pennsylvanians, who performed it on the radio, in concerts, and on records. In 1947 Julia Lee revived it as a jazz piece, in 1954 it was a hit for Georgia Gibbs, and soon after Patti Page made a recording that was a bestseller. Belle Baker, Franklyn Baur, Jesse Crawford, and Peggy Lee were among those who also made discs of it.

"My Sweet Adair" (1915) is a barbershop quartet favorite that is not dissimilar to the earlier "Sweet Adeline" (1903) in temperament and subject. Anatol Friedland composed the facile music that lends itself readily to harmonizing, and L. Wolfe Gilbert wrote the sentimental lyric praising the qualities of the adored Adair, the words playing off variations of her name ("I dare . . . declare . . ."). Unlike the earlier tune, "Sweet Adair" is not widely recognized anymore.

"My Time Is Your Time" (1925), the theme song for crooner Rudy Vallee, originated in Great Britain, where it was written for the music hall. Eric Little (a.k.a. R.S. Hooper) penned the lyric offering all of one's daylight and nighttime hours to a true love, and Leo Dance (a.k.a H.M. Tennant) composed the smooth music that is comprised almost entirely of whole notes and half notes, yet it moves along nicely. Young Vallee heard the song in London and shrewdly bought up the American rights, planning to use it later in his career. He first sang the ballad in a dining hall at Yale University when he was still a student. Vallee later sang it on his first radio broadcast in 1929 and kept it in his repertoire for decades, recording it a few times, using it as the title of his autobiography, and singing it on the soundtrack of the movies *Margie* (1946) and *The Helen Morgan Story* (1957). The number can also be heard in *Change of Heart* (1934) and *Danger on the Air* (1938). Because it was so firmly associated with Vallee, few others performed it, but the Hi-Lo's later made a distinctive recording of it.

"My Wild Irish Rose" (1899) was one of the earliest Irish-American ballads to become a Tin Pan Alley hit, and it remains one of the most recognized of all Hibernian numbers. Chauncey Olcott wrote the gliding music and the sprightly lyric about an Irish lass who once gave a lad a rose, then left him. Now he dreams of both the girl and the rose, hoping someday that "she may let me take the bloom from my wild Irish rose." Olcott introduced it himself in the Broadway musical *A Romance of Athlone* (1899), but it attracted little attention until it was picked up by tenor favorite John McCormack in concert and later records. When Olcott interpolated the song into *The Isle o' Dreams* (1913) and sang it again, it brought down the house. Over the years the ballad has been heard in sing-alongs, holiday celebrations, parades, radio broadcasts, films, and just about every media available. In addition to nearly every Irish band and singing group, it also received notable recordings by Al Jolson, Chick Webb, Mario Lanza, Dennis Day, the Ink Spots, Connie Francis, John Gary, and even a ragtime version by Rod Mill. The song was featured in several Irish-flavored movies, most memorably in *Doughboys in Ireland* (1943), and Dennis Day sang it in the Olcott bio *My Wild Irish Rose* (1947).

N

"Nagasaki" (1928), a spirited number that celebrates the goings-on in the bustling Japanese port city, was very popular before World War Two but was infrequently heard after the bombing of Nagasaki at the end of the war. Harry Warren composed the bright, honky-tonk music, and Mort Dixon wrote the playful, suggestive lyric about a place where the men chew "tobaccy" and the women "wicky-wacky-woo." Paul Mares and his Friars' Society Orchestra introduced the number on record, but it began to catch on when Bill Robinson performed it at the Cotton Club in Harlem, and the Ipana Troubadours had a successful disc version. The odd song was also a hit for the Mills Brothers, Gene Krupa, and Django Reinhardt. Among the other artists to record it were Glen Gray and the Casa Loma Orchestra, Benny Goodman, Fletcher Henderson, Fats Waller, the Manhattan Rhythm Kings, Basil Fromeen, Don Redman, Jesse Price and his Blues Band, and Cab Calloway. Doris Day sang "Nagasaki" in the movie *My Dream Is Yours* (1949), and Dick Hyman and the Three Deuces performed it on the soundtrack of *Bullets Over Broadway* (1994).

"Nature Boy" (1948) is an offbeat but intriguing ballad by Eden Ahbez about a wandering lad who is quiet, shy, and "sad of eye" but nevertheless is full of wisdom about the nature of love. Ahbez, a follower of Eastern religions, wrote the exotic number and left a copy of it at the stage door where Nat King Cole was performing. Cole was taken with the haunting quality of the song and recorded it, the disc going to the top of the charts, selling over a million copies and putting the ballad on the *Hit Parade* for eighteen weeks. Over the years "Nature Boy" has been interpreted in various ways, from jazz to pop to Latin, as seen in records by Frank Sinatra, Sarah Vaughan, George Benson, the John Coltrane Quartet, Zoot Sims, Stan Getz, Bill Evans, Art Pepper, Bobby Darin, Shirley Bassey, Don McLean, Natalie Cole, José Feliciano, and a parody version by Red Ingle. It can be heard in the films *Boy With Green Hair* (1948) and *Moulin Rouge* (2001).

"The Naughty Lady of Shady Lane" (1954) is a bouncy Latin number by Sid Pepper and Roy C. Bennett about a quiet town turned upside down by the arrival of a gal with lots of admirers. The Ames Brothers popularized the song with a 1955 disc with Hugo Winterhalter's Orchestra that sold over a million copies. Dean Martin, the Beverley Sisters, Archie Bleyer, and Ray Charles are among those who also recorded the lively, suggestive number.

"Navajo" (1903), the first successful Tin Pan Alley song about Native Americans, started a vogue for Indian songs early in the century, usually portraying the native peoples and their lifestyle in a romanticized manner. Henry H. Williams wrote the atmospheric lyric about Navajo life, and Egbert Van Alstyne composed the gently rhythmic music, his first of many hit songs over a long career. Marie Cahill interpolated "Navajo" into her Broadway show *Nancy Brown* (1903) after its opening and sang it to acclaim. Noteworthy discs of the ballad have been made by Billy Murray, J. W. Myers, Harry MacDonough, Julia Begaye, Joe Maphis, Bob Mintzer, Alistair Galbraith, and the New Christy Minstrels.

"Near You" (1947) is a slightly swinging ballad that declares the only place for a loved one is close by. Francis Craig composed the uptempo music, and Kermit Goell wrote the adoring lyric that asked a dearie to "never stray more than two lips away." Craig and his Orchestra introduced the song on record with Craig at the piano, and it reached the top of the charts. The Andrews Sisters, Larry Green and his Orchestra, and Alvino Rey and his Orchestra all had hit records as well, and Roger Williams revived it in 1958 with a successful disc. For many Americans "Near You" became familiar because Milton Berle used it as his theme song on his very popular television show sponsored by Texaco. Among the artists who also recorded it over the years were Billy Connolly, Marlene Dietrich, Wayne King, Boz Scaggs, Nat King Cole, B. Bumble and the Stingers, Liberace, Dwight Yoakam, Andy Williams, and Tammy Wynette.

"The Nearness of You" (1938) is an intoxicating ballad by Ned Washington (lyric) and Hoagy Carmichael (music) about losing one's reason and resistance when one's paramour is close by. James R. Morris points out that "the melody's architecture is flawless . . . its opening phrase traverses a downward path for six measures, then arches gracefully upward for two measures in a gesture that neatly rounds off the idea." The songwriters wrote it for one film only to see it cut and put in another, *Romance in the Dark* (1938), where it was sung by Gladys Swarthout. But the song didn't find fame until Glenn Miller and his Orchestra recorded it with success in 1940, and there were also hit discs by Bob Manning and Connee Boswell. Of the many memorable recordings made over the years were those by Dinah Shore, Larry Clinton, Guy Lombardo, Eddy Howard, Sarah Vaughan, the Dorsey Brothers, Charlie Parker, Ray Herbeck, Patti Page, Vic Damone, Mitzi Gaynor, John Gary, Pat Boone, Eartha Kitt, Chad and Jeremy, Tom Jones, and Shirley Bassey. Stella Stevens sang it in the movie *Girls! Girls! Girls!* (1962), it was heard in *Ash Wednesday* (1973), and it was sung on the soundtrack of *Indecent Proposal* (1993) by Bryan Ferry and in *The Impostors* (1998) by Steve Buscemi.

"Nevertheless (I'm in Love With You)" (1931) is a ballad of indecision that has resurfaced several times to become popular all over again. Harry Ruby wrote the gently swinging fox trot music, and Bert Kalmar penned the fatalistic lyric, the wooer vacillating over whether he is right or wrong to love such a person but always concluding with the title phrase and admitting, "I put my own head in the noose." Jack Denny and his Orchestra popularized the song, but it gained wider recognition when both Rudy Vallee and Bing Crosby featured it in their radio shows and each recorded it. The Mills Brothers revived "Nevertheless" with success in 1949, and the next year it became a hit again when Fred Astaire, Red Skelton, and Vera-Ellen (dubbed by Anita Ellis) performed it in the Kalmar-Ruby movie bio *Three Little Words* (1950). Popular records by Frank Sinatra and Paul Weston's Orchestra followed soon after. Among the many other discs made over the years were those by Astaire, Leo Reisman, Ray Anthony, Frankie Laine, Guy Lombardo, Ralph Flanagan (vocal by Harry Prime), Dick Haymes, Kay Starr, Joe Williams, and more recently, Liza Minnelli, Harry Nilsson, Anne Murray, and Karen Akers.

"Niagara Falls" (1841) is long forgotten now, but in its day it was so popular that it was largely responsible for making the Falls the honeymoon destination of choice. Mrs. W. Winchell is credited as the author, and sheet music sales before and after the Civil War were extraordinary, though no accurate statistics exist. The song relates a trip from Buffalo to see the famous Falls, and the homey lyric describes the water and compares the spray to "Aunt Deborah's washing day."

"The Night Is Young and You're So Beautiful" (1936) is probably the most famous song ever to come out of a local historical pageant. Dana Seusse composed the waltz music, and Billy Rose and Irving Kahal wrote the lyric in which a beau suggests they drop the talk about the World's Fair or Grover Cleveland and pleads for a kiss in the moonlight with the title phrase as his reason. It was written for the 1936 Frontier Days Celebration in Fort Worth, Texas, where it was introduced at Rose's Casa Mañana. Jan Garber and his Orchestra popularized the number on disc, and there were successful records by Wayne King and Cliff "Ukelele Ike" Edwards as well. In 1951 the song was revived by Ray Anthony and his Orchestra. Other well-known discs were made by Dick Haymes, Buddy Cole, Russ Case, Dinah Shore, Johnny Otis, Louis Prima, Ziggy Elman, Paula Kelly and the Modernaires, Frank Sinatra, and Dean Martin.

"Night Wind" (1935) is an atmospheric ballad about a lonely and loveless evening by Rob Rothberg (lyric) and David A. Pollack (music) that was later picked up by jazz musicians and often recorded by them over the years. Early discs by Taft Jordan, Fats Waller, Benny Goodman (vocal by Helen Ward), and the Dorsey Brothers (vocal by Bob Crosby) popularized the ballad. Other records of note were made by Cosy Cole, Leon Barry, Ella Fitzgerald, Billy Taylor's Big Eight, and David Arkenstone.

"A Nightingale Sang in Berkeley Square" (1940) is a British ballad by Eric Maschwitz (lyric) and Manning Sherwin (music) that was in demand in the States even though few Americans knew of the square or how to pronounce its name correctly. The song recalls a night long ago when a bird was singing while a beau met his sweetheart in the London square. The number was introduced by Judy Campbell in the London revue *New Faces* (1940) and popularized in America by a bestselling record by Glenn Miller (vocal by Ray Eberly). It was particularly beloved during the war years with successful discs by Guy Lombardo (vocal by Carmen Lombardo), Ray Noble (vocal by Larry Stewart), and Sammy Kaye (vocal by Tommy Ryan). Mel Tormé made it a specialty of his, as did Vera Lynn and Frank Sinatra. Among the many others who recorded the ballad were Ted Heath, Rosemary Clooney, Anita O'Day, Bob Crosby, Acker Bilk, Nat King Cole, the Demon Brothers, Tony Bennett, and Bobby Darin. "A Nightingale Sang in Berkeley Square" has enjoyed renewed interest of late, with recent recordings by Lainie Nelson, Andrea Marcovicci, Vicki Stuart, Karen Akers, Marlene Ver Planck, Harry Connick Jr., and others. It was also sung in the Off-Broadway revue *Swingtime Canteen* (1995).

"Nina Never Knew" (1952) is an echoing ballad by Milton Drake (lyric) and Louis Alter (music) about a naive gal who knew nothing of love or sex, but when romance finally came, it swept her off her feet. The gliding fox trot keeps repeating the title phrase, creating a hypnotic effect. The number was popularized by a bestselling record by the Sauter-Finegan Orchestra (vocal by Joe Mooney), and Johnny Desmond also had a hit with it. Other versions were made by Les Brown, the Jimmie Rowles

Trio, Vic Damone, Steve Jordan, Jack Jones, Bill Easley, Kenny Ball, Matt Monro, and John Pizzarelli.

"No Arms Can Ever Hold You (Like These Arms of Mine)" (1955) is a fervent ballad by Art Crafer and Jimmy Nebb that managed to resurface with success a couple of times. The ardent plea to a sweetheart to remain faithful was popularized by bestselling records by George Shaw, then Pat Boone. In 1965 the Bachelors revived it with a hit disc, and Bobby Vinton did the same in 1970.

"No Greater Love" (1936) is a bombastic song in which a wooer proclaims that no existing love comes close to that which he holds for her. Marty Symes wrote the confident lyric, and bandleader Isham Jones composed the lilting music. Jones and his Orchestra introduced the number with a popular record with Woody Herman providing the vocal. Soon after Guy Lombardo and the Royal Canadians also had a hit with it. Subsequent records of note were made by Billy May, Jimmy Dorsey (vocal by Bob Carroll), Billie Holiday, Al Hibbler with Johnny Hodges' Orchestra, Frankie Carle, Duke Ellington, Dick Haymes, Teddy Powell, Stan Getz, the Eddie Thompson Trio, Anita Ellis, Dizzy Gillespie, the Ray Brown Trio, Jan Pearce, and Ahmad Jamal. The song is sometimes listed as "There Is No Greater Love."

"No! No! A Thousand Times No! (You Shall Not Buy My Caress)" (1934) is a merry pastiche of sentimental ballads, nineteenth-century sing-along songs, and early silent films. Al Sherman, Al Lewis, and Abner Silver wrote the slapstick number in which "desperate Desmond" pursues an innocent gal who always resists him with the title phrase, even though he does such dastardly deeds as tying her to the railroad tracks. Subtitled "a melodrama in song," the number is very playful as it encourages everyone to join in on the repeated title phrase. Ozzie Nelson (vocal by Harriet Hilliard) and George Hall (vocal by Loretta Lee) popularized the waltzing spoof in clubs and on records, and it was a favorite around the family piano and in community sings during the depression.

"No Other Love (Have I)" (1953) is a Rodgers and Hammerstein song that took an unusual road to Tin Pan Alley. Richard Rodgers composed the enticing music, marked with a "slow habanera tempo," for a tango section called "Beneath the Southern Cross" that was part of his soundtrack score for the television documentary *Victory at Sea* (1952). The catchy rhythm song was given a romantic lyric by Oscar Hammerstein that pledged all of one's dreams and love for another. The new number was interpolated into the Broadway musical *Me and Juliet* (1953), where it was sung by Bill Hayes and Isabel Bigley. But the show was not one of Rodgers and Hammerstein's successes, so the ballad didn't gain favor until Perry Como recorded it and the disc went to the top of the charts. Among the artists who also made estimable recordings of it were Jo Stafford, Bing Crosby, Keely Smith, Margaret Whiting, Sonny Til and the Orioles, Mindy Carson, Julius LaRosa, the Ray Conniff Singers, Barry Manilow, and Michael Feinstein.

"No Regrets" (1936) is a fatalistic number about not turning back or being sorry one fell into a certain romance. Harry Tobias (lyric) and Roy Ingraham (music) wrote the ballad, and it was popularized by Glen Gray and the Casa Loma Orchestra. Tommy Dorsey (vocal by Jack Leonard), Billie Holiday, Edith Piaf, Frances Faye, Artie Shaw, Wingy Manone, Joe Haymes, the Walker Brothers, and Tom Rush are among those who recorded it with success.

"Nobody" (1905), one of the greatest of all seriocomic songs, was most associated with Bert Williams, the African American performer who cowrote it and performed it many times. Alex Rogers wrote the piercing lyric about a man whom no one seems to see or care about. The verse is a series of questions (Who soothes my "thumping, bumping brain?" Who gives me a handout when I'm hungry?), all of which are answered by the blunt title. In the refrain the tone gets bitter as the outcast proclaims that he has never harmed anyone, and until someone gives him something he has no intention of doing anything for anyone else. Williams composed the quiet, almost nonexistent melody that lends itself to talk-singing except on the long *o* of "nobody" that is both a comic punch and also a tragic wail. The comedy team of Walker and Williams introduced the song in vaudeville, and then Williams recorded it as a solo. Over the next few years, Williams and the song became famous, and he was asked to perform it in the *Ziegfeld Follies* (1910), the first time a black performer was starred alongside white stars. Among those who have also recorded the bittersweet number were Phil Harris, Bing Crosby, Dick Curless, Benny Goodman, Nina Simone, Carol Burnett, and Perry Como. On Broadway it was sung by Avon Long in *Bubbling Brown Sugar* (1976) and Lynn Thigpen in *Tintypes* (1980), and Bob Hope and Milly Vitale performed it in the movie *The Seven Little Foys* (1955).

"Nobody Else But Me" (1946), the last song by the renowned composer Jerome Kern, was written for the 1946 Broadway revival of *Show Boat*, where it was sung by Jan Clayton and the chorus. Oscar Hammerstein wrote the zesty lyric that celebrates the fact that, with all of one's faults, a darling thinks I'm grand and wishes for no one else. Kern's music is bouncy and easygoing with a slight swing to it. "Nobody Else But Me" was interpolated into many subsequent productions and recordings of *Show Boat*, and it also enjoyed many recordings, including those by Paul Weston (vocal by Lou Dinning), Stan Getz, Sylvia Syms, the Gerry Mulligan Quartet, Dinah Shore, Barbara Lea, Bill Evans, Morgana King, Mitzi Gaynor, Sylvia McNair, Tony Bennett, and more recently, Barbara Cook, Andrea Marcovicci, and Bobby Short.

"Nobody Knows (And Nobody Seems to Care)" (1919) was one of Irving Berlin's biggest sellers of sheet music (over a million copies), yet it is little known today. The tearful lament, a cry of pain by a lonesome soul who is "tired of being on-my-own-some," was sung by Berlin himself at the Palace Theatre during a one-week engagement in 1919. There were three successful recordings the year it was published: by the Art Hickman Trio, Irving and Jack Kaufman, and Esther Walker. It was not until years later that some artists picked up on it, and discs were made by Eddie Condon, Count Basie, the Dukes of Dixieland, Jimmy Rushing, Victoria Hamilton, and Cleo Laine.

"Nobody Knows De Trouble I've Seen" (c. 1865) is the traditional Negro spiritual that laments that only God sees and knows one's ups and downs. Its authorship and origins are unknown, but the slow, rolling ballad became widespread after the Civil War. A favorite of gospel singers and choral groups, the song has also enjoyed jazz and blues interpretations. Prominent recordings have been made by Paul Robeson, Louis Armstrong, Gene Autry, Harry James, Benny Carter and Dizzy Gillespie, Lena Horne, Jack Teagarden, Kay Starr, Red Garland, Mahalia Jackson, and Leontyne Price. The Hall Johnson Choir sang it in the films *Hearts in Dixie* (1929) and *Way Down South* (1939), and it was performed by Dick Foran in *Private Buckaroo* (1942). As painful and majestic as the song is, it has also been parodied on more than one occasion.

"Nobody Knows You When You're Down and Out" (1923) is a blues standard by Jimmie Cox in which a poor man notes how many friends he had when he was rich, but now they don't know him at all. But, he philosophizes, he knows they would become his "long-lost friends" if he ever got back in the money. Cox introduced the number in vaudeville, and it started to become popular when Bobby Baker made the first recording of it. Bessie Smith's 1929 disc revived interest in the ballad, and there were later hit records by Pinetop Smith, Julia Lee, and Nina Simone. Among the many artists who also recorded it were Leadbelly, Eddie Condon, LaVern Baker, Sidney Bechet, Ruth Brown, Louis Jordan, Sam Cooke, Buddy Greco, Otis Redding, Kenny Ball, Joe Williams, Dorothy Loudon, Barbra Streisand, and Don McLean. On Broadway, Linda Hopkins sang it in the musical bio *Bessie and Me* (1975), and it was performed by Leslie Uggams, Debbie Shapiro, and Jean Du Shon in the revue *Blues in the Night* (1982).

"Nobody's Sweetheart" (1923) is a plaintive lament about losing the love of a girl who was once simple and honest but now has become a classy lady with painted lips and eyes and wearing a "bird of paradise" hat. Gus Kahn, Ernie Erdman, Billy Myers, and Elmer Schoebel collaborated on the number, and it was introduced by Ted Lewis in the Broadway revue *The Passing Show of 1923*. Isham Jones and his Orchestra popularized the woeful ballad, and it was revived with success by Red Nichols in 1928, Cab Calloway in 1931, and the Mills Brothers in 1932, their disc selling over a million copies. The oft-recorded song also had discs by Duke Ellington, Benny Goodman, Frankie Trumbauer, Aker Bilk, Tiny Hill, Chet Atkins, Louis Prima, the Washboard Rhythm Kings, Bud Freeman, Muggsy Spanier, Max Morath, and Johnnie Ray. "Nobody's Sweetheart" has been used in at least a dozen films, performed by Rudy Vallee and his Connecticut Yankees in The *Vagabond Lover* (1929), Constance Moore in *I'm Nobody's Sweetheart Now* (1940), Ernest Whitman in *Stormy Weather* (1943), Belle Baker in *Atlantic City* (1944), Doris Day in *I'll See You in My Dreams* (1951), as well as being heard in *The Cuban Love Song* (1931), *Red-Headed Woman* (1932), *Stage Door Canteen* (1943), *Hit Parade of 1943* (1943), and others.

"Now's the Time to Fall in Love" (1931) is a novelty number by Al Lewis and Al Sherman that was popular during the depression, arguing that now, while prices for everything have dropped so low, is the perfect time for romance. Eddie Cantor introduced the comic ditty on his radio show and it became a specialty of his, performing it throughout the rest of his career. He also recorded it and sang it on the soundtrack for Keefe Brasselle in the film bio *The Eddie Cantor Story* (1953). Other discs were made by Gene Gardos, David Allen Coe, and Carroll Gibbons. The song is sometimes titled by the opening line "Potatoes Are Cheaper, Tomatoes Are Cheaper."

O

"The Object of My Affection" (1934) is a breezy song of total commit-
ment, the wooer willing to wait around while his sweetheart does what
she likes, as long as she says she is his. Pinky Tomlin, Coy Poe, and
Jimmy Grier collaborated on the catchy tune, and it was popularized on
record by Tomlin with Grier's Orchestra. There were also early hits by
the Boswell Sisters, Jan Garber (vocal by Lee Bennett), and Lionel Hampton. The bouncy ballad was a favorite throughout the depression and
remained a standard for decades. Among the many memorable recordings over the years were those by Archie Bleyer, Paul Pendarvis (vocal
by Patricia Norman), Teddy Powell, Joe Richardson (vocal by Paul
Small), Dick Haymes, Russ Morgan, Ruby Wright, Elaine Stritch, Faron
Young, and Django Reinhardt. Tomlin reprised the number in the film
Times Square Lady (1935), and his recording with Grier was heard in *Paper
Moon* (1973). Janet Blair sang it with the Dorsey Brothers' Band in *The
Fabulous Dorseys* (1947), and the song was heard in *One More Spring*
(1935) and *The Object of My Affection* (1998).

"Oh, Babe!" (1950) is a boogie-woogie standard by Louis Prima and
Milton Kabak that celebrates a sweetie with wild abandon. Prima intro-
duced the song on a record with Keely Smith that climbed the charts,
and it was also a hit for Kay Starr with Frank DeVol's Orchestra, the
Ames Brothers, Ralph Flanagan (vocal by Steve Benoric), and the Benny
Goodman Sextet. Al Cook, Johnny Watson, Elvin Bishop, Colin James,
Roy Milton, and Furry Lewis were among the artists who also made
discs of the number.

"Oh! Didn't He Ramble" (1902), a favorite of jazz bands in New Orleans
funeral processions, began as a minstrel number but was soon adopted

by jazz artists and was second only to "When the Saints Go Marching In" for bittersweet musical sendoffs for the deceased. The song was written by Bob Cole and J. Rosamond Johnson (the two together using the pseudonym Will Handy) and introduced by George Primrose in his minstrel act. Soon minstrel troupes across the country were using it. Of the many notable recordings made over the decades were those by Dan Quinn, Kid Ory's Creole Jazz Band, Jelly Roll Morton, Sidney Bechet, Louis Armstrong, Papa Celestin, Teddy Buckner, Al Hirt, Peggy Lee, and Max Collie. Lee sang it in the movie *Pete Kelly's Blues* (1955) with Dick Cathcart providing the trumpet playing for Jack Webb.

"Oh, Happy Day" (1953) is the rhythmic gospel number that has a touch of both rock-and-roll and country-western in it, finding popularity in concerts as well as in churches. Seventeen-year-old Don Howard Koplow collaborated with Nancy Binns Reed on the joyous number that celebrates the moment, and it became famous with Koplow's record that sold over a million copies. Other early hits versions were made by the Four Knights and Lawrence Welk (vocal by Larry Cooper). The spirited song was also recorded by the Imperials, Big Mama Thornton, the Prophets, Quincy Jones, the Statler Brothers, Edwin Hawkins, Ray Anthony, Dion, Tennessee Ernie Ford, Joan Baez, Glen Campbell, and Ladysmith Black Mambazo. "Oh, Happy Day" was heard in the movies *Sister Act* (1992) and *Sister Act 2: Back in the Habit* (1993).

"Oh, How She Could Yacki, Hacki, Wicki, Wacki, Woo" (1916), subtitled "Love in Honolulu," is a spoof of the kind of Hawaiian songs that were all the rage on Tin Pan Alley. Stanley Murphy, Charles McCarron (lyric), and Albert Von Tilzer (music) wrote the risible number about an island gal who could dance the hula and, as the silly suggestive lyric implies, make love with panache. Eddie Cantor introduced the number at the rooftop terrace of the New Amsterdam Theatre in New York, making his Broadway debut with his own kind of panache. He sang the song, then invited dandy Diamond Jim Brady, producer Charles B. Dillingham, and newspaper mogul William Randolph Hearst up on stage and did card tricks with them while he encored the number. Cantor recorded the ditty, and there was an early duet version by Arthur Collins and Bryon Harlan that was popular. But the song had pretty much disappeared by the depression.

"Oh, Johnny! Oh, Johnny! Oh!" (1914) is a vivacious love song that swept the nation in the late teens, selling over a million copies of sheet music and later spawning several hit records. Ed Rose wrote the energetic music, and Abe Olman penned the exclamatory lyric about a guy who is not handsome, but he can "make my sad heart jump for joy."

The songwriters originally meant the song as a morale booster for World War One, the lyric shouting, "Oh, Johnny! How you can fight!" But no one seemed interested in it, so they changed it to "how you can love!" and the song was soon being sung by Al Jolson, Sophie Tucker, Eddie Cantor, and Ted Lewis in vaudeville. It was interpolated into the Broadway musical *Follow Me* (1916), where it was sung with success by Henry Jackson. Connee Boswell had a hit recording in the 1930s, and a disc by "Wee" Bonnie Baker with Orrin Tucker's Orchestra sold over a million copies in 1940, putting the number on the *Hit Parade* for fourteen weeks. Other records of note were made by the American Quartet, the Joseph C. Smith Orchestra, Benny Goodman, the Andrews Sisters, Glenn Miller, Ella Fitzgerald, Lawrence Welk, Peggy Lee, the Moms and Dads, and Al Hirt. The rousing number was used in the films *Oh Johnny, How You Can Love!* (1940), *You're the One* (1941), *For Me and My Gal* (1942), and *Spotlight Scandals* (1943), and a recording by Miriam Gulager was heard on the soundtrack of *Red Sky at Morning* (1970).

"Oh, Promise Me" (1889), the wedding song of choice for five decades or so, was written by Clement Scott (lyric) and Reginald De Koven (music) when the star Jessie Bartlett Davis insisted on a new number for her to sing in the operetta *Robin Hood* (1890) after the show had been running a while. The songwriters provided a solemn number pleading for everlasting love to use for the wedding ceremony, and it became the hit of the show. Davis didn't think much of the song at first, but once it was identified with her, she sang it in public appearances for years. It didn't take long before the number was sung at millions of weddings across America, so much so that to sing it without nuptials seemed out of place. Regardless. it was often recorded, most notably by John McCormack, Conrad Thibault, Nelson Eddy, Phil Spitalny's Orchestra (featuring Evelyn and "her magic violin"), Jesse Crawford, Dick Leibert and Lucille Lawrence, Tommy Dorsey, Vaughn Monroe, and the Platters. "Oh, Promise Me" was heard in the wedding ceremony in *Rosalie* (1937) and dozens of other movies.

"Oh! Susanna" (1847) was one of Stephen Foster's first hits and the first time he received money for any of his songs: a cash payment of $100. The rousing travel song urges lonely Susanna not to weep, for he is returning from Alabama "with a banjo on my knee." The tuneful number was introduced in an ice cream parlor in Pittsburgh in 1847 and published the following year. When it was picked up by traveling minstrel shows, the song's fame quickly spread, and it seemed all America was soon singing it. "Oh! Susanna" was a particular favorite of the prospecting "Forty-Niners" heading to California, and it soon became the unofficial theme song for any pioneer heading to new lands. The ditty was also a staple in the repertoire of barbershop quartets. Sometimes titled "Banjo on My Knee," it was given well-known recordings by the Sons of the Pioneers, Al Jolson, the Boston Pops Orchestra, Tommy Dorsey, the Augustana Choir, the New Orleans Rhythm Kings, Morton Gould, Andre Kostelanetz, Carson Robison and his Old Timers, and Judy Garland. There have even been two classical pieces based on the song: Alan Shulman's symphonic piece and Lucien Cailliet's "Fantasia and Fugue on *Oh, Susanna.*" It was sung by the cast of the Broadway revue *Sing Out, Sweet Land!* (1944) and was heard in some dozen films, including *Babes in Arms* (1939) where it was performed by Garland and Mickey Rooney, *Colorado* (1940), *Go West!* (1940), *Coney Island* (1943), *Meet Me at the Fair* (1953), *Fighter Attack* (1953), and the three Foster movie bios, *Harmony Lane* (1935), *Swanee River* (1939), and *I Dream of Jeanie* (1952).

"Oh! What It Seemed to Be" (1946) is an expansive ballad by Bennie Benjamin, George David Weiss, and Frankie Carle in which the love for a certain someone can turn a neighborhood dance into a fancy dress ball and a ride on a train into a journey to the stars. Pianist Carle's record with a vocal by his daughter Marjorie Hughes was a bestseller, and Frank Sinatra's disc with Alex Stordahl's Orchestra was also a big hit, putting the song on *Your Hit Parade* for seventeen weeks. The upbeat love song was also given significant recordings by Charlie Spivak (vocal by Jimmy Saunders), Patti Page, Helen Forrest and Dick Haymes, Ted Heath, Jim Reeves, Roger Williams, and Jimmy Roselli.

"Oh, You Beautiful Doll" (1911) is the ragtime standard by A. Seymour Brown (lyric) and Nat D. Ayer (music) that extols the virtues of one's "great big beautiful" sweetie. The vivacious number was popularized by the American Quartet, and soon it was a favorite on the vaudeville circuit. During the Roaring Twenties the ditty was even more popular, as it was used for dancing to many of the new and wild steps then in vogue. The number remains one of the most recognized of Tin Pan Alley hits, performed by everyone from Dixieland jazz bands to country-western singers. Among the many recordings were those by Eddie Cantor, Frankie Vaughn, Claude Thornhill, Rosemary Clooney, Bob Wills, Hank Williams, Mike Douglas, Mel Tormé, Max Bygraves, Nancy Sinatra, Jessica Molansky, and Terry Waldo. On screen it was performed by George Murphy and Lucille Norman in *For Me and My Gal* (1942) and Charles Winninger in *Broadway Rhythm* (1944), and Cantor providing the singing for Keefe Brasselle in *The Eddie Cantor Story* (1953). It can also be heard in *Cavalcade* (1933), *The Best of Enemies* (1933), *Wharf Angel* (1934), *The Story of Irene and Vernon Castle* (1939), *Oh, You Beautiful Doll* (1949), and *The I-Don't-Care Girl* (1953).

"Oh, You Crazy Moon" (1939) was the first collaboration between composer Jimmy Van Heusen and lyricist Johnny Burke and the first of their many hits together. The uptempo number was introduced and popularized by Tommy Dorsey (vocal by Jack Leonard) with other successful discs by Bea Wain and the orchestras of Bob Crosby, Al Donahue, and Glenn Miller (vocal by Ray Eberly). Other noteworthy recordings were made by Artie Shaw, George Shearing (vocal by Mel Tormé), Peggy Lee, Art Tatum, Frank Sinatra, Chet Baker, Bing Crosby, Wes Montgomery, Ella Mae Morse, Sarah Vaughan, and Chris Connor.

"Old Black Joe" (1860) is a Stephen Foster song about an old slave, yet the number is not written in the Negro dialect that characterizes much of the composer-lyricist's work. When Foster was courting his future wife Jane McDowell, he was always greeted by Joe, an elderly house servant who smiled and welcomed him. The songwriter promised the old man he would write a song about him someday, but the servant died before "Old Black Joe" was finished. The lyric is quite moving as an old slave hears voices from his past as he lays dying. Rather than coming across as morose, the ballad has an inspirational flavor to it, partly because of Foster's lilting melody. Among the artists that recorded the song many years later were Lawrence Tibbett, Tommy Dorsey, Andre Kostelanetz, the London String Quartet, Morton Gould, Clay Everhart, Jerry Lee Lewis, Gene Krupa, and Redd Foxx. The number was included in the three Foster film bios, *Harmony Lane* (1935), *Swanee River* (1939), and *I Dream of Jeanie* (1952), as well as in *Young Eagles* (1930), *King of Jazz* (1930), *Hollywood Hotel* (1938), and the German movie *The Trapp Family* that was released in the United States in 1961.

"Old Fashioned Love" (1923) is a sassy number about down-home loving that was written in the Harlem jazz style but was later recorded in a variety of music genres. Cecil Mack (lyric) and James P. Johnson (music) wrote it for the all-Negro Broadway revue *Runnin' Wild* (1923), where it was performed by Adelaide Hall, Ina Duncan, and Arthur D. Porter. It became a specialty of Lena Horne's years later, and her rendition is considered the definitive one. All the same, there were also accomplished discs by Red Norvo, the Mills Brothers, Frank Crumit, Noble Sissle and Eubie Blake, Clyde McCoy, Bob Wills, Cliff Bruner and his Texas Wanderers, Sidney Bechet, Eva Taylor, Billy Cotton, Art Hodes, Eddy Howard, Max Morath, and Johnson himself. The song was heard in the movie *Sweet and Lowdown* (1999), with Howard Alden providing the guitar playing for Sean Penn.

"Old Folks at Home" (1851), arguably Stephen Foster's most popular and beloved song, combines a love for home and for the South in an appealing manner that has never dated. Foster wanted to write a song about a homestead by a river and went to an atlas to find a melodic name. He found the Suwanee River in Florida, shortened it to the Swanee, and wrote his unforgettable lyric about being tired of roaming the countryside and longing to return south to the "old folks." (Foster never saw the real river in his lifetime.) Edward Christy offered to pay Foster $500 to use it in his famous minstrel show but insisted his name appear as the author. Foster agreed, Christy was credited, and it is believed that Foster only ended up with $15. His name would not appear on printed copies of the music until 1879, fifteen years after his death. Christy's Minstrels introduced the number, and after it was published in 1852, it quickly became a nationwide hit. Two printing companies worked around the clock to keep up with the demand for sheet music. From minstrel shows it spread to vaudeville, community sings, and concerts. It was so popular that many other songs were written to capitalize on the original, from "The Old Folks Are Gone" to "Young Folks at Home." (George Gershwin's biggest hit song "Swanee" is a later example.) The ballad was first recorded in 1891 by Len Spencer, and after many other discs, it was revived by Jimmie Lunceford in 1936 and again by Tommy Dorsey in 1945. Among the many recordings made over the decades were those by Al Jolson, Bing Crosby with the Crinoline Choir, Fritz Kreisler and Carl Lawson, Andre Kostelanetz, the Mills Brothers, Frankie Carle, and Paul Robeson. Crosby reprised it with the Cabin Kids in the movie *Mississippi* (1935), Jolson reprised it in the Foster bio *Swanee River* (1939), Deanna Durbin sang it in *Nice Girl* (1941), and Harpo Marx played it on the harp in *Love Happy* (1949). The familiar tune can be heard in *Babes on Broadway* (1942), *Coney Island* (1943), *Hi, Buddy* (1943), and in *Gone With the Wind* (1939) and other Civil War–era films. At different times in its long history, the song has gone under different titles, including "Swanee River" and "Way Down Upon the Swanee River."

"The Old Lamp-Lighter" (1946) is a nostalgic ballad by Charles Tobias (lyric) and Nat Simon (music) that sold over a million copies of sheet music (in an era where radio and records prevailed) and over 2 million discs, yet it is little known today. Tobias recalled the lamplighters who went about his hometown of Worcester, Massachusetts, each evening at dusk, and he wrote a tender lyric about a particular old man who goes about his job every day without fail. A record by Sammy Kaye (vocal by Billy Williams) popularized the number by reaching the top of the charts, and soon after Kay Kyser (vocal by Mike Douglas) also had a bestselling disc. It was revived by the Browns in 1960 with a record that reached the Top 10. Other versions were made by Hal Derwin with Frank DeVol's Orchestra, Morton Downey with Jimmy Lytell's Orchestra, Russ Morgan (vocal by Kenny Baker), Gene Autry, Mac Wiseman, and Bing Crosby. Autry reprised it in the movie *Twilight on the Rio Grande* (1947).

"Old MacDonald Had a Farm" (1917), perhaps the most sung children's song in American popular culture, has obscure origins that go back much further than its publication in 1917. The simple ditty that lists and imitates various farm animals has no known author and cannot even be traced to a particular region of the country. But every child has learned it, often the first song that is learned. In addition to many children's records, the ditty has also been recorded by such varied artists as Gene Autry, Nat King Cole, Flatt and Scruggs, Ella Fitzgerald, the Three Stooges, and Spike Jones and his City Slickers. Randy Starr adapted the traditional tune into an uptempo number for Elvis Presley who recorded it and sang it in the movie *Double Trouble* (1967). It was also sung by William Holden and Susan Strasberg in *Picnic* (1955).

"The Old Master Painter" (1950) is a hymnlike number with a sprightly beat and a reverent but hardly solemn lyric. Beasley Smith composed the spirited music, and Haven Gillespie penned the lyric about God, the old master "from the faraway hills," who created a perfect setting in which a loving couple find themselves. Snooky Lanson introduced the ballad on record with Smith's band, but the big seller was a disc by Dick Haymes. Other recordings were made by Phil Harris, Peggy Lee and Mel Tormé, Bob Crosby and the Bobcats, the Fontane Sisters, Frank Sinatra with Paula Kelly and the Modernaires, and the Browns. The number can be heard in the movie *Panic in the Streets* (1950).

"The Old Piano Roll Blues" (1950) is a ragtime-blues by Cy Coben written decades after the ragtime era but capturing the period with nostalgic flair. The song of yearning asks for the old songs that one used to hear on a player piano, lamenting their loss and celebrating their memory. A record by Hoagy Carmichael and Cass Daley with Matty Matlock's All Stars was the most popular of the many recordings, though there were chart records by Lawrence "Piano Roll" Cook and Eddie Cantor with Lisa Kirk and Sammy Kaye's Orchestra. Other notable discs were made by the Andrews Sisters, Jan Garber, Jo Stafford, Floyd Cramer, Liberace, Beatrice Kay, Jan August, Cliff Stewart, the Jubilaires, and Johnny Maddox. Jane Powell and Vic Damone sang the number in the movie *Rich, Young and Pretty* (1951).

"Ole Buttermilk Sky" (1946) is a country-flavored ballad in which a suitor asks the sky to be moonlit and magical tonight because he is going to pop the question to his beloved. Hoagy Carmichael and Jack Brooks wrote the number for the film *Canyon Passage* (1946), where Carmichael sang it. The ballad was nominated for an Oscar and was given a successful recording by Kay Kyser (vocal by Mike Douglas), which hit the top of the charts. Other notable discs were made by Carmichael, Connee Boswell, Paul Weston (vocal by Matt Dennis), the Campus Kids, Bing Crosby, Nellie Lutcher, Anthony Perkins, the Mello-Larks, and more recently, Willie Nelson, Crystal Gayle, and Cory Jamison.

"On a Slow Boat to China" (1948) is the moderate swing standard that Frank Loesser wrote as a Tin Pan Alley entry, a rarity for the Broadway-Hollywood songwriter at this point in his career. The titles comes from an old gambling expression: "If I could get you on a slow boat to China, I'd get rich." Loesser struggled with ten different versions of the song until he came up with a lyric that turned the expression into a romantic one, wishing to be alone with a sweetheart on a long boat ride, away from her many admirers on shore. A recording by Kay Kyser (vocals by Harry Babbitt and Gloria Wood) sold a million copies, and there were also successful discs by Freddie Martin (vocal by Glen Hughes), Benny Goodman (vocal by Al Hendrickson), and Eddy Howard. The number was interpolated into the movie *Neptune's Daughter* (1949), where it was used behind a fashion show sequence. Other recordings were made by Bing Crosby, Rosemary Clooney, Snooky Lanson, Larry Clinton, Ella Fitzgerald, Art Lund, the Four Lads, Sonny Rollins, the Platters, Dean Martin, Jimmy Buffett, and more recently, Dee Dee Bridgewater, Al Saxon, Tommy Tune, Cleo Laine, Jackie Cain and Roy Kral, Liz Callaway, and Jimmy Roselli.

"On a Sunday Afternoon" (1902) is the familiar waltz by Andrew B. Sterling (lyric) and Harry Von Tilzer (music) that sold over 2 million copies of sheet music the first year it was published. Von Tilzer was at the beach one weekend, watching the working-class folk enjoy themselves after a hard week's work and the phrase "the one day that's fun day is Sunday" came to him. He persuaded Sterling to elaborate on it, so he wrote a lyric listing some of the pleasures of a Sunday in New York in June, from a trolley ride to the sea to a boat ride down the river. The tinkling number was soon sung in thousands of parlors on the piano, and it became a favorite of bands who played it at the sort of recreation places mentioned in the song. While there were many recordings, one by Blue Barron and his Orchestra was the biggest seller. Buddy and Vilma Ebsen performed it in the film *Broadway Melody of 1936* (1935), and Constance Moore sang it in *Atlantic City* (1944). The waltz was often used on the soundtrack for period movies, such as *Man-Proof* (1938) and *The Naughty Nineties* (1945).

"On Moonlight Bay" (1912), one of the most durable of Tin Pan Alley numbers about an idyllic setting for romance, is still widely recognized because of its dreamy but lively melody and picturesque lyric. Edward Madden (lyric) and Percy Wenrich (music) wrote the sublime ballad about sailing across the bay at night in the moonlight and losing one's heart to a true love. The number was introduced in vaudeville and was nationally known by the time World War One broke out. An early record by the American Quartet was a bestseller, and the song was revived in 1951 by a duet disc by Bing and Gary Crosby that climbed the charts. Other successful versions were made by Glenn Miller, the Mills Brothers, Claude Thornhill, Harry James and his Music Makers, Tony Martin, the Drifters, Billy Vaughn, the Champs, and the Mormon Tabernacle Choir. On screen it was sung by Alice Faye in *Tin Pan Alley* (1940), Frank Sinatra and the Pied Pipers with Tommy Dorsey's Orchestra in *Ship Ahoy* (1942), Deanna Durbin in *For the Love of Mary* (1948), and Doris Day in *On Moonlight Bay* (1951), as well being heard in *The Broadway Hoofer* (1929), *Babes in Arms* (1939), *Is Everybody Happy?* (1943), *April Showers* (1948), *By the Light of the Silvery Moon* (1953), and other films. Very often the song is simply listed as "Moonlight Bay."

"On the Banks of the Wabash (Far Away)" (1897), the official state song of Indiana since 1913, is Paul Dresser's most famous work. Dresser was born in Terre Haute, Indiana, and wrote the nostalgic lyric about his youth there. The atmospheric lyric recalls a mother standing at the door, the smell of fresh mown hay, and strolling along the river with Mary who now lies in the graveyard. The song was an immediate hit, selling over a million copies of sheet music during its first year and becoming a particular favorite with barbershop quartets, community bands, and the soldiers going off to fight in the Spanish-American War. Memorable recordings of the number were made by the Mills Brothers, Guy Lombardo and the Royal Canadians, Bing Crosby, Freddy Martin and the Martin Men, and William Bolcom and Joan Morris. The ballad can be heard in the Dresser film bio *My Gal Sal* (1942), as well as such films as *The Floradora Girl* (1930), *The Jolson Story* (1946), *Gilda* (1946), and *Wait Till the Sun Shines, Nellie* (1952).

"On the Sunny Side of the Street" (1930) was one of the earliest and most resiliant of the many depression-chasing songs to come out of the 1930s. Jimmy McHugh composed the bouncy music that sounds like the strutting down the street of a happy-go-lucky optimist, and Dorothy Fields's energetic lyric about getting out from the shade and walking in the sun has a lift to it that is still contagious. Harry Richman introduced the number in the Broadway show *The International Revue* (1930), and it has been a favorite of singers and musicians ever since. Richman re-

corded it first, and after many other discs it was revived by Tommy
Dorsey in 1945. Other artists who made recordings include Ted Lewis,
Louis Armstrong, Duke Ellington, Billie Holiday, Coleman Hawkins,
Frankie Laine, Judy Garland, Lionel Hampton, Ivie Anderson, Count Ba-
sie, Jo Stafford, Erroll Garner, Helen Forrest, Dizzy Gillespie, Keely
Smith, Maynard Ferguson, Pat Flowers, Ella Fitzgerald, Eddie Condon,
Roy Eldridge, and more recently, Bobby Short, Weslia Whitfield, Willie
Nelson, and Barbara Cook. Laine sang it in the movies *Make Believe Ball-
room* (1949) and *Sunny Side of the Street* (1951), and his recording was
heard in *House Calls* (1978). The song was also performed on screen by
Teddy Wilson in *The Benny Goodman Story* (1956), Ann Blyth (dubbed by
Gogi Grant) in *The Helen Morgan Story* (1957), and Dean Martin in *The
Silencers* (1966), and the Willie Nelson recording was heard in *Rich and
Famous* (1981). Other films that used the number include *Is Everybody
Happy?* (1943), *Nobody's Darling* (1943), *Swing Parade of 1946* (1946); *Two
Blondes and a Redhead* (1947), and *A League of Their Own* (1992).

"On Top of Old Smokey," the traditional folk ballad about a lost love
in the Smokey Mountains, dates back to the early 1800s when it was
sung by pioneers on Conestoga wagons heading west. The song probably
originated in England and was brought over by settlers in the Southern
Highlands. Although it tells the sad tale of a suitor who didn't get the
girl of his dreams because of "courting too slow," the tender ballad is
more remembered for evoking the misty Appalachian mountains. Various versions of the song had been published and recorded over the past
two centuries, but the biggest hit was a 1951 adaptation by Pete Seeger
that was recorded by the Weavers with Gordon Jenkins and his Orchestra, selling over a million discs. In addition to plenty of children's records, other versions were made by Burl Ives, Vaughn Monroe, Bing
Crosby, Dick Curless, Kate Smith, Connie Francis, Harry Belafonte, Gene
Autry, Minnie Pearl, and the group ABBA. In 1963 Tom Glazer wrote
and recorded a parody version called "On Top of Spaghetti" that was
also very popular. Autry sang the original ballad in the movies *Valley of
Fire* (1951) and *On Top of Old Smokey* (1953), and Elvis Presley performed
the Seeger version in *Follow That Dream* (1962).

"Once in a While" (1937) is a poignant ballad by Bud Green (lyric) and
Michael Edwards (music) that pleads with an adored one to give him a
little thought once in a while, even though she says she loves somebody
else. The gentle fox trot was popularized by Tommy Dorsey and his
Orchestra (vocal by Jack Leonard) with other leading records by Frances
Langford, Ozzie Nelson (vocal by Harriet Hilliard), and Louis Armstrong, helping the number stay in the top spot on the *Hit Parade* for
seven weeks. Harry James revived the number when his orchestra per-

formed it with a quintet in the film *I'll Get By* (1950) and recorded it with success. Years later Liza Minnelli did the same thing when she sang it in *New York, New York* (1977). Among the many artists who also made discs were Patti Page, Clifford Brown, Nat King Cole, Faron Young, the Dinning Sisters, Earl Hines, the Ravens, Acker Bilk, Ace Cannon, Oscar Perry, Chet Baker, Aretha Franklin, Dean Martin, Cleo Laine, and Willie Nelson. "Once in a While" is also remembered as the last song Bing Crosby ever sang; he recorded it in 1977, three days before he died.

"One Dozen Roses" (1942) is a cheerful love song that asks for roses to put with one's heart and have them sent to his beloved. Roger Lewis, Country Washburn (lyric), Dick Jurgens, and Walter Donovan (music) wrote the tuneful ballad that Jurgens popularized on record with his band and a vocal by Buddy Moreno. Other successful discs by Harry James (vocal by Jimmy Saunders), Dinah Shore, and Glen Gray and the Casa Loma Orchestra (vocal by Pee Wee Hunt) kept the number on *Your Hit Parade* for fourteen weeks. Glenn Miller, the Mills Brothers, Connee Boswell, Jim Reeves, Kate Smith, and George Morgan also made commendable recordings of the song. It can be heard in the movies *Miracle at Morgan's Creek* (1944) and *You Came Along* (1945).

"The One I Love (Belongs to Someone Else)" (1924) is the troubled lament of one who suspects that his inamorata has designs on another, leaving him "alone on the shelf." Gus Kahn (lyric) and Isham Jones (music) wrote the ballad, and Jones introduced it with a hit recording with his Orchestra. Other early discs were made by Al Jolson and Sophie Tucker, and the number was revived in 1938 by Tommy Dorsey and his Orchestra. Later there were bestsellers by Bing Crosby and Ella Fitzgerald, as well as other records by June Christy, Nellie Lutcher, Frankie Carle, the Dell Trio, Count Basie, Frank Sinatra, Eddie Condon, Paul Desmond, Jimmie Noone, Sarah Vaughan, Steve Allen, and Pete Fountain. On screen it was sung by Judy Garland in *Everybody Sing* (1938), Danny Thomas and Doris Day in *I'll See You in My Dreams* (1952), and Ann Blyth (dubbed by Gogi Grant) in *The Helen Morgan Story* (1957).

"One Morning in May" (1934), an atypical Hoagy Carmichael song yet one of his personal favorites, recalls that morning long ago when two lovers first met, though sadly they are not together anymore. Carmichael's music has a long, flowing musical line with lots of half notes, almost in the style of Jerome Kern. The rhythm is also unusual for him, using strong beats and afterbeats to create surprising pauses throughout the fluent melody. Mitchell Parish wrote the tender lyric, and the number was intended for a musical that was never produced. Instead it was popularized by Carmichael's recording, followed soon after by discs by

Lanny Ross and Wayne King's Orchestra. Tommy Dorsey, Mel Tormé, and Sarah Vaughan all had standout recordings of the ballad, and there were notable versions by Ray Noble (vocal Al Bowlly), Bert Kaempfert, George Shearing, and the Charlie Byrd Trio. Recently the song has become admired again with new recordings by Johnny Varro, Crystal Gayle, John Eaton, Matt Monro, Dave McKenna, and Carol Sloane.

"One Sweet Letter From You" (1927) is a soft and tearful plea for communication that has appealed to soloists, Big Bands, jazz musicians, and even rock-and-rollers. Lew Brown and Sidney Clare wrote the romantic lyric, and Harry Warren composed the graceful music. Ted Lewis and his Band introduced it, but it was Sophie Tucker who started the song on the road to success. In the 1930s there were successful records by Ethel Waters, Gene Austin, Kate Smith, and others; then it was revived by several bands in the late 1930s and 1940s, including Benny Goodman, Lionel Hampton, and Jimmy Dorsey (vocal by Helen O'Connell). Other noteworthy discs were made by Bunk Johnson, Norrie Cox, Miff Mole, Chris Barber, Cliff Bruner and his Texas Wanderers, Spade Cooley, and Bill Haley and the Comets.

"Our Love" (1939) is a lush ballad based on a lush musical theme by Tchaikovsky. Larry Clinton, Buddy Bernier, and Bob Emmerich adapted parts of the *Romeo and Juliet* overture into a rhapsodic number that compares one couple's romance to all the beauty in nature. Clinton and his Orchestra introduced the song, but the leading record was made by Tommy Dorsey (vocal by Stuart Foster). The haunting ballad was also recorded by Glenn Miller, Willie Clayton, Bebe Daniels, Red Nichols, the Dells, Dinah Washington, Jack Hylton, Jim Nabors, and Natalie Cole.

"Out in the Cold Again" (1934) is a torchy number by Ted Koehler (lyric) and Rube Bloom (music) that sings the blues after losing at the game of love once again. Glen Gray and the Casa Loma Orchestra (vocal by Kenny Sargent) featured the number for years and made it famous, and there were early successful records by Ruth Etting, Rudy Vallee, and the Dorsey Brothers (vocal by Bob Crosby). Among the many later discs were those by Red Nichols, Mindy Carson, Sam Donahue, Billy Eckstine, the Earls, Eddie Howard, Frankie Lymon and the Teenagers, Joe Loss, Sam Cooke, and Johnnie Ray.

"Out of Nowhere" (1931) is a very distinctive 1930s ballad that contains a sense of mystery in both its words and its music. Johnny Green composed the intoxicating music, the refrain using nine repeated notes that are played in different variations before the melody bursts forth. Edward Heyman wrote the quixotic lyric about a new love who came out of nowhere, captured one's heart, and is more than likely to disappear into nowhere. Guy Lombardo and the Royal Canadians introduced the song, and it was soon followed by a successful disc by Leo Reisman and his Orchestra. Bing Crosby's 1931 recording was his first hit as a solo singer; it went to the top of the charts and launched his remarkable career. Other records of note were made by Lena Horne with Teddy Wilson, Harry James, Artie Shaw, Jack Denny, Red Norvo, Martha Tilton, Art Tatum, Toots Thielemans, Charlie Parker, Dick Hyman, and a parody version by Red Ingle. Helen Forrest sang it in the film *You Came Along* (1945), Frank Sinatra performed a version (with an altered lyric by Harry Harris) in *The Joker Is Wild* (1957), and Red Nichols provided the cornet playing for Danny Kaye in *The Five Pennies* (1959). "Out of Nowhere" can also be heard in *Dude Ranch* (1931) and *They Shoot Horses, Don't They?* (1969).

"Over There" (1917), one of the greatest of all patriotic numbers, is George M. Cohan's biggest hit song not written for a Broadway show. Cohan wrote the rousing march after opening his morning newspaper one day and read that America had declared war on Germany. He took his opening phrase from a popular 1886 song titled "Johnny Get Your Gun" and expanded the idea in a lyric that was both a call to arms and a vow to not come home until "it's over over there" in Europe. Sigmund Spaeth points out that "the steady irresistible movement of the bass down the scale, under the sustained bugle notes, [gives the] inevitable impression of marching feet." Songwriter-performer Cohan introduced the song himself before an audience of soldiers at Ft. Myers, but it seemed to have little impact. Yet when Charles King sang it at a Red Cross benefit performance at the Hippodrome Theatre in New York, the response was overwhelming. Nora Bayes performed it to acclaim in vaudeville and recorded it, as did Ernestine Schumann-Heink and Enrico Caruso (in English and Italian). It quickly became the most popular song of World War One, selling over a million records and 2 million copies of sheet music. "Over There" was just as beloved during World War Two, prompting Franklin Roosevelt to give Cohan the Congressional Medal of Honor. In addition to many marching and military bands, the song has been recorded by Fred Waring's Pennsylvanians, Glenn Miller, Bob Crosby, the Mormon Tabernacle Choir, and George M. Cohan Jr. James Cagney and Frances Langford sang the patriotic number in the Cohan movie bio *Yankee Doodle Dandy* (1942), and it was featured in such films as *The Cock-Eyed World* (1929), *Tin Pan Alley* (1940), *For Me and My Gal* (1942), *Four Jills in a Jeep* (1944), *What Price Glory* (1952), and the British satire *Oh! What a Lovely War* (1969). On Broadway it was sung by Joel Grey and the cast of the Cohan bio musical *George M!* (1968).

P

"Pack Up Your Troubles in Your Old Kit Bag and Smile, Smile, Smile" (1915) is the bestselling English song that was just as popular in America, especially during World War One. Felix Powell composed the slow but deliberate march music, and George Asaf penned the optimistic lyric about forgetting your problems and joining the army to help save democracy. American doughboys heard the number when they arrived in Europe, and soon it spread back to the States, helped by performances in war rallies and early hit records by James F. Harrison and the Knickerbocker Quartet and Reginald Werrenrath. Adele Rowland and Felix Powell sang it in the Broadway musical *Her Soldier Boy* (1916), and many years later it was heard again on the Great White Way in the musicals *Oh! What a Lovely War* (1964) and *Dancin'* (1978) and in the Off-Broadway revue *Swingtime Canteen* (1995). Judy Garland sang the number in the movie *For Me and My Gal* (1942), Julie Andrews performed it in *Darling Lili* (1970), and it can be heard in many other films, including *Cavalcade* (1933), *The Perfect Gentleman* (1935), *What's Cookin'* (1942), *The Dolly Sisters* (1945), *On Moonlight Bay* (1951), *Wait Till the Sun Shines, Nellie* (1952), and *So This Is Love* (1953). Bob Crosby, Victoria Jackson, the Bluebirds, Max Bygraves, and Mary Cleere Haran are among the varied artists who have recorded the patriotic ballad.

"The Pagan Love Song" (1929) is an exotic ballad that has been performed in a variety of ways over the years, from a dreamy love song to a spirited Dixieland jazz number. Nacio Herb Brown composed the pseudonative music, and Arthur Freed wrote the atmospheric lyric about the hills calling a couple to starlit waters where they will be soothed by the sounds of a pagan love chant. It was written as the theme song for the movie *The Pagan* (1929), where Ramon Novarro sang it, but Bob Haring and his Orchestra were responsible for popularizing it on record. Other discs were made by Ray Kinney's Hawaiians, Alvino Rey, Jo Stafford, Harry James, the Andrews Sisters, Glenn Miller, Annette Hanshaw, Bob Crosby and the Bobcats, Eddie Miller, the King Sisters, Chet Atkins, Bert Kaempfert, Jaye P. Morgan, and Jo Ann Castle. The ballad was heard in the films *Devil May Care* (1929) and *Night Club Girl* (1944), and it was sung by Howard Keel and the chorus in *Pagan Love Song* (1950).

"Paper Doll" (1930), one of Tin Pan Alley's all-time champs with over 6 million records sold, sat idle for a decade before it was published and then took another decade before it became famous. Johnny S. Black wrote the affecting ballad about a man, thwarted by a lover, who decides he will buy a paper doll to cherish, the only kind of female who is sure to remain faithful and stay with him. Black wrote the number sometime in the late 1910s but put it aside when his "Dardenella" (1919) became a huge hit. But before long he had squandered all his earnings from the bestseller and was desperate to sell "Paper Doll." Although he didn't think much of it, publisher E.B. Marks paid Black $50 for it so he could buy some food. The number wasn't published until 1930, and it was performed on occasion, most memorably by Tommy Lyman in night-clubs. But it never was a hit until a dozen years later when Marks's son Herbert was looking through the company files, came across the song, and passed it on to the Mills Brothers. Their 1942 recording quickly went to the top of the charts, put the number on the *Hit Parade* for an unheard-of twenty-three weeks, and sold millions of discs and copies of sheet music. Bing Crosby, Louis Prima, Frank Sinatra, the Picketts, Cliff Edwards, Louis Armstrong, the Ink Spots, Lena Horne, Hank Thompson, the Clark Sisters, and Perry Como were among the many who also recorded it. On screen, it was heard in *Cowboy Canteen* (1944), the Delta Rhythm Boys performed it in *Hi, Good Lookin'* (1944), Horne reprised it in *Two Girls and a Sailor* (1944), the Mills's recording was heard in *Red Sky at Morning* (1970) and in *The Majestic* (2001), and Buddy Knox was heard singing it in *American Graffiti* (1973).

"Paradise" (1932) is a humming waltz number by Gordon Clifford and Nacio Herb Brown that some deemed a bit too suggestive for radio play. The passionate ballad about ideal romance in an ideal place has sections where the singer hums with self-satisfied contentment. Interpreted as the moaning of sexual excitement, the humming caused the song to be banned from the airwaves for a while. But as times changed, it found itself in the mainstream of popular music, and few could find anything suggestive about it today. The ballad was introduced in the film *A Woman Commands* (1932), where it was sung by Pola Negri. Early successful records were made by Guy Lombardo and the Royal Canadians,

Morton Downey, Phil Spitalny, and Russ Morgan, who used it as his theme song for a time. Later records were made by Frank Sinatra, Hal Kemp (vocal by Nan Wynn), Eddy Howard, Ray Anthony, Dorothy Lamour, Helen Forrest, Frances Langford, and Nat King Cole. In the movies it was performed by Belita in *The Gangster* (1947), Gloria Grahame in *A Woman's Secret* (1949), Valentina Cortesa in *Malaya* (1949), and Bob Crosby in *The Five Pennies* (1959).

"Peaceful Valley" (1925) is a lazy song of contentment by Willard Robison that found success in both the pop song category and with country-western artists. The lyric looks back at growing up in Peaceful Valley where even a turtle lying dead in a dried-up creek has a satisfied look on its face. The song was introduced by Robison's Deep River Five but popularized by Paul Whiteman and his Orchestra, who used it as their theme song for a while. Interest in "Peaceful Valley" was revived when it was featured in the film *Arkansas Judge* (1941). Charlie Barnet, Red Nichols and his Five Pennies, Fletcher Henderson, Mildred Bailey, and Christine and the Rangers are among those who also recorded it.

"The Peanut Vendor" (1930) is a rhumba standard from Cuba that crossed over to become a Tin Pan Alley hit recorded by a wide variety of artists. "El Manisero," with its rhythmic music by Moises Simons, was a popular number in Cuba, and the tune was brought to the States by visiting marimba bands. But when Marion Sunshine and L. Wolfe Gilbert wrote an English lyric and the new song was introduced by Don Azpiazu and his Havana Casino Orchestra at the Palace Theatre in New York, it immediately found favor, and there were major sheet music sales and many records, including hits by Paul Whiteman, Louis Armstrong, Guy Lombardo, and Xavier Cugat. The lyric is a silly sales pitch with the peanut vendor hawking his wares by proclaiming that 50 million "little monkeys can't be wrong." In addition to many Spanish recordings, there were noteworthy discs by Stan Kenton, Perez Prado, Ted Heath, Desi Arnaz, Morton Gould, Duke Ellington, Billy Vaughn, Tex Beneke, Woody Herman, Jimmy Dorsey, Ralph Marterie, and Chet Baker. The zesty number was interpolated into the movie *The Cuban Love Song* (1931), where it was sung by Lawrence Tibbett, and years later it was performed by Jane Powell in *Luxury Liner* (1948) and Judy Garland in *A Star Is Born* (1954). More recently it was played on the soundtrack of *Sweet and Lowdown* (1999) by guitarist Howard Alden, and the Prado recording was heard in *Office Space* (1999).

"Peg o' My Heart" (1913) was associated with actress Laurette Taylor for many years even though she never sang the song. Taylor's performance as the spunky Irish girl Peg in the Broadway play *Peg o' My Heart* (1912) inspired Alfred Bryan (lyric) and Fred Fisher (music) to write the catchy tune that gushes over Peg, proclaiming that "it's your Irish heart I'm after." Taylor's picture was printed on the sheet music cover, and she was identified with it for all of her life. Charles Harrison was the performer to popularize the ballad, and it was interpolated into the *Ziegfeld Follies of 1913*, where it was sung by José Collins. In the 1920s, Red Nichols and his Five Pennies made a jazz version that became a hit. After many more records it was revived in yet a new format, as an instrumental piece by Jerry Murad's Harmonicats in 1947, and the recording went to the top of the charts. "Peg o' My Heart" became a harmonica standard and has been thought of that way ever since. Of the many well-known recordings were those by Henry Burr, Lester Young, Josephine Baker, Glenn Miller, Bunny Berigan, Phil Regan, Clark Dennis, the Three Suns, Eddie Howard, Buddy Clark, Peggy Lee, Dean Martin, Joni James, and Andy Williams. Ann Blyth sang the ballad in the movie *Babes on Swing Street* (1944), and it can be heard in *Peg o' My Heart* (1933) and *Oh, You Beautiful Doll* (1949).

"Pennsylvania 6–5000" (1940) is Tin Pan Alley's most celebrated phone number, the telephone exchange for Manhattan's Hotel Pennsylvania from which Glenn Miller and his Orchestra played and broadcast for years. Carl Sigman (lyric) and Jerry Gray (music) wrote the swinging number saluting the famous landmark, and it was a regular feature on Miller's broadcast. A recording by Miller with the band doing the vocals sold over a million discs, and they reprised it in the film bio *The Glenn Miller Story* (1954). Even though the number was identified with Miller, there were also successful recordings by the Andrews Sisters, Ted Heath, Tex Beneke, Jive Bunny and the Mastermixers, the Brian Setzer Orchestra, and Max Greger.

"Penthouse Serenade (When We're Alone)" (1931) is a soothing ballad by Will Jason and Val Burton that pictures a penthouse apartment in the sky where two lovers can live like "heavenly hermits." The graceful music consists of a series of descending notes that create a highly romantic aura, and the lyric seems to whisper to one. Anita O'Day, Vera Lynn, Erroll Garner, Eddie Heywood, Sarah Vaughan, Dick Haymes, Les Brown, and Tony Bennett are among the many who had successful discs of the song, and recently there have been recordings by Bobby Short, Tommy Tune, and Chris Flory. Vera Miles (dubbed by Imogene Lynn) sang it in the movie *Beau James* (1957), and it can also be heard in *Strange Love of Molly Louvain* (1932), *Sweetheart of Sigma Chi* (1946), and *Sarge Goes to College* (1947).

"Perdido" (1942) is a Spanish instrumental piece that became a hit song on Tin Pan Alley when brought to America. Juan Tizol composed the lilting music, which was introduced in the States with a popular record by Duke Ellington and his Orchestra. Other discs followed (most memorably one by Flip Phillips and Illinois Jacquet), but the number found greater renown when Hans Lengsfelder and Ervin Drake added a tearful lyric about a love that has been "lost" (*perdido*). Among the numerous recordings made were those by Louis Armstrong, Dave Lambert and Buddy Stewart, Gene Krupa, Oscar Pettiford, Stan Freeman, Ella Fitzgerald, Ray Anthony, Count Basie, Gloria Lynn, Erroll Garner, the Dave Brubeck Quartet, Woody Herman, Carmen McRae, Sarah Vaughan, Dizzy Gillespie, Art Tatum, the Three Suns, and Joe Augustine, as well as many Spanish artists.

"Perfidia" (1941) is a slightly swinging song from Mexico that was popular as a Big Band number in the 1940s and a crooning ballad in the 1950s. Alberto Dominquez wrote the rhythmic ballad that was translated into English by Milton Leeds into an upbeat lament about a beloved who is fascinating but far from faithful. (*Perfidia* is Spanish for unfaithfulness or betrayal.) The English version was first heard in the film *Father Takes a Wife* (1941) and popularized by Glenn Miller with a bestselling record with vocals by Dorothy Claire and the Modernaires. More successful records followed, as well as major sheet music sales, and the song remained on *Your Hit Parade* for sixteen weeks. Xavier Cugat, Benny Goodman (vocal by Helen Forrest), and Jimmy Dorsey were among those who had hits with it the 1940s; then it was revived in 1952 by a disc by the Four Aces that climbed the charts. Other artists who have recorded the ballad include Fats Waller, Billy May, Perez Prado, Nat King Cole, Mantovanni's Orchestra, the Ventures, Ethel Smith, Susan and the Surftones, Jerry Murad's Harmonicats, Trini Lopez, and Julio Iglesias. "Perfidia" can be heard in the movies *Stardust on the Stage* (1942), *Casablanca* (1942), *Masquerade in Mexico* (1945), and *The Mambo Kings* (1992). David Engel and the cast of the Off-Broadway revue *Forever Plaid* (1990) sang the song in English and Spanish.

"Peter Cottontail" (1950), one of the few secular songs about Easter to become a hit, is a bouncy ditty by Steve Nelson and Jack Rollins that was popular throughout the 1950s and is still recognized today. The happy number celebrates the coming of spring when the Easter rabbit Peter is sighted "hoppin' down the bunny trail." The music seems to hop as well, as the lyric lists some of the goodies he has in his basket. Gene Autry popularized the song with a hit record, and country singer Mervin Shiner had even more success with it, his disc selling over a million copies. Fran Allison, Jimmy Wakely, Rosemary Clooney, Hank Snow, and Bob Crosby and the Bobcats are among the many who also recorded it. Autry reprised the song in the film *Hills of Utah* (1951), and it was heard in *Loving You* (1957).

"The Picture That Is Turned to the Wall" (1891) is a melodramatic narrative ballad that is all but a cliché today, but it reduced listeners to tears at the end of the nineteenth century. Charles Graham was inspired to write the song after seeing the hit play *Blue Jeans* (1890) in which a farmer renounces his wayward daughter by turning her picture over so that it faces the wall. The number was first heard when Irish tenor Andrew Mack interpolated it into the Broadway show *The City Directory* (1891). Graham was only paid $15 for the song, and it went on to sell thousands of copies of sheet music and became a staple in vaudeville for years. Julie Witmark performed it in variety and on the minstrel circuit and was long associated with the ballad. There were also early records by George J. Gaskin and the Manhansett Quartet that were successful. June Haver sang the number in the period film *The Daughter of Rosie O'Grady* (1950).

"Pink Elephants" (1932), a novelty song about the nasty side effects of drinking, found popularity in post-Prohibition America and popularized the cliché about seeing pink elephants when intoxicated. Mort Dixon (lyric) and Harry Woods (music) wrote the odd song, and it found fame when featured on the radio by Ben Bernie and Rudy Vallee. Recordings were made by the Joe Venuti–Eddie Lang Blue Five, Gene Kardos (vocal by Harry Goldfield), Phil Harris, Ernie Carson, Mick Harvey, and Bertrand Burgalat. The number is not to be confused with the song "Pink Elephants on Parade" that was written for the animated film *Dumbo* (1941) to illustrate a surreal alcoholic stupor, though it was no doubt inspired by the earlier ditty.

"Pistol Packin' Mama" (1943) is the hillbilly classic that crossed over to all markets and was a familiar favorite for years. Al Dexter got the idea for the song when he was in a Texas honky-tonk saloon and saw one woman chase another female with a gun, warning her to keep her hands off her husband. The lyric is a mocking narrative about an unfaithful husband named Al Dexter whose jealous wife is after him with a gun. Although he pleads several times to "lay that pistol down, babe," she ends up shooting him dead. The uptempo music is in a blues format yet bounces along like a travel song, so the number never gets too serious. "Pistol Packin' Mama" was introduced on record by Dexter and his Troopers, but it found wider recognition when Bing Crosby and the Andrews Sisters teamed up for a disc that sold over a million copies. Other well-known recordings were made by Boxcar Willie, Arthur Godfrey, Jo

Stafford, Harry James, the Pied Pipers, Big Jack Johnson, Charlie Walker, Roy Rogers, Hoyt Axton, Bill Haley, Jack Mudurian, and Jo Ann Castle. The novelty number can be heard in the movies *Pistol Packin' Mama* (1943) and *Beautiful But Broke* (1944).

"Play That Barbershop Chord" (1910), a perennial favorite with barbershop quartets, is a spirited number in which a lady beseeches the pianist Jefferson to play some of those harmonizing songs she loves so well. Lewis Muir composed the lively music, but there is some dispute over who wrote the lyric. Ballard MacDonald was the hired lyricist, but it is believed that the words used were by William Tracey, whose name appeared on the sheet music. When the song became a hit, MacDonald sued and got $37,000 in damages; yet the true authorship has never been determined. Bert Williams introduced the song at Hammerstein's Victoria Theatre in New York, and he reprised it in the *Ziegfeld Follies of 1910*. Sheet music sales were considerable, and choral groups of all kinds sang it throughout the 1910s. As the interest in barbershop quartets waned in the depression, the song seemed to disappear until Judy Garland sang it with a male quartet in the movie *In the Good Old Summertime* (1949). Garland's record was a hit, and there was a later disc by Chris Tyle's Silver Leaf Jazz Band that is distinctive.

"Please Be Kind" (1938) is an apologetic ballad by Sammy Cahn (lyric) and Saul Chaplin (music) that was an immediate hit when introduced by Red Norvo and his Orchestra (vocal by Mildred Bailey) on record. Other leading discs were made by Benny Goodman (vocal by Martha Tilton), Bob Crosby (vocal by Kay Weber), and the Original Dixieland Band, and the number was revived in 1946 with a hit record by Charlie Ventura and his Orchestra. Other versions were made by Carmen McRae, June Christy, Art Tatum, Gloria Lynne, Stan Kenton, Peggy Lee, Maxine Sullivan, Ella Fitzgerald, Bobby Hackett, Django Reinhardt, and Sarah Vaughan.

"Please Don't Eat the Daisies" (1960) is a repetitive little ditty by Joe Lubin that has long been associated with Doris Day. The silly title comes from a book by Jean Kerr that was fashioned into a movie in 1960 where Day sang it with some children. Day's disc version was very popular, and the number still shows up on children's records.

"Please, Mr. Sun" (1952), one of the heartbreaking "crying" ballads that were so popular in the 1950s, takes the form of a sentimental prayer to nature. Sid Frank (lyric) and Ray Getzov (music) wrote the number for Tommy Edwards who recorded it with modest success. But Johnnie Ray's disc with Jimmy Carroll's Orchestra sold a million copies and prompted subsequent hits for Perry Como and Doris Day. The number resurfaced in 1966 when the Vogues had success with it as well. Keely Smith, Les Baxter, the Innocents, Buddy Morrow, and Paul Peterson were among those who also recorded it. The Ray version can be heard in the film *The Last Picture Show* (1971).

"Poinciana (Song of the Tree)" (1943) is a passionate Spanish song by Manuel Cliso (lyric) and Nat Simon (music) that has a driving but romantic beat. Buddy Bernier wrote the English lyric about a song of love that comes from the trees and creates a "rhythmic savage beat" inside of one. Bing Crosby popularized the ballad in America, and there were also hit instrumental versions by the orchestras of Benny Carter and David Rose. Among the many artists who also recorded the song are Kay Kyser, Tex Beneke with Garry Stevens, George Shearing, Frank Sinatra, Glenn Miller, Nat King Cole, the Four Freshmen, Art Van Damme, the Starlighters, Dorothy Kirsten, Dave Brubeck, Chet Atkins, Robert Goulet, Ethel Smith, Steve Lawrence, the Manhattan Transfer, and Ahmad Jamal.

"Polka Dots and Moonbeams" (1940) is a domestic ballad with a strong rhythmic pattern that makes it both cozy and lively. Jimmy Van Heusen composed the radiant music that uses a series of ascending and descending notes as its main musical strain. Johnny Burke wrote the warm lyric about seeing polka dots and moonbeams at the dance when they first met; now that they are long married and settled down, they still see them. The song was popularized by hit records by Tommy Dorsey (vocal by Frank Sinatra) and Glenn Miller (vocal by Ray Eberly). Subsequent discs were made by Bill Evans, Sylvia Syms, Mel Tormé, Jerry Murad's Harmonicats, Dexter Gordon, Sarah Vaughan, Count Basie, Chet Baker, the Ray Brown Trio, Harry Allen, Paul Desmond, John Denver, and Marian McPartland.

"Polly Wolly Doodle" (c. 1883), one of the earliest and most popular nonsense songs in American music, is a farewell song about leaving for the South to see a gal who sings "polly wolly doodle" all day long. The authorship is unknown, but the song goes back to the post–Civil War years when it was a traditional number in minstrel shows. The merry ditty was most often associated with minstrel Billy Emerson, but it seemed everyone was singing it by the end of the century. Later "Polly Wolly Doodle" was mostly thought of as a children's song, especially when it was performed on screen by child stars Shirley Temple in *The Littlest Rebel* (1935) and Bobby Breen in *Make a Wish* (1937). It can also be heard in the movies *Colorado* (1940), *My Wild Irish Rose* (1947), and *Pocketful of Miracles* (1961). In addition to many children's records, there were discs by Red Norvo, Lawrence Welk, Burl Ives, Boxcar Willie, and the Carter Family.

"Poor Butterfly" (1916) is an unusual Tin Pan Alley hit in that it is about an opera character and was much admired by the public, many of whom were not even familiar with *Madame Butterfly*. John Golden (lyric) and Raymond Hubbell (music) wrote the sympathetic ballad about Puccini's heroine who waits for her American lover to return to Japan, knowing she will die if he doesn't come back. It was introduced by Haru Onukie in a Hippodrome spectacular called *The Big Show* (1916) but caused no stir, not even when Onuke was replaced by Sophie Bernard. It was early recordings by Edna Brown, the Joseph C. Smith Orchestra, and the Victor Military Band that popularized the song, and soon the whole country was "butterfly" crazy. Over 2 million copies of sheet music were sold, dozens of recordings flooded the market, and it seemed the number was included in every dance and concert. Among the most notable of the later recordings were those by Sarah Vaughan, Red Nichols and the Five Pennies, Count Basie, Carmen McRae, Nat King Cole, the Benny Goodman Sextet, Paul Desmond, Deanna Durbin, Al Hibbler, the Pied Pipers, Fritz Kreisler, Zoot Sims, the Three Suns, Sonny Rollins, the Hilltoppers, Teddy Wilson, Vikki Carr, and Kenny Burrell. Julie Andrews sang "Poor Butterfly" in the movie *Thoroughly Modern Millie* (1967), and the Nichols recording was heard on the soundtrack of *Bullets Over Broadway* (1994).

"Pop Goes the Weasel" (1853), the famous nonsense song that has been sung by children and adults since the seventeenth century, originated in England and is believed to have been brought to America by the Pilgrims. It was widely known and sung in the colonial days, and is still recognized today. While there have been many versions of the song, one by Charles Twiggs that was published in 1853 is the most familiar. The silly lyric contains many verses about money disappearing when it is needed for necessities, and it is taken as a nonsense song today. But in England "pop" was slang for "pawn," and "weasels" were one's tools of the trade, so the number is really about having to pawn your means of livelihood when funds are low. Somewhere over the years the song became associated with the toy jack-in-the-box, the puppet popping out on the title phrase. Deanna Durbin sang the ditty in the film *Lady on a Train* (1945), and maestro Arthur Rubinstein played it on the piano for his children in *Of Men and Music* (1951). The tune can still be heard on many children's records.

"Powder Your Face With Sunshine (Smile! Smile! Smile!)" (1948) is a sing-along favorite that looks at life optimistically and encourages one to face adversity with a smile. The sunny lyric was written by Stanley

Rochinski, a paraplegic who practiced what he preached: When Guy Lombardo's Orchestra was in town, Rochinski went to Carmen Lombardo's hotel room in a wheelchair and presented it to him. Lombardo polished the lyric in a few spots and composed the tuneful music. Guy Lombardo and the Royal Canadians introduced the number in a Washington, D.C. concert, with Carmen Lombardo doing the vocals. But it was a record by Evelyn Knight with the Stardusters that reached the top of the charts and turned the song into a familiar favorite. The Lombardos also had a successful disc, followed by well-known recordings by Sammy Kaye (vocals by the Three Kaydets), Doris Day and Buddy Clark, Blue Barron, Orrin Tucker and Bonnie Baker, Dean Martin, and Kay Starr. Gene Autry sang the number in the movie *Cow Town* (1950).

"Praise the Lord and Pass the Ammunition" (1942) is the popular World War Two ditty that launched Frank Loesser's career as a composer as well as a lyricist. Right after the attack on Pearl Harbor, Loesser wrote a simple lyric based on a phrase attributed to U.S. Navy chaplain William McGuire during the Honolulu battle. Since the entire lyric consisted of repeating the title phrase with the tag "and we'll all be free," he created a rhythmic "dummy" tune to hold the song together until he enlisted the aid of a composer. But when Loesser played the number for friends, they suggested he keep the melody as it was. Kay Kyser (vocal by the Glee Club) recorded it, and it quickly sold a million copies—Loesser's first hit as a composer-lyricist and the first successful patriotic song of the war. Other records followed, selling over 2 million discs, and sheet music sales topped a million as well. The song was so popular that the Office of War Information requested that radio stations not play it more frequently than every four hours so that it would not become overdone and lose its potency. The Merry Macs, Nelson Eddy, Bob Grant, the Southern Sons Quartette, Joan Edwards, Jimmy Carroll, the Young Pioneers, and Loesser himself are among those who made major recordings. The revivallike number was also sung by the cast of the Off-Broadway revue *Swingtime Canteen* (1995).

"Pretty Baby" (1915) is an adoring love song by Gus Kahn (lyric), Tony Jackson, and Egbert Van Alstyne (music) that uses baby and child images to describe and worship a sweetheart, asking her to "let me rock you in my cradle of love." The jazzy number was interpolated into the Broadway musical *A World of Pleasure* (1915) and was used the next year in the *Passing Show of 1916*, where it was performed by Dolly Brackett and the girls' chorus. Early hit records by Al Jolson and Eddie Cantor brought recognition to the song, and by the 1920s it was performed everywhere, from concerts to speakeasies. Notable records were also made by Jelly Roll Morton, Bob Scoby's Frisco Band, Doris Day, Earl

Hines, Bo Carter, Betty Grable, Willie Dixon, Jimmie Rogers, the Five
Satins, Brenda Lee, Tiny Tim, and Perry Como. "Pretty Baby" has been
used in no less than fourteen films, sung by Jolson in *Rose of Washington
Square* (1939) and on the soundtrack of *Jolson Sings Again* (1949), Gloria
DeHaven and Charles Winninger in *Broadway Rhythm* (1944), Grable in
Coney Island (1943), Robert Alda in *April Showers* (1948), Danny Thomas
in *I'll See You in My Dreams* (1952), and Eddie Cantor providing the
singing for Keefe Brasselle in *The Eddie Cantor Story* (1953). The song can
also be heard in *Applause* (1929), *She Done Him Wrong* (1933), *Ruggles of
Red Gap* (1935), *Is Everybody Happy?* (1943), *Shine On Harvest Moon* (1944),
The I-Don't-Care Girl (1953), and *Pretty Baby* (1978).

"Prisoner of Love" (1931) is a bombastic ballad that found success in the
1930s and 1940s, then again in the 1960s. Russ Columbo and Clarence
Gaskill composed the lush music that builds to a crescendo a couple of
times, and Leo Robin wrote the passionate lyric that compares being in
love to a prisoner in chains. Columbo introduced the number with his
orchestra on record, and it enjoyed some popularity throughout the decade. But a Perry Como disc in 1946 sold a million copies and put the
song on *Your Hit Parade* for fifteen weeks. James Brown revived it in
1963 with the Fabulous Flames, and their record climbed the charts also.
Other memorable recordings were made by Billy Eckstine, the Ink Spots,
Jo Stafford with Red Ingle, Benny Carter, Lena Horne, Frank Sinatra,
Teddy Wilson, Etta James, Art Tatum, Keely Smith, the Platters, Ace
Cannon, Connie Francis, and Pat Benatar. "Prisoner of Love" can be
heard in the movies *Night World* (1932) and *Raging Bull* (1980).

"The Prisoner's Song" (1924) was a giant Tin Pan Alley hit by Guy
Massey who sent it to a publisher, earned a substantial royalty, yet never
wrote another song. The morose ballad is the painful lament of a prisoner
being transferred to a different jail, thinking about his faraway darling,
and contemplating resting his head on "a pillow of stone." Massey had
never been in prison, but the song promoters sent out word that the
songwriter was a jailbird in order to create human interest. They needn't
have bothered, for the ballad was an immediate hit when Vernon Dalhart's nasal country-flavored recording sold 2 million discs, prompting
sheet music sales over a million. Dalhart sang the song throughout his
career, even recording it again under different labels and using a pseudonym. A 1938 disc by Bunny Berigan is considered the definitive recording, but there were also significant discs by Eddy Arnold, Rosemary
Clooney, Fats Domino, Sonny Burgess, the Osborne Brothers, Chet Atkins, Adam Wade, Warren Storm, Louis Armstrong, Wingy Manone, the
Dave Brubeck Octet, and Bill Monroe. Sometimes titled "If I Had the

Wings of an Angel," the number was heard in the films *Honey* (1930) and *Dangerous Nan McGrew* (1930).

"P.S. I Love You" (1934) is a love song in the form of a letter, most of which is filled with banal trivialities about the family and the weather but concluding with an affectionate postscript. Johnny Mercer wrote the clever lyric, and bandleader Gordon Jenkins composed the gentle music. Although Jenkins recorded it, discs by Rudy Vallee, Glen Gray and the Casa Loma Orchestra, Jack Fulton, and Eddie Stone were much more successful. Billy Vaughn had his first hit record with the ballad, and the Hilltoppers revived it in 1953, selling a million copies. Other recordings of note were made by Rosemary Clooney, Dick Haymes, Red Nichols, Billie Holiday, Woody Herman, Bing Crosby, Kay Starr, and George Shearing. Bette Midler sang "P.S. I Love You" in the film *For the Boys* (1991) and the number has recently been recorded by Vicki Stuart, Susannah McCorkle, and Diana Krall.

"Put On Your Old Gray Bonnet" (1909) is a stimulating march number that later became popular in several genres, from jazz to country. Percy Wendrich composed the lively music, and Stanley Murphy wrote the lyric, a marriage proposal asking a sweetheart to put on her bonnet, he'll hitch up the wagon, and they'll drive to Denver for their wedding. The original lyric referred to her "sun" bonnet (which makes more sense for a wedding), but the publishers thought the songwriters sang "gray bonnet" when they auditioned it, and so it was published that way. The number was a sing-along favorite in the early decades of the century, and later there were recordings by such varied artists as the Mills Brothers, Coleman Hawkins, Jimmy Durante and Helen Traubel, the Sons of the Pioneers, Jimmie Lunceford, Frank Sinatra, Percy Humphrey, and Glen Gray and the Casa Loma Orchestra. The uptempo song can be heard in the movies *It All Came True* (1940), *Here Comes Elmer* (1943), and *April Showers* (1948).

"Put the Blame on Mame" (1946) is a tongue-in-cheek number by Doris Fisher and Allan Roberts that is most remembered for Rita Hayworth's sexy slinky rendition of it in the film *Gilda* (1946). Although the song was written for Hayworth to sing in the movie, Anita Ellis provided the vocal on the soundtrack for the star. The droll lyric suggests that the femme fatale Mame can be blamed for the Chicago fire, the San Francisco earthquake, the California gold rush, and other historic events. Jeanette Davis with Archie Blyer's Orchestra, Quinn Lemley, Nat Gonella and his New Georgians, Christiane Noll, Cheryl Serio, and Mark Murphy also recorded the wry number. It can also be heard in the films *Betty Co-Ed* (1946) and *Senior Prom* (1958).

"Put Your Arms Around Me, Honey" (1910) is a warm "cuddle-up" standard by Junie McCree (lyric) and Albert Von Tilzer (music) that is equally effective when performed as a slow and sincere ballad as when played as a lively, uptempo number. The lyric is both affectionate and slangy, yet the slang doesn't seem to date the song at all. It was introduced by Byron Collins and Arthur Harlan in vaudeville and on record, then was interpolated into the Broadway musical *Madame Sherry* (1910) after opening, where it was performed by Elizabeth Murray. When the show toured across the country, the song became popular, helped by Blossom Seeley who took it on the vaudeville circuit. Dick Haymes revived the ballad with a hit record in 1943, and Fats Domino did the same in 1961. Other artists to make disc versions include Al Jolson, Tiny Hill, Glenn Miller with the Crew Chiefs, Ella Mae Morse, Judy Garland, Perry Como, Hank Snow, the Vamps, the Moms and Dads, Merle Travis, and Vikki Carr. On screen it was sung by Betty Grable in *Coney Island* (1943), Judy Canova in *Louisiana Hayride* (1944), and Garland with Van Johnson in *In the Good Old Summer Time* (1949). It was also used in *In Old Oklahoma* (1943), *Slightly Terrific* (1944), *Mother Wore Tights* (1947), and *Ever After* (1998).

"Put Your Dreams Away (For Another Day)" (1942), Frank Sinatra's theme song on the radio for several years, is a flowing ballad by Ruth Lowe (lyric), Stephen Weiss, and Paul Mann (music) about a real love replacing one's dreams. The tender lyric asks a beloved to take one's love and put it in her heart when she finds her dreams fade away at night. Sinatra's record with Alex Stordahl's Orchestra was the leading disc, but there were others by Eileen Farrell, the Cliff Adams Singers, Charlie Schaffer, the Hi-Lo's, Barry Manilow, and Frank Sinatra Jr. The number can also be heard in the film *Lolita* (1962).

"Put Your Head on My Shoulder" (1958) is an old-fashioned fox trot number by Paul Anka that managed to become a hit even as rock-and-roll was overtaking the market. The slow and dreamy ballad simply asks a loved one to come close and be comforted. Anka's recording was a hit, but just as successful were later discs by the Lettermen in 1969 and by sixteen-year-old Leif Garrett in 1978. The Beach Boys and Jerry Vale also made discs, and lately it has been recorded by Linda Ronstadt, Maureen McGovern, and P.J. Proby.

Q–R

"Que Sera, Sera (Whatever Will Be, Will Be)" (1956) is the Oscar-winning song of acceptance that became Doris Day's theme song later in her career. Jay Livingston and Ray Evans wrote the cheerful number about taking what life brings you, noting that the future is "not ours to see." It was introduced by Day in the movie *The Man Who Knew Too Much* (1956), and her record sold over a million copies. She reprised it in the films *Please Don't Eat the Daisies* (1960) and *The Glass Bottom Boat* (1966). In addition to many Spanish artists and children's discs, the song was also recorded by the Shirelles, Connie Francis, the Killarney Singers, Holly Cole, Anton Karas, and Johnny Thunders.

"Quien Sabe? (Who Knows?)" (1947) is a questioning ballad by Jimmy O'Keefe, Jack Fulton, and Dick Cunliffe that was, despite its Spanish title, a homegrown hit. Jimmy Dorsey and his Orchestra (vocals by Dee Parker and Bob Carroll) popularized the song with a successful record, and there were also noteworthy discs by Johnny Blas and Stan Kenton and his Orchestra.

"Racing With the Moon" (1941), the theme song for singer-bandleader Vaughn Monroe, is a dreamy ballad about flying high in the sky at midnight, pursuing both the moon and a love that always seems to fade from view. Monroe wrote the sublime lyric with Pauline Pope, and Johnny Watson composed the gliding fox trot music. Monroe and his Orchestra recorded the number with success and he sang it throughout his career on the radio and in concert. A distinctive jazz version was made by Bob Wilber years later.

"Rag Mop" (1950) is one of the most popular nonsense songs of the 1950s, a cheerful ditty that is actually about a rag mop and not much else. Johnnie Lee Wills and Deacon Anderson wrote the silly spelling song that rhythmically bounces through the alphabet to reach the correct letters to spell out "rag mop." The Ames Brothers popularized the novelty number with a record that sold over a million copies. There were other hit discs by Wills, Ralph Flanagan (vocal by Harry Prince), and Lionel Hampton (vocal by the Hamptones). Other records of note were made by Pee Wee King, the Davis Sisters, Jimmy Dorsey, Bob Crosby and the Bobcats, Joe Lutcher, the Mighty Blue Kings, Joe Liggins and the Honeydippers, and Johnny Carroll. The vigorous song can be heard in the movie *Honeychile* (1951) and was sung by the cast of the Off-Broadway revue *The Taffetas* (1988).

"Rags to Riches" (1953) is an upbeat love song that has a cha-cha beat in sections of the music yet can be sung in a crying manner typical of the "wailing" ballads popular at the time. Richard Adler and Jerry Ross, before they found fame as Broadway songwriters with *The Pajama Game* (1954), wrote the catchy number in which a suitor exclaims that her love for him has made a millionaire out of a pauper. Tony Bennett introduced the song, and his record with Percy Faith's Orchestra sold over 2 million copies, hitting the top of the charts and the Number One spot on the *Hit Parade*. Among the other artists who recorded it were Elvis Presley, Keely Smith, Billy Ward and the Dominoes, Jack Jones, Norman Hedman, Quint Black, Lenny Welch, Jackie Wilson, and Gene Pitney. David Engel sang the ballad in the Off-Broadway revue *Forever Plaid* (1990), and it was heard in the film *Goodfellas* (1990).

"Ragtime Cowboy Joe" (1912), a ragtime standard that was also a favorite of barbershop quartets, tells the story of an Arizona cowpoke who sang "raggy" music to his cattle and wowed all the girls in town with his "basso" singing voice. Lewis F. Muir, Grant Clarke, and Maurice Abrahams collaborated on the piquant number that was introduced by Bob Roberts with a hit record. The oft-revived song also saw hits by Pinky Tomlin in 1939, Eddy Howard in 1947, Jo Stafford in 1949, and the Chipmunks in 1959. Among the other artists to record it were the Pied Pipers, Dale Evans, Tiny Hill, Alice Faye, Jimmy Durante, Russ Conway, Ronnie Kemper, Jo Ann Castle, and Jack Mudurian and a parody version by Spike Jones and his City Slickers. Faye sang it with Jack Oakie and June Haver in the movie *Hello, Frisco, Hello* (1943), and Betty Hutton performed it in *Incendiary Blonde* (1945).

"The Ragtime Violin" (1911) is an early Irving Berlin number that enjoyed some fame until it was surpassed by his own similar song "Alexander's Ragtime Band" that same year. The sparkling song about a violinist who plays in tempo with the new sound was popularized by a hit record by the American Quartet. By World War One it was pretty much forgotten, though it did reappear in the movies years later, sung by Alice Faye, Dixie Dunbar, and Wally Vernon in *Alexander's Ragtime Band* (1938) and by Fred Astaire and Judy Garland in a medley in *Easter Parade* (1948).

"Rainbow Valley" (1939) is an atmospheric ballad by Edgar Leslie (lyric) and Joe Burke (music) about a peaceful and dreamy location. The song was popularized on the radio and on records by Sammy Kaye (vocal by Tommy Ryan) and Dick Jurgens (vocal by Eddy Howard). There were other well-known discs by Guy Lombardo, Joseph Sudy, the Shirelles, the Statler Brothers, and the Heptones.

"Rambling Rose" (1948) is a gentle rhythm song by Joseph Allen Mc-Carthy (lyric) and Joe Burke (music) about a wild and carefree gal ("mother nature's favorite child") that a beau hopes to win and train to become "a clinging vine." A record by Perry Como with Russ Case's Orchestra brought attention to the song, and there were also successful discs by Gordon MacRae with the Starlighters, Phil Brito with Richard Maltby's Orchestra, and Dean Martin. The ballad is not to be confused with the 1962 hit "Ramblin' Rose" popularized by Nat King Cole.

"Ramona" (1927) is a delicate ballad with a Latin tempo that sings the praises of Ramona, a departed beauty whom one hopes to meet again someday by a waterfall. L. Wolfe Gilbert (lyric) and Mabel Wayne (music) wrote the number to promote the silent film *Ramona* (1928), but the song caught on before the movie was released because of a unique radio broadcast: Paul Whiteman's Orchestra played it in New York, while Dolores Del Rio sang it in Los Angeles. Whiteman recorded the ballad with Gene Austin doing the vocal, and it sold over 2 million discs, which led to the sales of over 2 million copies of sheet music. Never completely forgotten, "Ramona" was revived by Billy Walker in 1968 with a country-western record that climbed the charts. Other artists to make major records include Gordon MacRae, Bob Grant, Jimmie Davis, Benny Goodman, George Shearing, Les Brown, Bix Beiderbecke, Jack Smith, Eddie Fisher, the Bachelors, and Jim Reeves.

"Reaching for Someone (And Not Finding Anyone There)" (1929) is a tearful lament by Edgar Leslie (lyric) and Walter Donaldson (music) that was popularized by a celebrated recording by Paul Whiteman and his Orchestra featuring Bix Beiderbecke on cornet and the vocal by Bing Crosby. Other successful discs were made by George Olsen (vocal by

Fran Frey), Frankie Trumbauer, Cliff Edwards, Vaughn Deleath, and Leon Redbone.

"Red Hot Mama" (1924) was written for Sophie Tucker who billed herself as the "last of the red hot mamas" and sang this number as a sort of signature tune. Gilbert Wells, Bud Cooper, and Fred Rose collaborated on the sassy song about a liberated lady who is always ready for partying and loving, and Tucker introduced it on record before adding it to her act. The jazzy number was also recorded by Jimmy O'Bryant, Freddie "Schnickelfritz" Fisher, Beatrice Kay, the Coon-Sanders Nighthawks Orchestra, Fletcher Henderson, Ray Miller, Paul James, George Clinton, Rue Davis, and Ronnie Dawson. Libi Staiger sang it in the short-lived Broadway musical *Sophie* (1963).

"Red River Valley" (1896), the traditional American folk song standard, did not come from the prairie or the Southwest but from Tin Pan Alley. James J. Kerrigan wrote a number called "In the Bright Mohawk Valley" about upstate New York, and its sheet music was widely distributed. Settlers out west took the song and rewrote it, simplifying the music and changing the lyric so that it was set in the Texas Panhandle. That version caught on quickly, and it is the folk song most know and love today. The ballad is a simple but poignant farewell to a beloved who is leaving the valley, asking if the departing one will remember both the place and person left behind. Although it was never out of favor, the number enjoyed a revival of interest when it was used throughout the classic film *The Grapes of Wrath* (1940) as a leitmotif. It was also featured in *Red River Valley* (1936), *Git Along Little Dogies* (1937), and other westerns. Among the many to record it were Gene Autry, the Sons of the Pioneers, Jo Stafford, Marty Robbins, Boxcar Willie, Bob Wills and his Texas Playboys, Lester Lanin, Dick Curless, Ace Cannon, Woody Guthrie, the Andrews Sisters, and Roy Rogers. There have also been successful variations of the song over the years. The Firehouse Five Plus Two jazzed it up as "Red Hot River Valley," Johnny Cash sang a ditty called "Please Don't Sing Red River Valley," and in 1959 Tom King, Ira Mack, and Fred Mendelsohn adapted it into a rock number called "Red River Rock" that was a hit record for Johnny and the Hurricanes.

"Red Roses for a Blue Lady" (1948) is a soothing fox trot number by Sid Yepper and Roy Brodsky in which a beau orders flowers from a florist, hoping to cheer up his depressed darling. The gentle ballad was popularized by Guy Lombardo and the Royal Canadians, but Vaughn Monroe's subsequent record climbed to the Top 10. The song was revived in 1965 by two highly successful discs: Bert Kaempfert's instrumental version and Vic Dana's vocal solo. Notable records were also made by Wayne Newton, Al Martino, Floyd Cramer, Eddy Arnold, Duke Ellington, Woody Herman, Roger Whitaker, the Moms and Dads, Ace Cannon, and the Ray Conniff Singers.

"Red Sails in the Sunset" (1935) is a British song that was equally popular on both sides of the Atlantic during the 1930s, and it is still widely known. Hugh Williams (a.k.a. Will Grosz) composed the gliding music that brings sailing to mind, and Jimmy Kennedy penned the potent lyric about a girl watching the boats in the harbor, their sails turned to red in the setting sun, and hoping one such ship will bring her beloved back home safely to her. America was introduced to the English ballad when it was interpolated into the revue *Provincetown Follies* (1935), where it was sung by Phyllis Austin. Bing Crosby's subsequent recording sold a million discs, prompted plenty of radio play, and pushed sheet music sales over the million mark. There were also early successful discs by Ray Noble and Guy Lombardo and the Royal Canadians. "Red Sails in the Sunset" was revived with a hit record by Nat King Cole in 1951. Prominent discs by other artists include those by Les Brown, Louis Armstrong, Fats Domino, the Platters, Sil Austin, the Mound City Blue Blowers, Mantovanni's Orchestra, the Cleftones, Kim Kahuna and the Royal Palms Orchestra, Slim Whitman, Frances Langford, Gracie Fields, Lanny Ross, Engelbert Humperdinck, the Browns, and "Whistling" Fred Lowery. Dean Martin sang the ballad in the movie *The Silencers* (1966), and it was heard in *The Way We Were* (1973).

"Remember" (1925), one of Irving Berlin's early but indelible ballads, seemed to be fading from memory, but recent recordings have revealed it to be as potent as his best work. The very simple lyric recalls a promise to hold one dear in memory, but as time has gone by, the beloved one "forgot to remember." The music meanders up and down the scale carefully and ends with a tentative but effective musical phrase. Berlin wrote the torchy number while courting the heiress Ellin Mackay, and there is no question that much of the song is autobiographical. Isham Jones and his Orchestra were the first to record it, but Ruth Etting made it her specialty in clubs and helped popularize the ballad. Memorable discs over the years were made by Jean Goldkette (vocal by Seymour Simon), Kenny Baker, Isham Jones, Erskine Hawkins, Basil Fromeen, Al Goodman, and Dinah Shore. More recently it has been recorded by Andrea Marcovicci, Michael Feinstein and Liza Minnelli, and Vicki Stuart. On screen, "Remember" was sung by Alice Faye in *Alexander's Ragtime Band* (1938), Bing Crosby in *Blue Skies* (1946), Kathryn Grayson in *So This Is Love* (1953), and Ethel Merman and Dan Dailey in *There's No Business Like Show Business* (1954). The song is sometimes listed by its original copyright title "You Forgot to Remember."

"Rhythm in My Nursery Rhymes" (1935) is a swinging number by Sammy Cahn, Don Raye (lyric), Jimmie Lunceford, and Saul Chaplin (music) that Lunceford and his Orchestra introduced with a hit record. The effervescent song about telling childhood tales with the new swing sound was also recorded with success by Tommy Dorsey's Clambake Seven (vocal by Edythe Wright). Count Basie, Joe Haymes, Wingy Manone, Teddy Wilson, and the Mound City Blue Blowers were among the other artists to make discs of it, and recently it has been recorded by Janis Siegel and Ann Hampton Callaway. The number is sometimes listed as "If I Had Rhythm in My Nursery Rhymes."

"Rhythm King" (1928) is a Roaring Twenties jazz favorite that is treasured by jazz enthusiasts as the first record made by Bix Beiderbecke and his Gang. Jo Trent wrote the lyric about a jiving musician, and J. Russel Robison (a.k.a. Joe Hoover) composed the vibrant music. There were hit discs by Ben Bernie and his Hotel Roosevelt Orchestra (vocals by Bernie and the High Speed Boys) and the Coon-Sanders Nighthawks Orchestra (vocal by Carlton Coon). Other artists to make significant records include the Dukes of Dixieland, the Original Salty Dogs Jazz Band, Kenneth Arnstrom, the Paradise City Jazz Band, Brian White, Dan Weiner, and Bricktop's Jazz Babes.

"Rhythm Saved the World" (1936) is a musical salute to the emerging swing sound on Tin Pan Alley that Bunny Berigan and his Orchestra popularized. Sammy Cahn (lyric) and Saul Chaplin (music) wrote the spirited number, and there were records of note by Louis Armstrong, Tommy Dorsey and the Clambake Seven (vocal by Edythe Wright), the Mills Brothers, and Wingy Manone.

"Riders in the Sky (A Cowboy Legend)" (1949) is Stan Jones's driving folk song that is often titled "Ghost Riders in the Sky." The cautionary ballad is about the ghosts of cowboys heard yelling at night as they chase the devil across the heavens, warning a lone cowpoke who watches them that he best mend his ways or he will end up like them. Burl Ives introduced the haunting song on record, but a disc by Vaughn Monroe and his Orchestra (vocal by Monroe) that same year was the big hit, selling over a million discs in less than ten weeks (a record at the time). Bing Crosby and Peggy Lee also had successful versions, and the song was revived by the Ramrods in 1961, the Baja Marimba Band in 1966, and the Outlaws in 1981. Among the other artists to make memorable discs were Eddy Arnold, Marty Robbins, the Ventures, Scatman Crothers, the Sons of the Pioneers, Frankie Laine, the Shadows, Dean Martin, Roy Clark, Vic Damone, Johnny Cash, and a group that took the title and called themselves Riders in the Sky. Gene Autry sang the ballad in the movie *Riders in the Sky* (1949).

"Ridin' Around in the Rain" (1934) is a freewheeling number by Gene Austin and Carmen Lombardo that both songwriters recorded, but it was discs by Bing Crosby, Glen Gray and the Casa Loma Orchestra (vocal by Pee Wee Hunt), and Isham Jones (vocal by Eddie Stone) that popularized it. Other well-known records were made by Guy Lombardo and the Royal Canadians, Vincent Lopez, Earl Burtnett, and Guy Mitchell.

"Riptide" (1934) is a ballad written by Gus Kahn (lyric) and Walter Donaldson (music) to promote the film *Riptide* (1934). While the song boasted no one major hit record, there were successful discs in the 1930s and 1940s by the Pickins Sisters, Vincent Lopez, Guy Lombardo, Benny Kruger, and others. It was revived fifty years later by Robert Palmer with a hit 1985 record. Eddy Duchin, Nye Mayhew, Lou Reed, Mike Post, Lee Nestor, and Ian Whitcomb and the Hotel Roosevelt Orchestra were among those who also recorded it.

"River, Stay 'Way From My Door" (1931), a Tin Pan Alley number written in the style of a Negro spiritual, has been interpreted as a prayerlike song and as a farcical ditty. Harry MacGregor Woods composed the majestic, rolling music, and Mort Dixon wrote the lyric that pleads with the river not to rise and wash away one's cabin, even as he prays to the Lord to have the river heed his request. Kate Smith popularized the song on disc with Guy Lombardo and the Royal Canadians, and there were also early records by Ethel Waters, Paul Robeson, and others who sang it as a serious lament. Comedian Jimmy Savo, on the other hand, turned the number into a pantomime routine, singing to the river while farcically trying to ward off the water. Savo performed it in vaudeville, clubs, on record, in the Broadway revue *Mum's the Word* (1931), and on screen in *Merry-Go-Round of 1938* (1937). Among the many other artists to record the song were Phil Harris, Ray Noble with Al Bowlly, Erno Rapee, Frank Sinatra, Bob Chester, Art Jarrett with Jimmie Noone's Band, Charlie Rich, Tex Williams, Dave Brubeck, and Singin' Sam the Barbasol Man. The number can also be heard in the movies *George White's Scandals* (1934) and *The Way We Were* (1973).

"Robins and Roses" (1936) is an idyllic nature ballad by Edgar Leslie (lyric) and Joe Burke (music) that Bing Crosby introduced and popularized on record. That disc and ones by Tommy Dorsey (vocal by Edythe Wright) and Jimmy Dorsey (vocal by Kay Weber) kept the song on *Your Hit Parade* for eleven weeks. Other memorable versions were made by

Stuff Smith's Combo featuring Jonah Jones, Dolly Dawn, Orville Knapp, Red Nichols, Pat Boone, and Rebecca Kilgore.

"Rock Around the Clock" (1954), the only true rock-and-roll number included in this encyclopedia, is generally considered the first mainstream rock song and the beginning of the end of Tin Pan Alley as it was traditionally known. With this and other rock hits of the 1950s, the music business splintered off into various directions, singer-writers replacing songwriters and pop music becoming separate and distinct from that written for Broadway and films. Max C. Freedman and Jimmy McKnight (a.k.a. James E. Myers) wrote the pulsating song that bounced through all the numbers on the clock to illustrate how one was going to dance away twenty-four hours. It was written for the film *Blackboard Jungle* (1955) (it was the first rock song to be included in a movie soundtrack), but the recording by Bill Haley and the Comets was released before the film and was already a hit, climbing the charts and selling millions of discs. Haley and his group reprised the number in the movies *Rock Around the Clock* (1956) and *Don't Knock the Rock* (1956), their recording was heard in *American Graffiti* (1973) and *Let the Good Times Roll* (1973), and they recorded it again in 1974 with success. As for the song itself, it would eventually be recorded in over thirty languages and sell over 25 million discs worldwide. Other recordings of note were made by the Isley Brothers, Pat Boone, the Platters, Myron Floren, Carl Perkins, Joey Weltz, Jack Mudurian, and Harry Nilsson. Sometimes listed as "We're Gonna Rock Around the Clock," it was also heard in the movies *The Girl Can't Help It* (1956) and *Superman* (1978).

"Rock-a-Bye Your Baby With a Dixie Melody" (1918), both a "mammy" number and a sentimental song about the South, was long associated with Al Jolson. Sam Lewis, Joe Young (lyric), and Jean Schwartz (music) wrote the Stephen Foster–like ballad about the wish to return home and have "mammy" sing to you again as she once did in childhood. Foster's "Old Black Joe" and "Swanee River" are even mentioned in the lyric as examples of the type of song one longs to hear. Jolson introduced the number when he interpolated it into his Broadway vehicle *Sinbad* (1918), and he kept it in his repertoire for decades. His initial recording of the song was a bestseller; he reprised it on the soundtrack for three movies— *Rose of Washington Square* (1939), *The Jolson Story* (1946), and *Jolson Sings Again* (1949); and he recorded it again in 1946, selling another million copies. An odd but successful recording by Jerry Lewis with Jack Pleis's Orchestra revived the song in 1956, and Aretha Franklin made it popular again in 1961. Among the many noteworthy discs made over the years were those by Judy Garland, Louis Prima, Sonny Rollins, Woody Herman, the Vagabonds, Brenda Lee, Sammy Davis Jr., Eddie Fisher, Connie

Francis, Leslie Uggams, David Campbell, Cher, and Mandy Patinkin. Sid Silvers sang it in the film *The Show of Shows* (1929), and it was heard in *On the Avenue* (1937) and *The Merry Monahans* (1944).

"Rockin' Chair" (1930), one of Hoagy Carmichael's favorites of his own songs, was long associated with Mildred Bailey, who introduced it, recorded it three times, used it as her theme song, and was even billed as the "Rockin' Chair Lady." Carmichael's music is lazy and peaceful with a country-blues flavor, while his lyric gently describes an old lady who sits in a rocker on the porch of her cabin, dreaming of the days of happiness long past, and reflecting how she is "chained to my rockin' chair" until Judgment Day. Carmichael got the idea for the song one day when Bailey was sitting in a child's rocker and talking to him. When she rose to stand up, the small chair came with her, and she commented, "This old rockin' chair's got me, I guess." Carmichael made a historic recording of the song in 1930 in which he was accompanied by Bix Beiderbecke, Joe Venuti, Eddie Lang, Gene Krupa, and other renowned musicians. He also made a disc with Louis Armstrong's All-Stars that is considered a classic. Red Nichols, Roy Eldridge, Paul Robeson, Larry Clinton, Lee Sims, Jack Teagarden, Duke Ellington, and the Mills Brothers are among the other artists to record the song. It was featured in the Broadway play *Side Man* (1999) about musicians of yesteryear.

"Room Full of Roses" (1949) is a flowing fox trot by Tim Spencer with unusual imagery in the lyric. An unrequited lover figures that if he sent his sweetheart a rose every time she made him blue and every time she made him cry all night, she would have a room filled with flowers. Yet all he longs for his "arms full of you." The ballad was popularized on record by Sammy Kaye (vocal by Don Cornell), and there were successful discs by Eddy Howard, Dick Haymes with Sonny Burke's Orchestra, and George Morgan as well. Mickey Gilley revived the number in 1974 with a country version that went to the top of the chart. Major records were also made by Gene Autry, Dick Curless, the Sons of the Pioneers, Jim Reeves, Roy Rogers, the Moms and Dads, and Jerry Lee Lewis. Autry also sang it in the film *Mule Train* (1950).

"Rose O'Day" (1941), more often remembered as "The Filla-Ga-Dusha Song," is an animated paean to an Irish gal that Charles Tobias and Al Lewis wrote one night when having dinner at Eddie Cantor's house. When Tobias asked the Irish maid serving them what her name was, she replied "Rose O'Day," and it struck the songwriters as an ideal title for a song. By the end of the evening the number was roughed out, and Cantor introduced it soon after. Early recordings by the Merry Macs and the team of Flanagan and Allen helped popularize the song, but the biggest hit records were made by Freddie Martin (vocal by Eddie Stone) and Kate Smith, each selling over a million discs. Within a few weeks, the song was in the Top 10 in both record and sheet music sales, as well as jukebox and radio play. Other estimable recordings were made by Woody Herman (vocals by Herman and Carolyn Grey), the King Sisters with Alvino Rey's Orchestra, Claude Thornhill, and Jack Mudurian.

"Rose of Washington Square" (1920) was the theme song for Fanny Brice, singing it in the 1919 and 1920 editions of Ziegfeld's *Midnight Frolics*, recording it, and performing the number throughout her long career. James F. Hanley composed the sprightly music, and Ballard Mac-Donald penned the wry lyric about a gal from lower Manhattan who is "withering there in basement air" because she has had too many dud affairs with Broadway dandies. Her future is questionable, she states, but "oh, what a past!" Although it was always identified with Brice, the ditty was also recorded by Alice Faye, Kaye Ballard, Holly Shelton, Benny Goodman, Bert Kaempfert, Bobby Hackett, Pee Wee Russell, Red Nichols, Bob Crosby, Clancy Hayes, and Barbra Streisand. Faye sang it as a Brice-like character in *Rose of Washington Square* (1939), and Ann Dee performed it in *Thoroughly Modern Millie* (1967). It was also sung by Millie Slavin in the show *To Broadway With Love* (1964) at the New York World's Fair.

"Rose Room" (1918) is an intriguing song by Harry Williams (lyric) and Art Hickman (music) that was ahead of its time, featuring harmonic changes in the music that foreshadowed the jazz sound of the 1920s. The passionate number about pining to be with a darling in "roseland" was introduced by Hickman at the New Amsterdam roof theater as part of Ziegfeld's *Midnight Frolics* (1918). The song would be picked up later by several bands, in particular jazz improvisors, and there were notable records made by Joseph C. Smith, Duke Ellington, Fletcher Henderson, Jimmie Lunceford, Teddy Wilson, Artie Shaw, Phil Harris, the Benny Goodman Sextet, Glenn Miller, and Woody Herman (vocal by Ruby Braff). Louis Armstrong performed "Rose Room" in the movie *The Strip* (1951), Betty Hutton sang it in *Somebody Loves Me* (1952), and it was heard in *The Story of Vernon and Irene Castle* (1939), *Ziegfeld Girl* (1941), and *The Merry Monahans* (1944).

"Rosetta" (1933) is a jazz standard using a woman's name to stretch out into interesting riffs and musical improvisations. Earl "Fatha" Hines and Henri Woode wrote the number, and Hines recorded it in 1933 and 1935. Memorable discs were also made by Red Allen, Dexter Gordon, Charlie Shavers, Muggsy Spanier, Benny Goodman, Teddy Wilson, Fats Waller, Art Tatum, Bob Wills, and Frankie Newton.

"Rosie the Riveter" (1943) is a salute to the women who worked in the factories making equipment for the war effort while many of the men were away. Redd Evans and John Jacob Loeb wrote the jive number that was popularized by a recording by the Four Vagabonds. The King Sisters sang the song with Alvino Rey's Orchestra in the movie *Follow the Band* (1943), and it was also interpolated into *Rosie the Riveter* (1944). Being such a topical number, it was seldom heard after World War Two.

"Route 66" (1946) is a mellow but catchy song by Bobby Troup about America's most famous highway and the places you can see (and the "kicks" you will get) if you take it west from Chicago to Los Angeles. Troup recorded the number, but it was a bestselling disc by the Nat King Cole Trio that popularized the offbeat song. There was also a hit record by Bing Crosby with the Andrews Sisters. Other accomplished discs were made by Perry Como, Keely Smith and Louis Prima, Buddy Rich, Roy Hamilton, Ted Heath, the Pied Pipers, Joe Carroll, the Four Freshmen, Curtis Mayfield, Grady Tate, the Rolling Stones, Little Willie Littlefield, Natalie Cole, Ann Hampton Callaway, and the Manhattan Transfer. José Iturbi played it on the piano in the movie *Three Darling Daughters* (1948). "Route 66" remained well known for decades and, with the help of a popular television show of the same name in the 1960s, immortalized the highway; years after the interstate system replaced it, the existing route 66 still holds a fascination for many. The song is often listed as "Get Your Kicks on Route 66."

"Row, Row, Row" (1912) is a vigorous travel song by William Jerome (lyric) and James V. Monaco (music) about a "rowing Romeo" named Johnny who rowed his sweetie up the river for kissing and spooning. Lillian Lorraine introduced the rousing number in the *Ziegfeld Follies of 1912*, and an early hit record by Ada Jones brought the song a great deal of attention. Eddie Cantor and other headliners sang it in vaudeville for years, Bing Crosby's later recording was popular, and Spike Jones and his City Slickers did a merry parody version as well. On screen, it was performed by Betty Hutton in *Incendiary Blonde* (1945), Debbie Reynolds and Carleton Carpenter in *Two Weeks With Love* (1950), Keefe Brasselle (dubbed by Cantor) in *The Eddie Cantor Story* (1953), and Bob Hope and a group of children in *The Seven Little Foys* (1955) and heard in *The Story of Vernon and Irene Castle* (1939). On Broadway, "Row, Row, Row" was sung by the ensemble in the British musical *Oh! What a Lovely War!* (1964).

"Rudolph the Red Nosed Reindeer" (1949) follows "White Christmas" as the second most popular song in the history of Tin Pan Alley. The character of Rudolph, a member of Santa's reindeer crew not included in the famous poem "A Visit From St. Nicholas," was created by Robert L. May in a 1939 pamphlet that was given to department store customers at Christmastime. The story of Rudolph was widely circulated and far from obscure when Johnny Marks put it into narrative ballad form and set it to music. The verse, not always performed, sets up the tale well, then the refrain relates the story of Rudolph from childhood to the Christmas Eve when he saved the holiday by lighting Santa's sleigh through the foggy night. Marks couldn't get any publisher to buy the song, so he published it himself under the St. Nicholas Music Company. He also approached Gene Autry to record it, and the singing star turned him down until Autry's wife urged him to do it. The disc was released in September of 1949, and by Christmas it had sold a million copies. Over the years the Autry record has sold 43 million discs, and over 300 other versions (in dozens of languages) have racked up sales of over 50 million copies. The ballad has also sold about 3.5 million copies of sheet music. Every major artist who has made any kind of Christmas album has probably recorded it, and it is still sung in schools, holiday concerts, television specials, and every other form of entertainment.

"Rum and Coca-Cola" (1944) is a sparkling calypso number about workers from Trinidad who go to the United States to work and earn "the Yankee dollar." Morey Amsterdam heard the rhythmic song played by a Trinidad band when he was visiting the West Indies. Thinking it was an old folk tune in public domain, he wrote a lyric and had Jeri Sullavan adapt the music into song format. Sullavan introduced it at a New York City nightclub; then it was recorded by the Andrews Sisters, becoming a bestseller. Soon it seemed every band was playing it, and sheet music sales were considerable. But the success of the song brought forth various songwriters claiming to have written it years before. The strongest case was that of Maurice Baron who had copyrighted and published the music in a book called *Songs of the Lesser Antilles*. Ironically, the tune for "Rum and Coca-Cola" had been written by Lionel Belasco back in 1906 when he was a boy in Trinidad. The courts sided with Belasco and Baron, damages were enormous, and all existing copies of the sheet music were destroyed. Other recordings of note have been made by Xavier Cugat, Vaughn Monroe, the Chenille Sisters, and Julio Iglesias.

"Runnin' Wild" (1922) is an archetypal Roaring Twenties song, a vibrant number that celebrates the newfound freedom of the era. A. Harrington Gibbs wrote the vibrant jazz music, and Joe Grey and Leo Wood collaborated on the sassy lyric about an abandoned lover who vows not to be lonesome and plans to live a reckless and carefree life. Ted Lewis and his Band made an early recording of the song, but it was Art Hickman and his Orchestra that popularized it. The number was interpolated into the Broadway revue *Runnin' Wild* (1923) and soon became a favorite in dance halls and speakeasies. Jimmie Lunceford revived it in 1938, and it enjoyed renewed popularity during the Big Band era. Among the other artists who made disc versions were Duke Ellington, the Benny Goodman Quartet, Glenn Miller, Pee Wee Crayton, Lionel Hampton, the Ventures, Sidney Bechet, Marilyn Monroe, and Mary Clare Haran. The Dorsey Brothers' band played "Runnin' Wild" in the film bio *The Fabulous Dorseys* (1947), Monroe sang it in *Some Like It Hot* (1959), and it was heard in *The Five Pennies* (1959) and *The Purple Gang* (1960).

"Russian Lullaby" (1927) is one of the very few Irving Berlin songs that reveals his Eastern European roots. Berlin's boyhood in Russia is recalled in both the tender, folk melody and the poignant lyric about a simple lullaby used to soothe crying children and let them dream of a faraway and better land. The song was first heard in vaudeville, then became more known through a recording by Roger Wolfe Kahn and his Orchestra (vocal by Henry Garden). Early discs were also made by Ernie Golden, Franklyn Baur, and Jesse Crawford. In 1938 Bunny Berigan (vocal by Kathleen Lane) revived it, and Teddy Wilson's recording was very popular during World War Two. Other noteworthy discs were made by Paul Whiteman (vocal by Joan Edwards), Guy Lombardo and the Royal Canadians, Red Nichols, Bob Grant, Dinah Shore, Benny Goodman, Dave Pell, Marylou Williams, and Helen Stuart. Bing Crosby sang the "Russian Lullaby" with a male quartet in the movie *Blue Skies* (1946).

S

"Sail Along, Silv'ry Moon" (1937) is a later version of a Tin Pan Alley "moon" ballad in the tradition of "Shine On, Harvest Moon," but it is an effective number all the same. Harry Tobias wrote the atmospheric lyric, and Percy Wenrich composed the graceful music. Gene Austin was the first to record it, and it was a hit for Red McKenzie, Horace Heidt and his Musical Knights, and Bing Crosby. Billy Vaughn revived the song in 1958 with a successful instrumental disc that climbed the charts. Other artists to record the ballad include Ace Cannon, Andy Williams, the Moms and Dads, Pete Tex, Sil Austin, and Max Greger.

"Sailboat in the Moonlight" (1937) is a dreamy ballad by John Jacob Loeb and Carmen Lombardo that paints a romantic picture and found success first with dance bands and then with jazz artists. Guy Lombardo and the Royal Canadians (vocal by Carmen Lombardo) introduced the song on record, and it was a hit, as were early discs by Billie Holiday and Dick Robertson. Later recordings by Duke Ellington, Johnny Hodges (vocal by Buddy Clark), and Lester Young established the number as a jazz favorite. Emery Deutsch, Arthur Tracy, Teddi King, Dick Jurgens, Ruby Braff, and Scott Hamilton were among those who also recorded it. "Sailboat in the Moonlight" can be heard in the movie *Stage Door* (1937).

"Sailing Over the Bounding Main" (1880) is the sailor chantey by Godfrey Marks that was rarely recorded over the years (except on children's records) but was familiar to several generations through sing-alongs and other informal gatherings. The rousing folk song encourages the sailors to withstand the perils of the stormy seas, promising that the wind will "blow ere Jack comes home again." The zesty travel ditty, sometimes listed as "Sailing, Sailing," was used countless times in films as background music for nautical sequences.

"Sam, the Old Accordion Man" (1927) is a tuneful number that was introduced, recorded, and popularized by Ruth Etting, an atypically upbeat song for the famous torch singer yet one suited to her particular style. Composer Walter Donaldson provided his own lyric for the catchy number, which was used in the films *The Dance of Life* (1929) and *Glorifying the American Girl* (1930). Years later Doris Day sang it on screen in the Etting bio *Love Me or Leave Me* (1955), and her recording enjoyed some popularity.

"Sam, You Made the Pants Too Long" (1933), a comic novelty number that parodies the hymnlike ballad "Lawd, You Made the Night Too Long" (1932), was long associated with Joe E. Lewis, who introduced it and sang it in nightclubs until the mob destroyed his singing career. Isham Jones wrote the soft-shoe music (which had the same melody as he wrote for the earlier hymn), and Fred Whitehouse and Milton Berle penned the amusing lyric about a customer complaining to his tailor. The suit that Sam made him fits fine, he says, except for the trousers that are so large he can feel "the winter breeze up and down the knees." Vaughn Monroe and his Orchestra (vocal by Ziggy Talent), Al Simmons, and Barbra Streisand each made distinctive recordings of the risible number.

"Sam's Song" (1950) is a Tin Pan Alley number about the song being sung, an odd conceit but one that works very well. Lew Quadling composed the merry music with a peppy soft-shoe tempo, and Jack Elliott wrote the lyric that was dedicated to music publisher Sam Weiss. The song celebrates itself, a happy tune that makes you grin because it is "catchy as can be" and "they call it Sam's song." "The Happy Tune," as it is sometimes titled, was popularized by a hit record by Bing Crosby and his son Gary (billed as "Gary Crosby and friend") that sold over a million copies. In 1962 Dean Martin and Sammy Davis Jr. made a duet version that was also a hit. Martin sang it with Frank Sinatra in concert, and it was recorded as well. Other discs were made by Joe "Fingers" Carr (a.k.a. Lou Busch), Artie Traum, Russ Conway, and Chris Rice.

"San Antonio Rose" (1940) is an early example of country swing, a number that uses brass and percussion in addition to the traditional guitar and other country strings. Bob Wills wrote the sensitive music in 1938 and recorded it as an instrumental. In 1940 he added a moving lyric about calling back a girl that one met in the moonlight near the Alamo. Wills and his Texas Playboys introduced the new song (which was titled

"New San Antonio Rose" at first to distinguish it from the instrumental version) but the number was popularized in 1941 with a bestselling disc by Bing Crosby that managed to sell 84,000 copies inside of a month. Dozens of recordings followed, including ones by Tex Ritter, Gene Autry, Tito Guizar, the Dinning Sisters, Floyd Cramer, the Firehouse Five Plus Two, Ken Griffin, Ernest Tubb, Pee Wee King, the Sons of the Pioneers, Chet Atkins, Johnny and the Hurricanes, Jim Nabors, and Patsy Cline. The song was featured in the movie *San Antonio Rose* (1941), Ray Price was heard singing it on the soundtrack of *Honkytonk Man* (1982), and Jessica Lange (dubbed by Cline) sang it in the Cline bio *Sweet Dreams* (1985).

"Santa Claus Is Comin' to Town" (1934), the cautionary holiday standard by Haven Gillespie and J. Fred Coots that warns children to behave because Christmas is approaching, was turned down by several publishers because they felt it was too much a kiddie record to sell to the general public. After two years of hawking the number, the songwriters convinced Eddie Cantor to sing it on the radio. Cantor didn't think much of the song, but his wife Ida persuaded him to add it to his holiday broadcast; it immediately caught the attention of the public. The first recording was made by George Olsen and his Orchestra (vocal by Ethel Shutta), and there was an early hit disc by George Hall (vocal by Sonny Schuyler). Before long, over 4 million copies of sheet music and several millions of records were sold. The most popular of all the discs was a 1947 version by Bing Crosby with the Andrews Sisters, followed by a hit record by Perry Como. As late as 1985 a disc by Bruce Springsteen managed to make the charts. The perennial favorite remains one of the most performed songs on Christmas albums, television specials, school concerts, and other forms of entertainment. The number is sometimes listed as "You Better Watch Out."

"Satin Doll" (1953) enjoyed success first as an instrumental and later as a vocal. Duke Ellington and Billy Strayhorn composed the smooth jazz number that uses repeated musical phrases but varies them just enough to avoid repetition or monotony. Ellington's record with his Orchestra and himself at the piano was an instrumental hit, and Earl "Fatha" Hines also made a distinctive version as well. In 1958 Johnny Mercer added a lyric consisting of short but potent phrases about wooing a chic, elusive gal who is "nobody's fool." Alec Wilder describes the number as "a soft-spoken, underplayed little song with a marvelous, perfect Mercer lyric, and it truly swings." Of the many vocal versions that followed, a disc by Ella Fitzgerald was the most popular. Other artists that recorded "Satin Doll" include Blossom Dearie, Nina Simone, George Shearing, Ernie Andrews, Joe Williams, Russ Conway, Oscar Peterson, the Impressions, Eddie Layton, Mel Tormé, and Mercer himself. More recently there have been versions by Stephane Grappelli, Ernestine Anderson, Bobby Short, and Kenny Blake. On Broadway, P.J. Benjamin sang it in the Ellington revue *Sophisticated Ladies* (1981), and it was performed by Susan Misner and the male chorus in the Mercer revue *Dream* (1997).

"Saturday Night (Is the Loneliest Night in the Week)" (1944) is the melancholy lament of a soul alone without a Saturday night date. Jule Styne wrote the gentle music, and Sammy Cahn penned the heartfelt lyric that came to him when he was trying to explain to someone outside of show business that for performers Saturday is always a workday. Frank Sinatra introduced the ballad on record with Alex Stordahl's Orchestra, and it was a bestseller. Sammy Kaye (vocal by Nancy Norman), Frankie Carle (vocal by Phyllis Lynne), Woody Herman (vocal by Frances Wayne), and the King Sisters all had hit records as well. Other notable discs were made by Bing Crosby, Oscar Peterson, Barry Manilow, and more recently, Ross Tompkins and Judy Kuhn. The song was also used in the movie *All-Star Bond Rally* (1945).

"Save the Last Dance for Me" (1931) is a tender fox trot by Walter Hirsch (lyric), Frank Magine, and Phil Spitalny (music) that was often played by dance bands at the end of the evening. Russ Columbo popularized the number on radio and records, and Arthur Tracy had a successful disc as well. Among the other artists to record it were Morton Downey, Erno Rapee, Al Bowlly, Eddy Arnold, and Jerry Lee Lewis. The song is not to be confused with a 1960 hit by the Drifters.

"Say It Isn't So" (1932) is one of Irving Berlin's finest ballads, a direct and painfully colloquial plea to save a romance that is rumored to be in trouble. The song gets right to the point as the lyric acknowledges the possibility that a dearie has stopped loving one, then asking the other party to please deny it. The music's effective use of repeated notes supports the straightforward words yet gives a tentative flavor to the ballad. Berlin wrote the song soon after he lost a fortune in the stock market crash and was in a long dry spell without any hits. The success of this number revitalized his career, with some of his best work coming in the following decade. Rudy Vallee introduced the ballad on the radio. A show business tale (probably apocryphal) relates that Vallee and his wife were on the verge of a divorce but were reconciled after he sang it for her over the airwaves. Early records by Connee Boswell, Ozzie Nelson, and George Olsen (vocal by Paul Small) were successful, and though it never produced a top-selling disc, the song was often recorded and highly esteemed. Records of note were made by Dick Haymes with Carmen Cavallaro, Annette Hanshaw, Al Goodman, Sam Coslow, Coleman

Hawkins, Peggy Lee, Stan Kenton, Georgia Gibbs, and Lawrence Welk. More recently "Say It Isn't So" has found new recognition with recordings by Andrea Marcovicci, Jimmy Roselli, Kiri Te Kanawa, and Michael Feinstein. Bing Crosby sang the ballad in the movie *Blue Skies* (1946).

"Say 'Si Si' " (1936), a Latin American standard in which language and romance intertwine, was originally written as "Paro Vigo Me Voy" by Francia Luban (Spanish lyric) and Ernesto Lecuona (music). Al Stillman wrote an English lyric in 1936 in which a beau teaches his dearie how to say "yes" in various languages, hoping that she will say "yes" to him as well. Xavier Cugat (vocal by Lina Romay) introduced the new version in the States with a successful record, but the song was even more popular in the 1940s because of hit versions by the Andrews Sisters, Glenn Miller (vocal by Marian Hutton), and rerelease of the Cugat record. "Say 'Si Si' " was revived in 1953 with popular discs by the Mills Brothers and Eugenie Baird, and there were also well-known records by Bing Crosby and Rosemary Clooney, Bert Kaempfert, and Chet Atkins. The number can be heard in the movies *Carolina Moon* (1940), *It Comes Up Love* (1943), *Samba-Mania* (1948), and *When My Baby Smiles at Me* (1948).

"Says My Heart" (1938) is a glowing ballad by Frank Loesser (lyric) and Burton Lane (music) about the call of love from within. Harriet Hilliard introduced it with Harry Owens' Orchestra in the film *Cocoanut Grove* (1938), and her record with Ozzie Nelson's Orchestra popularized the number, keeping it on *Your Hit Parade* for twelve weeks. Among the prominent recordings over the years were those by Billie Holiday, Jimmie Greer, Tommy Dorsey, Eddie Cantor, George Hall (vocal by Dolly Dawn), the Andrews Sisters, Maxine Sullivan, Bing Crosby, Mildred Bailey, Ruby Braff, Larry Clinton, Mary Stahl, and Loesser himself.

"Scarlet Ribbons (For Her Hair)" (1949) is a tender narrative ballad that has a fantastic flavor to it. Evelyn Daniz composed the folk song melody, and Jack Segal wrote the magical lyric about a mother whose special wish is to buy a red ribbon for her little girl's hair. She searches all over town without success, but when she returns home she finds scarlet ribbons in the girl's hair. Early recordings by Juanita Hall, Dinah Shore, and Jo Stafford were successful, but it was Harry Belafonte who made the song a standard in 1952 by singing in concerts and recording it as well. In 1959 the Browns revived the number with a disc that climbed the charts. Other major recordings were made by the Kingston Trio, Perry Como, Gracie Fields, the Brothers Four, Jim Reeves, Roger Whittaker, and the Lennon Sisters.

"School Days" (1907) was one of the biggest hits of the new century, selling over 3 million copies of sheet music and Bryon C. Harlan's recording becoming one of the biggest sellers yet seen on Tin Pan Alley. Gus Edwards composed the insistent but catchy music, and Will D. Cobb penned the nostalgic lyric that looked back to one's youth, recalling "the dear old golden rule days" and the time a girl wrote "I love you, Joe" on her chalk slate. Edwards introduced the number in vaudeville with his kiddie act, and soon it seemed everyone was humming it. In addition to many children's records, there are distinctive versions by Dizzy Gillespie, Archie Bleyer, Johnny Mercer with the Pied Pipers, Louis Jordan and the Tympani Five, William Bolcom and Joan Morris, and Teresa Brewer. On screen the number was featured in the Edwards bio *The Star Maker* (1939), *Hi, Buddy!* (1943), and *Sunbonnet Sue* (1945), where it was sung by Gale Storm and Phil Regan. It is sometimes listed as "When We Were a Couple of Kids."

"Second Hand Rose" (1921), one of Fanny Brice's signature songs, is a delightful ditty by Grant Clarke (lyric) and James Hanley (music) about a gal from Second Avenue whose life has been a series of hand-me-downs, from her clothes to the piano in her parlor to her beau, Jake the plumber, who has been previously married. Brice introduced the number in the 1921 edition of the *Ziegfeld Follies*, recorded it, sang it in the movie *My Man* (1928), and performed it throughout her career. Barbra Streisand revived the song in 1966 when she recorded it after playing Brice in the Broadway musical *Funny Girl* (1964). Streisand also sang it briefly in the 1968 film version. Kay Ballard, Dean Martin, Paul Tripp, and Marie Michuda also made records of "Second Hand Rose," and there were novelty versions by the Mazeltones and Mrs. Miller.

"See See Rider Blues" (1925) is the quintessential Gertrude "Ma" Rainey song, a blues number that she wrote and recorded and best typifies her unique talent. The lyric laments how a cad named C.C. Rider has taken up her heart and, at the same time, put her down. While there were only a few other recording made in Rainey's day, the song was revived on several occasions. Bea Booze had a hit with it in 1943, a Chuck Willis record in 1957 started "The Stroll" dance craze, La Vern Baker had a successful disc in 1963, and it was a hit for Eric Busdon and the Animals in 1966. Louis Armstrong, Helen Humes, Eddie Condon, Bunk Johnson, Big Bill Broonzy, and Jimmy Rushing were among those who made memorable recordings as well. The number is sometimes listed as "See See Rider" or "C.C. Rider."

"See You in September" (1959) is a mellow but moving farewell song by Sid Wayne (lyric) and Sherman Edwards (music) in which two lovers must part at the coming of summer and agree to be reunited in the fall, all the time worrying that one might lose the other "to a summer love." The ballad was popularized by a hit disc by the Tempos, and in 1966 it was revived with success by the Happenings with a chart record. There were also discs of note made by Jeremy Wallace, Shelley Fabares, Mike Curb, and Maryanne. The Tempos' recording was heard in the film *American Grafitti* (1973).

"Seems Like Old Times" (1946) is a delicate ballad about two former loves meeting again after a long period of time and how comfortable and familiar it seems to be back together. John Jacob Loeb and Carmen Lombardo wrote the gentle song, and it was introduced by Guy Lombardo and the Royal Canadians (vocal by Carmen Lombardo) on a record that was moderately successful. It was Arthur Godfrey who popularized the number, using it to open and close his radio show five times a week. The McGuire Sisters revived the song with success in 1957. Kate Smith, Mildred Bailey, Bob Allison, Vaughn Monroe, Rosemary Clooney, Betty Carter, Rob McConnell, and Lawrence Welk are among the many who also recorded it. Diane Keaton sang the ballad in the movie *Annie Hall* (1977), and it was heard in *Seems Like Old Times* (1980).

"Sent For You Yesterday and Here You Come Today" (1939) is a swinging blues number questioning a sweetheart's sincerity when he arrives too late. Count Basie, Ed Durham, and Jimmy Rushing collaborated on the rhythmic lament, and it was introduced on a hit record by Basie and his Orchestra with Rushing doing the vocal. Benny Goodman (vocal by Johnny Mercer) also had success with it, and Basie later rerecorded it with Al Hibbler. Among the other artists to make successful recordings were Joe Williams, Floyd McDaniel, Mel Tormé, Duke Ellington, Della Reese, Pee Wee Crayton, and Johnnie Ray.

"Sentimental Gentleman From Georgia" (1932) is a wry blues song about a smooth operator from the South who seems to steal all the girls' hearts. Frank Perkins composed the zesty music, and Mitchell Parish wrote the droll lyric about the "Mason-Dixon valentine" who is a "real professor" when it comes to love. The number was popularized by a hit record by Isham Jones and his Orchestra (vocal by Eddie Stone), and for some reason it became a favorite of sister groups, the Boswell, Pinkins, Dinning, and Pfister Sisters all having success with it. Other noteworthy discs were made by Marty Grosz and Destiny's Tots, Charlie Palloy, and the Mills Blue Rhythm Band. The song can be heard in the film *George White's Scandals* (1934).

"Sentimental Journey" (1944) is a slow, lazy, yet intoxicating Big Band ballad by Bud Green, Les Brown, and Ben Horner that was responsible for launching Doris Day's career. The music repeats the notes of C and E in a way that shouldn't work at such a casual tempo; yet the music has an engaging quality, and it never gets monotonous. The lyric is about the longing for home, hoping to travel back to "renew old memories." Brown introduced it and made it his theme song. He chose Day to do the vocal when he recorded it with his band, but the disc sat idle for a year before it caught on, eventually selling over a million copies, staying on the *Hit Parade* for sixteen weeks, and making Day famous. In 1947 there was a successful record by Ella Fitzgerald with Eddy Howard's Orchestra, and the Ames Brothers revived it in 1951 with a record with Les Brown and the Band. Among the other notable discs were those made by Tommy Dorsey, the Platters, Louis Prima, Kay Starr, Julie London, the Lennon Sisters, Boots Randolph, Marian McPartland, Ringo Starr, Roger Whittaker, and more recently, Brian Evans, Ian Cruickshank, and Andrea Marcovicci. The song was featured in the movie *Sentimental Journey* (1946) and was sung in the Off-Broadway revue *Swingtime Canteen* (1995).

"September in the Rain" (1935) is the romantic standard by Al Dubin (lyric) and Harry Warren (music) that took over a dozen years to catch on but has remained a beloved favorite ever since. The affecting lyric recalls a romance during a wet autumn when "raindrops seemed to play a sweet refrain." It was written for James Melton to sing in the film *Stars Over Broadway* (1935), but the vocal was cut and only the music was heard in the background. Melton got to sing it in *Melody for Two* (1937), and he recorded it as well, but it made little impact. It was not until a 1949 disc by the George Shearing Trio that the song caught on and became widely recognized. Dinah Washington revived the number with a hit record in 1961. Among the other significant recordings were those by Guy Lombardo, Lionel Hampton, Al Hibbler, Johnny Hartman, Doris Day, the Norman Luboff Choir, Frankie Laine, and Chad and Jeremy.

"Shadows on the Swanee" (1933) is a soothing lullaby that takes the form of a southern song aching for the homeland. Harold Spina wrote the fluent music, and Joe Young and Johnny Burke collaborated on the nostalgic lyric. Leading records by Irving Aaronson and his Commanders (vocal by Dick Robertson), the Allen "Red" Hawkins Orchestra, and Hal Kemp (vocal by Skinnay Ennis) popularized the song. There were also distinctive versions by Ethel Waters, Irene Taylor, and Paul Ash.

"Shaking the Blues Away" (1927) is a vivacious rhythm song by Irving Berlin that urges one to toss off your worries by way of vigorous dancing. The driving number has sharp rhythmic accents in the music and rhyming open-vowel contractions in the lyric that work together for a potent dance song. It was introduced by Ruth Etting and the chorus in the 1927 edition of the *Ziegfeld Follies*, and many recordings followed, including those by Etting, Edgar Fairchild and Ralph Rainger, Franklin Baur, Paul Whiteman, Ben Selvin, Anita O'Day, Harry Reser, Doris Day, Erroll Garner, and Mel Tormé. More recently it has been recorded by Cheryl Serio, Betsy Bruce Osmun, and Rob Fisher and the Coffee Club Orchestra. Ann Miller performed the number in the movie *Easter Parade* (1948), and Day sang it in the Etting bio *Love Me or Leave Me* (1955).

"Shame On You" (1944) is a country-western standard by Spade Cooley that crossed over to become popular in the pop and jazz fields as well. The scolding ballad was introduced on record by Cooley, followed by successful discs by Peggy Lee, Lisa Kirk, and Red Foley with Lawrence Welk's Orchestra. Other well-known records were made by Fats Domino, Alice Faye, Tex Beneke, Sonny Rhodes, Gene Autry, Faron Young, Tex Williams, Cliff Richard, Bob Wills and his Texas Playboys, Jerry Lee Lewis, and Roy Acuff. Autry reprised "Shame On You" in the movie *Trail to San Antone* (1947).

"Shanghai" (1951) is a warm ballad by Bob Hilliard and Milton DeLugg about running away to a distant land to escape the pains of love. Doris Day popularized the number with a record with Paul Weston's Orchestra. The Billy Williams Quartet, Bob Crosby, and Bing Crosby each had hit discs of it as well. Among the other artists to record it were Peggy Lee, Buddy Morrow, Chuck Loeb, and Pam Munter. The song is sometimes listed as "Why Did I Tell You I Was Going to Shanghai?"

"Shangri-La" (1946) is a bombastic song about a kiss that can transport one to the most exotic of places. Harpist Robert Maxwell and bandleader Matty Malneck composed the piece as an instrumental, and they introduced it on record. In 1956 Carl Sigman added a passionate lyric about a love so great that "anywhere you are is Shangri-La." (The title comes from the fictional land of bliss described in James Hilton's bestselling novel *Lost Horizon*.) The Four Coins had a hit record of the new version in 1957, and it was revived in 1964 by Vic Dana and again in 1969 by the Lettermen. Even Maxwell's rerecording in 1964 was a success. The ballad became familiar to millions of viewers in the 1960s as the theme song for Jackie Gleason's television show. Among those who also made noteworthy discs were Freddie Martin, Nelson Riddle, Sonny Stitt, Peggy Lee, Wayne Newton, Count Basie, Duane Eddy, Esther Phillips, the Four Freshmen, Johnny Mathis, the Kinks, and the Electric Light Orchestra.

Jason Graae, David Engel, Guy Stroman, and Stan Chandler performed "Shangri-La" in the Off-Broadway revue *Forever Plaid* (1990).

"Sh-Boom (Life Could Be a Dream)" (1954) is a breezy rhythm number that was written and introduced by a group called the Chords (James Keys, Claude and Carl Feaster, Floyd F. MacRae, and James Edwards). The song, in which the lyric as well as the music imitates the muted sounds of a percussionist, is very tuneful and caught on immediately. When a group titled the Crew-Cuts recorded it a few years later, they gave it a strong rock-and-roll beat, and the disc went to the Number One spot on the charts, the first "rock" song to do so. The Everly Brothers, Kenny Vance and the Planotones, Alton Ellis, the Alley Cats, Johnny Otis, and the trio Sharon, Lois, and Bram were among those who also recorded it. There was also a popular parody version in 1955 by Stan Freberg with the Toads and Billy May's Orchestra. The merry number can be heard in the films *Train Ride to Hollywood* (1978) and *Cry-Baby* (1990), and it was performed by the cast of the Off-Broadway revue *The Taffetas* (1988).

"She Is More to Be Pitied Than Censured" (1895) is a sentimental ballad by William B. Gray about a fallen woman that brought many a tear to the eye in the 1890s but was the subject of ridicule by later generations. The melodramatic lyric observes a girl flirting with men on the Bowery and explains that it was a callous man who led her to such a life. The song's title became a cliché in later years and satiric "mellerdramas" would quote sections of the lyric, such as "She is only a lassie who ventured on life's stormy path ill-advised." The number was published and sheet music sales were strong even before the ballad was introduced in vaudeville by Imogene Comer. It remained a favorite in variety for years, and there was an early record by vaudevillian Steve Porter that was popular. In 1951 a campy version of the song by Beatrice Kay with a male quartet was a hit, and in the movie *Cruisin' Down the River* (1953) the ballad was sung sarcastically by the chorus.

"She Wore a Yellow Ribbon" (1917) is the traditional American folk song that was handed down orally for several generations before it was finally written down and published. Its origins date back to a dialect song called "All 'Round My Hat" that was published in Britain in 1838, a number going back a hundred years or so that had a repeating "far away" in the refrain. In America a version called " 'Round Her Neck She Wears a Yellow Ribbon" (after the first line of the verse) was being sung by the middle of the nineteenth century. The lyric told of a sweetheart who misses her intended one while he is away, so she wears a ribbon all year long to remind her of him. A version by George A. Norton in

1917 was very popular and most resembles the song as we know it today. For the film *She Wore a Yellow Ribbon* (1949), M. Otter and Leroy Parker adapted it, and their version became hit records for Eddie Miller and the Andrews Sisters with Russ Morgan's Orchestra. There was also a popular sing-along version by Mitch Miller. The folk song was also sung by Roy Rogers in the movie *The Cowboy and the Senorita* (1944).

"The Sheik of Araby" (1921) is a sensuous ballad by Harry B. Smith, Francis Wheeler (lyric), and Ted Snyder (music) that was inspired by Rudolph Valentino in the silent film *The Sheik* (1921). The exotic number tells of a sheik who creeps into the tent of a maiden at night, seduces her, then promises her that she'll "rule this land with me." The movie's popularity and a record by the Club Royal Orchestra made the song a hit in the 1920s, and it was revived with success by Jack Teagarden in 1939. Ironically, the number is just as well known as a comic piece spoofing the "sheik" craze. Eddie Cantor sang it with glee in the Broadway show *Make It Snappy* (1921), Betty Grable, Alice Faye, Billy Gilbert, and the Nicholas Brothers spoofed it in *Tin Pan Alley* (1940), and a parody version by Spike Jones and his City Slickers was a hit record in 1943. Among the other artists to record the song were Benny Goodman, Fats Waller, Coleman Hawkins, Django Reinhardt, the Firehouse Five Plus Two, George Lewis, Sammy Rimington, Johnny and the Hurricanes, and Max Bygraves and a comic version by Lou Monte. An Andrews Sisters recording was heard in the film *The Story of Us* (1999).

"She'll Be Comin' Round the Mountain" (1899) is the traditional singalong song of uncertain origin that has as many versions as it has verses. The number is probably descended from a Negro spiritual called "When the Chariot Comes," which became more secular as it was adopted by workers laying railroad tracks in the last years of the nineteenth century. The merry ballad lists all the things the local folk will do when a certain person comes around the mountain and arrives in town. From early days it was a specialty of banjo players, and it remains a favorite on children's records and for school and camp sing-alongs. Joe Williams, Fats Waller, Connie Francis, Phil Haynes, Pete Seeger, Steve Brannen, and Buffy Sainte-Marie are among those to record it. The folk song was heard in the movie *I'll Take Romance* (1937), and Gene Autry sang it in *The Last Round-Up* (1947).

"She's Funny That Way" (1928) is a "bittersweet late-at-night song," as Alec Wilder describes it, in which a swain marvels at how his darling gave up the high life and a wealthy family to work for and worship him. Neil Moret wrote the intriguing music, a series of five similar phrases that moves into a release that climbs up the scale to break up the repetition. Composer Richard A. Whiting wrote one of his few lyrics for the number, and it was introduced by a hit record by Gene Austin. Interest in the song was revived when it was heard in the movie *The Postman Always Rings Twice* (1946), and it was popular all over again when Frank Sinatra sang it in *Meet Danny Wilson* (1952), his record climbing the charts. Other artists to make disc versions include Ted Lewis, Connie Haines, the Benny Goodman Sextet, Art Tatum, Lester Young, Bud Freeman, Zoot Sims, Martha Stewart, Eddie Condon, Mary Lou Williams, and Jimmie Noone. It was also sung by Frankie Laine in the film *Rainbow 'Round My Shoulder* (1952). The number is sometimes listed as "I Got a Woman, Crazy for Me."

"Shine" (1924) is a vaudeville ditty by Richard C. McPherson (a.k.a. Cecil Mack), Lew Brown (lyric), and Ford Dabney (music) that later became a jazz standard. The team of Van and Schenck and other vaudeville performers did a soft-shoe step to the song for years before Louis Armstrong popularized it as a jazz piece. Ella Fitzgerald revived it in 1938 with a hit record, and Frankie Laine's 1948 disc sold over a million copies. Other memorable recordings were made by Jack Teagarden, the Benny Goodman Sextet, Stan Getz, Eddy Duchin, and Art Hodes with Sidney Bechet. On screen it was performed by Bing Crosby in *Birth of the Blues* (1941), John "Bubbles" Bublett in *Cabin in the Sky* (1943), Harry James in *The Benny Goodman Story* (1956), and Howard Alden on the guitar for Sean Penn in *Sweet and Lowdown* (1999), as well as in *The Eddy Duchin Story* (1956). The number is often listed as "S-H-I-N-E."

"Shine On, Harvest Moon" (1908), perhaps the most famous and most durable of the many "moon" ballads, remains one of the most recognized of American popular songs even though its style is decidedly old-fashioned and a product of turn-of-the-century innocence. Vaudevillian Nora Bayes and her husband, dancer Jack Norworth, wrote the resplendent song about nocturnal romance and introduced it in variety before Bayes made a hit of the number when she sang it in the 1908 edition of the *Ziegfeld Follies*. It became her trademark song, and she sang it throughout her long career. Sheet music sales were considerable, and it remained a favorite around the parlor piano and of barbershop quartets for decades. Ada Jones, Billy Murray, and other stars helped popularize it on stage, it was interpolated into the Broadway musical *Miss Innocence* (1908) where it was sung by Lillian Lorraine, and Ruth Etting impersonated Bayes and performed it in the 1931 edition of the *Ziegfeld Follies*. A disc by Ethel Waters that same year was popular, and Kate Smith revived the ballad in 1943 with success. Of the many recordings made over the years, noteworthy ones were by Vera Lynn, Judy Garland, the Buffalo Bills, Billy Vaughn, Glenn Miller, the Pied Pipers, Artie Shaw, the

Platters, Gisele MacKenzie, and Nancy Dussault. Frequently used in the movies, the song was performed by Ann Sheridan and Dennis Morgan as Bayes and Norworth in *Shine On, Harvest Moon* (1944), and it was sung and danced by Jane Powell, Ann Sothern, and Louis Calhern in *Nancy Goes to Rio* (1950). "Shine On, Harvest Moon" can also be heard in *The Broadway Hoofer* (1929), *The Great Ziegfeld* (1936), *Ever Since Eve* (1937), *Look for the Silver Lining* (1949), *I'll See You in My Dreams* (1951), *The Eddy Duchin Story* (1956), and other movies.

"Shoo Shoo Baby" (1943) is a gently rhythmic farewell song by Phil Moore that was very popular during World War Two. The lyric expresses the sentiments of a beau "off to the seven seas" as he bids goodbye with a slangy and affectionate "shoo shoo." The song caught on when Lena Horne and Georgia Gibbs each sang it in clubs. Sheet music sales quickly reached 300,000, and a recording by the Andrews Sisters managed to stay in the Number One spot for nine weeks. Ella Mae Morse also had a hit with it, and the ballad stayed on the *Hit Parade* for seventeen weeks. Bing Crosby, Glenn Miller, Dinah Shore, the Nat King Cole Trio, Stan Kenton, Jan Garber, Joe Loss, the Golden Gate Quartet, and Tennessee Ernie Ford were among the many who also made successful discs. On screen it was sung by Jane Frazee and Judy Clarke in *Beautiful But Broke* (1944), the Andrews Sisters in *Follow the Boys* (1944), Ida James in *Trocadero* (1944), Morse in *South of Dixie* (1944), Betty Grable in *Diamond Horseshoe* (1945), and the Page Cavanaugh Trio in *Big City* (1948).

"Short'nin' Bread" (1928), the rhythmic Negro spiritual that is a specialty of baritone singers, is not an authentic spiritual at all but a pastiche of the style written and popularized in the twentieth century. Jacques Wolfe is the credited author, though many have claimed to have written it, and a song by Reece d'Pree in 1905 is very likely the origin of the song known today. The simple lyric about how "mammy's little baby" loves shortening bread has several nonsense verses about the magical powers of the baked confection, how a thief went to jail for stealing the bread, and even details about the skillet used in the making of the bread. The number was introduced in vaudeville, and soon it was a favorite in concerts of deep-voiced performers. Opera singer Lawrence Tibbett included the piece in his recitals for many years, and there were early records by Paul Robeson and Nelson Eddy that were popular. Both singers reprised the song on film, Robeson singing it in *Jericho* (1937) and Eddy providing the voice for Willie, the opera-singing whale, in the animated *Make Mine Music* (1946). The rhythmic ditty was also heard in the movie *Louisiana Hayride* (1944). Fats Waller, Conrad Thibaut, Elliott Lawrence, the Andrews Sisters, Mississippi John Hurt, the DeJohn Sisters, the Carter Family, Taj Mahal, and the Cramps are among the many who recorded it as well.

"Show Me the Way to Go Home" (1925), the unofficial anthem of singing drunks as they leave a bar at closing time, probably originated as a folk song. Musicologist Sigmund Spaeth discovered an old English ballad that opens with the lyric "Oh Mister, won't you show me the right way home?" British publishers Reg Connelly and Jimmy Campbell, using the pseudonym Irving King, adapted the music and wrote the now-famous lyric about being tired and wanting to go to bed because all the alcohol "went right to my head." The silly ditty was introduced to Americans by Vincent Lopez and his Orchestra, and it was soon a popular staple of the Happiness Boys (Billy Jones and Ernie Hare). Notable recordings were made by Bert Kaempfert, Al Hirt, Johnny Otis, Mitch Miller, Max Bygraves, Rufus Thomas, and Alison Fraser.

"Siboney" (1929) is a Latin favorite, especially of guitarists, by Ernesto Lecuona that was originally titled "Canto Siboney" when it was first published in Cuba. Dolly Morse wrote an English lyric, and it was popularized in the States by leading records by Jessica Dragonette, Enric Madriguera, and Nick Lucas with the Anglo-Persians. It was revived with success in the 1950s by Frances Wayne with Neal Hefti's Band. In addition to many Spanish artists, "Sibony" was also recorded by Percy Faith, the Platters, Desi Arnaz, Mantovanni's Orchestra, Xavier Cugat, Slim Gaillard, Chet Atkins, Stan Getz, Martin Denny, Don Azpiazu, and Placido Domingo. Grace Moore sang the ballad in the movie *When You're in Love* (1937), Gloria Jean performed it in *Get Hep to Love* (1942), and it was heard in *Vogues of 1938* (1937) and *Babes on Swing Street* (1944).

"Side By Side" (1927), the familiar companion song by Harry MacGregor Woods, became popular in vaudeville first, then became one of the top sellers of sheet music and records in the late 1920s. The verse refers to a romantic couple, but when the refrain is sung alone, the song is about friends without wealth ("we ain't got a barrel of money") but rich in companionship as they travel along singing. Nick Lucas and Paul Whiteman (vocals by the Rhythm Boys) made early popular recordings, and Kay Starr revived it with a hit disc in 1953. Other major records were made by Cliff Edwards, Dick Jurgens, Gene Krupa, the Hoylman Quartet, Aileen Stanley and Johnny Marvin, Duke Ellington, the Primo Scala String Band, and Betty Garrett with Larry Parks. Frankie Laine and Keefe Brasselle performed it in the movie *Bring Your Smile Along* (1955), and Dean Martin sang it in *The Silencers* (1966).

"The Sidewalks of New York" (1894), perhaps the most resiliant of all New York City songs, is a contagious waltz by Charles B. Lawlor (lyric) and James W. Blake (music) about a gang of friends gathered on a stoop who plan to "trip the light fantastic." All of the names mentioned in the lyric were actual people Blake knew from his East Eighteenth Street neighborhood. Lottie Gibson introduced the number in the Old London Theatre in the Bowery, and New Yorkers immediately took a shine to it. Dan Quinn and other vaudeville stars performed it on stage, and soon it was heard everywhere from restaurants to block parties to concerts. Quinn made an early recording, as did J.W. Myers and George J. Gaskin, and sheet music sales remained steady for years. The song became the unofficial anthem for New York by the time Alfred E. Smith used it as his campaign song during his bids for the presidency in 1920 and 1924. The tune was revived with a trio version by Alan Dale, Buddy Greco, and Johnny Desmond in 1954, and there were other expert records by Duke Ellington, Dale Miller, Mel Tormé, Mitch Miller, Caterina Valente, and more recently, Bobby Short, Mary Cleere Haran, and Jimmy Roselli. The song has been used in the background of *Rose of Washington Square* (1939), *Sweet Rosie O'Grady* (1943), and dozens of other movies set in New York. It was performed on screen by Lynn Overman in *Little Miss Marker* (1934), Betty Grable and June Haver in *The Dolly Sisters* (1945), and Bob Hope and Jimmy Durante (with a Yiddish lyric by Sammy Cahn) in *Beau James* (1957). The number was also featured in the Broadway show *The Sidewalks of New York* (1927).

"Sierra Sue" (1916) is the sorrowful plea of a cowboy to his gal Sue to leave the big city and come back to him and to "the hills that love you." Joseph Buell Carey wrote the folklike number that found its greatest success in the 1940s, making it to the top spot on *Your Hit Parade* because of hit recordings by Elliot Shapiro, Bing Crosby, Glen Gray and the Casa Loma Orchestra (vocal by Kenny Sargent), and Glenn Miller (vocal by Ray Eberly). Other notable discs were made by Gene Autry, Eddy Arnold, Gene Krupa, and the team of Flanagan and Allen. Autry reprised it in the movie *Sierra Sue* (1941), and the song was heard in *Country Fair* (1941).

"Silver Threads Among the Gold" (1873) is a domestic ballad by Eben E. Rexford (lyric) and Hart P. Danks (music) that proved to be one of the most successful sentimental songs of its era, selling over a million copies of sheet music by the end of the century. Rexford wrote the lyric as a poem about an old couple, their hair turning to gray and their lives "fading fast." But the two are still in love as they admit that the other never seems to have grown any older. The poem was published in a Wisconsin farm journal, where Danks saw it and paid Rexford $3 for it.

Danks made a fortune off the song, and Rexford got close to nothing, even his marriage (which had inspired his poem) ending in divorce soon after. Vaudeville performers and barbershop quartets made the ballad famous, and it was further popularized when John McCormack sang it in concerts and on record. Later discs were made by Vaughn Monroe, the Banjo Kings, Dick Curless, Daniel O'Donnell, Mitch Miller, and Jerry Lee Lewis.

"Since I Fell for You" (1948) is an adoring ballad by Buddy Johnson that became popular because of a jazz recording by pianist Paul Gayten and his Trio (vocal by Annie Laurie) that climbed the charts. Lenny Welch revived the song in 1963 with a chart record as well. Among the other artists to make disc versions were Mel Tormé with George Shearing's Orchestra, Charlie Rich, Laura Lee, Etta Jones, Doris Day, the Ramsey Lewis Trio, Barbara George, Nina Simone, and Tom Jones. The number was heard in the film *The Sergeant* (1968).

"Sincerely" (1955), a hit on the pop as well as the rhythm-and-blues charts, is a gushing pledge of love by Harvey Fuqua and Alan Freed that was introduced with success by the Moonglows. But an even bigger hit was a disc by the McGuire Sisters that reached the Number One spot in all four categories. The number was revived by the Four Seasons in 1964, and Paul Anka had success with it in 1969. Connie Francis, the Platters, Johnny Otis, the Persuasions, Bobby Vee, and the Tokens were among the others to record it. The Five Satins sang it in *Let the Good Times Roll* (1973), the Moonglows' recording was used in *American Hot Wax* (1978), and it was heard in *Sparkle* (1976) and *Goodfellas* (1990). "Sincerely" was also sung by the cast of the Off-Broadway revue *The Taffetas* (1988).

"Sing, Sing, Sing" (1936), one of the most recognized of all swing numbers, celebrates the urge to sing, but the song is more famous as a dance piece with a lot of scat singing involved. Louis Prima wrote and introduced the song, and there were other early records by Tommy Dorsey and Fletcher Henderson, but it was Benny Goodman who popularized the number by playing it at the renowned Carnegie Hall jazz concert in 1938 and stopping the show. Goodman's recording with featured solos by Harry James, Vido Musso, and Gene Krupa is considered a classic, a fifteen-minute rendition of the song that had to be recorded in two parts to fit onto discs. Hollywood often used the song in the background to recreate the swing era, and the number was featured in *After the Thin Man* (1936), *Strike Up the Band* (1940), and *The Benny Goodman Story* (1956), where it was reprised by James and Krupa. On Broadway "Sing, Sing, Sing" was performed by the casts of *Dancin'* (1978), *Fosse* (1999), and *Swing* (1999), the Goodman recording was used in *Contact* (2000), and it was sung by the cast of the Off-Broadway revue *Swingtime Canteen* (1995).

"Singin' the Blues (Till My Daddy Comes Home)" (1920) is a Dixieland blues number by Sam M. Lewis, Joe Young (lyric), Con Conrad, and J. Russell Robinson (music) that has been a favorite of all kinds of bands over the years. The song was popularized by the Original Dixieland Jazz Band, but the most successful version of all was a record by Fletcher Henderson's Connie's Inn Orchestra. Other commendable discs were made by Lionel Hampton, Adrian Rollini (vocal by Pat Hoke), Frankie Trumbauer featuring Bix Beiderbecke, Nat Gonella, Flip Phillips, and Rick Fay. The Beiderbecke recording was used effectively in the film *Bullets Over Broadway* (1994).

"Sioux City Sue" (1945) is a simpleminded but sincere cowboy song by Ray Freedman (lyric) and Dick Thomas (music) about a cowpoke driving cattle from Nebraska who meets up with a gal in Iowa and is smitten with her red hair and blue eyes, admitting, "I'd swap my horse and dog for you." Thomas introduced the ballad on record with success, but it was Bing Crosby who had the biggest hit with it, his record with the Jesters and Bob Haggart's Orchestra climbing the charts. Tony Pastor and his Orchestra also had a hit with the song, and there was a popular country-western version by Zeke Manners. Merle Travis, Bob Wills and his Texas Playboys, Gene Autry, the Original Memphis Five, Spade Cooley and Tex Williams, and Willie Nelson were among the artists also to record it. Autry also sang it in the movie *Sioux City Sue* (1946).

"Sister Susie's Sewing Shirts for Soldiers" (1914) is a tongue-twisting ditty by R.P. Weston (lyric) and Herman E. Darewski (music) about making "such silly silken shirts" and other alliterative doings. The British song was introduced right before the outbreak of World War One, and it was a favorite of soldiers throughout the war years. In America Al Jolson featured it in his act and recorded it, and Billy Murray had a popular disc as well. The novelty number was pretty much forgotten by the depression but was somewhat revived when it was used on Broadway as a sing-along led by Barbara Windsor in the British import *Oh! What a Lovely War!* (1964).

"Sittin' on a Log (Pettin' My Dog)" (1934) is a baby-talk number by Byron Gay (lyric) and Edward "Zez" Confrey (music) that was popular during the depression. Jack Denny and his Orchestra introduced the song on record with baby-voiced Jeanie Long doing the vocals. There were also major discs by Fran Frey, Sam Robbins, Isham Jones, and Anson Weeks (vocal by Bob Crosby).

"Sixteen Tons" (1947) is the rhythmic lament of a muscular worker who does hard labor all day and is always in debt because "I owe my soul" to the company's store. Merle Travis, the son of a Kentucky coal miner, wrote the number based on his background and recorded it, but the disc was only a modest success. It was Tennessee Ernie Ford's 1955 record that sold a million copies and hit the top spot in all categories. Ford sang it on his television show and used it as a signature song throughout his career. Tom Jones revived the number in 1967, and Don Harrison had success with it in 1976. Other artists to record the woeful ballad include Frankie Laine, the Weavers, Big Bill Broonzy, the Platters, the Tombstones, Lorne Greene, and Johnny Cash. Jason Graae sang "Sixteen Tons" in the Off-Broadway revue *Forever Plaid* (1990).

"Skip to My Lou" (c. 1844) is a carefree American folk song of unknown origin and author, but it is estimated that settlers were dancing to it several years before the Civil War. The nonsense lyric is a series of comments ("flies in the buttermilk . . . shoo, fly, shoo") and questions ("lost my partner . . . what'll I do?") to be sung while dancing. In addition to many children's records, the song was recorded by such artists as Pete Seeger, Judy Garland, Leadbelly, Frances Faye, Lawrence Welk, and Liza Minnelli. Garland sang and danced the number with Lucille Bremer, Henry Daniels Jr., and Tom Drake in the movie *Meet Me in St. Louis* (1944), and it was performed by the ensemble in the 1989 Broadway version of the movie musical.

"Skylark" (1942) is an indelible ballad by Johnny Mercer (lyric) and Hoagy Carmichael (music) that asks a bird if it knows where one's lover is and if it will lead the way there. Carmichael's music starts in an unusual way, a cry already in progress, and the melody is "loaded with chromatic shifts and changing emphasis," as described by James R. Morris. "The harmony is complex and daring . . . overall it is a strange song, but one that never loses its appeal." Glenn Miller and his Orchestra (vocal by Ray Eberly) popularized the ballad, and an early recording by Harry James (vocal by Helen Forrest) was also a hit, keeping the ballad on the *Hit Parade* for three months. Over the years there have been dozens of memorable discs, including those by Dinah Shore, Rosemary Clooney, Bing Crosby, Ella Fitzgerald, Woody Herman, Jack Jones, Tony Bennett, Bette Midler, Andrea Marcovicci, Linda Ronstadt, Annie Ross, George Cables, Chuck Hedges, and Carmichael himself. K.D. Lang sang it on the soundtrack of the film *Midnight in the Garden of Good and Evil*

(1997), and on Broadway it was performed by Jessica Molaskey in the Mercer revue *Dream* (1997).

"Sleep" (1923), the theme song for Fred Waring's Pennsylvanians for sixty years, is a graceful but uptempo lullaby by Earl Lebieg that he adapted from his earlier piano piece "Visions of Sleep." The Pennsylvanians popularized the song that urges one to sleep and dream in a hit recording with Fred and Tom Waring doing the featured vocals. Although it was always identified with the singing group, "Sleep" was recorded by many other artists as well, including Benny Goodman, Tommy Dorsey, Benny Carter, Les Paul and Mary Ford, Duke Ellington, Bobby Hackett, Earl Bostic, Ray Noble, the Moms and Dads, and Little Willie John.

"Sleepy Lagoon" (1930) was a symphonic composition, then a popular instrumental before it became a Tin Pan Alley song. British composer Eric Coates wrote a piece called "By a Sleepy Lagoon" that he adapted into a band arrangement in 1930. In 1942 Jack Lawrence added a lyric that described an idyllic spot for two lovers to meet, and the new number was introduced by Xavier Cugat and his Orchestra (vocal by Buddy Clark). An instrumental version by Harry James and a disc by Tommy Dorsey (with a trumpet solo by Red Seal) were both hits and put the song on *Your Hit Parade* for eighteen weeks. The Platters revived it with success in 1960. Well-known records were also made by Dinah Shore, Toots Thielemans, Ray Anthony, Meredith Willson's Orchestra, Beryl Davis with David Rose's Orchestra, Ralph Marterie, the Norman Luboff Choir, Al Hirt, and Coates himself. The song can be heard in the movies *Du Barry Was a Lady* (1943) and *Sleepy Lagoon* (1943).

"Sleepy Time Gal" (1925) is the comic lament of a husband who can't get his party-loving wife to stop dancing and come home to bed, complaining to her that "you're turning night into day." Joseph R. Alden and Raymond Egan wrote the wry lyric and Richard A. Whiting and Ange Lorenzo composed the lazy, early morning music that becomes a flapper's dance number when speeded up. Ben Bernie and his Orchestra introduced the song with a hit record, and it was an early success for Gene Austin, Glen Gray and the Casa Loma Orchestra, and Nick Lucas. Harry James revived the number in 1944, and many of the Big Bands played it during the 1940s. Distinctive recordings were made by Jimmie Lunceford, Paul Weston, the Mills Brothers, Josephine Baker, Eddie Condon, Art Lund, Roy Lanham and the Whippoorwills, Ken Griffin, Buddy Cole, and Bob Wilson and his Varsity Rhythm Boys. The number was heard in the film *Sleepytime Gal* (1942), and Frances Langford sang it in *Never a Dull Moment* (1943).

"Slow Poke" (1951), a country ballad about a happily contented slow-motion sweetie, crossed over to become a hit for various kinds of artists. The droll lyric complains about how one's dearie is always late, has no sense of time, and cannot be changed; so one had just better learn to be a slow poke, too. Mrs. Chilton, a Louisville housewife, wrote an early version of the song and sent it to bandleader Pee Wee King. He and Redd Steward made some refinements, then introduced it on a record with King's band and Stewart doing the vocal. The disc sold a million copies, and there were also successful records by Roberta Lee with Neal Hefti's Orchestra, Helen O'Connell, Arthur Godfrey, and Ralph Flanagan's Orchestra. The number remained an audience favorite at the Grand Ole Op'ry in Nashville for many years. Tennessee Ernie Ford, Doris Day, Gisele MacKenzie, Billy Vaughn, Hawkshaw Hawkins, the Ray Conniff Singers, and the group Riders in the Sky were among those who also recorded it. The King version was heard on the soundtrack of the film *The Last Picture Show* (1971).

"Smile" (1936) is a sublime ballad that is low key in its optimism, urging one to smile even if your heart is aching because the sun always has a way of shining through. Charles Chaplin composed the poignant music as the theme for his film classic *Modern Times* (1936), and the lyric was added later by John Turner and Geoffrey Parsons. Although it was recorded several times in the 1930s and 1940s, the song didn't become a chart hit until Tony Bennett revived it in 1959. There were also successful records by Timi Yuro in 1961, the team of Ferrante and Teicher in 1962, and Jerry Butler and Betty Everett in 1965. Nat King Cole's disc with Nelson Riddle's Orchestra is considered a ballad classic, and there were other laudable records by Frank Sinatra, Judy Garland, Sunny Gale, Peggy Lee, Ruth Brown, Dexter Gordon, David Whitfield with Eric Rogers' Orchestra, Dean Martin, David Axelrod, Herb Alpert and the Tijuana Brass, Johnny Mathis, and Natalie Cole. "Smile" was sung by the cast of the Off-Broadway revue *The Taffetas* (1988).

"Smiles" (1917) is a rousing cheer-up song that became a particular favorite during World War One even though the number has nothing to do with victory or fighting. Lee Roberts composed the sparkling music, and J. Will Callahan penned the zestful lyric that lists the various kinds of smiles there are and concludes that the best ones are those that "you give to me." The songwriters couldn't get any publishing house interested in the number, so they published it themselves, and it sold over 2 million copies of sheet music within six months. The song was introduced by Joseph C. Smith's Orchestra and was then interpolated into the Broadway revue *The Passing Show of 1918*, where it was sung by Neil Carrington and the girls' chorus. It later became the theme song for the

Ipana Troubadours, and major records were also made by Claude Thorn-
hill, Benny Goodman, Eddy Duchin, Charlie Barnet, Lou Reed, Lionel
Hampton, Gil Evans, Stan Getz, Oscar Peterson, and Coleman Hawkins.
Judy Garland sang "Smiles" in the movie *For Me and My Gal* (1942), Betty
Hutton and the chorus performed it in *Somebody Loves Me* (1952), and it
was heard in *Applause* (1929), *Tin Pan Alley* (1940), *The Dolly Sisters* (1945),
Pete Kelly's Blues (1955), and *The Eddy Duchin Story* (1956). On Broadway,
Jerry Zaks and Catherine Wright led the cast of the revue *Tintypes* (1980)
in singing it as the finale. The song is sometimes listed as "There Are
Smiles That Make Me Happy."

"Smoke Dreams" (1937) is a romantic ballad that uses that now-
unromantic image of a cigarette to create a picture of sweet melancholy.
Nacio Herb Brown composed the soft, dreamy music, and Arthur Freed
wrote the lyric about a thwarted lover smoking a cigarette in the dark,
the smoke rings rising up and dissolving like unfulfilled dreams. The
number was written for the film *After the Thin Man* (1937), but it got little
attention until Benny Goodman (vocal by Helen Ward) popularized it
on record and it was used as the theme song for the *Chesterfield Supper
Club* on radio. Other artists who made notable discs include Johnny
Hamp, Red Norvo, Abe Lyman (vocal by Sunny Schuyler), Jo Stafford,
Frankie Carle, Mildred Bailey, and more recently, K.D. Lang.

"Smoke! Smoke! Smoke! (That Cigarette)" (1947) is a honky-tonk country song by Tex Williams and Merle Travis that complains about being
addicted to cigarettes, wanting to murder the guy who invented the dang
things and knowing that everyone is going to smoke themselves right
up to St. Peter's gate. The lively, cantankerous number was introduced
by Williams and Travis with a record that sold 2 million copies. Phil
Harris also had a hit with the hoedown piece. Among those who also
recorded it were Jimmy Dean, Commander Cody and his Lost Planet
Airmen, the Blue Mountain Boys, Bambi and the Boys, Johnny Bond,
Sammy Davis Jr., Johnny Duncan, and Willie Nelson.

"Snookey Ookums" (1913) is a funny novelty number by Irving Berlin
about a local couple who drive all the neighbors crazy with their inces-
sant baby talk to each other. Natalie Normandy introduced the farcical
ditty filled with irritating endearments (such as the title phrase), and
there were early hit records by the team of Arthur Collins and Bryan
Harlan and Billy Murray. The silly song had been pretty much forgotten
when it was revived in the movie *Easter Parade* (1948), with Fred Astaire
and Judy Garland performing it with panache.

"Snuggled on Your Shoulder (Cuddled in Your Arms)" (1932) is a warm romantic ballad by Joe Young (lyric) and Carmen Lombardo (music), one of the best of the "cuddle" songs that Tin Pan Alley has always produced. The cozy ballad was introduced on record by Guy Lombardo and the Royal Canadians (vocal by Carmen Lombardo), and it was also a hit for Kate Smith, Jack Denny, Morton Downey, and Eddy Duchin. Kay Starr revived it with success in the late 1950s, and there were also noteworthy versions by Doris Day, Red Norvo, and Marty Grosz and Destiny's Tots.

"So Blue" (1927), a rare nonproduction song by the celebrated Broadway team of DeSylva, Brown, and Henderson, is a somber but effective ballad about the loneliness of lost love. B.G. DeSylva and Lew Brown wrote the tender lyric, Ray Henderson composed the graceful music, and it was popularized with a record by Harry Richman. "So Blue" was also a success for Annette Hanshaw with J. Russell Robinson, Nick Lucas, and Paul Whiteman, and provided a hit for Pee Wee Hunt and his Band when they revived it in 1954. Peggy Lee, the Revelers, and the Statler Brothers were among those who also recorded it.

"So Help Me" (1934), one of Irving Berlin's many ballads that use an everyday expression to convey a hidden feeling, is a moving portrait of one helplessly smitten by love. Freddy Martin (vocal by Elmer Feldkamp) made the first notable disc of the song, and it was also recorded with success by Emil Coleman and Paul Hamilton (vocal by Chick Bullock). A popular record by Paul Weston's Orchestra (with a whistling solo by Fred Lowery) revived the number in the mid-1950s, and there were also discs of note by the Five Willows and Bunny Berigan.

"So Long" (1940) is a soothing farewell song that was used by many bands as their closing number at dances and concerts in the 1940s and 1950s. Russ Morgan, Remus Harris, and Irving Melsher collaborated on the ballad, and Morgan and his Orchestra introduced it with a popular record. Gene Krupa and the Charioteers each had hit versions, and the song was revived in 1954 by the Four Aces.

"So Long (It's Been Good to Know You)" (1951) is a sincere farewell song by Woody Guthrie that is directed to friends and neighbors rather than to a true love. Guthrie wrote the number in the 1930s when he was forced to leave his home in the Oklahoma Dust Bowl and head for California, saying good-bye to the "Oakies" staying behind. The folk song borrows liberally from other classics in the genre, the verse echoing "The Ballad of Billy the Kid" and the refrain quoting from "Goodnight, Irene." Although Guthrie sang the song in concert on occasion, it was not published or recorded until 1951 with a disc by the Weavers, the group's first hit. The orchestras of Ralph Martiere and Paul West also made successful records at the time, and there were later well-known versions by Pete Seeger, the Cumberland Three, James Talley, Ernest Tubb, Jack Elliott, and Guthrie himself. David Carradine sang the ballad in the Guthrie film bio *Bound for Glory* (1976).

"So Many Times" (1939) is one of a handful of songs Tommy Dorsey composed as well as performed. Don De Vito penned the quiet lyric about the frequency of one's thoughts about a sweetheart, and Dorsey wrote the mellifluous melody. He recorded it with his Orchestra as an instrumental and again with a vocal by Jack Leonard. There were also hit versions of the number by Jack Teagarden (vocal by Kitty Kallen) and Tommy Tucker (vocal by Amy Arnell). Glenn Miller, Ernest Tubb, and Stephen Stills are among those who also recorded the ballad.

"So Tired" (1943) is a slow and lazy number about being weary of waiting for a beloved to call. Russ Morgan and Jack Stuart wrote the meandering song that complains of forever longing for and saving one's heart for an uncommunicative lover. Morgan and his Orchestra introduced the song on record in 1943, but it was a failure. Still he was convinced of its quality, so in 1949 he put the old recording on the reverse side of one of his new numbers. The record was a hit, and the neglected song was finally applauded. Kay Starr had one of her first successes with the ballad, and it was a hit for Freddy Martin (vocal by Merv Griffin) as well. Among the many others who recorded it were Hoagy Carmichael, Harry James, Orrin Tucker and Bonnie Baker, Art Blakey and the Jazz Messengers, Etta Jones, the Chambers Brothers, Johnny Griffin, Cliff Bruner, and Arthur Collins.

"Some of These Days" (1910) is an important turning point for Tin Pan Alley, a number Alec Wilder calls "perhaps *the* landmark song" of the era because it is "completely unlike most songs of the time. . . . [I]t is derived from none of the elements then current." Shelton Brooks, an African American singer, wrote the bluesy number in 4/4 time as a slow march, yet it has some jazz in it as well. The music is uniquely sophisticated for its day, using an ABCD structure that James R. Morris points out as "each section introducing new melodic ideas avoiding the traditional practice of repeating previously heard material." This unusual quality opened the door for improvisation and formed the basis for later jazz interpretations of popular songs. The lyric uses repeated identities ("hugging . . . kissing; lonely . . . honey") to tell a departing lover that he'll regret leaving and will miss her someday. Sophie Tucker introduced the number at the White City Park in Chicago, recorded it a few times, and sang it for decades as a torch song, a sentimental ballad, a seriocomic novelty number, and a dramatic character song. Of the hundreds of recordings over the years, memorable discs were made by such artists as Louis Armstrong, Bing Crosby, Paul Whiteman, Earl Hines, Joe Venuti, Ted Lewis, Harry James, Jan August, Judy Garland, Orrin Tucker and Bonnie Baker, Cab Calloway, Bobby Darin, and Dorothy Loudon with Buddy Barnes' All-Stars. Tucker sang it in three films—*Honky Tonk* (1929), *Broadway Melody of 1938* (1937), and *Follow the Boys* (1944). "Some of These Days" was also performed by Lillian Roth in *Animal Crackers* (1930), Jeanette MacDonald and Gilda Gray in *Rose Marie* (1936), Erzsebet Foldi in *All That Jazz* (1979), and it was heard in *Broadway* (1942) and other movies. Also, Barbara Rubenstein performed it in the Broadway revue *Bubbling Brown Sugar* (1976).

"Somebody Else Is Taking My Place" (1937) is a heart-tugging lament about a scorned lover who is miserable knowing that his former sweetie has found someone else, and she goes around "with a smile on [her] face." Dick Howard, Russ Morgan, and Bob Ellsworth collaborated on the number, and Morgan introduced it with his orchestra with modest success. The song was much more popular four years later, reaching the top spot on the *Hit Parade* because of a record by Benny Goodman (vocal by Peggy Lee) and the Morgan disc finally catching on. Al Martino revived the ballad in 1965, and there were other notable records by Kate Smith, Claude Thornhill, Percy Humphrey, Gene Autry and the Sons of the Pioneers, Bunny Berigan, Joni James, the Rag Pickers, Dinah Washington, the Preservation Hall Jazz Band, Bill Haley and the Comets, Connie Francis, Mose Allison, Spiegle Wilcox, and Steve Lawrence. The number was heard in the movies *Strictly in the Groove* (1942) and *Call of the Canyon* (1942), and Morgan and his band reprised it in *Sarge Goes to College* (1947).

"Somebody Loves Me" (1924) is an early George Gershwin hit that is still heard today and doesn't seem to date at all. B.G. DeSylva and Ballard MacDonald wrote the nimble lyric about a true love who has not yet appeared on the scene, but one is confident that such a person exists. Gershwin's music is unusual for its nebulous harmony and the distinctive "blue note" on the word "who." Winnie Lightner introduced the song in the Broadway revue *George White's Scandals of 1924*, and there were early records by Marion Harris and Paul Whiteman. Blossom Seeley featured it in her act for decades, and the Four Lads revived it with a hit record in 1952. Other major discs were made by Al Jolson, Dinah Shore, Benny Goodman, Bing Crosby, Erroll Garner, Helen Morgan, Lee Wiley, Nat King Cole, Peggy Lee, Art Tatum, Eddie Fisher, and more recently, Maureen McGovern and Mary Cleere Haran. "Somebody Loves

Me" can be heard in several movies, including renditions by Lena Horne in *Broadway Rhythm* (1944), Oscar Levant and Tom Patricula in the Gershwin bio *Rhapsody in Blue* (1945), Doris Day and Gene Nelson in *Lullabye of Broadway* (1951), Betty Hutton and Ralph Meeker (dubbed by Pat Morgan) in the Seeley bio *Somebody Loves Me* (1952), Peggy Lee in *Pete Kelly's Blues* (1955), and Ann Blyth (dubbed by Gogi Grant) in *The Helen Morgan Story* (1957).

"Somebody Stole My Gal" (1918) is an uptempo torch song by Leo Wood that took a while to catch on but eventually became a standard for jazz and pop artists. Wood's lyric might be considered maudlin as it bemoans the loss of a sweetie, but the music remains robust and cheerful even as its descending notes tumble into the lower register. Although the song was published in 1918, it did not find an audience until Ted Lewis and his Orchestra made a successful disc in 1922. It was revived with success by Johnnie Ray in 1953. Of the many recordings over the years, there were significant ones by Fats Waller, Ted Weems, Fletcher Henderson, Bix Beiderbecke, Larry Adler, Benny Goodman, Cab Calloway, Billy Cotton, Buddy Cole, Milton Brown, Bobby Darin, Count Basie, and Jimmy Rushing. The catchy number can be heard in the film *When Willie Comes Marching Home* (1950).

"Someday (You'll Want Me to Want You)" (1940) is an ambiguous ballad by Jimmie Hodges that is both a boast and a lament. He fears that by the time his darling comes around to loving him back, he'll be in love with someone else; yet the lyric can be interpreted as a threat as well. Elton Britt introduced and popularized the song on record, but a 1949 disc by Vaughn Monroe was a much bigger hit, reaching the top of the charts. Eddy Arnold, the Ames Brothers, Ricky Nelson, and the Mills Brothers also had success with the ballad. There were later recordings by Dean Martin, Jim Reeves, Patsy Cline, Ray Charles, and Sonny and Cher. Gene Autry sang the number in the movie *Sioux City Sue* (1946).

"Someday I'll Find You" (1930), probably Noel Coward's most well-known ballad, was written for the London comedy *Private Lives* (1930) where he and Gertrude Lawrence sang it briefly. The simple but entrancing number yearns to find an ideal mate, one "true to the dream I am dreaming." The play was a hit, and the flowing ballad became famous. Coward and Lawrence recorded it together and separately and performed it in the Broadway production of *Private Lives* in 1931. It was sung by Norma Shearer and Robert Montgomery in the 1931 film version and by Julie Andrews in the Lawrence bio *Star!* (1968). In the Off-Broadway bio *If Love Were All* (1999), "Someday I'll Find You" was performed by Harry Groener and Twiggy as Coward and Lawrence. Of the many others who recorded it, there were distinctive versions by Doris Day, Mel Tormé with George Shearing's Orchestra, Sonny Rollins, Barbara Lea, Marian McPartland, and Bobby Short.

"Someday Sweetheart" (1919) is a jazz standard by John and Benjamin Spikes in which a suitor dreams of a future with his beloved. Early successful discs were made by Mildred Bailey, King Oliver, Gene Austin, Bing Crosby, and Count Basie. Of the dozens that followed were commendable recordings by Woody Herman, Art Hodes, Red Allen, Eddie Condon. Ethel Waters, Benny Goodman, Jelly Roll Morton, Les Brown, the Dukes of Dixieland, Muggsy Spanier, Pete Fountain, Chet Atkins, Les Paul, and Della Resse.

"Sometimes I Feel Like a Motherless Child" (1918) is a traditional American spiritual that was sung as early as the Civil War but wasn't published until 1918. The moaning ballad about being alone and unloved, feeling like an orphan "a long ways from home," has a touch of the blues in it, and later it was interpreted by jazz artists as well. Among the many memorable recordings were those by Paul Robeson, Artie Shaw, Louis Armstrong, Helen Merrill, Marian Anderson, Fats Waller, the Golden Gate Quartet, Sarah Vaughan, Jessye Norman, Elvis Presley, the Clayton Brothers, Lena Horne, Jimmy Scott, and Mahalia Jackson. The song can be heard in *Way Down South* (1939) and other movies set in the Deep South, and it was sung by Lynn Thigpen in the Broadway revue *Tintypes* (1980).

"The Song From Moulin Rouge" (1953), just as well known as "Where Is Your Heart?," was based on the sorrowful French song "Le Long de la Seine" by Jacques Larue (French lyric) and Georges Auric (music). Bill Engvick wrote an English lyric for the Toulouse-Lautrec film bio *Moulin Rouge* (1952), where it was performed by Zsa Zsa Gabor (dubbed by Muriel Smith). The lyric is about a woman who is suspicious of her intended one's faithfulness, observing that when they kiss he closes his eyes and seems to dream of someone else. The English version of the song caught on right away, helped by a recording by Percy Faith and his Orchestra (vocal by Felicia Sanders) that sold a million copies. The orchestras of Henri Rene and Mantovani also had hits with the ballad. Among the other artists to record it were Andy Williams, Gisele MacKenzie, Bing Crosby, Connie Francis, Pete Fountain, Coleman Hawkins, Joni James, Pat Suzuki, Floyd Cramer, Jerry Vale, Erroll Garner, Les Brown, Gene Pitney, Michel Legrand, and Willie Nelson.

"The Song Is Ended (But the Melody Lingers On)" (1927), an Irving Berlin standard whose title has been called the theme of all popular music, is a chilling number in which both a lover and the ballad that was "their song" are gone; yet neither can be forgotten because they remain in one's memory. Ruth Etting popularized the number in clubs and on record, and it was revived in 1948 by Nellie Lutcher and her Rhythm. Other standout records were made by Jack Smith, Dick Haymes with Carmen Cavallaro, Jeri Southern, Ella Fitzgerald, Dizzy Gillespie, Louis Armstrong, the Randy Johnston Trio, Nat King Cole, Bob Barnard, Dinah Washington, and more recently, Andrea Marcovicci and Gerry Mulligan. Oddly, the song was not included in any of the Berlin-scored movies except *Blue Skies* (1946), where it was only heard in the background in one scene.

"Song of the Islands" (1915) is one of the most popular of all songs about Hawaii, an atmospheric number that paints an idyllic picture of the islands where the "skies of blue are calling me." Charles E. King wrote the ballad, which was first published in Honolulu and eventually made its way to the mainland, where it became a hit. Wayne King and his Orchestra revived the song in 1930, and Bing Crosby had a hit record of it in 1936. Ben Pollack's Band recorded it twice and used it as their theme song for years. Other discs of note include those by Frankie Laine, Count Basie, Harry Owens, Bobby Breen, Jesse Crawford, Burl Ives, Louis Armstrong, Hank Snow, Bob Crosby, Earl Bostic, Les Paul, Marty Robbins, and Andy Williams, as well as many Hawaiian bands and musicians. Owens' Band reprised it in the movie *Song of the Islands* (1942), and it can be heard in several other films, including *Melody Lane* (1929), *Flirtation Walk* (1934), *'Til We Meet Again* (1940), *Ice-Capades Revue* (1942), and *Cheaper By the Dozen* (1950).

"Sophisticated Lady" (1933), the song most often associated with Duke Ellington, is a cool jazz number about a gal who seems "nonchalant" as she smokes and drinks, but underneath she is longing for a long-lost love. The music is known for its "intense harmonic textures," according to James R. Morris, and its "rich chromatic tonalities which color the melody unforgettably." Ellington composed the number as an instrumental piece and even recorded a version of it in 1932, but it was never released. Mitchell Parish and Irving Mills added the lyric in 1933, and hit records by Ellington and his Orchestra and Glen Gray and the Casa Loma Orchestra popularized the song. While some argue that the piece makes a better instrumental than a vocal song, citing instances where the words have trouble keeping up with the gliding melody, it has been equally successful as both. Billy Eckstine revived the number in 1948, and Rosemary Clooney did the same in 1956 with a recording with Ellington. Morton Gould, Buddy Cole, the Boswell Sisters, Jimmie Lunceford, George Shearing, Andre Kostelanetz, Stan Kenton, Art Tatum,

Willie Smith, and Quincy Jones are among the many to make effective discs of the song. More recently there have been recordings by Phyllis Hyman, Linda Ronstadt, and Natalie Cole. Ellington reprised "Sophisticated Ladies" in the film *Paris Blues* (1961), and on Broadway it was sung by Chip Garnett and Vernon Washington in *Bubbling Brown Sugar* (1976), Gregory Hines in *Sophisticated Ladies* (1981), and Michele Bautier in *Stardust* (1987).

"Sound Off" (1941) is probably the most famous of the many nonsense songs sung by soldiers while doing close order training drills. This one was originally published in a training manual in Harrisburg, Pennsylvania, and it is believed to come from a counting chant sung by black troops in World War Two. Willie Lee Duckworth is the credited author, and the number is sometimes titled "The Duckworth Chant." The song became popular outside of the military when Vaughn Monroe and his Orchestra recorded it with success. The ditty was also familiar to civilians because it was used in radio and television commercials for Chesterfield cigarettes. The U.S. Marine Band and other marching ensembles recorded it, as well as Mickey Katz, Slim Gaillard, Jerry Gray, and Michael Brecker. It can also be heard in the movie *Sound Off* (1952).

"South of the Border (Down Mexico Way)" (1939) is a Spanish-flavored ballad that was written by two British songwriters, and it became a Tin Pan Alley hit on more than one occasion. Jimmy Kennedy and Michael Carr wrote the romantic number that recalls a love affair in Mexico, and it was introduced in the States by a Gene Autry recording that sold 3 million discs. Shep Fields and his Orchestra also had a record that went to the top of the charts, and Frank Sinatra revived it in 1953 with a bestseller. That year it was also the top seller of sheet music in the country. Country, jazz, and pop artists have all recorded it, including Kenny Baker, Tony Martin, Benny Goodman, Count Basie, Horace Heidt, the Champs, the Norman Luboff Choir, Bob Wills, Acker Bilk, the Doobie Brothers, Sammy Kaye, Herb Alpert and the Tijuana Brass, Willie Nelson, Patsy Cline, and a novelty version by Alec Templeton called "Opera Presentation of 'South of the Border.' " Autry reprised it in the movies *South of the Border* (1939) and *Down Mexico Way* (1941), Bing Crosby and Cantinflas performed it in *Pepe* (1960), and Dean Martin sang it in *The Silencers* (1966).

"Sparrow in the Tree Top" (1951) is a peppy little ditty by Bob Merrill about a very cheerful bird. Arthur Godfrey popularized it on his television show, and Guy Mitchell with Mitch Miller's Orchestra made a very successful disc version. The novelty number was also recorded by Bing Crosby and the Andrews Sisters, Rex Allen, and Jack Mudurian.

"S'posin' " (1929) is a lighthearted love song that provided Rudy Vallee with his first hit record. Paul Denniker composed the playful music, and Andy Razaf wrote the slangy lyric that asked a sweetie a series of questions: Suppose I fell in love with you? Would you return it? Would it "distress you" or would it "impress you?" Vallee's record popularized the song, and Fats Waller's wry version was also a hit. Years later it was revived with a successful 1953 disc by Don Cornell. Among the many others who recorded it were Andy Kirk, Seger Ellis, Doris Day, Erskine Hawkins, Jack Leonard, Al Hibbler, Helen Humes, Ruby Braff, Maxine Sullivan, Debbie Reynolds, Jane Jarvis, and the Miles Davis Quintet. Donald O'Connor sang it in the movie *Feudin', Fussin' and a-Fightin'* (1948).

"Spreadin' Rhythm Around" (1935) is a sassy song about Harlem night life that was most often associated with Fats Waller. Ted Koehler (lyric) and Jimmy McHugh (music) wrote the strutting number about an island (e.g., Manhattan) where everyone is swinging and "out high-hattin' " each night. Waller introduced it with Alice Faye in the film *King of Burlesque* (1935) and then recorded it with success. Billie Holiday, Teddy Wilson, the Mound City Blue Blowers, Pat Flowers, and Bob Howard are among those who also made memorable disc versions. The song was heard in the movie *The First Baby* (1936), and on Broadway it was sung by the cast of the Waller revue *Ain't Misbehavin'* (1978).

"Spring Will Be a Little Late This Year" (1944) is a poignant Frank Loesser ballad about the cold of winter lingering longer than usual since one's love is gone. The music consists of rising and falling musical lines that work potently with the words, giving the song an expansive yet intimate feeling. Deanna Durbin introduced the ballad on record and in the film *Christmas Holiday* (1944), but it was a disc by Morton Downey that popularized the song. Leslie Uggams's 1963 recording revived the number with success. Other notable discs were made by Ralph Flanagan, Dinah Shore, Johnny Johnston, the Red Garland Trio, Sonny Dunham, Joni James, the Four Lads, Eydie Gorme, Wynton Marsalis, and Loesser himself. The ballad can also be heard in the movie *Because of You* (1952).

"Squeeze Me" (1928) is a sexy, suggestive number by Clarence Williams (lyric) and Thomas "Fats" Waller (music) that invites a gal's "daddy" to squeeze her and kiss her every time she says so. Williams and his Blue Five (vocal by Eva Taylor) introduced the sly ballad, but the most popular recording came years later with a disc by Lena Horne. Bessie Smith, Mildred Bailey, Frank Froeba, Louis Armstrong, Bob Crosby, Chick Webb, Red Nichols, Earl Hines, Joe Pass, and Art Hodes are among the many who made major recordings. On Broadway, Amelia McQueen sang the number in the Waller revue *Ain't Misbehavin'* (1978).

"St. James Infirmary" (1930) is a morose ballad by Joe Primrose that was based on a traditional folk song with a morbid tale to tell. A beau is called to the hospital of the title where he looks upon his dead sweetheart stretched out on a table and looking white as a ghost. Primrose's version was first recorded by King Oliver, then popularized in 1931 with a hit record by Cab Calloway. A decade later Artie Shaw made a distinctive recording that took both sides of the record, and there was a successful disc in 1948 by Louis Armstrong with Earl Hines at the piano. Among the artists who also made disc versions were Teddy Wilson, Red Garland, Bob Scobey, Scatman Crothers, Jack Teagarden, the Dukes of Dixieland, Pete Fountain, Lou Rawls, and Bobby "Blue" Bland. The song was interpolated into the Broadway revue *Lew Leslie's Blackbirds of 1934*, it was sung by Bing Crosby in the movie *Birth of the Blues* (1941), and it was heard in *Henry and June* (1990).

"St. Louis Blues" (1914) is probably the "most popular and most imitated blues song ever written," according to Denes Agay, and there is no question it is a landmark in American popular music. W.C. Handy, who wrote both words and music, later told an interviewer that he tried to take the "humor of the coon song, the syncopation of ragtime, and the spirit of Negro folk songs and called it a blues." Recalling his days of destitution in St. Louis when he had to sleep on the cobblestones near the river each night, Handy began his lyric with "I hate to see the evening sun go down" and created a format that would dominate subsequent blues songs. The torchy lyric is a woman's lament for a man with a heart "like a rock cast in the sea," yet she loves him all the same. Sophie Tucker first sang it in vaudeville; then later Gilda Gray did a shimmy dance to it. But it was an orchestral version on the Victor label that prompted the sale of piano rolls and sheet music, millions of each sold over the years. It is also one of the few popular songs to be transmitted for just about every possible musical instrument. Marion Harris's early recording went to the top of the charts, followed by prominent revivals of the number by Bessie Smith in 1925, Louis Armstrong and Cab Calloway in 1930, the Mills Brothers in 1932, the Boswell Sisters in 1935, Benny Goodman in 1936, and Billy Eckstine in 1953. Of the hundreds of other recordings, mention must be made of those by the Original Dixieland Jazz Band, Paul Robeson, Ted Lewis, Bing Crosby with Duke Ellington's Orchestra, Larry Adler, Dinah Shore, Count Basie, Leo Reisman, Lena Horne, Bob Wills and his Texas Playboys, Guy Lombardo, Maxine Sullivan, Pearl Bailey, Johnny Mercer with the Pied Pipers, Andre Kostelanetz, Danny Kaye, and Handy himself who recorded it three times playing the trumpet. The blues standard was heard in over a dozen films, performed by Ted Lewis in *Is Everybody Happy?* (1929), Etta Moten in *Ladies They Talk About* (1933), the Hall Johnson Choir in *Banjo on My Knee* (1936), Maxine Sullivan in *St. Louis Blues* (1939), Ruby Elzy in *Birth of the Blues* (1941), Nan Wynn in *Is Everybody Happy?* (1943). Armstrong in *Jam Session* (1944), and Nat King Cole as Handy in the bio *St. Louis Blues* (1958). "St. Louis Blues" can also be heard in *Dancers in the Dark* (1932), *Baby Face* (1933), *Stella Dallas* (1937), *Do You Love Me?* (1946), *Glory Alley* (1952), and *The Glenn Miller Story* (1954), where it was turned into a "St. Louis Blues March." On Broadway, the song was interpolated into *George White's Scandals of 1926*, the all-Negro revue *Change Your Life* (1930), and *Black and Blue* (1989), where it was sung by Ruth Brown, and it was performed by Gretha Boston in *It Ain't Nothin' But the Blues* (1999).

"Stairway to the Stars" (1939) is a dreamy ballad by Mitchell Parish (lyric), Matt Malneck, and Frank Signorelli (music) about a romance that takes one up into the sky. The piece was written as an instrumental called "Park Avenue Fantasy" in 1935, and Malneck recorded it with his Orchestra. The lyric was added in 1939, and the new version was popularized by Paul Whiteman and his Orchestra. Leading records by Glenn Miller (vocal by Ray Eberly), Kay Kyser, Sammy Kaye, Al Donahue, Martha Raye, and Kenny Baker kept the number on *Your Hit Parade* for twelve weeks. Ella Fitzgerald, Eddie Layton, Erroll Garner, Chet Baker, and Johnny Mathis also recorded the song, and it was heard in the movie *The Glenn Miller Story* (1954).

"Star Dust" (1929), one of the most recorded of all American songs with over 500 different recordings in over forty languages, is a scintillating number in which one recalls a starry night and a lost love, the song itself being part of the memory. Hoagy Carmichael wrote the delicate music that only spans ten notes but is very tricky in its chord changes and is very difficult to sing accurately. The melody was written in 1927 when Carmichael was inspired by the memory of a girl he had loved while a college student at the University of Indiana; the romance ended because he was to pursue the career of a traveling musician, and she longed for security and a home. At a college reunion, Carmichael played the melody and a fellow alumnus, Stuart Gorrell, told the composer that the tune sounded like the dust from the stars falling down on a summer night. Carmichael titled the piano piece "Star Dust," but when it was recorded for the first time by Emil Seidel's Band, it was played as an uptempo, ragtimelike instrumental. A publisher suggested it might do better as a slow and moody torch song, so Mitchell Parish wrote the famous lyric in 1929 with such unforgettable phrases as "stardust melody" and "the meadow of my heart," concluding that love is "the stardust of yesterday." The vocal version was introduced at the Cotton Club in Harlem but didn't catch on until the mid-1930s when Artie Shaw's record sold 2.5 million copies. A disc by Isham Jones and his Orchestra (with Carmichael at the piano) went to the top of the charts, and there were also early hits by Bing Crosby, Louis Armstrong, and Wayne King. Never out of favor and often revived, the ballad enjoyed renewed popularity with records by Jimmie Lunceford in 1935, Benny Goodman and Tommy Dorsey (on opposite sides of the same disc) in 1936, Glenn Miller in 1941, Bill Ward and his Dominoes (vocal by Jackie Wilson) in 1957, Nat King Cole in 1957; Frank Sinatra in 1962, and Nino Tempo and April Stevens in 1964. There were also memorable recordings by Paul Whiteman, Eddy Duchin, Frankie Carle, Fred Lowery, Dick Haines, Guy Lombardo, Victor Borge, Larry Adler, Coleman Hawkins, Phil Baker, Dave Apollon, Elvira Rios (in Spanish), Tex Beneke, and the Pied Pipers. "Star Dust" can be heard in the movies *Hi, Buddy* (1943) and *The Perfect Marriage* (1946), Mary Healy sang it in *Star Dust* (1940), David Essex performed it in the British film *Stardust* (1975), the Nat King Cole recording was heard in both *My Favorite Year* (1982) and *Sleepless in Seattle* (1993), and Rob Wasserman and Aaron Neville performed it on the soundtrack of *Rain Man* (1988). On Broadway, Michele Bautier sang the ballad in the Parish revue *Stardust* (1987).

"The Star Spangled Banner" (1814), the official national anthem of the United States, has the most famous background story of any American song. During the War of 1812, the young lawyer Francis Scott Key was sent to Baltimore to negotiate the release of an American officer who was being held prisoner on a British warship. While there he witnessed the attack on the American Fort McHenry on September 13, 1814, waiting until dawn with others to see if the flag was still waving or if the fort had fallen. The sight of Old Glory on that morning prompted Key to write a poem entitled "The Defense of Fort McHenry," which was published that same year. A Baltimore music publisher brought it out as a song soon after, using a melody by John Stafford Smith, that he based on an English tune called "To Anacreon in Heaven." Although sung by millions of people in schools and ball parks each year, the anthem is one of the most difficult of all patriotic songs to sing. Not only does it have a wide range (a thirteen-step vocal span), but there are some sections with tricky rhythm changes, not to mention the very flowery lyric that is filled with outdated verbiage. But stirring phrases like "the land of the free and the home of the brave" are still effective, and some of the expressions in the lyric, such as "twilight's last gleaming," "dawn's early light," and "rockets' red glare," are much beloved clichés. The new song, sometimes listed as "Oh, Say Can You See?" was introduced by Ferdinand Durang in a Baltimore tavern and has been heard ever since. Probably no one sang it as much as opera singer Lucy Monroe, who racked up over 5,000 performances at concerts and public gatherings during World War Two. Oddly, the popular ballad was not made the official national anthem until an act of Congress in 1931.

"Stars Fell on Alabama" (1934) is an evocative ballad by Mitchell Parish (lyric) and Frank Perkins (music) about two lovers embracing in an Alabama field at night. The number was long associated with Jack Teagarden, who recorded it twice with his Orchestra and often performed it in concert, sometimes playing the trumpet, sometimes singing it, sometimes both. The sonorous ballad was given dozens of recordings, including notable ones by Guy Lombardo (vocal by Carmen Lombardo), Freddy Martin (vocal by Buddy Clark), Richard Himber, Billie Holiday, Benny Goodman, Woody Herman, the Lennon Sisters, Eddie Condon, Stan Getz, Toots Thielemans, Mantovanni's Orchestra, Al Haig, Alberta Hunter, and Johnny Guarnieri. On Broadway it was sung by Jim Walton and Maureen Brennan in the Parish revue *Stardust* (1987).

"Stein Song" (1910) is the official state song of Maine, probably the only such honor bestowed on a drinking ditty. E.A. Fenstad wrote the rousing march in 1901 as an instrumental piece to be played at festivities at the University of Maine. In 1910 students Lincoln Colcord (lyric) and A.W. Sprague (music) adapted the number into a song and added a lyric about filling one's stein and shouting and saluting the college. The number was titled "The Maine Stein Song," was used in a campus variety show, and soon after was adopted as the school song. The number never traveled off the campus until Rudy Vallee and his Connecticut Yankees performed it on the radio in the 1920s, and quickly 350,000 copies of sheet music and a half million records were sold. The song was so popular that Vallee's rival Will Osborne sang a novelty number called "I'd Like to Break the Neck of the Man Who Wrote the Stein Song." During Prohibition, the Maine legislature faced difficulties in declaring such a ribald drinking number the official state song until someone pointed out that the lyric did not say that it was alcohol in the stein, that it could very well be milk, and the proposition passed. "Stein Song" can be heard in the film *College Holiday* (1936), and Susan Hayward (dubbed by Jane Froman) sang it in *With a Song in My Heart* (1952). It has been performed and recorded by many marching bands over the years.

"Stella By Starlight" (1946) is a romantic standard by Ned Washington (lyric) and Victor Young (music) that was based on a musical theme Young had composed for the soundtrack of the movie *The Uninvited* (1944). Young introduced the new number on record, but the most successful disc was a 1947 one by Harry James and his Orchestra (vocal by

Frank Sinatra). Other artists to make recordings of the dreamy song include Buddy Greco, Charlie Parker, Billy Butterfield, Dick Haymes, Al Hibbler, Coleman Hawkins, Chet Baker, Miles Davis, Tom Pierson, Bill Evans, Don Friedman, Steve Smith, Charlie Mariano, and Eddie "Lockjaw" Davis. The ballad can be heard in the movie *Sabrina* (1995).

"Stompin' at the Savoy" (1934) is an early swing number about a romantic interlude at the Savoy Hotel ballroom that Benny Goodman cowrote and popularized. Edgar Samson and Chick Webb collaborated with Goodman on the music that is not a stomp at all but a smooth and gently swinging piece that is dreamlike at times. Although it is usually done as an instrumental, the song has an intriguing lyric by Andy Razaf that repeats the word "Savoy" throughout as a kind of punctuation mark. Webb introduced the number with his Orchestra, but it was the Goodman record that became a bestseller, and the song was more often associated with him. A classic disc by Ella Fitzgerald and Louis Armstrong that uses a lot of scat singing is also very distinctive. Among the other artists to record the song were Jimmy Dorsey, Teddy Wilson, Ben Pollock, Jonah Jones, Woody Herman, the Chicago Rhythm Kings, Art Tatum, Babs' Three Bips and a Bop, Judy Garland, Charlie Ventura, and Eddie South. On Broadway, it was performed by the ensemble of the revue *Bubbling Brown Sugar* (1976), Jimmy Slade in *Black and Blue* (1989), and Ann Hampton Callaway and Laura Benanti in *Swing!* (1999). Louis Prima sang it in the film bio *The Benny Goodman Story* (1956), and Harry Connick Jr. performed it on the soundtrack of *When Harry Met Sally* (1989).

"Stormy Monday Blues" (1941) is a slow and lazy blues by Earl Hines, Billy Eckstine, and Bob Crowder about a rejected lover left lonesome in the rain. The song was introduced on a record by Hines and his Orchestra (vocal by Eckstine) that climbed the charts, and Isaac Hayes revived the ballad with success in 1973. Big Joe Turner, T-Bone Walker, Count Basie, Buddy Guy, Gene Ammons, Lou Rawls, Jimmy Rushing, Smiley Lewis, Bobby "Blue" Bland, John Baldry, and Eric Clapton are among the artists to also record it. "Stormy Monday Blues" was featured in the Broadway revue *Bubbling Brown Sugar* (1976).

"Stormy Weather" (1933), the penetrating torch song most associated today with Lena Horne, has a fruitful history before she adopted it as her trademark song. Ted Koehler wrote the masterful lyric, a lament about the unfriendly weather that torments a woman when a lover has left and she "ain't together." The language is slangy and yet poetic, particularly when she worries that "old rockin' chair will get me." Harold Arlen composed the heart-wrenching music that is as unusual as it is unforgettable. There is no verse, the song breaking into the main theme with a powerful wail. Then instead of the expected structure, Arlen adds two measures in the second and fourth section, which at first threw off musicians used to the traditional eight-bar structure. (When the uneven numbers were pointed out to Arlen, he said he never noticed it, letting the melody dictate the form instead of the other way around.) The song-writers intended the number for Cab Calloway, but it was introduced instead on record by Leo Reisman and his Orchestra (vocal by Arlen), and the song slowly started to catch on. It was widely popularized when Ethel Waters sang it in the revue *Cotton Club Parade* (1933), the singer insisting that she only sing it once a night because she found the torch song so disturbing. For a decade or so Waters sang it in clubs, and it was considered her signature song. But Horne added it to her nightclub act and recorded it in 1941, and it was in her repertoire for decades. Horne sang it with Bill Robinson in the movie *Stormy Weather* (1943) and was still singing it when she did her one-woman show on Broadway in 1981. Other notable recordings were made by Waters, Guy Lombardo, Duke Ellington, Frank Sinatra, Eddy Duchin, Morton Gould, Peggy Lee, Connie Haines, Tex Beneke, Larry Adler, and Rickey Jordan. In the film *Swing Parade of 1946* (1946) the ballad was sung by Connee Boswell.

"Strange Fruit" (1939), sometimes cited as the first protest song of the civil rights movement, is a potent number about racial persecution that managed to become quite popular despite the fact that it received limited exposure on the radio. The title phrase refers to the victims of Negro lynchings in the South, a term author Lillian Smith used to describe a black man hanging from a tree. Abel Meerpool, a Jewish schoolteacher in the Bronx, saw a picture of just such a lynching in the newspaper and was inspired to write a poem about the "Southern trees [that] bear strange fruit" with their "blood on the leaves . . . blood at the roots." The poem was published in 1937, and two years later he composed the eerie and morose music, publishing the new song under the pseudonym Lewis Allan. Billie Holiday introduced the number in Manhattan in the inte-grated nightclub Cafe Society in 1939 and recorded it soon after with trumpeter Frankie Newton. The song is more a sorrowful lament than a racial anthem, yet the effect was very potent all the same. Few radio stations would play the number, and it could not be performed or broad-cast in the South. Yet standout recordings were made by Josh White, Nina Simone, Carmen McRae, Willie Smith, Webster Young, Terence Blanchard, Sidney Bechet, Mary Coughlan, and others. Awareness of the song was revived when Diana Ross sang it on screen in the Holiday bio *Lady Sings the Blues* (1972), and in the 1990s there were new recordings by Dee Dee Bridgewater, Abbey Lincoln, Sting, Cassandra Wilson, Si-ouxsie and the Banshees, and the group UB40. In the Broadway revue *It*

Ain't Nothin' But the Blues (1999), "Strange Fruit" was sung by Gretha Boston.

"Street of Dreams" (1932) is an intriguing ballad that found favor during the depression for its odd mixture of optimism and gritty reality. Victor Young wrote the uptempo music, and Sam M. Lewis penned the complex lyric about a place where "no one is poor" as long as "love is sure." But as much as one yearns for such a street, it is just about impossible to get there, so you may as well "trade in your old dreams for new." James R. Morris describes the strange songs as "more fatalistic than sentimental; the combination of bleak lyric and danceable melody might almost be saying, like it or not, buddy, life goes on." Russ Columbo popularized the number on a disc with his Orchestra, and there were also successful records in the 1930s by Bing Crosby and Morton Downey. Tommy Dorsey (vocal by Frank Sinatra) revived the ballad in 1943. Among the many other artists to record it were the Ink Spots, Stan Kenton, Gene Ammons, Patti Austin, Les Elgart, Peggy Lee, the Ray Brown Trio, Johnny Bothwell, Doris Day, Ella Fitzgerald, Chet Baker, Hank Crawford, Ahmad Jamal, and Johnny Mathis.

"Strip Polka" (1942) is a silly, sexy novelty number by Johnny Mercer that was a favorite on jukeboxes in the 1940s, particularly on military bases at home and abroad. The ribald song, sometimes titled by its refrain lyric "Take It Off, Take It Off!," tells about the burlesque stripper Queenie who stops "always just in time" from going too far. Someday, when she finally marries, the wedding bells will ring "in strip polka time." The number is more foolish than vulgar, but several radio stations chose not to play it. Hit records by Mercer, the Andrews Sisters, Kay Kyser (vocal by Jack Martin), and Alvino Rey (vocals by the King Sisters) made it one of the most popular songs of the era, yet the producers of *Your Hit Parade* decided not to include it in their weekly listing. The Andrews Sisters reprised it in the movie *Follow the Boys* (1944), and there were later records of note by Myron Floren with Lawrence Welk, Frankie Yankovic and his Yanks, Leon Berry, and Bobby Vinton.

"Struttin' With Some Barbecue" (1927) is a Dixieland classic that Louis Armstrong wrote with his wife Lillian and was introduced by the two of them on record. The freewheelin' jazz piece celebrating hot food and hot music was recorded by such artists as Bobby Hackett, Turk Murphy, Jimmy Dorsey, Pete Fountain, Art Hodes, Jack Teagarden, Eddie Condon, Ruby Braff, Bud Freeman, Teddy Buckner, the Dukes of Dixieland, Sammy Duncan, Willie Murphy, Doc Cheatham, Willie Nelson, and Louis Armstrong, who made a solo disc in 1938 that is highly prized.

"Stumbling" (1922) is a Roaring Twenties number by Zez Confrey that makes fun of Roaring Twenties dances. While the syncopated melody lampoons the new sound, the lyric tells about a klutzy dancer who trips and falls all over his partner; but when he tells her it's the latest dance craze, she willingly joins him in the new step. Confrey introduced the number as a piano solo; then the song was popularized by hit recordings by Paul Whiteman, Billy Murray, and Frank Crumit. Later discs were made by Russ Morgan, Bob Crosby, Billy May, Ernie Felice, the Three Suns, Dinah Shore, Jimmie Barnes, Lawrence Welk, Dave "Fingers" Mc-Kenna, and Johnny Costa. "Stumbling" was heard in the movie *Mother Wore Tights* (1947), and it was performed by Julie Andrews and Mary Tyler Moore in *Thoroughly Modern Millie* (1967).

"Such a Night" (1954) is a rhythm-and-blues number by Lincoln Chase that became a hit record three times running. The celebratory song was introduced by Clyde McPhatter and the Drifters on a disc that rose to the top of the charts. Not long after Johnnie Ray made a pop record with Leo Reisman's Orchestra, and it also was a bestseller. Elvis Presley recorded it in 1960 as part of a new album, but little happened until it was rereleased as a single in 1964 and it too became a hit. Other artists to make disc versions include Bunny Paul with Sy Oliver's Orchestra, Dinah Washington, Tommy Sands, Chris Barber, Tom Jones, David Bromberg, and Conway Twitty.

"Sugar" (1928) is a bluesy standard by Maceo Pinkard, Sidney D. Mitchell, and Edna Alexander that Ethel Waters introduced on record with success. The number, sometimes listed as "That Sugar Baby o' Mine," was also recorded by such artists as Count Basie, Bennie Moten, Paul Whiteman with Bix Beiderbecke, Louis Armstrong, Teddy Wilson, Jo Stafford, Billie Holiday, Coleman Hawkins, Lee Wiley, and more recently, Mary Stahl and Jeanie Bryson. In the film *Pete Kelly's Blues* (1955), it was performed by Peggy Lee with Matty Matlock's Dixielanders.

"Sugar Blues" (1932) is a lowdown blues number by Lucy Fletcher (lyric) and Clarence Williams (music) that calls for lots of brass in its sound, the lyric refusing to settle for "St. Louis blues" or "heigh-de-hoo." Sara Martin introduced the song, and Leona Williams and her Dixie Band were the first of many to record it. The number is most associated with trumpeter Clyde McCoy who was famous for his "wah-wah" sound. He made it his theme song and recorded it with his band four times, the first time in 1936 and his 1946 version climbing the charts. Other distinctive versions were made by Williams himself in 1934, Ella Fitzgerald in 1940, Johnny Mercer with Paul Weston's Orchestra in 1947, and Ace Cannon in 1962. Ray Anthony, Tommy Dorsey, Harry James, Count Basie, Chick Webb, Barney Kessel, the Mills Blue Rhythm Band, Bob Wills and his Texas Playboys, Marty Grosz, and the Clark Sisters were among the other artists to record it. There was even a version by Benny Carter called "Boogie Woogie Sugar Blues." The song can be heard in the movie *Some Like It Hot* (1959).

"Sugar Foot Stomp" (1925) is a Dixieland favorite by Walter Melrose (lyric) and Joseph "King" Oliver (music) that originated as an instrumental piece called "Dipper Mouth Blues." When the lyric about a new dance step was added, the song was recorded by both swing and jazz artists. The definitive disc is one by Fletcher Henderson and his Orchestra with a trumpet solo by Louis Armstrong. Benny Goodman's 1937 record is also considered a classic. Other prominent versions were made by Oliver, Jan Savitt, Larry Clinton, Art Hodes, Artie Shaw, Harry James, Glenn Miller, Kid Ory, Bob Crosby, Coleman Hawkins, Muggsy Spanier, and Jimmie Noone. Crosby and his Orchestra reprised it in the movie *Sis Hopkins* (1941).

"Sunbonnet Sue" (1906) is a gushing love song ("sunshine and roses ran second to you") about a swain who confesses he first fell in love with Sue when they were both kids and he kissed her under her sunbonnet. Will D. Cobb wrote the sentimental lyric, Gus Edwards composed the glowing music, and the song sold over a million copies of sheet music in its day. The Hayden Quartet was responsible for popularizing the number, but it was even more popular in 1937 when Bob Wills made a recording that became a bestseller. Other well-known records were made by Bing Crosby, the Fort Worth Doughboys, Milton Brown, Cliff Bruner and his Texas Wanderers, and Tennessee Ernie Ford. On screen, Crosby reprised the song in the Edwards bio *The Star Maker* (1939), and Gale Storm and Phil Regan sang it in the period piece *Sunbonnet Sue* (1945).

"Sunday" (1926) is the ballad that launched Jule Styne's sixty-year songwriting career. Styne was a pianist and arranger for Arnold Johnson's Orchestra in Chicago, but when he collaborated with Ned Miller, Chester Cohn, and Bennie Krueger on this number and it became a hit, he took up composing full-time. The heartfelt ballad concerns a beau who is blue all week long because he misses his darling, but he can always look forward to Sunday, the only day he gets to be with her. Early hit records by Cliff Edwards, Gene Austin, and Jean Goldkette and his Orchestra popularized the number, and later it became very familiar as the theme song for the Phil Harris–Alice Faye radio show. Other artists to record the ballad include Bunny Berigan, Eddie Condon, Carmen McRae, Doris Day with Les Brown, Bix Beiderbecke, Louis Jordan, Kay Starr, Art Blake-ley and the Jazz Messengers, Ben Webster, and near the end of his life, Styne with Michael Feinstein.

"A Sunday Kind of Love" (1946) is the bluesy lament that asks not for love at first sight but for a long-term love that "lasts past Saturday nite." Barbara Belle, Anita Leonard, Stan Rhodes, and Louis Prima collaborated on the ballad, and it was introduced by Claude Thornhill and his Orchestra (vocal by Fran Warren) on a hit record. Decades later it was revived by the duo Jan and Dean with a 1962 bestseller, Lenny Welch had success with it in 1972, and a 1986 disc by Reba McEntire climbed the country music charts. There were other commendable versions by Prima, Kay Starr, Billy Eckstine, Anita Ellis, Roy Rogers, Jo Stafford, Buddy Rich, Etta James, the Dell-Vikings, Oscar Peterson, Kenny Rankin, Dion, and Quincy Jones.

"Sunflower" (1949) is a merry love song by Mack David that is more famous today for the plagiarism suit it prompted than the song itself. The uptempo number praises a girl from Kansas, the Sunflower State, that one hopes to marry. The tuneful number was popularized by Russ Morgan and his Orchestra with a bestselling record. There were also successful discs by Jack Fulton, Frank Sinatra, and Jack Smith. The number was popular enough that it was made the official state song for Kansas. Years later, when Jerry Herman's "Hello, Dolly!" (1964) became one of the biggest hit songs to come out of Broadway in the 1960s, David sued Herman for plagiarism. Because the first four measures of the refrain in "Sunflower" and "Hello, Dolly!" are almost identical, even sharing the same rhythmic tempo, David won a $250,000 settlement. But it was only a fraction of the millions "Hello, Dolly!" earned, and few remember "Sunflower" today.

"Sunrise Serenade" (1939) is a romantic, gently swinging ballad that became a hit first as an instrumental and then as a vocal. Pianist Frankie Carle wrote the glowing music, and it was popularized by Glen Gray and the Casa Loma Orchestra with a hit record. Even more successful was an instrumental by Glenn Miller that sold a million discs. Jack Lawrence added a dreamy lyric about the morning sun coming up, and the new song was recorded by Connee Boswell successfully. Hers and other popular discs kept the number on the *Hit Parade* for fifteen weeks, and when Carle started his own band, "Sunrise Serenade" became his theme song. Archie Bleyer, Hank Snow, Lawrence Welk, Floyd Cramer, Chet Atkins, Tex Beneke, Hank Thompson, Bobby Hackett, Roger Williams, Marty Grosz, and Max Greger were among those who also recorded it. In the film bio *The Glenn Miller Story* (1954), Joseph Gershenson's Orchestra performed it as the Miller band.

"Swanee" (1919) was George Gershwin's first major hit, and no other song he wrote after it sold as much sheet music or records. Gershwin's music is a jazzed-up version of a southern ballad with syncopation rather than sentiment in its approach. Irving Caesar wrote the sparkling lyric, a paean to a southern home that has more than a passing nod to Stephen Foster's "Old Folks at Home." The song was introduced by Muriel DeForrest in the show *Demi-Tasse Revue* (1919) in New York, but the staging was so lush and dazzling that the song itself was little noticed. It was Al Jolson who popularized the number when he interpolated it into the tour of his Broadway musical *Sinbad* (1919), then continued to perform it in concert, on film, and on records. Jolson's disc sold 2 million copies, and sheet music sales topped 1 million within a year. When Jolson rerecorded the song for the movie *Rhapsody in Blue* (1945), the new version sold another million copies. Of the hundreds of recordings over the years, notable ones were made by Judy Garland, Eddie Condon, Ted Straeter, Paul Whiteman, Liberace, Andre Watts, Sarah Vaughan, Johnny Costa, John Arpin, Michael Feinstein, and Mandy Patinkin, as well as numerous banjo musicians. Jolson also sang it for the films *The Singing Kid* (1936), *The Jolson Story* (1946), and *Jolson Sings Again* (1949), and Garland performed it in *A Star Is Born* (1954).

"Sweet Adeline" (1903), a sentimental ballad that became a barbershop quartet standard, is an unabashed serenade to a gal who is "the flower of my heart." Henry W. Armstrong, a barbershop quartet enthusiast, wrote the music in 1890, providing an echo effect in the melody that he thought would suit singing foursomes. He asked Richard H. Gerard to provide a lyric, but the new song, titled "You're the Flower of My Heart, Sweet Rosalie," was turned down by several publishers. When the girl's name and the title were changed to "Sweet Adeline," it was published in 1903, but sales were meager and it took a year before the Quaker City Four performed it at Hammerstein's Victoria Theatre and it was a hit. The song was further popularized by the Peerless Quartet, and soon it seemed everyone was singing it. The way the title phrase is echoed by "my Adeline" makes the number a harmonizing gold mine. The song was just as popular with female quartets, and to this day, such groups are still called Sweet Adelines. As for Adelina herself, both prima donna Adeline Gerard and Italian opera diva Adeline Patti have been cited as the inspiration for the title name. In 1906 John F. "Honey" Fitzgerald made "Sweet Adeline" the campaign song for his bid for the mayor of Boston, and after he won, he used it in his 1910 and 1914 reelection bids. The Mills Brothers revived the song with a hit record in 1939. Aside from the many discs by quartet groups such as the Buffalo Bills, the ballad has been recorded with success by Artie Shaw, Tommy Dorsey, the Tempo Kings, Coleman Hawkins, the Golden Gate Quartet, and

Mitch Miller. On Broadway, it was heard in the musical *Sweet Adeline* (1929), and it was used in the films *Thunderbolt* (1929), *Doughboys* (1930), *Monkey Business* (1931), and *Sweet Adeline* (1935). The song is sometimes listed as "You're the Flower of My Heart, Sweet Adeline."

"Sweet and Lovely" (1931) is a rather overblown love song by Gus Arnheim, Harry Tobias, and Jules Lemare in which one's mistress is compared to a dove, May roses, summer breezes, and so on. Arnheim and his Orchestra introduced the ballad at the Cocoanut Grove nightclub in Los Angeles, and it was an immediate audience pleaser. Arnheim adopted it as his theme song and performed it on radio and in clubs for years. There were popular recordings in the 1930s by Bing Crosby, Russ Columbo, and Guy Lombardo and the Royal Canadians, and other noteworthy discs were made by Eddie Cantor, Dick Haymes, Coleman Hawkins, Ike Quebec, Roy Haynes, the Flamingos, Thelonious Monk, the Gerry Mulligan Sextet, and Bob Ackerman. June Allyson and Gloria DeHaven performed "Sweet and Lovely" with Harry James' Orchestra in the movie *Two Girls and a Sailor* (1944), and it was heard in *Battleground* (1949) and *This Earth Is Mine* (1959).

"Sweet Dreams" (1956) is a country-flavored lullaby that is most associated with Patsy Cline. Don Gibson wrote the tender ballad, and it was popularized by country-western singer Faron Young. Cline revived it in 1963, and her disc crossed over to become a hit on the pop as well as the country charts. Tommy McLain had success with the song in 1966, and Emmylou Harris's 1976 record was a bestseller. Roy Buchanan, Doris Day, the Everly Brothers, Jerry Lee Lewis, Chet Atkins, Ace Cannon, Floyd Cramer, Willie Nelson, Barbara Cook, and Loretta Lynn were among those who also recorded it. On screen, Beverly D'Angelo played Cline and performed it in *Coal Miner's Daughter* (1980), and Jessica Lange (dubbed by Cline) sang it in the Cline bio *Sweet Dreams* (1985).

"Sweet Genevieve" (1869), perhaps the most popular ballad between the Civil War and the prolific 1890s, is a highly sentimental lament in which a teary fellow tries to relive in his mind the brief time he and his sweetheart had together before she passed away. George Cooper wrote the heartbreaking lyric as a poem after his young wife Genevieve died. He sold the lyric for $5 to Henry Tucker, who composed the solemn music. The song first became popular with minstrel troupes, then later developed into a favorite of barbershop quartets and social sing-alongs. Memorable recordings were made by John McCormack, Bob Crosby, the Banjo Kings, the Sons of the Pioneers, and more recently, a cajun version by Doug Kershaw. Alice Brady, Tyrone Power, Don Ameche, Tom Brown, and June Storey performed it in the movie *In Old Chicago* (1938), it was performed by Mickey Rooney, Fay Bainter, George Bancroft, and Virginia Weilder in *Young Tom Edison* (1940), Barry Fitzgerald crooned it with the chorus in *Incendiary Blonde* (1945), Danny Kaye sang it in *A Song Is Born* (1948), and it was heard in *Juke Box Jenny* (1942) and *Meet Me at the Fair* (1953).

"Sweet Georgia Brown" (1925) is an early jazz classic that also foreshadows the swing sound to come along a decade later. Ben Bernie, Ken Casey, and Maceo Pinkard collaborated on the scintillating number about a new gal in town who comes from Georgia, upsetting all the women because all the men are dazzled by her. The wry lyric is very playful, noting that the only men she can't get are "fellers she ain't met yet." The bright and bouncy music is deceptively tricky, using chord lines with all sorts of key changes. As difficult as it is to sing accurately, the song has been whistled and hummed by the person on the street for decades. The number also lends itself to improvisation and later became a favorite of jazz musicians. Bernie and his Orchestra introduced the song with success, and there were also early hit discs by Isham Jones and his Orchestra and Ethel Waters and her Ebony Four. Bing Crosby revived it in 1932, Brother Bones did likewise in 1949, and there were other records of note made by the Mills Brothers, Red Nichols, Lester Young, Ella Fitzgerald, Harry James, Django Reinhardt, Eddie Condon, Benny Goodman, Chris Barber, Carol Burnett, and Jo Ann Castle. The uptempo ditty is still familiar to audiences today because it has been used as the theme song for the basketball-playing Harlem Globe Trotters on television and in exhibitions. Used often in the movies, "Sweet Georgia Brown" was performed by Louis Jordan and his Orchestra in *Follow the Boys* (1944), Cara Williams in *The Helen Morgan Story* (1957), and Mel Brooks and Anne Bancroft in *To Be or Not to Be* (1983). Also on screen, the Bones recording was used in *Harlem Globetrotters* (1951), and the song was heard in *Ann Carver's Profession* (1933), *Broadway* (1942), *Some Like It Hot* (1959), *Jazz on a Summer's Day* (1959), and *Sweet and Lowdown* (1999). Lonnie McNeil, Vivian Reed, and Newton Winters performed the number in the Broadway revue *Bubbling Brown Sugar* (1976).

"Sweet Lorraine" (1928) is an enticing slow rhythm number that was most associated with Nat King Cole even though the song had hundreds of other recordings. Mitchell Parish wrote the tripping lyric about one's wish to marry Lorraine, a girl who makes him feel like a child with a "brand new choo-choo toy." Cliff Burwell composed the felicitous music that seems to move along in a casual, almost meandering manner. The number was first heard in vaudeville, then Rudy Vallee popularized it on records. The ballad was responsible for turning the Nat King Cole Trio from an instrumental group to a singing sensation. Cole was playing with his band in a Los Angeles nightclub one night in 1940 when a drunk in the audience insisted he sing "Sweet Lorraine." To avoid a confrontation, Cole sang it, the first time he had ever sung in public, and the reaction was overwhelming. He recorded it soon after and again in 1943 and sang it in concerts for years after. Other effective disc versions were made by Frank Sinatra, Joe Venuti, Count Basie, George Shearing, Bob Wilson and his Varsity Rhythm Boys, Al Cohn, Tony Bennett, Bobby Henderson, Jimmie Noone, Matt Monro, and Stephane Grappelli. The ballad was heard in the film *Sweet Lorraine* (1987) and was sung on Broadway by Jim Walton in the Parish revue *Stardust* (1987).

"Sweet Rosie O'Grady" (1896), the Irish waltz favorite by Maude Nugent, is a simple, tuneful proposal of marriage to "my steady lady" named Rosie. Vaudevillian Nugent introduced the song at the Abbey Theatre in New York, but it was popularized by George J. Gaskin, and soon it was a staple on the vaudeville circuits. Nugent had trouble getting a publisher to buy the song because they feared the market was already overrun with ballads with girls' names. But one of them liked the melody so much he paid Nugent $100 for the number, then went on to make a fortune in sheet music sales. There is some question as to whether Nugent really wrote the song. Her husband Billy Jerome was a successful songwriter, and Nugent never wrote another well-known song. It is widely believed that he wrote it for Nugent to sing and put her name on the sheet music as a gift. There were notable recordings made by Betty Grable, Tony Kenny, Mitch Miller, Tiny Tim, and many Irish groups, such as MacNamara's Singers and the Killarney Singers. Grable sang it with Robert Young and Adolphe Menjou in the movie *Sweet Rosie O'Grady* (1943), and it was heard in *Little Miss Marker* (1934). A sequel to the song, "The Daughter of Rosie O'Grady" (1918) by Monty C. Brice (lyric) and Walter Donaldson (music), was also a hit.

"Sweet Sue (Just You)" (1928) is a simple, rhythmic love song that was inspired by silent screen star Sue Carol whose picture was printed on the cover of the sheet music. Will J. Harris wrote the direct and adoring lyric, and Victor Young composed the straightforward, unadorned music that is short (only sixty-one notes) and has a range of only an octave but uses repeated notes and phrases effectively. The number quickly became a steady staple of bands, singers, choral groups, and in particular, ukelele players. The Mills Brothers revived it with success in 1932, Tommy Dorsey did the same in 1939, and Johnny Long and his Orchestra had a hit with it in 1949. Other major recordings were made by Ben Pollock, Bob Wilson and his Varsity Rhythm Boys, Artie Shaw, Lionel Hampton, Georges Metaxa, Benny Goodman, Bill Coleman, Jimmie Noone, and Ruby Braff. Shaw revived "Sweet Sue" in the movie *Second Chorus* (1940), the Mills Brothers sang it in *Rhythm Parade* (1942) and that recording was also a hit, Carmen Cavallaro provided the piano playing on the sound-track for Tyrone Power in *The Eddy Duchin Story* (1956), and the number was heard in *Some Like It Hot* (1959) and *They Shoot Horses, Don't They?* (1969).

"The Sweetest Music This Side of Heaven" (1934) was the musical slo-gan for Guy Lombardo and the Royal Canadians for several years. His brother Carmen Lombardo and Cliff Friend wrote the gently swinging ballad, and the Lombardos performed it in concerts, on records, and in the film *Many Happy Returns* (1934). Maurice Winnick and Chris Bartley also recorded the gliding number.

"Sweetheart of All My Dreams (I Love You, I Love You, I Love You)" (1928) is a repetitive love song by Art and Kay Fitch and Bert Lowe that was popular in the 1920s and again in the 1940s. Rudy Vallee made the first recording of the ballad, using the pseudonym of Frank Mater, and there were early successful discs by Irving Aaronson and his Command-ers and Art Gillham. It was also interpolated into the movie *Applause* (1929), where Helen Morgan sang it. When a group of dancing couples sang the number in the film *Thirty Seconds Over Tokyo* (1944), audiences latched on to the song again, and there were popular recordings by Benny Goodman, Carmen Cavallaro, the King Sisters, and Charlie Spi-vak. Other expert records were made by Dizzy Gillespie, Tennessee Ernie Ford, Sammy Rimington, Thelonious Monk, Camille Howard, and Jes-sica Williams.

"The Sweetheart of Sigma Chi" (1912), perhaps the most famous of all fraternity songs and a favorite on college campuses for several decades, was written by Bryan Stokes (lyric) and F. Dudleigh Vernor (music), two freshmen at Albion College in Michigan. (Strangely, neither went into songwriting professionally.) The music is almost hymnlike in its solem-nity, yet it easily allows for impromptu harmonizing. The lyric is a heart-felt paean to a coed of one's dreams, describing her blue eyes, golden yellow hair, and so on. Rudy Vallee was the first professional entertainer to sing it in clubs, on the radio, and in records. Fred Waring's Pennsyl-vanians had the first hit disc, followed by other recordings by Tommy Dorsey, Tex Beneke, Dick Haymes, Martin Bogan and the Armstrongs, Hank Snow, Ian Whitcomb, and Dean Martin. The song was heard in the two movies titled *The Sweetheart of Sigma Chi*, one in 1933 and the second in 1946, and in *Mother Is a Freshman* (1949).

"Swing, Brother, Swing" (1936) is a vibrant swing standard by Walter Bishop, Lewis Raymond, and Clarence Williams that urges one not to waste time with "foolish talk" but instead to keep dancing because "deep rhythm captivates me." The fast and energetic number was popularized by recordings by Wingy Manone and his Orchestra and Willie "the Lion" Smith. Later discs were made by Billie Holiday, Count Basie, George Freeman, the Chazz Cats, Ray Condo and his Ricochets, and the Manhattan Transfer. It was sung and danced by the cast of the Broadway revue *Swing!* (1999).

"Swing High, Swing Low" (1937) is a zesty dance number that Ralph Freed (lyric) and Burton Lane (music) wrote for Dorothy Lamour to sing in the film *Swing High, Swing Low* (1937), but her recording was cut and only an instrumental version was heard. Lamour did make a successful record version of the song, and there were other discs by the Ink Spots, Phil Harris, Ruby Newman (vocal by Ray Heatherton), Benny Goodman, Ambrose and his Orchestra, and Rico Bell and the Snakehandlers. The number can be heard in the movie *Cruisin' Down the River* (1953).

"Swing Low, Sweet Chariot" (1917), one of the most fervent and beloved of all Negro spirituals, has unknown origins but was well known enough before the Civil War that it was often sung in stage versions of *Uncle Tom's Cabin* (1853). The hymnlike song is about dying yet is filled with peace and hope as one waits for a chariot to come and take one up to paradise. The repeated expression "comin' fo' to carry me home" is both conversational and reverent, and the phrase "my soul feels heavenly bound" is still potent. Although the song had been sung in churches and other gatherings for decades, it wasn't formally put onto sheet music until a version by Henry Thacker Burleigh in 1917. A variety of artists have made recordings over the years, including Judy Garland, Boxcar Willie, Glenn Miller, Peggy Lee, Valaida Snow, the Sons of the Pioneers, the Lennon Sisters, Leadbelly, the Norman Luboff Choir, and many other choral groups. More recently there have been recordings by Glenn Yarbrough, Eric Clapton, Joan Baez, B.J. Thomas, and Ladysmith Black Mambazo. "Swing Low, Sweet Chariot" was also heard in at least a dozen films, including *Cruisin' Down the River* (1953), *Nashville* (1975), and *Pastime* (1991). It was sung on screen by the Hall Johnson choir in *Dimples* (1936), Groucho and Chico Marx with Donald McBride and Cliff Dunston in *Room Service* (1938), Garland in *Everybody Sing* (1938), Bing Crosby in *Dixie* (1943), Charlie Spivak and his Orchestra in a jazz version in *Follow the Boys* (1944), and Elvis Presley and the Jordanaires in *The Trouble With Girls* (1969). Carolyn Byrd and the company sang it in the Broadway revue *Bubbling Brown Sugar* (1976).

"Swingin' Down the Lane" (1923), a tripping dance song that is more in the style of a soft shoe than a swing number, recalls dancing with a sweetheart whom one later lost. Gus Kahn (lyric) and Isham Jones (music) wrote the sprightly standard that was introduced by Cliff Edwards before Jones and his Orchestra popularized it on record. Of the many artists to record the song were Bing Crosby, Frankie Carle, Ben Bernie, Primo Scala, Rose Murphy, Frank Sinatra, the Kirby Stone Four, Charles Brown, the Musettes, the Columbians, and Vic Damone. It was heard in the movie *The Great American Broadcast* (1941) and performed on screen by Vivian Blaine in *Greenwich Village* (1944), Mona Freeman and the chorus in *Mother Wore Tights* (1947), and Danny Thomas and Doris Day in the Kahn bio *I'll See You in My Dreams* (1952).

T

"T'Aint Nobody's Bizness If I Do" (1922), the first song recorded by Thomas "Fats" Waller, is a breezy number by Graham Prince, Clarence Williams, and Porter Grainger that lists some of the many things one might do (jump into the ocean, dance on the ceiling, party all night, go to church, and so on), and it would be no one else's concern. The Waller disc is perhaps definitive, but there were also memorable records by Bessie Smith, Frank Froeba, Alberta Hunter, Betty Joplin, Billie Holiday, Ernestine Anderson, Dinah Washington, the M 'n' M Trio, and Jay McShane. Diana Ross sang it in the Holiday film bio *Lady Sings the Blues* (1972), and on Broadway it was performed by Linda Hopkins in *Bessie and Me* (1975), Andre DeShields in *Ain't Misbehavin'* (1978), and Ruth Brown and Hopkins in *Black and Blue* (1989).

"Take It Easy" (1943) is a catchy ditty about carefree living that was very popular in the war-weary 1940s. Albert DeBrue, Irving Taylor, and Vic Mizzy collaborated on the merry number, and it was introduced by Guy Lombardo and the Royal Canadians. Earl Hines, Duke Ellington, Bing Crosby, Fats Waller, Glenn Frey, Xavier Cugat, Freddie McGregor, Lightnin' Hopkins, Bobby Bell, and Crystal Gayle are among the artists to make recordings. The song was heard in the movie *Meet Miss Bobby Sox* (1944) and was sung by Virginia O'Brien and Lina Romay with Xavier's band in *Two Girls and a Sailor* (1944), Marion Hutton with Freddy Slack's Orchestra in *Babes on Swing Street* (1944), and Roy Rogers and the Sons of the Pioneers in *The Yellow Rose of Texas* (1944).

"Take Me Back to My Boots and Saddle" (1935) is a cowboy standard by Walter G. Samuels, Leonard Whitcup, and Teddy Powell that yearns for the Old West as it recalls the local general store, roping cattle, playing on the banjo, and the "Cherokee gal" who waits for one there. The song has a yodeling flavor with plenty of "ooh-ooh-ooh" in the lyric. Gene Autry introduced the ballad with a hit record, and there were subsequent discs by Red Allen, Art Tatum, Jimmy Ray, John Charles Thomas, Victor Young's Orchestra, Fred Lowery, Tommy Dorsey, Tex Ritter, and Jimmy Wakely. Autry reprised the song in the movie *Boots and Saddles* (1937), and it was also heard in *The Witness Chair* (1936), *Pepper* (1936), *Merry-Go-Round of 1938*, and *Call of the Canyon* (1942).

"Take Me in Your Arms" (1932) is a poignant ballad, based on a German farewell song by Fritz Rotter (lyric) and Fred Markush (music), asking for one more caress before parting. Mitchell Parish wrote the English lyric, and the new version was popularized by Ruth Etting. The song became widely known when Frank Parker featured it often on the radio, also making a disc with Marion Marlowe and Arthur Tracy. Other notable records were made by Doris Day, Hazel Scott, Stan Kenton, Mel Powell, Les Paul and Mary Ford, Perry Como, the Platters, Vic Damone, Don Cornell, and Robert Goulet. "Take Me in Your Arms" can also be heard in the movies *Hi, Buddy* (1943) and *On Stage Everybody* (1945).

"Take Me Out to the Ball Game" (1908), the national anthem of American baseball, was co written by vaudevillian Albert Von Tilzer who never saw a baseball game until twenty years after his song became a hit. Von Tilzer's music is a tinkling soft shoe in the hoofer style with no hint of a march or rousing anthem. Jack Norworth penned the catchy lyric, only the famous refrain being recognized today. The first verse concerns Katie Carson whose beau wants to take her out to a show. But Katie prefers the bleachers at the ball park and sings the title request. In the second verse, the team is losing the game so Katie repeats the refrain to cheer the players on. Von Tilzer introduced the song on stage, but it was vaudeville stars Billy Murray, Nora Bayes, and Sadie Jansell who popularized it in variety. Over the years the ditty has been recorded by such varied artists as Doris Day and Frank Sinatra, Frank Zappa, Bob McGrath, Tiny Tim, the Ray Brown Trio, Eddie Layton, Mandy Patinkin, the Nuclear Whales Saxophone Orchestra, Raffi, and Carly Simon. Ann Sheridan and Dennis Morgan sang it in the film *Shine On, Harvest Moon* (1944), Gene Kelly performed it with Sinatra and Esther Williams in *Take Me Out to the Ball Game* (1949), and it has been heard in dozens of baseball movies from *Thunderbolt* (1929) to *The Winning Team* (1952) to *Bad News Bears Go to Japan* (1978).

"Take the 'A' Train" (1941) is, according to its composer-lyricist Billy Strayhorn, "a swinging riff tune," and the number has always appealed to singers and musicians because of its multiple opportunities for scat singing and improvisation. The lyric is about the Eighth Avenue subway line in Manhattan, instructing one to take the train labeled "A" as the fastest way to reach Sugar Hill in Harlem. Strayhorn wrote the number for Duke Ellington and his Orchestra, who had a bestselling record and made it their theme song. Of the dozens of discs made over the years were distinctive ones by Ella Fitzgerald, Cab Calloway, Woody Herman, Teddy Wilson, George Shearing, John Coltrane, Joe Pass, Jonah Jones, Ray Brown, Ernie Andrews, Oscar Peterson, the Gerry Beaudoin Trio, Mel Tormé, Doc Severinson, the Rolling Stones, and Marian McPartland. Ellington reprised the number in the movie *Reveille With Beverly* (1943), his recording was heard in *Radio Days* (1987), and the song was played in *Paris Blues* (1961). On Broadway it was performed by the cast of the revue *Bubbling Brown Sugar* (1976), Gregory Hines and Phyllis Hyman in the Ellington revue *Sophisticated Ladies* (1981), and Cheryl Freeman and the company in *Play On!* (1997).

"Takes Two to Tango" (1952) is a moderate tango by Al Hoffman and Dick Manning about the necessity of two to make a romance. The nimble lyric lists some of the things you can do by yourself (sail a boat, get into debt, haunt a house, "go to pot on your own," and so on), but it takes two to "do the dance of love." Pearl Bailey popularized the ballad on record with Don Redman and his Orchestra, and Louis Armstrong had an early hit disc as well. Bing Crosby, Lester Young, Dean Martin, Ray Charles and Betty Carter, Ranee Lee, and Todd Rundgren were among the other artists to make commendable recordings. The song, sometimes listed as "It Takes Two to Tango," was heard in the film *The Karate Kid* (1984).

"Tammy" (1957), an innocent little ditty that is mostly forgotten today, was the most popular song in America in 1957, staying at the top of the charts for eight months and spawning 10 million records. Jay Livingston and Ray Evans wrote the love song in which an admirer compares the beauty of the backwoods (cottonwood trees that whisper, the "old hootie owl hootie-hoos," and such) to the gal he loves who comes from there. The Oscar-nominated ballad was introduced by Debbie Reynolds in the movie *Tammy and the Bachelor* (1957), and her recording alone sold a million discs. The Ames Brothers had a bestseller, and over one hundred other versions were made, most notably those by Brenda Lee, Sam Cooke, the Platters, Floyd Cramer, Jane Morgan, Liberace, Earl Bostic, Noleen Batley, Hank Snow, Duanne Eddy, John Gary, the Ray Conniff Singers, Andy Beb, and Tom Prin.

"Teach Me Tonight" (1953) is an easygoing standard by Sammy Cahn (lyric) and Gene De Paul (music) that requests a dearie to teach one the

ABC's and the XYZ's of love. Cahn's lyric is both coy and sexy as many schoolroom images (the sky is a blackboard on which one writes "I love you") are used to express lovemaking. The ballad was introduced on record by Janet Brace, but it got no reaction from the public until the DeCastro Sisters made a disc in 1954 that was on the charts. Jo Stafford's hit record further popularized the number, and it was revived by George Maharis in 1962, by Phoebe Snow in the 1970s, by Al Jarreau in 1982, and by Frank Sinatra the next year. Other standout recordings were made by Joe Williams, Nat King Cole, Blossom Dearie, Erroll Garner, Ella Fitzgerald, the Four Freshmen, Louis Armstrong, Sarah Vaughan, Brenda Lee, Sammy Davis Jr., Dinah Washington, Joe Augustine, Anne Murray, Liza Minnelli, Toni Tennille, Natalie Cole, and Ann Hampton Callaway.

"Tell Me Why" (1952) is a romantic ballad by Al Alberts (lyric) and Marty Gold (music) that asks a series of questions of one's heartthrob: Why did we dance until three in the morning? Why did our romance never have a chance? Why isn't it too late to try again? The song was popularized by a recording by the Four Aces (featuring Albert as the lead singer) that sold 1 million discs. Eddie Fisher's record with Hugo Winterhalter's Orchestra also sold a million copies, and it was a hit for Bobby Vinton when he revived it in 1964. Keely Smith, Dinah Washington, the Orioles, Bert Kaempfert, Eddie Cochran, and Steve Williams were among the other artists to record it.

"Ten Cents a Dance" (1930) is an unusual torch song by Rodgers and Hart in which a gal is not rejected by a lover but is wooed by too many men, none of whom offer true love. Richard Rodgers's music has a languid, honky-tonk flavor to it, and Lorenz Hart's narrative lyric is sordid and vivid. A taxi dancer at the Palace Ballroom quietly relates her disgust at the patrons whom she must dance with for money, hoping someday to escape and find a better life. Ruth Etting introduced the ballad in the Broadway musical *Simple Simon* (1930), and her recording was a bestseller. Other memorable discs were made by Doris Day, Ella Fitzgerald, Anita O'Day, Shirley Horn, Carol Burnett, Dorothy Loudon, and more recently, Chris Connor and Weslia Whitfield. The number was heard in the film *Ten Cents a Dance* (1946), and Day sang it in the Etting bio *Love Me or Leave Me* (1955).

"Tenderly" (1946) is a haunting waltz standard that recalls a tender kiss that is compared to a breeze through the trees and a wave that caresses the shore. Walter Gross wrote the lilting music to apologize to Margaret Whiting for his rude behavior to her when he was drunk. Whiting contacted Jack Lawrence and had him write the lyric, and the new song was

introduced on record by Clark Dennis. Of the subsequent hit records by
Sarah Vaughan, Nat King Cole, and others, the most popular was a disc
by Rosemary Clooney that sold a million copies. Oddly enough, Whiting
never recorded the song she had helped to create. But among the many
who did were Duke Ellington, Stan Getz and Lionel Hampton, Billie
Holiday, Tony Bennett, Kenny Burrell, Louis Armstrong, Bill Evans, Stan
Kenton, Billy Ward and the Dominoes, Oscar Peterson, Pat Boone, Bobby
Dukoff, Chet Baker, the Norman Luboff Choir, Jack Jones, Natalie Cole,
Ann Hampton Callaway, and Carol Sloane. Joan Crawford can be heard
singing the ballad under the opening titles of the movie *Torch Song*
(1953).

"Tennessee Waltz" (1948) is a narrative ballad by Redd Stewart and Pee
Wee King that is sometimes mistaken for a traditional folk song, but it
is pure Tin Pan Alley. The slow and lilting number recalls dancing with
one's sweetheart to the "Tennessee Waltz" one night at a dance. But he
also recollects how he introduced her to a friend who later stole her
away. King and his Orchestra introduced the song on a record with
Stewart doing the vocal, and it was successful. But Patti Page's 1950 disc,
in which she sang the number contrapuntally with her own recorded
voice, sold over 3 million copies and kept the song on *Your Hit Parade*
for fifteen weeks. Bobby Comstock and Jerry Fuller each revived the
ballad in 1959, and Sam Cooke made it a hit again in 1964. Other significant versions were made by Erskine Hawkins, Cowboy Copas, Sonny
Rollins, Elvis Presley, Floyd Cramer, Ace Cannon, Connie Francis,
Sammy Kaye, the Mills Brothers, Louis Prima, Ella Fitzgerald, Billy
Vaughn, Jimmy Martin and the Sunny Mountain Boys, Roy Acuff, the
Moms and Dads, LaVern Baker, John Gary, Ramsey Lewis, and Davis
Gaines. "The Tennessee Waltz" was heard in the film *Zabriskie Point*
(1970) and was sung by Jody Abrahams in the Off-Broadway revue *The
Taffetas* (1988). The waltz became the official state song of Tennessee in
1965.

"Tenting on the Old Camp Ground" (1863), a Civil War song little
known today, was one of the most widely recognized ballads of the
second half of the nineteenth century and one of the first American songs
to take a less-than-glorious view of war. Walter Kittredge, a professional
singer about to be drafted into the Union army, was grieved at the
thought of having to leave his wife and daughter, and wrote this gentle
folk song about the thoughts that go through a soldier's mind during a
lull in the battle, yearning for an end of the war and returning home.
Ironically, Kittredge was rejected by the military for medical reasons, but
he brought the song to the popular singing group, the Hutchinson Fam-

ily, and Asa Hutchinson got music publisher Oliver Ditson to buy it with the understanding that he and Ditson would share in the royalties. The number quickly caught on, and Kittredge, Hutchinson, and Ditson all made a considerable amount of money. Kittredge joined the Hutchinsons and toured with them for years, often singing the famous ballad. The group was asked to perform the song at such illustrious occasions as the 1866 celebration at the end of the war, the Philadelphia Exposition in 1876, and a soldiers' reunion in 1893. At the next year's Columbian Exposition in Chicago, a chorus of 500 sang the beloved ballad. In addition to several choral renditions such as that by the Robert Shaw Chorale, the song has been recorded by Mississippi John Hurt, Douglas Jimerson, and William and Carla Coleman. Tex Ritter sang it in the film *Tenting Tonight on the Old Camp Ground* (1943).

"Thank You for a Lovely Evening" (1934) is a warm ballad by Dorothy Fields (lyric) and Jimmy McHugh (music) that was introduced by Phil Harris and his Band in a New York City nightclub. Harris's recording, with vocals by himself and Leah Ray, was popular, and there were other successful recordings by Don Bestor and his Orchestra, Faron Young, and Peter Mintun. The good-bye song can be heard in the movies *Have a Heart* (1934) and *Girl From Missouri* (1934).

"Thank You So Much, Mrs. Lowsborough-Goodby" (1934) is a party song by Cole Porter that was never put in one of his shows but became well known all the same. The novelty number is in the form of a thank-you letter one wishes one could write to an overbearing hostess after a dreadful weekend together. The comic lyric politely but sarcastically thanks her for the warm cocktails, the cold bath, the dull company, and even the "ptomaine I got from your famous tin salmon." Porter sang it often at social gatherings and later recorded the farcical ditty. Fred Astaire also included it in his concerts late in his career and recorded it as well.

"That Certain Party" (1925) is a lively fox trot by Gus Kahn (lyric) and Walter Donaldson (music) that uses a series of questions (Does she have "naughty eyes?") and answers (She sure does!) about a certain girl of the title. The song was popular in the 1920s and was featured by Ted Lewis and his Orchestra and the team of Ernest Hare and Billy Jones. Benny Strong and his Orchestra revived interest in the number in 1948, and there were subsequent duet versions by Buddy Clark and Doris Day and by Dean Martin and Jerry Lewis, each taking the form of questions and answers. Isham Jones, the Hot Temperance Seven, and Louis Prima also made noteworthy recordings.

"That Lucky Old Sun (Just Rolls Around Heaven All Day)" (1949) is a quiet yet effective ballad by Haven Gillespie (lyric) and Beasley Smith (music) that is similar in tone and subject to "Ol' Man River." A hardworking laborer looks up to the lazy sun who doesn't have to work and wonders when he will be able to cross the river to paradise and be as free as the sun is. Frankie Laine's recording hit the Number One spot on all the charts, and there were also successful discs by Vaughn Monroe, Sarah Vaughan, Frank Sinatra, and Louis Armstrong with Gordon Jenkins's Orchestra. Ray Charles revived the number with a popular 1964 record. Other artists to make disc versions include the Isley Brothers, Dick Haymes, Dean Martin, Liberace, the Velvets, Jerry Lee Lewis, and Keely Smith.

"That Old Gang of Mine" (1923), the first hit for songwriters Billy Rose and Ray Henderson, is a sentimental lament about four friends each going separate ways and the longing for the old days when the quartet used to sing "Sweet Adeline" and other harmonizing numbers. Mort Dixon and Rose based their lyric on a poem entitled "Old Familiar Faces" and had an unknown composer write a melody. But the song was not working out, so they discarded the music and asked Henderson, a fledging composer who worked as a court stenographer, to come up with a better melody. He composed the graceful tune and even made substantial changes to the lyric. The revised version was introduced by the team of Van and Schenck in vaudeville, and the number went over so well that the duo and the song were both interpolated into the *Ziegfeld Follies of 1923*. "That Old Gang of Mine" sold 30,000 copies of sheet music each week for several months, Rose broke into the big time, and Henderson had a new career. The song was revived with success by Dick Robertson in 1938, and it is still widely recognized today. Among the many who recorded it were Ted Weems, Frank Froeba, Buddy Clark, Kay Starr, the Four Aces, Frank Novak, Keith Ingham, the Ravens, Bobby Hackett, Perry Como, Sammy Fain, and Jimmy Roselli. The number is not to be confused with the similar "Wedding Bells Are Breaking Up That Old Gang of Mine" (1929).

"That Tumble-Down Shack in Athlone" (1918) is a sentimental Irish ballad by Richard W. Pascoe (lyric), Monte Carlo, and Alma M. Sanders (music) that recalls with nostalgia a place back home in Ireland. The song was popularized by early recordings by John McCormack and the Sterling Trio, and there were later discs of note by Bing Crosby, Phil Regan, and various Irish singers and musicians.

"That's How Much I Love You" (1947) is a country-flavored ballad that managed to cross over and find success with pop artists as well. Eddy

Arnold, Wally Fowler, and J. Graydon Hall collaborated on the number, and Arnold introduced it on record. Much more successful were discs by Bing Crosby with Bob Crosby's Orchestra, Louis Prima, and Frank Sinatra with the Page Cavanaugh Trio. Later recordings were made by Charlie Rich, Pat Boone, Patsy Cline, the Manhattans, Chris Bartley, Mac Curtis, and Kathy Troccoli.

"That's My Desire" (1931) is the song that made Frankie Laine famous, although both the song and his career were nearly lost. Carroll Loveday (lyric) and Helmy Kresa (music) wrote the tender ballad about a spurned lover who wishes that he could meet with his former sweetheart one last time in a cozy little café where they can drink wine and dance together. Lanny Ross introduced the song on the radio in 1931, but nothing came of it and the number was pretty much forgotten. Near the end of World War Two, Laine's singing career was going nowhere, and he was earning his living working in a defense plant in Cleveland. One night he heard a woman sing "That's My Desire" in a little nightclub and was so taken with the song that he found a copy of the sheet music and used it in his next audition. Soon Laine was singing it in clubs, and his 1947 record sold 1.5 million copies, making him a singing star. (Laine later went back to Cleveland to try and find the unknown singer and thank her, but he never found out who she was.) Louis Armstrong, Ella Fitzgerald, Helen Forrest, LaVern Baker, Claude Thornhill, Al Saxon, Dion and the Belmonts, and Jim Reeves were among the other artists to record the song. The Laine version can be heard in the film *Raging Bull* (1980).

"That's My Weakness Now" (1928), the ditty that made Helen Kane a star and introduced "boop-oop-a-doop" to the world, was written by Bud Green and Sam H. Stept for a show at the Paramount Theatre in New York. The coy number explains how a guy never cared for blue eyes, dimpled cheeks, and billing and cooing until he met a certain gal; now he has a weakness for all of those things. Kane introduced the number in the show with Paul Ash's Orchestra, adding a couple of "boop-oop-a-doop's" to her interpretation. The audiences immediately adored Kane and the song, her recording becoming a bestseller and everyone imitating her baby-voiced cooing. Cliff Edwards and Paul Whiteman with the Rhythm Boys each had early successful discs as well, and the song was revived by Russ Morgan (vocals by the Modernaires) in 1949. Other standout recordings were made by Bing Crosby with Bix Beiderbecke, "Whispering" Jack Smith, the Cliff Adams Singers, Nat Shilkret, and the Four Lads. "That's My Weakness Now" can also be heard in the film *Applause* (1929).

"That's What You Think" (1935) is a peppy number by Truman "Pinky" Tomlin, Coy Poe, and Raymond Jasper with an "I-told-you-so" attitude. Tomlin introduced the song in the movie *King Solomon of Broadway* (1935) and recorded it with success. Other notable discs were made by Gene Krupa (vocal by Anita O'Day), Red McKenzie, Will Osborne, the Swarf Sisters, Freddie King, Mike Stern, and Carl Smith.

"That's Why They Call Me 'Shine' " (1924) is "one of the most telling comments on prejudice in popular song," as described by Robert Gottlieb and Robert Kimball. The African-American songwriter Cecil Mack had a friend nicknamed "Shine" who was hurt in a Negro race riot in New York in 1900. Recalling the man years later, Mack wrote a potent lyric about an African American whose name was Samuel Johnson Brown but was called everything from "Sambo" to "Choc'late Drop" by white folks. But he likes it when they call him "Shine" because it puts him in mind of diamonds and other valuable gems, and he can easily ignore their taunting. Ford Dabney wrote the bluesy music, and the song was popularized by the California Ramblers. Both black and white performers have made records of the number over the years. Bing Crosby and Louis Armstrong each had hits in 1932, and Frankie Laine revived it in 1948 with a disc that made the Top 10. There are also distinctive recordings by Ella Fitzgerald and Ry Cooder.

"Them There Eyes" (1930) is a steady rhythm song that is somewhat torchy, somewhat happy. Maceo Pinkard, William Tracey, and Doris Tauber collaborated on the lucid number about a sweetie who has such enticing eyes that one fell in love looking into them the first time. Yet the lyric complains about the flirting eyes as well, cautioning the lover that "them there eyes" are going to "get you in a lot of trouble." Gus Arnheim and his Orchestra made the first recording, but it was Louis Armstrong's 1931 disc that became a hit. In 1939 Billie Holiday revived the uptempo ballad, her record was a bestseller, and the song has been associated with her ever since. Other artists to record it include Anita O'Day, Lester Young, Sarah Vaughan, Bing Crosby, the McGuire Sisters, Peggy Lee, Doc Cheatham, Roy Fox, and Carol Sloane. Diana Ross sang "Them There Eyes" on screen in the Holiday bio *Lady Sings the Blues* (1972).

"Then You've Never Been Blue" (1929) is a torchy ballad by Sam M. Lewis, Joe Young (lyric), and Ted Fio Rito (music) about the signs of romantic heartbreak. Fio Rito and his Band introduced it on record, and there were other early discs by Frances Williams and Roger Wolfe Kahn's Orchestra that were successful. Frances Langford sang it in the movie *Every Night at Eight* (1935) and recorded it as well. Kay Starr, Erroll

Garner, Ella Fitzgerald, and Martha Lou Harp also made noteworthy discs of the number.

"There Are Such Things" (1942) is an optimistic number that appealed to Americans during the early dark days of World War Two. Stanley Adams, Abel Baer, and George W. Meyer collaborated on the flowing fox trot that looks at the sky above and at love blossoming all around and concludes that there are still good things in life. The song became well known because of a record by Tommy Dorsey and his Orchestra with vocals by Frank Sinatra and the Pied Pipers. The disc stayed on the charts for six months (in the Number One spot for six weeks) and was featured on *Your Hit Parade* for eighteen weeks. Other notable versions were made by Sarah Vaughan with Count Basie, Al Hibbler, Sonny Rollins, the Modernaires, Etta Jones, Jerry Vale, and Ann Shelton.

"There Goes That Song Again" (1944) is a torchy serenade with up-tempo music that swings slightly, creating an unusual yet effective ballad. Jule Styne composed the sparkling music, and Sammy Cahn penned the moving lyric about recalling "our song" and a failed love affair, the song bringing back the memory of lost love every time one hears it. The ballad was introduced in the movie *Carolina Blues* (1944), where it was performed by Kay Kyser and his Orchestra (vocals by Harry Babbitt and Georgia Carroll). It was also recorded by Kyser and company and was an immediate hit. Russ Morgan, Sammy Kaye (vocal by Nancy Norman), Billy Butterfield (vocal by Margaret Whiting), and Kate Smith all had successful discs as well. Among the other artists to record it were Ginny Simms, Frankie Carle, Harry James, Dick Jurgens, and Eugenie Baird. Dick Haymes sang the ballad in the film *Cruisin' Down the River* (1953).

"There Is a Tavern in the Town" (1883) is a college sing-along favorite that became a Tin Pan Alley hit and is still a familiar tune to many. The authorship is hazy, although when it was first published as "The Students' Song" in 1883, the sheet music read "edited by William H. Hills." But the ditty's origins probably go back to Cornwall, England, where coal miners sang a song that began "There is an alehouse in our town . . ." The number we now know has a merry polka beat and an exaggerated lyric about drinking at the local tavern and trying to forget one who "never never thinks of me." In some ways it is a torch song ("I died of love"), but it is so cheerful and contagious that it is still known more as a party song. "There Is a Tavern in the Town" became popular on college campuses in America by the 1870s, and sheet music sales were steady for decades. Rudy Vallee revived further interest in the ditty in the late 1920s when he sang it on the radio and made a hit record of it. In addition to many polka bands, there have been successful discs by the Four Aces, Ted Heath and his Musicke, Connie Francis, Ace O'Donnell, Joey Miskulin, the Moms and Dads, Myron Floren with Lawrence Welk, Mitch Miller, and others. The song can be heard in the background in many films and was featured in *Cowboy in the Clouds* (1943) and *Malaya* (1949).

"There Is No Greater Love" (1936) is a fervent ballad by Marty Symes (lyric) and Isham Jones (music) that offers love that is sincere and everlasting. Jones and his Orchestra (vocal by Woody Herman) introduced the song on record with success, and there was an even more popular disc by Guy Lombardo and the Royal Canadians. Billie Holiday, Jimmy Dorsey (vocal by Bob Carroll), Al Hibbler with Johnny Hodges' Orchestra, and Billy May all had successful records later on, and there were also notable versions by Teddy Powell, Frankie Carle, Duke Ellington, Chet Baker, the Eddie Thompson Trio, the Miles Davis Quintet, and Jan Peerce.

"There, I've Said It Again" (1941) is a romantic fox trot in which a suitor cannot help letting the phrase "I love you" slip into the conversation, asking her to forgive him and understand how he feels. Redd Evans and Dale Mann wrote the warm ballad, which was introduced by Billy Carter and his Orchestra but seemed to get little attention. It was a 1945 record by Vaughn Monroe (vocals by the Norton Sisters) that caught the public's fancy, selling 3.5 million discs. Other hit versions in the 1940s were made by Jimmy Dorsey (vocal by Teddy Walters) and the Modernaires with Paula Kelly. Bobby Vinton revived the number in 1964 with a record that climbed to the top of the charts. Among the others to record it were Nat King Cole, Sam Cooke, Russ Morgan, the Lennon Sisters, Roger Whitaker, Joan Edwards, Vic Damone, Frankie Avalon, Johnny Mathis, and, more recently, Kathie Lee Gifford, Andrea Marcovicci, and Jimmy Roselli.

"There'll Be Some Changes Made" (1924) is a short (only eighteen measures) and simple song with a clever lyric about turning over a new leaf. Billy Higgins and W. Benton Overstreet wrote the easygoing number in which one vows to changes his ways, his address, his clothes, even his "long tall" sweetie for a "short fat" one. Higgins introduced the number in vaudeville, but when Ethel Waters sang it in clubs and made the first recording of the song, it became well known. Sophie Tucker had success with it in 1928, and it was revived by Benny Goodman in 1941 and by Ted Weems in 1947. Other noteworthy records were made by Ted Lewis, Marion Harris, Bunny Berigan, the Boswell Sisters, Art Tatum, Vaughn Monroe, Mildred Bailey, Artie Shaw, Gene Krupa (vocal by Irene Daye), the Dave Brubeck Quartet, and more recently, Mary Cleere Haran. On screen, the song was sung by Ida Lupino in *Road House* (1948), Joan Blondell in *The Blue Veil* (1951), Dolores Gray in *Designing Woman* (1957), and Ann Reinking in *All That Jazz* (1979), as well as heard in *Play Girl* (1941) and *Sweet and Lowdown* (1999). Josephine Premice performed the number in the Broadway revue *Bubbling Brown Sugar* (1976).

"There's a Broken Heart for Every Light on Broadway" (1915) is pretty much forgotten as a song, but its cautionary title is still part of show business jargon. Howard Johnson (lyric) and Fred Fisher (music) wrote the ballad that warns unsuspecting folk in the country that to leave the farm to find fame in New York means heartbreak and disillusionment. The number is of historic interest because it illustrates the Great White Way as a place glowing with outdoor lighting. Electricity enabled the theatre district (at the time of the song, centered on Broadway at Twenty-Third Street) to glow with hundreds of light bulbs; the title of the song, then, suggests a considerable number of broken hearts. The Avon Comedy Four introduced the number in vaudeville, and it was soon a favorite on the variety circuit. Elsie Baker made an early record that was successful, and years later Rosemary Clooney and Mel Tormé each recorded it as well. The song can be heard in the Fisher film bio *Oh, You Beautiful Doll* (1949).

"There's a Cabin in the Pines" (1933) is an atmospheric ballad by Billy Hill about a romantic and cozy retreat in the woods. It was introduced on the radio by George Hall's Orchestra (vocal by Loretta Lee), and later there were hit records by Mildred Bailey, Ray Noble (vocal by Al Bowlly), and Johnny Mercer. Louis Armstrong and the Classic Jazz Quartet each made memorable discs as well.

"There's a Gold Mine in the Sky" (1938) is a simple but charming cowboy ballad by Charles and Nick Kenny that Gene Autry introduced in the movie *Gold Mine in the Sky* (1938). Autry's recording was popular, and Bing Crosby, Kate Smith, and Isham Jones had success with it as well. Other accomplished versions were made by Horace Heidt, Smokey Greene, Pat Boone, and Jimmie Davis.

"There's a Long, Long Trail" (1913) is one of the most beloved of all World War One ballads, though it was written before the war broke out, and there is nothing in the song about war. Stoddard King (lyric) and Zo Elliott (music) were students at Yale University when they wrote the haunting number for a fraternity banquet. While Elliott's music is aching and solemn, it is far from morose. King's flowing lyric is about a long winding road that travels through one's dreams and about the dawn that comes after a long night of waiting. The committee in charge of the banquet turned down the song, as did several music publishers. When Elliott went to study at Cambridge in England, he finally got a British publisher interested, but he had to pay the cost of the initial printing. Elliott was traveling in Germany when the war broke, and it took him time to escape to Switzerland. There he found a sizable royalty check waiting for him, as the ballad had started to catch on in Great Britain. When the song was finally published in the States, sales were sluggish until America got into the war. Then the hopeful ballad sold 2.5 million copies of sheet music and was sung in all kinds of public and private gatherings. President Woodrow Wilson was a particular fan of the song and often sang it to White House guests after dinner. Though never forgotten, the number was popular again during World War Two, and it was often sung as a countermelody to the other "great war" ballad "Keep the Home Fires Burning." Jeannette MacDonald sang "There's a Long, Long Trail" in the movie *Smilin' Through* (1941), the King's Men were heard singing it on the soundtrack of *For Me and My Gal* (1942), and partygoers sang it in *Thirty Seconds Over Tokyo* (1944). On Broadway, Ian Paterson performed the number in the British revue *Oh! What a Lovely War!* (1964), and it was heard in the 1969 film version as well. While many choral groups have recorded it, the most celebrated disc is one by Frank Sinatra.

"There's No Tomorrow" (1949) is a bombastic ballad that Al Hoffman, Leo Corday, and Leon Carr fashioned out of the Italian favorite "O Solo Mio" by Edoardo di Capua. The passionate lyric argues that when love is new, there is no future to worry about and tonight is all that matters. While the new version was sung and recorded on occasion, it did not become a hit until Tony Martin performed it with Henri René and his Orchestra in the movie *Two Tickets to Broadway* (1951), and their subsequent record was popular. Other artists to make well-known versions of the ballad include Dean Martin, the Clovers, Tony Bari, and Emile Ford and the Checkmates.

"These Foolish Things (Remind Me of You)" (1935) is the indelible British ballad by Holt Marvell (lyric), Jack Strachey, and Harry Link (music) that was given dozens of recordings in America and remained in the top spot of *Your Hit Parade* for thirteen weeks. The music has a leisurely flavor to it, in some ways more like a French café song than an English one, and the poignant lyric lists the many little details (a cigarette with lipstick marks on it, an airline ticket, a telephone ring, a certain table in a candle-lit café, and so on) that remind one of a lost lover. Marge Elliott and Cyril Ritchard introduced the song in the London musical *Spread It Abroad* (1935), and spread it did. In America a record by Benny Goodman (vocal by Helen Ward) was the first hit, and Billie Holiday's disc with

Teddy Wilson was also very popular. Other notable versions were made by Nat Brandwynne, Lester Young, Martha Tilton, Joe Sanders, Lee Sims, Ella Fitzgerald, Gene Krupa, Rosemary Clooney, Art Pepper, Coleman Hawkins, Thelma Carpenter, a parody version by Red Ingle, and more recently, Ken Peplowski, Vicki Stuart, and Andrea Marcovicci. "These Foolish Things" can be heard in the movies *A Yank in the R.A.F.* (1941), *Ghost Catchers* (1944), and *Tokyo Rose* (1946), and it was sung by Leslie Uggams in the Broadway revue *Blues in the Night* (1982).

"They Didn't Believe Me" (1914) is the masterful ballad by Herbert Reynolds (lyric) and Jerome Kern (music) that served as one of the earliest and most influential models for the thirty-two-bar Tin Pan Alley ballad. Martin Gottfried points out that it "invented stage ballads" by creating an American kind of song that broke completely away from the European operettalike number. The lyric is a smooth yet conversational commentary on a beloved one, describing all of his fine qualities and yet repeating the title phrase that no one else sees those qualities. While not exactly slangy, Reynolds's lyric has an everyday speech pattern to it, such as "Well, who can say" and the famous section "And I'm cert'nly am goin' to tell them," the word *certainly* sung with only two syllables and sitting on the music beautifully. Much has been written about Kern's unique accomplishments in the music: the unusual harmonic influence on the melody, the use of quarter notes in the refrain to build up to the climax that is a key change, and a melody line that is, as Alec Wilder states, "as natural as walking." The song was written for the London musical *The Girl From Utah* when it was brought to Broadway in 1914, and it was sung by Donald Brian and Julia Sanderson. While few critics pointed out the number, audiences were intrigued by the unusual song and eventually over 2 million copies of sheet music were sold. An early recording was made by Grace Kerns and Reed Miller, followed over the years by memorable discs by Billy May, Bing Crosby, Gloria Lynne, Stan Kenton, Tommy Dorsey, Dick Haymes, Ray Anthony, Margaret Whiting, Gogi Grant, Dinah Washington, Charlie Byrd, Johnny Mercer, Marni Nixon, Oscar Peterson, Pearl Bailey, Leontyne Price, Barbra Streisand, Sylvia McNair, Curtis Fuller, Robert Clary, and Julie London. On screen it was sung by Dinah Shore in *Till the Clouds Roll By* (1946), Kathryn Grayson and Mario Lanza in *That Midnight Kiss* (1949), and Vanessa Redgrave in *Agatha* (1979).

"Thinking of You" (1926) is a bluesy torch song by Paul Ash (lyric) and Walter Donaldson (music) about a melancholy wooer who cannot get his beloved out of his mind. Early successful records by Ash and his Orchestra, Ruth Etting, and Willard Robison popularized the song, and Kay Kyser and his Orchestra revived it in 1935 with a hit version, making the number their theme song. Other significant records were made by Lee Wiley, Dick Haymes, George Shearing, Annette Hanshaw, Count Basie, Fats Domino, Eddie Fisher, Sarah Vaughan, and Connie Francis. The ballad, sometimes listed as "I've Grown So Lonesome Thinking of You," can be heard in the movies *You'll Find Out* (1940) and *Du Barry Was a Lady* (1943).

"This Could Be the Start of Something (Big)" (1956), the most famous of the many songs written by Steve Allen, is about the realization that hits one walking down the street or at a party when you see the someone that you know will be that special love of your life. Allen introduced it with Les Brown and his Band of Renown on his television show, and it was Allen's theme song for the rest of his long career. The Brown recording was a modest success, and a duet version by Steve Lawrence and Eydie Gorme was also popular. Because of radio play, television, and numerous recordings, the ballad was widely known and became a standard even though it never had a single disc that reached bestseller status. Among the other artists to record it were Joni James, Count Basie, Buddy Greco, Lionel Hampton, Lester Lanin, the Oscar Peterson Trio, Aretha Franklin, the Four Freshmen, Jack Jones, the Ray Charles Singers, and George Bugatti.

"This Is My Country" (1940), the rousing chorale favorite about the land of one's birth being the grandest land of all, was written by Don Raye and Al Jacobs and popularized by Fred Waring's Pennsylvanians who were long associated with the number. Woodie Guthrie, Lawrence Welk, the Impressions, the Mormon Tabernacle Choir, Eric Donaldson, and Curtis Mayfield were among the others to made laudable recordings of the patriotic song.

"This Is Romance" (1933) is a dreamy romantic ballad by Edward Heyman (lyric) and Vernon Duke (music) that describes the feelings of lovers in love. Glen Gray and the Casa Loma Orchestra (vocal by Kenny Sargent) brought attention to the number with their popular record, and there were successful discs by the orchestras of Ben Bernie, Jack Fulton, and Ray Noble (vocal by Al Bowlly) as well. Artie Shaw revived the ballad in 1941 with a hit record. Distinctive versions were also made by Nye Mayhew and June Christy with the Kentones.

"This Land Is Your Land" (1945) is the popular folk song celebrating America that Woody Guthrie wrote because he thought Irving Berlin's "God Bless America" was vulgar and phony. Guthrie's music is based on an old Baptist hymn, and his lyric lists various natural landmarks, from prairies and valleys to forests and oceans, that make the country great. Both songs are appropriate anthems: Berlin, a city dweller, praises the people and philosophy of the nation, while Guthrie, a country boy, celebrates the varied natural gifts from God. (Guthrie's original title was "God Blessed America.") Although written around 1940 and sung by Guthrie in various places, the song was not written out until he recorded it in 1945. Nothing much happened to the ballad until the Weavers' 1956 disc made it popular. The New Christy Minstrels revived it in 1963, and that same year there was a bestselling record by Ketty Lester. Other effective versions were made by Peter, Paul and Mary, Paul Anka, Flatt and Scruggs, Pete Seeger, the Wee Turtles, the Kingston Trio, the Lime-liters, Harry Belafonte, the Brothers Four, the Travellers, Trini Lopez, the Browns, and Wanda Jackson. David Carradine and a chorus sang the song in the Guthrie movie bio *Bound for Glory* (1976).

"This Little Piggy Went to Market" (1933) is a silly ditty by Sam Coslow (lyric) and Harold "Lefty" Lewis (music) based on the familiar nursery rhyme. Ruth Etting popularized the number in clubs and on record, and there were early discs by Annette Hanshaw, George Olsen and his Or-chestra (vocal by Ethel Shutta), and Victor Young (vocal by Peg La Cen-tra under the pseudonym of Jane Vance). The Andrews Sisters revived the amusing number in 1939, and it can be heard in the movies *Eight Girls in a Boat* (1934) and *She Made Her Bed* (1934).

"Three Coins in the Fountain" (1954) is the Oscar-winning ballad by Sammy Cahn (lyric) and Jule Styne (music) that was inspired by the Trevi Fountain in Rome. The music is lilting and catchy, and the lyric asks which of the three Americans who threw a coin in the fountain will see his or her wish come true. Frank Sinatra introduced the song on the soundtrack of the film *Three Coins in the Fountain* (1954), and his record with Nelson Riddle's Orchestra was a bestseller. The Four Aces also had a popular disc that went to the top of the charts. The success of the song (and the film itself) made the Roman fountain a must-see destination for thousands of Americans. Among the other artists to record the lovely ballad were Doris Day, Mantovanni's Orchestra, Al Martino, Rene Paulo, the Platters, Dinah Washington, the Ray Conniff Singers, the Dominoes, the Vince Guaraldi Trio, Earl Bostic, Henry Mancini, Frank Chacksfield, Connie Francis, Skitch Henderson, Julius LaRosa, and the Gatlin Broth-ers. Guy Stroman led the cast in singing it in the Off-Broadway revue *Forever Plaid* (1990).

"Three Little Fishes (Itty Bitty Poo)" (1939) is the ridiculous but catchy novelty number by Saxie Dowell that remained familiar for decades be-cause of its contagious silliness. The lyric about a mother fish and her children who swim over a dam is filled with nonsense words such as "dit dit ditty" and "itty bitty poo." The number was introduced on a successful record by Hal Kemp and his Orchestra with Dowell doing the vocals with the Smoothies. But even more popular was a disc by Kay Kyser (vocal by Ish Kabibble) that sold a million copies and went to the top of the charts. The number was revived in 1967 by Mitch Ryder and the Detroit Wheels on a record that combined the song with "Too Many Fish in the Sea." While most novelty songs are recorded a few times and then fade away, "Three Little Fishes" has had dozens of recordings over the years. A sampling would include those by Paul Whiteman (vocal by the Modernaires), Spike Jones, the Hoosier Hot Shots, Glenn Miller, Ambrose and his Orchestra, Guy Lombardo, Red Norvo, Bebe Daniels, Mitch Ryder, Maurice Denham, and Shelley Duvall. The number can also be heard in the film *Spring Reunion* (1957).

"Three O'Clock in the Morning" (1921) is a waltzing ballad that for many years was traditionally played as the last number at a dance. Julian Robledo wrote the gliding music as a piano piece in 1918. Dorothy Terriss (a.k.a. Dolly Morse) added a lyric in 1921, and the song was introduced in the revue *Greenwich Village Follies of 1921*, where it was performed by Richard Bold and Rosalind Fuller. The lyric is about two lovers still dancing when the clock strikes 3:00 A.M., the couple unaware of the rest of the world and willing to dance on forever. The music even echoes the famed chimes of Westminster in the middle section. Paul Whiteman's recording in 1922 sold 3.5 million discs and encouraged the sale of over a million copies of sheet music. Monty Kelly and his Orchestra revived the number in 1953 with a successful record, and there were discs by Lou Rawls and Bert Kaempfert in 1965 that were also hits. Among the many others who made recordings were Frank Crumit, John McCormack, Eddy Duchin, Erroll Garner, Dexter Gordon, Don Byas, Chet Atkins, Oscar Peterson, Sergio Mendez, and Stephane Grappelli. The song was heard in the movies *Margie* (1946), *Belles on Their Toes* (1952), and *The Eddy Duchin Story* (1956), and it was sung by Judy Garland in *Presenting Lily Mars* (1943) and J. Carroll Naish in *That Midnight Kiss* (1949).

"Tiger Rag" (1917), just as familiarly known as "Hold That Tiger!," is not about the jungle beast but instead is a vivacious plea to the dance band to play "The Tiger Rag." The pulsating rag comes across as much as a cheer ("choke him, poke him, kick him, and soak him!") as a dance song, but it proved to be ideal material for jazz musicians. Henry Spargo wrote the vigorous lyric, and the music was by Jelly Roll Morton with Nick La Rocca and Larry Shields, members of the Original Dixieland Jazz Band. The number was introduced by the authors and was immediately popular. The Mills Brothers revived it in 1931 with their first

record. Other disc versions of note were made by Louis Armstrong, Is-
ham Jones, Ted Lewis, Tommy Dorsey, Djando Reinhardt, Kid Ory,
Larry Adler, Les Paul and Mary Ford, Valaida Snow, Sidney Bechet, and
Morton as a solo. "Tiger Rag" has been used in some dozen movies,
including *Night Club Girl* (1944), *Variety Girl* (1947), *Let's Dance* (1950),
Has Anybody Seen My Gal? (1952), *Jazz on a Summer's Day* (1959), and
Pretty Baby (1978). Ted Lewis reprised it in *Is Everybody Happy?* (1929),
Bing Crosby sang it in *Birth of the Blues* (1941), and the Mills Brothers
performed it in *The Big Broadcast* (1932), and their recording was heard
in *King of the Hill* (1993). The song was also featured in the Off-Broadway
musical *Jelly Roll* (1996).

"Till the End of Time" (1945) is a flowing ballad that Buddy Kaye and
Ted Mossman adapted from Chopin's Polonaise in A Flat Minor (Opus
53). The list song is filled with hyperbolic images ("till the well runs
dry") of how long a wooer will love his darling. The new-old song was
featured in the Chopin movie bio *A Song to Remember* (1945) but got more
attention when Perry Como recorded it, selling 2 million discs and
prompting the sale of 1.5 million copies of sheet music. Other hit records
were made by Les Brown (vocal by Doris Day) and Dick Haymes, helping the song to stay on the *Hit Parade* for nineteen weeks. Among the
other artists to make notable discs were Frank Sinatra, Caterina Valente,
Billy Vaughn, the Flamingos, Jerry Vale, Della Reese, Dave Specter and
the Bluebirds, Gene Pitney, Bonnie Tyler, Jim Nabors, Matt Monro, and
Mariah Carey. Como was heard on the soundtrack of the film *Till the
End of Time* (1946), where it was used as the theme song.

"Till We Meet Again" (1918), one of the most successful (and arguably
the finest) of all World War One ballads, is a heartfelt farewell song in
which a beau promises to return and wed her, guaranteeing that "ev'ry
tear will be a memory." Raymond B. Egan (lyric) and Richard A. Whiting
(music) wrote the delicate waltz after America entered the war but were
so displeased with the song that they threw it into the trash basket. A
secretary fished it out and sent it to a publisher, and it ended up selling
over 15 million copies of sheet music over the years. Of the many recordings were those by Rosemary Clooney, Bing Crosby, Helen Forrest
and Dick Haymes, Frankie Laine, Eddy Duchin, the Mills Brothers, the
Ray Benson Orchestra, Kay Starr, Al Goodman, Patti Page, Jaye P. Morgan, Joni James, Bunk Johnson, Frank Novak and the Rootin' Tootin'
Boys, and Mitch Miller. The ballad can be heard in the movies *Ride 'Em
Cowboy* (1942), *Tomorrow Is Forever* (1946), and *Auntie Mame* (1958), was
sung by Judy Garland and Lucille Norman in *For Me and My Gal* (1942)
and Doris Day and Gordon MacRae in *On Moonlight Bay* (1951), and
played on the soundtrack by pianist Carmen Cavallaro for Tyrone Power

in *The Eddy Duchin Story* (1956). For many years "Till We Meet Again" was sung in the halls of the U.S. Congress at adjournment.

"Time on My Hands" (1930) is a gentle yet intoxicating standard that lists in short descriptive phrases the expansive feeling one has with a sweetheart in one's arms and love in one's heart. Harold Adamson, Mack Gordon (lyric), and Vincent Youmans (music) wrote the ballad for Marilyn Miller to sing in the Broadway musical *Smiles* (1930), but the star didn't like it, so her leading man Paul Gregory sang it instead. The show was short-lived and the song took quite a while to catch on. In fact, it was a hit in England before it found success in the States. But it would go on to be recorded hundreds of times, including memorable discs by Count Basie, Glenn Miller, Ray Noble (vocal by Al Bowlly), Billie Holiday, Mario Lanza, Benny Goodman, Paul Weston, Duke Ellington, the Boswell Sisters, Sonny Rollins, Oscar Peterson, Russ Columbo, Marlene Dietrich (in German), Billy Eckstine, Miles Davis, and Quincy Jones. On screen it was sung by June Haver in the Miller bio *Look for the Silver Lining* (1949) and Kathryn Grayson in *So This Is Love* (1953).

"To Each His Own" (1946), the first hit for the successful songwriting team of Jay Livingston and Ray Evans, is an engaging ballad about how all things need something to stay alive: Flowers need sun, a door needs a key, words need music, and "I need you." It was written for the film *To Each His Own* (1946) but was never used. Instead the song was introduced by Eddy Howard with a record that sold 2 million copies. The number also provided hits for Tony Martin and for the Modernaires with Paula Kelly, and both the Ink Spots and Freddy Martin (vocal by Stuart Wade) had discs that sold a million copies each. The ballad was revived with success by the Platters in 1961, the Tymes in 1964, and Frankie Laine in 1968. Other versions were made by Al Martino, Joni James, Keely Smith, Pat Boone, and Willie Nelson. "To Each His Own" can be heard in the movie *Saigon* (1948).

"To Love Again" (1956), another Tin Pan Alley hit based on a classical piece of music, is a gushing ballad by Ned Washington (lyric), Morris Stoloff, and George Sidney (music) that borrowed liberally from Chopin's E-Flat Nocturne. Eddy Duchin used an instrumental version for his theme song, and there was a hit record of the vocal version by the Four Aces. Roger Williams, Sil Austin, Hank Crawford, Jerry Vale, and Jane Olivor were among those who also recorded it. In the movie bio *The Eddy Duchin Story* (1956), Carmen Cavallaro provided the piano playing on the soundtrack for Tyrone Power.

"Together" (1928), a rare independent song from the Broadway team of DeSylva, Brown, and Henderson, took nearly twenty years to become a hit but then stayed popular for four decades. Ray Henderson wrote the tuneful music, and Lew Brown and B.G. DeSylva collaborated on the lyric about all the things two lovers did together: laughing at the rain, singing love songs, pretending that it would never end, and so on. Now they are separated, but in one's memory they will always be together. Paul Whiteman and his Orchestra (vocal by Jack Fulton), Nick Lucas, Cliff Edwards, and Franklyn Baur each made early recordings of the song, but it never got widespread attention. Not until it was used in the film *Since You Went Away* (1944) did it become well known and stay on the *Hit Parade* for twelve weeks. Clark Dennis recorded "Together" in the 1940s, Connie Francis revived it with success in 1961, and it returned again in 1967 with a record by the Intruders and in 1980 thanks to Septet Tierra. Dan Dailey (as Ray Henderson) sang the ballad in the movie *The Best Things in Life Are Free* (1956).

"Tonight You Belong to Me" (1926) is an embracing ballad by Billy Rose (lyric) and Lee David (music) that was popular in the 1920s and then again in the 1950s. There were early successful recordings by Gene Austin, Franklyn Baur, Sam Lanin, and Irving Kaufman (who recorded it three more times during his career). The song was revived in 1956 by a popular Frankie Laine disc and one by Patience and Prudence that sold a million copies. Other noteworthy versions were made by the Lennon Sisters with Lawrence Welk's Orchestra, Karen Chandler and Jimmy Wakely, Erskine Hawkins, Cliff Brunner and his Texas Wanderers, Frances Faye, and Paul Stanley. Tia Speros and Jody Abraham performed the number in the Off-Broadway revue *The Taffetas* (1988).

"Too Young" (1951) is a delicate ballad by Sylvia Dee (lyric) and Sidney Lippman (music) about the power of youthful love. The lyric is the complaint by a couple who have been told by those older and wiser that they are too young to know the meaning of love. But the youths are convinced of their sincerity, are determined that it will last, and look forward to the day when others will realize that they "weren't too young at all." The graceful number was introduced by Johnny Desmond but popularized by Nat King Cole, whose record with Les Baxter's Orchestra was Number One in all categories and sold a million copies. The song was so beloved across the country that it remained in the top position on *Your Hit Parade* for twelve weeks, a feat never again repeated. Donny Osmond revived the ballad with success in 1972. Other versions were made by Sam Cooke, the Lettermen, Lewis Lymon and the Teenagers, Connie Francis, Floyd Cramer, and Natalie Cole.

"Toolie Oolie Doolie (The Yodel Polka)" (1948) is a happy-go-lucky nonsense song from Switzerland that translated into a Tin Pan Alley hit with little difficulty. Arthur Beul wrote the Swiss-German number as "Nach em Rage Schint Sunne," and soon it was being yodeled across Europe. Vaughn Horton wrote an amusing English lyric cautioning Swiss suitors that they cannot win the girl of their hearts unless they learn to yodel "toolie oolie doo" and make all their dreams come true. The merry song was introduced in America by Horton and his Polka Debs, and there were hit records by the Andrews Sisters and the Sportsmen. Eddie Cantor, the Larkin Sisters, Mary Schneider, and Kenny Roberts also made successful discs. Gene Autry sang the echoing number in the movie *Riders of the Whistling Pines* (1949).

"Too-Ra-Loo-Ra-Loo-Ral (That's an Irish Lullaby)" (1913) is the Irish American favorite that came from Tin Pan Alley rather than the old country, but it has enough Gaelic touches to sound authentic. James R. Shannon wrote the soothing lullaby for the musical extravaganza *Shameen Dhu* (1913), where it was introduced by Chauncey Olcott with great success. Sheet music sales remained healthy for decades, and there were many recordings by Irish singers and musicians. The song became even more popular when Bing Crosby sang Barry Fitzgerald to sleep with it in the movie *Going My Way* (1944). Crosby's disc version sold over a million copies, and then it seemed everyone was making recordings of the song, including Kate Smith, Dennis Day, Rosemary Clooney, Gene Tracy, Ruby Braff, Dick Haymes, Ruby Murphy, Frances Faye, Joni James, Connie Francis, John Gary, Mitch Miller, and Tony Kenny. It can also be heard in the films *Nob Hill* (1945) and *At War With the Army* (1950).

"Toot Toot Tootsie (Goodbye)" (1922), the rapid farewell song that is far from gloomy, was long associated with Al Jolson who interpolated it into his Broadway show *Bombo* (1922), recorded it, and sang it in four movies. Gus Kahn, Ernie Erdman, and Dan Russo wrote the slaphappy number that bids good-bye to a sweetie as her beau takes off on a "choo-choo," telling her that if she doesn't get a letter she'll "know I'm in jail." Over the years there have been enjoyable versions by Eddie Cantor, Judy Garland, Eddy Howard, Lester Lanin, Bing Crosby, Woody Herman, Sonny Rollins, Tony Bennett, Spike Jones, Dean Martin, Eddie Fisher, Tony Martin, Vic Damone, Mitch Miller, Wayne Newton, and Liza Minnelli. On screen, Jolson either sang or dubbed "Toot Toot Tootsie" in *The Jazz Singer* (1927), *Rose of Washington Square* (1939), *The Jolson Story* (1946), and *Jolson Sings Again* (1949), and his recording was heard in *Bullets Over Broadway* (1994). Doris Day performed it in *I'll See You in My Dreams*

(1952), June Allyson and Van Johnson did a duet version in *Remains to Be Seen* (1953), and it was heard in *The Sand Pebbles* (1966).

"The Trail of the Lonesome Pine" (1913) is a nostalgic ballad by Ballard MacDonald (lyric) and Harry Carroll (music) about longing to return to the mountains where a loved one lives in a cabin under a single pine tree, their names once carved into the tree trunk. While the title came from a novel by John Fox Jr., set in the Cumberland Mountains of Kentucky, the song is set in the Blue Ridge Mountains of Virginia. The "ear-caressing tune," as David Ewen describes it, was popularized in vaudeville by Henry Burr and Albert Campbell, then interpolated into the Broadway revue *Passing Show of 1914*, where it was sung by Muriel Window. Fuzzy Knight performed the ballad in the movie *The Trail of the Lonesome Pine* (1936), and Stan Laurel (dubbed by Chill Wills) sang it in *Way Out West* (1937). A distinctive record was made by Russ Morgan and his Orchestra.

"Trees" (1922) is a concert song, based on the beloved poem by Joyce Kilmer, that crossed over to Tin Pan Alley with success. Otto Rasbach composed the elegant music that was set to the short but memorable poem about the beauty and dignity of nature, and it was sung in concert by John Charles Thomas, Paul Robeson, Nelson Eddy, and others. "Trees" was revived in 1931 with a hit record by Isham Jones and his Orchestra. Other artists to make disc versions include Bunny Berigan, the Sons of the Pioneers, Claude Hopkins, Les Elgart, Louis Armstrong, Donald Novis, Al Hibbler, the Platters, Benny Goodman, the Spaniels, and Sarah Vaughan. Novis reprised the song in the film *The Big Broadcast* (1932), and it was performed by Fred Waring's Pennsylvanians on the soundtrack of the animated *Melody Time* (1948).

"Trouble in Mind" (1926) is an anguished blues number by Richard M. Jones in which the dejected one is so depressed he considers putting his head on "some lonesome railroad iron" and letting the "2:19 train ease my troubl'd mind." Jones introduced the number on record with his band, but the most renowned version is a blues classic disc by Bertha "Chippie" Hill with Louis Armstrong on the cornet. The song was popular in the 1920s with hits by Jay McShann (vocal by Julia Lee) and Victoria Spivey, then was revived in the 1950s with prominent records by Ray Charles and Ella Fitzgerald. Disc versions were also made by Sister Rosetta Tharpe with Lucy Millinder's Band, Nina Simone, Aretha Franklin, Red Garland, and Hank Williams Jr. Marianne Faithful sang the slow blues number on the soundtrack of the film *Trouble in Mind* (1985).

"Truckin' " (1935) may sound like a country-western road song from the 1960s, but it is a depression-era number about a new Harlem dance that everyone in town is supposedly doing, even the Park Avenue set. Ted Koehler (lyric) and Rube Bloom (music) wrote the piquant number, and it was introduced by Cora La Redd in a Cotton Club revue. Major recordings were made by Fats Waller, Duke Ellington (vocal by Ivie Anderson), Johnny "Scat" Davis, Red Allen, the Mills Blue Rhythm Band, the Little Ramblers, and Mel Tormé. The song can be heard in the movie *The Cotton Club* (1984).

"True Confession" (1937) is a teary ballad that Sam Coslow and Frederick Hollander wrote as the theme song for the film *True Confession* (1937). Among the many artists to record it were Dorothy Lamour, Sammy Kaye, Larry Clinton (vocal by Bea Wain), Don Bestor, Russ Morgan, Louis Armstrong, Fats Waller, Benny Goodman, and Fats Domino.

"Trust in Me" (1937) is a loving ballad that found modest success in the 1930s but became a major hit in the 1950s. Ned Wever (lyric), Milton Ager, and Jean Schwartz (music) wrote the warm plea for companionship, and it was given an early recording by Mildred Bailey. But little happened to the song until Eddie Fisher revived it in 1952 with a chart disc. Other hit versions in the 1950s and early 1960s were made by Roy Rogers, Chris Connor, Patti Page, and Etta James. Among those who also recorded the ballad were Bobby Hayes (vocal by Don Cornell), Wayne King, Abe Lyman (vocal by Sonny Schyler), Billy Eckstine, Fats Domino, Louis Jordan, the Orioles, Dinah Washington, Hank Crawford, Holly Cole, and Harry Nilssen.

"Try a Little Tenderness" (1933) is the cautionary ballad by Harry Woods, Jimmy Campbell, and Reg Connelly that asks one to be particularly careful when dealing with moody or sullen young ladies, for they are all waiting for love. The song became a hit first in England (Campbell and Connelly were British), then in America where it was introduced and recorded by Ruth Etting. Although it never fell out of favor, it was revived in the late 1960s with hit records by Otis Redding and Three Dog Night. Among the notable versions made over the years were those by Frank Sinatra, Ray Noble, Ted Lewis, Eddie Cantor, Bing Crosby, Jimmy Durante, Gloria Lynne, Eddy Duchin, Ella Fitzgerald, Aretha Franklin, Percy Sledge, Tom Jones, Shirley Bassey, and Michael Bolton. The gentle number was played under the opening credits of the film *Dr. Strangelove* (1964) for ironic effect, and it was also heard in *The Mirror Has Two Faces* (1996).

"Tuxedo Junction" (1939) found success first as an instrumental, then as a vocal, becoming a favorite in both forms during the Big Band era. Erskine Hawkins, William Johnson, and Julian Dash composed the swinging music in 1939, and Hawkins and his Band introduced the instrumental at the Savoy Ballroom in New York. His recording was a success, but a disc by Glenn Miller was an even bigger hit. In 1940 Buddy Feyne added a smooth lyric about a railroad junction in Alabama, and the Andrews Sisters introduced the new version on record. Other well-known discs were made by Jan Savitt, Harry James, Bob Crosby, Ernie Fields, Duke Ellington, Ray Anthony, Glen Gray and the Casa Loma Orchestra, Stan Kenton, Duane Eddy, Gene Krupa, the Four Freshmen, Joe Augustine, Chet Atkins, and the Manhattan Transfer. The vibrant number can be heard in the movies *Tuxedo Junction* (1941) and *The Glenn Miller Story* (1954).

"Twilight Time" (1944) is a romantic ballad about meeting one's darling in the light of a setting sun. Buck Ram, Morty Nevins, and Artie Dunn wrote the affecting number, and it was introduced by the Three Suns, whose record was so successful they made it their theme song. There were popular instrumental versions made by Les Brown in 1945 and Johnny Maddox in 1953, but the biggest hit record was a vocal by the Platters in 1958 that went to the top of all the charts and put the song in the Number One position on *Your Hit Parade*. The Impressions, Earl Bostic, Ray Anthony, Louis Prima, Carmen Cavallaro, Billy Vaughn, Jerry Murad's Harmonicats, Ted Heath, the Lennon Sisters, Andy Williams, Gene Pitney, and Willie Nelson were among the artists who also made recordings. The atmospheric song was used in the movie *Sparkle* (1976).

"Two Cigarettes in the Dark" (1934) is a moody late-night song by Paul Francis Webster (lyric) and Lew Pollack (music) about a couple in the dark, he striking a match to light their cigarettes and the flame being compared to their love. Gloria Grafton introduced the song in the film *Kill That Story* (1934), and there were popular records by Morton Downey and Glen Gray and the Casa Loma Orchestra (vocal by Kenny Sargent). Other discs of note were made by Joe Morrison, Bing Crosby, Johnny Green, Ted Straeter, Skitch Henderson, Alberta Hunter, Betty Carter, and more recently, Marlene Ver Planck and Peter Mintun.

"Tzena, Tzena, Tzena" (1950) is a rhythmic little ditty from Israel that was popular in the States in the 1950s and is still heard in schools and performed by klezmer bands. Issachar Miron and Julius Grossman wrote the Hebrew song, which was published in 1947 and became well known in Israel. When a group of Israeli students were visiting New York, they sang the song in a club where members of the Weavers heard it and liked it. They got Mitchell Parish to write an English lyric that playfully asks all the girls in the village to come out and greet the brave soldiers, and the Weavers recorded it with Gordon Jenkins' Band. The disc sold a million copies, and the folk-singing group had their first hit. Among the other artists to record the zesty number were Mitch Miller, the Barry Sisters, Vic Damone, Chet Atkins, Mantovanni's Orchestra, Bruce Kaminsky, the Modern Klezmer Quartet, and the children's songs trio Sharon, Lois, and Bram.

U–V

"Unchained Melody" (1955) is the passionate lament of an amorist who waits for a sweetheart, having "hungered for your touch" too long. Hy Zaret (lyric) and Alex North (music) wrote the throbbing ballad for the film *Unchained* (1955), and it was popularized by an instrumental record by Les Baxter and his Orchestra and a vocal version by Al Hibbler. The Righteous Brothers revived it with success in 1965. Other artists to record the lush number include Andy Williams, the Platters, Liberace, Tom Jones, Gisele MacKenzie, Roger Whittaker, Henry Mancini, Richard Clayderman, James Galway, and more recently, Paul Mauriat and Karen Akers.

"Undecided" (1939) got its name when composer Charlie Shavers wired to his publishers that he was undecided about the title, and they thought that was the title, so they asked Sid Robin to write a lyric around the word. The result is an enticing ballad in which a lover laments over his sweetie's indecisiveness, keeping him "sitting on the fence." Shavers's music has an unusual rhythmic pattern, almost an early form of bebop, and the melody fluctuates nicely with the uncertain lyric. The song was introduced on record by John Kirby and "the biggest little band in the world" with Shavers on trumpet. Much more successful was a disc by Chick Webb (vocal by Ella Fitzgerald) that was a bestseller. The number was revived in 1951 with an even bigger hit, a recording by the Ames Brothers with Les Brown that sold a million copies. Of the many records over the years, significant ones were made by Louis Armstrong, George Shearing, Joe Venuti, Benny Goodman, Nat King Cole, the Clark Sisters, Fats Waller, Don Redman, Erroll Garner, Coleman Hawkins, Louis Prima, Gene Ammons, Dave Brubeck, John Coltrane, Acker Bilk, Ray Charles, and Dee Dee Bridgewater. Jason Graae sang "Undecided" in the Off-Broadway revue *Forever Plaid* (1990).

"Under a Blanket of Blue" (1933) is a cozy ballad by Marty Symes, Al Neiberg (lyric), and Jerry Livingston (music) about a couple snuggled together under a deep blue evening sky. The song was introduced with a successful record by Glen Gray and the Casa Loma Orchestra (vocal by Kenny Sargent). Among the artists to record it were George Hall, Don Bestor, Will Osborne, Art Tatum, Ella Fitzgerald and Louis Armstrong, Coleman Hawkins, Maxine Sullivan, Connee Boswell, the Three Suns, and Doris Day.

"Under the Anheuser Bush" (1904) is the hit vaudeville song by Andrew B. Sterling (lyric) and Harry Von Tilzer (music) that is a sequel of sorts to Von Tilzer's earlier "Down Where the Wurzburger Flows" (1902). The catchy number is a beau's plea to his beloved Sue to come and "make eyes with me" at the local beer garden where they can drink "Budwise" and listen to the German band. The song was a favorite on the variety circuits, and there were early records by Billy Murray and the team of Arthur Collins and Bryon Harlan. It was also popular in London, where it was titled "Down at the Old Bull and Bush," and British comic Stanley Holloway recorded it and sang it for years in clubs and concerts. "Under the Anheuser Bush" can be heard in the movie *Meet Me in St. Louis* (1944).

"Under the Bamboo Tree" (1902), an early ragtime classic originally titled "If You Lak-a Me," is an oddball novelty number about a Zulu and a maiden who decide that two can live as cheaply as one in the jungle. Robert Cole and J. Rosamond Johnson wrote the number that musically is a syncopated variation of the Negro spiritual "Nobody Knows de Trouble I've Seen." The number uses 4/4 time in the verse and 2/4 time in the refrain, an uncommon practice at the time. The two songwriters fashioned the song for their vaudeville act, but it was Arthur Collins who popularized it first on stage and then on record. The merry number went over so well that Tin Pan Alley was saturated with other animal songs for the next ten years. Marie Cahill interpolated it into her Broadway musical *Sally in Our Alley* (1902), reprised it in *Nancy Brown* (1903), recorded it, and made it her signature song. On the screen, Lillian Albritton sang it in *Bowery to Broadway* (1944), and it was performed by Judy Garland and Margaret O'Brien in *Meet Me in St. Louis* (1944). Donna Kane and Courtney Peldon sang it in the 1989 Broadway version of the film musical. Enjoyable recordings of the ditty were made by Garland, Ian Whitcomb and the Bungalow Boys, the Buffalo Bills, the Jelly Roll Kings, Kid Ory and his Creole Jazz Band, Hal Smith, William Bolcom and Joan Morris, the St. Louis Ragtimers, and Liza Minnelli.

"Underneath the Arches" (1933), a British sing-along number popular in pubs, is an easygoing song about a carefree life. Reg Connelly and Bud Flanagan wrote the gentle soft-shoe ballad about a free spirit who likes to sleep under the arches of a bridge, content to "dream my dreams away." The songwriters introduced the song in London, but it didn't become a hit in the States until 1948 when Joseph McCarthy revised the lyric for Americans. Hit records by George Olsen and his Band (vocal by Ethel Shutta) and Primo Scala's Banjo and Accordion Orchestra popularized the number, and there were also successful discs by the Andrews Sisters and Andy Russell with the Pied Pipers. Connee Boswell, Gracie Fields, Flanagan and Allen, Phil's Liverpool Band, Max Bygraves, and Vicki Stuart were among the other artists to record it.

"Underneath the Harlem Moon" (1932) is a jazzy ballad by Mack Gordon (lyric) and Harry Revel (music) that was popularized by Joe Rines and his Orchestra. The rhythmic serenade was recorded by such artists as Don Redman, Chick Bullock, Bunny Berigan, Fletcher Henderson, the Washboard Rhythm Kings, Peter DeRose, the Spirits of Rhythm, and Randy Newman.

"Unforgettable" (1951) is the hit ballad by Irving Gordon that is about the song being sung. The intoxicating music is a contagious fox trot, and the smooth lyric describes a beloved who is like a song that clings to one and cannot be forgotten. The ballad is most associated with Nat King Cole whose recording with Nelson Riddle's Orchestra was a bestseller. Dinah Washington revived the number in 1959, and her disc was also a hit. Among the other artists to make memorable versions were Peggy Lee, Pete Fountain, Vera Lynn, Johnny Hartman, Teddi King, Ella Fitzgerald, Billy May, the Four Freshmen, Aretha Franklin, Lou Rawls, Vikki Carr, James Galway, Sammy Davis Jr., Engelbert Humperdinck, and the Dick Hyman Trio. In 1991 Natalie Cole made a distinctive recording, using her father's original track in order to sing it as a duet with him. The disc revived interest in the number and prompted more recent versions by Cleo Laine, Dean Fraser, Kenny Rogers, Frank Pellico, and Roberta Flack.

"Until the Real Thing Comes Along" (1931) is a sublime declaration of love in which a suitor is willing to slave for a beloved; if such behavior isn't love, it will have to do until the real thing appears. Sammy Cahn, Saul Chaplin, L.E. Freeman, Mann Holiner, and Alberta Nichols all collaborated at different times on the enticing ballad, which was introduced as "Till the Real Thing Comes Along" in the revue *Rhapsody in Black* (1931), where it was sung by Ethel Waters. Cahn and others made changes in the song, and it was reintroduced in 1936 with a record by Andy Kirk and his Clouds of Joy (vocal by Pha Terrell) that became a bestseller. Other early hits versions were made by Fats Waller and Leo Reisman and his Orchestra (vocal by Larry Stewart). The number was a particular favorite of jazz musicians because of its subtle but driving rhythm. Notable records were also made by Carmen McRae, Dexter Gordon, Billie Holiday, Erskine Hawkins, the Ink Spots, Nat King Cole, Lillian Roth, Erroll Garner, Ella Fitzgerald, the Clark Sisters, Dean Martin, and more recently, Mark Murphy, Larry Elgart, and Weslia Whitfield. The Reisman recording was heard in the film *Paper Moon* (1973).

"Uska Dara (A Turkish Tale)" (1953) is a spirited novelty number by Stella Lee that is adapted from a Turkish song sometimes titled "Uska-dara." Although Eydie Gorme introduced the song with a successful record, the piece is most associated with Eartha Kitt, who sang it both in English and Turkish, had a bestselling disc, and kept it in her nightclub act for years. Kitt reprised the number in the movie *New Faces* (1954).

"The Very Thought of You" (1934) is a sparkling ballad by bandleader Ray Noble in which one thinks of his darling all day long, wherever he is, whatever he is doing, sometimes forgetting where he is and what he is doing. The lyric is effortless and calm, while the music seems to keep climbing up the scale all the time, even though the song is not all that rangy. Noble and his Orchestra popularized the ballad on record, and there were also major discs by Dick Haymes, Billie Holiday, Carmen Cavallaro, Al Bowlly, Jeri Southern, Kitty Carlisle, Benny Carter, Joe Reichman, Nat King Cole, Oscar Peterson, Tony Bennett, Ricky Nelson, and more recently, Michael Feinstein, Natalie Cole, and Betty Buckley. Doris Day sang it in the movie *Young Man With a Horn* (1950), and it can be heard in *Casablanca* (1942), *The Very Thought of You* (1944), and *Hotel* (1967).

"Vict'ry Polka" (1943) is a merry number, written during the dark days of World War Two, that anticipates victory with a polka beat. Sammy Cahn (lyric) and Jule Styne (music) wrote the cheer-up song, and it was popularized by a hit record by Bing Crosby and the Andrews Sisters. The bands of Glenn Miller and Kay Kyser also had success with it. On screen, the ditty was sung by Ann Miller and the chorus in *Jam Session* (1944), and the Andrews Sisters reprised it in *Follow the Boys* (1944).

"Vieni Su (Say You Love Me Too)" (1949) is a romantic ballad that Johnny Cola based on an old Italian song in the public domain. The emotive number, sung in English and Italian, was popularized by a hit record by Vaughn Monroe and his Orchestra. Dean Martin's disc with Paul Weston's Orchestra was popular, and Carl Ravazza and his Orchestra had enough success with it to make it their theme song. Other noteworthy versions were made by Phil Brito with Walter Gross's Orchestra, Frankie Carle (vocal by Marjorie Hughes), and Jerry Vale.

"Volare" (1958), a Tin Pan Alley giant with over 3 million records sold in the States, is unusual in that two different versions with different titles were both hits. Franci Migliacci (Italian lyric) and Domenico Modugno (music) wrote the expansive ballad as "Nel Blu, Dipinto di Blu," and it sold a million records in Italy. When it came to America some artists sang it in its original form, and others used a version called "Volare" with some English phrases added by Mitchell Parrish. Both songs are about the lighter-than-air feeling one has when in love ("volare" is Italian for "to fly"), and the public responded to both, though "Volare" was a lot easier to remember. Bobby Vinton, Dean Martin, and the McGuire Sisters all had early hit records, and Bobby Rydell revived it with success in 1960. In addition to many Italian singers and bands, there were other discs of note by Modugno, Al Martino, the Platters, Louis Armstrong, Leadbelly, the Gipsy Kings, Chet Atkins, Oscar Peterson, Trini Lopez, Earl Grant, Petula Clark, and more recently, Richie Cole, Alejandre Guzman, and Luciano Pavarotti. The song was heard in the British film *Absolute Beginners* (1986), and on stage it was sung by Jim Walton and the company in the Broadway revue *Stardust* (1987) and by the cast of the Off-Broadway revue *The Taffetas* (1988).

W

"Wait 'Til the Sun Shines, Nellie" (1905) is a comforting ballad by Andrew B. Sterling (lyric) and Harry Von Tilzer (music) in which a beau tries to cheer up his sweetie, telling her tomorrow will be a brighter day. Sterling got the lyric idea when he overheard a man say the title phrase to his new wife when their trip to Coney Island was canceled because of rain. Von Tilzer wrote the slow march melody that, years later, would become a jazz favorite with a faster tempo. Winona Winter introduced the ballad in vaudeville, and it was further popularized by Bryon Harlan, Harry Talley, and various male quartets, selling over a million copies of sheet music. The number has always been a banjo favorite as well. Harry James, Jo Stafford with Paul Weston's Orchestra, the Sons of the Pioneers, Louis Nelson, the Buffalo Bills, Frank Novak and his Rootin' Tootin' Boys, Buddy Holly, Max Bygraves, and Teresa Sterne are among the artists who recorded it, but the biggest seller was a jazzed-up duet version by Mary Martin and Bing Crosby taken from the movie *Birth of the Blues* (1941). Also on screen, Dennis Morgan sang it in *My Wild Irish Rose* (1947), and the song can also be heard in *The Strawberry Blonde* (1941), *Rhythm Parade* (1942), *Bowery to Broadway* (1944), *In the Good Old Summertime* (1949) and *Wait Till the Sun Shines, Nellie* (1952).

"Waitin' for the Train to Come In" (1945) is a slow blues number about a woman who stands at the depot and waits for her man to return, deep in melancholy since he left. Sunny Skylar and Martin Block wrote the poignant number, and it was popularized by Peggy Lee in her first solo record to climb the charts. There were other early hits by Harry James (vocal by Kitty Kallen) and Johnny Long (vocal by Dick Robertson). There were also discs by Louis Prima, Dick Haymes, the Pied Pipers, Sam Donahue, Rex Stewart, and Ruth Cameron.

"Waiting for the Robert E. Lee" (1912), one of the most vibrant and durable of all ragtime hits, is a contagious rhythm number about an assembly of folks waiting for a riverboat to come in. L. Wolf Gilbert got the idea for the lyric one day when he was watching Negro dockworkers unloading the *Robert E. Lee* at the Mississippi levee at Baton Rouge. Lewis F. Muir composed the vigorous music that is in the key of C for the verse but moves into F for the refrain, an unusual practice at the time. The song is beautifully unified, a musical theme from the verse repeated within the B section. The number was introduced with a bang when Al Jolson sang it in a concert one night at the Winter Garden Theatre in New York. Belle Baker, Ruth Royce, and other vaudeville headliners helped popularize it, and the Heidelberg Quintet made an early recording. Eddie Cantor sang the number as a boy in Gus Edwards's kiddie act, then sang it as an adult in concerts in a southern-Yiddish accent that made him a comic favorite. Notable record versions were made by Jolson, Louis Jordan, Bing Crosby, Benny Goodman, Alan Dale, Beatrice Kay, the Dukes of Dixieland, Lu Waters, Woody Herman, the Vagabonds, Will Bill Davison, the Basin Street Six, Dean Martin, and many others. Jolson sang it on the soundtrack for Larry Parks in *The Jolson Story* (1946) and *Jolson Sings Again* (1949), and it was also performed by Bobby Gordon in *The Jazz Singer* (1927), Fred Astaire and Ginger Rogers in *The Story of Vernon and Irene Castle* (1939), and Mickey Rooney, Judy Garland, and the chorus in *Babes on Broadway* (1942). "Waiting for the Robert E. Lee" can also be heard in *Applause* (1929), *Hellzapoppin'* (1941), *Cairo* (1942), and *Lake Placid Serenade* (1944).

"Walkin' My Baby Back Home" (1930) is the lighthearted, gently swinging song about a couple walking "arm in arm" through a bucolic setting late at night. Roy Turk and Fred Ahlert wrote the engaging number that was most associated with Harry Richman, who introduced it and sang it in clubs and on records for years. When Johnnie Ray, abandoning his usual wailing style, revived it in 1952, his disc sold a million copies. The uptempo ballad was also a hit for Nat King Cole. Other well-known discs were made by Jo Stafford, Ted Weems (vocal by Parker Gibbs), Louis Armstrong, Annette Hanshaw, the Page Cavanaugh Trio, Maurice Chevalier, Ray Anthony, Dean Martin, Jerry Vale, and more recently, Joe Pass, Steve Hall, Don Shirley, and Toni Carroll. Donald O'Connor sang it in the movie *Walkin' My Baby Back Home* (1953).

"Waltz Me Around Again, Willie (Around, Around, Around)" (1906) is a merry dance song by Will D. Cobb (lyric) and Ren Shields (music) about ribbon salesman Willie Fitzgibbons and his sweetie Madeline Mooney who would "rather be dancing than eat." So she brings Willie to the music hall and pleads the title phrase to him. The number was popularized by Billy Murray and the Hayden Quartet, who later recorded it, and in vaudeville it was performed by Della Fox, Willie Devere, and a performer actually named Willie Fitzgibbons. On Broadway, Blanche Ring sang the waltz in *His Honor, The Mayor* (1906), and years later it was performed by the cast of the revue *Tintypes* (1980). William Bolcom and Joan Morris made a standout recording of the waltz.

"Wanderin' " (1950) is a traditional folk song from Minnesota that was turned into a Tin Pan Alley hit in 1950 when Sammy Kaye and Edward Jackson adapted it and set it to a poem Carl Sandburg had written in 1926. The travel-weary number is about a man jilted by a red-headed woman, so he journeys from New York to "the Golden Gate" and works until he is exhausted and sore, but all his wandering can't make him forget her. Kaye and his Orchestra (vocal by Tony Alamo) had a hit record of the song, and there were other successful discs by Peter, Paul and Mary, Frank Sinatra, Gale Garnett, Acker Bilk, the Great American String Band, and Chris Isaak. The ballad can be heard in the movies *Heart of the Rockies* (1951), *Sweethearts on Parade* (1953), and *How the West Was Won* (1962).

"Washboard Blues" (1926), Hoagy Carmichael's first major song, began as a jazz instrumental that was popularized by Curtis Hitch's Happy Harmonists on a record with Carmichael doing the piano solo. Although the song has verse, refrain, and release sections, it all seems like one continuous melodic line. The music also makes a leap of an octave and a fourth, a challenge that would seem to keep the number from being a pop vocal. The piece caught on with jazz musicians, and there were discs by Miff Mole, the Jim Cullum Jazz Band, Red Nichols and his Five Pennies, and others. But a recording by the Wolverines with Bix Beiderbecke is considered a classic in the field. Fred B. Callahan, a Native American stonecutter, heard the music and wrote an unsentimental blues lyric about a woman so weary of washing clothes and so tired of life that she considers throwing herself into the river the next time she goes down to fetch water. Callahan sent the Negro dialect lyric to Carmichael, who liked it and rerecorded the song as a vocal. Other discs made of the number, vocal and instrumental, include those by Paul Whiteman, Mildred Bailey, Tommy Dorsey, Phil Harris, Art Hodes, Connee Boswell, Glen Gray and the Casa Loma Orchestra, John Eaton, and Pete Fountain.

"Way Back Home" (1935) is a nostalgic number that became famous because of a radio contest. Al Lewis and Tom Waring wrote the homesick ballad, and it was introduced by Fred Waring's Pennsylvanians on their network radio program and on record. Then Waring held a contest in which listeners could send in additional lyrics, the winning entries being performed by the singers on his program. The response was overwhelming, and different variations of the number were heard on the air for weeks. Bing Crosby, the Crusaders, Bob Crosby and the Bobcats, Ray Noble, Wallace Coleman, Jimmy Bowen, and Vince Gill are among the artists to record the ballad.

"Way Down Yonder in New Orleans" (1922), a Dixieland jazz classic and arguably the best of the many songs written about the Louisiana city, has been recorded hundreds of times and is still a favorite during Mardi Gras. J. Turner Layton composed the pulsating music that uses repeated notes so effectively it can be described as a stomp. Henry Creamer wrote the vibrant lyric about the yearning to return south to the city with the "Creole babies with flashing eyes." The repeated use of "Guess!" and "Stop!" in the lyric punctuates the musical line and gives the number a bounce beloved by jazz musicians. The songwriters intended the song for the all-Negro revue *Strut Miss Lizzy* (1922), but it was cut from the show and introduced instead by Creamer and Layton in *Spice of 1922*. Blossom Seeley helped popularize the number by singing it in vaudeville, on record, and in her nightclub act for years. Interest in the song was revived in 1960 when Freddie Cannon's country-rock version became a bestseller. Significant recordings over the years were made by Louis Armstrong, Paul Whiteman, Lester Young, Tommy Dorsey, Bobby Hackett, Bix Beiderbecke, Bob Wilson and his Varsity Rhythm Boys, Jan Garber, Buddy Clark, Coleman Hawkins, Louis Prima, Pete Fountain, Gene Krupa, Juanita Hall, Dean Martin, and Jan and Dean. Fred Astaire and Ginger Rogers danced to the number in the movie *The Story of Vernon and Irene Castle* (1939), it was sung by Bob Haymes in *Is Everybody Happy?* (1943), Betty Hutton performed it in the Seeley bio *Somebody Loves Me* (1952), and it was played by Krupa's Orchestra in *The Gene Krupa Story* (1959).

"We Could Make Such Beautiful Music (Together)" (1940) is a gliding fox trot by Robert Sour (lyric) and Henry Manners (music) that uses musical imagery to describe a couple's romantic possibilities. The number became popular in 1941 with a recording by Buddy Clark with Wayne King's Orchestra, and in 1947 Vaughn Monroe and his Orchestra had a bestselling disc. Other artists to record it include Frankie Carle, Billy Butterfield, Chet Baker, Barbara Lea, Judy Garland, and more recently, Marlene Ver Planck and Sandra King. The song can be heard in the film *Abroad With Two Yanks* (1944).

"We Just Couldn't Say Goodbye" (1932) is a torchy ballad by Harry Woods that brings inanimate objects to life in order to describe the sorrow when two lovers break up (the chair and sofa "broke right down and cried") and the rejoicing (the room was "singin' love songs") when they are reunited. There were popular 1930s discs by Paul Whiteman (vocal by Mildred Bailey), Russ Carlson, and Freddy Martin; then the song was revived in the early 1950s with a hit record by Hal Derwin. Chick Bullock, the Boswell Sisters, Annette Hanshaw, Rosemary Clooney, Sylvia Syms, and Max Bygraves are among the others to record it.

"We Shall Overcome" (1946), the unofficial anthem of the civil rights movement for African Americans, originated as a religious folk song of unknown authorship. In 1901 C. Albert Tindler adapted it into a Baptist hymn called "I'll Overcome Someday" that over the years took on its present title and added the lyric "deep in my heart I do believe that we shall overcome." It was first used as a protest song in 1946 when black workers in Charleston, South Carolina, went on strike, and it was sung on the picket lines. Also in the 1940s, coal miners in West Virginia sang it when they went on strike. Various versions with differing lyrics were used at rallies, marches, and meetings throughout the 1950s and 1960s. The version most familiar today is one written by Zilphia Horton, Frank Hamilton, Guy Carawan, and Pete Seeger in 1960. Joan Baez sang this version in a concert at Mills College in Birmingham, Alabama, in 1963 and later made a hit recording; from that point on the song was associated with civil rights. Other major discs were made by Seeger, Mahalia Jackson, Louis Armstrong, Paul Winter, the Turtle Creek Chorale, Solomon Burke, Toots and the Maytals, and Peter, Paul and Mary.

"We Three (My Echo, My Shadow and Me)" (1940) is an easygoing swing number by Dick Robertson, Nelson Cogane, and Sammy Mysels about a lonely and forsaken one who misses an ex-lover and has only his own voice and shadow to keep him company. The Ink Spots popularized the song with a record that went to the top of the charts, and there was also a popular disc by Tommy Dorsey (vocal by Frank Sinatra). Among those who also recorded it were Vera Lynn, Kay Starr, Brenda Lee, Ann Shelton, and more recently, Paul Costentio and Alex Pangman.

"Weary River" (1929) is a bluesy lament that Grant Clarke (lyric) and Louis Silvers (music) wrote for the film *Weary River* (1929), where it was sung by Richard Barthelmess (dubbed by an unknown singer). The melancholy number about the drudgery of life became popular because of recordings by Gene Austin, Rudy Vallee, and Joe Venuti (vocal by Smith Ballew), and later there were discs by Jan Garber, Bob Haring, Hank Snow, and Roy Acuff.

"Wedding Bells Are Breaking Up That Old Gang of Mine" (1929) is a torchy ballad about the loss of friends and the lack of love as a lonely fellow watches all his friends marry and move away, leaving the town quiet and his heart aching. Irving Kahal and Willie Raskin wrote the heartfelt lyric, and Sammy Fain composed the gentle music. Gene Austin first popularized the song on record; years later it was revived by Steve Gibson and the Redcaps with a hit disc in 1948 and again in 1954 by the Four Aces. Memorable versions were also made by Fain, Kay Starr, Tennessee Ernie Ford, Gene Vincent, Fingerle and Schutt, and Ralph Hodges. Kahal's later song "When I Take My Sugar to Tea" (1931) expresses an opposite sentiment.

"We'll Meet Again" (1939), a favorite in both America and England during World War Two, is an optimistic ballad by British songwriters Ross Parker and Hughie Charles in which a separating couple hopes for a reunion "some sunny day." Because the music is determined and forceful and the lyric is convincingly upbeat, the song was beloved of parting couples and separated dear ones. Vera Lynn, the "British Kate Smith," introduced the ballad on radio and record (she rerecorded it in 1954 with success), and it was long identified with her. In the States, there were early hit discs by Kay Kyser (vocals by Harry Babbitt and Ginny Simms), Guy Lombardo (vocal by Carmen Lombardo), and Benny Goodman (vocal by Peggy Lee). Other leading recordings were made by Frank Sinatra, the Ink Spots, Rosemary Clooney, Sammy Kaye, Kate Smith, the Andrews Sisters, Jack Hylton, the Cliff Adams Singers, Chris Barber, Barry Manilow, and more recently, Andrea Marcovicci and Vicki Stuart. "We'll Meet Again" was heard in the film *Mister Big* (1943), and the Lynn recording was used for satiric effect at the end of *Dr. Strangelove* (1964).

"What a Difference a Day Made" (1934) is a Latin favorite that traveled from Mexico to Tin Pan Alley and remained a familiar staple there for decades. Maria Grever wrote the ballad as "Cuando Vuelva a Tu Lado," and Stanley Adams wrote an English lyric about how much one's life has changed in the twenty-four hours since falling in love. The Dorsey Brothers' Orchestra (vocal by Bob Crosby) popularized the new version in the States, and it was revived with success in 1941 by Benny Carter (vocal by Maxine Sullivan), in 1944 by Charlie Barnet (vocal by Kay Starr), in 1959 with a soul version by Dinah Washington that sold a million discs, and in 1975 by Little Esther Phillips. Richard Himbler (vocal by Joey Nash), Dick Haymes, Freddy Martin (vocal by Elmer Feldkamp), Art Kassell, Django Reinhardt, Sarah Vaughan, Aretha Franklin, Sonny Rollins, and Milt Jackson are among the many artists to record it as well. The song can be heard in the movie *The Racers* (1955).

"What a Little Moonlight Can Do" (1935) is a slightly swinging ballad about the role moonlight played in making one fall for a dearie. It was written by the American Harry Woods for the British film *Roadhouse Nights* (1930) but it became popular because of a classic recording by Billie Holiday with Teddy Wilson's Band. Benny Goodman (vocal by Helen Ward) revived the number with success in 1950. Other major recordings were made by Peggy Lee, Etta Jones, Ben Webster, Betty Carter, Tony Bennett, Frankie Lymon and the Teenagers, Terry Blaine, Nancy Wilson, and more recently, Jackie Ryan, Dee Dee Bridgewater, and Carol Sloane. Diana Ross sang it as Holiday in the movie bio *Lady Sings the Blues* (1972).

"What Are You Doing New Year's Eve?" (1947), probably the most famous New Year's song after "Auld Lang Syne," is a smooth and romantic invitation for a date to welcome the new year. Frank Loesser wrote the quiet ballad, and it was introduced by Margaret Whiting with a hit record. Widely recorded over the years, there have been discs by such artists as Mel Tormé, Joe Williams, Dick Haymes, Lena Horne, Patti LaBelle and the Bluebells, the Orioles, Kay Kyser, Spike Jones, Gladys Knight and the Pips, Holly Near, Spider Saloff, John Pizzarelli, Barbra Streisand, Liz Callaway, and Loesser himself.

"What Do You Want to Make Those Eyes at Me For?" (1916) is a questioning ballad by Joseph McCarthy, Howard Johnson (lyric), and James Monaco (music) in which a gal asks her sweetie why his eyes promise devotion when she knows "they don't mean what they say." Emma Carus introduced the song in vaudeville, and there was an early hit record by Ada Jones and Billy Murray. The number was interpolated into the Broadway show *Follow Me* (1916), where it was sung by Henry Lewis. Decades later it was added to the 1973 Broadway revival of *Irene*. Mindy Carson, Bob Howard, Johnny Otis, Ray Peterson, Emile Ford and the Checkmates, Paul Barnes, Joe Meek, and Ruby Wright were among the artists also to record the song. It can be heard in the movies *Follow the Band* (1943), *The Merry Monahans* (1944), and *Incendiary Blonde* (1945), where it was performed by Betty Hutton.

"What'll I Do?" (1924), one of Irving Berlin's most beloved ballads, has remained popular for eighty years, and it is still frequently performed and recorded. The quiet lyric, asking how one will survive without a sweetheart's love, is distinguished by its intricate but subtle internal rhymes and the soft tones the words create. Almost all the rhymes in the refrain are a delicate "oo" sound. The long-lined and flowing music has a haunting quality that remains warmly hypnotic as it waltzes along with suspenseful hesitations throughout. In many ways it is Berlin's most perfectly constructed and emotionally moving ballad. Written and published as an individual song, it was quickly interpolated into the 1923 edition of the *Music Box Revue* after opening, where it was sung by Grace Moore and John Steel. Alice Faye sang the song in the movie *Alexander's Ragtime Band* (1938), Danny Thomas performed it in *Big City* (1948), and it was used as a recurring theme in *The Great Gatsby* (1974). Of the hundreds of records over the years were prominent ones by Paul Whiteman, Frank Sinatra, Lena Horne, Art Lund, Gloria Lynn, Henry Burr and Marcia Freer, Nat King Cole, Ruth Brown, Gisele MacKenzie, Julie London, Judy Holliday, Johnny Mathis, Max Bygraves, Eydie Gorme, Ann Shelton, and Sarah Vaughan. There have also been dozens of recordings just during the past two decades, including those by Cleo Laine, Barbara Cook, Karen Akers, Linda Ronstadt, Liza Minnelli and Michael Feinstein, Andrea Marcovicci, Jessica Molasky, and Harry Nilssen.

"What's New?" (1939) is a subtle ballad by Johnny Burke (lyric) and Bob Haggart (music) that takes the form of a casual conversation, yet so much is implied in the subtext. When two former lovers meet after a length of time, they ask each other a series of innocent questions. But soon it becomes clear that their love for each other is still strong and their facades are fooling no one. The piece was written in 1938 as an instrumental called "I'm Free" and was recorded by the bands of Bob Crosby and Jess Stacy (trumpet solo by Billy Butterfield). Burke added the lyric the next year, and several bands and vocalists recorded it during the 1940s. Notable discs were made by Benny Goodman, Bing Crosby, Stan Getz, Kay Kyser (vocal by Ginny Simms), Billie Holiday, Maynard Ferguson, Red Garland, Dexter Gordon, Art Pepper, Frank Sinatra, Milt Jackson, Frank Ifield, Quincy Jones, and Miles Davis. "What's New?" was revived in 1983 by a successful record by Linda Ronstadt with Nelson Riddle's Orchestra. The ballad can be heard in the movie *Dive Bomber* (1941).

"What's the Reason (I'm Not Pleasin' You)?" (1935) is the jazzy lament of an unrequited lover that Coy Poe, Jimmie Grier, Truman "Pinky" Tomlin, and Earl Hatch collaborated on together. Tomlin introduced the number in the movie *Times Square Lady* (1935) and his record with Grier's Orchestra was a hit. Fats Waller, the Mills Brothers, Jimmy Dorsey, Guy Lombardo, the Mound City Blue Blowers, and Della Reese were among the artists to also record it.

"When Day Is Done" (1926) is a ballad from Vienna that found success in America when B.G. DeSylva wrote an English lyric about a lonely soul who finds that the night has "lost its charms" because all he can think of at the end of the day is the one he is separated from. Robert Katscher wrote the animated music and German lyric as "Madonna" in 1924, and the DeSylva version was popularized in the States by Paul Whiteman and his Orchestra, featuring trumpeter Henry Busse. When he later started his own band, Busse used the number as his theme song. Other early recordings were made by Mildred Bailey, Jesse Crawford, Dennis Day, Lee White, Hal Derwin, and Arthur Tracy. Jack Fulton, Dinah Shore, Coleman Hawkins, Guy Lombardo, Mario Lanza, Django Reinhardt, and Gene Autry also made discs of the ballad. "When Day Is Done" can also be heard in the movies *King of Jazz* (1930) and *Shadows and Fog* (1992).

"When Francis Dances With Me" (1921) is a charming novelty number by Ben Ryan (lyric) and Sol Violinsky (music) that gently mocks the Tin Pan Alley dance songs of the era. The lyric playfully explains how delightful it is dancing the latest steps with Frank and going to the various dance halls, though the Bowery is passé and "we don't go there anymore." There was an early recording by Ada Jones and Billy Murray that was popular, and years later Benay Venuta made a successful disc. The song can be heard in the film *Give My Regards to Broadway* (1948).

"When I Fall in Love" (1952) is a solemn ballad that dreams of total and lasting love or none at all. Victor Young wrote the hymnlike music, and Edward Heyman penned the ardent lyric claiming that one's first love will be forever because he will give his heart away completely. The song was introduced in the movie *One Minute to Zero* (1952) but popularized by Doris Day with a hit record. Nat King Cole's disc soon after was also very successful. The Lettermen revived the ballad in 1962 with their best-selling record. Other successful versions were made by Jeri Southern, Dinah Washington, Lena Horne, Chet Baker, Patti Page, Miles Davis, and more recently, Linda Ronstadt, Celine Dion, and Julio Inglesias. Cole sang it in the film *Istanbul* (1957), his recording was heard in *Mona Lisa* (1986), Celine Dion and Clive Griffin sang it on the soundtrack of *Sleepless in Seattle* (1993), and a version by Victor Sylvester's Orchestra was used in *Eyes Wide Shut* (1999). The song is also remembered as the ballad that Marilyn Monroe sang to John F. Kennedy at a celebrated birthday bash.

"When I Lost You" (1912) was Irving Berlin's first successful ballad, a poignant and tender song that was unlike all the ragtime and dance songs the public had associated with him previously. It was also one of his most autobiographical works, inspired by the death of his young wife Dorothy Goetz when she contracted typhoid while on their honeymoon in Cuba. The lyric is a simple, unadorned lament about how the world has ceased to sparkle since her death, and Berlin's music is so straightforward and plaintive that the notes seem to ache with remorse. Henry Burr first sang the ballad in clubs, and it quickly caught on, selling over 2 million copies of sheet music. Over the years memorable recordings include an early one by Frank Froeba and his Rhythm Boys (which included Bing Crosby, who did a solo version later), Manuel Romain, Kay Starr, Frank Sinatra, Jimmy Durante, the Mills Brothers, Tony Bennett, and, more recently, Jimmy Rosselli, Jessica Molasky, and Andrea Marcovicci.

"When I Take My Sugar to Tea" (1931) is a dapper number about a swain who is dating a gal who is so high-class that he doesn't want to bring her to his old hangouts and meet his low-class buddies. Sammy Fain, Irving Kahal, and Pierre Norman Connor collaborated on the number that is a reverse situation from Kahal's "Wedding Bells Are Breaking Up That Old Gang of Mine," which takes the point of view of the discarded old friends. Early successful records by Glen Gray and the Casa Loma Orchestra (vocal by Pee Wee Hunt), Bert Lown, and Joe Mooney and the Melotone Boys made the song popular. Among those who made later discs were Connee Boswell, Frank Sinatra, the King Cole Trio, Don Cornell, the Clark Sisters, and Billy May. The number can be heard in the movies *Monkey Business* (1931) and *The Mating Game* (1959).

"When Irish Eyes Are Smiling" (1912), the perennial favorite that was beloved by Irish immigrants (and everyone else) in the years before World War One, remains one of the most recognized of all American ballads. Chauncey Olcott and George Graff Jr. wrote the sentimental lyrics about the contagious quality of a smile in an Irish lass's eyes, filled with such lyrical blarney as "the lilt of Irish laughter" and "sure they steal your heart away" that became clichés. Ernest R. Ball composed the waltzing melody that sounds like a real Irish folk song but has the dramatic structure of a Tin Pan Alley number. Olcott introduced the ballad in the Broadway musical *The Isle o' Dreams* (1913), and it was immediately acclaimed. Olcott recorded it and sang it throughout his career, as did many other Irish performers. Years later the song became even more familiar to radio listeners when Morton Downey featured it on his network show, singing it on the air over a thousand times. Prominent records were made by John McCormack, Harry MacDonough, Dennis Day, Phil Regan, Peggy Lee, Gracie Fields, Bing Crosby, Kate Smith, Connie Francis, Bradley Kincaid, Roger Whittaker, and even Frank Zappa. The song has been heard in some two dozen movies, sung by Betty Grable in *Coney Island* (1943), Dick Haymes in *Irish Eyes Are Smiling* (1944), Dennis Morgan in the Olcott bio *My Wild Irish Rose* (1947), and Crosby in *Top o' the Morning* (1949), as well as in *Stage Mother* (1933), *Let Freedom Ring* (1939), *It All Came True* (1940), *Tear Gas Squad* (1940), *Moonlight in Havana* (1942), *Doughboys in Ireland* (1943), *Hey, Rookie* (1944), *Nob Hill* (1945), *Starlift* (1951), *Painting the Clouds With Sunshine* (1951), *Sincerely Yours* (1955), and others.

"When It's Apple Blossom Time in Normandy" (1912) is a sentimental ballad about the promise to return to one's beloved Rose Marie in France and to wed her in the springtime. Harry Gifford, Huntley Trevor, and Tom Mellor collaborated on the number, the music borrowed heavily from Beethoven's Minuet in G. Elsie Baker and James F. Harrison made early recordings, but the song became popular when it was interpolated into the show *Roly Poly* (1912), where Nora Bayes sang it with success. Interest in the ballad was revived when Ann Sheridan and Dennis Morgan sang it in the movie *Shine On, Harvest Moon* (1944). Leading records were made by Harry MacDonough and Marguerite Dunlap and, years later, the Sons of the Pioneers. In 1917 Jerome Kern (music) and P.G. Wodehouse (lyric) spoofed the song with their satirical "(When It's) Nesting Time in Flatbush."

"When It's Sleepy Time Down South" (1931) is a jazz standard by Leon and Otis René and Clarence Muse that yearns to return home and be back in a mother's arms again. Although the lyric is filled with southern clichés (banjos strumming, steamboats sailing by, the locals crooning songs in the moonlight), the music is vibrant and original. The number was popularized by early records by Paul Whiteman and Louis Armstrong, the latter recording it several times in his career. Later versions were made by Mildred Bailey, Benny Goodman, Ethel Waters, Harry James, Billie Holiday, Paul Robeson, Teddi King, Ruby Braff, the Ray Brown Trio, the Dukes of Dixieland, Frankie Laine, Louis Prima, Sidney Bechet, Wild Bill Davison, Dizzy Gillespie, Jimmy Dean, Al Hirt, Pete Fountain, and Wynton Marsalis.

"When Johnny Comes Marching Home" (1863), one of the most recognized songs to come out of the Civil War, was actually more popular during the Spanish-American War forty years later. Patrick Gilmore (a.k.a. Louis Lambert), a Union army bandmaster, wrote the catchy tune about anticipating the celebration that will occur when the soldiers return home. While the music is thought to have been based on a Negro work song, the melody is much closer to some traditional Irish folk numbers. The march was so well known that many variations and parodies were written, including a ribald one titled "Johnny, Fill Up the Bowl" and the popular ditty "The Ants Go Marching One by One." Notable recordings of the song were made by Glenn Miller, Ed Sweeney, Charles Earland, Erroll Garner, Lee Michaels, Jimmy Smith, Barney Kessel, and Patti LaBelle and the Bluebelles. An orchestral version of the tune can be heard in Roy Harris's Fourth Symphony. Among the many films where it can be heard are *Cavalcade* (1933), *Gone With the Wind* (1939), *For Me and My Gal* (1942), *When Johnny Comes Marching Home*

(1942), *Golden Girl* (1951), and *How the West Was Won* (1962). The march was turned into a dance by the cast of the Broadway revue *Dancin'* (1978).

"When My Baby Smiles at Me" (1920) is the gushing description of traveling up to paradise and getting a glimpse of heaven every time a darling tosses off a smile. The song is most identified with Ted Lewis, who cowrote it with Andrew B. Sterling and Harry Von Tilzer, introduced it with his band in the revue *Greenwich Follies of 1919* (1920), recorded it with success, and used it as his theme song. Other artists to make disc versions include Benny Goodman, Clyde McCoy, Johnny Hodges, Lawrence Welk, Jo Ann Castle, Pete Fountain, and Bobby Darin. Lewis reprised the number in the movie *Hold That Ghost* (1941), it was used in *Behind the Eight Ball* (1942), the Ritz Brothers performed it in *Sing, Baby, Sing* (1936), and it was sung by Dan Dailey in *When My Baby Smiles at Me* (1948).

"When My Sugar Walks Down the Street (All the Little Birdies Go Tweet-Tweet)" (1924), the first hit for composer Jimmy McHugh, is a slaphappy love song that proudly boasts of a gal so special that when she kisses one, "I sure stay kissed." Gene Austin and Irving Mills wrote the playful lyric, and Austin introduced it on record with Aileen Stanley. The song is most associated with Phil Harris, who sang it with his orchestra in concert, on the radio, and on records throughout his career. Discs were also made by Eddie Cantor, Ivie Anderson, Eddie Condon, the Benny Strong Orchestra, Sy Oliver, Bix Beiderbecke, Ella Mae Morse, the Four Freshmen, Ella Fitzgerald, Roy Lanham and the Whippoorwills, Oscar Peterson, Max Morath, and Johnny Mathis. Judy Garland sang the uptempo number in the film *A Star Is Born* (1954), but it was cut before the movie was released; the footage was restored when it was rereleased thirty years later.

"When the Lights Go On Again (All Over the World)" (1942) is an inspiring ballad by Eddie Seiler, Sol Marcus, and Bennie Benjamin that was much loved during World War Two as it optimistically looked forward to when the soldiers return home, when ships can sail freely again, when all that will fall from the skies is rain or snow, and when there will be time for wedding rings and love rather than blackouts. The stirring number was popularized by Vaughn Monroe and his Orchestra with a bestselling record, and there were also noteworthy discs by Lucy Millinder, Vera Lynn, Dick Todd, Bob Grant, Abbey Lincoln, Joan Edwards, and Andrea Marcovicci. The song was featured in the movie *When the Lights Go On Again* (1944).

"When the Midnight Choo Choo Leaves for Alabam'" (1912) is a robust number about returning home to the South that Irving Berlin wrote in the uptempo Stephen Foster style. The lyric is bold and cheerful as one anticipates leaving an apartment in the city and going back to Alabama where Ma, Pa, and "my honey-lamb" await. The music is more raggy than Foster, and it foreshadows George Gershwin's later "Swanee" (1919) in its use of early jazz techniques. The team of Arthur Collins and Bryon Harlan popularized the number in vaudeville and on record, and there was also an early disc by the Victory Military Band that was successful. The song was heard in the film *Thunderbolt* (1929) and was sung by Alice Faye, Tyrone Power, and Don Ameche in *Alexander's Ragtime Band* (1938), Judy Garland and Fred Astaire in *Easter Parade* (1948), and Ethel Merman, Dan Dailey, Mitzi Gaynor, and Donald O'Connor in *There's No Business Like Show Business* (1954). Over the years there have been record versions by Faye, Bing Crosby, the Andrews Sisters, Francis Thorne, Tommy Dorsey and the Clambake Seven, Jackie Washington, Mary Cleere Haran, Michael Feinstein, and a parody version by Spike Jones and his City Slickers.

"When the Moon Comes Over the Mountain" (1931), Kate Smith's theme song for years on radio, film, television, and records, is a simple yet operatic ballad that looks forward to meeting one's beloved once the sun goes down and the moon comes up. Smith is sometimes credited with writing the song with Howard Johnson (lyric) and Harry Mac-Gregor Woods (music), but her authorship has always been questioned. Bunk Johnson, Carl Perkins, Lester Bowie, and the Ben Selvin Orchestra also recorded the ballad. On screen, Smith reprised it in both *The Big Broadcast* (1932) and *Hello, Everybody* (1933), and the ballad can be heard in *Dinner at Eight* (1933).

"When the Nylons Bloom Again" (1943) is a merry number that was so topical it pretty much disappeared once World War Two ended and nylon stockings were available again. George Marion Jr. (lyric) and Fats Waller (music) wrote the humorous song lamenting the scarcity of nylon during the war effort and complaining that cotton is too hard to mend. The song received a lot of airplay during the last years of the war, but few recordings. Interest in the comic number was revived when Armelia McQueen, Charlaine Woodard, and Nell Carter sang it in the Broadway Waller revue *Ain't Misbehavin'* (1978).

"When the Red, Red Robin Comes Bob, Bob Bobbin' Along" (1926) is a silly but contagious number celebrating the arrival of spring and chasing away the blues on a beautiful day. Harry MacGregor Woods wrote the chipper song, using repeated notes and syllables to create a bouncing effect. Sophie Tucker introduced the ditty at the Woods Theatre in Chicago, and Lillian Roth helped popularize it in vaudeville. Al Jolson also sang it on stage and made an early recording that was successful. Other accomplished discs were made by Eddy Howard, Anne Vincent, Barry Wood, Paul Whiteman, Dave Lambert, Jack Smith, Jo Stafford, Eva Taylor, Tennessee Ernie Ford, Mel Tormé and the Mel-Tones, Dion and the Belmonts, Mitch Miller, Mandy Patinkin, and Jessica Molasky. Jolson reprised it on the soundtracks for *The Jolson Story* (1946) and *Jolson Sings Again* (1949), the song was heard in *Has Anybody Seen My Gal?* (1952), Susan Hayward sang it in the Roth bio *I'll Cry Tomorrow* (1955), and Dick Hyman and the Three Deuces performed it on the soundtrack of *Bullets Over Broadway* (1994).

"When the Saints Go Marching In" (1896), the most famous and often performed of all Dixieland jazz pieces, is credited to Katherine E. Purvis (lyric) and James M. Black (music), though the authorship has long been questioned. It is known that the song was played by Negro bands in New Orleans by the late 1890s and was often used as a funeral hymn even though it is far from melancholy or solemn. The rousing number looks forward to joining along with all the saints that go parading by on Judgment Day. It is a favorite of jazz musicians because of the way its simple rising and falling rifts can be used to improvise endless variations on the melody. Over the years, the song has most often been associated with Louis Armstrong, who first recorded it in 1930 and performed it throughout his long career. In addition to concerts, parades, nightclubs, and an occasional funeral, "When the Saints Go Marching In" was used in several films, most prominently by the Hall Johnson Choir in *Green Pastures* (1936), Mario Lanza and company in *The Seven Hills of Rome* (1958), Armstrong and Danny Kaye in *The Five Pennies* (1959), Louis Prima and the chorus in *Hey Boy, Hey Girl* (1959), and Elvis Presley in *Frankie and Johnny* (1966) and on the soundtrack of *Lucky Lady* (1975). Among the many recordings over the years are those by such diverse talents as the New Orleans Jazz Band, the Isley Brothers, Fats Domino, the Weavers, Andy Griffith, Tiny Tim, Queen Esther Marrow with the Harlem Gospel Singers, Jerry Lee Lewis, Gladys Knight, the Kingston Trio, and Trini Lopez.

"When the Sun Comes Out" (1940), a companion piece of sorts to "Stormy Weather" by the same songwriters, is a powerful torch song that is very bluesy yet also swings a lot. Harold Arlen composed the delectable music that Richard R. Morris describes as having "the completely integrated use of musical materials—melody, harmony, and rhythm—to express emotion." Ted Koehler wrote the penetrating lyric that vows to pull oneself together and get over a lost lover as soon as the weather clears up. It was several years before the song caught on despite early recordings by Benny Goodman (vocal Helen Forrest), Harry James, Charlie Barnet (vocal by Bob Carroll), and Charlie Spivak. But a disc by Tommy Dorsey (vocal by Helen O'Connell) made it popular, and in 1956 Mel Tormé had a hit version as well. "When the Sun Comes Out" was revived again when Barbra Streisand sang it in clubs and recorded it in the 1960s. Among the other well-known versions were those by Peggy Lee, Billy Eckstine, June Christy, Judy Garland, Eileen Farrell, Ella Fitzgerald, Chet Baker, Julie London, Julius LaRosa, and Julie Wilson.

"When the Swallows Come Back to Capistrano" (1940) is a ballad by Leon René about the mysterious pull of nature that brings the migrating swallows back to a church in California. The number has been recorded dozens of times by everyone from Big Bands to country singers to early rock-and-roll groups. The biggest hits were those by the Ink Spots and Glenn Miller (vocal by Ray Eberly), but Gene Autry, Gene Krupa (vocal by Howard DuLany), Ray Herbeck, Guy Lombardo (vocal by Carmen Lombardo), and Xavier Cugat (vocal by Dinah Shore) all had successful discs as well. Other recordings of note were made by Harry James (vocal by Dick Haymes), the King Sisters, Billy May, Emil Ford and the Checkmates, the Satellites, Billy Ward and the Dominoes, and Pat Boone.

"When the World Was Young (Ah, the Apple Trees)" (1950) is a delectable French ballad by Angela Vannier (lyric) and M. Phillippe-Gerard (music) that was given a sterling English lyric by Johnny Mercer and became popular in the States. The nostalgic number recalls both quiet moments of the past and raucous memories of youth, the music shifting moods as the lyric moves dramatically back and forth. Mercer kept the French names and places in the new lyric, yet there is a universal quality to all the images. Peggy Lee's bestselling record popularized the song in America, and there were also commendable versions by Mel Tormé, Bing Crosby, June Christy, Nat King Cole, Julie London, Mabel Mercer, Jane Morgan, Nancy Wilson, Johnny Mathis, and Patti LuPone.

"When You and I Were Young, Maggie" (1866) is a sentimental ballad by George W. Johnson (lyric) and James Austin Butterfield (music) with a woeful tale behind it. Johnson had married Maggie Clark, a schoolteacher from Canada, but she died within a year. So he wrote a poem about an old man remembering his long-departed wife, a "creaking old mill" that they once walked past stirring up his memory. The poem was published in a book of verses, and Butterfield put it to music, the heart-tugging number selling plenty of sheet music for the rest of the century. The team of Van and Schenck revived the number in 1923 when they performed it in vaudeville and recorded it, and there was a popular version by Frank Stanley and Corrine Morgan as well. The ballad was also revived in 1951 with discs by Bing with Gary Crosby, Margaret Whiting with Jimmy Wakely, and a jazz version by Jack Frost and Jimmy McHugh. Other recordings were made by Teddy Wilson, Gene Autry, Bunk Johnson, the Sons of the Pioneers, Don Reno, Jo Ann Castle, and James Galway. The song can be heard in the films *Mammy* (1930) and *Sing a Jingle* (1943) and was performed by the Andrews Sisters in *Swingtime Johnny* (1943) and the Dorseys' band in *The Fabulous Dorseys* (1947).

"When You Were Sweet Sixteen" (1898), a longtime favorite of crooning tenors and barbershop quartets, is a rather formal and Victorian declaration of love, proclaiming to a wife after years of marriage that he still loves her as much as the day they met on the village green and she was only sixteen years old. James Thornton, a songwriter with gallavanting ways, was always being asked by his wife Bonnie if he still loved her, so he wrote the song to answer her. She must have believed him, for she introduced it in vaudeville and before long it sold over a million copies of sheet music. Decades later the ballad was revived by Perry Como, whose recording with the Satisfiers sold a million discs. The solemn number was also recorded with success by Shirley Temple, the Mills Brothers, Al Jolson, the Ink Spots, Bobby Darin, and Mitch Miller. Temple sang it with a male quartet in *Little Miss Broadway* (1938), the song was heard in *The Strawberry Blonde* (1941), Bing Crosby crooned it on the soundtrack of *The Great John L* (1945), and Scotty Beckett performed it in *The Jolson Story* (1946).

"When You Wore a Tulip and I Wore a Big Red Rose" (1914) is a nostalgic yet uptempo ballad by Jack Mahoney (lyric) and Percy Wenrich (music) that recalls a day long ago when a couple living in a small Kentucky town professed their love to each other. The music has a driving force for a sentimental song, and later there were many record versions that jazzed up the song. It was first popularized by the American Quartet, and soon it was heard frequently in vaudeville and burlesque. Later records of note were made by Eddie Cantor, Bing Crosby, Tiny Hill, Bunk Johnson, the Firehouse Five Plus Two, the Sportsmen, Sidney Bechet, Noeleen Batley, the Main Street Band, the Platters, John Fahey, a comic rendition by the Korn Kobblers, and a very popular duet version by Judy Garland and Gene Kelly from the film *For Me and My Gal* (1942). The song can be heard in other movies, such as *Hello, Frisco, Hello* (1943), *Chicken Every Sunday* (1948), *Cheaper By the Dozen* (1950), *Has Anybody Seen My Gal?* (1952), and *Belles on Their Toes* (1952). It was also sung on screen by Wallace Beery in *Stablemates* (1938), Allan Jones and the King Sisters in *Larceny With Music* (1943), Ann Blyth in *The Merry Monahans*

(1944), and Don Ameche, William Bendix, and the chorus in *Greenwich Village* (1944).

"When Your Lover Has Gone" (1931) is a bluesy ballad by E.A. Swan that uses a series of poetic comparisons ("like faded flowers") to express the loneliness after love turns sour. Louis Armstrong brought recognition to the song, and early records by Bert Lown, Harry Richman, and Johnny Walker helped popularize it as well. Among the other artists to record it were Frank Sinatra, Art Tatum, George Shearing, Roy Eldridge, Stan Kenton, Billie Holiday, Teddy Wilson, the Four Freshmen, Sarah Vaughan, Bobby Darin, and more recently, Linda Ronstadt, Dorothy Loudon, and Carly Simon. The number can be heard in the movie *Blonde Crazy* (1931).

"When You're Smiling (The Whole World Smiles With You)" (1928) is a cheerfully naive song of optimism by Mark Fisher, Joe Goodwin, and Larry Shay that believes that laughter is contagious, but tears only bring rain and sadness, so it is best to keep smiling. Seger Ellis popularized the tune, but it was Louis Armstrong who made it a standard. Cab Calloway, Clyde McCoy, King Oliver, Teddy Wilson, Skitch Henderson, Benny Carter, Jack Teagarden, Duke Ellington, Jimmy Rushing, Eddie Layton, and Dean Martin are among those to record it as well. Gene Autry sang "When You're Smiling" in the movie *Under Fiesta Stars* (1941), the Kings Men performed it in *You're a Lucky Fellow, Mr. Smith* (1943), Frank Sinatra crooned it in *Meet Danny Wilson* (1952), Roberta Flack sang it in *$* (1972), and the Armstrong recording was heard in *The Cotton Club* (1984). The song can also be heard in *Shantytown* (1943) and *When You're Smiling* (1950).

"Where Did You Get That Hat?" (1888) is a comic number by Joseph Sullivan that gave rise to a popular expression. Sullivan, a vaudeville comic, came across an old top hat of worn silk while going through his father's effects. When he wore it on the street, a boy laughed at him and asked, "Where did you get that hat?" From this Sullivan fashioned a novelty song about a man who inherit a silly hat from his grandfather and is forced to wear it if he hopes to inherits the old man's money. So he wears it, and everywhere he goes people ask him the title question. The wry lyric is supported by a catchy, bouncy melody that borrows a leitmotiv from Wagner's *Lohengrin*, another inside joke at the time. Sullivan introduced the number in vaudeville, and it caught on. Eventually across the country people used the catchphrase and laughed. The song still shows up in children's songbooks and records, and there are also discs by Al Simmons, Porter Grainger, the Ploughman's Lunch, Edith Perrin, and Anne Hills and the Raisin Pickers. The number was used in the movie *Give My Regards to Broadway* (1948) and Gene Kelly sang it in *Take Me Out to the Ball Game* (1949).

"Where Do We Go From Here?" (1917) is a World War One ditty that enlisted men sang quite frequently, then it was forgotten until World War Two. Howard Johnson (lyric) and Percy Wenrich (music) wrote the satiric number that took the point of view of the new draftee in the army, wondering what comes next. Jack Wise popularized it in vaudeville, but the song was rarely recorded and appealed mainly to those in the military. When Judy Garland and the chorus sang it in the film *For Me and My Gal* (1942), interest in the song was revived, and GIs started to sing it again. Bob Crosby, Tex Williams, the Dells, Peter Skellern, the Trammps, and Russ Ballard recorded it, and it was heard in the movie *Marianne* (1929).

"Where Was I?" (1939) is an indecisive ballad by Al Dubin (lyric) and Franke Harling (music) that was published, then interpolated into the movie *'Til We Meet Again* (1940) but didn't attract much attention until a bestselling record by Charlie Barnet and his Orchestra (vocal by Mary Ann McCall) in 1940. Other hit versions in the 1940s were made by Sammy Kaye (vocal by Clyde Burke) and Jan Savitt (vocal by Alan DeWitt) that helped keep the song on the *Hit Parade* for ten weeks. There were other later recordings by Tony Martin, Paul Thorn, Ricky Van Shelton, Kenny Wayne Shepherd, and Tim Rose.

"The Whiffenpoof Song" (1909), just as well known as "We Are Poor Little Lambs," has been the theme song of the singing Whiffenpoof Club at Yale University for nearly a century. Meade Minnigerode, George S. Pomeroy (lyric), and Tod B. Galloway (music), members of the Yale class of 1910, are the credited authors, though there is ample evidence to suggest it was really written by Guy Scull. The song originated when The Whiffenpoof Society (as it was then called) was founded in 1909 as a branch of the Yale Glee Club. The idea for the lyric came from Rudyard Kipling's poem "Gentlemen Rankers," and a "Whiffenpoof" was an imaginary character from Victor Herbert's operetta *Little Nemo* (1908). The number is actually a nonsense song about sheep who are lost, but the solemn music and harmonics make it sound more like a hymn. Rudy Vallee, who had heard the song while a student at Yale, adapted it into Tin Pan Alley format and sang it on the radio in 1936, the first time the old favorite was heard nationally. Vallee's record was popular, and soon every choral group seemed to be singing it. Other discs of note were made by Bing Crosby, Louis Armstrong, Tex Beneke, the Pied Pipers, the Sons of the Pioneers, the Statler Brothers, Slim Whitman, and the Browns. On screen, it was sung by Dennis Morgan in *My Wild Irish Rose*

(1947), Cary Grant and Ginger Rogers in *Monkey Business* (1952), and Elvis Presley in *The Trouble With Girls* (1969) and was heard in *Winged Victory* (1944) and *Riding High* (1950). The song featured prominently in the Off-Broadway play *Poor Little Lambs* (1982).

"While Strolling Through the Park One Day" (1884) is the widely recognized soft-shoe number that gave birth to a classic dance routine. Ed Haley wrote the bouncy song that recalls a day in May when one first saw the girl of his dreams with her "pair of roguish eyes." It was published as "The Fountain in the Park," but once the opening line became so familiar the number's title was changed. It was popularized in vaudeville by the DuRell Twin Brothers, who introduced it at Tony Pastor's in New York with a soft-shoe dance section in which they lifted their hats and said "Ahhhhh" near the end of the song. The routine was used by other artists when they performed it, and the dance became a much-imitated standard in variety. The DuRells kept the song in their act for decades, and publishers kept the sheet music in stock just as long. Cliff Edwards, Gus Edwards, Polly Moran, Marie Dressler, and Bessie Love performed the number in the movie *The Hollywood Revue of 1929* (1929), and in *Show Business* (1944) it was sung by Eddie Cantor, George Murphy, Joan Davis, and Constance Moore. It can also be heard in *Yankee Doodle Dandy* (1942), *Lake Placid Serenade* (1944), *Sunbonnet Sue* (1945), and *April Showers* (1948). Mitch Miller made a distinctive sing-along recording in the early 1960s.

"While We're Young" (1943) is a waltzing ballad by William Engvick, Morty Palitz (lyric), and Alec Wilder (music) about the ways in which youth enjoys life and everything is "all sweet surprise." The tender number was introduced by Mabel Mercer in clubs and soon was recorded by several singers and bands, most memorably a 1958 disc by Portia Nelson. Other artists to record it include Mercer, Tony Bennett, Georgia Gibbs, Peggy Lee, Meredith Willson's Orchestra, Dinah Washington, Coleman Hawkins, Rosemary Clooney, Ruth Brown, Carole Sloane, and Andrea Marcovicci.

"Whispering" (1920) is a cooing number that was popular with crooners and barbershop quartets because of its gentle melody and caressing words. John Schonberger, Richard Coburn, and Vincent Rose collaborated on the ballad that urges one's honey to come close and whisper words of tenderness into one's ear. Paul Whiteman and his Orchestra popularized the song with a record that sold 1.5 million copies. It was revived in 1951 with a hit disc by Les Paul. Of the many others who made versions of the song were Tommy Dorsey (vocal by Frank Sinatra), Al Bowlly, Louis Armstrong, Benny Goodman, the Dukes of Dixieland,

Spade Cooley, the Comedian Harmonists, Chet Atkins, Eddy Duchin, the Bachelors, Patti Page, and Miles Davis. "Whispering" was sung on screen by Vivian Blaine in *Greenwich Village* (1944) and Dan Dailey and Charles Winninger in *Give My Regards to Broadway* (1948), Carmen Cavallaro provided the piano version of it for Tyrone Power in *The Eddy Duchin Story* (1956), and it was heard in *Ziegfeld Girl* (1941), *The Clock* (1945), and *Belles on Their Toes* (1952).

"Whispering Grass (Don't Tell the Trees)" (1940) is a gentle nature ballad by Fred Fisher (lyric), at the end of his career, and his daughter Doris Fisher (music), at the beginning of hers. The atmospheric number was popularized by a bestselling record by the Ink Spots. Among the many discs to follow were those by Erskine Hawkins (vocal by Jimmy Mitchelle), Jimmy Dorsey (vocal by Bob Eberly), Duke Ellington, Orrin Tucker, Gloria Lynne, Tommy Reynolds, the Platters, Max Bygraves, and Ringo Starr.

"The White Cliffs of Dover" (1941) is an American song about peace in Great Britain, and the optimistic ballad was very popular in both countries during World War Two. Walter Kent composed the warm and gliding melody, and Nat Burton wrote the lyric that looks ahead to better days when bluebirds would once again fly over the coastline of England rather than German bombers. During the early days of the war, the Germans used the chalky white cliffs at Dover as a reference point to attack their inland targets. The American songwriters were inspired by the newspaper stories of the brave citizens of Britain during the blitz and wrote the number, one of the first written about looking toward a better world after the war. There were bestselling records by Kay Kyser (vocal by Harry Babbitt), Kate Smith, Glenn Miller (vocal by Ray Eberly), Vera Lynn, Jimmy Dorsey (vocal by Bob Eberly), and Sammy Kaye (vocal by Arthur Wright), and the song remained on *Your Hit Parade* for seventeen weeks. Other notable discs were made by Bing Crosby, Rosemary Clooney, Louis Prima, Acker Bilk, Jim Reeves, the Five Keys, the Righteous Brothers, and more recently, Andrea Marcovicci and Vicki Stuart. The Miller recording was heard in the movie *Radio Days* (1987). The song is sometimes listed as "There'll Be Bluebirds Over the White Cliffs of Dover."

"Who Takes Care of the Caretaker's Daughter (When the Caretaker's Busy Taking Care)?" (1924) is a novelty number that came from vaudeville where it was sung by comics and, later, recorded by Billy Jones with success. The ditty was interpolated into the Broadway musical *Lady Be Good* (1924), where it was sung by Cliff Edwards. Chick Endor and Paul Revere are the credited songwriters, but it has also been listed with

Edward Ward and Paul Specht as the authors. The merry song was revived in 1963 by a popular duet version by Johnny Mercer and Bobby Darin.

"Who Threw the Overalls in Mrs. Murphy's Chowder?" (1899) is a raucous Irish favorite by George L. Giefer, perhaps the most durable of the many songs written at the time about life among the immigrants, the Irish in particular. The farcical lyric tells about the time Mrs. Murphy gave a party and fell into a faint when she went to serve the chowder and found a pair of overalls in the pot. Tim Nolen is angered by the insult and demands to know who played such an old Irish trick on the hostess, promising he'd "lick the mick" who did it. The novelty number was introduced by Annie Hart in vaudeville, and it soon became a favorite of Irish comics, usually with a sing-along format. The popularity of the song was revived when Charles Winninger and the chorus sang it in the movie *Coney Island* (1943), and there were successful records by Bing Crosby and Pat Murphy. It is often listed as "Who Put the Overalls in Mrs. Murphy's Chowder?"

"Who's Afraid of the Big Bad Wolf?" (1933) is a seemingly innocent children's song that became internationally known and took on deeper significance during hard times in the depression. Frank Churchill and Ann Ronell collaborated on the simple song that the three pigs sing as they celebrate their victory over the wolf. It was written for the Disney film short *The Three Little Pigs* (1933) and soon everyone was singing or whistling it on the street. Americans in the 1930s saw the depression as the "big bad wolf," and the song was a form of defiance against the difficulties of the day. The number was translated and sung in several foreign countries, becoming popular for the same reason. In Russia it was so successful that it was turned into a popular children's book that claimed the tune was based on an old Russian folk song. Early successful recordings of the ditty were made by Ethel Shutta, Ben Bernie, and Harry Reser, with later discs by such varied artists as Wendy and the Wombats, Barbra Streisand, Jean Sablon (in French), the Mormon Tabernacle Choir, Massimo Farao, and L.L. Cool J. It can also be heard in the movies *Babes in Toyland* (1934), *Bottoms Up* (1934), and *Ship Cafe* (1935). The song inspired the punning title for Edward Albee's play *Who's Afraid of Virginia Woolf?* (1962).

"Who's Sorry Now?" (1923) is a slow ballad by Bert Kalmar, Harry Ruby, and Ted Snyder that takes the form of a revenge song, though an ambiguous one at that. When two lovers parted, he smiled while she wept. But as time passes he is distraught and she has learned to smile, telling him, "I'm glad you're sorry now." The team of Van and Schenck popularized the number in vaudeville, and before long a million copies of sheet music were sold. There were early successful records by Isham Jones and Marion Harris; then later Connie Francis revived the song with an upbeat 1958 disc that sold a million records and kept the number on the *Hit Parade* for six weeks. Significant versions over the years were made by Eddie Howard, Bing Crosby, Leo Reisman, Charles Baum, Harry James, Lee Wiley, Glen Gray and the Casa Loma Orchestra, Frank Novak, the Three Suns, Judy Garland with Liza Minnelli, Jimmy Roselli, and Willie Nelson. Lisette Verea sang it in the movie *A Night in Casablanca* (1946), Gloria DeHaven performed it in *Three Little Words* (1950), and it was sung and danced by the chorus in *All That Jazz* (1979), that production number later recreated in the Broadway revue *Fosse* (1999).

"Why Don't You Do Right?" (1942) is a swinging blues number by Joe McCoy that is sassy and sarcastic on the surface, hurt and aching underneath. A woman complains to her good-for-nothing beau that he's spent all his money on gin and other women, asking him the title question. Lil Green introduced the song on record, but it caught on the next year when Peggy Lee sang it with Benny Goodman's Orchestra in the film *Stage Door Canteen* (1943). The Lee-Goodman recording was a big hit, and Lee did a solo version a few years later that was also successful. The rhythmic number was also recorded by Helen Merrill, Mel Tormé, Fats Domino, Ella Fitzgerald, LaVern Baker, Kay Kyser, Shirley Horn, the Chazz Cats, Pat Morrissey, and Julie London.

"Why Should I Cry Over You?" (1925) is an uptempo torch song by Ned Miller (lyric) and Chester Conn (music) in which one wonders why all the tears, sighs, and blues over a departed lover who treated her so badly, admitting that the culprit "broke my heart in two." The ballad was popularized with a record by Billy Jones (using the pseudonym Victor Roberts), and many discs followed, including ones by Johnny Johnston, Curt Massey, Ace Brigode, Johnny Mercer with the Pied Pipers, Nat King Cole, Frank Sinatra, Peggy Lee, the King Sisters, the Moms and Dads, Adolf Hofner, Jerry Lee Lewis, Hank Engel and the Hoosier Daddies, and Brian Evans.

"Why Was I Born?" (1929), the celebrated torch song most associated with Helen Morgan, has been a favorite of female singers ever since Morgan introduced it in the Broadway musical *Sweet Adeline* (1929). Oscar Hammerstein wrote the piercing lyric that consists of a series of questions ending with "Why was I born to love you?" Jerome Kern composed the felicitous music that ingeniously uses a series of repeated notes without becoming predictable and has a delicate blues harmony that makes the number very beguiling. Morgan recorded the ballad and sang it throughout her career, but there were also memorable versions by Billie Holiday, Etta Jones, Sarah Vaughan, Art Tatum, Judy Garland, Lena Horne, Ambrose and his Orchestra, Ella Fitzgerald, Charlie Byrd, Aretha Franklin, Cher, Sonny Rollins, Kenny Burrell and John Coltrane, and Vic Damone. On screen the song was sung by Irene Dunne and Wini Shaw in *Sweet Adeline* (1935), Ida Lupino in *The Man I Love* (1946), Horne in *Till the Clouds Roll By* (1946), and Ann Blyth (dubbed by Gogi Grant) in *The Helen Morgan Story* (1957).

"Will You Love Me in December as You Do in May?" (1905) is a flowing ballad by James J. Walker (lyric) and Ernest R. Ball (music) in which a young couple asks each other if they will still be in love years from now when their hair turns gray. Walker, a young law student, came up with the title and sent it to composer Ball as a possible idea for a song. Ball suggested Walker write the lyric, which he did. The song was so successful that Walker finished law school on the $10,000 he earned from royalties the first year, later went into politics, used the number as his campaign song in 1926, and became one of the most famous mayors in New York City history. The song was introduced by Janet Allen in vaudeville. She later wed Walker, and the ballad was played at their wedding. Early records by the Haydn Quartet, Albert Campbell, and later the Knickerbocker Serenaders helped make the number widely known, and sheet music sales were considerable for several years. The song was heard in the movie *The Eddy Duchin Story* (1956) and was sung by Dennis Morgan in *My Wild Irish Rose* (1947), Keefe Brasselle (dubbed by Cantor) in *The Eddie Cantor Story* (1953), and Bob Hope in the Walker bio *Beau James* (1957).

"Willow Weep for Me" (1932) is a bluesy number by Ann Ronell that asks a willow tree to bend down, listen, and weep for one whose lover has left. The music has an intriguing shift from major to minor modes, and as originally written, the song doubles its tempo for one section, then returns to the original pace. (Many later singers and musicians omitted the unusual change and kept the tempo the same.) The song was introduced by Paul Whiteman's Orchestra (vocal by Irene Taylor) and popularized by early records by Ruth Etting and Ted Fio Rito. Later discs were made by Harry James, Cab Calloway, Frank Sinatra, Dizzy Gillespie, Duke Ellington, June Christy with Stan Kenton's Band, Ray Bryant, Zoot Sims, and Mary Stallings. The biggest hit record was made by the duo Chad and Jeremy in 1964. "Willow Weep for Me" can be heard in the movie *Love Happy* (1949), and it was sung by Debbie Shapiro in the Broadway revue *Blues in the Night* (1982).

"Winter Wonderland" (1934), a perennial favorite at Christmastime even though there is no mention of the holidays in the lyric, paints an idyllic picture of a loving couple strolling through the snow, building a snowman, and even proposing marriage. Richard B. Smith wrote the cheerful lyric, and Felix Bernard composed the sprightly music that seems to bounce up and down the scale. Guy Lombardo and the Royal Canadians popularized the song, and there were early successful records by Ted Weems (vocal by Parker Gibbs), Archie Bleyer, and Richard Himber (vocal by Joey Nash). Though hardly forgotten, the song was revived in 1950 with a disc by the Andrews Sisters with Lombardo that sold a million copies. Since then it seems every artist who ever put out a holiday album has recorded it. "Winter Wonderland" can be heard in the movie *Lake Placid Serenade* (1944), and Harry Connick Jr. sang it on the soundtrack of *When Harry Met Sally* (1989). Sometimes the song is listed as "Walking in a Winter Wonderland."

"Wishing (Will Make It So)" (1939), a rare case of lyricist B.G. DeSylva writing both words and music, is a musical argument that one should depend on dreamers, for they are the ones who make wishes come true. The Oscar-nominated ballad was introduced by Irene Dunne and a chorus of children in the movie *Love Affair* (1939), and it became popular with a bestselling record by Glenn Miller and his Orchestra. One of the song's most fondly remembered renditions was Skinnay Ennis singing it on Bob Hope's radio show. Rose Murphy revived it in the late 1940s, and there were other noteworthy versions made by Ennis, Russ Morgan, Vera Lynn, Ted Straeter, Orrin Tucker, Dick Haymes, Harry James, Larry Clinton, and Ruby Braff. Ethel Smith played "Wishing" on the organ in the film *George White's Scandals* (1945).

"Witchcraft" (1957) is an enticing ballad by the Broadway team of Carolyn Leigh (lyric) and Cy Coleman (music) describing the magic a paramour uses to seduce one's heart. The song was written for an Off-Broadway revue that was never produced, so it was introduced instead by Gerry Matthews in a nightclub show called *Take Five* (1957). Frank Sinatra had the lead record, but it was also recorded with success by Sarah Vaughan, Rosemary Clooney, Marilyn Volpe, Chet Baker, Julie Wilson, Oscar Peterson, Sara Zahn, Bill Evans, and George Maharis.

"With a Song in My Heart" (1929) is the Rodgers and Hart standard that is atypical of the team, being a rhapsodic ballad rather than the snappy, knowing kind of song the team often wrote. Richard Rodgers composed the soaring music, and Lorenz Hart penned the lush and hyperbolic lyric ("heaven opens it portals to me") about going through life carrying the song of a loved one in your heart. Like the team's other conventional hit "Blue Moon," there is not a trace of wit or cynicism in the lyric to counter the full-throttle emotion of the music. It was introduced by John Hundley and Lillian Taiz in the Broadway musical *Spring Is Here* (1929) and found favor rather quickly. Standout recordings were made by Margaret Whiting, Doris Day, Jane Froman, Bing Crosby, Hildegard, Mario Lanza, Ella Fitzgerald, Perry Como, Dinah Washington, Sammy Davis Jr., Jerry Vale, Sonny Rollins, Bobby Short, and more recently, Nicholas Payton, Weslia Whitfield, Holly Near, Mary Cleere Haran, and José Carreras. On screen it was sung by Bernice Claire and Frank Albertson in *Spring Is Here* (1930), Donald O'Connor and Susanna Foster in *This Is the Life* (1944), Como in *Words and Music* (1948), Day in *Young Man With a Horn* (1950), Dennis Morgan and Lucille Norman in *Painting the Clouds With Sunshine* (1951), and Susan Hayward (dubbed by Jane Froman) in *With a Song in My Heart* (1952).

"With These Hands" (1951) is an emotional ballad by Benny Davis (lyric) and Abner Silver (music) that offers long-term devotion. Nelson Eddy and Jo Stafford introduced the number on disc but little happened to it until 1953 when there were hit records by Eddie Fisher with Hugo Winterhalter's Orchestra, Johnnie Ray with the Four Lads, and Buddy Cole's Quintet. Welsh singer Tom Jones revived it with success in 1965, and his recording was heard in the film *Edward Scissorhands* (1990) for ironic effect. Other expert versions were made by Shirley Bassey, Ray Anthony, Les Elgart, the Bachelors, Les McCann, Matt Monro, Rusty Bryant, the Temptations, and P.J. Proby.

"Without a Song" (1929) is a lyrical ballad by Edward Eliscu, Billy Rose (lyric), and Vincent Youmans (music) that was a favorite of both pop and concert singers. The warm and affecting number comments that living, working, and even loving are not possible without music in your heart. It was written for the short-lived Broadway musical *Great Day!* (1929), where it was sung by Lois Deppe and Russell Wooding's Jubilee Singers. The song started to catch on when opera star Lawrence Tibbett sang it in the movie *The Prodigal* (1931). His recording was popular (he even made it his theme song for a while) and prompted other concert singers to perform it. "Without a Song" had successful pop records by Paul Whiteman (vocal by Bing Crosby), Nelson Eddy, Tommy Dorsey (vocal by Frank Sinatra), and Perry Como, and it was revived in 1983 by Willie Nelson. Other artists to make discs include Jan Peerce, Wild Bill Davis, Rex Stewart, Eddie Howard, and Ray McKinley.

"A Woman Is Only a Woman (But a Good Cigar Is a Smoke)" (1905) is a cynical comic number that used a popular catchphrase of the period to lampoon the male ego. The title comes from Rudyard Kipling's poem

"The Betrothed," and the lyric urges those men who have been deceived or rejected by a woman not to resort to drink but to "puff puff puff" on a good cigar, watch the smoke rings rise, and learn that "love is a practical joke." Harry B. Smith (lyric) and Victor Herbert (music) wrote the wry number for the musical *Miss Dolly Dollars* (1905), where it was sung by Melville Stewart. Sometimes listed as "A Good Cigar Is a Smoke," it was sung by the cast of the Off-Broadway musical satire *The Club* (1976).

"Wonderful One" (1922) is the waltzing paean to the girl one dreams of and wishes to hold close. Dorothy Terriss (a.k.a. Theodora Morse) penned the gushing lyric, and Paul Whiteman and Ferde Grofe wrote the music, basing it on a theme by Marshall Neilan. Whiteman and his Orchestra introduced the number in clubs and then recorded it with success. "Wonderful One" later became the theme song for radio singer Al Shayne, and there were notable discs made by Ray Noble (vocal by Al Bowlly), the McGuire Sisters, Doris Day, Glenn Miller, Frank Devol, Mel Tormé, Paul Weston, Jerry Vale, and Marty Robbins. Judy Garland sang it in the movie *Strike Up the Band* (1940) and it was heard in such films as *Margie* (1940), *The Great American Broadcast* (1941), *Flight for Freedom* (1943), and *Thirty Seconds Over Tokyo* (1944). The number is sometimes listed as "My Wonderful One."

"Woodman, Woodman, Spare That Tree!" (1911) is a sad-comic ditty that Irving Berlin wrote (with Vincent Bryan) as specialty material for Bert Williams, who sang it in the *Ziegfeld Follies of 1911* and in his act for years. The slapstick lyric is the lament of a beleaguered husband who mourns the loss of a particular tree, not because he loves nature but because he needs a place to hide from his shrewish wife. Berlin was lampooning an old song called "Woodman, Spare That Tree" (1837) about saving a tree remembered from one's childhood. Williams made a record of the farcical number, and there were later discs of note by Bob Roberts and Phil Harris.

"The Woodpecker Song" (1940) is a delightful novelty song from Italy that was popular in America during the Big Band era. C. Bruno (Italian lyric) and Eldo di Lazzaro (music) wrote the tuneful ditty "Reginella Campagnola," which was popular in Europe. Harold Adamson penned an English lyric about a rhythmic woodpecker, and the new number was introduced in the States by Will Glahe and his Musette Orchestra. Early hit records by Glenn Miller (vocal by Marion Hutton), the Andrews Sisters, and Kate Smith popularized it, and there were also discs by Kay Kyser, Gene Krupa, Gracie Fields, Gene Autry, Danny Kaye, Russ Morgan, and Billy Cotton. Autry sang it in the movie *Ride, Tenderfoot, Ride* (1940), and it was performed by Frank Ferrante in the Off-Broadway show *Groucho: A Life in Revue* (1994). The number is not to be confused with "The Woody Woodpecker Song" based on the popular cartoons.

"The World Is Waiting for the Sunrise" (1919) is a teary ballad by Eugene Lockhart (lyric) and Ernest Seitz (music) that later became a favorite of jazz musicians. Lockhart, who later turned to acting under the name Gene Lockhart, wrote the tender lyric that notices a whole new world with each day's sunrise, yet each new day finds one's heart calling for a sweetheart. There were early records by Isham Jones and John Steel, but later jazz versions by Benny Goodman, Duke Ellington with Al Hibbler, Jack Teagarden, Bob Crosby, and others were more successful. The song was revived in 1951 by Les Paul and Mary Ford with a disc that sold a million copies and put the number on *Your Hit Parade* thirty years after it was written. Other laudable records were made by Red Nichols, Coleman Hawkins, Acker Bilk, Chet Atkins, Frankie Newton, the Everly Brothers, Pete Fountain, the Three Suns, John Fahey, and Willie Nelson. The number can be heard in the film *Sweet and Low-down* (1944).

"Would I Love You (Love You, Love You)?" (1951) is an echoing love song by Bob Russell (lyric) and Harold Spina (music) that was a giant hit for Patti Page, her record selling over a million discs. It was also a bestseller for Doris Day, who sang it in the movie *Young Man With a Horn* (1950) and recorded it with Harry James and his Orchestra. Other notable versions were made by Helen O'Connell, Bing Crosby, Tony Martin, Tex Beneke, and Sonny Til and the Orioles.

"Wrap Your Troubles in Dreams (And Dream Your Troubles Away)" (1931) is an optimistic ballad that was popular in the 1930s as a depression chaser. Billy Moll and Ted Koehler wrote the comforting lyric that suggested dreaming away your woes, and Harry Barris composed the fluent music. Bing Crosby introduced the song on record and it was revived two decades later when Frankie Laine sang it in the movie *Rainbow 'Round My Shoulder* (1952), and his recording was a hit. Other discs of note were made by Dizzy Gillespie, Dick Haymes, June Christy, Earl Hines, Mildred Bailey, Maxine Sullivan, Jane Morgan, and more recently, Peter Yorke and Jessica Williams. The song was heard in the film *Top Man* (1943), and Howard Alden provided the guitar playing of it for Sean Penn in *Sweet and Lowdown* (1999).

"Wreck of the Old '97" (1923) is a moralistic ballad based on a true incident, warning women never to speak harshly to your husband because the next time he goes off to his job he may never live to return. The song was based on an 1856 narrative ballad by Henry C. Work called "The Ship That Never Returned." After a famous train wreck in 1903,

Charles K. Noell and Fred J. Lewey wrote a new version, about an engineer who died at the throttle while driving freight between Lynchburg and Danville, Kentucky. Little happened to the song until 1923 when singer Henry Whittier recorded his version, and it became one of the first country-western hits. Whittier's disc was so close to the earlier song that Noell and Lewey sued and won a settlement from Whittier, and all three names appeared in subsequent sheet music. There was another early disc by Vernon Dalhart that was a bestseller, and records were also made by Carl Fenton, Muggsy Spanier, Hank Snow, Kate Smith, Eddy Arnold, Boxcar Willie, the Osborne Brothers, Jenks Tex Carman, Woody Guthrie, and Johnny Cash. The song can be heard in the movie *Smokey River Serenade* (1947).

Y–Z

"Yaaka Hula Hickey Dula" (1916) is a ribald novelty number that spoofs Hawaiian ballads and allows for some pretty blatant double entendres as well. E. Ray Goetz, Joe Young, and Peter Wendling wrote the comic song in which an ardent amorist vows to return to his girl Hula Lou in Hawaii who will greet him with the title phrase. Al Jolson introduced it in his Broadway show *Robinson Crusoe Jr.* (1916) and recorded it that year, as did the team of Arthur Collins and Bryon Harlan, and the Avon Comedy Four. The number was revived when it was included in the film *Applause* (1929), and there were other recordings by Sammy Rimington, Felix Mendelssohn and his Hawaiian Serenaders, Jimmy Bryant and Speedy West, George Lewis, and Ken Coyler.

"Yankee Doodle (Went to Town)" (c. 1775), described by Denes Agay as "the first all-American hit song," is perhaps the earliest and most famous folk song in American music. The origin of the music has been explored by musicologists for years with no satisfactory results. It is said to be based on a Spanish sword dance, a Dutch folk song, a German farmer's chant, a French vineyard workers' song, or most likely, a British nursery rhyme called "Lucy Locket." Dr. Richard Shackburg wrote the nonsense lyric around 1775, but again there are different versions of where he got it. Some say he was taught the tune by farmers and settlers who sang it in 1753 as they went off to the French and Indian Wars, mocking the New Englanders. But the Yankees liked the tune and adopted it for themselves. During the American Revolution, British soldiers sang the number to mock the colonists (there are reports of its being sung by the Redcoats as they marched to Lexington), but it was sung just as often by the American troops. "Yankee Doodle" was sung at the surrender at Yorktown, and eventually the song became the national anthem for the new country (until "The Star-Spangled Banner" came along during the War of 1812). Throughout the nineteenth century the familiar ditty was turned into symphonic pieces, military marches, operetta numbers, and even a drinking song. Recordings have been made by Pete Seeger, Boxcar Willie, Ferrante and Teicher, the Robert Shaw Chorale, Tex Ritter, Myron Floren, Jack Teagarden, Linda Arnold, the Caledonian Heritage Pipes, Mickey Finn, and the Micanopy Brass Band and on many kids' records. Among the many films in which it can be heard are *For Me and My Gal* (1942), *Thousands Cheer* (1943), *Living in a Big Way* (1947), *Captain Newman, M.D.* (1963), *Rocky* (1976), *Out of Africa* (1985), and *Gettysburg* (1993).

"Yankee Doodle Blues" (1922) is a jazzed-up variation of "Yankee Doodle" by Irving Caesar, B.G. DeSylva (lyric), and George Gershwin (music). Written as an individual number, it was interpolated into the revue *Spice of 1922*, where it was sung by Georgie Price. The song also served as a recurring theme in the expressionistic Broadway play *Processional* (1925). The team of Van and Schenck made an early recording, and there were later discs by the Original Memphis Five, Lodd's Black Aces, Little Brother Montgomery, Mary Lou Williams, and William Bolcom and Joan Morris. On screen, it was sung by Joan Leslie with organist Hazel Scott in *Rhapsody in Blue* (1945) and by June Haver, Gloria DeHaven, and the chorus in *I'll Get By* (1950).

"Yankee Doodle Never Went to Town" (1935) is a breezy ballad by Ralph Freed (lyric) and Bernard Hanighen (music) that Benny Goodman popularized on a record with Helen Ward doing the vocal. Babs and her Brothers, a group that would later change its name to the Smoothies, made a noted recording as well. Other discs were made by Glen Gray and the Casa Loma Orchestra, Teddy Wilson, Claude Hopkins, Joe Venuti, and Billie Holiday.

"The Yellow Rose of Texas" (1858), the familiar sing-along staple, started as a minstrel number that was popular in both the North and the South during the Civil War. The earliest version was published in 1858 with "J.K." credited as the author. Later versions differed in the lyric, though most concerned one's plan to return to Texas to see a light-skinned Negress who "beats the belles of Tennessee." By the turn of the century the song fell out of favor and pretty much disappeared until the 1950s when Don George adapted the number into Tin Pan Alley format and there were bestselling discs by Mitch Miller and Johnny Desmond. The rhythmic march has also had memorable recordings by Gene Autry, Elvis Presley, the Blue Sky Boys, Roy Rogers and Dale Evans, Freddy Quinn, Jo Ann Castle, Frank De Vol, Ernest Tubb, the Moms and Dads,

Peter Nero, Mantovanni's Orchestra, Dick Curless, and Myron Floren and a parody version by Stan Freberg. "The Yellow Rose of Texas" was sung on screen by Presley in *Viva Las Vegas* (1964) and Paul Newman in *The Life and Times of Judge Roy Bean* (1972) and can be heard in such movies as *Riders of the Whistling Pines* (1949), *Night Stage to Galveston* (1952), and *Giant* (1956).

"Yes Indeed!" (1941) is a hand-clapping revival number that the composer-lyricist Sy Oliver calls "a jive spiritual." The music has a rhythmic march tempo with a touch of boogie-woogie, and the lyric urges one to shout "Hallelujah!" when the spirit moves you. Tommy Dorsey and his Orchestra (vocals by Jo Stafford and Oliver) introduced the number with a successful record, but it was Bing Crosby who popularized it with a bestselling disc. Connee Boswell's version was also a chart record. Other notable discs were made by Frank Sinatra, Peggy Lee, Dick Haymes, Count Basie, Connie Francis, Pete Fountain, the Isley Brothers, and Ray Charles.

"Yes, My Darling Daughter" (1940) is an unusual ballad by Jack Lawrence that takes the form of a conversation between a mother and her daughter. To a series of questions about romance posed by the daughter (culminating in one asking what to say if he proposes), the mother answers with the affirmative title phrase. Lawrence adapted an old Yiddish folk song from the Ukraine by updating the lyric and giving the Eastern European music a touch of the Big Band sound. The song launched Dinah Shore's career; she used it to audition for Eddie Cantor's radio show and got the job, her record version becoming a bestseller after she sang the number on the air. Other commendable discs were made by Benny Goodman (vocal by Helen Forrest), Glenn Miller (vocal by Marion Hutton), the Andrews Sisters, Ambrose and his Orchestra, the Barry Sisters, Gene Krupa, and Anne Shelton. The song was interpolated into the Broadway revue *Crazy With the Heat* (1941), where it was performed by Gracie Barrie.

"Yes, Sir, That's My Baby" (1925) is another 1920s song that was so popular that its title became a catchphrase for decades after. Gus Kahn wrote the spirited lyric that asks a series of questions ("Who's that walking down the street?") that are gleefully answered with the title phrase. Kahn uses short and deliberate phrases ("Don't mean maybe") that sit effectively on composer Walter Donaldson's vibrant, Charleston-like music. In fact, one of the reasons the ditty became popular is because one could dance the Charleston to it. Eddie Cantor popularized the number and was long associated with it. Other well-known recordings over the years were made by Ben Bernie, Gene Austin, Ace Brigode, the Coon-

Sanders Nighthawk Orchestra, the Nat King Cole Trio, Ruth Brown, Earl Hines, Frank Sinatra, Tiny Hill, Woody Herman, Buddy Greco, Charlie Charleston, Cliff Edwards, and Rick Nelson. The merry song can be heard in the films *The Dance of Life* (1929) and *Broadway* (1942) and was sung on screen by Donald O'Connor, Gloria DeHaven, Charles Coburn, Barbara Brown, and Joshua Shelley in *Yes Sir, That's My Baby* (1949), Doris Day, Danny Thomas, and a children's chorus in the Kahn bio *I'll See You in My Dreams* (1951), Keefe Brasselle (dubbed by Cantor) in *The Eddie Cantor Story* (1953), and Jason Robards in *A Thousand Clowns* (1965). In the Broadway musical *Big Deal* (1986), it was performed by Cleavant Derricks.

"Yes! We Have No Bananas" (1922), possibly the most popular nonsense song of Tin Pan Alley, was one of the top sellers in the 1920s, and it is still widely recognized today. Frank Silver and Irving Cohn got the idea for the silly number when they overheard a Greek fruit peddler say the title phrase to a customer on the street. The songwriters expanded the contradictory notion into a lyric and composed bright and vigorous music for it. Sigmund Spaeth has pointed out that the music is filled with sly little references to famous compositions, including Handel's "Hallelujah Chorus," "My Bonnie," "An Old-Fashioned Garden," and "I Dreamed That I Dwelt in Marble Halls." Silver's Music Masters introduced it in restaurants and clubs, but it was popularized when Eddie Cantor heard it and interpolated it into his Broadway revue *Make It Snappy* (1922) when it was trying out in Philadelphia. Cantor and the number stopped the show, his record went on to become a bestseller, and he kept it in his act for years. He even made a spoof version with Belle Baker called "I've Got the Yes! We Have No Bananas Blues." Billy May had an early hit disc, and there were other records of note made by Eva Taylor, Ray Noble (vocal by Al Bowlly), Benny Goodman and the Rhythm Makers, Louis Prima, Max Bygraves, and Spike Jones's own spoof version. On screen, Maurice Chevalier sang it in French in *Innocents of Paris* (1929), the Pied Pipers harmonized to it in *Luxury Liner* (1948), and Cantor provided the singing voice for Keefe Brasselle in *The Eddie Cantor Story* (1953). Another parody version, by Irving Berlin and the original songwriters, that spoofed famous opera arias was sung by Al Jolson in the movie *Mammy* (1930).

"A Yiddishe Momme" (1925) is a sentimental ballad that became popular even though the Yiddish title was very foreign to many admirers of the number. Lyricist Jack Yellen wrote the song, both music and lyric, after his mother had died and Lew Pollack helped him with the music. Sophie Tucker introduced it at the Palace Theatre in New York, and it was an immediate hit, Tucker keeping it in her repertoire for years and using it as one of her signature songs. In fact, she sang it so many times in Europe that it was this tender ballad and not "Some of These Days" that she was most associated with on the other side of the Atlantic. There were recordings made by various artists, including Johnny Desmond, Billie Holiday, Hazel Scott, Billy Daniels, Jackie Wilson, Connie Francis, Vic Damone, and Ann Shelton. The number is sometimes listed as "My Yiddishe Momme" or "My Yiddish Mamma."

"You Always Hurt the One You Love" (1944) is a fatalistic ballad about how one always seems to do the most harm to "the one you shouldn't hurt at all." Allan Roberts and Doris Fisher wrote the smooth number, and it was popularized by the Mills Brothers, whose record sold over a million copies. Kay Starr, Al Martino, the Ink Spots, Charlie Spivak, Earl Hines, Ace Cannon, Fats Domino, Brenda Lee, Connie Francis, Dave Bartholomew, Cynthia Sager, Spike Jones and his City Slickers, and Ringo Starr were among those who also recorded it.

"You and I" (1941) is a tender ballad of togetherness that was written by Meredith Willson; it was the bandleader's first hit and encouraged him to score other Tin Pan Alley and Broadway songs. The music flows with just the slightest swing to it, and the lyric claims that two lovers know the reason for blues skies and other miracles of life. Glenn Miller and his Orchestra (vocal by Ray Eberly) popularized the song on record, but it became widely familiar when the number was used as the theme song for the *Maxwell House Coffee Time* radio show. It remained on *Your Hit Parade* for nineteen weeks, thanks to successful discs by Bing Crosby and Tommy Dorsey (vocal by Frank Sinatra). The latter recording was heard in the movie *Radio Days* (1987).

"You and the Night and the Music" (1934) is a smoldering ballad with a moderate tango tempo, but it had a quite different origin. Arthur Schwartz wrote the music as the warm and domestic theme song for the radio serial *The Gibson Family*, and it was heard on the air often. Then Howard Deitz wrote a passionate lyric for it, and the new number was used in the Broadway musical *Revenge With Music* (1934), where it was sung by Georges Metaxa and Libby Holman. Schwartz's music was re-arranged as a Latin-flavored piece, and the lyric urged lovemaking once the three ingredients of the title were provided. The show was short-lived, but the song caught on, though some radio stations wouldn't play it, fearing the line "fill me with flaming desire" a bit too suggestive for the airwaves. Holman recorded it, but Conrad Thibault popularized the ballad. Among the many disc versions were those by Nelson Eddy, Mel Tormé, Joe Williams, the Phil Woods Quintet, Nelson Riddle, Chet Baker, Julie London, Clark Ingram, Barbra Streisand, and Louis Prima. The number was heard in the movies *When Johnny Comes Marching Home* (1942) and *The Band Wagon* (1953), and Anne Bancroft performed it in *To Be or Not to Be* (1983).

"You and Your Love" (1939) is a warm love song by Johnny Mercer (lyric) and Johnny Green (music) that displays affection without hyperbolizing in either the words or the melody. Green's music is particularly fine, the lengthy song (sixty-six measures) never getting monotonous and the release retaining enough elements of the main theme to keep the number unified and satisfying. Early records by Count Basie (vocal by Helen Humes), Bob Crosby (vocal by Teddy Grace), Gene Krupa (vocal by Irene Daye), and Ozzie Nelson (vocal by Harriet Hilliard) were successful and popularized the ballad. Other discs of note were made by Jo Stafford, Benny Goodman, and Mercer himself.

"You Are My Sunshine" (1940) is a simple country tune that crossed over to become a favorite in several categories. Jimmie Davis and Charles Mitchell wrote the homespun lament about how the sun hasn't shone since one's sweetie went away. It was introduced by Tex Ritter in the movie *Take Me Back to Oklahoma* (1940) and then enjoyed hit records by Bing Crosby, Bob Atcher, and Gene Autry (his first major disc). When Davis turned to politics, he used the number as his campaign song for his successful bid for the governorship of Louisiana in 1944. Ray Charles revived the ballad in 1962 with a chart record, and there was even a rock version called "Sunshine Twist" by the Jelly Roll Kings that was popular. Other notable discs were made by Patti Page, Joe Williams, Mike Douglas, Johnny and the Hurricanes, Andy Williams, Boxcar Willie, Les Brown, Betty Wright, Slim Whitman, the Banjo Kings, Sammy Rimington, and the Ames Brothers. The song has been heard in some dozen other movies, including *Back in the Saddle* (1941), *Ridin' on a Rainbow* (1941), *Cowboy Serenade* (1942), *Strictly in the Groove* (1942), *Du Barry Was a Lady* (1943), *I'm From Arkansas* (1944), *Mississippi Rhythm* (1949), *Beaches* (1988), and *O Brother, Where Art Thou?* (2000).

"You Belong to Me" (1952) is a catchy ballad that proved to be one of the biggest hits of the year and remained on the *Hit Parade* for nineteen weeks. Pee Wee King, Redd Stewart, and Chilton Price wrote the gliding number that lists all the places that one's true love may travel to (the pyramids on the Nile, a marketplace in Algiers, and other exotic locales) but reminds the darling that "you belong to me." Joni James introduced the song on record, but it was Jo Stafford's disc that sold over 2 million copies. Patti Page and Dean Martin each had versions that climbed the charts, and the Duprees revived it in 1962 with a bestselling record. Other successful discs were made by Bing Crosby, Anita Baker, Connie

Francis, Judy Garland, Pat Boone, Tennessee Ernie Ford, Johnny Mathis, the Orioles, the Doobie Brothers, the Alley Cats, Petula Clark, Patsy Cline, Tommy Tune, and Maureen McGovern. "You Belong to Me" was heard in the film *Forbidden* (1953), the Stafford recording was used in *The Last Picture Show* (1971), and it was sung by the company of the Off-Broadway revue *The Taffetas* (1988).

"You Call Everybody Darling" (1948) is a peppy, banjo-strumming number that warns a flirtatious beau who calls every girl "darling" and doesn't mean it that someday he just might find himself alone and no one will ever call him "darling." Sam Martin, Ben Trace, and Clem Watts collaborated on the zesty song, and it was popularized by a record by Trace and his Silly Symphonists that went to the top of the charts and kept the song on *Your Hit Parade* for sixteen weeks. Among the many other artists to record it were the Andrews Sisters, Anne Vincent, Jerry Wayne, Jack Smith, Art Lund, the Moms and Dads, Bruce Hayes, Jerry Lee Lewis, Bill Haley, and Faron Young.

"You Call It Madness (Ah, But I Call It Love)" (1931) is an easygoing ballad by Con Conrad, Gladys Du Bois, Russ Columbo, and Paul Gregory that recalls the night a couple met: She thought it was madness; he thought it was love. Now that she wants to break it off and dismisses the whole romance as madness, he still insists it was love. Columbo popularized the number with a hit record, and he made it his theme song on the radio. Other early successful discs were made by Smith Ballew, Bert Lown, Kate Smith, and Phil Spitalny. Later versions were made by Tony Martin, Nat King Cole, Mildred Bailey, Ernie Andrews, Billy Eckstine, Dick Stabile, Stuart Allen with Richard Himber's Orchestra, Don Byas, and Jerry Vale.

"You Can Depend on Me" (1932) is the musical promise of romantic security that Earl "Fatha" Hines, Charles Carpenter, and Louis Dunlap wrote and was often recorded over the years. Hines, Louis Armstrong, and Fletcher Henderson had the leading records, and in 1961 a disc by Brenda Lee climbed the charts. Among the artists to also record it were Count Basie (vocal by Jimmy Rushing), Art Jarrett, Orrin Tucker (vocal by Bonnie Baker), Pinky Tomlin, Frankie Laine, Lester Young, Peggy Lee, Dexter Gordon, Nat King Cole, Ruby Braff, Dave Brubeck, Dinah Washington, and Cliff Brunner.

"You Cannot Make Your Shimmy Shake on Tea" (1919) is a slapstick number that anticipated the effects of Prohibition on America. When the Volstead Act was passed in 1919 and liquor was outlawed, Irving Berlin and Rennold Wolf wrote the sassy number complaining about the inability of nonalcoholic beverages to put spice into life. It was introduced by Bert Williams in the *Ziegfeld Follies of 1919* and was mostly associated with him. While the number enjoyed modest popularity during the Roaring Twenties, it was quickly forgotten once Prohibition was repealed.

"You Don't Know What Love Is" (1941) is a melancholy song that argues one cannot understand the meaning of love unless you have suffered through the loss of love. Don Raye wrote the piercing lyric with vivid imagery (a lover who has "faced each dawn with sleepless eyes"), and Gene DePaul composed the brooding music with rising and falling sections that are very haunting. This cascading effect and the unusual harmonics made the number a favorite of jazz musicians. Carol Bruce introduced the song in the movie *Keep 'Em Flying* (1941) and reprised it in *Behind the Eight Ball* (1942). Her recording was followed by dozens of others, including a hit disc by Teddi King that revived the song in 1951 and two classic jazz improvisation versions by Miles Davis and Sonny Rollins in the mid-1950s. Other recordings of note were made by Dick Haymes, Billy Eckstine and Earl Hines, Billie Holiday, Ella Fitzgerald, Etta Jones, Harry James, Dinah Washington, Tony Bennett, Julius La-Rosa, Fran Warren, and Chris Connor. The number was also used in the movies *Butch Minds the Baby* (1942) and *Two Tickets to London* (1943).

"You Go to My Head" (1938) is a simple yet hypnotic ballad by Haven Gillespie (lyric) and J. Fred Coots (music) that used alcohol imagery to convey the effect a lover has on one. The music is very spare and concise yet manages to be mysterious. Gillespie's lyric is rich with potent phrases, relating how a smile "makes my temperature rise" and describing a sweetheart who is "spinning around in my brain." Because the song mentions champagne, mint juleps, and "burgundy brew," it took the songwriters two years to find a publisher because radio stations were discouraged from playing drinking songs. The standard was introduced with success by Glen Gray and the Casa Loma Orchestra (vocal by Kenny Sargent), and there were also hit records by Larry Clinton (vocal by Bea Wain) and Billie Holiday. Other noteworthy discs were made by Frank Sinatra, Mitchell Ayes and his Orchestra (who made it their theme song), Bob Grant, Marlene Dietrich, Teddy Wilson (vocal by Nan Wynn), Tallulah Bankhead, Bud Powell, Paul Weston, Kay Kyser (vocal by Ginny Simms), Mel Powell, Doris Day, Billy Eckstine, Zoot Sims, Lena Horne, Quincy Jones, and more recently, Tony Bennett, Ann Hampton Callaway, and Linda Ronstadt.

"You Made Me Love You (I Didn't Want to Do It)" (1931), the song that launched Al Jolson's career, has been associated with several stars over the years, from Jolson, Fanny Brice, and Ruth Etting on stage to

Judy Garland and Doris Day on the screen to Harry James and other bands on records. James Monaco composed the flowing music that hesitates at points in an affecting manner. Joseph McCarthy wrote the conversational lyric that both confesses and complains how an endeared one has captured one's heart, using short, stammering phrases ("Yes, I do . . . 'deed I do . . . you know I do") to make the sentiment all the more poignant. Written as an independent number, it was interpolated by Jolson into the Broadway show *The Honeymoon Express* (1913), where he sang it in blackface and went down on one knee for the first time in his career. Both the song and the new star were a sensation, and Jolson recorded it and kept it in his repertoire for decades. He reprised it on the soundtracks of the movies *The Jolson Story* (1946) and *Jolson Sings Again* (1949), and his 1946 rerecording sold a million copies. Brice sang the number in vaudeville with success, and Etting featured it in her concerts for years. It was revived by James and his Orchestra in 1941, one of the band's first records and one that sold a million discs as well. Other accomplished versions were recorded by Louis Armstrong, Hildegarde, Eddie Heywood, Erroll Garner, Eddie Fisher, Connie Francis, Julie London, Bobby Darin, Shirley Bassey, and more recently, Willie Nelson, Harry Nilsson, Cris Groenendaal, and Michael Ball. The ballad has been heard in some dozen films, most memorably when teenage Garland sang it to a photograph of Clark Gable in a version called "Dear Mr. Gable" in *Broadway Melody of 1938* (1937). Dorothy Dell performed it in *Wharf Angel* (1934), Helen Forrest sang it in *Private Buckaroo* (1942), James and the band reprised it in *Springtime in the Rockies* (1942), and Doris Day sang it as Etting in *Love Me or Leave Me* (1955). "You Made Me Love You" can also be heard in *Syncopation* (1942), *Three Daring Daughters* (1948), *Xanadu* (1980), and *The Lonely Guy* (1984).

"You Oughta Be in Pictures" (1934), the familiar favorite by Edward Heyman (lyric) and Dana Suesse (music) that compliments a sweetie by conferring movie star status, was heard on stage before it was put on screen. The number was interpolated into the *Ziegfeld Follies of 1934*, where it was sung by Jane Froman. Doris Day performed it in the film *Starlift* (1951), and it was also heard in *New York Town* (1941) and *You're My Everything* (1949). Guy Lombardo (vocal by Carmen Lombardo), George Hall, Little Jack Little, and the Boswell Sisters had the most popular recordings of the song, and there were also discs by Al Bowlly, Mel Tormé, Rudy Vallee, Andy Williams, and Connie Francis.

"You Showed Me the Way" (1937) is a ballad of appreciation and affection by Ella Fitzgerald, Chick Webb, Buddy McRae, and Bud Green that was introduced with a popular disc by Fitzgerald with Webb's Orchestra. There were also early hit versions by Fats Waller and Teddy

Wilson. Frankie Newton, Gene Kardos, Billie Holiday, Benny Goodman, Joe Williams, and Tony Bennett are among the other artists to record it.

"You Tell Me Your Dream (I'll Tell You Mine)" (1908) is the sentimental standard in which two children share their dreams, then, years later as adults, each tells the other that they dreamt of the other again. A.H. Brown and Seymour Rice wrote the doting lyric, and Charles N. Daniels composed the soft-edged music. The number was a big seller of sheet music and soon became a favorite of barbershop quartets. The Mills Brothers revived the song with success in 1931, and there were other recordings by Jimmie Davis, the Sons of the Pioneers, Connie Francis, and the Moms and Dads. Dennis Morgan sang the song in the movie *My Wild Irish Rose* (1947), and it was heard in *Walking My Baby Back Home* (1953) and *High Time* (1960).

"You Took Advantage of Me" (1928) is a lively torch song by Rodgers and Hart that has more sass in it than regret. Richard Rodgers's music hops along in a carefree manner, and Lorenz Hart's lyric makes all kinds of fatalistic similes (an apple shaken down from a tree, a goose that is cooked, all bridges burned, and so on), but they seem far from tragic. Joyce Barbour and Busby Berkeley introduced the song in the Broadway musical *Present Arms* (1928), and in the movie version of the show, called *Leathernecking* (1930), it was performed by Lilyan Tashman and Fred Santley. Morton Downey's record made the number a familiar favorite, and there were many other discs over the years, including well-known ones by Ella Fitzgerald, Carmen McRae, Teddy Wilson, Bud Freeman, Bunny Berigan, Dick Haymes, Art Tatum, Anita O'Day, Bix Beiderbecke, Oscar Peterson, Al Hirt, Tony Bennett, Neil Sedaka, and more recently, Linda Ronstadt and Bobby Short. The song was used in the film *Young Man With a Horn* (1950), Judy Garland sang it in *A Star Is Born* (1954), and Dick Hyman and the Three Deuces were heard performing it in *Bullets Over Broadway* (1994). Also, it was interpolated into the 1954 Broadway revival of *On Your Toes* where Elaine Stritch sang it.

"You, You, You" (1953) is a simple, memorable fox trot that came from a German song called "Du, Du, Du" with delectable music by Lotar Olias. Robert Mellin wrote the English lyric, a straightforward declaration of love using triplets ("true, true, true . . . do, do, do . . .") throughout. The new version was popularized by the Ames Brothers with Hugo Winterhalter's Orchestra, their disc selling over a million copies. Bert Kaempfert and his Orchestra also made a noteworthy record of the ballad. Tia Speros, Jody Abrahams, and Melanie Mitchell sang "You, You, You" in the Off-Broadway revue *The Taffetas* (1988).

"Young at Heart" (1954), one of the finest ballads of its era, has the quality of a lullaby as it nostalgically looks at youth and tries to carry such a quality into adulthood. Johnny Richards wrote the entrancing music as an instrumental called "Moonbeam," but it is Carolyn Leigh's sterling lyric that allows the song to soar. The number argues that those who can think optimistically like the young will weather the disappointments of the grown-up world, noting that even childhood fairy tales can come true. Richards's music builds quietly but firmly, and Leigh's rhymes are just as quiet and effortless. Frank Sinatra was the first to record the ballad, and its growing popularity encouraged movie producers to rename a recently completed Sinatra film *Young at Heart* (1954) and used his recording over the opening and closing titles. The disc went on to sell a million copies and was used on the soundtracks of the later movies *The Front* (1976) and *Sweet Dreams* (1985). Other significant recordings were made by Jimmy Durante, Perry Como, the Andy Williams Trio, Connie Francis, Bobby Vinton, Keely Smith and Louis Prima, Jack Jones, and more recently, Carol Sloane, Sara Zahn, Salome Bey, and Brian Evans.

"Your Cheatin' Heart" (1952), Hank Williams's most famous ballad, is a torch song that is very country yet has crossed over and been recorded successfully in other genres. The straightforward lyric warns an unfaithful lover that someday her dishonesty will keep her awake at night and she will be as miserable as her thwarted one is now. While the lyric is passionate and heartbreaking, the music is relaxed and even resigned. Williams introduced the song with a bestselling record, and the next year Joni James's disc sold over a million copies. Ray Charles revived the ballad with success in 1962. Other notable recordings were made by Frankie Laine, Patsy Cline, Fats Domino, Elvis Presley, Brenda Lee, Ernest Tubb, Del Shannon, Jerry Lee Lewis, Petula Clark, Glen Campbell, Pete Fountain, John Gary, Connie Stevens, and Boxcar Willie. On screen it was sung by George Hamilton (dubbed by Hank Williams Jr.) in the Williams bio *Your Cheatin' Heart* (1964), it was heard in *Rhinestone* (1984), and it was performed by Jessica Lange (dubbed by Patsy Cline) in the Cline bio *Sweet Dreams* (1985).

"Your Eyes Have Told Me So" (1919) is a crooning ballad by Gus Kahn (lyric), Walter Blaufuss, and Egbert Van Alstyne (music) that became a favorite of barbershop quartets. John McCormack popularized the song on record, and interest in the number was revived when James Melton sang it in the movie *Sing Me a Love Song* (1936). Kate Smith, Ted Straeter's Orchestra, Mario Lanza, Doris Day, and the Buffalo Bills are among those who also recorded it. The King's Men performed it in the film *You're a Lucky Fellow, Mr. Smith* (1943), Day sang it with Gordon MacRae in *By* *the Light of the Silvery Moon* (1953), and it was heard in *Here Comes Elmer* (1943) and *I'll See You in My Dreams* (1952).

"Your Feet's Too Big" (1935) is a ribald novelty song by Ada Benson and Fred Fisher that was introduced by and long associated with Thomas "Fats" Waller. The jazzy music is pounding and deliberate, and the ridiculous lyric complains about a gal whose large feet are ruining the romantic atmosphere when she goes out to a Harlem nightclub with her beau. Some of the lyric imitates musical instruments ("shwa-shwa-bo") that seem to do some complaining as well. Waller's record was popular, and later there were distinctive versions by the Ink Spots and the Detonators. The Beatles sang it in concert in Germany in 1967, and they recorded it. In the Broadway Waller revue *Ain't Misbehavin'* (1978), it was performed by Ken Page.

"You're Driving Me Crazy (What Did I Do?)" (1930) is a vibrant rhythm song and a very early version of a swing number. Composer Walter Donaldson wrote both words and music, both of them innovative. The lyric is a lament of one lost in love, the emotions being evoked more ambiguous than tragic. The music uses few notes yet manages with its short musical phrases to create a driving rhythm that foreshadows a swing tempo. This unusual quality later made the song a favorite of jazz musicians. The number was interpolated into the Broadway musical *Smiles* (1930), where it was performed by Adele Astaire, Eddie Foy Jr., and the chorus. When Guy Lombardo and the Royal Canadians played it on the radio, sheet music sales soared. Rudy Vallee's recording was a hit, and Kay Starr revived it in 1957 with success. Other discs of note were made by Teddy Wilson, Etta James, Jess Stacy, Dick Haymes, Django Reinhardt, Della Reese, and Louis Prima. Ava Gardner sang "You're Driving Me Crazy" in the movie *Pandora and the Flying Dutchman* (1951), it was performed by Jane Russell and Jeanne Crain (dubbed by Anita Ellis) in *Gentlemen Marry Brunettes* (1955), and it was heard in *Six Cylinder Love* (1931) and *The Marrying Man* (1991).

"You're in the Right Church But the Wrong Pew" (1908) is a comic number with a serious subtext, delivered with bittersweet style as only Bert Williams could. Chris Smith composed the lazy music, and R.C. McPherson (a.k.a. Cecil Mack) wrote the farcical lyric about a Negro who is welcome to a congregation as long as he sits in the designated section of the church. The comedy team of Williams and Walker popularized the number in vaudeville, and Williams interpolated it into the Broadway show *My Landlady* (1908), where he sang it in his devastatingly bittersweet manner. The Negro dialect song was also put into the musical *Bandana Land* (1908).

"You're Mine, You" (1933) is a romantic number about love as owner-ship, two lovers proclaiming they are in the possession of the other and are "chained and bound together." Edward Heyman (lyric) and Johnny Green (music) wrote the ardent song, and it was popularized by early records by Ray Noble, Guy Lombardo, and Gertrude Niesen. Among the many other artists to record it were Artie Shaw, the Delta Rhythm Boys, Mary Ann McCall, Carmen Cavallaro, Horace Henderson, Kay Thompson, Ziggy Elman, Jeri Southern, Lonnie Johnson, Billy Byers, and Sarah Vaughan.

"You're My Everything" (1931) is an expansive love song by Mort Dixon, Joe Young (lyric), and Harry Warren (music) in which one's sweetheart is every season, every song ever written, everything in the world. Jeanne Aubert and Lawrence Gray introduced the ballad in the Broadway show *The Laugh Parade* (1931), but it didn't catch on nationally until the 1940s. Russ Columbo, Anita O'Day, Zoot Sims (vocal by Jimmy Rowles), Louis Prima and Keely Smith, Eddy Duchin, Nat King Cole, Billy Eckstine, and Connie Francis are among the artists who recorded it with success. Dan Dailey sang it in the movie *You're My Everything* (1949), and it was heard in *Painting the Clouds With Sunshine* (1951) and *The Eddy Duchin Story* (1956).

"You're Nobody 'Til Somebody Loves You" (1944) is a fluent ballad by Russ Morgan, Larry Stock, and James Cavanaugh arguing that riches and power are useless unless one has love. Morgan and his Orchestra introduced it on record, but sales were slow and the sheet music sat idle for ten years. Then Roberta Sherwood started singing it in clubs in the mid-1950s, and it slowly caught the attention of various artists who recorded it. Dean Martin revived the ballad with a hit record in 1965, and it was long associated with him. Other significant discs were made by the Mills Brothers, Nat King Cole, Danny Davis, Kate Smith, Sammy Davis Jr. with Count Basie and Quincy Jones, Frank Sinatra, Gisele MacKenzie, Bobby Darin, Connie Francis, Wayne Newton, Eydie Gorme, and Boyd Gaines. The Martin recording was used in the Broadway dance musical *Contact* (2000).

"You're Not the Only Pebble on the Beach" (1896) is another one of those 1890s songs that were so popular that the title became a catch-phrase that outlived the number itself. Frederick J. Redcliffe (a.k.a. Stanley Carter) wrote the sprightly music, and Harry B. Berdan (a.k.a. Harry Braisted) penned the comic lyric that warns men not to spoil a girl with too much praise; remind her that she's not the only choice in the world. Lottie Gilbert introduced the ditty at Koster and Bial's Theatre in New York, and the merry number, also sung about men not being indispensable, was soon a favorite in vaudeville and around many parlor pianos. The song can be heard in the movie *Trail Street* (1947). Years later Johnny Burke (lyric) and Harold Spina (music) created their own version of the song called "You're Not the Only Oyster in the Stew," which Fats Waller recorded with success.

"You're So Desirable" (1939) is a gushing ballad that bandleader Ray Noble wrote both the words and the music for. He and his Orchestra introduced the song on a record with Howard Barrie doing the vocal, and it was popular. Other early discs by Red Norvo (vocal by Terry Allen), Red Nichols (vocal by Bill Darnell), and Gray Gordon (vocal by Cliff Grass) were also successful. There were also recordings by Jimmy Dorsey, Teddy Wilson, and Billie Holiday.

"You're the One (You Beautiful Son-of-a-Gun)" (1932) is a peppy song of adoration by Buddy Fields (lyric) and Gerald Marks (music) that originated in a very different vein. Marks wrote the number as a "schottische," a slow ballroom dance song in 2/4 time. Fred Waring heard Marks demonstrate the number in a publisher's office and suggested that the composer pick up the tempo. Marks rewrote it in 6/8 time, and the sparkling number was interpolated into the revue *George White's Music Hall Varieties* (1932), where Harry Richman sang it. Richman recorded it, but it was a disc by Waring's Pennsylvanians (featured vocal by Jimmy "Scat" Davis) that was a hit. Also, the song got widespread attention because Rudy Vallee often sang it on the radio.

"You're the Only Star (In My Blue Heaven)" (1938) is a genial cowboy ballad by Gene Autry in which a cowpoke sees the girl of his dreams as a star who is "shining just for me." Autry introduced the song in the movie *The Old Barn Dance* (1938), recorded it with success, and reprised it in *Mexicali Rose* (1939) and *Rim of the Canyon* (1949). George Morgan, Elvis Presley, Blue Barron, Patsy Montana, Roy Acuff, Jerry Lee Lewis, and Barry Wood are among those who also recorded it.

"Yours" (1931) is a fervent love song with a bolero beat that was a hit in Cuba and then on Tin Pan Alley. Augustin Rodriguez (Spanish lyric) and Gonzalo Roig (music) wrote the number as "Quierme Mucho," and it was given an English lyric by Jack Sherr and Albert Gamse in which a suitor pledges eternal love and devotion for all time. The bombastic ballad was introduced in the States in Spanish by Tito Schipa, and the new version was recorded first by Dinah Shore. It did not become a hit until Jimmy Dorsey made a disc in 1941 with vocals by Bob Eberly and Helen O'Connell, followed by successful records by Benny Goodman, Tito Guizar (in Spanish), and Vaughn Monroe. Vera Lynn revived the ballad in 1952 with a hit record, and there were other versions by Les Baxter, Ray Anthony, Gene Autry, Xavier Cugat, Bing Crosby, Billy Vaughn, and Vicki Stuart.

"You've Been a Good Old Wagon But You Done Broke Down" (1896), though little known today, is considered by many musicologists to be the first popular song to use ragtime. Called a "coon shout" song in its day, the music is in a blues format but with a ragtime tempo, "far from the typical pop song" of its day, according to Alec Wilder. Ben Harney wrote the music, putting it in 4/4 time (though it was later usually performed in 2/4 time), and the words are credited to a Mr. Biller. The lyric is a comic-sad lament about a wagon, but a longtime lover is implied as well. Harney introduced the song as a "stick dance" specialty in minstrel shows, then it was popularized in vaudeville by May Irwin. The number is believed to be responsible for starting an interest in coon songs and ragtime on Tin Pan Alley. When Bessie Smith revived it in the late 1920s, it was more in the blues mode. Later recordings were made by Lil Green, Juanita Hall, Dinah Washington, the Salty Dog Jazz Band, Teresa Brewer, Della Reese, Paula Lockheart, and Dave Van Ronk.

"You've Changed" (1942) is a haunting song of realization by Bill Carey (lyric) and Carl Fischer (music) that is most associated with Billie Holiday. The low-key, sad ballad lists the little things (no sparkle in the eyes, an insincere smile, kisses that are "blasé") that give evidence of a lover who is bored with one. Harry James (vocal by Dick Haymes) popularized the song, and in 1949 there were hit versions by Bill Farrell with Russ Case's Orchestra and Connie Russell with Harold Mooney's Orchestra. But Holiday's recording and her many performances in clubs and concert are considered definitive. Among the many who have made disc versions are Kay Starr, Ella Fitzgerald with Count Basie, Chet Baker, Sarah Vaughan, Nat King Cole, Frankie Laine, Dexter Gordon, Julie London, Johnny Griffin, Nancy Wilson, Bobby Dukoff, Hank Crawford, and more recently, Barney Kessel, Jesse Davis, and Andrea Marcovicci. Diana Ross sang the ballad in the Holiday film bio *Lady Sings the Blues* (1972).

"You've Got Me Crying Again" (1933) is the tearful standard by Charles Newman (lyric) and Isham Jones (music) that Jones introduced with a disc with Curt Massey doing the vocal. Ruth Etting popularized the song in clubs and on disc, and there were many other versions over the years, including lead records by Hal Kemp, Phil Harris, Teresa Brewer, and Sammy Kaye. Major discs were also made by Buddy Rich, Billy Eckstine, Coleman Hawkins, Boyd Raeburn, Brenda Lee, Lee Wiley, the Four Freshmen, Dean Martin, and Ray Charles.

"You've Got to See Mama Ev'ry Night or You Can't See Mama at All" (1923) is a funny, sassy demand for faithfulness that Sophie Tucker popularized and used as a specialty number for years. Con Conrad composed the hot jazz music, and Billy Rose wrote the hilarious lyric in which a suspicious gal insists that her beau include her in his night life plans or she "won't be home when you call." There is an amusing patter section in the song in which she goes through the days of the week listing all the excuses he gave her; and when he finally did call on Sunday he "brought three girls for company." Notable recordings of the ditty were made by Kay Starr, Carol Channing, Tiny Hill, Homer and Jethro, Lizzie Miles, Max Morath, Claude Williams, and Sid Phillips. Dick Hyman and the Three Deuces played it on the soundtrack of the movie *Bullets Over Broadway* (1994).

"Zing! Went the Strings of My Heart!" (1934) is a tangy song of romantic realization by James Hanley that explains how a symphony of music and a love of nature deep inside one burst out when that special someone came along. Hal Le Roy and Eunice Healey introduced the number in the Broadway revue *Thumbs Up!* (1934), but it really caught on when teenage Judy Garland sang it in the movie *Listen Darling* (1938) and recorded it as well. It was often recorded in the 1940s and 1950s, then revived again in 1972 with a disco version by the Trammps. Among the artists to make prominent discs were Dinah Shore, Frank Sinatra, Eddy Howard, Carmen Cavallaro, Billy Eckstine, Dick Haymes, Les Elgart, Brenda Lee, the Spaniels, Charlie Byrd, the Coasters, Petula Clark, and more recently, Stacey Kent, Loretta Cormier, Manny Alban, and P.J. Proby. Gene Nelson sang it in the film *Lullaby of Broadway* (1951), and the song was heard in *Thumbs Up!* (1943) and *Stonewall* (1995).

"Zing Zing, Zoom Zoom" (1950) is a merry little nonsense song by Charles Tobias (lyric) and Sigmund Romberg (music) that imitates the sounds created when "my little heart goes boom." The ditty was popularized by Perry Como on a record with Romberg's Orchestra. Les Baxter also made a successful disc, but the song remained familiar for years because it was sung in many schools.

"Zip Coon" (1834), a southern nonsense song that is long forgotten, still survives because its melody was later turned into the popular square dance tune "Turkey in the Straw." The original number was a minstrel song about a "zip coon," a slang term for a Broadway swell who wore fancy clothes, carried a walking stick, and claimed to be a "larned skolar." Much of the lyric is nonsense gibberish with a silly refrain about a "possum up a gum tree, coony on a stump." Bob Farrell introduced the ditty at the Bowery Theatre in New York; then it became a regular staple

Zizzy, Ze Zum, Zum

in minstrels shows, especially for George Washington Dixon, who performed it for years. Although both Farrell and Dixon each claimed to
have written the number, it is very unlikely; the melody probably came
from an Irish folk song. Although the number was a favorite for many
decades, it could never be performed today without giving offense.

"Zizzy, Ze Zum, Zum" (1898) was one of the most popular nonsense
songs at the turn of the century. Karl Kennett (lyric) and Lyn Udall
(music) wrote the animated number that called for facial contortions and
silly body positions in the singing of it. The ditty came from vaudeville,
where it was featured by many comics on the circuit, then later became
a popular party song. By World War One it faded away, replaced by
other ridiculous and just-as-unsophisticated numbers.

Alternate Song Titles

Song titles vary from the published sheet music to the record label to the listing in a playbill or on a movie's screen credits. Some songs have even been published with different titles over the years. The following are alternate titles for some of the songs discussed. The alternate title is followed by the title used in this book.

Ah, the Apple Trees	When the World Was Young
Ain't It a Shame	Ain't That a Shame
All I Want for Christmas Is My Two Front Teeth	My Two Front Teeth
Alla en El Rancho Grande	El Rancho Grande
The Alphabet Song	'A' You're Adorable
And the Band Played On	The Band Played On
Back Home Again in Indiana	Indiana
Back Home in Indiana	Indiana
Ballad for Uncle Sam	Ballad for Americans
Banjo on My Knee	Oh! Susanna
A Bicycle Built for Two	Daisy Bell
The Blue Tail Fly	Jimmy Crack Corn
Bury Me Not on the Lone Prairie	Carry Me Back to the Lone Prairie
By the Sleepy Lagoon	Sleepy Lagoon
C.C. Rider	See See Rider Blues
The Caisson Song	The Caissons Go Rolling Along
Caldonia Boogie	Caldonia
Camptown Races	De Camptown Races
Canto Siboney	Siboney

Careless Love Blues	Careless Love
Chattanooga Shoe Shine Boy	Chattanoogie Shoe Shine Boy
Chestnuts Roasting on an Open Fire	The Christmas Song
Chew Your Bubble Gum	Chew-Chew-Chew
A Cowboy Legend	Riders in the Sky
Dance, Ballerina, Dance	Ballerina
Dance with a Dolly with a Hole in Her Stocking	Buffalo Gals
Day-O	The Banana Boat Song
Dear Mr. Gable	You Made Me Love You
Deep River	Dear Old Southland
Dipper Mouth Blues	Sugar Foot Stomp
Dixieland	Dixie
Do Not Forsake Me	High Noon
Does Your Chewing Gum Lose Its Flavor..?	Does the Spearmint Lose Its Flavor..?
Down Mexico Way	South of the Border
Down Upon the Swanee River	Old Folks at Home
The Duckworth Chant	Sound Off
The Dying Cowboy	Carry Me Back to the Lone Prairie
East Side, West Side	The Sidewalks of New York
Eating Goober Peas	Goober Peas
El Rancho Rock	El Rancho Grande
Farewell to Thee	Aloha oe
The Filla-Ga-Dusha Song	Rose O'Day
The Fountain in the Park	While Strolling Through the Park One Day
From the Halls of Montezuma	The Marine's Hymn
The Gang That Sang Heart of My Heart	Heart of My Heart
Get Your Kicks on Route 66	Route 66
Ghost Riders in the Sky	Riders in the Sky
A Good Cigar Is a Smoke	A Woman Is Only a Woman
Gwine to Run All Night	De Camptown Races
The Happy Tune	Sam's Song
Has Anybody Seen My Girl?	Five Foot Two
The Hi-De-Ho Song	Minnie the Moocher
Hold That Tiger!	Tiger Rag

How Much Is That Doggie in the Window?	Doggie in the Window
I Ain't Gwine Study War No More	Down By the Riverside
I Don't Stand a Ghost of a Chance With You	Ghost of a Chance With You
I Dream of Jeanie With the Light Brown Hair	Jeanie With the Light Brown Hair
I Get Ideas	Adios Muchachos
I Got a Woman, Crazy for Me	She's Funny That Way
I Guess I'll Hang My Tears Out to Dry	Guess I'll Hang My Tears Out to Dry
I Know My Baby Is Cheatin' On Me	Cheatin' On Me
I Love You for Sentimental Reasons	For Sentimental Reasons
I Scream, You Scream, We All Scream for Ice Cream	Ice Cream
I Wish I Was in Dixie's Land	Dixie
If I Had Rhythm in My Nursery Rhymes	Rhythm in My Nursery Rhymes
If I Had the Wings of an Angel	The Prisoner's Song
If Jack Were Only Here	Mother Was a Lady
If You Believed in Me	It's Only a Paper Moon
If You Lak-a Me	Under the Bamboo Tree
I'll Take Manhattan	Manhattan
In Other Words	Fly Me to the Moon
It Takes Two to Tango	Takes Two to Tango
It Will Have to Do . . .	Until the Real Thing Comes Along
It's Later Than You Think	Enjoy Yourself
It's So Good	C'est Si Bon
I've Found a New Baby	I Found a New Baby
I've Got Spurs That Jingle, Jangle, Jingle	Jingle, Jangle, Jingle
I've Grown So Lonesome Thinking of You	Thinking of You
Jealousy	Jalousie
Johnny Get Your Gun	Over There
Just a Song at Twilight	Love's Old Sweet Song
Just Break the News to Mother	Break the News to Mother
Kiss Me, Honey, Do	Dinah
Kiss Me Once, Kiss Me Twice . . .	It's Been a Long, Long Time
Let Tyrants Shake Their Iron Rod	Chester

Life Could Be a Dream	Sh—Boom
Look Out for Jimmy Valentine	Jimmy Valentine
Love Everlasting	L'Amour, Tourjours, L'Amour
Love in Honolulu	Oh, How She Could Yacki, Hacki, Wicki, Wacki, Woo
Love Me Tender	Aura Lee
Loveless Love	Careless Love
Lubly Fan	Buffalo Gals
The Maine Stein Song	Stein Song
Mama Yo Quiero	I Want My Mama
The Man on the Flying Trapeze	The Daring Young Man on the Flying Trapeze
May Irwin's Bully Song	The Bully Song
Melancholy Baby	My Melancholy Baby
Merrily We Roll Along	Good Night, Ladies
Mon Homme	My Man
Moonlight Bay	On Moonlight Bay
Moritat	Mack the Knife
My Country 'Tis of Thee	America
My Grandfather's Clock in the Hallway	Grandfather's Clock
My Mother Was a Lady	Mother Was a Lady
My Two Front Teeth	All I Want for Christmas
My Wonderful One	Wonderful One
My Yiddish Mamma	My Yiddishe Momme
Nel Blu, DiPinto di Blu	Volare
New San Antonio Rose	San Antonio Rose
Nick Nack Paddy Whack	The Children's Marching Song
O, Bury Me Not on the Lone Prairie	Carry Me Back to the Lone Prairie
Oh, Dem Golden Slippers	Golden Slippers
Oh, My Darling Clementine	Clementine
Oh, Say Can You See?	The Star Spangled Banner
On the Bayou	Jambalaya
The One-Horse Open Sleigh	Jingle Bells
Over Hill, Over Dale	The Caissons Go Rolling Along
Paper Moon	It's only a Paper Moon
Potatoes Are Cheap, Tomatoes Are Cheaper	Now's the Time to Fall in Love

Pretty Little Poppy	Amapola
Put Another Nickel In	Music! Music! Music!
Roll Out the Barrel	Beer Barrel Polka
Rosie, You Are My Posie	Ma Blushin' Rosie
'Round Her Neck She Wears a Yellow Ribbon	She Wore a Yellow Ribbon
Sailing, Sailing	Sailing over the Bounding Main
Say You Love Me Too	Vieni Su
See See Rider	See See Rider Blues
S-H-I-N-E	Shine
The Ship That Never Returned	Wreck of the Old '97
Song of the Tree	Poinciana
The Stammering Song	K-K-K-Katy
The Suicide Song	Gloomy Sunday
Swanee River	Old Folks at Home
Take It Off! Take It Off!	Strip Polka
That Doggie in the Window	Doggie in the Window
That Sugar Baby o' Mine	Sugar
The Theme from *The Threepenny Opera*	Mack the Knife
There Are Smiles That Make Me Happy	Smiles
There Is No Greater Love	No Greater Love
There'll Be a Hot Time in the Old Town Tonight	A Hot Time in the Old Town
There'll Be Blue Birds Over . . .	The White Cliffs of Dover
There's a Cabin in the Cotton	Cabin in the Cotton
There's No Place Like Home for the Holidays	Home for the Holidays
They Called Her Frivolous Sal	My Gal Sal
This Is My Last Affair	My Last Affair
This Joint Is Jumpin'	The Joint Is Jumpin'
This Old Man	The Children's Marching Song
Till the Real Thing Comes Along	Until the Real Thing Comes Along
Tisket, A-Tasket	A-Tisket, A-Tasket
A Turkish Tale	Uska Dara
Val-De Ri, Val-De Ra	The Happy Wanderer
Walking in a Winter Wonderland	Winter Wonderland
Want Some Sea Food, Baby	Hold Tight—Hold Tight

Way Down Upon the Swanee River	Old Folks at Home
We Are Poor Little Lambs	The Whiffenpoof Song
We're Gonna Rock Around the Clock	Rock Around the Clock
What Did I Do to Be So Black and Blue?	Black and Blue
Whatever Will Be, Will Be	Que Sera, Sera
What's Become of Hinky Dinky Parlay Voo?	Hinky Dinky Parlay Voo
When It's Darkness on the Delta	Darkness on the Delta
When We Were a Couple of Kids	School Days
When We're Alone	Penthouse Serenade
Where Is Your Heart?	The Song from Moulin Rouge
Who Knows?	Quien Sabe?
Who Put the Overalls in Mrs. Murphy's Chowder?	Who Threw the Overalls in Mrs. Murphy's Chowder?
Why Did I Tell You I Was Going to Shanghai?	Shanghai
Wish I Were in the Land of Cotton	Dixie
The Year of Jubilo	Kingdom Coming
The Yodel Polka	Toolie Oolie Doolie
You Better Watch Out	Santa Claus Is Coming to Town
You Forgot to Remember	Remember
You're Not the Only Oyster in the Stew	You're Not the Only Pebble on the Beach
You're the Flower of My Heart, Sweet Adeline	Sweet Adeline

ASCAP's Hit Parade

In 1964, the American Society of Composers, Authors, and Publishers (ASCAP) celebrated its fiftieth anniversary and voted on a hit parade of the best songs written during the organization's lifetime. The following sixteen songs were deemed the best of the best:

Alexander's Ragtime Band*

April Showers**

Begin the Beguine**

The Birth of the Blues**

The Darktown Strutters' Ball*

God Bless America*

Happy Days Are Here Again*

I Wonder Who's Kissing Her Now*

Night and Day**

Over the Rainbow***

Rudolph the Red Nosed Reindeer*

September Song**

Star Dust*

Tea for Two**

White Christmas***

You Made Me Love You*

*Discussed in this volume.
**Discussed in *The American Musical Theatre Song Encyclopedia*.
***Discussed in *The American Musical Film Song Encyclopedia*.

NEA's Hit Parade

In 2001, the National Endowment for the Arts (NEA) and the recording industry compiled a list of the 365 "Songs of the Century" and the recordings of those songs they felt were the best. The top 20 songs, followed by the favored recording artist, were:

1. Over the Rainbow (Judy Garland)***
2. White Christmas (Bing Crosby)***
3. This Land Is Your Land (Woody Guthrie)*
4. Respect (Aretha Franklin)
5. American Pie (Don McLean)
6. Boogie Woogie Bugle Boy (Andrews Sisters)***
7. *West Side Story* cast recording (1957)**
8. Take Me Out to the Ball Game (Billy Murray)*
9. You've Lost That Lovin' Feeling (Righteous Brothers)
10. The Entertainer (Scott Joplin piano roll)
11. In the Mood (Glenn Miller)*
12. Rock Around the Clock (Bill Haley and the Comets)*
13. When the Saints Go Marching In (Louis Armstrong)*
14. You Are My Sunshine (Jimmie Davis)*
15. Mack the Knife (Bobby Darin)*
16. Satisfaction (Rolling Stones)

*Discussed in this volume.
**Discussed in *The American Musical Theatre Song Encyclopedia*.
***Discussed in *The American Musical Film Song Encyclopedia*.

17. Take the 'A' Train (Duke Ellington)*
18. Blueberry Hill (Fats Domino)*
19. God Bless America (Kate Smith)*
20. Stars and Stripes Forever (John Philip Sousa)

Tin Pan Alley Standards from Stage and Screen

BROADWAY

Broadway started providing song hits for Tin Pan Alley in the 1880s. The following theatre songs written before 1960, as well as hundreds of others, can be found in *The American Musical Theatre Song Encyclopedia*.

After You, Who?

Ah, Sweet Mystery of Life

Alice Blue Gown

All Alone Monday

All of You

All Through the Night

Allah's Holiday

Almost Like Being in Love

Alone Together

Always True to You in My Fashion

Any Place I Hang My Hat Is Home

Anything Goes

Anything You Can Do (I Can Do Better)

April Showers

As Time Goes by

At Long Last Love

Auf Wiedersehn

Babes in Arms

Babes in the Woods

Bali Ha'i

Bambalina

Baubles, Bangles and Beads

Because You're You

Begin the Beguine

Bess, You Is My Woman

The Best Things in Life Are Free

Bewitched (Bothered and Bewildered)

Bidin' My Time

The Birth of the Blues

Black Bottom

Blow, Gabriel, Blow

The Blue Room

The Bowery

Brown October Ale

Brush Up Your Shakespeare

Buckle Down, Winsocki

A Bushel and a Peck

But Not for Me

By Myself

Cabin in the Sky

Can't Help Lovin' Dat Man

Castle of Dreams

C'est Magnifique

Clap Yo' Hands

Climb Ev'ry Mountain

Close as Pages in a Book

Come Rain or Come Shine

Come to Me, Bend to Me

Could You Use Me?

Crazy Rhythm

Cuddle Up a Little Closer

Dancing in the Dark

Deep in My Heart, Dear

The Desert Song

Diamonds Are a Girl's Best Friend

Diga Diga Doo

Do Do Do

Doin' the New Low-Down

Don't Ever Leave Me

Do-Re-Mi

Down in the Depths (On the Ninetieth Floor)

The Drinking Song

D'Ye Love Me?

Eadie Was a Lady

Embraceable You

Everybody Step

Everything's Coming Up Roses

Falling in Love With Love

Fascinating Rhythm

Feeling I'm Falling

Forty-five Minutes From Broadway

Friendship

Funny Face

The Gentleman Is a Dope

Get Me to the Church on Time

Getting to Know You

Giannina Mia

A Girl Is on Your Mind

Girl of the Moment

The Girl That I Marry

Give My Regards to Broadway

Glad to Be Unhappy

Glitter and Be Gay

Golden Days

Good News

Goodnight, My Someone

Gypsy Love Song

Happy Talk

Harlem on My Mind

Harrigan

Haunted Heart

Have You Met Miss Jones?

He Loves and She Loves

(You Gotta Have) Heart

Heat Wave

The Heather on the Hill

Hello Young Lovers

Here in My Arms (It's Adorable)

Hernando's Hideaway

Hey, There

Honey Bun

Honey in the Honeycomb

How Are Things in Glocca Morra?

How'd You Like to Spoon With Me?

I Can Cook Too

I Can't Get Started With You

I Could Have Danced All Night

I Could Write a Book

I Didn't Know What Time It Was

I Don't Know How to Love Him

I Feel Pretty

I Found a Million Dollar Baby (In a Five and Ten Cent Store)

I Get a Kick Out of You

I Got Lost in His Arms

I Got Lucky in the Rain

I Got Plenty o' Nuthin'

I Got Rhythm

I Got the Sun in the Morning

I Guess I'll Have to Change My Plan

I Had Myself a True Love

I Happen to Like New York

I Have Dreamed

I Like the Likes of You

I Love Paris

I Love Thee, I Adore Thee

I Loves You, Porgy

I Married an Angel

I See Your Face Before Me

I Still Get Jealous

I Talk to the Trees

I Want to Be Happy

I Whistle a Happy Tune

I Wish I Were in Love Again

If Ever I Would Leave You

If I Loved You

If I Were a Bell

If Love Were All

If This Isn't Love

I'll Be Hard to Handle

I'll Build a Stairway to Paradise

I'll Know (When My Love Comes Along)

I'll See You Again

I'm Falling in Love With Someone

Imagine

Indian Love Call

It Ain't Necessarily So

It Never Entered My Mind

Italian Street Song

It's a Long Way to Tipperary

It's a Lovely Day Today

It's All Right With Me

It's De-Lovely

It's Got to Be Love

I've Confessed to the Breeze

I've Got Rings on My Fingers

I've Grown Accustomed to Her Face

I've Never Been in Love Before

I've Told Ev'ry Little Star

Joey Joey Joey

Johnny One-Note

June Is Bustin' Out All Over

Just in Time

Just One of Those Things

Keep Smiling at Trouble

Kiss Me Again

The Lady Is a Tramp

The Lambeth Walk

Leave It to Jane

Let Me Entertain You

Let's Be Buddies

Let's Do It (Let's Fall in Love)

Let's Have Another Cup of Coffee

Lida Rose

Life Is Just a Bowl of Cherries

Life Upon the Wicked Stage

Limehouse Blues

A Little Bit in Love

Little Girl Blue

A Little Girl From Little Rock

Liza

Look for the Silver Lining

Look to the Rainbow

Lost in the Stars

Love for Sale

Love Is Sweeping the Country

Love, Look Away

The Love Nest

Lover, Come Back to Me

Luck Be a Lady

Lucky in Love

Maggie Murphy's Home

Make Believe

Make Someone Happy

Makin' Whoopee

March of the Toys

Maria

Marian the Librarian

Mary's a Grand Old Name

Moanin' Low

Moonbeams

Moonshine Lullaby

The Most Beautiful Girl in the World

Mr. Gallagher and Mr. Shean

My Beautiful Lady

My Darling, My Darling

My Favorite Things

My Funny Valentine

My Heart Belongs to Daddy

My Heart Stood Still

My Man's Gone Now

My One and Only

My Romance

My Ship

Naughty Marietta

'Neath the Southern Moon

Nellie Kelly, I Love You

Never, Never Land

New Sun in the Sky

New York, New York

Night and Day

The Night Was Made for Love

Of Thee I Sing, (Baby)

Oh! How I Hate to Get Up in the Morning

Oh, Lady Be Good!

Oh, What a Beautiful Mornin'

Ohio

Oklahoma

Ol' Man River

Old Devil Moon

On the Street Where You Live

Once in Love With Amy

One Alone

One Kiss

Out of My Dreams

Pack Up Your Sins and Go to the Devil

Papa, Won't You Dance With Me?

The Party's Over

People Will Say We're in Love

A Picture of Me Without You

A Pretty Girl Is Like a Melody

Put on a Happy Face

Quiet Night

The Rain in Spain

Reuben and Cynthia

Ridin' High

The Riff Song

Rise 'n' Shine

Romany Life

Rose-Marie

'S Wonderful

The Saga of Jenny

Say It With Music

Sentimental Me

September Song

Serenade

Seventy-six Trombones

Shall We Dance?

(Play) A Simple Melody

Sing for Your Supper

Sit Down, You're Rockin' the Boat

Small World

Smoke Gets in Your Eyes

So in Love

Softly, as in a Morning Sunrise

Some Enchanted Evening

Some Other Time

Some Sort of Somebody

Someone to Watch Over Me

Something to Remember You By

Something Wonderful

Sometimes I'm Happy

Somewhere

The Song Is You

The Sound of Music

South American Way

Speak Low

Spring Is Here

Standing on the Corner

Steam Heat

Stouthearted Men

Strange Music

Stranger in Paradise

The Streets of New York

Strike Up the Band

Summertime

Sunny

Supper Time

The Surrey With the Fringe on Top

Sweet and Low-Down

Take Back Your Mink

Take Me Along

Take Me Back to Manhattan

Taking a Chance on Love

Tea for Two

Tell Me, Pretty Maiden

There Is Nothin' Like a Dame

There's a Small Hotel

There's No Business Like Show Business

They Call the Wind Maria

They Say It's Wonderful

This Can't Be Love

This Funny World

This Nearly Was Mine

Thou Swell

Till the Clouds Roll by

Till There Was You

To Keep My Love Alive

Tonight

Too Darn Hot

The Touch of Your Hand

Toyland

Try to Remember

Two Lost Souls

The Varsity Drag

Way Out West (On West End Avenue)

We Kiss in a Shadow

Whatever Lola Wants

What's the Use of Wond'rin'?

When I'm Not Near the Girl I Love

Where or When

Whip-Poor-Will

Who?

Who Cares?

Why Do I Love You?

Will You Remember?

With a Little Bit of Luck

A Wonderful Guy

Wunderbar

The Yankee Doodle Boy

Yesterdays

You Are Love

You Can't Get a Man With a Gun

You Do Something to Me

You Say the Nicest Things, Baby

You Were Meant for Me

You'll Never Walk Alone

Young and Foolish

Younger Than Springtime

You're a Builder-Upper

You're a Grand Old Flag

You're Just in Love

You're the Cream in My Coffee

You're the Top

Zip

HOLLYWOOD

Hollywood musicals have introduced hundreds of songs that went on to become Tin Pan Alley standards. Among those written before 1960 are the following, all of which can be found in *The American Musical Film Song Encyclopedia*.

About a Quarter to Nine

Ac-cent-tchuate the Positive

All God's Chillun Got Rhythm

All I Do Is Dream of You

All the Way

Am I Blue?

Animal Crackers in My Soup

Anniversary Song

April Love

At the Codfish Ball

Baby, It's Cold Outside

Be a Clown

Be Careful, It's My Heart

Be My Love

Beginner's Luck

Better Luck Next Time

Beyond the Blue Horizon

Blue Hawaii

Blues in the Night

Bojangles of Harlem

Boogie Woogie Bugle Boy

The Boy Next Door

Broadway Melody

Broadway Rhythm

Buttons and Bows

Californ-i-ay

The Carioca

Change Partners

Chattanooga Choo-Choo

Cheek to Cheek

Cocktails for Two

The Continental

Count Your Blessings

A Couple of Swells

Cuban Love Song

Dames

Dearly Beloved

Did You Ever See a Dream Walking?

Ding Dong! The Witch Is Dead!

Do You Know What It Means to Miss New Orleans?

The Donkey Serenade

Evergreen

Everyone Says I Love You

A Fine Romance

Flirtation Walk

Flying Down to Rio

A Foggy Day (In London Town)

The Folks Who Live on the Hill

Forty-second Street

Gigi

Give Your Baby Lots of Lovin'

Going My Way

Good Morning

Hallelujah, I'm a Bum

Happiness Is (Just) a Thing Called Joe

Happy Holiday

Have Yourself a Merry Little Christmas

Heigh-Ho

Hit the Road to Dreamland

Hooray for Hollywood

How About You?

I Can't Be Bothered Now

I Can't Begin to Tell You

I Concentrate on You

I Couldn't Sleep a Wink Last Night

I Don't Want to Walk Without You

I Dream Too Much

I Feel a Song Comin' On

I Had the Craziest Dream

I Know Why (and So Do You?)

I Only Have Eyes for You

I Remember It Well

I Remember You

I Won't Dance

If I Had a Talking Picture of You

I'll String Along With You

I'll Walk Alone

I'm a Dreamer (Aren't We All?)

I'm an Old Cowhand (From the Rio Grande)

I'm in the Mood for Love

I'm Old Fashioned

In the Cool, Cool, Cool of the Evening

In the Still of the Night

Isn't It Romantic?

Isn't This a Lovely Day (To Be Caught in the Rain)?

It Might as Well Be Spring

It Only Happens When I Dance With You

It's a Grand Night for Singing

It's a Most Unusual Day

It's Magic

I've Got a Feeling You're Fooling

I've Got a Girl in Kalamazoo

I've Got My Love to Keep Me Warm

I've Got You Under My Skin

I've Heard That Song Before

Jeepers Creepers

A Journey to a Star

June in January

Just Let Me Look at You

Just You, Just Me

The Lady in Red

Learn to Croon

Let Me Sing and I'm Happy

Let Yourself Go

Let's Call the Whole Thing Off

Let's Face the Music and Dance

Let's Fall in Love

Long Ago (And Far Away)

Louise

Love in Bloom

Love Is Here to Stay

Love Is Just Around the Corner

Love Is Where You Find It

Love Me Tonight

Love Walked In

The Loveliest Night of the Year

Lovely to Look At

Lover

Lullaby of Broadway

Make 'Em Laugh

The Man That Got Away

Mimi

Moonlight Becomes You

More and More

Music Is Better Than Words

My Baby Just Cares for Me

My Dreams Are Getting Better All the Time

My Old Flame

My Shining Hour

Never Gonna Dance

Nice Work If You Can Get It

Night Over Shanghai

The Night They Invented Champagne

No Love, No Nothin'

No Strings (I'm Fancy Free)

No Two People

Now It Can Be Told

On the Atchison, Topeka and the Santa Fe

On the Good Ship Lollipop

Once and for Always

One for My Baby

One Hour With You

Orchids in the Moonlight

Our Love Affair

Over the Rainbow

Painting the Clouds With Sunshine

Pennies From Heaven

Personality

Pick Yourself Up

Please

Put Me to the Test

Puttin' on the Ritz

A Rainy Night in Rio

Remember My Forgotten Man

Remind Me

Rosalie

San Francisco

Secret Love

September in the Rain

Serenade in Blue

Shadow Waltz

Shall We Dance?

She's a Latin from Manhattan

Should I (Reveal)?

Shuffle Off to Buffalo

Silver Bells

Sing, You Sinners

Singin' in the Rain

Slap That Bass

Slumming on Park Avenue

Small Fry

Some Day My Prince Will Come

Something's Gotta Give

Sonny Boy

Steppin' Out With My Baby

Straighten Up and Fly Right

Sunny Side Up

Sure Thing

Sweepin' the Clouds Away

Sweet Leilani

Swinging on a Star

Tangerine

Temptation

Thank Heaven for Little Girls

Thanks for the Memory

That Old Black Magic

That's Amore

That's Entertainment

That's for Me

There Will Never Be Another You

There's a Lull in My Life

They All Laughed

They Can't Take That Away From Me

Things Are Looking Up

Three Little Words

Time After Time

Tip Toe Through the Tulips With Me

Too Late Now

Too Marvelous for Words

The Trolley Song

True Love

Two Dreams Met

The Way You Look Tonight

The Wedding of the Painted Doll

We're in the Money

What Wouldn't I Do for That Man

When I Grow Too Old to Dream

When You Wish Upon a Star

Whistle While You Work

White Christmas

With Plenty of Money and You

Wonderful Copenhagen

Wonderful, Wonderful Day

The Words Are in My Heart

You Are My Lucky Star

You Are Too Beautiful

You Belong to My Heart

You Brought a New Kind of Love to Me

You Don't Know What Love Is

You Keep Coming Back Like a Song

You Make Me Feel So Young

You Must Have Been a Beautiful Baby

You Say the Sweetest Things, Baby

You Stepped Out of a Dream

You Were Meant for Me

You'd Be So Nice to Come Home To

You'll Never Know

Your Head on My Shoulder

You're Getting to Be a Habit With Me

Zip-a-Dee-Doo-Dah

Selected Bibliography

WORKS ON TIN PAN ALLEY AND AMERICAN POPULAR MUSIC

Blesh, Rudi, and Harriet Janis. *They All Played Ragtime*. New York: Knopf, 1950.

Burton, Jack. *The Blue Book of Tin Pan Alley*. Watkins Glen, N.Y.: Century House, 1951.

Case, Brian, and Stan Britt. *The Harmony Illustrated Encyclopedia of Jazz*. New York: Harmony Books, 1986.

Clifford, Mike, ed. *The Illustrated Encyclopedia of Black Music*. New York: Harmony Books, 1982.

Courlander, Harold. *Negro Folk Music U.S.A.* New York: Columbia University Press, 1963.

Crawford, Richard. *America's Musical Life: A History*. New York: W.W. Norton, 2001.

Dachs, David. *Anything Goes: The World of Popular Music*. Indianapolis: Bobbs-Merrill, 1964.

Ewen, David. *All the Years of American Popular Music*. Englewood Cliffs, N.J.: Prentice-Hall, 1977.

———. *American Popular Songs*. New York: Random House, 1966.

———. *History of Popular Music*. New York: Barnes and Noble, 1961.

———. *The Life and Death of Tin Pan Alley: The Golden Age of American Popular Music*. New York: Funk and Wagnalls, 1964.

Freeman, Graydon Lavern. *The Melodies Linger On*. Watkins Glen, N.Y.: Century House, 1951.

Gammond, Peter. *The Oxford Companion to Popular Music*. New York: Oxford University Press, 1991.

Goldberg, Isaac, and Edward Jablonski. *Tin Pan Alley*. New York: F. Unger, 1961.

Hamm, Charles. *Yesterdays: Popular Song in America*. New York: W.W. Norton, 1979.

Jacobs, Dick, and Harriet Jacobs. *Who Wrote That Song?* Cincinnati, Ohio: Writer's Digest Books, 1994.

Jasen, David A. *Tin Pan Alley: The Composers, the Songs, the Performers, and Their Times.* New York: Donald I. Fine, 1988.

Jasen, David A., and Gene Jones. *That American Rag.* New York: Schirmer Books, 2000.

Jasen, David A., and Trebor Jay Tichenor. *Rags and Ragtime: A Musical History.* New York: Seabury Press, 1978.

Lax, Roger, and Frederick Smith. *The Great Song Thesaurus.* 2nd ed. New York: Oxford University Press, 1989.

Lissauer, Robert. *Lissauer's Encyclopedia of Popular Music, 1888 to the Present.* New York: Paragon House, 1991.

Malone, Bill C. *Southern Music—American Music.* Lexington: University Press of Kentucky, 1979.

Merlis, Bob, and Davin Seay. *Heart & Soul: A Celebration of Black Music Style in America, 1930–1975.* New York: Stewart, Tabori and Chang, 1997.

Morgan, Thomas L., and William Barlow. *From Cakewalks to Concert Halls: An Illustrated History of African American Popular Music From 1895 to 1930.* Washington, DC: Elliott and Clark, 1992.

Morris, James R., J.R. Taylor, and Dwight Blocker Bowers. *American Popular Song: Six Decades of Songwriters and Singers.* Washington, D.C.: Smithsonian Institution Press, 1984.

Murray, Albert. *Stomping the Blues.* New York: Da Capo Press, 1976.

Murrells, Joseph. *Million Selling Records From the 1900s to the 1980s.* New York: Arco, 1984.

Otfinoski, Stan. *The Golden Age of Novelty Songs.* New York: Billboard Books, 2000.

Palmer, Tony. *All You Need Is Love: The Story of Popular Music.* New York: Grossman, 1976.

Paymer, Marvin E., gen. ed. *Facts Behind the Songs: A Handbook of American Popular Music From the Nineties to the 90s.* New York: Garland, 1993.

Popular Music: An Annotated Index of American Popular Songs. 18 vol. Editors: Nat Shapiro (1964–1973); Bruce Pollock (1984–1994). New York: Adrien Press, 1964–1973; Detroit: Gale Research, 1984–1994.

Robinette, Richard. *Historical Perspectives in Popular Music: A Historical Outline.* Dubuque, Iowa: Kendall-Hunt, 1980.

Scheurer, Timothy E. *Born in the U.S.A.: The Myth of America in Popular Music From Colonial Times to the Present.* Jackson, Miss: University Press of Mississippi, 1991.

Shaw, Arnold. *Dictionary of American Pop/Rock.* New York: Schirmer Books, 1982.

———. *The Jazz Age: Popular Music in the 1920's.* New York: Oxford University Press, 1987.

———. *Let's Dance: Popular Music in the 1930's.* New York: Oxford University Press, 1998.

Spaeth, Sigmund. *A History of Popular Music in America.* 1948. New York: Random House, 1971.

Stambler, Irwin. *Encyclopedia of Popular Music.* New York: St. Martin's Press, 1965.

Tawa, Nicholas E. *The Way to Tin Pan Alley: American Popular Song, 1866–1910.* New York: Schirmer Books, 1990.

Whitcomb, Ian. *After the Ball: Pop Music From Rag to Rock*. New York: Simon and Schuster, 1973.

Williams, John R. *This Was Your Hit Parade*. Camden, Maine: John R. Williams, 1973.

WORKS ON SONGS AND SONGWRITERS

Adler, Richard, with Lee Davis. *You Gotta Have Heart: An Autobiography*. New York: Donald I. Fine, 1990.

Agay, Denes. *Best Loved Songs of the American People*. Garden City, N.Y.: Doubleday, 1975.

Arbold, Elliot. *Deep in My Heart: Sigmund Romberg*. New York: Duell, Sloane and Pearce, 1949.

Armitage, Merle. *George Gershwin: Man and Legend*. New York: Duell, Sloane and Pearce, 1958.

Bach, Bob, and Ginger Mercer, eds. *Our Huckleberry Friend: The Life, Times and Lyrics of Johnny Mercer*. Secaucus, N.J.: Lyle Stuart, 1982.

Barrett, Mary Ellin. *Irving Berlin: A Daughter's Memoir*. New York: Simon and Schuster, 1994.

Bergreen, Laurence. *As Thousands Cheer: The Life of Irving Berlin*. New York: Viking Press, 1990.

Bloom, Ken. *American Song: The Complete Companion to Tin Pan Alley*. New York: Facts On File, 2001.

———. *American Song: The Complete Musical Theatre Companion, 1900–1984*. New York: Facts On File Publications, 1985.

———. *Hollywood Song: The Complete Film & Musical Companion*. New York: Facts On File Publications, 1995.

Bordman, Gerald. *Days to Be Happy, Years to Be Sad: The Life and Music of Vincent Youmans*. New York: Oxford University Press, 1982.

———. *Jerome Kern: His Life and Music*. New York: Oxford University Press, 1980.

Brahms, Caryl, and Ned Sherrin. *Song By Song: The Lives and Work of 14 Great Lyric Writers*. Egerton, Bolton (United Kingdom): R. Anderson Publications, 1984.

Cahn, Sammy. *I Should Care: The Sammy Cahn Story*. New York: Arbor House, 1974.

Carmichael, Hoagy. *Sometimes I Wonder*. New York: Da Capo Press, 1976.

———. *The Stardust Road*. 1946. Bloomington: Indiana University Press, 1983.

Citron, Stephen. *Noel and Cole: The Sophisticates*. New York: Oxford University Press, 1993.

———. *The Wordsmiths: Oscar Hammerstein II and Alan Jay Lerner*. New York: Oxford University Press, 1995.

Cohan, George M. *Twenty Years on Broadway*. New York: Harper and Brothers, 1924.

Collier, James Lincoln. *Duke Ellington*. New York: Oxford University Press, 1987.

Coslow, Sam. *Cocktails for Two: The Many Lives of the Giant Songwriter Sam Coslow*. New Rochelle, N.Y.: Arlington House, 1977.

Craig, Warren. *Sweet and Low Down: America's Popular Somgwriters*. Metuchen, N.J.: Scarecrow Press, 1978.

David, Lee. *Bolton and Wodehouse and Kern*. New York: James H. Heineman, 1993.

Dietz, Howard. *Dancing in the Dark*. New York: Quadrangle Books/New York Times Book Co., 1974.

Donaldson, Frances. *P.G. Wodehouse: A Biography*. New York: Alfred A. Knopf, 1982.

Dreiser, Theodore. *The Story of Paul Dresser*. New York: Boni and Liveright, 1927.

Duke, Vernon. *Passport to Paris*. Boston: Little, Brown, 1955.

Eells, George. *The Life That Late He Led: A Biography of Cole Porter*. New York: G.P. Putnam's Sons, 1967.

Ewen, David. *American Songwriters*. New York: H.W. Wilson, 1987.

———. *George Gershwin: His Journey to Greatness*. Westport, Conn.: Greenwood Press, 1977.

———. *Richard Rodgers*. New York: Holt, 1957.

———. *The World of Jerome Kern*. New York: Holt, 1960.

Fordin, Hugh. *Getting to Know Him: A Biography of Oscar Hammerstein II*. New York: Random House, 1977.

Freedland, Michael. *Irving Berlin*. New York: Stein and Day, 1974.

———. *Jerome Kern*. New York: Stein and Day, 1981.

Furia, Philip. *Ira Gershwin: The Art of the Lyricist*. New York: Oxford University Press, 1996.

———. *Irving Berlin: A Life in Song*. New York: Schirmer Books, 1998.

———. *The Poets of Tin Pan Alley: A History of America's Great Lyricists*. New York: Oxford University Press, 1990.

Gershwin, Ira. *Lyrics on Several Occasions*. New York: Viking Press, 1973.

Gordon, Eric A. *Mark the Music: The Life and Work of Marc Blitzstein*. New York: St. Martin's Press, 1989.

Gottlieb, Robert, and Robert Kimball, eds. *Reading Lyrics*. New York: Pantheon Books, 2000.

Grafton, David. *Red, Hot and Rich: An Oral History of Cole Porter*. New York: Stein and Day, 1987.

Grattan, Virginia L. *American Women Songwriters: A Biographical Dictionary*. Westport, Conn.: Greenwood Press, 1993.

Green, Benny. *P.G. Wodehouse: A Literary Biography*. New York: Rutledge Press, 1981.

Green, Stanley. *Rodgers and Hammerstein Fact Book*. Milwaukee, Wis.: Lynn Farnol Group/Hal Leonard Publishers, 1986.

———. *The Rodgers and Hammerstein Story*. New York: John Day, 1963.

Groce, Nancy. *New York: Songs of the City*. New York: Watson-Guptill Publications, 1999.

Hamm, Charles. *Irving Berlin—Songs from the Melting Pot: The Formative Years, 1907–1914*. New York: Oxford University Press, 1997.

Hammerstein, Oscar, II. *Lyrics*. Rev. ed. Milwaukee, Wis.: Hal Leonard Books, 1985.

Handy, William C. *Father of the Blues: An Autobiography*. New York: Macmillan, 1941.

Harris, Charles K. *After the Ball: Forty Years of Melody*. New York: Frank Maurice, 1926.

Hart, Dorothy. *Thou Swell, Thou Witty: The Life and Lyrics of Lorenz Hart*. New York: Harper and Row, 1976.

Hart, Dorothy, and Robert Kimball, eds. *The Complete Lyrics of Lorenz Hart*. New York: Alfred A. Knopf, 1986.

Hischak, Thomas S. *The American Musical Film Song Encyclopedia*. Westport, Conn.: Greenwood Press, 1999.

———. *The American Musical Theatre Song Encyclopedia*. Westport, Conn.: Greenwood Press, 1995.

———. *Word Crazy: Broadway Lyricists From Cohan to Sondheim*. New York: Praeger Publishers, 1991.

Hyland, William G. *Richard Rodgers*. New Haven, Conn.: Yale University Press, 1998.

———. *The Song Is Ended: Songwriters and American Music, 1900–1950*. New York: Oxford University Press, 1995.

Jablonski, Edward. *Gershwin*. Garden City, N.Y.: Doubleday, 1987.

———. *Harold Arlen: Happy With the Blues*. Garden City, N.Y.: Doubleday, 1961.

Jablonski, Edward, and Lawrence D. Stewart. *The Gershwin Years*. Garden City, N.Y.: Doubleday, 1958.

Kahn, E.J. *The Merry Partners: The Age and Stage of Harrigan and Hart*. New York: Random House, 1955.

Kaye, Joseph. *Victor Herbert*. New York: Crown Publishers, 1931.

Kendall, Alan. *George Gershwin: A Biography*. New York: Universe Books, 1987.

Kimball, Robert ed. *Cole*. New York: Holt, Rinehart and Winston, 1971.

———. *The Complete Lyrics of Cole Porter*. New York: Alfred A. Knopf, 1983.

———. *The Complete Lyrics of Ira Gershwin*. New York: Alfred A. Knopf, 1993.

———. *The Complete Lyrics of Irving Berlin*. New York: Alfred A. Knopf, 2001.

Kimball, Robert, and Linda Emmet. *The Complete Lyrics of Irving Berlin*. New York: Random House, 2000.

Kimball, Robert, and William Bolcom. *Reminiscing With Sissle and Blake*. New York: Viking Press, 1973.

Kimball, Robert, and Alfred Simon. *The Gershwins*. New York: Atheneum, 1973.

Lees, Gene. *Inventing Champagne: The Worlds of Lerner and Loewe*. New York: St. Martin's Press, 1990.

Lerner, Alan Jay. *A Hymn to Him: The Lyrics of Alan Jay Lerner*. Ed. Benny Green. New York: Limelight Editions, 1987.

———. *The Street Where I Live*. New York: W.W. Norton, 1978.

Lewine, Richard, and Alfred Simon. *Encyclopedia of Theatre Music*. New York: Random House, 1961.

———. *Songs of the Theater*. New York: H.W. Wilson, 1984.

Loesser, Susan. *A Most Remarkable Fella: Frank Loesser and the Guys and Dolls in His Life*. New York: Donald I. Fine, 1993.

Marx, Samuel, and Jan Clayton. *Rodgers and Hart: Bewitched, Bothered and Bewildered*. New York: G.P. Putnam's Sons, 1976.

McCabe, John. *George M. Cohan: The Man Who Owned Broadway*. Garden City, N.Y.: Doubleday, 1973.

McGuire, Patricia Dubin. *Lullaby of Broadway: The Life of Al Dubin*. Secaucus, N.J.: Citadel Press, 1983.

Meyerson, Harold, and Ernie Harburg. *Who Put the Rainbow in* The Wizard of
    Oz? *Yip Harburg, Lyricist.* Ann Arbor: University of Michigan Press, 1993.
Mordden, Ethan. *Rodgers and Hammerstein.* New York: Harry N. Abrams, 1992.
Morehouse, Ward. *George M. Cohan, Prince of the American Theatre.* New York:
    J.B. Lippincott, 1943.
Morley, Sheridan. *A Talent to Amuse: Noel Coward.* New York: Doubleday, 1970.
Nolan, Frederick. *Lorenz Hart: A Poet on Broadway.* New York: Oxford University
    Press, 1994.
———. *The Sound of Their Music: The Story of Rodgers and Hammerstein.* New York:
    Walker, 1978.
Raymond, Jack. *Show Music on Record.* New York: Frederick Ungar, 1981.
Rodgers, Richard. *Musical Stages: An Autobiography.* New York: Random House,
    1975.
Root, Deane L. *American Popular Stage Music, 1860–1880.* Ann Arbor: UMI Re-
    search Press, 1987.
Rose, Al. *Eubie Blake.* New York: Schirmer Books, 1979.
Rosenberg, Deena. *Fascinating Rhythm: The Collaboration of George and Ira Gersh-
    win.* New York: Dutton, 1991.
Schwartz, Charles. *Cole Porter: A Biography.* New York: Dial Press, 1977.
———. *Gershwin, His Life and Music.* Indianapolis: Bobbs-Merrill, 1973.
Secrest, Meryle. *Somewhere for Me: A Biography of Richard Rodgers.* New York:
    Alfred A. Knopf, 2001.
Simon, William Lo, ed. *Festival of Popular Songs.* (Song Introductions by John S.
    Wilson.) Pleasantville, N.Y.: Readers Digest Assn., 1977.
Singer, Barry. *Black and Blue: The Life and Lyrics of Andy Razaf.* New York: Schir-
    mer, 1992.
Suskin, Steven. *Berlin, Kern, Rodgers, Hart and Hammerstein: A Complete Song Cat-
    alogue.* Jefferson, N.C.: McFarland, 1990.
Taylor, Deems. *Some Enchanted Evenings: The Story of Rodgers and Hammerstein.*
    New York: Harper and Brothers, 1953.
Taylor, Theodore. *Jule: The Story of Composer Jule Styne.* New York: Random
    House, 1979.
Thomas, Tony. *Harry Warren and the Hollywood Musical.* Secaucus, N.J.: Citadel
    Press, 1975.
Vaché, Warren W. *The Unsung Song Writers.* Metuchen, N.J.: Scarecrow Press,
    1999.
Waller, Maurice, and Anthony Calabrese. *Fats Waller.* New York: Schirmer Books,
    1977.
Waters, Edward. *Victor Herbert: A Life in Music.* New York: Macmillan, 1955.
Whitcomb, Ian. *Irving Berlin and Ragtime America.* New York: Limelight Editions,
    1988.
White, Mark. *"You Must Remember This . . .": Popular Songwriters, 1900–1980.* New
    York: Charles Scribner's Sons, 1985.
Wilder, Alec. *American Popular Song: The Great Innovators, 1900–1950.* New York:
    Oxford University Press, 1972.
Wilk, Max. *They're Playing Our Song.* New York: Atheneum, 1973.
Willson, Meredith. *But He Doesn't Know the Territory.* New York: G.P. Putnam's
    Sons, 1959.

Winer, Deborah Grace. *On the Sunny Side of the Street: The Life and Lyrics of Dorothy Fields*. New York: Schirmer Books, 1997.

Wodehouse, P.G., and Guy Bolton. *Bring on the Girls! The Improbable Story of Our Life in Musical Comedy*. New York: Simon and Schuster, 1953.

Index

Aaronson, Irving, 208, 210, 315, 351
Abarbanell, Lina, 100
ABBA, 247, 278
Abbott, Diahnne, 143
Abel, Walter, 169
Above Suspicion, 40
Abrahams, Jody, 358, 373, 421
Abrahams, Maurice, 296
Abroad With Two Yanks, 387
Absolute Beginners, 383
Ackerman, Bob, 174, 348
Acuff, Roy, 2, 33, 34, 49, 81, 129, 192, 193, 212, 231, 316, 358, 388, 425
Adair, Tom, 101
Adams, A. Emmett, 38
Adams, Edie, 134
Adams, Frank R., 165
Adams, India, 43
Adams, Stanley, 214, 363, 389
Adamson, Harold, 21, 67, 78–79, 83, 104, 186, 229, 372, 409
Adkins, Paul, 134
Adler, Larry, 183, 243, 332, 337, 339, 342, 371
Adler, Richard, 296
Adrian, Iris, 183
Adventures of Priscilla, Queen of the Desert, 154
Affairs of Dobie Gillis, The, 177
Affairs of Susan, The, 169

Africana, 84
After the Thin Man, 323, 328
Agatha, 366
Ager, Milton, 7, 110, 130, 132, 138, 165, 176, 225, 376
Ahbez, Eden, 261
Ahlert, Fred E., 154, 171, 175, 234, 245, 385
Ain't Misbehavin', 6, 7, 41, 105, 140, 143, 152, 175, 186, 189, 195, 199, 234, 336, 337, 354, 396, 423
Akers, Karen, 6, 92, 147, 257, 263, 264, 379, 391
Akst, Harry, 26, 84, 126
Alamo, Tony, 110, 250, 386
Alban, Manny, 427
Albert, Eddie, 82
Alberts, Al, 357
Albertson, Frank, 408
Albrecht, Elmer, 98
Albritton, Lillian, 380
Alda, Alan, 168
Alda, Frances, 38
Alda, Robert, 56, 100, 239
Alden, Howard, 172, 174, 197, 273, 284, 319, 410
Alden, Joseph R., 326
Alexander, Edna, 344
Alexander, Joe, 136
Alexander, Van, 167, 196, 244

Alexander's Ragtime Band, 10, 44, 96, 101, 146, 207, 231, 297, 299, 391, 396
Alexandria, Lorez, 30
Alias Jimmy Valentine, 194
Alice Doesn't Live Here Anymore, 189
Alice's Restaurant, 16
All Hands on Deck, 24
All Star Bond Rally, 311
All That Jazz, 5, 331, 365, 405
All the Fine Young Cannibals, 119
All Through the Night, 61
Allen, Barclay, 230
Allen, Bob, 95, 97, 108
Allen, Fred, 131
Allen, Harry, 95, 244, 252, 289
Allen, Janet, 406
Allen, Johnny, 75
Allen, Lewis, 145
Allen, Peter, 85, 161
Allen, Red, 64, 77, 79, 178, 180, 238, 255, 304, 333, 355, 376
Allen, Rex, 205, 335
Allen, Robert, 59, 141, 187
Allen, Rosalie, 193
Allen, Steve, 105, 210, 220, 279, 368
Allen, Terry, 146, 157, 218, 425
Allen, Woody, 177
Alley Cats, The, 317, 418
Allison, Bob, 314
Allison, Fran, 286
Allison, Mose, 150, 167, 331
Allyson, June, 23, 178, 348, 375
Almeida, Laurindo, 3
Along the Navajo Trail, 14
Alpert, Herb, 18, 19, 107, 243, 327, 335
Alter, Louis, 229, 235, 264
Altman, Arthur, 12
Always Leave Them Laughing, 51
Ambrose and his Orchestra, 45, 352, 370, 406, 414
Ameche, Don, 96, 193, 210, 348, 396, 400
American Graffiti, 8, 124, 135, 283, 302, 314
American Hot Wax, 323
American in Paris, An, 147, 189
American Me, 110

American Quartet, The, 57, 63, 67, 126, 272, 277, 297, 399
American Werewolf in London, An, 43
Americana, 48
Ames Brothers, The, 43, 134, 151, 176, 269, 296, 315, 332, 356, 379, 417, 421
Ames, Leon, 234
Ammons, Albert, 178
Ammons, Gene, 44, 60, 122, 253, 341, 343, 379
Anchors Aweigh, 18, 169, 191
And the Angels Sing, 194
Anders, Tiffany, 2
Anderson, Carl, 158
Anderson, Deacon, 296
Anderson, Edmund, 107
Anderson, Ernestine, 311, 354
Anderson, Ivie, 106, 130, 158, 184, 243, 278, 376, 395
Anderson, Marian, 56, 82, 138, 258, 333
André, Fabian, 92
Andrews, Ernie, 112, 158, 310, 356, 418
Andrews, Julie, 10, 26, 50, 130, 147, 282, 290, 332, 344
Andrews, Lee, 38
Andrews Sisters, The, 10, 11, 14, 18, 33, 37, 46, 49, 71, 87, 88, 89–90, 91, 99, 104, 108, 133 137, 140, 158, 164, 170, 193 194, 196, 208, 234, 262, 271, 275, 283, 285, 287, 298, 305, 310, 312, 318, 320, 335, 343, 369, 374, 377, 381, 382, 389, 396, 399, 407, 409, 414, 418
Andy Hardy Meets Debutante, 176
Angela's Ashes, 84
Angel's Holiday, 124
Anglo-Persians, 321
Animal Crackers, 258, 331
Anka, Paul, 83, 294, 323, 369
Ann Carver's Profession, 349
Annie Hall, 185, 314
Ann-Margaret, 38, 163
Anthony, Ray, 3, 19, 33, 43, 44, 68, 73, 76, 78, 82, 92, 93, 95, 99, 107, 126, 132, 150, 161, 163, 165, 167, 172, 177, 186, 236, 237, 252, 258, 263,

264, 270, 284, 286, 344, 367, 377, 385, 408, 426

Anything Goes, 97, 211

Apache Country, 66

Applause, 189, 292, 328, 351, 361, 385, 412

Applewhite, Charlie, 98

Apollo 13, 43

Apollon, Dave, 339

April in Paris, 20

April Showers, 56, 100, 188, 277, 293, 292, 402

Arcaraz, Luis, 29

Arden-Ohman Orchestra, 239

Arkansas Judge, 284

Arkenstone, David, 264

Arlen, Harold, 21, 38, 114, 130, 158, 181, 187, 190, 204, 210, 341–42, 397

Armen, Kay, 67

Armour, Steve, 69

Arms, Russell, 8

Armstrong, Henry W., 347

Armstrong, Lillian, 343

Armstrong, Louis, 3, 5, 6, 18, 27, 33, 39, 40, 41, 42, 44, 45, 58, 63, 75, 77, 80, 84, 87, 90, 92, 100, 102, 105, 108, 111, 114, 127, 141, 146, 147, 149, 151, 152, 153, 156,158, 160, 162, 163, 167, 181, 182, 184, 186, 189, 190, 197, 199, 200–201, 207, 208, 215, 224, 228, 231, 232, 237, 243, 250, 256, 267, 270, 278, 283, 284, 286, 292, 299, 304, 313, 319, 331, 333, 334, 336, 337–38, 339, 341, 343, 344. 345, 356, 357, 358, 360, 361, 362, 365, 371, 375, 376, 379, 380, 383, 385, 387, 388, 394, 397, 400, 401, 402, 418, 420

Arnaz, Desi, 48, 126, 284, 321

Arnaz, Lucie, 253

Arnell, Amy, 330

Arnell, Ann, 155

Arnheim, Gus, 153, 162, 198, 348, 362

Arnold, Eddy, 28, 57, 82, 93, 133, 136, 137, 150, 155, 208, 236, 292, 300, 311, 322, 332, 360–61, 411

Arnold, Linda, 413

Arnold, Malcolm, 63

Arnstrom, Kenneth, 300

Arodin, Sidney, 207

Around the World in Eighty Days, 21

Arpin, John, 347

Arthur, 43

As Long as They're Happy, 69

As Thousands Cheer, 96

Asaf, George, 282

Ash, Paul, 7, 315, 361, 367

Ash, Sam, 35, 136

Ash Wednesday, 263

Astaire, Adele, 226, 423

Astaire, Fred, 92, 161, 216, 233, 241, 263, 297, 328, 359, 385, 387, 396

At Long Last Love, 210

At the Circus, 37, 43

At War With the Army, 374

Atcher, Bob, 417

Atlee, John Yorke, 212

Atkins, Chet, 25, 34, 35, 38, 73, 75, 117, 133, 137, 162–63, 171, 178, 186, 242, 244, 258, 268, 283, 289, 292, 310, 312, 321, 333, 346, 348, 370, 377, 378, 383, 403, 410

Atlantic City, 56, 76, 149, 241, 268, 276

Atwell, Winifred, 203

Aubert, Jeanne, 424

August, Jan, 43, 224, 275, 331

Augustana Choir, The, 272

Augustine, Joe, 86, 92, 174, 178, 237, 246, 286, 357, 377

Auld, George, 164

Auntie Mame, 371

Auric, Georges, 333

Austin, Gene, 2, 5, 7, 51, 56, 60, 106, 110, 115, 126, 145, 152, 193, 215, 218, 251, 280, 297, 301, 308, 319, 326, 333, 345, 373, 388, 389, 395, 414

Austin, Patti, 2, 243, 343

Austin, Sil, 299, 308, 372

Autry, Gene, 14, 16, 17, 27, 33, 44, 56, 57, 66, 68, 75, 79, 81–82, 84, 87, 91, 98, 110. 112. 116, 122, 124, 133, 137, 142, 178, 189, 194, 199, 204–205, 208, 209, 238, 249–50, 267, 274, 275, 278, 286–87, 291, 298, 301, 303, 306, 310, 316, 318, 322, 324, 331, 332,

335, 355, 365, 374, 392, 398, 399, 400, 409, 413, 417, 425, 426
Autumn in New York, 24
Autumn Leaves, 24
Avalon, Frankie, 11, 187, 364
Avery, Betty, 15
Avon Comedy Four, The, 365, 412
Awakening, The, 230
Awful Truth, The, 142
Axelrod, David, 327
Axton, Hoyt, 87, 163, 288
Ayer, Nat D., 272
Ayers, Mitchell, 66, 141, 419
Aznavour, Charles, 161
Azpiaza, Don, 125, 284, 321

Babbitt, Harry, 68, 194, 276, 363, 389, 403
Babe, 43
Babes in Arms, 76, 79, 153, 167, 175, 272, 277
Babes in Toyland, 180, 404
Babes on Broadway, 9, 28, 51, 164, 274, 385
Babes on Swing Street, 285, 321, 354
Baby Face, 26, 75, 159, 338
Bachelor of Arts, 96
Bachelors, The, 60, 83, 150, 171, 180, 231, 245, 253, 297, 403, 408
Back in the Saddle, 4, 27, 417
Bad News Bears Go to Japan, 355
Baer, Abel, 221, 363
Baez, Joan, 16, 42, 214, 270, 352, 388
Bagdasarian, Ross, 67
Bailey, Benny, 141, 200
Bailey, Buster, 160
Bailey, Jim, 131
Bailey, Mildred, 23, 45, 75, 77, 88, 108, 114, 127, 141, 143, 151, 177, 190, 196, 208, 215, 244, 247, 255, 258, 284, 288, 303, 312, 314, 328, 333, 336, 364, 365, 376, 386, 388, 392, 394, 410, 418
Bailey, Pearl, 33, 40, 97, 98, 233, 256, 337, 356, 367
Bainter, Fay, 349
Baird, Eugenie, 88, 254, 312, 363
Baja Marimba Band, The, 300

Baker, Anita, 150, 417
Baker, Belle, 12, 15, 43, 91, 109, 132, 259, 268, 385
Baker, Bobby, 267
Baker, Bonnie, 99, 271, 291, 330, 331, 418
Baker, Chet, 13, 43, 73, 77, 79, 81, 82, 101, 105, 122, 146, 157, 177, 214, 244, 253, 255, 273, 279, 284, 289, 338, 341, 343, 358, 364, 387, 392, 398, 407, 416, 426
Baker, Don, 82
Baker, Elsie, 71, 161, 365, 394
Baker, Josephine, 3, 38, 44, 47, 48, 84, 156, 285, 326
Baker, Kenny, 25, 38, 124, 195, 236, 274, 299, 335, 338
Baker, LaVern, 28, 267, 313, 358, 361, 405
Baker, Phil, 170, 339
Baldridge, Fanny, 209
Baldry, Long John, 28, 341
Baldwin, Renee Busbee, 210
Ball, Ernest R., 212, 218, 248, 393, 406
Ball, Kenny, 33. 136, 243, 267
Ball, Lucille, 37, 48
Ball, Michael, 10, 69, 101, 104, 420
Ballard, Kay, 107, 200, 304, 313
Ballard, Pat, 241
Ballard, Russ, 401
Ballew, Smith, 131, 388, 418
Bancroft, Anne, 135, 349, 417
Bancroft, George, 349
Band Wagon, The, 417
Bandana Land, 423
Banjo Kings, The, 8–9, 41, 50, 73, 75, 87, 137, 142, 179, 181, 193, 323, 348, 417
Banjo on My Knee, 338
Bankhead, Tallulah, 232, 419
Barbed Wire, 238
Barber, Chris, 90, 243, 280, 344, 349, 389
Barbour, Dave, 225, 227
Barbour, Joyce, 421
Barcelata, Lorenzo, 230
Bare, Bobby, 133
Barnard, Bob, 4, 334

Barnes, Jimmy, 344
Barnes, Paul, 90, 390
Barnet, Charlie, 14, 44, 61, 65, 76, 77, 81, 105, 108, 116, 122, 182, 186, 284, 328, 389, 398, 401
Barnez, Liz, 216
Barrie, Gracie, 414
Barrie, Howard, 425
Barris, Harry, 162, 410
Barron, Blue, 20, 22, 113, 158, 167, 230, 276, 291, 425
Barroso, Ary, 47
Barry, Donald, 252
Barry, Gracie, 138
Barry, Leon, 264
Barthelmess, Richard, 388
Bartholomew, Dave, 8, 96, 183, 416
Bartley, Chris, 351, 361
Barton, Eileen, 168
Barton, John, 120
Basie, Count, 12, 18, 20, 25, 46, 51, 65, 81, 84, 86, 87, 89, 96, 99, 102, 103, 106, 107, 110, 111, 117, 151, 156, 160, 162, 167, 172, 173, 174, 178, 214, 216, 237, 243, 247, 252, 255, 267, 278, 279, 286, 289, 290, 300, 314, 316, 332, 333, 334, 335, 337, 341, 344–45, 350, 352, 363, 368, 372, 414, 417, 418, 424, 426
Bass, Paul, 6
Bassey, Shirley, 10, 69, 97, 171, 178, 184, 256, 261–62, 263, 376, 408, 420
Bassman, George, 174
Bates, Alan, 90
Bates, Charles, 132
Bates, Katherine Lee, 17
Bathing Beauty, 153
Batley, Noleen, 110, 182, 356, 399
Battle, Kathleen, 178
Battleground, 163, 348
Bauer, Bill, 233
Baum, Bernie, 250
Baum, Charles, 32, 405
Baur, Franklyn, 246, 259, 307, 316, 373
Bautier, Michele, 129, 335, 339
Baxter, Ann, 227
Baxter, Les, 9, 34, 289, 373, 379, 426, 427

Bayes, Nora, 91, 132, 147, 170, 192, 234, 281, 319, 355, 394
Baylor, Helen, 38
Beach Boys, The, 170, 294
Beaches, 117, 417
Beatles, The, 7, 423
Beatty, Ethel, 237
Beau, Hinie, 209
Beau James, 131, 229, 322, 406
Beaudoin, Gerry, 356
Beautiful But Broke, 288, 320
Beautiful Thing, 92
Beb, Andy, 356
Because of You, 336
Because You're Mine, 13
Bechet, Sidney, 22, 41, 44, 59, 63, 80, 90, 111, 140, 156, 167, 168, 228, 243, 267, 270, 273, 307, 319, 342, 371, 394, 399
Beckett, Scotty, 4, 50, 399
Beckett, T. A., 66
Bedelia, Bonnie, 39
Bee, Molly, 162
Beery, Wallace, 399
Beetlejuice, 30
Begaye, Julia, 262
Behind the Eight Ball, 395, 419
Bei Mir Bist Du Schoen, 37
Beiderbecke, Bix, 31, 63, 65, 75, 101, 114, 121, 127, 179, 207, 216, 240, 297, 300, 303, 324, 332, 344, 345, 361, 386, 387, 395, 421
Belafonte, Harry, 19, 30, 74, 191, 195, 278, 312, 369
Bell, Bobby, 354
Bell, Rico, 352
Bellamy, Ralph, 142
Belle, Barbara, 346
Belle of the Nineties, 238
Belles on Their Toes, 207, 212, 370, 399, 403
Bells of Capistrano, The, 23, 110
Bells of St. Mary's, The, 38
Belmonts, The, 177, 361
Benanti, Laura, 69, 115, 181, 341
Bendix, William, 400
Beneke, Tex, 42, 43, 60, 88, 99, 103,

150, 167, 196, 213, 284, 285, 289,
  316, 339, 342, 346, 351, 401, 416
Benjamin, Bennie, 155, 272, 395
Benjamin, P. J., 311
Bennett, David, 51
Bennett, Lee, 187, 269
Bennett, Roy C., 262
Bennett, Tony, 12, 20, 36, 38, 43, 44,
  62, 66, 89, 107, 133, 160, 161, 167,
  169, 173, 182, 185, 196, 204, 228,
  243, 249, 254, 264, 267, 285, 296,
  325, 327, 350, 358, 374, 382, 390,
  393, 402, 419, 421
Benny Goodman Story, The, 18, 25, 63,
  122, 124, 210, 237, 245, 278, 319,
  323, 341
Benoric, Steve, 269
Benson, Ada, 423
Benson, George, 261
Benson, Ray, 371
Benton, Brooks, 108, 111
Berdan, Harry B., 424
Bergantine, Borney, 254
Bergen, Polly, 97, 102
Bergere, Roy, 145
Bergman, Henry, 15
Bergman, Ingrid, 63
Berigan, Bunny, 7, 54, 81, 105, 153,
  178, 219, 231, 235, 285, 292, 329,
  331, 345, 364, 374, 381, 421
Berkeley, Busby, 421
Berle, Milton, 262, 309
Berlin, Irving, 5, 9, 10, 12, 15, 19, 43,
  54, 77, 96, 101, 118, 126, 145, 160,
  189, 207, 227, 230, 233, 267, 296,
  299, 307, 311, 315, 329, 333, 368–69,
  392, 396, 409, 415, 418
Bernadine, 218
Bernard, Felix, 74, 407
Bernard, Sophie, 290
Bernie, Ben, 7, 61, 81, 153, 176, 184,
  207, 208, 209, 210, 211, 252, 287,
  300, 307, 326, 349, 353, 368, 404, 414
Bernier, Buddy, 28, 289
Berry, Chu, 202
Berry, Chuck, 191
Berry, Leon, 343
Bert Rigby, You're a Fool, 92, 106

Bessie and Me, 144, 267
Best of Enemies, 272
Best of Everything, 6
Best Things in Life Are Free, The, 184,
  197, 373
Best, William, 109
Best Years of Our Lives, The, 18, 207
Bestor, Don, 359, 376, 380
Betsy, 43
Betti, Henri, 58
Betty Co-Ed, 293
Beul, Arthur, 374
Bevel, Charles, 123
Beverley Sisters, The, 162, 214, 262
Bey, Salome, 422
Beyond the Forest, 62
Beyond the Purple Hills, 79
Big Boy, 169, 184
Big Broadcast, The, 84, 122, 239, 371,
  375, 396
Big Broadcast of 1936, 124
Big City, 87, 118, 320, 391
Big Deal, 7, 8, 33, 63, 100, 131, 141,
  233, 250, 415
Big Show, The, 232, 290
Big Sombrero, The, 65
Big Store, The, 164
Big T.N.T. Show, The, 114
Big Town, The, 104, 224
Bigard, Barney, 54, 62, 243
Bigelow, Bob, 132
Bigley, Isabel, 266
Bilk, Acker, 160, 241, 264, 268, 279,
  335, 379, 386, 403, 410
Billings, Bud, 93
Billings, William, 61–62
Billion Dollar Scandal, 53
Billy's Hollywood Screen Kiss, 219
Bingham, G. Clifton, 220
Bird, 12, 20, 151
Birth of the Blues, 22, 50, 238, 257, 319,
  337, 338, 371, 384
Bishop, Elvin, 269
Bishop, Henry, 142
Bishop, Joe, 43
Bishop, Walter, 351
Black and Blue, 5, 40, 46, 152, 178, 237,
  338, 341, 354

Black, Ben, 245
Black, Frances, 4, 103
Black, James M., 397
Black, Johnny S., 74, 283
Black, Quint, 296
Black, Ted, 178
Blackbirds of 1928, 152
Blackbirds of 1930, 84
Blackboard Jungle, The, 302
Blackburn, John, 246
Blackburn, Tom, 28
Blaine, Terry, 23, 212
Blaine, Vivian, 353, 403
Blair, Janet, 231
Blair Witch Project, The, 200
Blake, Eubie, 175, 236–37, 273
Blake, James W., 322
Blake, Kenny, 311
Blake, Norman, 57
Blakey, Art, 47, 168, 188, 255, 330, 345–46
Blanc, Mel, 19
Blanchard, Terrence, 342
Bland, Bobby, 58, 337, 341
Bland, James, 56, 119, 180
Blas, Johnny, 295
Blaufuss, Walter, 255, 422
Blazing Sun, The, 14
Bledsoe, Jules, 215
Bleyer, Archie, 54, 179, 224, 236, 241, 246, 262, 269, 293, 313, 346, 407
Blitzstein, Marc, 224
Bloch, Ray, 41, 120, 177
Block, Dan, 64
Block, Martin, 158
Blonde Crazy, 400
Blonde in Black, The, 154
Blondell, Joan, 71, 365
Blood, Sweat and Tears, 119
Bloom, Marty, 86
Bloom, Rube, 78, 89, 108, 151, 280, 376
Bloom, Vera, 191
Blue, Ben, 50, 180
Blue Hawaii, 14
Blue Jeans, 287
Blue Ridge Rangers, 192

Blue Skies, 10, 15, 19, 44, 118, 146, 147, 190, 207, 228, 307, 312, 334
Blue Sky Boys, The, 4, 89–90, 120, 413
Blue Veil, The, 71, 365
Blue Velvet, 44, 218
Blues Brothers, The, 239
Blues for Lovers, 55, 69
Blues in the Night, 158, 220, 268, 366, 405
Blyth, Ann, 20, 25, 39, 45, 48, 152, 171, 189, 197, 226, 247, 257, 278, 279, 285, 332, 399, 406
Bob and Jean, 55
Bocage, Peter, 60
Body and Soul, 46
Bogan, Martin, 351
Boland, Clay, 127
Bolcom, William, 5, 41, 73, 123, 155, 161, 211, 220, 277, 313, 380, 386, 413
Bold, Richard, 370
Boles, John, 3
Bolger, Ray, 80, 168
Boll Weevil Jazz Band, The, 200
Bolton, Michael, 376
Bombo, 53, 256, 374
Bon Bon, 18, 127, 186
Bond, Carrie Jacobs, 161
Bond, Johnny, 14, 28, 57, 133, 135, 140
Bonime, Joseph, 209
Bonney, Betty, 101, 139
Booker, James, 38
Boone, Pat, 7, 8, 10, 15, 24, 45, 58, 60, 61, 82, 85, 89, 93, 98, 110, 136, 137, 150, 170, 172, 192, 209, 215, 218, 235, 254, 263, 265, 302, 358, 361, 365, 372, 398, 418
Boots and Saddles, 355
Booze, Bea, 313
Border G-Man, 27
Bordman, Gerald, 6
Bordoni, Irene, 256
Borge, Victor, 339
Borgnine, Ernest, 184
Bori, Lucrezia, 159
Born to Dance, 97
Born to Sing, 28
Bostic, Earl, 54, 61, 82, 107, 218, 236, 244, 326, 334, 356, 369, 377

Boston, Gretha, 338, 343
Boston Pops Orchestra, 191, 272
Boswell, Connee, 10, 12, 16, 32, 81, 98, 102, 135, 143, 152, 175, 209, 214, 216, 222, 233, 244, 257, 263, 271, 276, 279, 311, 342, 346, 380, 381, 386, 393, 414
Boswell Sisters, The, 10, 39, 84, 89, 100, 129, 175, 184, 206, 209, 243, 250, 253, 256, 269, 314, 334, 337, 364, 372, 388, 420
Bothwell, Johnny, 64, 343
Botsford, George, 126
Bottoms Up, 404
Boulanger, Georges, 258
Boulden, Alice, 105
Bound for Glory, 91, 123, 330, 369
Boutelje, Phil, 63
Bow, Clara, 26
Bowen, Jimmy, 387
Bower, Arthur De Courcey, 227
Bowers, Kenny, 167
Bowery to Broadway, 73, 380, 384
Bowie, Lester, 396
Bowlly, Al, 3, 8, 45, 96, 124, 126, 131, 133, 135, 136, 151, 168, 175, 183, 196, 203, 214, 217, 231, 280, 301, 311, 365, 368, 372, 382, 402, 409, 415, 420
Bowman, Brooks, 95
Boy With Green Hair, 262
Boyd, Jimmy, 162
Boyer, Anita, 77, 129, 259
Boyer, Lucienne, 129
Brace, Janet, 357
Bradford, Barker, 65
Bradley, Everett, 12
Bradley, Kitty, 187
Bradley, Will, 33–34, 46, 106, 108, 115, 215
Brady, Alice, 348
Brady Bunch, The, 112
Braff, Ruby, 15, 84, 96, 136, 143, 153, 169, 182, 211, 214, 216, 304, 308, 312, 336, 343, 350, 374, 394, 407, 418
Braisted, Harry, 424
Brammer, Julius, 197
Branch, Gretchen, 159

Brand, Oscar, 126–27
Brando, Marlon, 82
Brandow, Jerry, 140
Brandwynne, Nat, 155, 171, 175, 192, 205, 230, 367
Brannen, Steve, 318
Brascia, John, 228
Brasselle, Keefe, 51, 167, 169, 224, 230, 268, 272, 305, 321, 406, 415
Braxton Brothers, The, 19
Brazil, 47
Brecht, Bertolt, 224
Brecker, Michael, 335
Breen, Bobby, 14, 185, 247, 289, 334
Bremer, Lucille, 325
Brennan, J. Keirn, 212
Brennan, Maureen, 340
Brennan, Walter, 141
Brent, George, 169
Brent, Jack, 93
Bresler, Jerry, 106
Breuer, Ernest, 86
Brewer, Clyde, 183
Brewer, Teresa, 77, 105, 120, 182, 250, 313, 426
Brian, Donald, 367
Brice, Fanny, 256, 313, 419
Brice, Monty C., 77, 350
Bricktop's Jazz Babes, 300
Bridgewater, Dee Dee, 276, 342, 379, 390
Briggs, Bunny, 178
Brigh, Teresa, 134
Brigode, Ace, 405, 414
Brine, Mary D., 136
Bring on the Girls, 64
Bring Your Smile Along, 87, 321
Bringing Up Baby, 152
Brito, Phil, 68, 186, 297, 383
Britt, Addy, 6
Britt, Albert, 111
Broadway, 9, 76, 84, 175, 331, 349, 415
Broadway Hoofer, The, 51, 277, 320
Broadway Hostess, 74
Broadway Melody of 1936, 276
Broadway Melody of 1938, 331, 420
Broadway Rhythm, 13, 167, 229, 272, 292, 332

Broadway Serenade, 220
Broadway to Hollywood, 36, 66, 144, 223
Brockman, James, 89, 156, 174
Brodsky, Roy, 298
Bromberg, David, 344
Bronson, George, 201
Bronx Tale, A, 110
Brooke, Bobby, 85
Brooke, Tyler, 56
Brooks, Arthur, 110
Brooks, Beryl, 217
Brooks, Bobby, 23
Brooks, Garth, 118, 141, 209
Brooks, Harry, 6, 41
Brooks, Jack, 275
Brooks, Leslie, 121
Brooks, Mel, 349
Brooks, Randy, 56, 93, 200
Brooks, Richard, 110
Brooks, Robert, 213
Brooks, Shelton, 76, 330
Broonzy, Big Bill, 28, 313, 325
Brother Bones, 349
Brothers Cazimero, The, 14
Brothers Four, The, 34, 191, 312, 369
Brown, A. H., 421
Brown, A. Seymour, 272
Brown, Barbara, 415
Brown, Clifford, 61, 96, 151, 168, 217, 279
Brown, Edna, 71, 290
Brown, James, 7, 114, 243, 292
Brown, Kay, 200
Brown, Les, 7, 16, 18, 23, 54, 64, 78, 89, 92, 93, 101, 107, 108, 124, 139, 158, 163, 179, 182, 185, 186, 205, 213, 216, 231, 245, 264, 285, 297, 299, 315, 333, 345, 368, 371, 377, 379, 417
Brown, Lew, 37, 88, 163, 177, 184, 197, 259, 280, 319, 329, 373
Brown, Milton, 89, 332, 345
Brown, Nacio Herb, 282, 283, 328
Brown, Ray, 178, 243, 265, 289, 343, 355, 356, 394
Brown, Ruth, 46, 113, 121, 150, 258, 267, 327, 338, 354, 391, 402, 415
Brown, Tom, 230, 348

Browne, Kirk, 120, 198
Browne, Louis, 248
Browne, Roscoe Lee, 24, 200
Browns, The, 45, 91, 133, 140, 255, 274, 275, 299, 369, 401
Brox Sisters, The, 147, 207
Brubeck, Dave, 13, 22, 38, 41, 43, 45, 49, 79, 98, 101, 107, 135, 188, 210, 221, 286, 289, 292, 301, 364, 379, 418
Bruce, Carol, 3, 158, 174, 419
Brunies, Henry, 19
Brunies, Merritt, 19
Brunner, Cliff, 169, 273, 280, 330, 345, 373, 418
Bruns, George, 28
Bryan, Alfred, 67, 153, 285
Bryan, Vincent P., 69, 91, 179, 409
Bryant, Anita, 118
Bryant, Boudleaux, 11
Bryant, Jimmy, 93, 244, 412
Bryant, Ray, 150, 406
Bryson, Jeanie, 344
Bublett, John "Bubbles," 319
Bubbling Brown Sugar, 119, 143, 158, 184, 266, 331, 335, 341, 349, 352, 356, 365
Buchanan, Roy, 139, 348
Buck, Gene, 71, 136
Buck Privates, 46, 171
Buck, Richard Henry, 80, 199
Buckley, Betty, 69, 206, 382
Buckner, Teddy, 270, 343
Buddy Holly Story, The, 99
Buffalo Bills, The, 19, 36, 41, 80, 121, 150, 167, 181, 253, 319, 347, 380, 384, 442
Buffett, Jimmy, 170, 191, 276
Bugatti, George, 368
Bullets Over Broadway, 207, 211, 261, 290, 374, 397, 421, 427
Bullock, Chick, 2, 75, 235. 329, 381, 388
Bunny, Jive, 7, 11, 59, 88, 285
Burgalat, Bertrand, 287
Burge, Gregg, 54
Burgess, Sonny, 129, 292
Burgie, Irving, 191
Burke, Clyde, 401

Burke, Joe, 22, 56, 73, 109, 212, 244, 297, 301
Burke, Johnny, 137, 177, 242, 273, 289, 315, 391, 424
Burke, Solomon, 34, 91, 388
Burke, Sonny, 55, 225, 303
Burleigh, Henry Thacker, 82, 352
Burnett, Carol, 126, 266, 349, 357
Burnett, Earl, 162
Burnett, Ernie, 256
Burnette, Johnny, 58
Burns, George, 184
Burns, Ralph, 95
Burr, Harry, 181
Burr, Henry, 15, 20, 35, 72, 143, 166, 174, 235, 247, 285, 375, 391, 392
Burrell, Kenny, 107, 113, 149, 168, 189, 204, 290, 358, 406
Burris, Jim, 29
Burstyn, Ellen, 189
Burton, Ann, 205
Burton, Fred, 208
Burton, Val, 285
Burtnett, Earl, 113, 301
Burwell, Cliff, 349
Buscemi, Steve, 263
Busch, Lou, 246, 309
Busdon, Eric, 313
Bushkin, Joe, 147, 178, 226
Busse, Henry, 177, 185, 391–92
Butch Minds the Baby, 419
Butera, Sam, 104
Butler, Bill, 249
Butler, Jerry, 110, 327
Butterfield, Billy, 2, 60, 246, 341, 363, 387, 391
Butterfield, Erskine, 77
Butterfield, James Austin, 398
Butterworth, Donna, 40
By the Beautiful Sea, 180
By the Light of the Silvery Moon, 8, 50, 235, 277, 423
Byas, Don, 61, 370, 418
Bye Bye Braverman, 91
Byers, Billy, 424
Bygraves, Max, 5, 31, 60, 81, 85, 133, 135, 155, 169, 254, 272, 282, 318, 321, 381, 384, 388, 391, 403, 415

Byington, Spring, 181
Byng, Douglas, 240
Byrd, Carolyn, 350
Byrd, Charlie, 38, 201, 280, 367, 406, 427

Caan, James, 188, 233
Cabin in the Sky, 319
Cabin Kids, The, 274
Cables, George, 325
Cadillacs, The, 89
Cadman, Charles Wakefield, 22
Caesar, Irving, 94, 183, 197, 347, 413
Cagney, James, 31, 155, 281
Cahill, Marie, 73, 262, 380
Cahn, Sammy, 37, 78, 111, 126, 139, 183, 186, 209, 216, 288, 300, 311, 322, 356, 363, 369, 381, 382
Cailliet, Lucien, 272
Cain and Mabel, 203
Cain, Jackie, 50, 112, 245, 276
Caine Mutiny, The, 151
Cairo, 35, 142, 385
Caldwell, Anne, 159
Caldwell, Bobby, 13, 38
Caledonia Heritage Pipers, The, 413
Calhern, Louis, 320
California Ramblers, The, 53, 106, 362
California Swing Cats, The, 80, 182, 201
Call of the Canyon, 331, 355
Callahan, Fred B., 386
Callahan, J. Will, 327
Callaway, Ann Hampton, 12, 13, 38, 46, 88, 97, 102, 121, 138, 146, 170, 178, 181, 190, 253, 300, 305, 341, 357, 358, 419
Callaway, Liz, 276, 390
Callen, Michael, 122
Calloway, Cab, 27, 39, 45, 51, 52, 81, 89, 103, 114–15, 145, 149, 158, 169, 190, 196, 239, 240, 243, 245, 261, 268, 331, 332, 337, 342, 356, 400, 406
Calvanes, The, 89
Calvert, Carter, 104
Calypso Heat Wave, 30
Camarata, Tutti, 47
Cameron, Ruth, 384

Campbell, Albert, 174, 181, 375, 406
Campbell, David, 303
Campbell, Glen, 11, 16, 112, 137, 270, 422
Campbell, James, 123, 167, 321, 376
Campbell, Judy, 264
Campo, Del, 120
Campus Kids, The, 276
Candido, Candy, 5
Cannon, Ace, 85, 215, 243, 258, 279, 292, 298, 299, 308, 344, 348, 358, 416
Cannon, Freddy, 53, 56, 60, 109, 387
Cannon, Hughie, 40, 111
Canova, Judy, 149, 224, 294
Can't Help Singing, 16, 118, 142, 220
Can't Stop the Music, 74
Cantinflas, 335
Cantor, Eddie, 7, 8, 26, 29, 31, 50, 51, 53, 67, 75, 84, 91, 94, 109, 147–48, 156, 162, 164, 166, 185, 190, 212, 223–24, 228, 229–30, 251, 256, 268, 270, 271, 272, 275, 291, 292, 303, 305, 310, 312, 318, 348, 374, 376, 385, 395, 399, 402, 414, 415
Canyon Passage, 276
Capehart, Jerry, 34
Captain Carey, USA, 243
Captain Newman, M.D., 413
Carawan, Guy, 388
Careless Lady, 12
Carey, Bill, 426
Carey, Bob, 30
Carey, Joseph Buell, 322
Carey, Mariah, 371
Carle, Frankie, 42, 82, 84, 98, 103, 116, 117, 140, 143, 151, 164, 171, 182, 208, 230, 241, 265, 272, 274, 279, 311, 328, 339, 346, 353, 363, 364, 383, 387
Carlisle, Elsie, 214
Carlisle, Kitty, 382
Carlo, Monte, 360
Carlson, Russ, 52, 131, 206, 388
Carlton, Larry, 143
Carlyle, Russ, 22
Carman, Jenks Tex, 52, 411
Carmichael, Hoagy, 1, 18, 29–30, 31, 76, 113–14, 134–35, 156–57, 195, 204,

207, 208, 214, 243–44, 262, 275–76, 279, 303, 325, 330, 338–39, 386
Carnival in Flanders, 137
Carol, Sue, 350
Carolina Blues, 363
Carolina Moon, 56, 312
Carpenter, Carlton, 1, 163, 305
Carpenter, Charles, 418
Carpenter, Thelma, 102, 116, 156, 169, 175, 367
Carpenters, The, 141, 162, 209
Carr, Helen, 125
Carr, Jimmy, 178
Carr, Joe "Fingers," 14, 309
Carr, Joyce, 253
Carr, Leon, 366
Carr, Michael, 335
Carr, Vikki, 12, 51, 258, 290, 294, 381
Carradine, David, 330, 369
Carreras, José, 13, 16, 36, 243, 408
Carrington, Neil, 327
Carroll, Barbara, 2, 114, 122, 148, 161, 249
Carroll, Bob, 29, 265, 295, 364, 398
Carroll, David, 178
Carroll, Georgia, 363
Carroll, Harry, 50, 173, 375
Carroll, Jimmy, 242, 288, 291
Carroll, John, 296
Carroll, Toni, 385
Carson, Doris, 189
Carson, Ernie, 287
Carson, Fiddlin' John, 81
Carson, Jenny Lou, 192
Carson, Mindy, 90, 151, 176, 214, 252, 280, 390
Carter, Benny, 7, 82, 120, 122, 137, 151, 162, 189, 190, 235, 244, 326, 382, 389, 400
Carter, Betty, 23, 45, 98, 135, 141, 155, 178, 231, 258, 314, 356, 377, 390
Carter, Billy, 364
Carter, Caitlin, 115
Carter, Calvin, 124
Carter Family, The, 57, 104, 163, 188, 290, 320
Carter, John, 34, 213

Carter, Nell, 105, 143, 185, 189, 234, 396
Carter, Stanley, 424
Carus, Emma, 9, 36, 390
Caruso, Enrico, 35, 281
Casablanca, 185, 286, 382
Case, Russ, 426
Casey, Ken, 349
Cash, Johnny, 5, 45, 57, 65, 66, 111, 122, 139, 163, 236, 298, 300, 325, 411
Cass, Mama, 151
Cassard, Jules, 19
Castle, Jo Ann, 9, 54, 89, 117, 144, 176, 224, 283, 288, 296, 349, 395, 399, 413
Casucci, Leonello, 197
Cates, George, 245
Cathcart, Dick, 270
Cattle Town, 31
Cavalcade, 272, 282, 394
Cavallaro, Carmen, 8, 24, 102, 146, 151, 172, 210, 259, 311, 334, 351, 371, 372, 377, 380, 403, 424, 427
Cavanaugh, James, 198, 424
Cavanaugh, Jessie, 46
Cha-Cha-Cha Boom!, 114, 215
Chabrier, Alexis, 144
Chacksfield, Frank, 97, 140, 243, 369
Chad and Jeremy, 263, 315, 406
Challis, Bill, 245
Chaloff, Serge, 129
Chamberlain, Richard, 11, 23, 54
Chambers Brothers, The, 330
Chambers, Craig, 68
Chambers-Ketchum, Annie, 46
Champagne Waltz, The, 59
Champion, Gower, 189
Champion, Marge, 189
Champs, The, 98, 277, 335
Chance, Slim, 41
Chances Are, 59
Chandler, Gene, 110
Chandler, Karen, 157, 373
Chandler, Stan, 69, 203, 217, 317
Change of Heart, 259
Change Your Life, 338
Channing, Carol, 6, 427
Chantels, The, 58, 233
Chaplin, Charles, 327

Chaplin, Saul, 37, 288, 300, 381
Chapman, Graham, 84, 192, 233
Chapman, Topsy, 100
Charioteers, The, 68
Charles, Dick, 14
Charles, Hughie, 389
Charles, Ray, 3, 9, 11, 17, 27, 53, 55, 58, 69, 81, 91, 114, 126, 132, 139, 147, 166, 177, 178, 231, 241, 245, 257, 262, 332, 356, 360, 368, 375, 379, 414, 417, 422, 426
Charleston Chasers, 32, 59, 103, 106
Charo, 38
Chasing Rainbows, 130–31
Chateaus, The, 76
Chatman, Peter, 99
Chazz Cats, The, 101, 106, 352, 405
Cheap Trick, 8
Cheaper By the Dozen, 334, 399
Cheatham, Doc, 151, 201, 237, 242, 343, 362
Checker, Chubby, 29
Checkmates, The, 1, 201, 243, 366, 390
Chenille Sisters, The, 1, 306
Cher, 147, 256, 303, 406
Chescoe, Laurie, 182
Chester, Bob, 98, 196, 301
Chevalier Brothers, The, 53, 106, 195
Chevalier, Maurice, 115, 167, 176, 255, 385, 415
Chicago, 62
Chicago Rhythm Kings, The, 156, 341
Chicken Every Sunday, 399
Chinatown, 96
Chipmunks, The, 11, 17, 112
Chittison, Herman, 45
Choates, Harry, 216
Chordettes, The, 109, 241
Chords, The, 317
Christian, Charlie, 156
Christie, Lou, 224
Christmas Holiday, 15, 336
Christy, E. P., 121, 257
Christy, Edward, 274
Christy, June, 2, 13, 21, 89, 97, 102, 107, 111, 114, 122, 137, 147, 148, 151, 162, 178, 184, 186, 188, 221, 279, 288, 368, 398, 406, 410

Churchill, Frank, 404
Churchill, Savannah, 89
City Directory, The, 287
Claire, Bernice, 408
Claire, Dorothy, 286
Claire, Ina, 136
Clarice, June, 174
Clambake Seven, 396
Clapton, Eric, 85, 341, 352
Clarc, Sidncy, 223, 280
Clare Sisters, The, 143, 163, 223, 283,
   345
Clark, Buddy, 29, 64, 93, 97, 116, 129,
   166, 171, 172, 185, 198, 201, 285,
   291, 308, 340, 359, 360, 387
Clark, Gladys, 15
Clark, Judy, 320
Clark, Petula, 157, 236, 418
Clark, Roy, 92, 120, 300
Clark, Sanford, 7
Clark Sisters, The, 26, 37, 92, 174, 379,
   382, 393
Clark, Thais, 5
Clarke, Gordon, 28
Clarke, Grant, 228, 296, 313, 388
Clarkson, Geoff, 141
Clarkson, Harry, 141
Clary, Robert, 205, 367
Clayderman, Richard, 38, 379
Clayton Brothers, The, 333
Clayton, Jan, 266
Clayton, Lee, 27
Clayton, Willie, 280
Cleftones, The, 109, 135, 299
Clemen, Bettine, 103
Clements, Vassar, 61
Cleveland, Phyllis, 200
Cliff Adams Singers, The, 28, 76, 109,
   140, 159, 180, 181, 201, 247, 294,
   361, 389
Clifford, Gordon, 162, 283
Cline, Maggie, 91
Cline, Patsy, 40, 90, 133, 218, 221, 310,
   332, 335, 348, 361, 418, 422
Clinton, George, 298
Clinton, Larry, 36, 55, 62, 82, 84, 135,
   151, 156, 157, 215, 218, 258, 263,
   276, 280, 303, 312, 376, 407, 419

Cliquot Club Eskimos, The, 25, 238
Clock, The, 403
Clooney, Rosemary, 1, 15, 19, 20, 34,
   38, 49, 62, 67, 89, 98, 101, 108, 109,
   110, 111, 115, 119, 121, 122, 140,
   146, 147, 149–50, 157, 158, 169, 170,
   184,186, 189, 209, 224, 228, 237, 240,
   247, 264, 272, 276, 286, 292, 293,
   312, 314, 325, 334, 358, 365, 367,
   371, 374, 388, 389, 402, 403, 407
Closer You Get, 201
Clouds of Joy, The, 73
Clough, Arthur, 90
Clovers, The, 366
Clowns in Clover, 86
Club Royal Orchestra, The, 318
Club, The, 409
Coal Miner's Daughter, 16, 133, 348
Coasters, The, 427
Coates, Eric, 326
Cobb, Arnett, 60, 108
Cobb, Will D., 313, 345, 385
Coben, Cy, 275
Coburn, Charles, 227, 415
Coburn, Richard, 402
Cochran, Dorcas, 3, 5
Cochran, Eddie, 357
Cocker, Joe, 51
Cockeyed Cavaliers, 68
Cockeyed World, The, 140, 201, 281
Coco, 5
Cocoanut Grove, 312
Cocoanuts, The, 15
Coe, David Allan, 268
Cogane, Nelson, 388
Cohan, George M., 281
Cohn, Irving, 415
Cola, Johnny, 382
Colcord, Lincoln, 340
Cole, Buddy, 190, 243, 245, 264, 326,
   332, 334, 408
Cole, Cozy, 198, 264
Cole, Holly, 295, 376
Cole, Nat "King," 3, 5, 6, 11, 21, 24,
   25, 27, 29, 30, 33, 38, 54, 55, 61, 64,
   68, 76, 78, 87, 90, 92, 101, 107, 108,
   109, 112, 113, 123, 141, 146, 150,
   151, 155, 156, 160, 163, 167, 168,

170, 171, 177, 184, 185, 187, 205,
206, 211, 212, 216, 217, 218, 222,
226, 230, 233, 238, 240, 242, 243,
244, 251, 254, 261, 262, 264, 275,
279, 284, 286, 289, 290, 297, 299,
305, 320, 327, 331, 334, 338, 339, 349–
350, 357, 358, 364, 373, 379, 381,
382, 385, 391, 392, 393, 398, 405,
415, 418, 424, 426
Cole, Natalie, 24, 25, 34, 76, 88, 109,
121, 134, 188, 218, 222, 243, 262,
280, 305, 327, 335, 357, 358, 373,
381, 382
Cole, Paula, 25
Cole, Richie, 383
Cole, Robert, 380
Coleman, Bill, 87, 156, 238, 350, 359
Coleman, Cy, 38, 407
Coleman, Desiree, 7, 131
Coleman, Emil, 214, 238, 329
Coleman, Wallace, 387
College Coach, 198
College Holiday, 340
College Humor, 163
Collegiate, 125
Collete, Buddy, 58, 76, 205
Collie, Max, 270
Collins, Arthur, 1, 9, 40, 57, 69, 101,
126, 270, 294, 328, 330 380, 396,
412
Collins, Dorothy, 147
Collins, Judy, 16, 49, 170, 209
Collins, Sam, 176
Colorado, 272, 289
Colquhoun, Christopher, 143
Coltrane, John, 13, 102, 111, 168, 214,
222, 261, 356, 379, 406
Columbia Stellar Quartet, The, 32, 101
Columbians, The, 353
Columbo, Russ, 12, 126, 155, 198, 218,
292, 311, 343, 348, 372, 418, 424
Colville, John, 73
Come and Get It, 24
Come See the Paradise, 88, 217
Comedian Harmonists, The, 403
Comer, Imogene, 179, 317
Como, Perry, 1, 11, 19, 36, 44, 56, 58,
67, 77, 79, 81, 93, 96, 109, 110, 113,

116, 133, 138, 141, 144, 150, 156,
159, 161, 162, 165, 166, 170, 173,
186, 187, 188, 208, 214, 217, 218,
219, 232, 243, 247, 249, 251, 252,
266, 283, 289, 292, 294, 297, 305,
310, 312, 355, 360, 371, 399, 408,
422, 427
Comstock, Bobby, 192, 358
Comstock, Frances, 146
Condon, Eddy, 53, 63, 103, 121, 151,
162, 165, 174, 228, 235, 247, 251,
267, 278, 279, 313, 319, 326, 333,
340, 343, 347, 349, 395
Coney Island, 40, 50, 76, 209, 272, 274,
292, 294, 393, 404
Confrey, Edward, 324
Confrey, Zez, 344
Conley, Larry, 68
Conn, Chester, 405
Connelly, Reg, 123, 167, 321, 376, 381
Connick, Harry, Jr., 24, 25, 69, 88, 97,
185, 208, 250, 264, 341, 407
Connolly, Billy, 262
Connor, Chris, 64, 108, 273, 357, 376,
419
Connor, Pierre Norman, 393
Connor, Tommie, 162
Conrad, Con, 31, 59, 223, 229, 237,
324, 418, 427
Conrad, Richard, 249
Contact, 424
Conte, Dick, 174
Controllers, The, 31
Conway, Julie, 194
Conway, Russ, 296, 309, 310
Cooder, Ry, 64, 67, 362
Cook, Al, 269
Cook, Barbara, 56, 87, 102, 132, 134,
152, 161, 173, 209, 267, 278, 348,
391
Cook, Joe, 105
Cook, Lawrence, 275
Cooke, Sam, 43, 58, 109, 111, 267, 280,
356, 358, 364, 373
Cool, Harry, 68, 98, 259
Cooley, Eddie, 104
Cooley, Spade, 204–5, 211, 280, 316,
324, 403

Coolidge, Edwina, 15
Coolidge, Rita, 104
Coon-Sanders Nighthawk Orchestra,
    199, 201, 298, 300, 414–15
Cooney, Andy, 162
Cooper, Bud, 298
Cooper, George, 348
Coots, J. Fred, 35, 108, 122, 218, 310,
    419
Copas, Cowboy, 358
Coquette, 68
Corday, Leo, 366
Corey, Wendell, 82
Cormier, Loretta, 427
Cornell, Don, 55, 135, 185, 217, 303,
    336, 355, 376, 393
Cortesa, Valentina, 284
Cory, George, 160
Cosgrove, Jim, 120
Coslow, Sam, 198, 311, 369, 376
Costa, Don, 163
Costa, Johnny, 344, 347
Costello, Bartley, 98
Costello, Dolores, 227
Costello, Elvis, 197
Costentio, Paul, 388
Cotton, Billy, 28, 229, 273, 332, 409
Cotton Club, The, 39, 152, 208, 239,
    243, 376, 400
Cotton Club Parade, 21, 89, 130, 190,
    342
Cotton, James, 99
Cotton, Joseph, 227
Cotton, Larry, 155, 208
Coughlan, Mary, 342
Coulter, Phil, 16, 34, 173, 220
Countdown, 20
Country Fair, 322
Country Music Holiday, 198
Courtney, Del, 124
Coutet, Henri, 11
Cow Town, 49, 57, 91, 291
Cowan, Stanley, 85
Coward, Noel, 15, 88, 205, 249, 332
Cowboy and the Indians, The, 137
Cowboy and the Senorita, 318
Cowboy Canteen, 207, 283
Cowboy in the Clouds, 364

Cowboy Serenade, 68, 417
Cox, Ida, 225
Cox, Jimmie, 267
Cox, Norrie, 164, 232, 280
Coy, Jimmy, 145
Coyler, Ken, 412
Coyne, Jeannie, 111
Craig, Francis, 262
Crain, Jeanne, 6, 7, 71, 163, 172, 207,
    423
Cramer, Floyd, 34, 54, 110, 133, 135,
    139, 215, 243, 275, 299, 310, 333,
    346, 348, 356, 358, 373
Cramps, The, 321
Crane, Cynthia, 110
Cranshaw, Patrick, 99
Crawford, Hank, 87, 167, 343, 372,
    376, 426
Crawford, Jesse, 4, 22, 56, 161, 203,
    220, 259, 271, 307, 334
Crawford, Joan, 41, 43, 59, 167, 358
Crayton, Pee Wee, 100, 307, 314
Crazy House, 27, 172, 247
Crazy With the Heat, 414
Creamer, Henry, 5, 80, 82, 167, 387
Creole Serenaders, The, 60
Crew-Cuts, The, 317
Crinoline Choir, 274
Criss, Sonny, 9
Criswell, Kim, 43, 247
Croakley, Tom, 95
Crocker, Joe, 69
Crooks, Richard, 34, 35, 193, 220, 248
Crooner, 179
Crosby, Bing, 3, 7, 8, 10, 12, 14, 15,
    18, 19, 21, 23, 28, 29, 32, 33, 34, 38,
    43, 44, 48, 50, 52, 55, 60, 67, 74–75,
    76, 77, 78, 79, 80, 81, 82, 84, 85, 87,
    90, 92, 93, 96, 98, 109, 111, 112, 114,
    117, 118, 122, 125, 131, 132, 133,
    137, 139, 140, 142, 144, 145, 149,
    150, 151, 153, 156, 159, 161, 162,
    163, 164, 167, 168, 169, 170, 171,
    172, 173, 177, 178, 180, 182, 183,
    186, 189, 190, 193, 194, 197, 198,
    199, 203, 204, 207, 209, 210, 211,
    213, 215, 220, 223, 225, 228, 232,
    233, 236, 238, 239, 240, 241, 243,

244, 245, 249, 251, 252, 255, 256, 257, 258, 263, 266, 273, 274, 275, 276, 277, 278, 279, 281, 283, 287, 289, 293, 297, 299, 300, 301, 305, 307, 308, 309, 310, 311, 312, 316, 319, 320, 322, 324, 325, 331, 333, 334, 335, 337, 339, 343, 345, 348, 349, 352, 353, 354, 356, 360, 361, 362, 365, 367, 371, 374, 376, 377, 382, 384, 385, 387, 391, 393, 396, 398, 399, 401, 403, 404, 405, 408, 410, 414, 416, 417, 426

Crosby, Bob, 9, 18, 19, 33, 39, 52, 68, 78, 79, 81, 88, 89, 95, 99, 102, 124, 140, 167, 172, 176, 207, 208, 212, 215, 240, 251, 264, 273, 275, 280, 281, 282, 283, 284, 287, 288, 296, 304, 316, 325, 334, 336, 344, 345, 348, 361, 377, 387, 389, 391, 401, 410, 417

Crosby, Gary, 90, 277, 309, 399

Cross, Douglass, 160

Crothers, "Scat Man," 102, 175, 300, 337

Crowder, Bob, 341

Cruickshank, Ian, 315

Cruisin' Down the River, 162, 317, 352, 363

Crumit, Frank, 10, 111, 163, 176, 230, 249, 273, 344, 370

Crusaders, The, 214, 387

Cry Baby, 242, 317

Csupo, Gabor, 93

Cuban Love Song, The, 231, 268

Cuban Pete, 48

Cugat, Xavier, 3, 16, 30, 38, 47, 61, 64, 120, 125, 164, 183, 191, 225, 256, 284, 286, 306, 312, 321, 326, 354, 398, 426

Cullum, Jim, 22, 33, 82, 244, 386

Cumberland Three, The, 23, 120, 330

Cummings, Robert, 210

Cummins, Bernie, 2, 68, 169

Cunliffe, Dick, 295

Cunningham, Tom, 46

Curb, Mike, 314

Curiel, Gonzalo, 112

Curlee, Karen, 58

Curless, Dick, 34, 38, 57, 110, 140, 149, 163, 188, 191, 213, 266, 278, 298, 303, 323, 414

Curtis Hitch's Happy Harmonists, 386

Curtis, King, 40, 104, 140

Curtis, Loyal, 93

Curtis, Mac, 361

Cushing, Catherine Chisholm, 203

Czibulka, Alphonse, 136

Dabney, Ford, 319, 362

Dacre, Henry, 72, 99

Daddy Long Legs, 92

Dailey, Dan, 6, 7, 161, 168, 171, 184, 187, 208, 251, 299, 373, 395, 396, 403, 424

Dale, Alan, 61, 102, 135, 196, 322, 385

Dale, Carlotta, 115, 219

Daley, Cass, 1, 275

Dalhart, Vernon, 57, 80, 81, 221, 292, 411

Damerell, Stanley J., 203, 209

Damita, Lili, 211

Damnation Alley, 6

Damone, Vic, 6, 18, 47, 60, 69, 82, 87, 97, 98, 110, 116, 129, 130, 137, 151, 160, 171, 176, 186, 206, 211, 228, 231, 239, 243, 244, 253, 257, 263, 265, 275, 300, 353, 355, 364, 374, 378, 406, 416

Dana, Vic, 113, 245, 246, 298, 316

Dance, Girl, Dance, 37

Dance of Life, The, 78, 171, 309, 415

Dancers in the Dark, 203, 338

Dancin', 282, 323, 395

Dancing Sweeties, 73

Dandridge, Dorothy, 189

Dandridge, Putney, 35, 212

Dandridge Sisters, The, 77

D'Angelo, Beverly, 92, 348

Danger on the Air, 259

Dangerous Nan McGrew, 293

Daniels, Bebe, 280, 370

Daniels, Billy, 13, 95, 416

Daniels, Charles, 27, 135, 421

Daniels, Eddie, 35

Daniels, Henry, Jr., 325

Daniels, Maxine, 68

Daniz, Evelyn, 312
Danks, Hart P., 322–23
Danson, Ted, 124
Darby, Ken, 166
Darewski, Herman E., 324
Darin, Bobby, 9, 26, 33, 34, 40, 44, 65,
    107, 118, 149, 166, 174, 176–77, 207,
    224, 252, 261, 264, 331, 332, 395,
    399, 400, 404, 420, 424
*Daring Young Man on the Flying Tra-
    peze, The,* 75
Darling, Erik, 30
Darling Lili, 282
Darnell, Bill, 220, 425
Dash, Julian, 140, 377
Date with Judy, A, 142
Daughter of Rosie O'Grady, The, 78,
    223, 287
Davenport, John, 104
David, Hal, 110
David Harum, 91
David, Lee, 373
David, Mack, 61, 103, 154, 244, 346
Davidson, John, 145
Davies, Bill, 201
Davis, Benny, 26, 56, 176, 229, 408
Davis, Beryl,
Davis, Bette, 14
Davis, "Wild " Bill, 221, 385, 408
Davis, Danny, 424
Davis, Eddie "Lockjaw," 45, 341
Davis, Gussie, 104, 179
Davis, Henry C., 231
Davis, Jackie, 117
Davis, Jeanette, 293
Davis, Jesse Bartlett, 271, 426
Davis, Jimmie, 166, 208, 219, 235, 251,
    297, 365, 417, 421, 425
Davis, Joan, 71, 84, 164, 402
Davis, Johnny "Scat," 376
Davis, Mack, 244
Davis, Miles, 51, 77, 87, 178, 188, 336,
    341, 364, 372, 391, 392, 403, 419
Davis, Meyer, 215
Davis, Rue, 298
Davis, Sammy, Jr., 36, 38, 51, 62, 97,
    111, 113, 127, 149, 153, 186, 199,

219, 224, 233, 302, 309, 328, 357,
    381, 408, 424
Davis Sisters, The, 296
Davis, Skeeter, 120
Davis, Sterling, 213
Davison, Wild Bill, 156, 163, 228, 394
Davy Crockett and the River Pirates, 28
*Davy Crockett, King of the Wild Fron-
    tier,* 28
Dawes, Charles Gates, 186
Dawn, Dolly, 77, 185–86, 245, 302, 312
Dawson, Ronnie, 249, 298
Day, Dennis, 82, 171, 195, 225, 248,
    260, 374, 392, 393
Day, Doris, 6, 8, 10, 12, 16, 20, 21, 23,
    50, 63, 64, 77, 78, 79, 89, 92, 97, 99,
    100, 105, 106, 112, 127, 137, 139,
    148, 158, 160, 161, 165, 167, 169,
    170, 171, 172, 174, 176, 178, 179,
    184, 185, 209, 216, 219, 226, 234,
    243, 251, 252, 261, 268, 277, 279,
    288, 289, 291, 295, 309, 315, 316,
    323, 327, 329, 332, 333, 336, 343,
    345, 353, 355, 357, 359, 369, 371,
    374, 380, 382, 392, 408, 409, 410,
    415, 419, 420, 422
Day Dreamers, 189
*Day in Hollywood—A Night in the
    Ukraine, A,* 8, 97, 192
Daye, Irene, 102, 364, 417
De Castro Sisters, The, 357
De Fore, Don, 169
De Koven, Reginald, 271
De Lugg, Milton, 316
De Lys, Helene, 210
De Marco Sisters, The, 96
De Niro, Robert, 43
De Paul, Gene, 138, 356, 419
De Rose, Peter, 82, 133, 237, 381
De Shields, Andre, 82, 152, 354
Dead End, 46
Dead Reckoning, 98
Dean, Eddie, 66
Dean, Jimmy, 328, 394
Dearie, Blossom, 228, 310, 357
DeBrue, Albert, 354
Dee, Joey, 58
Dee, Sylvia, 373

Deep in the Heart of Texas, 82
Deep River Boys, The, 77
Deer Hunter, 118
Defender, The, 180
DeForrest, Muriel, 347
DeHaven, Gloria, 12, 23, 152, 171, 178,
   187, 190, 348, 405, 413, 415
Dehr, Richard, 236
DeJohn Sisters, 320
Del Corso, Geralyn, 115
Del Rio, Dolores, 297
DeLange, Eddie, 14, 77, 81, 245
Deleath, Vaughn, 20, 298
Delettre, Jean, 129
Deliverence, 103
Dell, Dorothy, 420
Dell Trio, The, 279
Dell-Vikings, The, 346
Dells, The, 8, 117, 280, 401
Delmar, Elaine, 253
Delmore, Alton, 34
Delta Rhythm Boys, The, 13, 109, 145,
   283, 424
Demarest, Frances, 100
Demi-Tasse Revue, 347
Demon Brothers, The, 264
Dempsey, James E., 2
Denniker, Paul, 336
Dennis, Clark, 101, 191, 211, 285, 358,
   373
Dennis, Matt, 23, 234, 276
Denny, Jack, 59, 198, 246, 263, 281,
   324, 329
Denny, Martin, 255, 321
Denton, William L., 219
Denver, John, 188, 289
Deppe, Lois, 152, 408
Der Fuehrer's Face, 83
Derricks, Cleavant, 415
Derwin, Hal, 29, 274, 388, 392
Designing Woman, 365
Desmond, Johnny, 15, 36, 58, 126, 135,
   264, 322, 373, 413, 416
Desmond, Paul, 101, 178, 279, 289,
   290
Destiny, 172
DeSylva, B. G., 8, 25, 53, 168, 184,

   197, 200, 237, 259, 329, 331, 373,
   391, 407, 413
Detonators, The, 423
Detour, 151
Deutsch, Emery, 105, 132, 308
Devol, Frank, 67, 110, 244, 269, 274,
   409, 413
DeWitt, Alan, 401
DeWolfe, Billy, 59, 190
Dexter, Al, 287
Dey, Tracy, 120
di Capua, Edoardo, 366
di Lazzaro, Eldo, 104, 409
Diamond Horseshoe, 1, 63, 209, 257, 320
Diamond, Leo, 201
Dickens, Little Johnny, 144
Dietrich, Marlene, 152, 197, 201, 206,
   251, 262, 371, 419
Dietz, Howard, 168, 416
Dillard, Douglas, 38
Dillon, Will, 163
Dimbleby, Kate, 155, 227
Dimples, 352
Diner, 104
Dinner at Eight, 396
Dinning, Mark, 42
Dinning Sisters, The, 47, 166, 198, 218,
   279, 310, 314
Dion, 104, 177, 270, 346, 361, 397
Dion, Celine, 119, 392
DiPardo, Patti, 245
Ditson, Oliver, 359
Dive Bomber, 391
Dixie, 352
Dixie Stompers, The, 7, 65, 166
Dixie Symphony Four, 199
Dixie to Broadway, 228
Dixieland Ramblers, 40, 112
Dixon, Floyd, 73
Dixon, George Washington, 428
Dixon, Mort, 51, 175, 261, 287, 301,
   360, 424
Do You Love Me?, 338
Doctor, Sam, 4
Dodds, Johnny, 5
Dodge City, 213
Dodridge, Phillip, 143
Dokuchitz, Jonathan, 206

$ (Dollars), 400

Dolly Sisters, The, 56, 76, 140, 173, 282, 322, 328

Domingo, Placido, 16, 36, 230, 321

Domino, Antoine "Fats," 8, 10, 29, 44–45, 68, 81, 124, 129, 150, 179, 183, 192, 251, 254, 292, 294, 299, 316, 368, 376, 397, 398, 405, 416, 422

Dominoes, The, 214, 296, 339

Dominquez, Alberto, 286

Don Juans, The, 155

Donahue, Al, 78, 244, 273, 338

Donahue, Sam, 84, 186, 280, 384

Donald, B. B., 156

Donald Duck in Nutzi Land, 83

Donaldson, Eric, 368

Donaldson, Walter, 3, 22, 27, 55, 83, 147, 215, 219, 251, 252, 255, 297, 301, 309, 350, 359, 367, 414, 423

Dondi, 194

Donegan, Lonnie, 86

Donnie Brasco, 135

Donovan, Jason, 99

Donovan, Walter, 1, 279

Don't Bother to Knock, 229, 302

Don't Fence Me In, 14, 87, 205

Doobie Brothers, The, 335, 418

Dorris, Red, 86

Dorsey, Jimmy, 1, 12, 13, 14, 16, 18, 22, 23, 29, 38, 42, 46, 47, 55, 64, 65, 68, 78, 82, 92, 99, 100, 106, 112, 126, 129, 140, 143, 150, 151, 178, 183, 188, 196, 200, 204, 207, 215, 228, 229, 230, 245, 252, 255, 263, 264, 265, 269, 280, 284, 286, 295, 296, 301, 307, 341, 343, 364, 389, 391, 403, 425

Dorsey, Tommy, 13, 14, 20, 22, 23, 31, 33, 54, 62, 63, 64, 68, 77, 78, 81, 82, 83, 84, 85, 95, 101, 106, 108, 109, 129, 133, 134, 138, 143, 145, 150, 151, 154, 155, 156, 158, 170, 172, 174, 176, 177–78, 182, 188, 196, 199, 204, 207, 209, 215, 218, 228, 229, 230–31, 245, 246, 250, 263, 264, 266, 269, 271, 272, 273, 274, 277, 278, 279, 280, 289, 300, 301, 307, 312, 315, 323, 326, 330, 339, 343, 344, 347,

350, 351, 355, 363, 367, 371, 386, 387, 388, 389, 396, 398, 402, 408, 416

Dosher, George, 49

Double Trouble, 275

Doughboys, 180

Doughboys in Ireland, 13, 225, 248, 260, 393

Douglas, Donna, 111

Douglas, Kirk, 114

Douglas, Mike, 1, 137, 145, 272, 274, 276, 417

Dove, Ronnie, 69, 213

Dowell, Saxie, 250, 369–70

Down Among the Sheltering Palms, 12, 89

Down Argentine Way, 164

Down Mexico Way, 230, 335

Downey, Morton, 56, 108, 198, 217, 274, 284, 311, 329, 336, 343, 377, 393, 421

Doyle, Buddy, 169

d'Pree, Reece, 320

Dr. Strangelove, 376, 389

Dragon, Rusty, 120

Dragonette, Jessica, 203, 321

Drake, Alfred, 146

Drake, Claudia, 151

Drake, Ervin, 121, 150, 286

Drake, Milton, 59, 225, 264

Drake, Tom, 325

Dream, 19, 78, 92, 108, 206, 311, 326

Dresser, Paul, 70, 198, 253, 277

Dressler, Marie, 402

Drew, Doris, 138

Drew, Kenny, 39, 103, 188

Dreyer, Dave, 233

Drifters, The, 38, 58, 236, 277, 311, 344

Du Bois, Gladys, 418

Du Shon, Jean, 268

DuBarry Was a Lady, 174, 326, 368, 417

Dubin, Al, 15, 73, 109, 182, 315, 401

Duchin, Eddy, 7, 39, 45, 47, 96, 129, 148, 152, 153, 159, 172, 185, 210, 211, 226, 228, 235, 238, 244, 301, 319, 328, 329, 339, 342, 370, 371, 372, 376, 403, 424

Duckworth, Willie Lee, 335

Dude Ranch, 281
Duel in the Sun, 189
Duke, Vernon, 20, 368
Dukes of Dixieland, The, 75, 90, 117, 144, 201, 267, 300, 333, 337, 343, 385, 394, 402
Dukoff, Bobby, 188, 358, 426
Dulany, Howard, 68, 218, 398
Dumbo, 287
Dunbar, Dixie, 101, 297
Duncan, Ina, 273
Duncan Sisters, The, 159, 208
Duncan, Tommy, 60
Dunham, Sonny, 97, 115, 237, 336
Dunlap, Louis, 418
Dunlap, Marguerite, 394
Dunn, Artie, 377
Dunne, Irene, 4, 142, 406, 407
Dunstan, Cliff, 352
Duprees, The, 185, 417
Durand, Paul, 11
Durante, Jimmy, 40, 117, 169, 293, 296, 322, 376, 393
Durbin, Deanna, 15, 16, 36, 115, 118, 142, 173, 220, 274, 277, 290, 336, 422
DuRell Brothers, The, 402
Durham, Ed, 155, 314
Dussault, Nancy, 320
Duvall, Shelly, 370
Dvorak, Ann, 36
Dvorsky, George, 205
Dylan, Bob, 43
Dyrenforth, James, 113

Eade, Dominique, 133
Earl Carroll Sketchbook, 158
Earl Carroll's Vanities, 123, 158, 164
Earland, Charles, 398
Earls, The, 150, 280
Easley, Bill, 265
East Side of Heaven, 257
East Side, West Side, 43
Easter Parade, 96, 101, 161, 297, 316, 328, 396
Easy Living, 96
Easy to Love, 68, 97
Eaton, Jimmy, 42, 49, 155–56
Eaton, John, 208, 280, 386

Eaton, Mary, 26
Eberhart, Nelle Richmond, 22
Eberly, Bob, 13, 14, 16, 22, 38, 42, 47, 54, 68, 78, 103, 112, 126, 129, 229, 230, 235, 252, 403, 425
Eberly, Ray, 15, 44, 99, 103, 108, 129, 158, 177, 182, 204, 258, 264, 273, 289, 322, 325, 338, 398, 403, 416
Ebsen, Buddy, 97, 276
Ebsen, Vilma, 276
Eckstine, Billy, 43, 54, 68, 89, 113, 116, 150, 169, 174, 178, 217, 219, 252, 259, 280, 292, 334, 337, 341, 346, 372, 376, 398, 418, 419, 426, 427
Ed Blackwell Trio, The, 101
Eddie Cantor Story, The, 8, 36, 51, 148, 167, 169, 219, 224, 230, 235, 268, 272, 292, 305, 405, 415
Eddy, Duane, 45, 74, 140, 249, 316, 356, 377
Eddy, Nelson, 18, 22, 53, 56, 112, 220, 258, 271, 291, 320, 375, 408, 416
Eddy Duchin Story, The, 7, 46, 47, 102, 152, 210, 229, 319, 320, 328, 351, 370, 372, 403, 406, 424
Eder, Linda, 112, 170
Edmonds, Kenny "Babyface," 99
Edward Scissorhands, 142, 408
Edwards, Cliff, 4, 22, 53, 75, 84, 109, 132, 152, 153, 163, 166, 169, 185, 187, 264, 283, 298, 321, 345, 353, 361, 373, 402, 403, 415
Edwards, Don, 28, 238
Edwards, Gus, 50, 179, 193–94, 313, 345, 385, 402
Edwards, James, 317
Edwards, Joan, 77, 145, 244, 291, 307, 364, 395
Edwards, Michael, 278
Edwards, Sherman, 313
Edwards, Tommy, 186, 247, 257, 288
Egan, Raymond B., 8, 162, 192, 326, 371
8 ½, 43
Eight Girls in a Boat, 369
Eldridge, Roy, 8, 41, 108, 113, 155, 168, 174, 189, 244, 278, 303, 400
Electric Light Orchestra, The, 316

Elgart, Larry, 51, 382
Elgart, Les, 92, 109, 135, 155, 169, 213,
  235, 343, 375, 408, 427
Eliscu, Edward, 247, 408
Ellington, Duke, 12, 14, 18, 32, 42, 54,
  62, 64, 65, 78, 80, 85–86, 87–88, 89,
  97, 104, 106, 108, 115, 122, 130, 149,
  151, 152, 157–58, 173–74, 178, 181,
  182, 183, 184, 197, 211, 216, 220,
  222, 238, 239, 242, 243, 254, 265,
  268, 278, 284, 286, 299, 303, 304,
  307, 308, 310–11, 314, 321, 322, 326,
  334–35, 337, 342, 354, 356, 358, 364,
  372, 376, 377, 400, 403, 406, 410
Elliot, Don, 77
Elliott, Jack, 31, 116, 309, 330
Elliott, Mama Cass, 92
Elliott, Zo, 365–66
Ellis, Alton, 317
Ellis, Anita, 6, 71, 109, 163, 244, 263,
  265, 293, 346, 423
Ellis, Bobbie, 56
Ellis, Seger, 6, 115, 336, 400
Ellsworth, Bob, 331
Elman, Mischa, 239
Elman, Ziggy, 18, 171, 177, 216, 217,
  233, 264, 424
Elvis, 21, 33, 85
Elvis on Tour, 24, 33
Elvis: That's the Way It Is, 24
Elzy, Ruby, 338
Embarrassing Moments, 49
Emerson, Billy, 289
Emerson, Ida, 123, 136
Emmett, Daniel Decatar, 84, 193
Emperor Jones, The, 195
Emperor Waltz, The, 159
Endangered Species, 34
Endor, Chick, 403
Engel, David, 191, 217, 286, 296, 317
Engel, Hank, 405
Engelmann, H., 235
Engvick, William, 46, 333, 402
Ennis, Skinnay, 81, 124, 129, 315, 407
Erbsen, Wayne, 195, 200
Erdman, Ernie, 268, 374
Errico, Melissa, 211
Erstrand, Lars, 23

Ertegun, Ahmet, 58
Erwin, Ralph, 159
Eskew, Doug, 53
Essex, David, 339
Etting, Ruth, 6, 22–23, 68, 74, 81, 102,
  110, 114, 126, 167, 171, 176, 179,
  180, 184, 185, 198, 219, 233–34, 280,
  309, 316, 319, 334, 355, 357, 367,
  369, 376, 406, 419, 420, 426
Eubie, 175, 237
Evans, Bill, 20, 35, 45, 97, 101, 174,
  178, 253, 261, 267, 289, 341, 358, 407
Evans, Brian, 175, 216, 224, 315, 405,
  422
Evans, Dale, 33, 96, 98, 142, 296, 413
Evans, George, 180, 254
Evans, Gil, 204, 328
Evans, Ray, 119, 242, 295, 356, 372
Evans, Redd, 138, 305, 364
Evans, Tolchard, 203, 209
Evelyn and her Magic Violin, 161
Eve of St. Mark, 36
Ever After, 294
Ever Since Eve, 320
Everett, Betty, 327
Evergreen, 73
Everhart, Clay, 273
Everly, Brothers, 11, 87, 163, 317, 348,
  410
Every Night at Eight, 362
Everybody Sing, 279, 352
Everyone Says I Love You, 64, 99, 168,
  177
*Everything You Wanted to Know About
  Sex . . .* , 210
Ewen, David, 48, 61, 136
Eyes Wide Shut, 158, 168, 392
Eyton, Frank, 45

Fabares, Shelly, 186, 314
Fabian, 7, 175
Fabulous Dorseys, The, 23, 101, 126,
  231, 269, 307, 399
Fagan, Barney, 253
Fahey, John, 5, 399, 410
Fain, Sammy, 20, 79, 150, 170, 208,
  216–17, 360, 389, 393
Fairchild, Edgar, 316

Faith, Percy, 3, 12, 35, 47, 82, 98, 159, 191, 239, 296, 321, 333
Faithful in My Fashion, 155, 203
Faithful, Marianne, 375
Falkenburg, Jinx, 71
Fallen Angel, 70
Farao, Massimo, 404
Fargo, Donna, 242
Farley, Ed, 250
Farmer, Frances, 105
Farmer's Daughter, The, 193
Farrell, Bill, 426
Farrell, Bob, 427
Farrell, Eileen, 15, 18, 88, 126, 157, 177, 204, 222, 231, 249, 294, 398
Farrell, Skip, 218
Fay, Rick, 156, 324
Faye, Alice, 4, 10, 36, 44, 50, 56, 66, 70, 101, 126, 132, 136, 172, 173, 175, 201, 256, 277, 296, 297, 299, 304, 316, 318, 336, 345, 391, 396
Faye, Frances, 104, 266, 325, 373, 374
Faye, John, 73
Fearon, Clinton, 210
Feaster, Carl, 317
Feaster, Claude, 317
Feinstein, Michael, 10, 15, 126, 146, 147, 151, 161, 170, 171, 186–87, 221, 226, 266, 299, 312, 346, 347, 382, 391, 396
Feldkamp, Elmer, 185, 233, 235, 329, 389
Felice, Ernie, 56, 344
Feliciano, José, 262
Fenstad, E. A., 340
Fenton, Carl, 411
Fenton, Stan, 186
Ferguson, Maynard, 278, 391
Ferrante and Teicher, 327, 413
Ferry, Bryan, 263
Fetchit, Stepin, 215
Feudin', Fussin' and A-Fightin', 233, 336
Feyne, Buddy, 377
Fiedler, Arthur, 190
Fielding, Jerry, 225
Fields, Arthur, 1, 54, 157
Fields, Benny, 257

Fields, Buddy, 425
Fields, Dorothy, 42, 86, 102, 122, 152, 215, 277, 359
Fields, Ernie, 59, 84, 181, 186, 258, 377
Fields, Gracie, 60, 68, 74, 105, 110, 183, 185, 214, 251, 299, 312, 381, 393, 409
Fields, Herbie, 61, 75
Fields, Shep, 83, 97, 179, 214, 238, 244, 335
Fighter Attack, 272
Fighting Coast Guard, 142
Fine and Dandy, 105
Fingerle, Marlene, 48
Fingerle and Schutt, 189
Finn, Mickey, 413
Fio Rito, Ted, 75, 115, 209, 362, 406
Fireballs, The, 178
Firehouse Five Plus Two, The, 18, 22, 32, 50, 63, 116, 135, 140, 161, 164, 183, 203, 298, 310, 318, 399
First Baby, The, 336
First Love, 16, 142
Fischer, Carl, 426
Fisher, Dan, 121
Fisher, Doris, 19, 98, 120, 182, 293, 403, 416
Fisher, Eddie, 21, 28, 110, 154, 203, 212, 216, 232, 297, 302, 331, 357, 368, 374, 376, 408, 420
Fisher, Fred, 62, 72, 74–75, 285, 365, 403, 423
Fisher, Freddie "Schnickelfritz," 298
Fisher, Mark, 400
Fisher, Rob, 316
Fitzgibbons, Willie, 386
Fitzgerald, Barry, 349, 374
Fitzgerald, Ella, 2, 3, 10, 13, 18, 20, 21, 23, 32, 33, 37, 38, 39, 40, 43, 44, 45, 54, 62, 65, 69, 73, 76, 78, 81, 82, 84, 86, 92, 95, 97, 99, 101, 102, 106, 108, 109, 111–12, 114, 119, 124, 126, 127, 129, 132, 134, 138, 143, 146, 147, 149, 151, 153, 158, 173, 174, 177, 178, 182, 184, 186, 187, 189, 196, 200, 206, 207, 215, 216, 222, 224, 226, 228, 233, 234, 240, 242, 246, 249, 250, 254, 255, 256, 258, 264,

271, 275, 276, 278, 279, 286, 288, 310, 315, 319, 325, 334, 338, 341, 343, 344, 349, 356, 357, 358, 361, 362, 363, 367, 375, 376, 379, 380, 381, 382, 395, 398, 405, 406, 408, 419, 420, 421, 426

Five Guys Named Moe, 7, 53, 106

Five Keys, 117, 403

Five Pennies, The, 5, 33, 40, 182, 194, 250, 251, 281, 284, 386, 397

Five Satins, The, 170, 323

Five Willows, The, 329

Flack, Roberta, 68, 138, 381, 400

Flame, The, 219

Flame of the Barbary Coast, The, 51, 70, 80, 144

Flaming Bullets, 33

Flamingo Road, 167

Flamingos, The, 38, 48, 74, 124, 246, 250, 348, 371

Flanagan and Allen, 303, 322, 381

Flanagan, Bud, 381

Flanagan, Ralph, 132, 143, 263, 269, 296, 327, 336

Flanagan, Roger, 35

Flap, 203

Flatt and Scruggs, 92, 103, 120, 134, 163, 195, 212, 275, 369

Fleeson, Neville, 170

Fleet's In, The, 16

Fletcher, Lucy, 234, 344

Fletcher, Robert, 87

Flippen, Jay C., 147

Flirtation Walk, 334

Flirtations, The, 242

Floren, Myron, 37, 59, 213, 225, 302, 343, 364, 413, 414

Florodora Girl, The, 47, 144, 248, 277

Flory, Chris, 121, 285

Flowers, Pat, 56, 105, 195, 278, 336

Flying Colors, 88

Flying Down to Rio, 197

Flynn, Allan, 232

Flynn, Joe, 91

Foldi, Erzsebet, 331

Foley, Joe, 13

Foley, Red, 123, 316

Folies Bergere, 115

Follow Me, 271, 390

Follow That Dream, 278

Follow the Band, 6, 138, 252, 257, 305, 390

Follow the Boys, 37, 38, 140, 145, 171, 172, 320, 331, 343, 349, 352, 382

Follow Your Heart, 195

Fomeen, Basil, 56, 84, 93

Fontaine, Jacqueline, 117

Fontaine Sisters, The, 1, 30, 168, 275

For Me and My Gal, 5, 29, 50, 109, 140, 148, 271, 272, 281, 282, 328, 366, 371, 394, 399, 401, 413

For the Boys, 293

For the Love of Mary, 173, 277

Foran, Dick, 267

Forbert, Steve, 212

Forbidden, 418

Forbidden Hollywood, 164

Ford, Emile, 1, 166, 201, 243, 390, 398

Ford, Glenn, 82

Ford, Mary, 50, 51, 75, 93, 123, 146, 174, 176, 181, 193, 198, 210, 242, 326, 355, 371, 410

Ford, Tennessee Ernie, 28, 116, 139, 148, 149, 162, 166, 169, 223, 249, 270, 320, 325, 327, 345, 351, 389, 396, 418

Forest Rangers, The, 194

Forever Plaid, 58, 69, 135, 191, 203, 217, 296, 286, 317, 325, 369, 379

Forrest, Helen, 3, 6, 13, 39, 78, 82, 95, 138, 139, 146, 151, 153, 173, 176, 185, 226, 229, 255, 256, 258, 272, 278, 281, 284, 286, 325, 361, 371, 398, 414, 420

Fort Worth Doughboys, The, 345

Fosdick, W. W., 23

Fosse, 51, 161, 233, 323, 405

Fosse, Bob, 63, 111

Foster, Stephen, 9, 34, 79, 193, 257–58, 271–72, 273–74, 302, 347, 396

Foster, Stuart, 129, 231, 280

Foster, Susannah, 203, 408

Fountain, Pete, 20, 32, 40, 44, 103, 165, 230, 231, 251, 279, 333, 337, 343, 381, 386, 387, 394, 395, 410, 414, 422

Four Dusty Travelers, 215

Four Freshmen, The, 30, 60, 78, 102, 108, 112, 125, 172, 173, 174, 188, 204, 221, 239, 243, 289, 305, 316, 357, 368, 377, 381, 395, 400, 426

Four Hits and a Miss, 215

Four Jills in a Jeep, 53, 281

Four Knights, The, 270

Four Lads, The, 48, 207, 276, 331, 336, 361, 408

Four Lovers, The, 164

Four Seasons, The, 8, 162, 323

Four Tops, The, 12, 143, 160, 186

Four Tunes, The, 55

Four Vagabonds, The, 67, 305

Fowler, Wally, 361

Fox, Cody, 176

Fox, Della, 213, 386

Fox, Harry, 161, 173

Fox, Roy, 132, 203, 362

Foxx, Redd, 273

Foy, Eddie, 63

Foy, Eddie, Jr., 423

Francis, Connie, 2, 10, 18, 21, 23, 31, 34, 49, 56, 65, 69, 91, 118, 136, 139, 140, 142, 150, 151, 153, 161, 167, 173, 176, 181, 187, 192, 213, 241, 254, 260, 278, 292, 295, 302–303, 318, 323, 331, 333, 358, 364, 368, 369, 373, 374, 393, 405, 414, 416, 417–18, 420, 421, 422, 424

Francois, Jacqueline, 11

Frank, Sid, 288

Frankel, Harry, 52

Frankie and Johnny, 90, 111, 116, 397

Franklin, Aretha,147, 205, 242, 279, 302, 368, 375, 376, 381, 389, 406

Franklin, Dave, 238

Franks, Laurie, 35, 199, 210

Fraser, Alison, 50, 321

Fraser, Dean, 381

Fraser, Jeri Lynn, 27

Frawley, Lillian, 55

Frawley, William, 255

Frazee, Jane, 320

Freberg, Stan, 30, 317, 414

Freddie Steps Out, 87

Freed, Alan, 323

Freed, Arthur, 105, 153, 282, 328

Freed, Ralph, 133, 218, 219, 352, 413

Freedman, Max C., 302

Freedman, Ray, 324

Freelon, Nenna, 168

Freeman, Al, 23

Freeman, Bud, 23, 63, 64, 132, 155, 156, 207, 237, 254, 268, 319, 343, 421

Freeman, Cheryl, 88, 158, 356

Freeman, George, 352

Freeman, L. E., 381

Freer, Marcia, 391

Frey, Fran, 113, 298, 325

Friedland, Anatol, 259

Friedman, Don, 158, 341

Friedman, Leo, 209

Friend, Cliff, 220, 238, 351

Friganza, Trixie, 161

Friml, Rudolf, 203

Frisco Sal, 2

Froeba, Frank, 51, 166, 196, 336, 354, 360, 393

From Here to Eternity, 37

Froman, Jane, 17, 43, 56, 82, 83, 85, 113, 114, 150, 177, 182, 216, 247, 340, 408, 420

Fromeen, Basil, 261, 299

Front, The, 422

Frost, Jack, 399

Full Metal Jacket, 231

Fuller, Curtis, 48, 229, 367

Fuller, Jerry, 358

Fuller, Jessie, 164

Fuller, Rosalind, 370

Fuller's Novelty Orchestra, 117

Fulson, Lowell, 99

Fulton, Jack, 17, 45, 185, 217, 293, 295, 346, 368, 373, 392

Funny Face, 147

Funny Girl, 256, 313

Funny Lady, 65, 125, 157, 188, 233, 247

Fuqua, Harvey, 323

Furber, Douglas, 38

Furia, Philip, 9, 136, 210, 219

Gable, Clark, 50, 75, 420

Gabor, Zsa Zsa, 333

Gade, Jacob, 191

Gaillard, Slim, 107, 115, 321, 335

Gaines, Boyd, 424
Gaines, Davis, 358
Gaines, Roy, 57
Galbraith, Alistair, 262
Gale, Sunny, 124, 327
Gallagher, Ed, 241
Gallop, Sammy, 98
Galloway, Tod B., 401
Galway, James, 173, 379, 381, 399
Gambale, Frank, 225
Gammon, Peter, 146
Gamse, Albert, 15, 425
Gang's All Here, The, 47, 210
Gangster, The, 284
Gannon, Kim, 93, 106, 169
Garber, Jan, 26, 35, 36, 84, 169, 186, 187, 230, 235, 247, 264, 269, 275, 320, 387, 388
Gardell, Carlos, 3
Garden, Henry, 307
Garden, Mary, 22
Gardiner, Reginald, 97
Gardner, Ava, 39, 423
Gardner, Donald, 11
Gardner, Freddy, 27, 140, 156
Gardner, Jack, 100
Gardner, Kenny, 99, 195
Gardos, Gene, 268
Garland, Joe, 181
Garland, Judy, 5, 10, 18, 29, 50, 56, 68, 78, 87, 96, 100, 101, 107, 109, 111, 114, 127, 131, 137, 148, 153, 154, 160, 161, 162, 171, 173, 175, 176, 181, 184, 196, 204, 233, 234, 235, 237, 239, 247, 257, 272, 278, 279, 282, 284, 288, 294, 297, 302, 319, 325, 327, 328, 331, 341, 347, 352, 370, 371, 374, 380, 385, 387, 395, 396, 398, 399, 401, 405, 406, 409, 418, 420, 421, 427
Garland, Red, 10, 23, 44, 76, 106, 129, 149, 160, 267, 336, 337, 375, 391
Garner, Erroll, 15, 44, 60, 68, 87, 101, 105, 109, 112, 122, 206, 220, 221, 242, 247, 256, 278, 285, 286, 316, 331, 333, 338, 357, 362–63, 370, 379, 382, 394, 420
Garnett, Chip, 335

Garrett, Betty, 87, 321
Garnett, Gale, 386
Garrett, Leif, 294
Garrett, Lloyd, 73, 93
Garrick Gaieties, The, 228, 249
Garry, Sid, 197
Gary, John, 107, 112, 260, 263, 356, 358, 374, 422
Gary, Sid, 42
Gaskill, Clarence, 151, 239, 292
Gaskin, George J., 36, 287, 322, 350
Gaster, Marvin, 183
Gatlin Brothers, The, 369
Gaul, James, 74, 93
Gauthier, Eva, 226
Gaxton, William, 97, 238
Gay, Byron, 324
Gay Senorita, The, 98
Gayle, Crystal, 69, 119, 208, 276, 280, 354
Gaylor, Ruth, 244
Gaylord, Charles, 17
Gaylords, The, 183
Gaynor, Mitzi, 10, 33, 85, 120, 154, 207, 263, 267, 396
Gayten, Paul, 323
Gee, Lottie, 175
Geibel, Adam, 199
Genaro and Bailey, 22
Gene and Debbe, 236
Gene Krupa Story, The, 61, 102, 181, 182, 237
Gentlemen Marry Brunettes, 6, 71, 163, 423
Gentry, Bobbie, 11
George, Don, 149, 173, 413
George M!, 281
George White's Music Hall Follies, 52
George White's Music Hall Varieties, 211, 425
George White's Scandals, 20, 52, 75, 93, 105, 206, 237, 301, 314, 331, 338, 407
Gerard, Adeline, 347
Gerard, Richard H., 347
Gerry and the Pacemakers, 192
Gershenson, Joseph, 181, 346
Gershwin, George, 93, 146–47, 189,

200, 226, 238, 239, 274, 331, 347,
    396, 413
Gershwin, Ira, 146–47, 189, 200, 226,
    238, 239
Gerson, Roy, 168
Gerun, Tom, 2
Get Hep to Love, 321
Gets, Malcolm, 67, 152
Gettysburg, 16, 85, 142, 198, 413
Getz, Stan, 24, 89, 95, 96, 120, 122,
    129, 155, 178, 182, 221, 252, 265,
    267, 319, 321, 328, 340, 358, 391
Getzov, Ray, 288
Geva, Tamara, 45
Ghost Catchers, 5, 30, 366
Ghost World, 114
Giant, 414
Gibb, Andy, 11
Gibbons, Carol, 52
Gibbons, Carroll, 113, 268
Gibbs, A. Harrington, 306
Gibbs, Georgia, 29, 168, 206, 212, 259,
    312, 320, 402
Gibbs, Parker, 385, 407
Gibbs, Terry, 210
Gibson, Banu, 196
Gibson, Don, 2, 348
Gibson, Lottie, 322
Gibson, Steve, 155, 389
Giefer, George L., 404
Gifford, Harry, 394
Gifford, Kathie Lee, 109, 155, 364
Gilbert, Billy, 318
Gilbert, Fred, 227
Gilbert, J. Wolfe, 91, 221, 259, 284,
    297, 385
Gilbert, Lottie, 424
Gilbert, Ronnie, 201
Gilchrist, Connie, 100
Gilda, 277, 293
Gilkyson, Terry, 236
Gill, Vince, 387
Gillespie, Dizzy, 24, 51, 54, 114, 137,
    155, 168, 179, 222, 257, 258, 265,
    267, 278, 286, 313, 334, 351, 394,
    406, 410
Gillespie, Haven, 35, 48, 93, 143, 275,
    310, 360, 419

Gilley, Mickey, 58, 303
Gillham, Art, 2, 19, 351
Gilmore, Patrick, 394
Gilson, Lottie, 213. 234, 248
Giltrap, Gordon, 235
Gimbel, Norman, 54
Gimble, Johnny, 77
Gipsy Kings, The, 383
Girl Behind the Counter, The, 117
Girl Can't Help It, The, 69, 165, 302
Girl From Missouri, The, 148, 359
Girl From Rectors, The, 69
Girl From Utah, The, 29, 366
Girls! Girls! Girls!, 263
Git Along Little Doggies, 5, 64, 116,
    121, 131, 298
Give My Regards to Broadway, 208, 211,
    392, 401, 403
Glahe, Will, 37, 409
Glass Bottom Boat, The, 295
Glazer, Tom, 235–36, 278
Gleason, Jackie, 316
Glenn Miller Story, The, 3, 32, 181, 213,
    247, 285, 338, 346, 377
Glickman, Fred, 249
Glorifying the American Girl, 23, 26,
    309
Glory Alley, 338
Gluck, Alma, 56
Gluskin, Lud, 129, 134, 245
Go Chase Yourself, 105
Go West, 34, 272
Godfrey, Arthur, 80, 109, 176, 287,
    314, 327, 335
Godfrey, Lynnie, 175
Goell, Kermit, 262
Goetschius, Marjorie, 156
Goetz, E. Ray, 108, 412
Going My Way, 374
Going Up!, 136
Gold, Lew, 211
Gold, Marty, 357
Gold Mine in the Sky, 365
Goldberg, Kenny, 112
Golden Earrings, 119
Golden Gate Quartet, The, 56, 67, 84,
    320, 333, 347
Golden Girl, 34, 56, 85, 120, 395

Goldfield, Harry, 287
Goldie, Don, 162
Goldkette, Jean, 115, 299, 345
Gone With the Wind, 85, 120, 232, 274, 394
Gonella, Nat, 164, 183, 194, 244, 293, 324
Gonsalves, Paul, 184
Good Boy, 163
Goodfellas, 296, 323
Goodhart, Al, 105, 131, 150, 195
Goodman, Al, 10, 120, 299, 311, 371
Goodman, Benny, 5, 10, 15, 18, 21, 25, 31, 32, 37, 39, 43, 44, 45, 46, 51, 53, 56, 63, 64, 65, 76, 77, 80, 84, 90, 99, 102, 107, 108, 112, 114, 117, 122, 124, 125, 129, 143, 145, 146, 148, 152, 153, 155, 156, 158, 159, 160, 161, 167, 176, 178, 181, 182, 185, 187–88, 189, 192, 194, 196, 207, 209–10, 211, 218, 219, 221, 222, 226, 237, 245, 250, 251, 254, 261, 264, 266, 268, 269, 271, 276, 280, 286, 288, 290, 297, 304, 307, 314, 318, 319, 323–24, 326, 328, 331, 332, 333, 335, 337, 339, 340, 341, 345, 349, 351, 352, 364, 366, 372, 375, 376, 379, 385, 389, 390, 391, 394, 395, 398, 402, 405, 410, 414, 415, 417, 421, 425
Goodman, Lillian Rosedale, 61
Goodman, William, 142
Goodwin, Joe, 400
Goofus Five, The, 103
Gordon, Bobby, 131, 182, 253, 385
Gordon, Dexter, 65, 69, 77, 109, 115, 221, 289, 304, 327, 370, 382, 418, 426
Gordon, Gray, 104, 167, 187, 425
Gordon, Irving, 381
Gordon, Mack, 134, 254, 372, 381
Gordon, Odette Felicious, 195
Gordon, Sheila, 30
Gore, Lesley, 242
Gorman, Ross, 61
Gorme, Eydie, 18, 37, 38, 105, 119, 126, 127, 147, 154, 171, 218, 231, 259, 336, 368, 382, 391, 424
Gorney, Jay, 48
Gorrell, Stuart, 113, 338

Gottfried, Martin, 367
Gottlieb, Alex, 111
Gould, Morton, 82, 258, 272, 273, 284, 334, 342
Goulet, Robert, 98, 141, 245, 289, 355
Graae, Jason, 58, 191, 217, 317, 325, 379
Grable, Betty, 56, 143, 145, 165, 173, 189, 201, 245, 251, 254, 294, 318, 320, 322, 350, 383, 393
Grace of My Heart, 2
Grace, Simon and Verity, 23
Grace, Teddy, 417
Graff, George, Jr., 393
Graham, Charles, 287
Graham, Irvin, 150
Graham, Roger, 149
Grahame, Gloria, 284
Grainger, Porter, 354. 400
Grande, Tex, 133
Grafton, Gloria, 377
Grant, Bob, 53, 56, 67, 76, 87, 88, 100, 109, 208, 233, 251, 252, 291, 297, 395, 419
Grant, Cary, 83, 142, 152, 402
Grant, Earl, 58, 104, 383
Grant, Gary, 86
Grant, Gogi, 20, 25, 39, 45, 48, 152, 171, 174, 189, 197, 226, 247, 256, 257, 278, 279, 332, 367, 406
Grant, Kirby, 188
Granville, Bernard, 136
Grapes of Wrath, The, 298
Grappelli, Stephane, 63, 156, 311, 350, 370
Grass, Cliff, 167, 425
Gray, Chauncey, 51
Gray, Dolores, 137, 365
Gray, Gilda, 164, 331, 337
Gray, Glen, 42, 43, 59, 73, 87, 88, 109, 131, 140, 148, 151, 153, 177, 188, 196, 198, 207, 208, 211, 214, 217, 235, 237, 244, 245, 254, 261, 266, 279, 280, 293, 301, 322, 326, 334, 346, 368, 377, 380, 386, 393, 405, 413, 419
Gray, Jerry, 113, 285, 335
Gray, Lawrence, 424

Gray, Wardell, 182
Gray, William B., 317
Graydon, Joel, 6
Grayson, Carl, 83
Grayson, Kathryn, 4, 79, 165, 191, 299, 367, 372
Grease, 43, 217
Great American Broadcast, The, 9, 162, 167, 174, 212, 352, 409
Great American String Band, The, 386
Great Caruso, The, 36
Great Day, 125, 408
Great Gatsby, The, 8, 33, 106, 391
Great John L, The, 399
Great Magoo, The, 187
Great Ziegfeld, The, 169, 256, 320
Greco, Buddy, 174, 185, 199, 267, 322, 341, 368, 415
Green, Bud, 8, 107, 278, 315, 361, 420
Green, Eddie, 121
Green, Harold, 158
Green, Jesse, 201
Green, Johnny, 45, 68, 96, 152, 280, 377, 417, 424
Green, Larry, 262
Green, Lil, 6, 145, 405, 426
Green Mile, The, 60, 152
Green Pastures, The, 397
Green, Slim, 175
Greene, Joe, 2
Greene, Lorne, 249, 325
Greene, Richard, 59
Greene, Smokey, 365
Greenwich Village, 175, 353, 400, 403
Greenwich Village Follies, 370, 395
Gregor, Max, 213, 236, 285, 308, 346
Gregory, Paul, 372, 418
Grever, Maria, 389
Grey, Clifford, 124, 128
Grey, Joe, 306
Grey, Joel, 281
Grier, Jimmy, 269, 391
Griffin, Clive, 392
Griffin, Johnny, 42, 330, 426
Griffin, Ken, 21, 38, 93, 115, 204, 209, 218, 245, 310
Griffin, Merv, 135, 159, 247, 330
Griffith, Andy, 397

Grissom, Dan, 105, 255
Grissom Gang, The, 152
Grodin, Charles, 168
Groenendaal, Chris, 26, 420
Groener, Harry, 249, 332
Grofé, Ferde, 78, 409
Gross, Walter, 357, 383
Grossman, Julian, 377
Grouya, Ted, 107
Grosz, Marty, 2, 45, 83, 90, 101, 132, 165, 183, 217, 314, 329, 345, 346
Grosz, Will, 15, 299
Groucho: A Life in Revue, 223, 241, 410
Gruber, Edmond L., 52
Guadacanal Diary, 164, 231
Guaraldi, Vince, 369
Guarnieri, Johnny, 32, 108, 340
Guess Who's Coming to Dinner, 117
Guitar, Bonnie, 244
Guizar, Tito, 98, 310, 425
Gustufson, Wylie, 86
Gutenberg, Steve, 124
Guthrie, Woody, 49, 116, 149, 195, 298, 329–30, 368–69, 411
Guy, Helen, 35
Guy Named Joe, A, 171
Guzman, Alejandre, 383
Gywnne, Fred, 187

Habermann, Robert, 13
Hackett, Bobby, 3, 12, 23, 65, 115, 156, 164, 168, 190, 288, 304, 326, 343, 346, 360, 387
Hackett, Charles, 93
Hagan, Paul, 61
Hagar, Sammy, 139
Hagen, Carl, 196
Haggard, Merle, 21, 110
Haggart, Bob, 324, 391
Haig, Al, 245, 340
Haines, Connie, 176, 319, 342
Haldeman, Oakley, 137
Hale, Sonny, 73
Haley, Bill, 53, 60, 150, 193, 218, 245, 280, 288, 302, 331, 418
Haley, Ed, 402
Hall, Adelaide, 152, 239, 273
Hall, Fred, 156, 157

Hall, George, 43, 94, 185–86, 218, 245, 265, 310, 312, 365, 380, 420

Hall, Henry, 123

Hall, J. Graydon, 361

Hall Johnson Choir, The, 267, 338, 352, 397

Hall, Juanita, 3, 121, 247, 312, 387, 426

Hall, Rich, 68

Hall, Steve, 213

Hall, Wendell, 183

Hallet, Mal, 46

Halls of Montezuma, 231

Hamilton, Arthur, 69

Hamilton, Frank, 388

Hamilton, George, 66, 139, 192, 422

Hamilton, Lawrence, 174

Hamilton, Nancy, 146

Hamilton, Roy, 98, 145, 258, 305

Hamilton, Scott, 13, 45, 101, 182, 221, 308

Hamilton, Victoria, 267

Hamm, Fred, 51

Hammerstein, Arthur, 36

Hammerstein, Oscar, 13, 39, 123, 159, 200, 205, 265–66, 405

Hamp, Johnny, 52, 328

Hampton, Lionel, 5, 41, 63, 73, 107– 108, 115, 146, 156, 159, 160, 184, 196, 237, 247, 255, 256, 269, 278, 280, 296, 307, 315, 324, 328, 350, 358, 368

Hampton, Ruth, 247

Hanby, Benjamin Russell, 77

Hancock, Herbie, 228

Handman, Lou, 20

Hands Across the Table, 129

Handy, W. C., 33, 55, 195, 237, 337

Haney, Carol, 111

Hanighen, Bernard, 413

Hanley, James F., 182, 304, 313, 427

Hanlon, Clare, 215

Hannon, Bob, 7, 94, 219

Hanshaw, Annette, 7, 106, 153, 156, 163, 189, 283, 311, 368, 369, 385, 388

Happenings, The, 256

Happy Birthday, 159

Happy Days, 45

Haran, Mary Cleere, 228, 282, 307, 322, 331, 364–65, 396, 408

Harbach, Otto, 100

Harburg, E. Y., 20, 48, 181, 187, 204, 214

Hard to Hold, 160

Hardeman, Rick, 186

Hardin, Ty, 51

Hardwick, Mark, 258

Hardy, Francoise, 58

Hare, Ernest, 86, 137, 140, 147, 170, 241, 321, 359

Harford, Harold, 159

Harford, John, 23

Hargraves, Robert, 209

Haring, Bob, 282, 388

Harlan, Bryon, 1, 9, 57, 69, 101, 253, 270, 294, 313, 328, 380, 384, 396, 412

Harlem Globe Trotters, The, 349

Harlem Globe Trotters, The, 349

Harlem Gospel Singers, The, 397

Harling, Franke, 401

Harlow, Jean, 42, 83

Harmonicats, The, 60, 104, 128, 198, 230, 285, 286, 289, 377

Harmony Lane, 258, 272, 273

Harnell, Joe, 107, 160

Harney, Ben, 426

Harp, Mary Lou, 363

Harper, Janice, 69

Harptones, The, 205

Harrell, Bill, 58

Harriot, Derrick, 85

Harris, Ace, 53

Harris, Charles K., 4, 47

Harris, EmmyLou, 242, 348

Harris, Gene, 223

Harris, HiTide, 123

Harris, Marion, 5, 6, 20, 42, 121, 145, 149, 175, 176, 185, 226, 331, 337, 364, 405

Harris, Phil, 7, 49, 54, 60, 106, 121, 125, 182, 207, 266, 275, 287, 301, 304, 328, 345, 352, 359, 386, 395, 409, 426

Harris, Remus, 329

Harris, Roy, 394

Harris, Will J., 350

Harris, Woody, 65
Harrison, Charles, 170, 213, 285
Harrison, Don, 325
Harrison, James F., 282, 394
Harrow, Nancy, 121, 233
Harry Delmar's Revels, 152, 233
Hart, Annie, 404
Hart, Jimmy, 60
Hart, Lorenz, 42, 73, 134, 228, 248–49, 357, 407, 421
Hartman, George, 76
Hartman, Johnny, 172, 222, 315, 381
Harvey, Mick, 287
Harvey, Morton, 154
Has Anybody Seen My Gal?, 106, 115, 177, 183, 371, 397, 399
Hatch, Earl, 391
Have a Heart, 216, 359
Havens, Richie, 119
Haver, June, 56, 126, 171, 187, 190, 287, 296, 322, 372, 413
Haverly, Charles, 253
Havoc, June, 136
Hawaii Calls, 14
Hawkins, Coleman, 22, 45, 47–48, 54, 62, 88, 111, 133, 143, 146, 149, 162, 179, 182, 198, 216, 225, 232, 251, 252, 255, 278, 293, 311–12, 318, 328, 333, 339, 341, 344, 345, 347, 348, 367, 377, 379, 380, 387, 392, 410, 426
Hawkins, Dale, 53
Hawkins, Edwin, 270
Hawkins, Erskine, 53, 106, 156, 299, 336, 358, 373, 382, 403
Hawkins, Hawkshaw, 327
Hawkins, Ronnie, 8, 81
Hawn, Goldie, 177
Hay, Mary, 189
Hayden, Joe, 144
Haydn Quartet, The, 36, 80, 181, 345, 386, 406
Hayes, Bill, 28, 266
Hayes, Clancy, 2, 304
Hayes, Edgar, 181
Hayes, Gabby, 98
Hayes, Helen, 159
Hayes, Isaac, 186, 341
Hayes, Roland, 138

Hayman, Richard, 224
Haymes, Bob, 112, 387
Haymes, Dick, 12, 13, 42, 78, 79, 95, 108, 120, 127, 146, 157, 158, 162, 165, 166, 171, 173, 185, 206, 207, 209, 212, 215, 217, 219, 220, 231, 248, 254, 257, 263, 264, 265, 269, 272, 275, 285, 293, 294, 300, 303, 311, 334, 341, 348, 351, 360, 363, 367, 368, 371, 374, 382, 384, 389, 390, 393, 398, 407, 410, 414, 419, 421, 423, 426, 427
Haymes, Joe, 130, 266, 300
Haynes, Phil, 34, 318
Haynes, Roy, 348
Hays, Lee, 201
Hayton, Lennie, 52
Hayward, Susan, 17, 53, 56, 82, 85, 114, 177, 182, 252, 340, 397, 408
Hayworth, Rita, 31, 253, 293
He Laughed Last, 74
Healy, Dan, 163
Healy, Eunice, 427
Healy, Mary, 339
Healy, Ted, 200
Hearst, William Randolph, 154
Heart of Paddy Whack, 213
Heart of the Golden West, 56
Heart of the Rio Grande, 82
Heart of the Rockies, 386
Heartaches, 136
Heath, Hy, 249
Heath, Ted, 38, 42, 71, 78, 134, 156, 246, 264, 272, 284, 285, 305, 364, 377
Heatherton, Ray, 352
Heat's On, The, 53
Hedges, Chuck, 325
Hedman, Norman, 296
Hefti, Neil, 52, 60, 159, 222, 321, 327
Hegamin, Lucille, 9, 132
Heidelberg Quintet, The, 50, 385
Heidt, Horace, 36, 81, 89, 103, 120, 122, 155, 175, 219, 238, 244, 308, 335, 365
Heifetz, Jascha, 239
Helen Morgan Story, The, 20, 25, 39, 46, 48, 51, 152, 170, 189, 197, 226, 247, 257, 259, 278, 279, 322, 349, 406

Hello Everybody, 84, 396

Hello, Frisco, Hello, 36, 41, 50, 126, 132, 136, 137, 181, 188, 296, 399

Hellzapoppin', 385

Henderson, Bobby, 350

Henderson, Chick, 230

Henderson, Fletcher, 6, 7, 8, 27, 45, 65, 84, 122, 130, 132, 143, 165, 188, 202, 228, 261, 284, 298, 304, 324, 332, 345, 381

Henderson, Horace, 2, 424

Henderson, Ray, 8, 51, 106, 184, 197, 259, 329, 360, 373

Henderson, Skitch, 60, 135, 140, 146, 205, 215, 217, 246, 369, 377, 400

Henderson, Wayne, 242

Hendricks, Barbara, 87–88

Hendrickson, Al, 276

Henhouse Five Plus Two, The, 181

Henry and June, 337

Henry, O., 193

Henson, Deborah, 199

Hepburn, Audrey, 147

Hepburn, Katharine, 152

Heptones, The, 297

Her Highness and the Bellboy, 143

Her Jungle Love, 219

Her Kind of Man, 46

Her Lucky Night, 49

Her Master's Voice, 90

Herbeck, Ray, 112, 263, 398

Herbert, Victor, 22, 182, 401, 409

Herbert, Victoria, 93

Here Comes Elmer, 293, 423

Here Comes the Band, 233

Here's Love, 187

Herman, Jerry, 346

Herman, Reba Nell, 200

Herman, Woody, 39, 43, 46, 53, 54, 73, 81, 86, 95, 99, 103, 106, 107, 149, 153, 156, 184, 190, 200, 206, 209, 217, 221, 234, 257, 265, 284, 286, 293, 299, 302, 304, 311, 325, 333, 340, 341, 356, 374, 385, 415

Herron, Fiddlin' Red, 212

Hers to Hold, 118

Hershey, June, 81

Herzog, Arthur, 119

Herth, Milt, 84, 107

He's My Guy, 138

Hey, Boy! Hey, Girl!, 25, 104, 207, 397

Hey, Rookie, 393

Heyman, Edward, 3, 45, 46, 77, 96, 152, 217, 235, 246, 258, 280, 285, 368, 392, 420, 424

Heyward, Ronnie, 156

Heywood, Eddie, 54, 126, 153, 245

Heywood, Phil, 67, 420

Hi, Buddy, 79, 148, 274, 313, 339, 355

Hi Diddle Diddle, 240

Hi, Good Lookin', 108, 283

Hi, Neighbor, 82

Hi Ya, Chum, 138

Hibbler, Al, 13, 36, 79, 86, 87, 149, 265, 290, 314, 315, 336, 341, 363, 364, 375, 379, 410

Hickman, Art, 267, 304, 306

Hickman, Sara, 23

Higgins, Billy, 364

Higgins, Eddie, 129

High Level Ranters, The, 31

High Noon, 139

High Society, 211

High Time, 421

Higley, Brewster, 141

Hildegarde, 76, 102, 109, 117, 127, 159, 168, 170, 205, 226, 408, 420

Hill, Benita, 21

Hill, Bertha, 220, 375

Hill, Billy, 117, 133, 179, 204, 211

Hill, Dedette Lee, 2

Hill, Mildred J., 130

Hill, Patty Smith, 130

Hill, Tiny, 7, 19, 26, 77, 169, 176, 223, 253, 268, 294, 296, 399, 415, 427

Hilliard, Bob, 55, 79, 80, 316

Hilliard, Harriet, 94, 211, 265, 278, 312, 417

Hillman, Roc, 252

Hills of Utah, 287

Hills, Anne, 400

Hills, William H., 363

Hilltoppers, The, 167, 290, 293

Hilton, Jack, 73

Hiltzik, Scott, 200

Himber, Richard, 180, 185, 205, 217, 218, 340, 389, 407, 418
Hines, Earl "Fatha," 15, 19, 40, 44, 62, 89, 100, 149, 158, 167, 174, 178, 185, 189, 211, 221, 228, 242, 279, 291–92, 304, 310, 331, 336, 337, 341, 354, 410, 415, 416, 418, 419
Hines, Gregory, 86, 88, 174, 184, 335, 356
Hirsch, Louis, 136
Hirsch, Walter, 81, 221, 311
Hirt, Al, 16, 25, 32, 61, 80, 99, 100, 120, 223, 270, 271, 321, 326, 394, 421
His Butler's Sister, 183
His Honor, the Mayor, 386
Hit Parade of 1943, The, 268
Hit Parade of 1941, The, 84, 230
Hit the Deck, 129, 130, 160, 247
Ho, Don, 14
Hodes, Art, 237, 273, 319, 333, 336, 343, 345, 386
Hodes, Johnny, 86, 208
Hodges, Eddie, 139
Hodges, Jimmie, 332
Hodges, Johnny, 44, 80, 173, 197, 265, 308, 364, 395
Hodges, Joy, 230
Hodgson, Red, 250
Hoey, Evelyn, 20, 42
Hoffman, Al, 105, 131, 135, 144, 150, 168, 214, 225, 356
Hofner, Adolf, 405
Hogan, Claire, 1
Hogan, Ernest, 11
Hogan, Louella, 24
Hold That Ghost, 233, 395
Holden, William, 275
Hole in the Head, A, 139
Holiday, Billie, 12, 13, 43, 55, 77, 78, 83, 86, 95, 96, 97, 101, 114, 115, 116, 119, 121, 151, 152, 153, 158, 169, 171, 185, 187, 198, 219–20, 234, 246, 255, 256, 265, 266, 278, 293, 308, 312, 336, 340, 342, 344, 352, 354, 358, 362, 364, 366, 372, 382, 390, 391, 394, 400, 406, 413, 416, 419, 421, 425, 426
Holiday in Mexico, 124, 250

Holiday Inn, 96, 207
Holiday, Judy, 207, 210, 391
Holiner, Mann, 159, 381
Hollander, Frederick, 219, 376
Hollander, Rick, 30
Holliday, Jennifer, 181
Holliday, Michael, 144
Holloway, Stanley, 380
Holloway, Sterling, 228, 249
Holly, Buddy, 384
Hollywood Canteen, 87
Hollywood Hotel, 43, 53, 273
Hollywood Party, 42
Hollywood Revue of 1929, 402
Holman, Libby, 45, 138, 416
Holmes, Richard, 242
Holt, Dave, 58
Holt, Tim, 227
Holtz, Lou, 200
Holy Terror, The, 110
Holyman Quartet, The, 321
Home on the Prairie, 140
Homer and Jethro, 86, 427
Homer, Louise, 17
Honey, 293
Honeychile, 296
Honeymoon Express, The, 420
Honeymoon Lodge, 85, 162, 177
Honeysuckle Rose, 143
Honky Tonk, 138
Honky Tonk Man, 310
Hoodlum Saint, The, 168
Hooper, R. S., 259
Hoosier Hot Shots, The, 10, 48, 164, 230, 370, 405
Hootenanny Hoot, 42
Hope, Bob, 20, 64, 205, 229, 305, 322, 406, 407
Hopkin, Mary, 202, 217
Hopkins, Claude, 150, 181, 228, 374, 413
Hopkins, Lightnin', 166, 354
Hopkins, Linda, 5, 144, 267, 354
Horn, Shirley, 32, 35, 38, 104, 256, 357, 405
Horne, Lena, 21, 33, 39, 43, 54, 55, 78, 81, 88, 102, 111, 143, 147, 149, 150, 152, 158, 177, 190, 195, 217, 219,

226, 238, 251, 267, 273, 281, 283,
   292, 320, 332, 333, 336, 337, 341–42,
   390, 391, 392, 406, 419
Horne, Marilyn, 193
Horner, Ben, 315
Hornez, Andrez, 58
Horrocks, Jane, 27, 92, 114, 163, 184
Horse Soldiers, The, 46
Horton, Vaughn, 242, 374
Horton, Walter, 195
Horton, Zilphia, 388
Hoschna, Karl, 100
Hot Chocolates, 6, 40
Hot Temperance Seven, The, 359
Hough, Will H., 165
House Calls, 278
House I Live In, The, 145
Houston, Cisco, 34, 57, 58
How the West Was Won, 33, 250, 386,
   395
How to Make an American Quilt, 155
How to Marry a Millionaire, 82
Howard, Bart, 107
Howard, Bob, 163, 336, 390
Howard, Camille, 351
Howard, Dick, 331
Howard, Eddy, 54, 68, 97, 109, 183,
   207, 234, 263, 273, 276, 280, 284,
   285, 296, 297, 303, 315, 372, 374,
   397, 405, 408, 427
Howard, Esther, 200
Howard, Joseph E., 123, 136–37, 165–
   66
Howard, Ron, 45
Howard, Willie and Eugene, 55, 204
Howe, Julia Ward, 32
Hudson, James, 124
Hudson, Will, 107, 244, 245
Hughes, Glen, 276
Hughes, Jimmy, 58
Hughes, Margorie, 98, 272, 383
Hughes, Mary Beth, 6
Hullabaloo, 56, 129
Humes, Helen, 18, 39, 81, 89, 121, 141,
   151, 167, 234, 313, 336, 417
Humperdinck, Engelbert, 21, 110, 150,
   170, 253, 299, 381

Humphrey, Percy, 23, 165, 166, 293,
   331
Humphrey, Willie, 32, 63, 143, 185,
   245
Hundley, John, 408
Hunt, Marsha, 5, 23
Hunt, Pee Wee, 32, 196, 208, 244, 279,
   301, 329, 393
Hunter, Alberta, 6, 33, 121, 138, 340,
   354, 377
Hunter, Ivory Joe, 150, 169, 245
Hunter, Jerry, 142
Hunter, Joe, 193
Hunter, Tab, 170, 192
Hupfield, Herman, 211
Hurfurt, Skeets, 81
Hurricanes, The, 92
Hurt, Mississippi John, 57, 111, 123,
   144, 320, 359
Husik, Lida, 155
Hutchinson, Asa, 359
Hutton, Betty, 176, 230, 296, 304, 305,
   328, 332, 387, 390
Hutton, Ina Ray, 129, 171
Hutton, June, 98
Hutton, Marion, 88, 106, 196, 409, 414
Hylton, Jack, 17, 131, 258, 280, 389
Hyman, Dick, 224, 261, 281, 381, 397,
   421, 427
Hyman, Phyllis, 158, 178, 184, 335,
   356

I Can't Give You Anything But Love,
   152
I Cover the Waterfront, 153
I-Don't-Care Girl, The, 33,136, 154, 272,
   292
I Dream of Jeanie, 34, 193, 258, 272, 273
I Love a Bandleader, 121
I Loved a Woman, 142
I Married an Angel, 14
I Surrender, Dear, 162, 163
I Walk the Line, 163
I Was an American Spy, 36
I Wonder Who's Kissing Her Now, 117–
   18, 123, 137, 166, 180
I Would If I Could, 37
Ice Capades, 195

Ice Capades Revue, 53, 334

Idiot's Delight, 50

If I Had My Way, 167

If Love Were All, 249, 332

If You Knew Susie, 169

Ifield, Frank, 47, 79, 83, 117, 135, 254, 391

Iglesias, Julio, 243, 286, 306, 392

I'll Cry Tomorrow, 177, 397

I'll Get By, 82, 171, 187, 190, 225, 279, 413

I'll See You in My Dreams, 8, 56, 165, 172, 177, 185, 219, 236, 252, 268, 279, 292, 320, 353, 374, 415, 423

I'll Take Romance, 318

I'm Nobody's Sweetheart Now, 268

Imperials, The, 270

Imposters, The, 63, 263

Impressions, The, 258, 310, 368, 377

In Old Chicago, 56, 348

In Old Monterey, 66, 252

In Old Oklahoma, 294

In Posterland, 180

In Society, 237

In the Good Old Summertime, 62, 154, 180, 204, 235, 288, 294, 384

In the Groove, 85

In the Mood, 181

Incendiary Blonde, 76, 167, 185, 230, 296, 305, 349, 390

Indecent Proposal, 263

Indian Territory, 60

Ingham, Keith, 30, 159, 235, 360

Ingle, Red, 106, 109, 162, 202, 262, 281, 292, 367

Inglez, Roberto, 64

Ingraham, Roy, 266

Ingram, Clark, 416

Ink Spots, The, 2, 9, 15, 60, 85, 109, 127, 153, 155, 161,167, 171, 173, 174, 179, 181, 182, 185, 186, 196, 232, 237, 258, 260, 283, 292, 343, 352, 372, 382, 388, 389, 398, 399, 403, 416, 422

Inn of the Sixth Happiness, The, 63

Innocents of Paris, 415

International Revue, The, 102, 277

Interrupted Melody, 18, 88, 231

Ipana Troubadors, The, 26, 42, 261, 328

Irene, 173, 390

Irish Eyes Are Smiling, 213, 219, 248, 393

Irwin, Gene, 106

Irwin, May, 49, 426

Is Everybody Happy?, 9, 64, 175, 185, 236, 277, 278, 292, 337, 371, 387

Isaak, Chris, 386

Island in the Sun, 6

Isle o' Dreams, The, 248, 260, 393

Isley Brothers, The, 138, 302, 360, 397, 414

Istanbul, 392

It Ain't Nothin' But the Blues, 104, 123, 338, 342–43

It All Came True, 236, 293, 393

It Comes Up Love, 220, 312

It Happened One Night, 75

It Should Happen to You, 210

It's a Great Life, 208

Iturbi, José, 18, 305

Ives, Burl, 14, 18, 34, 42, 50, 57, 111, 120, 142, 163, 193, 199, 238, 242, 244, 249, 253, 278, 290, 300, 334

Jackpot, 213

Jackson, Arthur, 93

Jackson, Eddie, 40, 386

Jackson, Ernestine, 21, 198

Jackson Five, The, 112, 162

Jackson, Freddie, 121

Jackson, Joe, 106, 196

Jackson, Mahalia, 16, 17, 90, 118, 138, 150, 267, 333, 388

Jackson, Milt, 23, 81, 389, 391

Jackson, Slim, 140, 183, 229

Jackson, Tony, 291

Jackson, Victoria, 282

Jackson, Wanda, 104, 369

Jacobs, Al, 368

Jacobs, Dick, 61, 104

Jacobs, Jacob, 37

Jacobson, Sascha, 239

Jacquet, Illinois, 237, 286

Jaffe, Moe, 127

Jaffe, Nat, 199

Jam Session, 47, 61, 152, 338
Jamal, Ahmad, 251, 265, 289, 343
James, Colin, 269
James, Etta, 116, 138, 221, 292, 346, 376, 423
James, Harry, 7, 12–13, 44, 60, 61, 71, 78, 85, 90, 96, 102, 108, 114, 116, 126, 136, 138, 151, 153, 155, 156, 158, 162, 167, 168, 171, 173, 174, 186, 188, 191, 196, 213, 221, 226, 229, 233, 237, 243, 244, 252, 254, 267, 277, 278, 279, 281, 283, 288, 319, 323, 325, 326, 330, 331, 340, 344, 345, 348, 349, 363, 377, 384, 394, 398, 405, 406, 407, 410, 419–20, 426
James, Ida, 320
James, Jimmy, 58
James, Joni, 18, 39, 78, 150, 151, 177, 188, 205, 209, 214, 232, 285, 331, 333, 336, 368, 371, 372, 374, 417, 422
James, Lewis, 26, 72, 172
James, Paul, 105, 298
Jamison, Cory, 244, 276
Jamison, Judith, 174
Jan and Dean, 11, 135, 144, 346, 387
Janis, Conrad, 90
Jansell, Sadie, 355
Jarreau, Al, 357
Jarrett, Art, 68, 169, 198, 210, 301, 418
Jason, Will, 285
Jasper, Raymond, 362
Jarvis, Jane, 336
Javor, Laszlo, 116
Jazz on a Summer's Day, 349, 371
Jazz Singer, The, 44, 48, 167, 176, 253, 374
Jean, Gloria, 4, 213, 321
Jeepers Creepers, 180, 212, 213
Jeffries, Herb, 28, 106, 110
Jelly Roll, 29, 371
Jenkins, Andrew, 80
Jenkins, Ella, 31, 63, 188
Jenkins, Gordon, 6, 15, 43, 45, 93, 121, 123, 151, 174, 215, 252, 278, 293, 360, 378
Jennings, Al, 49
Jennings, Waylon, 201

Jenny, Jack, 169, 214
Jericho, 320
Jerome Kern Goes to Hollywood, 204
Jerome, William, 27, 36, 63, 305, 350
Jersey Lily, The, 36
Jessel, George, 53, 109
Jesters, The, 31, 324
Jillian, Ann, 102
Jimerson, Douglas, 198, 359
Jinxed, 61
John, Little Willie, 104
John Murray Anderson's Almanac, 161
John, Scatman, 225
Johnny and the Hurricanes, 298, 310, 318, 417
Johnny Doughboy, 195
Johns, Glynis, 40
Johnson, Arnold, 122
Johnson, Betty, 13, 161
Johnson, Big Jack, 288
Johnson, Buddy and Ella, 92, 323
Johnson, Bunk, 10, 22, 29, 56, 64, 76, 90, 232, 280, 313, 371, 396, 399
Johnson, Chic, 31
Johnson, George W., 398
Johnson, Haven, 255
Johnson, Howard, 166, 247, 365, 390, 396, 401
Johnson, J. C., 195, 216
Johnson, J. Rosamond, 270, 380
Johnson, James P., 44, 59, 167, 175, 189, 199, 273
Johnson, Lonnie, 28, 424
Johnson, Marc, 41
Johnson, Mel, Jr., 7, 131
Johnson, Van, 181, 294, 375
Johnson, William, 377
Johnston, Arthur, 198, 228
Johnston, Johnny, 21, 35, 206, 336, 405
Johnston, Randy, 334
Joker Is Wild, The, 23, 62, 153, 167, 281
Jolly Bachelors, The, 132
Jolson, Al, 5, 8, 10, 21, 25, 26, 27, 34, 44, 48, 49, 53, 56, 62, 64, 79, 89, 91, 98, 106, 109, 164, 165, 167, 168–69, 175, 176, 183, 184, 190, 207, 223, 228, 233, 252, 255–56, 260, 271, 272, 274, 279, 291, 294, 302, 324, 331,

347, 374, 385, 397, 399, 412, 415, 419–
20
Jolson Sings Again, 5, 26, 53, 56, 64,
    109, 175, 176, 183, 223, 256, 292,
    302, 347, 374, 385, 397, 420
Jolson Story, The, 4, 25, 50, 53, 56, 100,
    164, 176, 223, 256, 277, 302, 347,
    374, 385, 397, 399, 420
Jones, Ada, 50, 67, 305, 319, 390, 392
Jones, Alan Rankin, 97
Jones, Allan, 35, 125, 152, 161, 399
Jones, Billy, 8, 86, 89, 115, 137, 140,
    147, 241, 321, 359, 403, 405
Jones, Dick, 29
Jones, Etta, 23, 54, 83, 109, 116, 121,
    138, 150, 170, 217, 220, 254, 256,
    323, 330, 363, 390, 406, 419
Jones, George, 242
Jones, Grandpa, 104
Jones, Hank, 188
Jones, Isham, 43, 75, 103, 108, 156,
    172, 176, 184–85, 196, 199, 206, 254,
    258, 265, 268, 279, 299, 301, 309,
    314, 325, 339, 353, 359, 364, 365,
    371, 375, 405, 410, 426
Jones, Jack, 107, 160, 189, 210, 265,
    296, 325, 358, 368, 422
Jones, Jonah, 201, 236, 302, 341, 356
Jones, Joni, 150
Jones, Palmer, 111
Jones, Quincy, 86, 206, 258, 335, 346,
    372, 391, 419, 424
Jones, Richard M., 375
Jones, Spike, 11, 32, 50, 57, 59, 64, 67,
    75, 79, 83, 90, 117, 134, 137, 159,
    162, 174, 202, 225, 250, 275, 296,
    305, 318, 370, 374, 396, 415, 416
Jones, Tom, 26, 49, 104, 108, 263, 323,
    325, 376, 379, 408
Jordan, Louis, 7, 12, 31, 53, 106, 109,
    115, 267, 313, 345, 349, 376, 385
Jordan, Rickey, 342
Jordan, Steve, 265
Joy Bells, 140
Joyce, Teddy, 179
Jubilaires, The, 275
Jubilee Singers, The, 6
Judge, Dick, 122

Juke Box Jennie, 56, 349
Juke Box Rhythm, 210
Jump for Joy, 158
Jurgens, Dick, 15, 54, 97, 98, 178, 238,
    259, 279, 297, 308, 321, 363
Just a Gigolo, 149, 159, 197

Kabibble, Ish, 370
Kaempfert, Bert, 46, 93, 110, 153, 208,
    242, 258, 280, 283, 298, 304, 312,
    321, 357, 370, 421
Kahal, Irving, 170, 208, 263, 389, 393
Kahn, Gus, 8, 55, 64, 68, 92, 126, 165,
    172, 177, 184, 218, 236, 252, 255,
    268, 279, 291, 301, 353, 359, 374, 414–
    15, 422
Kahn, Walter Wolfe, 18, 151, 208, 249,
    258, 307, 362
Kahuna, Kim, 14, 98, 132, 134, 244,
    255, 299
Kallen, Kitty, 38, 55, 124, 126, 139,
    173, 180, 186, 214, 242, 330, 384
Kalmar, Bert, 163, 200, 263, 404
Kaminsky, Bruce, 378
Kaminsky's Dixielanders, 168
Kanawa, Kiri Te, 44, 96, 205, 312
Kane, Bob, 73
Kane, Donna, 380
Kane, Helen, 163, 361
Karas, Anton, 295
Karate Kid, The, 356
Kardos, Gene, 287, 421
Karger, Fred, 111
Karl, Raymond, 225
Kassel, Art, 27, 250, 389
Katscher, Robert, 391
Katz, Mickey, 335
Kaufman, George S., 15
Kaufman, Irving, 128, 141, 208, 267,
    373
Kay, Beatrice, 41, 177, 209, 275, 298,
    317, 385
Kay, Dolly, 132
Kay, Mack, 122
Kay, Mary, 164
Kaye, Alma, 111
Kaye, Buddy, 1, 112, 371
Kaye, Danny, 11, 29, 33, 40, 44, 58, 84,

166, 182, 194, 239, 250, 281, 337, 349, 397, 409
Kaye, Judy, 138
Kaye, Sammy, 12, 14, 15, 37, 55, 71, 84, 89, 110, 120, 126, 127, 132, 143, 158, 185, 188, 205, 218, 250, 252, 258, 264, 274, 275, 291, 297, 303, 311, 335, 338, 358, 363, 376, 386, 389, 401, 403, 426
Keaton, Diane, 185, 314
Keel, Howard, 82, 283
Keene, Linda, 99
Keep 'Em Flying, 174, 419
Keever, Liz, 207
Kellem, Milton, 120
Kellette, John, 174
Keller, Greta, 45, 211
Kellerman, Fred, 201
Kelly, Daniel, 141
Kelly, Gene, 29, 105, 109, 169, 209, 355, 399, 401
Kelly, Monte, 370
Kelly, Patsy, 152, 196
Kelly, Paula, 88, 124, 143, 264, 275, 364, 372
Kelly, Willie, 67
Kemp, Hal, 89, 97, 108, 116, 124, 129, 143, 159, 185, 217, 250, 284, 315, 370, 426
Kemper, Ronnie, 296
Kenbrovin, Jean, 174
Kenin, Herman, 138
Kennedy, Edward, 157
Kennedy, Jimmy, 132, 183, 258, 299, 335
Kennett, Karl, 428
Kenny, Jack, 241
Kenny, Nick and Charles, 208, 218, 365
Kenny, Tony, 350, 374
Kent, Billy, 29
Kent, Leonard, 140
Kent, Stacey, 427
Kent, Walter, 169, 403
Kenton, Stan, 2, 3, 20, 86, 95, 102, 157, 162, 178, 206, 219, 220, 225, 246, 284, 288, 295, 312, 320, 334, 343, 355, 358, 367, 377, 400, 406

Kentones, The, 368
Kentucky Colonels, The, 212
Kentucky Headhunters, The, 28
Kern, Jerome, 13, 39, 74, 123, 205, 266, 279, 367, 394, 405
Kerr, Anita, 95, 157, 172
Kerr, Jean, 288
Kerrigan, James J., 298
Kershaw, Doug, 348
Kessel, Barney, 50, 89, 163, 216, 345, 394, 426
Kessinger Brothers, The, 229
Key, Francis Scott, 339
Keys, James, 317
Kid Boots, 84
Kid Millions, 228
Kilgore, Rebecca, 182, 302
Kill That Story, 377
Killarney Singers, The, 295, 350
Killen, Louis, 31
Kilmer, Joyce, 375
Kilmer, Val, 21
Kim Loo Sisters, The, 20
Kincaid, Bradley, 393
Kind of Loving, A, 90
King, Andrea, 66
King, B. B., 7, 53, 99, 237
King, Charles, 10, 131, 281, 334
King, Freddie, 362
King, Henry, 20, 26, 96, 116
King, Irving, 321
King, Morgana, 151, 249, 267
King of Burlesque, 336
King of Jazz, 1, 211, 240, 273, 292
King of the Cowboys, 82
King of the Hill, 148, 174, 201, 371
King, Pee Wee, 108, 236, 296, 310, 327, 358, 417
King, Robert A., 35, 166
King, Sandra, 387
King Sisters, The, 12, 23, 104, 139, 157, 162, 171, 217, 245, 252, 283, 304, 305, 311, 343, 351, 398, 399, 405
King Solomon of Broadway, 362
King, Stoddard, 365
King, Teddi, 145, 199, 253, 308, 381, 394, 419
King, Tom, 298

King, Vera, 234
King, Walter Woolf, 86
King, Wayne, 35, 74, 92, 103, 122, 124,
   155, 161, 166, 262, 264, 280, 334,
   339, 376, 387
King, Yvonne, 88
King's Men, The, 366, 400, 422
Kingston Trio, The, 120, 123, 191, 201,
   312, 369, 397
Kinks, The, 30, 316
Kipling, Rudyard, 401, 408
Kirby, John, 379
Kirby Stone Four, The, 181, 353
Kirk, Andy, 73, 115, 143, 217, 336, 382
Kirk, Lisa, 275, 316
Kirsten, Dorothy, 239, 289
Kiss Me, Kate, 111
Kitt, Eartha, 6, 33, 49, 55, 58, 154, 210,
   221, 224, 238, 255, 256, 263, 382
Kittredge, Walter, 358–59
Klein, Oscar, 27
Klenner, John, 135, 198, 215, 236
Kline, Olive, 136
Knef, Hildegarde, 207
Knickerbocker Serenaders, 4, 36, 406
Knight, Evelyn, 49, 291
Knight, Fuzzy, 235, 375
Knight, Gladys, 390, 397
Knight, June, 187
Knightsbridge Strings, The, 69
Knox, Buddy, 283
Koehler, Ted, 21, 38, 89, 114, 130, 151,
   158, 190, 210, 336, 341, 376, 397, 410
Koenig, Martha E., 55
Kohlam, Churchill, 68–69
Konitz, Lee, 196
Koplow, Don Howard, 270
Kornkobblers, The, 165, 399
Kosma, Joseph, 24
Kostelanetz, André, 3, 34, 52, 79, 107,
   125, 229, 243, 272, 273, 274, 334, 337
Kral, Roy, 50, 112, 245, 276
Krall, Diana, 13, 38, 69, 86, 115, 157,
   168, 293
Kramer, Alex, 7
Kreisler, Fritz, 35, 274, 290
Kresa, Helmy, 361
Kristien, Dale, 173

Krueger, Benny, 147, 165, 301
Krupa, Gene, 5, 10, 14, 31, 32, 41, 44,
   52, 61, 63, 68, 80, 90, 100, 102, 115,
   125, 135, 182, 193, 205, 207, 218,
   231, 243, 246, 255, 258, 261, 273,
   286, 303, 321, 322, 323, 329, 362,
   364, 367, 377, 387, 398, 409, 414, 417
Kuhn, Judy, 126, 186, 311
Kurtz, Manny, 178
Kyser, Kay, 44, 68, 88, 99, 104, 108,
   194, 195, 250, 274, 276, 289, 291,
   338, 343, 363, 370, 382, 389, 390,
   391, 403, 405, 409, 419

La Bamba, 124
La Belle, Patti, 74, 390, 394
La Centra, Peg, 77, 369
La Redd, Cora, 376
La Rocca, Nick, 370
Lacalle, Joseph M., 15
Ladies' Man, The, 164
Ladies They Talk About, 167, 338
Lady Be Good, 205, 226, 403
Lady Is a Square, The, 217
Lady on a Train, 115, 290
Lady Sings the Blues, 11, 119, 120, 153,
   220, 226, 234, 256, 342, 354, 362,
   390, 426
Ladysmith Black Mambazo, 270, 352
Lahr, Bert, 152, 211
Laine, Cleo, 5, 39, 93, 102, 151, 175,
   189, 267, 276, 279, 381, 391
Laine, Frankie, 14, 36, 41, 44, 51, 61,
   68, 87, 92, 114, 135, 136, 139, 150,
   155, 161, 191, 196, 221, 232, 246,
   250, 263, 278, 300, 315, 319, 321,
   325, 334, 360, 361, 362, 371, 372,
   373, 394, 410, 418, 422, 426
Lake Placid Serenade, 81, 255, 385, 402,
   407
Lamb, Arthur J., 40
Lambert, Dave, 134, 286, 397
Lambert, Louis, 394
Lambert, Mande, 218
Lamour, Dorothy, 14, 158, 210, 219,
   244, 284, 352, 376
Lampe, Del, 75
Lane, Abbe, 126, 178

Lane, Burton, 352
Lane, Kathleen, 307
Lane, Ken, 100
Lane, Priscilla, 37
Lane, Ronnie, 41, 49
Lang, Eddie, 33, 287, 303
Lang, K. D., 325, 328
Lange, Jessica, 221, 310, 348, 422
Lange, Johnny, 249
Langdon, Sue Ann, 111
Langford, Frances, 30, 97, 132, 159,
   170, 174, 183, 218, 245, 250, 251,
   257, 278, 281, 284, 299, 326, 362
Langford, Frank, 250
Lanham, Roy, 158, 326, 395
Lanin, Lester, 3, 59, 117, 169, 189, 241,
   298, 368, 374
Lanin, Sam, 147, 168, 185, 208, 225,
   246, 373
Lanson, Snooky, 112, 275, 276
Lanza, Mario, 13, 35, 36, 203, 217, 236,
   245, 247, 252, 260, 367, 372, 392,
   397, 408, 422
Larceny With Music, 399
Larkin Sisters, The, 374
Larkins, Ellis, 177
LaRosa, Julius, 51, 124, 150, 266, 369,
   398, 419
Larue, Jacques, 61, 333
Las Vegas Nights, 172
Las Vegas Story, The, 157
Last Picture Show, The, 44, 66, 139, 192,
   221, 289, 327, 418
Last Roundup, The, 205, 318
Last Time I Saw Paris, The, 205
Lathrop, Jack, 128
Latouche, John, 28
Laugh Parade, The, 424
Laugh Your Blues Away, 14, 138
Laughlin, Tim, 75
Laura, 206
Laurel, Stan, 375
Laurie, Annie, 323
Law of the Underworld, 105
Lawlor, Charles B., 323
Lawrence, Barbara, 7
Lawrence, Bill, 192
Lawrence, Elliot, 39, 320

Lawrence, Gertrude, 45, 71, 102, 332
Lawrence, Jack, 12, 129, 167, 326, 346,
   357, 414
Lawrence, Kate, 72
Lawrence, Steve, 18, 30, 37, 38, 126,
   171, 231, 289, 331, 368
Lawrence, Syd, 3
Laws, Herbert, 76
Lawson, Carl, 274
Layton and Johnstone, 183
Layton, Eddie, 311, 338, 355, 400
Layton, J. Turner, 5, 80, 82–83, 387
Layton, John, 154
Le Boy, Grace, 165
Lea, Barbara, 30, 42, 158, 210, 215,
   216, 222, 249, 254, 267, 333, 387
Leadbelly, 28, 73, 91, 123, 195, 201,
   325, 352, 383
Leadbelly, 123, 193
Leader, Mickey, 49
League of Their Own, A, 278
Leary, Ford, 105
Leathernecking, 421
Lebedeff, Aaron, 37
Lecuona, Ernesto, 47, 312, 321
Lee, Alfred, 75
Lee, Barron, 52
Lee, Brenda, 40, 44, 45, 69, 85, 112,
   114, 167, 187, 207, 302, 356, 357,
   388, 416, 422, 426, 427
Lee, Bryon, 110, 232
Lee, Julia, 167, 259, 267, 375
Lee, Laura, 323
Lee, Loretta, 43, 94, 265, 365
Lee, Mary, 57
Lee, Peggy, 3, 8, 38, 39, 51, 73, 78, 81,
   82, 96, 99, 104, 110, 112, 119, 122,
   127, 132, 138, 145, 147, 152, 155,
   158, 169, 171, 175, 186, 190, 198,
   210, 216, 219, 221, 224, 227, 233,
   256, 259, 270, 271, 273, 275, 285,
   288, 300, 312, 316, 327, 329, 331,
   332, 342, 343, 344, 352, 362, 381,
   384, 389, 390, 393, 398, 402, 405,
   414, 418
Lee, Ranee, 356
Lee, Roberta, 327
Lee, Stella, 382

Leeds, Milton, 286
Leff, Jeanette, 86
Legrand, Michel, 333
Lehrman Engel Singers, The, 118
Lehrman, Lotte, 118
Leigh, Carolyn, 38, 407, 421
Leigh, Janet, 118, 143
Leighton Brothers, The, 57
Leliohaku, 133
Lemare, Jules, 348
Lemley, Quinn, 207, 293
Lemon Drop Kid, The, 84
Lemmon, Jack, 145, 189, 210
Lemper, Ute, 224
Lengsfelder, Hans, 286
Lennon Sisters, The, 18, 24, 104, 141, 191, 312, 315, 340, 352, 364, 373, 377
Lenox, Jean, 154
Leonetti, Tommy, 131
Leonard, Anita, 346
Leonard, Eddie, 166
Leonard, Harlan, 155
Leonard, Jack, 13, 182, 231, 266, 278, 330, 336
Lerner, Sammy, 94, 195
LeRoy, Hal, 427
Leslie, Edgar, 17, 22, 108, 212, 244, 245, 297, 301
Leslie, Joan, 413
Lessack, Lee, 24, 206
Lester, Ketty, 217–18, 369
Let 'Em Eat Cake, 238–39
Let Freedom Ring, 142, 145, 188, 393
Let the Good Times Roll, 45, 170, 251, 302, 323
Let's Dance, 371
Let's Fall in Love, 210
Let's Make It Legal, 36
Letterman, The, 11, 21, 117, 186, 217, 294, 316, 373, 392
Letters, Will, 132
Levant, Oscar, 239, 332
Levey, Ethel, 9
Levine, Mark, 168
Levine, Sam, 229
Lew Leslie's Blackbirds, 148, 159, 236, 337
Lewey, Fred J., 411

Lewis, Al, 44, 265, 268, 303, 386
Lewis, Alde, Jr., 140
Lewis, Brenda, 192
Lewis, Diana, 34
Lewis, Furry, 269
Lewis, Gary, 11
Lewis, George, 29, 73, 75, 77, 90, 166, 212, 232, 318, 412
Lewis, Harold, 369
Lewis, Harry, 390
Lewis, Jerry, 115, 164, 177, 256, 302, 359
Lewis, Jerry Lee, 55, 66, 85, 111, 129, 179, 192, 214, 218, 221, 231, 238, 251, 273, 303, 311, 316, 323, 331, 348, 360, 397, 405, 422, 425
Lewis, Joe E., 309
Lewis, Monica, 24
Lewis, Morgan, 146
Lewis, Patti, 115, 214
Lewis, Ramsay, 323, 358
Lewis, Roger, 279
Lewis, Sam, 2, 35, 84, 106, 108, 116, 147, 159, 176, 178, 198, 206, 255, 302, 323, 343, 362
Lewis, Sheri, 208
Lewis, Smiley, 341
Lewis, Ted, 10, 19, 73, 103, 111, 121, 133, 165, 178, 183, 197, 211, 215, 230, 233, 237, 268, 271, 278, 280, 306, 319, 332, 337, 338, 359, 364, 371, 376, 395
Lewis, Vicki, 80
Leybourne, George, 75
Libbey, J. Aldrich, 4
Liberace, 37, 61, 96, 104, 214, 218, 233, 262, 275, 347, 356, 360, 379
Life and Times of Judge Roy Bean, The, 414
Life of Her Own, A, 97
Liggins, Joe, 296
Light, Enoch, 14, 225
Lightfoot, Terry, 166
Lightner, Winnie, 331
Liliuokalani, 14
Lilley, Joseph J., 194
Lillian Russell, 4, 31, 66, 223
Lillie, Beatrice, 160

Limeliters, The, 368
Linck, Paul, 117
Lincoln, Abbey, 256, 342, 395
Lind, Jenny, 142
Lindeman, Edith, 214
Lindsay, Jenny, 72
Link, Harry, 189, 366
Lippman, Sid, 1, 373
Lipscomb, Mance, 183
Listen Darling, 427
Little Anthony and the Imperials, 87, 153, 217
Little Bit of Heaven, A, 213
Little Giant, 62
Little, Little Jack, 20, 178, 211, 420
Little Lost Boy, 76
Little Miss Broadway, 130, 399
Little Miss Marker, 322, 350
Little Nellie Kelly, 74
Little Nemo, 401
Little, Rich, 216
Little Voice, 114, 163, 220
Little Willie John, 326
Littlefield, Little Willie, 305
Littlest Rebel, The, 289
Liverpool, Phil, 201
Living in a Big Way, 185, 413
Livingston, Jay, 119, 242, 295, 356, 372
Livingston, Jerry, 75, 177, 188, 225, 380
Lizzie, 187
Load of Coal, 143
Lockhart, Gene, 410
Lockheart, Paula, 426
Lodd's Black Aces, 413
Loder, John, 201
Loeb, John Jacob, 46, 187, 305, 314
Loesser, Frank, 133, 134–35, 194, 196, 244, 276, 291, 312, 336, 390
Logan, Ella, 20
Logan, Frederick Knight, 244
Lolita, 294
Lomax, John, 123
Lombardo, Carmen, 2, 46, 68, 116, 187, 264, 291, 301, 308, 314, 329, 340, 351, 389, 398, 420
Lombardo, Guy, 2, 5, 12, 15, 31, 33, 37, 40, 42, 46, 50, 56, 60, 68, 80, 81, 86, 93, 96, 97, 99, 108, 110, 111, 112, 115, 116, 123, 127, 128, 131, 132, 134, 144, 145, 155, 161, 172, 183, 187, 195, 204, 206, 215, 233, 237, 238, 250, 251, 263, 264, 265, 277, 281, 283, 284, 291, 297, 298, 299, 301, 307, 308, 314, 315, 329, 337, 339, 340, 342, 348, 351, 354, 364, 370, 389, 391, 392, 398, 407, 420, 423, 424
London, Julie, 43, 59, 67, 69, 71, 97, 101, 104, 119, 137, 172, 184, 189, 214, 218, 259, 315, 367, 391, 398, 405, 416, 420, 426
London String Quartet, The, 273
Lonely Guy, The, 420
Long, Avon, 21, 143, 266
Long, Jeanie, 324
Long, Johnny, 44, 139, 178, 185, 246, 350, 384
Long Gray Line, The, 24
Long Long Trailer, The, 48
Long Voyage Home, The, 132
Look for the Silver Lining, 197, 320, 372
Looking for Love, 151
Loos, Anita, 159
Lopez, Vincent, 15, 44, 99, 116, 147, 175, 197, 201–202, 301, 321
Lopez, Trini, 51, 107, 120, 286, 369, 383, 397
Lorenzo, Ange, 326
Lorraine, Lillian, 50, 71, 305, 319
Los Indios Tabajares, 230
Loss, Joe, 320
Lost Horizon, 316
Loudon, Dorothy, 134, 161, 179, 184, 185, 247, 267, 331, 357, 400
Louigay, M., 61
Louise, Tina, 129
Louisiana Hayride, 294, 320
Louisiana Washboard Five, The, 228
Love Affair, 407
Love and Hisses, 76
Love, Bessie, 131, 402
Love, Geoff, 138
Love Happy, 274, 406
Love, Honor and Behave, 37
Love in the Afternoon, 58, 103

Love Is a Many Splendored Thing, 216
Love Letters, 217
Love Me or Leave Me, 3, 23, 100, 106, 153, 177, 184, 219, 234, 251, 309, 316, 357, 420
Love Me Tonight, 144
Loveday, Carroll, 361
Lovell, Royal, 18
Lover, Come Back, 197, 215
Loving You, 287
Lowe, Ruth, 171–72, 294
Lowery, Fred, 161, 208, 299, 329, 339, 355
Lown, Bert, 45, 51, 153, 351, 393, 400, 418
Luban, Francia, 312
Lubin, Joe, 288
Lucas, Nick, 12, 15, 51, 74, 106, 108, 171, 176, 178, 321, 326, 329, 373
Lucky Boy, 53
Lucky Lady, 7, 144, 397
Luker, Rebecca, 87
Lullaby of Broadway, 179, 332, 427
Lunceford, Jimmie, 7, 25, 27, 60, 84, 90, 96, 97, 105, 107, 143, 163, 185, 228, 230, 238, 243, 251, 255, 274, 293, 300, 304, 307, 334, 339
Lund, Art, 128, 243, 276, 326, 391, 418
Lupino, Ida, 5, 45, 365, 406
Lupone, Patti, 7, 101, 222, 398
Lutcher, Joe, 296
Lutcher, Nellie, 40, 48, 133, 199, 276, 279, 334
Luther, Frank, 31, 79, 214
Luxury Liner, 284, 415
Lyman, Abe, 3, 10, 38, 48, 53, 153, 198, 214, 328, 376
Lyman, Arthur, 14
Lyman, Frankie, 7, 83, 117, 124, 280, 390
Lyman, Tommy, 2, 135, 251, 257, 283
Lymon, Lewis, 373
Lynch, Christopher, 248
Lynn, Imogene, 229, 285
Lynn, Loretta, 348
Lynn, Vera, 16, 18, 21, 38, 54, 79, 93, 133, 135, 155, 170, 171, 185, 233, 238, 258, 264, 319, 381, 388, 389, 395, 403, 407, 425
Lynne, Gloria, 20, 129, 252, 286, 288, 367, 376, 391, 403
Lynne, Phyllis, 311
Lynne, Shelby, 163
Lysinger, Pat, 136
Lytell, Jimmy, 274

M 'n' M Trio, The, 156, 179, 354
Ma! He's Making Eyes at Me, 224
MacDonald, Ballard, 35, 65, 182, 288, 304, 331, 375
MacDonald, Jeanette, 14, 25, 33, 35, 56, 84, 219, 331, 366
MacDonough, Harry, 80, 262, 393, 394
MacEwan, Fr. Sydney, 93
MacFarlane, George, 213
MacGill, Casey, 184
Mack, Andrew, 135, 287
Mack, Cecil, 59, 273, 319, 362, 423
Mack, Ira, 298
Mack the Knife, 224
MacKenzie, Gisele, 3, 61, 98, 327, 333, 379, 391, 424
MacKenzie, Leonard, 64
MacLaine, Shirley, 5
MacMurray, Fred, 41
MacNamara Singers, The, 350
MacRae, Floyd F., 317
MacRae, Gordon, 1, 8, 13, 45, 50, 78, 79, 80, 123, 124, 128, 163, 184, 197, 249, 297, 371, 422
Mad Dogs and Englishmen, 69
Madam Satan, 183
Madame Sherry, 100, 294
Madden, Edward, 50, 193, 277
Madden, Frank, 232
Maddox, Johnny, 135, 169, 275, 377
Madriguera, Enric, 3, 321
Magidson, Herb, 99, 120, 171, 250
Magine, Frank, 311
Magnificent Ambersons, The, 227
Mahal, Taj, 30, 320
Maharis, George, 357, 407
Mahogany, Kevin, 206
Mahoney, Jack, 399
Mahoney, Jerry, 41

Main Street Band, 399
Majestic, The, 283
Make a Wish, 289
Make Believe Ballroom, 177, 278
Make It Snappy, 318, 415
Make Mine Music, 5, 320
Make Way for Tomorrow, 248
Malaya, 43, 284, 364
Malcolm X, 108
Malneck, Matty, 124, 177, 316, 338
Maltby, Richard, 297
Mamas and the Papas, The, 92
Mambo Kings, The, 286
Mammy, 256, 399, 415
Man Called Peter, A, 225
Man From Oklahoma, The, 174
Man I Love, The, 45, 226, 406
Man of the Century, 241
Man-Proof, 276
Man Who Knew Too Much, The, 295
Mancini, Henry, 369, 379
Mandrell, Barbara, 150
Mangione, Chuck, 116
Manhansett Quartette, The, 287
Manhattan, 189, 239
Manhattan Mary, 197
Manhattan Melodrama, 42
Manhattan Transfer, The, 42, 159, 201, 289, 305, 352, 377
Manhattans, The, 361
Manilow, Barry, 18, 88, 171, 246, 266, 294, 311, 389
Mann, Carl, 243
Mann, Dale, 364
Mann, David, 80
Mann, Herbie, 108, 214
Mann, Marion, 81, 89, 176
Mann, Paul, 294
Mann, Peggy, 36, 102
Manners, Bernard, 5, 237
Manners, Henry, 387
Manners, Zeke, 324
Mannheim Steamroller, 28
Manning, Dick, 104, 144, 247, 356
Manone, Wingy, 33, 46, 57, 73, 94, 107, 149, 181, 183, 209, 250, 254, 266, 292, 300, 352
Mantovanni's Orchestra, 3, 16, 38, 60, 74, 107, 189, 217, 230, 286, 299, 321, 333, 340, 369, 377, 414
Many Happy Returns, 351
Maphis, Joe, 229, 262
Marcellino, Muzzy, 209
Marcels, The, 43, 135
March, Lucy Isabelle, 117
Marchetti, F. D., 103
Marcovicci, Andrea, 2, 12, 15, 24, 39, 44, 92, 146, 170, 174, 186, 205, 207, 220, 231, 245, 246, 264, 267, 299, 312, 315, 325, 334, 364, 367, 389, 391, 393, 395, 402, 403, 426
Marcus, Sol, 155, 395
Mares, Paul Joseph, 103, 261
Margie, 7, 23, 25, 59, 60, 172, 230, 259, 370, 409
Marianne, 401
Mariano, Charlie, 341
Marion, George, Jr., 253, 396
Marks, Edward B., 213, 248, 283
Marks, Gerald, 12, 94, 183, 425
Marks, Godfrey, 308
Marks, Johnny, 2, 306
Marks, Larry, 14
Markush, Fred, 355
Marley, Bob, 59, 118
Marlowe, Marion, 355
Marlowe, Mary, 127
Married Before Breakfast, 105
Married With Children, 216
Marrow, Esther, 397
Marrying Man, The, 143, 217, 423
Mars, Kenneth, 211
Marsala, Joe, 160
Marsalis, Wynton, 31, 101, 336, 394
Marsh, Bernard J., 33–34, 250
Marsh, Roy, 162
Marshall, Charles, 159
Marshall, Larry, 131, 239
Marterie, Ralph, 54, 206, 221, 284, 326, 330
Martin, Dean, 1, 2, 9, 12, 29, 51, 54, 56, 60, 76, 92, 98, 100–101, 106, 117, 124, 135, 148, 154, 155, 163, 169, 180, 183, 187, 198, 205, 209, 211, 227, 236, 237, 262, 264, 276, 278, 279, 285, 291, 297, 299, 300, 309,

313, 321, 327, 332, 335, 351, 356,
359, 360, 366, 374, 382, 383, 385,
387, 400, 417, 424, 426
Martin, Freddy, 1, 20, 33, 96, 124, 135,
156, 194, 206, 212, 233, 235, 240,
251, 276, 277, 304, 316, 329, 330,
340, 372, 388, 389
Martin, Jimmy, 34, 358
Martin, Johnny, 6
Martin, Mary, 172, 384
Martin, Sam, 418
Martin, Sara, 344
Martin, Tony, 3, 13, 35, 54, 68, 78, 97,
98, 107, 126, 129, 133, 150, 155, 158,
159, 171, 173, 205, 216, 228, 236,
244, 247, 250, 277, 335, 366, 372,
374, 401, 410, 418
Martino, Al, 104, 108, 110, 133, 236,
299, 331, 369, 372, 383, 416
Marvell, Holt, 366
Marvin, Johnny, 65, 81, 122, 233, 321
Marx Brothers, The, 15, 43, 164, 200,
258, 274, 352
Maschwitz, Eric, 264
M*A*S*H, 131, 251
Masquerade in Mexico, 286
Massey, Curt, 426
Massey, Guy, 292
Massey, Louise, 98
Mason, Barbara, 110
Mason, Rod, 223
Masters, Frankie, 13
Mathis, Johnny, 38, 59, 73, 82, 151,
178, 187, 206, 210, 228, 232, 242,
316, 327, 338, 343, 364, 391, 395,
398, 418
Mating Game, The, 393
Matlock, Matty, 275, 344
Matson, Vera, 23
Matthews, Gerry, 407
Matthews, Jessie, 72, 73, 134
Mauriat, Paul, 379
Maxwell, Robert, 97, 316
May, Allen, 213
May, Billy, 33, 60, 62, 97, 106, 120,
143, 213, 255, 259, 265, 286, 317,
344, 364, 367, 381, 393, 398, 415
Mayes, Sally, 152

Mayfair and Montmartre, 93
Mayfair, Mitzie, 214
Mayfield, Curtis, 110, 305, 368
Mayhew, Nye, 301, 368
Mayhew, Billy, 185
Mayhew, Stella, 129
Mays, Bill, 24, 126
Maytime, 56, 220
Mazeltones, The, 313
McAfee, Johnny, 78
McBride, Donald, 352
McBroom, Amanda, 30
McCall, Mary Ann, 81, 186, 401, 424
McCarron, Charles, 270
McCarthy, Henry, 46
McCarthy, Joseph, 173, 297, 381, 390,
420
McCartney, Linda, 242
McCauley, Jack, 111
McClintock, Poley, 166
McClure, George, 2
McConnell, Rob, 129, 314
McCorkle, Susannah, 44, 87, 93, 112,
146, 155, 255, 293
McCormack, John, 10, 22, 159, 173,
193, 213, 219, 236, 245, 248, 260,
271, 323, 348, 360, 370, 393, 395, 422
McCoy, Clyde, 43, 127, 165, 243, 273,
344, 400
McCoy, Joe, 405
McCoy, Viola, 28, 145
McCoys, The, 104
McCrane, Paul, 196
McCree, Junie, 294
McDaniel, Floyd, 314
McDermott, John, 52
McDonald, Audra, 39
McDonald, Marie, 185
McDonald, Skeets, 122
McDowell, Ronnie, 21
McEntire, Reba, 170, 346
McGill, Josephine, 93
McGillan, Howard, 97
McGimsey, Bob, 115
McGovern, Maureen, 56, 114, 120,
147, 294, 331, 418
McGrath, Bob, 355
McGregor, Freddie, 354

McGuire Sisters, The, 10, 21, 89, 124, 216, 236, 314, 323, 362, 383, 409

McHugh, Jimmy, 42, 67, 86, 102, 122, 140, 151, 152, 215, 277, 336, 359, 395, 399

McIntyre, Patience and Prudence, 120, 373

McKee, Lonette, 39

McKenna, Dave, 32, 96, 129, 207, 208, 233, 280, 344

McKenna, William C., 132

McKenzie, Red, 2, 76, 188, 190, 198, 206, 308, 362

McKinley, Ray, 33–34, 46, 106, 132, 159, 408

McKinney's Cotton Pickers, 3, 27, 62, 113, 156, 167

McLaren, Malcolm, 49

McLean, Don, 49, 221, 262, 267

McLerie, Allyn, 249

McMartin, John, 211

McNair, Sylvia, 39, 204, 367

McNeil, Lonnie, 349

McPartland, Joe, 173, 213, 219, 232

McPartland, Marian, 24, 43, 61, 87, 96, 105, 127, 169, 222, 289, 315, 333, 356

McPhatter, Clyde, 344

McPherson, R. C., 319, 423

McQueen, Amelia, 105, 337, 396

McRae, Carmen, 30, 39, 43, 45, 78, 101, 102, 107, 115, 134, 147, 160, 178, 204, 252, 253, 286, 288, 290, 342, 345, 382, 421

McShann, Jay, 81, 354, 375

Me and Bessie, 5

Me and Juliet, 265

Mecum, Dudley, 19

Meek, Joe, 390

Meeker, Ralph, 153, 332

Meerpool, Abel, 342

Meet Danny Wilson, 12, 121, 146, 189, 319, 400

Meet Me at the Fair, 40, 272, 349

Meet Me in Las Vegas, 111

Meet Me in St. Louis, 234, 325, 380

Mehldau, Brad, 92

Melachrino, George, 203

Melba, 142

Melchior, Lauritz, 36, 97

Mellin, Robert, 421

Mello-Larks, The, 276

Mellor, Tom, 394

Melody for Two, 315

Melody Lane, 212, 334

Melody Ranch, 27

Melody Time, 375

Melotone Boys, The, 393

Melrose, Walter, 345

Melton, James, 35, 57, 248, 315, 422

Melvin and Howard, 51

Memphis Belle, 74, 108, 126

Men With Wings, 174

Mendelsohn, Fred, 298

Mendez, Sergio, 125, 370

Mercer, Frances, 13

Mercer, Johnny, 10, 18–19, 24, 78, 79, 87, 92, 95, 108, 115, 117–18, 124, 175, 206, 208, 238, 241, 243, 293, 310–11, 313, 314, 325–26, 337, 343, 344, 365, 367, 398, 404, 405, 417

Mercer, Mabel, 2, 24, 53, 73, 107, 134, 228, 251, 398, 402

Mercer, Tommy, 24

Menjou, Adolphe, 350

Meringlo, Marieann, 59

Merman, Ethel, 10, 44, 80, 139, 145, 158, 168, 228, 299, 396

Merrick, Dick, 206

Merrill, Bob, 86, 168, 335

Merrill, Carol, 157

Merrill, Helen, 35, 42, 96, 113, 134, 333, 405

Merrill, Joan, 71

Merrill, Robert, 205

Merrill, Scott, 224

Merry-Go-Round of 1938, 165, 301, 355

Merry Macs, The, 81, 194, 205, 207, 225, 244, 291, 303

Merry Monahans, The, 56, 173, 179, 241, 303, 304, 390, 399

Metaxa, Georges, 168, 350, 416

Methot, Mayo, 247

Metropolitan, 204

Metz, Theodore M., 144

Mexicali Rose, 98, 238, 425

Mexicana, 98

Meyer, George, 108, 228, 363
Meyer, Joseph W., 53, 168, 196, 218, 254
Mezzrow, Mezz, 211, 235, 245
Micanopy Brass Band, The, 413
Michaels, Lee, 394
Michuda, Marie, 313
Midler, Bette, 117, 181, 209, 293, 325
Midnight Frolics, 304 ·
Midnight in the Garden of Good and Evil, 25, 92, 108, 206, 325
Midnight Rounders, The, 223, 230
Migenes, Julia, 47
Mighty Blue Kings, The, 296
Migliacci, Franci, 383
Milburn, Richard, 212
Miles, Alfred Hart, 18
Miles, Lizzie, 6, 427
Miles, Vera, 229, 285
Miller, Ann, 87, 111, 152, 316, 382
Miller, Big, 4, 12
Miller, Dale, 73, 322
Miller, Eddie, 9, 283, 318
Miller, Frank, 236
Miller, Glenn, 3, 14, 15, 18, 23, 33, 35, 37, 42, 44, 54, 61, 68, 71, 74, 84, 88, 99, 100, 103, 108, 115, 122, 125, 129, 140, 141, 156, 158, 167, 172, 176, 178, 181, 182, 193, 194, 196, 204, 213, 235, 241, 244, 246, 251, 252, 254, 255, 258, 263, 264, 271, 273, 277, 279, 281, 283, 285, 286, 289, 294, 304, 307, 312, 319, 320, 322, 325, 330, 338, 339, 345, 346, 352, 370, 372, 377, 382, 394, 398, 403, 407, 409, 414, 416
Miller, Henry S., 57
Miller, Marilyn, 39, 96, 228, 372
Miller, Mitch, 8, 31, 46, 51, 63, 67, 73, 90, 106, 135, 162, 169, 173, 176, 188, 209, 242, 318, 321, 322, 323, 335, 348, 350, 364, 371, 374, 378, 397, 399, 402
Miller, Mrs., 313
Miller, Ned, 345, 405
Miller, Ray, 19, 298
Miller, Sonny, 124
Miller, Woods, 123

Miller's Crossing, 124
Millinder, Lucy, 375, 395
Million Dollar Mermaid, 209
Millionaire for Christy, A, 115
Mills Blue Rhythm Band, The, 239, 244, 314, 345, 376
Mills Brothers, The, 2, 27, 54, 55, 56, 63, 77, 84, 99, 107, 117, 122, 155, 156, 167, 169, 181, 184, 187, 192, 207, 208, 214, 218, 235, 238, 240, 250, 253, 261, 263, 268, 273, 274, 277, 279, 283, 293, 300, 302, 312, 326, 332, 337, 347, 349, 350, 351, 358, 370–71, 391, 393, 399, 416, 421, 424
Mills, Florence, 228
Mills, Frederick Allen, 21–22
Mills, Haley, 17
Mills, Irving, 45, 54, 140, 178, 184, 220, 239, 243, 244, 245, 334, 395
Mills, Kerry, 234
Milton, Roy, 269
Mimms, Garnet, 110
Mingus, Charles, 116, 129, 174
Mingus, Eric, 2
Minnelli, Liza, 15, 51, 59, 119, 127, 161, 226, 256, 263, 279, 299, 325, 357, 374, 380, 391, 405
Minnevitch, Borrah, 75
Minnigerode, Meade, 401
Minoque, Kylie, 99
Minstrel Man, 257
Mintun, Peter, 359, 377
Mintzer, Bob, 262
Miracle at Morgan's Creek, The, 279
Miranda, Carmen, 47, 164, 175
Mirror Has Two Faces, The, 376
Miskulin, Joey, 364
Misner, Susan, 311
Miss Dolly Dollars, 409
Miss Innocence, 319
Miss Nobody From Starland, 166
Miss Susie Slagle's, 180
Missing, 13
Mississippi, 274
Mississippi Rhythm, 417
Mitchell, Charles, 417
Mitchell, George D., 2

Mitchell, Guy, 301, 335
Mitchell, Melanie, 421
Mitchell, Sidney D. 235, 344
Mizzy, Vic, 354
Modern Klezmer Quartet, The, 378
Modern Times, 327
Modernaires, The, 77, 88, 99, 124, 158,
    196, 204, 228, 264, 275, 286, 361,
    363, 364, 370, 372
Modugno, Domenico, 383
Moeller, Friedrich Wilhelm, 131
Molasky, Jessica, 8, 34, 272, 326, 391,
    393, 397
Mole, Miff, 10, 144, 253, 280, 386
Moll, Billy, 166, 410
Molloy, J. L., 220
Molly and Me, 209
Moments, The, 167
Moms and Dads, The, 2, 19, 21, 35,
    75, 90, 92, 218, 236, 238, 241, 242,
    255, 271, 294, 299, 308, 326, 358,
    364, 405, 413, 418, 421
Mona Lisa, 243, 392
Monaco, James V., 305, 390, 420
Mondello, Toots, 216
Monk, Thelonious, 10, 20, 56, 75, 174,
    235, 243, 348, 351
Monkey Business, 348, 393, 402
Monro, Matt, 108, 252, 265, 280, 350,
    371, 408
Monroe, Bill, 92, 176, 292
Monroe, Lucy, 340
Monroe, Marilyn, 5, 51, 163, 177, 207,
    307, 392
Monroe, Vaughn, 29, 71, 75, 93, 172,
    188, 197, 209, 236, 237, 244, 245,
    249, 252, 255, 271, 278, 295, 298,
    300, 306, 309, 314, 323, 332, 335,
    360, 364, 383, 387, 395, 425
Montana, Patsy, 208, 425
Montand, Yves, 58
Monte, Lou, 76, 135, 168, 318
Montgomery, Garth, 64
Montgomery, Marion, 138
Montgomery, Robert, 332
Montgomery, Wes, 48, 114, 189, 273
Montrose, Percy, 65
Moody, James, 216

Moon Over Miami, 245
Moon Over Parador, 38
Mooney, Art, 6, 26, 34, 106, 168, 176
Mooney, Harold, 426
Mooney, Joe, 264, 393
Moonglows, The, 44, 323
Moonlight and Cactus, 91, 141
Moonlight in Havana, 166, 393
Moonlight in Vermont, 246
Moonstruck, 245
Moore, Anthony, 58
Moore, Constance, 5, 50, 84, 158, 164,
    185, 268, 276, 402
Moore, Dudley, 43
Moore, Fleecie, 53
Moore, Grace, 10, 15, 61, 225, 239,
    321, 391
Moore, Lee, 57
Moore, Mary Tyler, 344
Moore, Phil, 320
Moorehead, Agnes, 227
Moran, Lois, 238
Moran, Polly, 402
Morath, Max, 8, 208, 217, 268, 273,
    395, 427
Moreno, Buddy, 279
Moreno, Rita, 113
Moret, Neil, 64, 245, 318
Morgan, Al, 192
Morgan, Corrine, 399
Morgan, Dennis, 31, 213, 320, 355,
    384, 393, 394, 401, 406, 408, 421
Morgan, George, 279, 303, 425
Morgan, Harry, 111
Morgan, Helen, 25, 39, 45, 111, 116,
    189, 197, 226, 233–34, 247, 257, 331,
    351, 405–406
Morgan, Jane, 3, 21, 104, 187, 356, 410
Morgan, Jaye P., 163, 184, 197, 283,
    371, 398
Morgan, Pat, 153, 332
Morgan, Russ, 49, 51, 68, 81, 110, 156,
    185, 192, 209, 242, 269, 274, 284,
    318, 329, 330, 331, 344, 346, 361,
    363, 364, 375, 376, 407, 409, 424
Morita, Pat, 192
Mormon Tabernacle Choir, The, 17,

23, 32, 52, 79, 193, 231, 277, 281, 368, 404

Morris, Elida, 136

Morris, James R., 13, 21, 48, 149, 169, 253, 330, 334, 343

Morris, Joan, 5, 41, 73, 123, 155, 161, 211, 220, 277, 313, 380, 386, 413

Morris, Johnny, 201

Morris, Lee, 44

Morris, Richard R., 397

Morrissey, Pat, 405

Morrison, Joe, 217, 377

Morrow, Buddy, 3, 24, 169, 289, 316

Morrow, Lisa, 200

Morse, Dolly, 321

Morse, Ella Mae, 8, 92, 124, 135, 138, 175, 250, 273, 294, 320, 395

Morse, Lee, 42, 44, 55, 134, 215, 243

Morse, Theodore F., 128, 247

Morton, Jelly Roll, 19, 29, 33, 76, 253, 270, 291, 333, 370–71, 380

Mosley, Roger E., 123

Mossman, Ted, 112, 371

Moten, Etta, 338

Mother Is a Freshman, 92, 351

Mother Wore Tights, 36, 72, 180, 248, 294, 344, 353

Moulin Rouge, 262, 333

Mound City Blue Blowers, The, 76, 212, 250, 299, 300, 336, 391

Mr. Big, 389

Mr. Blandings Builds His Dream House, 142

Mraz, George, 246

Muddy Waters, 53

Mudurian, Jack, 19, 31, 62, 64, 154, 169, 188, 251, 288, 296, 302, 304, 335

Muir, Lewis F., 288, 296, 385

Mulcays, The, 254

Muldaur, Maria, 1, 225, 242

Mule Train, 250, 303

Mulligan, Gerry, 141, 222, 267, 334, 348

Mum's the Word, 301

Munde, Alan, 229

Munn, Frank, 68, 197

Munsel, Patrice,142

Munson, Eddie, 166

Munter, Pam, 316

Muppet Movie, The, 17

Murad, Jerry, 60, 61, 75, 104, 185, 230, 285, 286, 289, 377

Murphy, C. W., 132

Murphy, George, 50, 84, 164, 185, 272, 402

Murphy, Mark, 7, 167, 293, 382

Murphy, Pat, 173, 248, 404

Murphy, Rose, 152,163, 179, 233, 353, 407

Murphy, Ruby, 374

Murphy, Stanley, 270, 293

Murphy, Turk, 90

Murray, Anne, 54, 104, 263, 357

Murray, Billy, 36, 50, 54, 57, 67, 69, 89, 138, 161, 185, 190, 201, 262, 319, 324, 328, 344, 355, 380, 386, 390, 392

Murray, Elizabeth, 294

Murray, J. F., 131

Murray, J. Harold, 24

Murray, Ruby, 133

Muse, Clarence, 394

Musettes, The, 353

Music Box Revue, 10, 391

Music for Millions, 23

Music Goes Round, The, 250

Music Man, The, 66, 121, 232

Musso, Vido, 323

My Blue Heaven, 251

My Buddy, 252

My Darling Clementine, 65

My Dream Is Yours, 261

My Favorite Year, 146, 339

My Foolish Heart, 252

My Gal Sal, 73, 253, 277

My Landlady, 423

My Man, 256, 313

My One and Only, 147, 200

My Pal Trigger, 98

My Wild Irish Rose, 66, 180, 213, 248, 260, 289, 384, 393, 401, 406, 421

Myers, Billy, 268

Myers, J. W., 80, 180, 262, 322

Myers, James E., 302

Myrow, Josef, 106

Mysels, Sammy, 388

Mystics, The, 188

Nabors, Jim, 16, 232, 280, 310, 371
Nagler, Eric, 225
Naismith, Laurence, 187
Naked Alibi, 2
Nancy Brown, 262, 380
Nancy Goes to Rio, 320
Napton, Johnny, 252
Nash, Clarence, 83
Nash, Joey, 217, 389, 407
Nashville, 352
Naudain, May, 117
Naughty Nanette, 76
Naughty Nineties, The, 223, 276
Nealy, Milton Craig, 7
Near, Holly, 390, 408
Nebb, Jimmy, 265
Neiburg, Al, 75, 188, 380
Nelson, Ed, 150
Nelson, Gene, 332, 427
Nelson, Laine, 88, 264
Nelson, Ozzie, 45, 94, 126, 134, 155,
    175, 183, 208, 211, 265, 278, 311, 417
Nelson, Portia, 24, 107, 402
Nelson, Ricky, 84, 108, 109, 116, 133,
    217, 251, 332, 382, 415
Nelson, Steve, 112, 286
Nelson, Willie, 12, 24, 37, 44, 92, 93,
    114, 119, 132, 133, 137, 143, 175,
    276, 278, 279, 324, 333, 335, 343,
    348, 372, 377, 405, 410, 420
Nemo, Henry, 88
Neptune's Daughter, 276
Nero, Peter, 116, 174, 249, 414
Nestor, Lee, 301
Never a Dull Moment, 138, 251, 326
Never Been Kissed, 58
Neville, Aaron, 110, 339
Neville Brothers, The, 90
Neville, Marcus, 102
Nevins, Morty, 377
New Christy Minstrels, The, 57, 201,
    262, 369
New Faces, 58, 255, 382
New Orleans, 32, 232
New Orleans Feetwarmers, The, 156
New Orleans Jazz Band, 397
New Orleans Rhythm Kings, 94, 103

New York, New York, 43, 86, 108, 143,
    186, 226, 279
New York Town, 420
Newberger, Eli, 100
Newman, Alfred, 244
Newman, Charles, 426
Newman, Joe, 63
Newman, Joel, 201
Newman, Lee, 167
Newman, Lionel, 6
Newman, Paul, 414
Newman, Randy, 258, 381
Newman, Ruby, 32, 76, 77, 219, 238,
    244, 258, 352
Newton, Eddie, 57
Newton, Frankie, 304, 342, 410, 421
Newton, John, 16
Newton, Juice, 11
Newton, Wayne, 40, 101, 160, 170,
    299, 316, 374, 424
Nice Girl, 274
Nicholas Brothers, The, 9, 164, 196,
    318
Nicholls, Horatio, 17
Nichols, Alberta, 159, 381
Nichols, Gary, 28
Nichols, Herbie, 239
Nichols, Red, 2, 10, 29, 33, 41, 42, 48,
    56, 63, 96, 116, 162, 167, 175, 182,
    253, 254, 265, 268, 280, 281, 284,
    285, 290, 293, 302, 303, 304, 307,
    336, 349, 386, 410, 425
Niesen, Gertrude, 424
Night and Day, 87, 97, 165, 240
Night at the Opera, A, 200
Night Club Girl, 283, 371
Night in Casablanca, A, 405
Night of the Iguana, The, 131
Night Stage to Galveston, 414
Night World, 292
Nilsson, Harry, 109, 173, 188, 207,
    263, 302, 376, 391, 420
9 ½ Weeks, 38
9:15 Revue, 114
Ninety-Eight Degrees, 170
1941, 90, 181
Nitty Gritty Dirt Band, The, 11, 92,
    192, 212

Nixon, Marni, 39, 118, 189, 367
No Leave, No Love, 53
Nob Hill, 64, 137, 374, 393
Noble, Johnny, 133
Noble, Ray, 3, 8, 15, 35, 45, 50, 56, 61,
    63, 112, 123–24, 126, 131, 133, 161,
    171, 183, 192, 203, 214, 217, 233,
    244, 246, 264, 280, 299, 301, 326,
    365, 368, 372, 376, 382, 387, 409,
    415, 424, 425
Nobody's Darling, 173, 278
Noell, Charles K., 411
Noll, Christiane, 293
Noonan, Paddy, 36
Noone, Jimmy, 138, 160, 279, 301, 319,
    345, 350
Norman, Jessye, 13, 118, 125, 333
Norman Luboff Choir, The, 42, 82, 87,
    92, 112. 172, 258, 315, 326, 335, 352,
    358
Norman, Lucille, 191, 272, 371, 408
Norman, Nancy, 121, 311, 363
Norman, Patricia, 269
Normandie, Natalie, 328
North, Alex, 379
North, Sheree, 184, 197
Norton, George A., 237, 257, 317
Norton Sisters, The, 364
Norworth, Jack, 319–20, 355
Novarro, Ramon, 282
Norvo, Red, 65, 108, 143, 151, 157,
    249, 250, 273, 281, 288, 290, 328,
    329, 370, 425
Novak, Frank, 360, 371, 384, 405
Novis, Donald, 35, 159, 375
Nuclear Whales Saxophone Orchestra,
    355
Nugent, Maude, 350

O Brother, Where Art Thou, 417
Oakie, Jack, 126, 132, 136, 142, 160,
    179, 201, 296
Oakland, Ben, 59, 171
Oberhamer, Douglas, 46
Object of My Affection, The, 269
O'Brien, Margaret, 118, 380
O'Brien, Virginia, 41, 178, 354
O'Bryant, Jimmy, 298

Ocean's Eleven, 54
O'Connell, Helen, 12, 16, 47, 99, 125,
    196, 229, 280, 327, 398, 410, 425
O'Connell, Maura, 159
O'Connor, Donald, 10, 105, 179, 207,
    233, 336, 385, 396, 408, 415
O'Connor, Shamus, 224
O'Day, Anita, 2, 42, 86, 95, 96, 102,
    107, 126, 185, 215, 220, 237, 264,
    285, 316, 357, 362, 421, 424
Odetta, 16, 118, 138
Odette, Marcelene, 112
O'Donnell, Ace, 4, 31, 73, 75, 161, 181,
    364
O'Donnell, Daniel, 173, 237
Of Men and Music, 290
Of Thee I Sing, 239
Office Space, 284
Officer, Philip, 201
Oh, Johnny, How You Can Love, 142,
    271
Ohrlin, Glenn, 31
Oh, Please!, 160
Oh, Lady! Lady!, 39
Oh, Look!, 173
Oh! What a Lovely War, 281, 282, 305,
    324, 366
Oh, You Beautiful Doll, 62, 67, 72, 75,
    89, 272, 285, 365
O'Hara, Geoffrey, 201
O'Keefe, Dennis, 169
O'Keefe, Jimmy, 295
O'Keefe, Johnny, 83
O'Keefe, Walter, 75, 137
Oklahoma Annie, 133
Oklahoma Kid, The, 155
Olcott, Chauncey, 213, 260, 374, 393
Old Barn Dance, The, 425
Olias, Lotar, 421
Oliver, King, 333, 337, 345, 400
Oliver, Sy, 344, 395, 414
Olivor, Jane, 371
Olman, Abe, 89, 270
Olsen, George, 15, 22, 44, 51, 93, 113,
    130, 156, 204, 222, 297, 310, 311,
    369, 381
Olsen, Ole, 31
O'Malley, Pat, 124

On Moonlight Bay, 8, 100, 174, 277, 282, 371
On Stage Everybody, 49, 355
On the Riviera, 29, 48
On Top of Old Smokey, 278
On Your Toes, 421
One Exciting Week, 46
One Flew Over the Cuckoo's Nest, 60
One Hour Late, 205
One Minute to Zero, 392
One Mo' Time, 5, 100, 144
One More Spring, 269
One Sunday Afternoon, 179, 180
O'Neill Brothers, The, 41
O'Neill, Dennis, 213
Orbison, Roy, 11, 34, 69
Original Dixieland Jazz Band, The, 6, 76, 190, 230, 288, 324, 337, 370
Original Memphis Five, The, 6, 138, 201, 254, 324, 413
Original Salty Dogs Jazz Band, The, 300
Orlob, Harold, 166
Ory, Kid, 22, 40, 89, 145, 164, 270, 371, 380
Osborne Brothers, The, 129, 249, 258, 292, 411
Osborne, David, 10, 59
Osborne, James, 230
Osborne, Will, 153, 340, 362, 380
Osmond, Donny, 21, 82, 247, 373
Osmond, Marie, 82, 247
Osmun, Betsy Bruce, 316
Osser, Edna, 156
Ossman, Vern, 22
Osterwald, Bibi, 57
Otis, Johnny, 154, 223, 254, 264, 317, 321, 323, 390
O'Toole, Peter, 251
Otter, M., 318
Our Dancing Daughters, 59
Our Town, 216
Out of Africa, 413
Out of the Past, 105
Out of This World, 111
Outlaws, The, 300
Overman, Lynn, 322
Overstreet, W. Benton, 364

Owens, Bonnie, 110
Owens, Harry, 14, 134, 211, 312, 334
Owens, Jack, 192
Oxman, Keith, 168

Padula, Marguerite, 129
Pagan, The, 282
Pagan Love Song, 283
Page Cavanaugh Trio, The, 126, 222, 320, 361, 385
Page, Hot Lips, 190
Page, Ken, 143, 175, 423
Page, Patti, 11, 41, 86, 101, 115, 117, 154, 155, 172, 180, 184, 191, 194, 208, 209, 218, 221, 242, 249, 259, 263, 272, 279, 358, 371, 376, 392, 410, 417
Paige, Janis, 187
Painting the Clouds With Sunshine, 191, 393, 408, 424
Paiva, Jararaca and Vincente, 164
Paley, William S., 162
Palitz, Morty, 402
Palloy, Charlie, 314
Palmer, Bee, 164
Palmer, Jack, 100,156, 196
Palmer, John E., 30
Palmer, Leland, 5
Palmer, Robert, 301
Palm Beach Story, The, 124
Palm Springs Weekend, 51
Pandora and the Flying Dutchman, 423
Pangman, Alex, 388
Panic in the Streets, 275
Papa's Delicate Condition, 40
Paper Moon, 5, 90, 114, 188, 198, 269, 382
Paradise City Jazz Band, The, 300
Paradise, Hawaiian Style, 40
Paragons, The, 44, 197
Pardon My Rhythm, 172
Pardon My Sarong, 85
Paris, 18, 210
Paris Blues, 243, 335, 356
Paris Holiday, 20, 205
Paris Honeymoon, 149, 191
Parish, Mitchell, 11, 52, 82, 129, 243,

246–47, 314, 338–39, 340, 349, 355, 378, 383
Parker, Bonnie, 183
Parker, Charlie, 13, 20, 68, 87, 95, 97, 107, 114, 127, 129, 146, 151, 162, 174, 198, 206, 220, 254, 257, 263, 281, 341
Parker, Dee, 295
Parker, Eleanor, 18, 88, 231
Parker, Fess, 28
Parker, Frank, 213, 225, 355
Parker, Leroy, 318
Parker, Ross, 389
Parks, Andrew, 80
Parks, Larry, 5, 25, 26, 53, 109, 164, 175, 176, 223, 256, 321, 385
Parsons, Geoffrey, 327
Parton, Dolly, 163
Pascoe, Richard W., 360
Pass, Joe, 20, 35, 61, 64, 81, 86, 96, 119, 141, 149, 186, 222, 224, 246, 336, 356, 385
Passing Show, The, 29, 50, 55, 174, 268, 291, 327, 375
Passport to Pimlico, 155
Pastime, 352
Pastor, Tony, 3, 49, 57, 72, 112, 324, 402
Patience and Prudence. See McIntyre, Patience and Prudence
Patinkin, Mandy, 10, 15, 31, 43, 49, 170, 173, 201, 231, 233, 256, 303, 347, 355, 397
Patricola, Tom, 332
Patterson, Ottilie, 90
Patti, Adelina, 142, 347
Paul, Les, 14, 47, 50, 51, 54, 75, 93, 123, 146, 174, 176, 181, 186, 193, 194, 198, 203, 210, 224, 242, 253, 255, 326, 333, 334, 355, 371, 402, 410
Pavarotti, Luciano, 160, 383
Paxton, George, 102
Payne, Bennie, 52
Payne, Jack, 203, 217
Payne, John, 136, 173, 201
Payne, John Howard, 142
Payton, Nicholas, 408
Peabody, Eddie, 65

Peaches and Herb, 210
Pearl, Minnie, 278
Peck, Gregory, 188
Peerce, Jan, 34, 36, 265, 364, 408
Peerless Quartet, The, 50, 154, 209, 347
Peg o' My Heart, 285
Peldon, Courtney, 380
Pell, Dave, 307
Pellico, Frank, 381
Pendarvis, Paul, 269
Penn, Sean, 172, 197, 273, 319, 410
Pennies From Heaven, 186, 210, 211
Pennington, Ann, 164
People Are Funny, 19
Pepe, 335
Pepper, 355
Pepper, Art, 13, 61, 77, 137, 151, 178, 261, 367, 391
Pepper, Sid, 262
Peretti, Hugo, 201
Perfect Gentleman, The, 282
Perfect Marriage, 339
Perfectly Frank, 196
Perkins, Anthony, 276
Perkins, Carl, 33, 53, 302, 396
Perkins, Frank, 52, 314, 340
Perkins, Pinetop, 58, 150
Perrin, Edith, 400
Perry, Kathryn, 148, 159
Perry, Oscar, 279
Persuasions, The, 11, 86, 323
Pete Kelly's Blues, 3, 48, 51, 132, 162, 270, 328, 332, 344
Peter and Gordon, 140, 217
Peter, Paul and Mary, 49, 201, 369, 386, 388
Peters, Bernadette, 155
Peterson, Betty, 254
Peterson, Oscar, 20, 23, 43, 45, 63, 87, 102, 106, 108, 112, 147, 151, 158, 174, 189, 209, 222, 223, 234, 251, 310, 311, 328, 346, 356, 358, 367, 368, 370, 372, 382, 383, 395, 407, 421
Peterson, Paul, 124, 289
Peterson, Ray, 390
Peterson, Russ, 73
Petkere, Bernice, 222

Petrie, H. W., 155
Pettiford, Oscar, 286
Pettis, Jack, 61
Petty, Norman, 115, 139, 192
Peyton, Dave, 149
Pfister Sisters, The, 314
Philharmonica Trio, The, 203
Philippe-Gerard, M., 398
Phillips, Esther, 316, 389
Phillips, Flip, 235, 286, 324
Phillips, Howard, 43, 130, 169
Phillips, Sid, 427
Piaf, Edith, 266
Piantadosi, Al, 153
Pickens, Jane, 176, 226
Pickhall, Marjorie, 93
Picnic, 7, 245, 275
Pied Pipers, The, 10, 25, 79, 92, 97, 98,
  100, 116, 118, 158, 172, 225, 238,
  253, 254, 257, 277, 288, 290, 296,
  305, 313, 319, 337, 339, 363, 381,
  384, 401, 405, 415
Pierce, Webb, 154
Pierpont, S. J., 194
Pierson, Tom, 341
Pillow, Sarah, 23
Pinetoppers, The, 242
Pingatore, Mike, 211
Pink Flamingos, 86
Pinkard, Maceo, 115, 344, 349, 362
Pinkins, Tonya, 88, 150, 243
Pinza, Ezio, 82
Pirates of Penzance, The, 128
Piron, Armand, 164
Pistol Packin' Mama, 288
Pitney, Gene, 119, 230, 242, 258, 296,
  333, 371, 377
Pitts, Tom, 162
Pizarelli, Bucky, 14
Pizzarelli, John, 3, 14, 67, 68, 95, 108,
  155, 170, 237, 265, 390
Place, Mary Kay, 43
Planotones, The, 317
Platters, The, 85, 98, 112, 117, 119,
  127, 132, 155, 161, 167, 168, 170,
  171, 182, 214, 217, 241, 245, 258,
  271, 276, 292, 299, 302, 315, 320,

321, 323, 326, 355, 356, 369, 372,
  375, 377, 379, 383, 399, 403
Play On!, 88, 150, 158, 174, 184, 243,
  356
Playboy of Paris, 255
Playgirl, 365
Pleis, Jack, 205, 214, 302
Please Don't Eat the Daisies, 295
Ploughman's Lunch, The, 400
Pocket Full of Miracles, 289
Pockriss, Lee, 58
Poe, Coy, 269, 362, 391
Point of No Return, 42
Pointer Sisters, The, 195
Pollack, Lew, 60, 377, 415
Pollock, Ben, 53, 81, 178, 244, 334,
  341, 350
Pollock, Channing, 256
Pollock, David A., 264
Pollyanna, 17
Pomeroy, George S., 401
Pons, Lily, 203
Pope, Pauline, 295
Porter, Arthur D., 273
Porter, Cole, 87, 97, 101, 111, 206, 210,
  240, 359
Porter, Steve, 317
Post, Mike, 301
Postman Always Rings Twice, The, 319
Poulton, George R., 23
Powell, Bud, 24, 95, 205, 252, 419
Powell, Dick, 75, 82, 157, 198
Powell, Eleanor, 97
Powell, Felix, 282
Powell, Jane, 50, 142, 160, 275, 284,
  320
Powell, Janet, 175
Powell, Mel, 7, 108, 355, 419
Powell, Teddy, 54, 115, 122, 212, 259,
  265, 269, 354, 364
Power, Tyrone, 102, 210, 348, 351,
  371, 372, 396, 403
Powers Girl, The, 160, 210
Prado, Perez, 47, 58, 60, 61, 126, 225,
  284, 286
Premice, Josephine, 143, 365
Present Arms, 421
Presenting Lily Mars, 100, 370

Preservation Hall Jazz Band, The, 40, 166, 331
Presley, Elvis, 14, 17, 21, 23–24, 33, 43, 45, 85, 90, 104, 108, 111, 133, 137, 154, 170, 173, 189, 218, 275, 278, 296, 333, 344, 352, 358, 397, 402, 413, 422, 425
Pretty Baby, 22, 292, 371
Prevert, Jacques, 24
Previn, André, 39, 96, 137, 161, 206, 210
Price, Boyd, 2
Price, Chilton, 417
Price, Georgie, 32, 50, 51, 53, 413
Price, Leontyne, 267, 367
Price, Lloyd, 242
Price, Ray, 74, 310
Price, Toni, 196
Pride, Charley, 221
Pride of the Yankees, The, 15
Prima, Louis, 18, 24, 31, 37, 50, 53, 59, 64, 99, 104, 106, 108, 109, 131, 146, 152, 154, 158, 159, 161, 162, 175, 196, 197, 203, 207, 210, 222, 231, 245, 250, 264, 268, 283, 302, 305, 315, 323, 341, 346, 358, 359, 361, 377, 379, 384, 387, 397, 403, 415, 416, 422, 423, 424
Primary Colors, 79
Prime, Harry, 263
Primo Scala String Band, The, 321, 353, 381
Primrose, George, 56, 270
Primrose, Joe, 337
Prin, Tom, 356
Prince, Graham, 354
Prince, Hugh, 33, 46
Prince of Tonight, The, 166
Prince's Orchestra, 10, 27, 29, 33, 50, 69
Principal, Victoria, 11
Private Buckaroo, 88, 267, 420
Private Lives, 332
Proby, P. J., 117, 294, 408, 427
Processional, 413
Prodigal, The, 142, 408
Profit, Clarence, 221
Prophets, The, 270

Provincetown Follies, 299
Pruett, Eddie, 87
Pryor, Arthur, 36, 101, 181, 219
Puck, Eva, 123
Pullout, JoAnne, 73
Purcell, Charles, 160
Purple Gang, The, 307
Pursuit of Happiness, 28
Purvis, Katherine E., 397
Puttin' on the Ritz, 171

Quadling, Lew, 54, 98, 309
Quaker City Four, The, 347
Quebec, Ike, 49, 348
Queen, John, 40
Quiet Man, The, 173
Quinn, Dan, 31, 72, 144, 270, 322
Quinn, Freddy, 413
Quintones, The, 62

Racers, The, 289
Radford, Dave, 188
Radio Days, 46, 122, 156, 174, 181, 356, 403, 416
Raeburn, Boyd, 43, 426
Raffi, 355
Raging Bull, 292, 361
Rain Man, 339
Rain or Shine, 183
Rainbow Round My Shoulder, 51, 319, 410
Rainey, Gertrude "Ma," 313
Rainger, Ralph, 96
Raisin Pickers, The, 400
Raleigh, Ben, 98, 205
Rall, Tommy, 111
Ram, Buck, 62, 169, 377
Ramirez, Roger, 219–20
Ramona, 297
Ramona, 211
Ramos, Silvano R., 98
Ramrods, The, 300
Ramsey, Kevin, 7, 237
Rancho Grande, 98
Randall, James Ryder, 231
Randolph, Boots, 206, 231, 315
Rankin, Kenny, 36, 63, 346
Rapee, Erno, 60, 301, 311

Rappolo, Leon, 103
Rapson, Steve, 52
Rasbach, Otto, 375
Raskin, Willie, 389
Ravazza, Carl, 383
Ravens, The, 188, 231, 279, 360
Rawls, Lou, 44, 58, 114, 119, 150, 237, 337, 341, 370, 381
Ray Conniff Singers, 3, 38, 59, 69, 73, 81, 101, 112, 163, 187, 201, 236, 246, 258, 266, 299, 327, 356
Ray, Jimmy, 355
Ray, Johnnie, 10, 12, 68, 129, 148, 184, 268, 280, 288–89, 314, 332, 344, 385, 408
Ray, Leah, 359
Raye, Don, 33, 46, 138, 300, 368, 419
Raye, Martha, 45, 120, 193, 338
Raymond, Harriet, 69
Raymond, Lewis, 351
Raymond, Robin, 183
Razaf, Andy, 6, 41, 44, 105, 113, 143, 181, 195, 199, 216, 236, 336, 341
Reardon, Caspar, 178
Re-Bops, The, 86
Reckless Age, The, 164
Red Headed Woman, The, 268
Red Hot Swing Cats, The, 210
Red River Valley, 298
Red Salute, 166
Red Sky at Morning, 88, 271, 283
Red, Tampa, 60
Redbone, Leon, 21, 144, 149, 208, 218, 221, 298
Redcliffe, Frederick J., 424
Redding, Otis, 91, 110, 117, 267, 376
Redgrave, Vanessa, 367
Redman, Don, 3, 62, 75, 113, 206, 261, 356, 379, 381
Reds, 155
Reed, Dave, Jr., 218
Reed, Lou, 26, 301, 328
Reed, Nancy Binns, 270
Reed, Vivian, 119, 349
Reese, Della, 10, 40, 67, 71, 126, 133, 153, 173, 176, 244, 258, 314, 333, 371, 391, 423, 426
Reeves, Dianne, 61

Reeves, Jim, 33, 74, 79, 133, 232, 236, 245, 254, 272, 279, 297, 303, 312, 332, 361, 403
Reeves, Vic, 249
Regan, Phil, 248, 254, 285, 313, 345, 360, 393
Reid, Billy, 127
Reid, Lou, 2
Reinhardt, Django, 5, 59, 76, 103, 160, 192, 261, 269, 288, 318, 349, 371, 389, 392, 423
Reinking, Ann, 365
Reisman, Joe, 124, 129
Reisman, Leo, 45, 49, 51, 87, 96, 130, 131, 191, 216, 233, 263, 281, 337, 342, 382, 405
Remains to be Seen, 375
Remember the Night, 96
René, Henri, 58, 131, 192, 333, 366
René, Leon, 394, 398
René, Otis, 394
Reno, Don, 120, 399
Reser, Harry, 25, 164, 316, 404
Reveille With Beverly, 356
Revel, Harry, 134, 381
Revelers, The, 18, 26, 42, 48, 68, 118, 176, 178, 246, 329
Revenge of the Nerds, 229
Revenge With Music, 168, 416
Revere, Paul, 403
Rexford, Eben E., 322–23
Rey, Alvino, 75, 81, 88, 104, 140, 176, 252, 262, 283, 304, 305, 343
Reynolds, Burt, 7, 210
Reynolds, Debbie, 1, 8, 105, 163, 173, 245, 336, 356
Reynolds, Herbert, 367
Rhapsody in Black, 226, 381
Rhapsody in Blue, 239, 332, 347, 413
Rhinestone, 422
Rhodes, Sonny, 99–100, 316
Rhodes, Stan, 346
Rhythm Boys, The, 7, 162, 321, 361
Rhythm on the Range, 238
Rhythm Parade, 351, 384
Rhythm Round-Up, 34
Rhythmania, 39
Rice, Billy, 57

Rice, Chris, 309
Rice, Seymour, 421
Rich and Famous, 278
Rich, Buddy, 105, 107, 153, 162, 305, 323, 346, 426
Rich, Charlie, 8, 16, 17, 66, 139, 150, 301, 361
Rich, Young and Pretty, 82, 275
Richard, Cliff, 12, 45, 186, 316
Richard, Lisa, 67
Richard, Little, 26, 50
Richards, Johnny, 422
Richardson, Jerome, 178
Richman, Harry, 7, 44, 86, 102, 105, 197, 211, 238, 277, 329, 385, 400, 425
Richman, Jonathan, 159
Richmond, Jane, 151
Riddle, Nelson, 24, 29, 64, 100, 122, 131, 176, 182, 316, 327, 391, 416
Ride 'Em, Cowboy, 23, 371
Ride, Tenderfoot, Ride, 208, 409
Riders in the Sky, 301
Rider in the Sky, 27, 33, 301, 327
Riders of the Whistling Pines, 374, 414
Ridge, Antonia, 131
Ridgley, Tommy, 225
Ridin' Down the Canyon, 178
Ridin' High, 79, 402
Ridin' on a Rainbow, 33, 57, 417
Right This Way, 151, 170
Righteous Brothers, The, 98, 114, 379, 403
Riley, Mike, 250
Rim of the Canyon, 425
Rimbault, Edward F., 146
Rimes, LeAnn, 16
Rimmington, Sammy, 182, 318, 351, 412, 417
Rines, Joe, 381
Ring, Blanche, 36, 67, 154, 180, 386
Ring-a-Ding Rhythm, 33, 90, 100
Ringside Maisie, 41
Rio Grande, 85, 173
Rios, Elvira, 339
Riptide, 301
Ritchard, Cyril, 366
Ritchie Family, The, 47
Ritter, Tex, 33, 55, 91, 116, 133, 139, 187, 192, 194, 235, 310, 355, 359, 413, 417
Ritter, Thelma, 82
Ritz Brothers, The, 250, 395
Ritzel, Ricky, 23, 195
River of No Return, 51
Rivera, Anthony, 193
Rivera, E., 125
Riverdance, 225
Rivers, Jimmy, 146
Roach, Max, 117
Road to Rio, 47
Road House, 5, 365
Roadhouse Nights, 146, 390
Roaring Twenties, The, 179, 219
Robards, Jason, 51, 415
Robbins, Marty, 2, 18, 34, 35, 191, 230, 255, 298, 300, 334, 409
Robbins, Sam, 325
Robert Shaw Chorale, 18, 52, 118, 231, 359, 413
Roberta, 182
Roberts, Allan, 19, 98, 120, 182, 293, 416
Roberts, Bob, 296, 409
Roberts, Doris, 82
Roberts, Kenny, 212, 374
Roberts, Lee, 327
Robertson, Dale, 120
Robertson, Dick, 97, 185, 208, 211, 214, 223, 238, 308, 315, 360, 384, 388
Robeson, Paul, 16, 22, 28, 80, 116, 145, 195, 208, 214, 215, 258, 267, 274, 301, 303, 320, 333, 337, 375, 394
Robin Hood, 271
Robin, Leo, 96, 128, 254, 292
Robin, Sid, 108, 379
Robinson, Bill, 6, 39, 90, 261, 342
Robinson, Carson, 119
Robinson Crusoe, Jr., 412
Robinson, Earl, 28, 145
Robinson, Edward, 140
Robinson, Holly, 62
Robinson, J. Russell, 6, 229–30, 324
Robinson, Jim, 232
Robinson, Lilla Cayley, 117
Robinson, Scott, 59
Robinson, Smokey, 118, 218

Robison, Carson J., 31, 56–57, 93, 272

Robison, Willard, 68, 113, 115–16, 246, 284, 367

Robledo, Julian, 370

Rochinski, Stanley, 290–91

Rock Around the Clock, 302

Rock, George, 162

Rockapella, 141

Rocky, 231, 413

Rodemich, Gene, 230

Rodgers, Eileen, 211

Rodgers, Jimmie, 111, 201, 248

Rodgers, Richard, 42, 73, 134, 159, 228, 248–49, 265, 357, 407, 421

Rodney, Don, 110

Rodriquez, Augustin, 425

Rogers, Alex, 266

Rogers, Charles "Buddy," 131, 187, 219, 252, 253, 255

Rogers, Clyde, 194

Rogers, Ginger, 241, 385, 387, 402

Rogers, Jimmy, 74

Rogers, Kenny, 133, 138, 217, 256, 381

Rogers, Roy, 14, 33, 56, 57, 68, 87, 96, 98, 116, 142, 204–205, 235, 238, 246, 288, 298, 303, 318, 346, 376, 413

Rogers, Will, 91

Rogue Cop, 43

Rolling Stones, The, 305, 356

Rollini, Adrian, 43, 130, 169, 324

Rollins, Jack, 112, 286

Rollins, Sonny, 119, 178, 180, 205, 228, 244, 255, 257, 276, 290, 302, 333, 358, 363, 372, 374, 389, 406, 408, 419

Roly Boly Eyes, 166

Roly Poly, 394

Romain, Manuel, 393

Romance in the Dark, 263

Romance of Athlone, A, 260

Romano, Christy, 64

Romay, Lina, 312, 354

Romberg, Sigmund, 427

Ronell, Ann, 404, 406

Ronstadt, Linda, 11, 24, 109, 115, 122, 126, 157, 189, 220, 222, 234, 294, 325, 334, 391, 392, 400, 419, 421

Room Service, 352

Rooney, Mickey, 6, 152,164, 167, 175, 228, 272, 349, 385

Rooney, Pat, Jr., 78

Root, George Frederick, 197

Rootin' Tootin' Boys, 371

Rootin' Tootin' Rhythm, 238

Ros, Edmundo, 64, 164, 227

Rosa, Malia, 110

Rosalie, 18, 53, 147, 226, 271

Rose, The, 209

Rose, Billy, 31, 65, 86, 157, 187, 189, 247, 263, 360, 373, 408, 427

Rose, David, 217, 326

Rose, Ed, 270

Rose, Fred, 33, 81, 143, 298

Rose, Harry, 201

Rose Marie, 84, 331

Rose of Washington Square, 53, 172, 173, 175, 192, 248, 256, 292, 302, 304, 322, 374

Rose, Tim, 401

Rose, Vincent, 25, 44, 211, 402

Roselli, Jimmy, 19, 69, 80, 90, 164, 276, 322, 360

Rosie the Riveter, 305

Ross, Andy, 51, 203

Ross, Annie, 228, 325

Ross, Diana, 12, 16, 119, 121, 137, 153, 220, 226, 234, 256, 342, 354, 362, 390, 426

Ross, Don, 204

Ross, Jerry, 296

Ross, Lanny, 159, 205, 245, 280, 299, 361

Ross, Shirley, 42

Rosselli, Jimmy, 72, 116, 150, 223, 255, 256, 272, 313, 364, 393, 405

Roth, David Lee, 149, 197

Roth, Lillian, 7, 147, 155, 167, 168, 172, 186, 331, 382, 397

Roth, Tim, 168

Rothberg, Bob, 264

Rotter, Fritz, 159, 355

Round Midnight, 147

Round-Up in Texas, 84

Rovin' Tumbleweeds, 27

Rowles, Jimmy, 43, 264, 424

Roxie Hart, 62

Roy, Harry, 76
Roye, Ruth, 1, 8, 385
Royle, Selena, 142
Rubenstein, Arthur, 290
Rubenstein, Barbara, 331
Ruby, Harry, 163, 200, 263, 404
Ruby, Herman, 254
Rucker, Ellyn, 14
Ruggles of Red Gap, 51, 292
Rugolo, Pete, 227
Ruling Class, The, 251
Rundgren, Todd, 356
Runnin' Wild, 59, 273, 307
Rush, Tom, 266
Rushing, Jimmy, 46, 100, 136, 149,
    185, 267, 313, 314, 332, 341, 400, 418
Ruskin, Harry, 161
Russell, Andy, 3, 12, 38, 87, 96, 153,
    156, 172, 197, 198, 205, 381
Russell, Bob, 29, 85, 87, 112, 410
Russell, Connie, 426
Russell, Jane, 6, 71, 157, 163, 423
Russell, Kurt, 21, 33, 85
Russell, Leon, 125, 229
Russell, Lillian, 66
Russell, Luis, 259
Russell, Madely, 6
Russell, Pee Wee, 3, 121, 184, 199, 304
Russell, S. K., 47, 230
Russo, Dan, 374
Ryan, Ben, 135, 392
Ryan, Buck, 200
Ryan, Johnny, 7
Ryan, Peggy, 145, 179
Ryan, Rebecca, 147
Ryan, Tommy, 218, 264, 297
Rydell, Bobby, 83, 383
Ryder, Mitch, 370
Ryerson, Frank, 42

Sabel, Josephine, 144
Sablon, Jean, 404
Sabrina, 259, 341
Saddle Pals, 16
Sadie McKee, 5
Sadovy, Liza, 100
Safety in Numbers, 253
Saginaw Trail, 34

Saigon, 372
Sainte-Marie, Buffy, 318
Sakall, S. Z., 181
Sally, 39
Sally in Our Alley, 380
Saloff, Spider, 23, 195, 390
Salt and Pepper, 65
Salt City Six, The, 149
Salty Dogs Jazz Band, The, 426
Saludos Amigos, 47
Salvatore, Sergio, 141
Samba Mania, 312
Sambo Girl, The, 154
Same Time, Next Year, 168
Sampson, Edgar, 221, 341
Samuels, Walter G., 354
San Antonio Rose, 310
San Francisco, 22, 33, 144, 219
Sand Pebbles, The, 375
Sanders, Alma M., 360
Sanders, Felicia, 107, 333
Sanders, Joe, 367
Sanders, Julio, 3
Sanderson, Julia, 217, 367
Sands, Tommy, 1, 155, 344
Santa Fe Trail, 15
Santley, Fred, 421
Santley, Lester, 176
Sarge Goes to College, 285, 331
Sargent, Kenny, 109, 131, 150, 153,
    177, 188, 198, 217, 280, 322, 368,
    377, 380, 419
Sarno, Tony, 17
Sarong Girl, The, 77
Saroyan, William, 67, 75
Satellites, The, 398
Satisfaction, 119
Satisfiers, The, 399
Saunders, Jimmy, 109, 272, 279
Saunders, Karen, 234
Sauter-Finnegan Orchestra, The, 20,
    124–25, 246, 264
Savitt, Jan, 18, 98, 127, 167, 186, 219,
    246, 345, 377, 401
Savo, Jimmy, 87, 161, 301
Saxe, Emily, 224
Saxon, Al, 276, 361
Say It With Music, 217

Scaggs, Boz, 218, 262
Scared Stiff, 154, 164
Scarlett, Mose, 201
Scarlet Street, 257
Scatterbrain, 149
Schallen, Bill, 81
Schell, Jack, 230
Schipa, Tito, 425
Schmidt, Erwin, 93
Schneider, Mary, 374
Schoebel, Elmer, 103, 268
Schonberger, John, 402
Schulz, Bob, 164, 201
Schuman, William, 62
Schumann-Heink, Ernestine, 74, 281
Schutt, Arthur, 48, 161
Schuyler, Sonny, 94, 99, 214, 310, 328, 376
Schwandt, Wilbur, 92
Schwartz, Arthur, 3, 168, 416
Schwartz, Jean, 36, 63, 302, 376
Scobey, Bob, 2, 19, 62, 140, 291, 337
Scott, Clement, 271
Scott, Hazel, 226, 355, 413, 416
Scott, Jimmy, 2, 205, 333
Scott, Lizbeth, 98
Scott, Phil, 159
Scull, Guy, 401
Second Chorus, 350
Secunda, Sholom, 37
Sedaka, Neil, 170, 421
Sedric, Gene, 195
See My Lawyer, 170
Seeger, Pete, 49, 63, 90, 91, 116, 142, 188, 193, 195, 201, 278, 318, 325, 330, 369, 388, 413
Seelen, Jerry, 58
Seeley, Blossom, 8, 161, 207, 247, 294, 331–32, 387
Seems Like Old Times, 314
Segal, Jack, 312
Seibert, T. Lawrence, 57
Seidel, Emil, 338
Seidel, Toscha, 239
Seiler, Eddie, 155, 395
Seitz, Ernest, 410
Selleck, Tom, 124

Selvin, Ben, 18, 26, 44, 62, 74, 131, 174, 178, 198, 222, 228, 316, 396
Senior Prom, 293
Sentimental Journey, 315
Seress, Rezso, 116
Sergeant, The, 323
Serio, Cheryl, 293, 316
Serrato, Greg, 202
Setzer, Brian, 285
Seusse, Dana, 258, 263
Seven Hills of Rome, The, 236, 397
Seven Little Foys, The, 64, 266, 305
Seven Lively Arts, 102
Seven Sinners, 152
Severinson, Doc, 100, 356
Seymour, Carolyn, 251
Sha Na Na, 43
Shackburg, Richard, 412
Shade, Lillian, 158
Shadows, The, 300
Shadows and Fog, 224, 392
Shaffer, Charlie, 93
Shake, Rattle and Rock!, 8
Shameen Dhu, 374
Shand, Terry, 49, 156
Shank, Kendra, 41
Shannon, Del, 66, 139, 422
Shannon, Dick, 109
Shannon, James R., 241, 374
Shantytown, 400
Shapiro, Debbie, 196, 268, 406
Shapiro, Elliot, 322
Shapiro, Helen, 104
Shapiro, Ted, 129, 167
Sharon, Lois and Bram, 317, 378
Shattuck, Trudy, 218
Shavers, Charlie, 304, 379
Shaw, Artie, 10, 13, 15, 20, 44, 77, 81, 82, 86, 116, 129, 140, 146, 151, 153, 163, 168, 171, 174, 185, 192, 235, 245, 251, 266, 273, 281, 304, 319, 333, 337, 339, 345, 347, 350, 364, 368, 424
Shaw, David T., 66
Shaw, George, 265
Shaw, Hollace, 13
Shaw, Miriam, 89
Shaw, Oscar, 19

Shaw, Virgil, 110
Shaw, Winnifred, 22, 406
Shay, Larry, 400
She Done Him Wrong, 111, 292
She Loves Me Not, 3
She Made Her Bed, 369
She Wore a Yellow Ribbon, 318
Shea, George Beverly, 16, 17, 82, 138
Shean, Al, 241
Shearer, Norma, 332
Shearing, George, 13, 21, 33, 35, 54,
    61, 95, 97, 106, 109, 115, 131, 169,
    187, 215, 217, 221, 245, 259, 273,
    280, 289, 293, 297, 310, 315, 323,
    333, 334, 350, 356, 368, 379, 400
Sheehy, Eleanore, 33
Sheik, The, 318
Sheldon, Jack, 195
Shelley, Joshua, 415
Shelton, Ann, 67, 363, 388, 391, 414,
    416
Shepherd, Cybil, 210
Shepherd, Kenny Wayne, 401
Sheridan, Ann, 213, 320, 355, 394
Sherman, Al, 77, 265, 268
Sherman, Bobby, 162
Sherman, Hiram, 13
Sherman, Jimmy, 220
Sherr, Jack, 425
Sherrill, Joya, 173
Sherwin, Manning, 264
Sherwood, Roberta, 135, 424
*She's Working Her Way Through Col-
    lege*, 26
Shields, Larry, 370
Shields, Ren, 180, 385
Shilkret, Nat, 44, 74, 105, 114, 150,
    215, 221, 361
Shine On Harvest Moon, 48, 73, 100,
    179, 292, 320, 355, 394
Shiner, Mervin, 286
Ship Ahoy, 277
Ship Café, 404
Shirelles, The, 295, 297
Shirl, Jimmy, 150
Shirley, Don, 221, 385
Shondell, Troy, 122
Shoot the Moon, 11

Shore, Dinah, 12, 14, 15, 39, 47, 51, 54,
    64, 69, 73, 77, 79, 84, 85, 89, 97, 104,
    109, 110, 119, 126, 127, 134, 143,
    146, 151, 162, 170, 171, 177, 186,
    205, 215, 216, 219, 228, 229, 236,
    237, 240, 243, 256, 257, 263, 264,
    267, 279, 299, 307, 312, 320, 325,
    326, 331, 336, 337, 344, 367, 392,
    398, 414, 425, 427
Short, Bobby, 24, 36, 93, 96, 102, 112,
    151, 189, 200, 210, 228, 239, 267,
    278, 285, 311, 322, 333, 408, 421
Shot in the Dark, A, 110
Show Boat, 4, 22, 39, 82, 123, 215, 267
Show Business, 9, 78, 84, 164, 185, 402
Show Girl in Hollywood, 259
Show Is On, The, 214
Show of Shows, The, 303
Shuffle Along, 175
Shulman, Alan, 272
Shutta, Ethel, 310, 369, 381, 404
Side Man, 115, 303
Sidewalks of New York, The, 322
Sidney, George, 372
Siegel, Janis, 300
Sierra Sue, 33, 322
Sigler, Maurice, 214
Sigman, Carl, 29, 55, 97, 99, 186, 218,
    285, 316
Signorelli, Frank, 338
Silencers, The, 117, 169, 205, 278, 299,
    321, 335
Silver, Abner, 77, 265, 408
Silver, Frank, 415
Silvers, Louis, 388
Silvers, Sid, 303
Simmons, Al, 309, 400
Simms, Ginny, 13, 89, 108, 165, 235.
    363, 389, 391, 419
Simms, Margaret, 6
Simon and Garfunkle, 118
Simon, Carly, 74, 102, 134, 157, 189,
    204, 206, 355, 400
Simon, Nat, 274, 289
Simon, Simone, 76
Simone, Nina, 41–42, 108, 134, 138,
    158, 180, 184, 266, 267, 310, 323,
    342, 375

Simons, Moise, 284
Simons, Seymour, 12, 48, 143, 299
Simple Simon, 73, 219, 357
Sims, Lee, 45, 233, 303, 367
Sims, Zoot, 13, 43, 86, 89, 153, 163, 189, 244, 254, 261, 290, 319, 406, 419, 424
Sinatra, Frank, 3, 10, 12–13, 14, 17, 18, 20, 23, 24, 38, 60, 62, 68, 73, 78, 79, 81, 85, 89, 92, 95, 98, 100–101, 107, 108, 111, 112, 114, 115, 118, 119, 120, 121, 122, 123, 124, 126, 127, 128, 137, 139, 142, 145, 146, 148, 153, 155, 156, 157, 158, 160, 166, 167, 168, 169, 170, 171, 172, 173, 178, 182, 183, 184, 185, 186, 189, 190, 204, 215, 216, 218, 224, 231, 233, 236, 243, 244, 245, 246, 251, 254, 257, 259, 261, 263, 264, 272, 273, 275, 277, 279, 281, 283, 284, 289, 292, 293, 294, 301, 309, 319, 327, 335, 339, 341, 342, 343, 346, 350, 353, 355, 357, 360, 361, 363, 366, 369, 371, 376, 386, 388, 389, 391, 393, 400, 402, 405, 406, 407, 408, 414, 415, 416, 419, 421, 424, 427
Sinatra, Frank, Jr., 294
Sinatra, Nancy, 132, 210, 252, 272
Sinbad, 302, 346
Since You Went Away, 84, 373
Sincerely Yours, 393
Sing a Jingle, 35, 80, 399
Sing, Baby, Sing, 56, 182, 250, 395
Sing For Your Supper, 28
Sing Me a Love Song, 57, 422
Sing, Neighbor, Sing, 133
Sing Out, Sweet Land, 57, 111, 193, 251, 272
Singin' in the Corn, 224
Singin' in the Rain, 105
Singin' Sam, 178–79, 301
Singing Cowboy, The, 212
Singing Fool, The, 176, 184
Singing Guns, 249
Singing Hill, The, 44, 205
Singing Kid, The, 53, 2,6, 347
Sioux City Sue, 324, 332
Siouxsie and the Banshees, 342

Siras, John, 178
Siravo, George, 38
Sis Hopkins, 345
Sissle, Noble, 55, 175, 273
Sister Act, 270
Sister Act II, 270
Six Cylinder Love, 423
Six Fat Dutchmen, 37, 59, 241
Six Hits and a Miss, 51
Skellern, Peter, 167, 217, 401
Skylar, Sunny, 38, 115, 384
Skyliners, The, 151
Skelton, Red, 263
Slack, Freddie, 33, 138, 200, 354
Sledge, Percy, 376
Sleepless in Seattle, 27, 51, 201, 339, 392
Sleepy Lagoon, 326
Sleepytime Gal, 326
Slight Case of Murder, 238
Slightly French, 210
Slightly Terrific, 294
Sloane, Carol, 3, 45, 169, 174, 246, 259, 280, 358, 362, 390, 402, 422
Slow Drag, 41, 43, 100, 143, 247
Small, Paul, 68, 129, 150, 269, 311
Smeck, Roy, 197
Smiles, 372, 423
Smiley, Red, 120, 198
Smilin' Through, 366
Smith, Alfred E., 322
Smith, Arthur, 34, 120
Smith, Beasley, 275, 360
Smith, Bessie, 5, 6, 10, 22, 27, 28, 55, 80, 121, 144, 149, 267, 336, 337, 354, 426
Smith, Carl, 362
Smith, Chris, 29, 423
Smith, Edgar, 223
Smith, Ethel, 47, 48, 98, 203, 286, 289, 407
Smith, Gordon, 189
Smith, Harry B., 318, 409
Smith, Jack, 26, 100, 111, 115, 134, 159, 174, 233, 251, 297, 333, 346, 361, 397, 418
Smith, Jimmy, 150, 224, 394
Smith, Joseph C., 140, 271, 290, 304, 327

Smith, Kate, 12, 34, 37, 74, 87, 92, 96,
    118, 150, 160, 162, 167, 177, 185,
    187, 193, 205, 207, 217, 237, 252,
    278, 279, 280, 301, 304, 314, 319,
    329, 331, 363, 365, 374, 389, 393,
    396, 403, 409, 410, 418, 422, 424
Smith, Keely, 18, 24, 31, 37, 54, 87,
    104, 107, 108, 109, 137, 186, 207,
    210, 231, 236, 250, 252, 266, 269,
    278, 289, 292, 296, 305, 357, 360,
    372, 422, 424
Smith, Muriel, 333
Smith, Pinetop, 267
Smith, Queenie, 123, 166
Smith, Richard B., 66, 407
Smith, Samuel Francis, 16
Smith, Something, 185
Smith, Steve, 341
Smith, Stuff, 202, 302
Smith, Willie, 59, 335, 342, 352
Smoky River Serenade, 411
Smoothies, The, 48, 89, 230, 370, 413
Snow, Hank, 2, 34, 103, 125, 133, 150,
    208, 236, 242, 254, 255, 286, 294,
    334, 346, 351, 356, 388, 411
Snow, Phoebe, 357
Snow, Valaida, 239, 352, 371
Snyder, Ted, 9, 318, 404
So This Is Love, 159, 165, 236, 282, 299,
    372
So This Is Paris, 152
Solar, Willie, 1
Some Came Running, 5
Some Like It Hot, 50, 89, 135, 163, 177,
    307, 345, 349, 351
Somebody Loves Me, 153, 304, 328, 332,
    387
Son, 67
Song Is Born, A, 108, 174, 231, 349
Song o' My Heart, 159
Song of Nevada, 142
Song of Texas, 238
Song of the Islands, 142, 334
Song of the Range, 15
Song of the Sarong, 79
Song to Remember, A, 371
Sonny and Cher, 332
Sons of the Pioneers, The, 49, 56, 57,

    80, 87, 116, 120, 125, 129, 133, 142,
    173, 198, 200, 212, 235, 238, 258,
    272, 293, 298, 300, 303, 310, 331,
    348, 352, 354, 374, 384, 394, 399,
    401, 421
Soo, Jack, 192
Sophie, 298
Sophisticated Ladies, 54, 86, 88, 158,
    174, 178, 184, 311, 335, 356
So's Your Uncle, 88
Sosenko, Anna, 76
Sothern, Ann, 56, 205, 210, 228, 320
Sound Off, 335
Sour, Robert, 45, 387
Sousa, John Philip, 4, 22, 52, 128
South, Eddie, 341
South of Dixie, 75, 320
South of the Border, 116, 122, 335
South Sea Rose, 91
South Sea Sinner, 177
Southern, Jeri, 24, 81, 102, 127, 134,
    255, 334, 382, 392, 424
Southern Sons Quartette, The, 291
Spaeth, Sigmund, 218, 321, 415
Spain, Irene, 80
Spaniels, The, 124, 135, 375, 427
Spanier, Muggsy, 19, 63, 73, 228, 254,
    268, 304, 333, 345, 411
Spargo, Henry, 370
Sparkle, 323, 377
Sparks, Larry, 122
Spears, Billie Jo, 11
Specht, Paul, 176, 237, 404
Specter, Dave, 371
Spencer, Len, 11, 274
Spencer, Lew, 144
Spencer, Tim, 303
Spencer, Tracie, 36
Spice of 1922, 387, 413
Spicer, Willie, 83
Spier, Larry, 237
Spikes, Benjamen, 333
Spikes, John, 333
Spina, Harold, 410, 424
Spinners, The, 169
Spirits of Rhythm, The, 190, 196, 381
Spitalny, Phil, 150, 161, 255, 271, 284,
    311, 418

Spivey, Victoria, 375
Spotlight Scandals, 271
Spread It Abroad, 366
Sprigate, Sylvester, 185
Speros, Tia, 69, 107, 373, 421
Sportsmen, The, 181, 233, 374, 399
Spottswood, Willie, 140
Spring Is Here, 2, 408
Spring Reunion, 370
Springfield, Dusty, 169
Springsteen, Bruce, 310
Springtime in the Rockies, 420
St. John, Bridget, 58
St. Louis Blues, 33, 55, 238, 338
St. Louis Ragtimers, The, 380
Stablemates, 399
Stabile, Dick, 138, 418
Stacy, Jess, 423
Stafford, Jo, 1, 24, 27, 41, 43, 56, 78,
    79, 80, 95, 108, 109, 123, 138, 139,
    170, 171, 179, 190, 192, 212, 229,
    266, 275, 283, 287–88, 292, 296, 298,
    312, 328, 344, 346, 357, 384, 385,
    397, 408, 414, 417–18
Stage Door, 308
Stage Door Canteen, 124, 231, 268, 404
Stage Fright, 207
Stage Mother, 393
Stahl, Mary, 312, 344
Staiger, Libi, 298
Staines, Bill, 131
Stallings, Mary, 406
Stallion Road, 158
Stamford, John J., 224
Stamper, Dave, 71
Stand Up and Cheer, 205
Stanley, Aileen, 171, 185, 233, 321, 395
Stanley Brothers, The, 187
Stanley, Frank, 399
Stanley, Paul, 373
Stanley, Ralph, 212
Stansfield, Lisa, 7
Staple Singers, The, 125
Stapleton, Cyril, 63
Stapp, Jack, 60
Star!, 4, 332
Star Dust, 339

Star Is Born, A, 171, 257, 284, 347, 395,
    421
Star Maker, The, 179, 194, 313, 345
Stardust, 82, 129, 247, 335, 339, 340,
    350, 383
Stardust on the Sage, 124, 286
Stargazers, The, 144, 224
Starlift, 161, 393, 420
Starlings, The, 250
Starliters, The, 58, 289, 297
Starr, Edwin, 237
Starr, Kay, 6, 19, 89, 106, 109, 138,
    143, 153, 167, 177, 182, 225, 241,
    253, 263, 267, 269, 291, 293, 315,
    321, 329, 330, 345, 346, 360, 362,
    371, 388, 389, 393, 416, 423, 426, 427
Starr, Randy, 275
Starr, Ringo, 44, 133, 315, 403, 416
Stars and Stripes Forever, The, 33, 85
Stars Are Singing, The, 36, 67
Stars on Ice, 196
Stars on Parade, 46, 196
Stars Over Broadway, 57, 315
Statler Brothers, The, 60, 71, 126, 237,
    270, 297, 329, 401
Stauffer, Teddy, 238
Stealing Home, 11
Steel, John, 391
Steele, Blue, 115
Steele, John, 254, 410
Steele, Sandra, 254
Stella Dallas, 75, 174, 230, 338
Stept, Sam, 88, 361
Sterling, Andrew B., 54, 91, 234, 276,
    380, 384, 395
Stern, Joseph W., 213, 248
Stern, Mike, 362
Sterne, Teresa, 384
Stevens, April, 82, 115, 339
Stevens, Connie, 66, 139, 192, 422
Stevens, Garry, 252, 289
Stevens, Leonard, 156
Stevens, Mark, 166
Stevens, Ray, 242
Stevens, Rise, 96, 220, 226
Stevens, Stella, 263
Stevens, Trudy, 228
Stewart, Al, 182

Stewart and Gillen, 180

Stewart, Billy, 99

Stewart, Buddy, 14, 115, 286

Stewart, Cliff, 275

Stewart, Freddie, 87, 156

Stewart, Helen, 259

Stewart, James, 97

Stewart, Larry, 264, 382

Stewart, Martha, 319

Stewart, Melville, 409

Stewart, Redd, 358, 417

Stewart, Rex, 8, 384, 408

Stewart, Rod, 16

Stillman, Al, 47, 59, 141, 150, 164, 187, 196, 312

Stills, Stephen, 330

Sting, 224, 342

Sting, The, 77

Stitt, Sonny, 96, 174, 215, 247, 252, 316

Stock, Larry, 44, 247, 424

Stolen Harmony, 136

Stoloff, Morris, 245, 372

Stone, Eddie, 196, 214, 293, 301, 304, 314

Stone, Gregory, 209

Stone, Henry, 60, 238

Stone, Lew, 94, 183

Stoner, Mickey, 158

Stonewall, 427

Stooge, The, 198

Stop! Look! Listen!, 161

Stop, You're Killing Me, 26

Stordahl, Alex, 78, 272, 294, 311

Storey, June, 348

Stork Club, The, 30, 63, 181

Storm, Gale, 236, 313, 345

Storm, Warren, 292

Stormy Weather, 6, 79, 152, 196, 268, 342

Story of Us, The, 88, 199, 318

Story of Vernon and Irene Castle, The, 50, 51, 62, 67, 76, 117, 136, 213, 241, 272, 304, 305, 385, 387

Stothart, Herbert, 163

Strachey, Jack, 366

Straeter, Ted, 347, 377, 407, 422

Straight Is the Way, 148

Strait, George, 11

Strange Love of Molly Louvain, 285

Strasberg, Susan, 275

Stratas, Teresa, 39

Strawberry Blonde, The, 31, 40, 180, 219, 234, 384, 399

Strayhorn, Billy, 222, 310, 355

Streisand, Barbra, 58, 69, 105, 119, 125, 131, 133, 157, 170, 173, 184, 185, 188, 226, 241, 247, 254, 256, 257, 267, 304, 309, 313, 367, 390, 398, 404, 416

Strictly Dynamite, 122

Strictly in the Groove, 33, 49, 162, 240, 331, 417

Strike Up the Band, 189, 226, 323, 409

Strip, The, 6, 32, 87, 200, 304

Stripling Brothers, The, 255

Stritch, Billy, 21, 210, 249

Stritch, Elaine, 18, 20, 97, 209, 269

Stroman, Guy, 135, 217, 317, 369

Stromberg, John, 66, 223

Strong, Benny, 359, 395

Strong, Buddy, 168

Stroud, Claude, 177

Strut Miss Lizzie, 387

Strutter, Ted, 75

Stuart, Jack, 330

Stuart, Ralph, 13

Stuart, Vicki, 88, 170, 218, 264, 293, 299, 367, 381, 389, 403, 426

Stutz, Carl, 214

Styne, Jule, 126, 186, 209, 311, 345–46, 363, 369, 382

Sudy, Joseph, 297

Suessdorf, Karl, 246

Sugar Babies, 87, 102, 152

Sullavan, Jeri, 306

Sullivan, Henry, 161

Sullivan, Joseph, 153, 244, 400

Sullivan, K. T., 126, 134, 158, 247

Sullivan, Maxine, 21, 39, 44, 49, 60, 77, 97, 102, 114, 120, 157, 170, 177, 193, 199, 203, 251, 255, 288, 312, 336, 337, 338, 380, 389, 410

Summer Stock, 114

Sun Valley Serenade, 181

Sunbonnet Sue, 51, 313, 345, 402

Sunny Side of the Street, 161, 278

Sunset in Wyoming, 57
Sunshine, Marion, 284
Superman, 302
Susan and the Surftones, 286
Sutton, Harry O., 154
Sutton, Ralph, 199, 218
Suzy, 83
Suzuki, Pat, 105, 333
Swan, E. A., 400
Swander, Don, 81
Swanee River, 34, 79, 193, 258, 272, 273, 274
Swarf Sisters, The, 362
Swarthout, Gladys, 226, 263
Sweeney, Ed, 394
Sweet Adeline, 347, 348, 404, 405
Sweet and Lowdown, 12, 54, 156, 172, 174, 184, 197, 210, 273, 284, 319, 349, 365, 410
Sweet Bird of Youth, 98
Sweet Dreams, 310, 348, 422
Sweet Lorraine, 350
Sweet Rosie O'Grady, 254, 322, 350
Sweetheart of Sigma Chi, 285, 351
Sweetheart of the Fleet, 163
Sweethearts on Parade, 386
Swift, Kay, 105
Swing!, 12, 46, 54, 69, 88, 115, 181, 184, 341, 352
Swing High, Swing Low, 352
Swing It, Soldier, 257
Swing Parade of 1946, 53, 278, 342
Swinger, The, 163
Swingin' the Dream, 76
Swingtime Canteen, 71, 87, 146, 170, 171, 264, 282, 291, 315, 324
Swingtime Johnny, 31, 121, 161, 399
Sylvester, Victor, 156, 392
Symes, Marty, 75, 188, 265, 364, 380
Syms, Sylvia, 95, 124, 129, 170, 249, 267, 289, 388
Syncopation, 420

Tabackin, Lew, 14
Tabrar, Joseph, 72
Taffetas, The, 21, 58, 69, 86, 197, 131, 137, 218, 242, 251, 296, 323, 327, 358, 373, 383, 418, 421

Tahiti Honey, 65
Tait, John, 31
Taiz, Lillian, 408
Take a Chance, 187
Take Five, 407
Take It Big, 37
Take Me Back to Oklahoma, 417
Take Me Out to the Ball Game, 204, 355, 401
Talent, Ziggy, 309
Talley, Harry, 384
Tamara, 151, 170
Tamblin, Russ, 129, 130
Tammy and the Bachelor, 356
Tanguay, Eva, 27, 154
Tanner, Elmo, 135
Tarrirers, The, 30
Tashman, Lilyan, 421
Tate, Buddy, 200–201
Tate, Grady, 305
Tatum, Art, 35, 78, 105, 108, 120, 153, 158, 160, 178, 214, 220, 222, 234, 244, 245, 250, 255, 273, 281, 286, 292, 304, 319, 331, 334, 341, 355, 364, 380, 400, 406, 421
Tauber, Doris, 362
Tauber, Richard, 36, 159, 203, 220
Taylor, Billy, 264
Taylor, Eva, 27, 64, 103, 164–65, 167, 228, 273, 336, 397, 415
Taylor, Irene, 315, 406
Taylor, Irving, 87, 100, 354
Taylor, Johnny, 60, 110
Taylor, Larry, 14
Taylor, Laurette, 284–85
Taylor, Sam, 245
Taylor, Tell, 90
Tea for Two, 59, 160
Teagarden, Jack, 5, 32, 33, 41, 57, 63, 74, 81, 82, 99, 148, 156, 158, 159, 167, 196, 207, 267, 303, 318, 319, 330, 337, 343, 400 410, 413
Teahouse of the August Moon, 82
Tear Gas Squad, 393
Teenagers, The, 373
Tell It to a Star, 219
Tell It to the Judge, 210
Tell Me More, 200

Temey, Jack B., 238
Temperance Seven, The, 100
Temple, Shirley, 130, 289, 399
Templeton, Alec, 335
Templeton, Fay, 223
Tempo Kings, The, 347
Tempo, Nino, 82, 339
Tempos, The, 314
Temptations, The, 209, 408
10, 130
Ten Cents a Dance, 357
Tennant, H. M., 259
Tennile, Toni, 357
*Tenting Tonight on the Old Camp
    Ground*, 359
Terrell, Clyde, 150
Terris, Dorothy, 370, 409
Terris, Norma, 4
Tesca, Gary, 216
Teschemacher, Edward, 35
Texas Rangers, The, 98
Texas Wanderers, The, 169, 373
Texas Troubadours, The, 31
Thanks a Million, 131
Tharpe, Rosetta, 375
That Midnight Kiss, 89, 367, 370
That's My Boy, 29
That's the Spirit, 27, 145
Thebom, Blanche, 248
There's a Girl in My Heart, 4, 73
There's No Business Like Show Business,
    5, 10, 207, 231, 299, 396
They Shoot Horses, Don't They?, 39, 46,
    49, 50, 53, 68, 96, 153, 192, 281, 351
Thibault, Conrad, 145, 205, 217, 271,
    320
Thielemans, Toots, 281, 326, 340
Thigpen, Lynn, 17, 40, 144, 266, 333
Third World Cop, 225
Thirty Seconds Over Tokyo, 82, 351,
    366, 409
This Could Be the Night, 43, 158
This Earth Is Mine, 131, 348
This Is the Army, 118, 228
This Is the Life, 13, 23, 203, 408
This Time for Keeps, 64, 97, 171
Thomas, B. J., 66, 352

Thomas, Danny, 48, 151, 165, 167,
    172, 176, 185, 279, 353, 391, 415
Thomas, Dick, 324
Thomas, George, 27
Thomas, John Charles, 22, 205, 355,
    375
Thomas, Rufus, 56, 321
Thompson, Eddie, 364
Thompson, Hank, 2, 60, 283, 346
Thompson, Jane Brown, 156–57
Thompson, Joe, 183
Thompson, Johnny, 192
Thompson, Kay, 146, 245, 424
Thompson, Lucky, 221
Thorn, Paul, 401
Thorne, Francis, 396
Thornhill, Claude, 3, 81, 85, 95, 120,
    132, 220, 237, 272, 277, 304, 328,
    331, 346, 361
Thornton, Bonnie, 99
Thornton, James, 399
Thornton, Teri, 42
Thoroughly Modern Millie, 26, 60, 151,
    177, 192, 290, 304, 344
Thorpe, Bo, 47
Thousands Cheer, 66, 79, 143, 178, 209,
    413
Three Coins in a Fountain, 368
Three Darling Daughters, 305
Three Dog Night, 258, 376
Three for the Show, 145, 189
Three Little Pigs, The, 404
Three Little Words, 163, 263, 405
Three Men and a Baby, 124
Three Peppers, The, 90
Three Smart Girls Grow Up, 36
Three Stooges, The, 1, 20, 63, 225, 238,
    275
Three Suns, The, 6, 12, 29, 74, 75, 88,
    106, 115, 117, 140, 174, 198, 237,
    245, 285, 286, 290, 344, 377, 380,
    405, 410
Threepenny Opera, The, 224
Three's a Crowd, 45
Thrill of a Romance, The, 36
Thumbs Up, 24, 427
Thunderbirds, The, 61
Thunderbolt, 348, 355, 396

Thunders, Johnny, 295
Tibbett, Lawrence, 204, 273, 284, 320, 408
Tierra, Septet, 373
Til, Sonny, 108, 153, 162, 180, 410
'Til We Meet Again, 334, 401
Till the Clouds Roll By, 13, 205, 367, 406
Till the End of Time, 371
Tiller, Ted, 111
Tillman, Floyd, 186
Tillotson, Johnny, 44
Tilsley, Henry J. 203, 209
Tilton, Martha, 12, 18, 29, 97, 152, 281, 288, 367
Tim, Tiny, 26, 109, 162, 215, 254, 350, 355, 397
Time, the Place and the Girl, The, 147, 166
Times Square Lady, 269, 391
Timm, Wladimir, A., 37
Tin Pan Alley, 143, 164, 201, 236, 245, 277, 281, 318, 328
Tindley, C. Albert, 388
Tintypes, 17, 40, 41, 144, 154, 173, 179, 199, 235, 266, 328, 333, 386
Tiomkin, Dimitri, 139
Tipton, Bill, 201
Titanic, 10, 67
Tizol, Juan, 54, 286
Tjader, Cal, 222
To Be or Not To Be, 135, 349, 417
To Broadway With Love, 304
To Each His Own, 372
To Have and Have Not, 30
Toast of New York, The, 105
Tobani, Theodore Moses, 136
Tobias, Charles, 3, 88, 237, 274, 303, 427
Tobias, Harry, 308, 348
Todd, Dick, 14, 155, 395
Tofflemire, Anne, 207
Tokens, The, 323
Tokyo Rose, 367
Tombes, Andrew, 131
Tomlin, Pinky, 269, 362, 391, 418
Tomorrow Is Forever, 371
Tompkins, Ross, 311

Toney, Oscar, Jr., 110
Too Many Blondes, 75
Too Young to Know, 188
Toots and the Maytals, 388
Top Man, 410
Top o' the Morning, 393
Top Secret, 21
Torch Song, 43, 358
Torchy Blane in Panama, 53
Tormé, Mel, 5, 6, 14, 19, 24, 29, 36, 38, 43, 55, 64, 68, 78, 102, 105, 106, 110, 117, 120, 126, 129, 135, 147, 153, 157, 170, 172, 173, 184, 215, 237, 249, 250, 264, 272, 273, 275, 280, 289, 311, 314, 316, 322, 323, 333, 356, 365, 376, 390, 397, 398, 405, 409, 416, 420
Towers, Constance, 87
Towne, Charlie, 225
Trace, Al, 225
Trace, Ben, 418
Tracey, William, 288, 362
Tracy, Arthur, 95, 116, 141, 204, 308, 355, 392
Tracy, Gene, 374
Trail of the Lonesome Pine, 235, 375
Trail Street, 425
Trail to San Antone, 316
Train Ride to Hollywood, 317
Trammps, The, 401, 427
Trapp Family, The, 273
Traubel, Helen, 56, 161, 215, 293
Traum, Artie, 309
Travis, Merle, 28, 37, 51, 58, 73, 92, 140, 168, 172, 218, 224, 294, 324, 325, 328
Travis, Randy, 89
Treasure Girl, 189
Tree, Maria, 142
Tremaine, Paul, 18, 129
Trevathan, Charles E., 49
Trevor, Huntley, 394
Trimble, Kenny, 19
Trip to Chinatown, A, 4
Tripp, Paul, 313
Tristano, Lennie, 196
Trocadero, 250, 320
Troccoli, Kathy, 361

Trotter, John Scott, 12, 32, 238
Trouble Along the Way, 248
Trouble in Mind, 375
Trouble With Girls, The, 76, 352, 402
Troup, Bobby, 71, 182, 242, 305
True to the Army, 152
Trumbauer, Frankie, 51, 143, 156, 206, 268, 298, 324
Tubb, Ernest, 123, 133, 182, 192–93, 232, 310, 330, 413, 422
Tucker, Bonnie, 147
Tucker, Henry, 348
Tucker, Marshall, 100, 135
Tucker, Orrin, 2, 93, 99, 100, 112, 147, 183, 271, 291, 330, 331, 403, 407, 418
Tucker, Sophie, 5, 6, 7, 9, 60, 69, 76, 91, 109, 121, 126, 129, 138, 147, 149, 205, 225, 247, 271, 279, 298, 330–31, 337, 364, 397, 415, 427
Tucker, Tommy, 36, 155, 205, 330
Tulsa Kid, 120
Tunbridge, Joseph, 124
Tune, Tommy, 147, 276, 285, 418
Turk, Roy, 3, 6, 20, 115, 154, 171, 228, 234, 385
Turk 182, 224
Turner, Claramae, 160
Turner, Ike and Tina, 8, 91
Turner, Joe, 58, 341
Turner, John, 327
Turner, Spyder, 110
Turtle Creek Chorale, The, 388
Tuxedo Junction, 377
Twenty Million Sweethearts, 56, 75, 205
Twiggs, Charles, 290
Twiggy, 147, 332
Twilight on the Prairie, 213
Twilight on the Rio Grande, 275
Twirly Whirly, 66
Twitty, Conway, 58, 74, 83, 150, 243, 344
Two Blondes and a Redhead, 278
Two for the Show, 146
Two Girls and a Sailor, 23, 60, 75, 283, 348, 354
Two Latins From Manhattan, 71
2001: A Space Odyssey, 73

Two Tickets to Broadway, 58, 228–29, 366
Two Tickets to London, 419
Two Tickets to Paris, 27
Two Weeks in Another Town, 1, 50, 87, 305
Twomey, Kay, 195
Tyle, Chris, 288
Tyler, Bonnie, 371
Tymes, The, 372

UB40, 342
Udall, Lyn, 428
Uggams, Eloise, 159
Uggams, Leslie, 86, 87, 114, 215, 220, 224, 268, 303, 336, 367
Unchained, 379
Uncle Tom's Cabin, 77, 352
Under Colorado Skies, 193
Under Fiesta Stars, 75, 400
Undercover Girl, 138
Underwater, 61
Unholy Partners, 5
University Six, The, 2
Uninvited, The, 340
Up and Down Broadway, 63
Up the River, 116, 247
Upshaw, Dawn, 73, 134, 228, 249
Ure, Midge, 66
Utrera, Adolfo, 125

Vagabond Lover, The, 268
Vagabonds, The, 58, 165, 207, 302, 385
Vale, Jerry, 27, 36, 112, 116, 133, 156, 160, 173, 217, 244, 333, 363, 371, 372, 383, 385, 408, 409, 418
Valente, Caterina, 58, 112, 124, 140, 191, 229, 258, 322, 371
Valentino, Rudolph, 318
Vallee, Rudy, 18, 48, 68, 73, 75, 87, 113, 117, 123, 132, 143, 145, 152, 159, 163, 168, 183, 201, 204, 207, 208, 211, 215, 216, 230, 240, 259, 263, 268, 280, 287, 293, 311, 336, 340. 349, 351, 363, 388, 401, 420, 423, 425
Valley of Fire, 278
Valli, Frankie, 8

Vamps, The, 150, 294

Van Alstyne, Egbert, 35, 93, 121, 181, 236, 262, 291, 422

Van and Schenck, 5, 8, 55, 89, 109, 165, 227–28, 319, 360, 398, 404, 413

Van, Bobby, 111, 177

Van Damme, Art, 24, 89, 127, 129, 188, 206, 226, 239, 289

Van Duser, Guy, 158

Van Dyke, Jerry, 51

Van Heusen, Jimmy, 14, 77, 81, 137, 139, 177, 216, 273, 289

Van Ronk, Dave, 426

Van Shelton, Ricky, 401

Van Steeden, Peter, 141

Vance, Kenny, 317

Vance, Paul J., 58

Vanderbilt Revue, The, 42

Vannier, Angela, 398

Variety Girl, 371

Varner, Tom, 200

Varro, Johnny, 167, 280

Vaughan, Sarah, 6, 12, 15, 30, 38, 40, 45, 87, 89, 95, 96, 104, 112, 115, 125, 138, 143, 145, 148, 153, 172, 175, 177, 189, 204, 211, 219, 220, 221, 222, 233, 242, 261, 263, 273, 279, 280, 285, 286, 288, 289, 290, 333, 347, 357, 358, 360, 362, 363, 368, 375, 389, 391, 400, 406, 407, 424, 426

Vaughn, Billy, 12, 14. 35, 47, 54, 93, 104, 112, 133, 134, 136, 140, 143, 182, 236, 241, 245, 254, 277, 293, 308, 319, 327, 358, 371, 377, 426

Vaughn, Frankie, 216, 217, 272

Vedani, Cesar, 3

Vee, Bobby, 26, 83, 123, 186, 242, 258, 323

Vejvoda, Jaromir, 37

Velazquez, Consuelo, 38

Veloz and Yolanda, 59

Velvets, The, 360

Velvetones, The, 117

Ventura, Charles, 32, 42, 98, 115, 177, 221, 288, 341

Ventures, The, 47, 54, 61, 83, 104, 110, 119, 126, 134, 193, 221, 222, 244, 286, 300, 307

Venuta, Benay, 392

Venuti, Joe, 5, 19, 31, 33, 65, 74, 140, 163, 207, 254, 287, 303, 331, 350, 379, 388, 413

Ver Planck, Marlene, 81, 150, 264, 377, 387

Vera-Ellen, 228, 263

Verea, Lisette, 405

Vereen, Ben, 65

Vern, Kaaren, 61

Vernon, Wally, 101, 297,

Verrill, Virginia, 83

Very Thought of You, The, 382

Very Warm for May, 13

Vibrations, The, 242

Victor, Floyd, 200

Victoria, Vesta, 72

Victory at Sea, 265

Victory Military Band, The, 396

Village People, The, 149

Village Stompers, The, 37, 111, 123, 249

Vincent, Ann, 397, 418

Vincent, Nat, 174

Vinton, Bobby, 36, 43, 44, 236, 265, 343, 357, 364, 383, 422

Violinsky, Sol, 392

Virginians, The, 58

Vitali, Milly, 266

Vitro, Rosemary, 150

Viva Las Vegas, 189, 414

Vogues of 1938, 321

Vogues, The, 289

Volpe, Marilyn, 407

Von Tilzer, Harry, 40–41, 54, 69, 91, 163–64, 170, 177, 270, 276, 294, 355, 380, 384, 395

Von Weber, Carl Maria, 209

Voorhees, Don, 177, 215

Vorse, Heaton, 155

Vye, Murvyn, 119

W. W. and the Divie Dancekings,124

Wabash Avenue,165, 181

Wade, Adam, 292

Wade, Stuart, 194, 372

Wagoner, Porter, 112

Wailers, The, 59, 118

Wain, Bea, 82, 85, 115, 135, 151, 157, 176, 177, 376, 419

Wainwright, Loudon, 2

Wait Till the Sun Shines, Nellie, 47, 212, 220, 277, 282, 384

Waitts, Tom, 49

Wake Up and Live, 79

Wakely, Jimmy, 34, 49, 179, 235, 286, 355, 373, 399

Walburn, Raymond, 131

Wald, Jerry, 206

Waldo, Terry, 247, 272

Waldron, Cliff, 103

Walk a Little Faster, 20

Walker, Billy, 34

Walker Brothers, The, 45, 266

Walker, Charlie, 288

Walker, Dianne, 237

Walker, James J., 255, 406

Walker, Johnny, 400

Walker, Polly, 60

Walker, T-Bone, 100, 122, 341

Walking My Baby Back Home, 79, 118, 143, 385, 421

Walking Stick, The, 98

Walkup, Cathi, 201

Wallace, Chester, 246

Wallace, G. Oliver, 83, 140

Wallace, Jeremy, 314

Waller, Jack, 124

Waller, Thomas "Fats," 5, 6–7, 23, 41, 44, 46, 50, 55, 60, 73, 76, 82, 84, 94, 100, 105, 107, 114, 120, 121, 129, 140–41, 143, 149, 152, 164, 171, 175, 185, 189, 195, 199, 212, 219, 228, 244, 261, 264, 286, 304, 318, 320, 332, 333, 336, 354, 376, 379, 382, 396, 423, 425

Wallflower, 161

Walls, Van, 58

Walters, Teddy, 364

Walton, Jim, 340, 350, 383

Wand, Hart A., 73

War of the Wildcats, 90, 179

Ward, Aida, 39, 151, 152, 190

Ward, Billy, 82, 296, 339, 358, 398

Ward, Charles B., 30

Ward, Edward, 404

Ward, Helen, 39, 43, 71, 78, 117, 122, 124, 153, 189, 264, 328, 366, 390, 413

Ward, Samuel A., 17

Ware, Leonard, 140

Warfield, Charles, 27

Waring, Fred, 61, 105, 166, 177, 215, 237, 251, 259, 281, 326, 351, 368, 375, 386, 425

Waring, Tom, 237, 326, 386

Warner, Jeanette, 29

Warren, Fran, 95, 102, 133, 158, 178, 346, 419

Warren, Harry, 2, 254, 261, 280, 315, 424

Warren, Leonard, 213

Warren, Shorty, 193

Warshauer, Frank, 185

Warwick, Dionne, 58, 187

Washboard Rhythm Kings, The, 130, 258, 269, 381

Washburne, Country, 109, 279

Washington, Dinah, 3, 6, 28, 41, 44, 66, 69, 79, 101, 107, 121, 132, 138, 150, 151, 185, 198, 199, 217, 228, 247, 252, 280, 315, 331, 334, 344, 354, 357, 367, 369, 381, 389, 392, 402, 408, 418, 419, 426

Washington, Jackie, 396

Washington, Ned, 114, 116, 139, 148, 169, 174, 217, 252, 262, 340, 372

Washington, Vernon, 335

Washington, Yvonne, 24

Wasserman, Rob, 339

Waters, Ethel, 41, 45, 55, 84, 87, 114, 148, 152, 159, 217, 236, 240, 245, 280, 301, 315, 319, 333, 342, 344, 349, 364, 381, 394

Watkins, Billy, 50

Watson, Deke, 109

Watson, Doc, 125

Watson, Johnny, 186, 269, 295

Watson, Milton, 123

Watters, Lu, 2, 22

Watts, Andre, 347

Watts, Clem, 168, 418

Watts, Grady, 42

Way Down South, 267, 333

Way Out West, 375

Way We Were, The, 299, 301
Wayne, Bernie, 44, 205
Wayne, Frances, 52, 159, 222, 311, 321
Wayne, Mabel, 93, 178, 214, 297
Wayne, Sid, 313
Weatherly, Fred, 74
Weatherwax Brothers Quartet, The, 213
Weary River, 388
Weavers, The, 49, 65, 116, 201, 278, 330, 369, 378, 397
Webb, Chick, 23, 45, 62, 65, 84, 167, 178, 215, 260, 336, 341, 345, 379, 420
Webb, Clifton, 45, 96, 189
Webb, Jack, 270
Weber, Kay, 129, 245, 288, 301
Weber, Rex, 48
Webster, Ben, 44, 45, 95, 147, 163, 174, 211, 346, 390
Webster, Paul Francis, 29, 157, 204, 216, 377
Wee Turtles, 369
Weekend Pass, 13
Weeks, Anson, 169, 325
Weeks, Harold, 140
Weems, Ted, 135, 140, 166, 175, 202, 332, 360, 364, 385, 407
Weilder, Virginia, 349
Weill, Kurt, 224
Weiner, Dan, 300
Weir, Frank, 131
Weisman, Ben, 111, 189
Weiss, George David, 221, 272
Weiss, Stephen, 250, 294
Welch, Elisabeth, 21, 59, 158
Welch, Lenny, 296, 323, 346
Welk, Lawrence, 16, 18, 29, 37, 44, 46, 54, 58, 61, 63, 98, 104, 125, 131, 136, 150, 161, 174, 178, 181, 209, 213, 224, 230, 236, 238, 241, 242, 253, 258, 270, 271, 290, 312, 314, 316, 325, 343, 344, 346, 364, 368, 373, 395
Welles, John Barnes, 236
Wellingtons, The, 28
Wells, Dickie, 211
Wells, Gilbert, 298
Wells, Robert, 64
Wells, Terry, 103

Welsh, Alex, 140
Weltz, Joey, 302
Wendy and the Wombats, 404
Wendling, Pete, 412
Wenrich, Percy, 277, 293, 308, 399, 401
Werrenrath, Reginald, 136, 282
West, Mae, 111, 238
West, Paula, 200
West, Speedy, 412
Westendorf, Thomas, 172
Westman, Theodore, 181
Weston, Paul, 23, 78, 82, 87, 95, 98, 120, 126, 146, 153, 171, 179, 205, 234, 238, 247, 251, 254, 259, 263, 267, 276, 316, 326, 329, 344, 372, 383, 384, 409, 419
Weston, R. P., 324
Wettling, George, 76, 165
Wever, Ned, 376
Wharf Angel, 126, 136, 272, 420
What Price Glory?, 60, 281
What Women Want, 38, 168, 190, 224
What's Cookin', 282
Wheeler, Francis, 208, 318
Wheetman, Dan, 123
When Harry Met Sally, 24, 88, 185, 341, 407
When Johnny Comes Marching Home, 126, 332, 394, 417
When My Baby Smiles at Me, 51, 78, 312, 395
When the Lights Go On Again, 395
When You're in Love, 239, 321
When You're Smiling, 81, 114, 196, 225, 400
Where the Buffalo Roam, 142
Whitaker, Forest, 151
Whitcomb, Ian, 125, 301, 351, 380
Whitcup, Leonard, 354
Whitman, Ernest, 268
White, Bob, 183
White, Brian, 156, 300
White Christmas, 44, 228
White, Cool, 49
White, Josh, 28, 145
White, Lew, 74
White, Robert, 79, 93, 159
White, Sammy, 123

Whitehill, Clarence, 220

Whitehouse, Fred, 309

Whiteman, Paul, 1, 5, 7, 10, 12, 17, 35, 45, 55, 59, 62, 77, 82, 103, 116, 125, 133, 143, 145, 159, 162, 178, 184, 185, 192, 197, 206, 207, 211, 216, 226, 228, 229, 240, 241, 244, 246, 256, 257, 284, 297, 307, 316, 321, 329, 331, 338, 339, 344, 347, 361, 370, 373, 386, 387, 388, 391, 394, 397, 402, 406, 409

Whitfield, David, 327

Whitfield, Weslia, 21, 35, 102, 156, 228, 278, 357, 382, 408

Whiting, George, 251

Whiting, Margaret, 8, 39, 66, 78, 110, 111, 126, 127, 132, 146, 168, 185, 210, 246, 252, 253, 255, 257, 263, 266, 367, 390, 399, 408

Whiting, Richard A., 8, 126, 143, 188, 192, 253, 254–55, 319, 326, 371

Whitley, Ray, 27

Whitman, Slim, 18, 34, 55, 91, 133, 173, 221, 242, 299, 401, 417

Whitney, Dave, 23

Whitney, Joan, 7

Whitson, Beth Slater, 209, 235

Whittaker, Roger, 21, 299, 312, 315, 364, 379, 393

Whittier, Henry, 411

Whoopee, 219

Who's on Bass?, 200

Whyte, Ronny, 50

Widow Jones, The, 49

Wieland, Clara, 253

Wilber, Bob, 295

Wilder, Alec, 14, 21, 26, 42, 76, 83, 137, 168, 169, 172, 217, 310, 318, 330, 367, 402, 426

Wiley, Lee, 2, 20, 55, 81, 96, 97, 129, 147, 148, 151, 188, 189, 210, 226, 228, 255, 331, 344, 368, 405, 426

Wilkinson, Dudley, 36

Willcox, Spiegle, 23, 188, 253, 331

Williams, Andy, 14, 24, 33, 38, 45, 54, 74, 101, 102, 160, 162, 185, 186, 201, 218, 244, 254, 262, 285, 308, 333, 334, 377, 379, 417, 420, 422

Williams, Bert, 149, 266, 288, 409, 419, 423

Williams, Billy, 12, 121, 171, 175, 205, 274, 316

Williams, Clarence, 27, 100, 228, 336, 344, 351, 354

Williams, Claude, 427

Williams, Cootie, 85

Williams, Esther, 355

Williams, Frances, 132, 362

Williams, Hank, 65–66, 191, 220–21, 272, 422

Williams, Hank, Jr., 6, 8, 66, 139, 192, 375, 422

Williams, Harry H., 121, 139, 181, 304

Williams, Henry, 130, 262

Williams, Jessica, 351, 410

Williams, Joe, 5, 87, 99, 113, 121, 149, 151, 158, 178, 182, 209, 255, 263, 267, 310, 314, 318, 357, 390, 416, 417, 421

Williams, Juanita, 100

Williams, Leona, 344

Williams, Mary Lou, 143, 307, 319, 413

Williams, Mason, 31, 241

Williams, Midge, 208

Williams, Mollie, 165

Williams, Roger, 24, 92, 160, 187, 217, 262, 272, 346, 372

Williams, Spencer, 32, 55, 100, 149, 156

Williams, Steve, 347

Williams, Tex, 301, 316, 324, 328, 401

Williamson, Tony, 23

Willie, Boxbar, 17, 85, 122, 123, 139, 249, 287, 290, 298, 352, 411, 413, 417, 422

Willing, Foy, 133

Willis Brothers, The, 28

Willis, Lynn, 96

Wills, Bob, 2, 10, 14, 32, 81, 99, 133, 152, 164, 253, 272, 273, 298, 304, 309, 316, 324, 335, 337, 345

Wills, Chill, 375

Wills, Johnny Lee, 296

Wills, Viola, 120

Willson, Meredith, 187, 203, 232, 326, 416
Willie and Joe in Back at the Front, 46
Wilson, Bob, 7, 59, 143, 163, 223, 230, 326, 350, 387
Wilson, Cassandra, 342
Wilson, Dooley, 185
Wilson, Edith, 41, 105
Wilson, Eileen, 39, 252
Wilson, Jackie, 36, 110, 256, 296, 339, 416
Wilson, Julie, 21, 39, 188, 190, 204, 207, 224, 398, 407
Wilson, Nancy, 38, 43, 137, 138, 178, 221, 390, 398, 426
Wilson, Patrick, 102
Wilson, Teddy, 5, 6, 25, 63, 68, 80, 89, 96, 97, 105, 129, 151, 152, 160, 168, 171, 234, 244, 255, 256, 257, 278, 281, 290, 292, 300, 304, 307, 336, 337, 341, 344, 356, 367, 390, 399, 400, 413, 419, 420–21, 423, 425
Wilson, Trey, 173
Winchell, W., 263
Winchell, Walter, 157
Windom, H. W., 104
Window, Muriel, 50, 375
Windjammer, 236
Windsor, Barbara, 101, 324
Wingate, Philip, 63, 155
Winged Victory, 402
Wings, 252
Winkler, Franz, 110
Winner, Joseph E., 213
Winnick, Maurice, 351
Winning Team, The, 355
Winninger, Charles, 173, 208, 241, 272, 403, 404
Winston, Sherry, 216
Winter, Johnny, 50
Winter, Paul, 388
Winter, Winona, 384
Winterhalter, Hugo, 54, 192, 200, 262, 357, 408, 421
Winters, Newton, 349
Winters, Shelley, 121
Wirges, William, 64
Wise, Fred, 1, 189

Wise, Jack, 401
Wiseman, Mac, 274
Wiseman, Scott, 133
With a Song in My Heart, 9, 43, 53, 62, 82, 85, 114, 177, 182, 340, 408
Witmark, Julie, 287
Witness, The, 104
Witness Chair, The, 355
Wodehouse, P. G., 39, 394
Wolf, Rennold, 418
Wolfe, Jacques, 320
Wolverines, The, 386
Womack, Bobby, 107
Woman Commands, A, 283
Woman's Secret, A, 284
Wonder, Stevie, 119
Wood, Barry, 19, 68, 118, 187, 208, 397, 425
Wood, Dell, 92, 99
Wood, Donna, 155
Wood, Gloria, 276
Wood, Leo, 143, 306, 332
Wood, Mrs. John, 85
Woodard, Charlaine, 140, 152, 199, 396
Woode, Henri, 304
Wooding, Russell, 6, 408
Woodruff, Henry, 165–66
Woods, Carol, 234
Woods, Eddie, 3, 125
Woods, Harry MacGregor, 175, 287, 301, 321, 376, 390, 396
Woods, Phil, 416
Wopat, Tom, 157
Words and Music, 43, 73, 228, 249, 408
Work, Henry Clay, 125, 200, 229, 410
World of Pleasure, A, 291
Worth, Bobby, 85
Wright, Arthur, 403
Wright, Catherine, 328
Wright, Edythe, 20, 81, 83, 84, 250, 300, 301
Wright, Lawrence, 17
Wright, Ruby, 390
Wrubel, Allie, 105, 120, 169, 250
Wyman, Jane, 161
Wymore, Patrice, 56, 59, 219
Wynette, Tammy, 232, 262

Wynn, Keenan, 89
Wynn, Larry, 106
Wynn, May, 151
Wynn, Nan, 47, 102, 151, 185, 221,
   253, 284, 338, 419

Xanadu, 420

Yale Glee Club, The, 55
Yank in the RAF, A, 367
Yankee Doodle Dandy, 281, 402
Yankee, Pat, 206
Yankovic, Frankie, 35, 37, 131, 241,
   343
Yarbrough, Glen, 74, 352
Yellen, Jack, 7, 20, 60, 89, 110, 130,
   132, 138, 165, 225, 415
Yellow Rose of Texas, 354
Yepper, Sid, 298
Yes, Giorgio, 160
Yes Sir, That's My Baby, 415
Yip Yip Yaphank, 118, 227
Yoakam, Dwight, 262
Yokel Boy, 37, 88
Yorke, Peter, 410
You Came Along, 255, 279, 281
You Were Meant for Me, 6, 7, 124, 168,
   171
Youmans, Vincent, 128, 160, 247, 372,
   408
Young at Heart, 422
Young Eagles, 273
Young, Austin, 17
Young, Alan, 6
Young, Eve, 168
Young, Faron, 140, 168, 180, 232, 269,
   279, 316, 348, 359, 418
Young, Joe, 2, 84, 106, 147, 148, 159,
   175, 176, 178, 222, 255, 302, 315,
   324, 329, 362, 412, 424

Young, Lester, 65, 115, 153, 160, 182,
   211, 285, 308, 319, 349, 356, 362,
   367, 387, 418
Young Man With a Horn, 64, 114, 161,
   226, 248, 382, 408, 410, 421
Young Man With Ideas, 155
Young, Neil, 142
Young Pioneers, The, 291
Young, Ralph, 158
Young, Rida Johnson, 248
Young, Robert, 25. 350
Young Tom Edison, 349
Young, Trummy, 60
Young, Victor, 21, 35, 116, 119, 148,
   211, 217, 252, 340, 343, 355, 369, 392
Young, Webster, 342
Your Cheatin' Heart, 66, 139, 192, 422
You're a Lucky Fellow, Mr. Smith, 400,
   422
You're My Everything, 53, 161, 420
Yuro, Timi, 150, 327
Yvain, Maurice, 256

Zabawa, Jule, 198
Zabriskie Point, 358
Zahn, Sara, 407, 422
Zaks, Jerry, 328
Zappa, Frank, 355, 393
Zaret, Hy, 379
Zavaroni, Lena, 223
Zeman, Vasek, 37
Zentner, Si, 207
Ziegfeld, Florenz, 147
Ziegfeld Follies, 50, 69, 71, 89, 136, 190,
   204, 227, 241, 251, 256, 266, 285,
   288, 305, 313, 316, 319, 360, 409,
   419, 420
Ziegfeld Girl, 173, 241, 304, 403
Ziemba, Karen, 77
Zimmerman, Charles A., 18

About the Author

THOMAS S. HISCHAK is Professor of Theater at the State University of New York College, Cortland. He is the author of *Film It with Music: An Encyclopedic Guide to the American Movie Musical* (Greenwood, 2001); *American Theatre: A Chronicle of Comedy and Drama, 1969–2000; The American Musical Film Song Encyclopedia* (Greenwood, 1999); *The Theatregoer's Almanac* (Greenwood, 1997); *The American Musical Theatre Song Encyclopedia* (Greenwood, 1995); *Stage It with Music: An Encyclopedic Guide to the American Musical Theatre* (Greenwood, 1993); and *Word Crazy: Broadway Lyricists from Cohan to Sondheim* (Praeger, 1991).